www.wadsworth.com

www.wadsworth.com is the World Wide Web site for Thomson Wadsworth and is your direct source to dozens of online resources.

At *www.wadsworth.com* you can find out about supplements, demonstration software, and student resources. You can also send email to many of our authors and preview new publications and exciting new technologies.

www.wadsworth.com
Changing the way the world learns®

RELATED TITLES

CogLab:

The *CogLab Reader* may be used in conjunction with *CogLab,* a set of cognitive experiments and demonstrations that are available either online or on CD-ROM. To order the *CogLab Reader* in conjunction with *CogLab,* contact your Thomson Learning sales representative.

CogLab Manual (with Acccess Code for Online Access)
by Greg Francis and Ian Neath

CogLab on a CD-ROM
by Greg Francis and Ian Neath

Cognitive Psychology In and Out of the Laboratory, 3rd edition
by Kathleen Galotti

Cognitive Psychology: Connecting Mind, Research, and Everyday Experience
by E. Bruce Goldstein

Cognition: Theory and Applications, 6th edition
by Stephen K. Reed

Cognitive Psychology, 3rd edition
by Robert J. Sternberg

Human Memory: An Introduction to Research, Data, and Theory, 2nd edition
by Ian Neath and Aimée M. Surprenant

Language:

Psychology of Language, 4th edition
by David W. Carroll

Language Development, 2nd edition
by Erika Hoff

Psycholinguistics, 2nd edition
by Jean Berko Gleason and Nan Bernstein Ratner

CogLab Reader

Aimée M. Surprenant
Purdue University

Greg Francis
Purdue University

Ian Neath
Purdue University

THOMSON
™
WADSWORTH

Australia • Canada • Mexico • Singapore • Spain
United Kingdom • United States

THOMSON

WADSWORTH

Publisher: *Vicki Knight*
Acquisitions Editor: *Marianne Taflinger*
Technology Project Manager: *Darin Derstine*
Editorial Assistant: *Justin Courts*
Marketing Manager: *Chris Caldeira*
Marketing Assistant: *Laurel Anderson*
Advertising Project Manager: *Brian Chaffee*
Project Manager, Editorial Production: *Paul Wells*
Print/Media Buyer: *Rebecca Cross*

Permissions Editor: *Stephanie Lee*
Production Service: *Scratchgravel Publishing Services*
Text Designer: *Anne Draus*
Copy Editor: *Toni Zuccarini Ackley*
Compositor: *Scratchgravel Publishing Services*
Cover Designer: *Roy Neuhaus*
Cover Image: *Chad Baker/Getty Images*
Printer: *Webcom*

Printed in Canada

2   3   4   5   6   7   08   07   06   05

For more information about our products, contact us at:
Thomson Learning Academic Resource Center
1-800-423-0563

For permission to use material from this text or product,
submit a request online at
http://www.thomsonrights.com.
Any additional questions about permissions can be submitted
by email to thomsonrights@thomson.com.

Library of Congress Control Number: 2004105876

ISBN 0-534-64120-2

Thomson Wadsworth
10 Davis Drive
Belmont, CA 94002-3098
USA

Asia
Thomson Learning
5 Shenton Way #01-01
UIC Building
Singapore 068808

Australia/New Zealand
Thomson Learning
102 Dodds Street
Southbank, Victoria 3006
Australia

Canada
Nelson
1120 Birchmount Road
Toronto, Ontario M1K 5G4
Canada

Europe/Middle East/Africa
Thomson Learning
High Holborn House
50/51 Bedford Row
London WC1R 4LR
United Kingdom

Latin America
Thomson Learning
Seneca, 53
Colonia Polanco
11560 Mexico D.F.
Mexico

Spain/Portugal
Paraninfo
Calle Magallanes, 25
28015 Madrid, Spain

BRIEF CONTENTS

DETAILED CONTENTS

PREFACE

This volume consists of 32 original articles, each of which corresponds to a demonstration in CogLab, the Cognitive Psychology Online Laboratory (www.coglab.wadsworth.com). The reason for developing CogLab was to provide a laboratory component for our Cognitive Psychology classes. As in a chemistry laboratory, the intent is to give the student a sense of how the experiment is conducted and how individual and group data look. *CogLab Reader* complements that goal by providing a context for the experiments both historically and in terms of the theoretical development in the area.

Each reading is accompanied by an introduction that clarifies some of the more obscure segments of the article and focuses the reader's attention on the important aspects of the article. At the end of the introduction some questions for discussion and a reference section encourage the reader to learn more about the topic.

Some of the articles are the original papers published on the use of a particular technique or experimental paradigm (for example, article 4, "Stroop Effect"; article 14, "Brown-Peterson Task"). Some are summaries of an entire area (for example, article 3, "Spatial Cueing"). Other articles are up-to-date examinations of the phenomenon (for example, article 11, "Metacontrast Masking"). Some of the phenomena are very old (article 4 was published in 1935), and some are rather recent (article 22, "Forgot It All Along," was published in 2002). Some articles encompass several CogLab demonstrations (for example, article 16, "Working Memory" covers the irrelevant speech, memory span, and phonological similarity demonstrations). Many of the readings are the "classic" papers in the area or are the papers upon which the CogLab demonstrations are based.

The articles are ordered in the same way that the demonstrations appear on the CogLab Web site.

We are particularly indebted to Professor Richard Gregory for generously providing the original photographs of some of the illusions in his paper.

ABOUT THE AUTHORS

Aimée M. Surprenant is currently an associate professor in the Department of Psychological Sciences at Purdue University in West Lafayette, Indiana. She received her Ph.D. in cognitive psychology from Yale University in 1992 and did postdoctoral work at Indiana University in the Department of Speech and Hearing Sciences. She regularly teaches Introduction to Cognitive Psychology as well as other courses on memory, psycholinguistics, and other aspects of cognition. She co-authored the textbook *Human Memory: An Introduction to Research, Data, and Theory,* 2nd edition, also published by Thomson Wadsworth.

Greg Francis is currently an associate professor in the Department of Psychological Sciences at Purdue University in West Lafayette, Indiana. He received his Ph.D. in cognitive and neural systems from Boston University in 1993. His research investigates properties of neural networks and visual perception. He regularly teaches Introduction to Cognitive Psychology and created CogLab to give students in this course the experience of being a subject in classic experiments.

Ian Neath is currently a professor in the Department of Psychological Sciences at Purdue University in West Lafayette, Indiana. He received his Ph.D. in cognitive psychology from Yale University in 1991. He regularly teaches Introduction to Cognitive Psychology as well as courses on introductory psychology, human memory, and simulation modeling. He co-authored the textbook *Human Memory: An Introduction to Research, Data, and Theory,* 2nd edition, also published by Thomson Wadsworth.

CogLab Reader

CHAPTER ONE

Attention

1

This paper is best known for its clever explanation of a variety of past and new experimental data. The basic idea is that processing some types of visual information will produce an attentional blink during which it is difficult to process other visual information. In addition to its empirical contribution, the introduction of the paper provides an excellent review of related studies, and introduces a technique that is often used to study the temporal properties of visual attention: rapid serial visual presentation (RSVP).

In the RSVP task, stimuli are shown briefly in rapid succession. The duration of each stimulus is often only 10 milliseconds (there are 1000 milliseconds in a second), and the observer's task is to identify the properties of some of the stimuli. At first glance, it might seem as if this task has nothing to do with how we interact with the real world; however, we actually face this problem all the time. As you move around the world, the stimuli that are processed by your visual system change constantly. You move, items in the world change, and your eyes make quick jumps as they focus on various objects. Thus, your visual system is constantly trying to identify the characteristics of stimuli from a steady stream of information. The RSVP task provides a methodology for an experimenter to control the properties of that stream, and thus can study how we interact with the real world.

As the introduction of this reading notes, other studies using the RSVP task have observed a "posttarget processing deficit." The first experiment using RSVP was a replication of an earlier study, in which one letter in a stream of letters is white (the target) and all the others are black. The observer's task was to report the target and the next three letters. As Figure 1.2A shows, observers were quite good at reporting the target (serial position zero), but were unlikely to report the next three letters correctly, and instead reported letters that actually came much later in the stream. It is as if the observers "blinked" after detecting the target, and letters that came much later appeared to be right after the target.

Experiment 2 is the most important empirical part of the paper. It attempts to determine the "level" at which the blink occurs. It is common in cognitive psychology to think in terms of levels of processing. Whenever a new result is found, psychologists want to know at what level it operates. The blink found in Experiment 1 could be at the sensory, attentional, or memory level.

One possibility is that the blink in Experiment 1 might have been the result of observers seeing the letters after the target, but then forgetting them as more items appeared. Experiment 2 was designed to rule out memory effects because the task was now simply to detect the presence of a single item. Observers did not have to remember very much information, so if the blink was still found, it seems unlikely that memory was involved.

A sensory-level blink would suggest that the visual system does not acquire information about the letters right after the target, perhaps because the properties of the target (a white letter among a stream of black letters) causes some sensory masking (see Chapter 11 on metacontrast masking). In Experiment 2, sensory effects were measured by having an experimental and a control condition. In both conditions there was a white letter and possibly a black X. In both conditions the observer's task was to report whether the black X was present. However, in the experimental condition observers also had to identify the white letter, whereas in the control condition, they were told to ignore the white letter. If the blink was due to sensory-level effects, these conditions should give similar results.

If the blink is found in the experimental condition but not the control condition, then by the process of elimination, we are forced to conclude that it is the attentional demand involved in identifying the target that causes the blink, rather than memory or sensory effects. This is exactly what was found and is reported in Figure 1.3A. Experiments 3 and 4 were designed to measure different properties of the attentional mechanisms.

Since this reading was published, a variety of techniques have been used to demonstrate an attentional blink. The results of the CogLab attentional blink experiment are most similar to Experiment 2 of this paper. The CogLab experiment combines the control and experimental conditions into a single RSVP stream. In this version, two targets are presented in the RSVP stream, and the attentional blink makes the second target harder to detect than the first target.

Since its discovery, the attentional blink has been used in a variety of contexts. For example, Kavcic and Duffy (2003) report on using the attentional blink paradigm to investigate the behavior of Alzheimer's patients.

REFERENCE

Kavcic, V., & Duffy, C. J. (2003). Attentional dynamics and visual perception: Mechanisms of spatial disorientation in Alzheimer's disease. *Brain, 126,* 1173–1181.

QUESTIONS

1. What do the numbers on the x-axis of Figure 1.2A mean?
2. Explain how the idea of an attentional blink can account for the data in Figure 1.3A.
3. What is the main dependent variable in the attentional blink task?
4. What is the main difference between the control and experimental conditions in Experiment 2?
5. How does the RSVP method compare to the visual search task? (See Chapter 8, "Visual Search.")

Temporary Suppression of Visual Processing in an RSVP Task: An Attentional Blink?

Jane E. Raymond, Kimron L. Shapiro, and Karen M. Arnell

University of Calgary, Calgary, Alberta, Canada

ABSTRACT

Through rapid serial visual presentation (RSVP), we asked Ss to identify a partially specified letter (target) and then to detect the presence or absence of a fully specified letter (probe). Whereas targets are accurately identified, probes are poorly detected when they are presented during a 270-ms interval beginning 180 ms after the target. Probes presented immediately after the target or later in the RSVP stream are accurately detected. This temporary reduction in probe detection was not found in conditions in which a brief blank interval followed the target or Ss were not required to identify the target. The data suggest that the presentation of stimuli after the target but before target-identification processes are complete produces interference at a letter-recognition stage. This interference may cause the temporary suppression of visual attention mechanisms observed in the present study.

During the course of many visual activities such as reading or scanning a visual scene, the eyes alternately fixate an area of the visual field and make a saccade to a different location. Because visual processing is suppressed during the rapid saccadic eye movement (for a review, see Volkmann, 1986), this oculomotor behavior presents a rapid succession of brief, complex images to the perceptual processing system. The limits governing the brain's ability to process such a stream of stimuli can be studied in the laboratory with rapid serial visual presentation (RSVP). In this paradigm, stimuli such as letters, digits, words, or pictures are presented briefly in the same location and in rapid succession, usually in the same location (from 6 to about 20 items/s). Typically one item in the stimulus

stream, the target, is differentiated in some way (e.g., presented in a different color), and the subject's task is to identify it. It is commonly known that processing a single briefly exposed target is substantially easier than processing the same stimulus embedded in a stream of complex stimuli (Lawrence, 1971). In this sense, RSVP tasks may be viewed as visual search tasks operating in the temporal rather than the spatial domain. Just as visual search studies have been useful in investigating how visual attention may be distributed spatially (e.g., Treisman & Gelade, 1980), the RSVP procedure may be used to examine the temporal characteristics of perceptual and attentional processes.

Single-task RSVP experiments (in which only one target is identified) have provided data with regard to the temporal characteristics of the processes involved in the identification of a single target item (e.g., Lawrence, 1971) and thus have been useful in developing theories of the attentional and perceptual mechanisms that mediate such a task (e.g., McLean, D. E. Broadbent, & M. H. P. Broadbent, 1982). We review these studies and theories in the following. In addition to single-task experiments, there are a number of studies that have used a multiple-task RSVP procedure (in which two or more targets are identified). The latter studies have demonstrated that the cost of identifying the first target in a multiple-task RSVP experiment is a temporary but relatively long-lasting deficit in the identification of stimuli presented after the first target (D. E. Broadbent & M. H. P. Broadbent, 1987; Kanwisher, 1987; Kanwisher & Potter, 1989, 1990; Reeves & Sperling, 1986; Weichselgartner & Sperling, 1987). The purpose of the present article is to explore

SOURCE: From Raymond, J. E., Shapiro, K. L., & Arnell, K. M. (1992). Temporary suppression of visual processing in an RSVP task: An attentional blink? *Journal of Experimental Psychology: Human Perception and Performance, 18*(3), 849–860. Copyright © 1992 by the American Psychological Association. Reprinted with permission.

further the nature of this posttarget processing deficit by determining (a) if perceptual or attentional factors underlie the reported deficits, (b) whether such deficits are observed in a simple detection task as opposed to the more complex identification tasks previously studied, and (c) what role other items in the RSVP stream (especially those in close temporal proximity to the target) play in producing the posttarget deficit.

RSVP procedures can be categorized on the basis of the information available to the subject for identification of the target(s). In studies that use target-identification tasks (as opposed to detection tasks), targets are partially (as opposed to fully) specified and are described by both a target-defining characteristic and a to-be-reported characteristic. For example, after the presentation of an RSVP stream of letters, each with a different color, a subject might be required to supply the letter name of the only red letter in the stream. The target-defining characteristic in this example is featural, the color *red*. The to-be-reported feature is the letter name.

Single-task RSVP studies have shown that even with very rapid stimulus presentation rates, subjects are able to identify the target on a significant proportion of trials (Gathercole & D. E. Broadbent, 1984; Lawrence, 1971; McLean et al., 1982). When target-identification errors are made, however, they tend to be systematic. Analysis of such errors has been useful in modeling the processes involved in target identification. Depending on the stimuli, presentation rate, and target-defining characteristics, target-identification errors tend to be of two types: pretarget intrusions, that is, naming the to-be-reported feature from an item immediately preceding the target by n items (designated as $-n$ errors), or posttarget intrusions, that is, naming the to-be-reported feature from an item succeeding the target by n items ($+n$ errors).

When the target-defining characteristic is featural (e.g., "name the red letter"), subjects typically produce posttarget intrusion errors only (Lawrence, 1971; McLean et al., 1982). The prevalence of $+n$ errors suggests that processing of features in the target to an output stage extends beyond the time during which the target is physically present by n times the stimulus onset asynchrony (SOA). The occurrence of posttarget intrusion errors has been interpreted to indicate that target identification in filtering tasks involves two

stages: an initial (early selection) stage in which the target-defining feature is detected and a subsequent stage in which the to-be-reported feature is identified from items in the available sensory store (D. E. Broadbent & M. H. P. Broadbent, 1986, 1987; Gathercole & D. E. Broadbent, 1984; Lawrence, 1971; McLean et al., 1982). If the to-be-reported feature is identified when posttarget letters are present in the store, a posttarget intrusion error may occur. To the extent that posttarget intrusion errors can be used to indicate target processing time, RSVP studies consistently suggest that target identification is complete on most trials in approximately 100 ms for both word and letter stimuli (Gathercole & D. E. Broadbent, 1984; Lawrence, 1971; McLean et al., 1982).

An alternative explanation for posttarget intrusion errors is a late-selection two-stage model in which codes associated with target-defining and to-be-reported features in each item develop concurrently but at different rates (Keele & Neill, 1978). Posttarget intrusions would occur when the target's code for the target-defining feature and a posttarget item's code for the to-be-reported feature arrive simultaneously for attentional coordination and are integrated into one percept. McLean et al. (1982) tested this possibility by using RSVP tasks with different target-defining features. First, color was used as the target-defining feature, and target name was used as the to-be-reported feature. In the second experiment, which used the same presentation rate, the roles were reversed. A predominance of posttarget intrusions was found for both conditions, which indicates that differential speed of code development alone cannot explain intrusion errors in feature-selection RSVP tasks.

This conclusion, however, cannot be applied equally to categorical selection tasks. McLean et al. (1982) reported that RSVP tasks that use categorically defined targets produce a pattern of adjacency intrusions; that is, both 1 and -1 intrusions were equally likely. Subjects were asked to name the color (to-be-reported feature) of a numeral (target-defining category) in a stream of colored letters and found adjacency errors. McLean et al. (1982) suggested that categorically defined targets may not provide enough specificity to define the target for successful operation of the detect-then-identify model. They proposed that in such a situation, a late-selection mechanism may be used in which the codes for both target-defining and to-be-reported characteristics develop in parallel with active codes being integrated at a later stage.

Intraub (1985) found adjacency errors by using a single-task picture RSVP paradigm. The pattern of errors was found to be related to the speed of target detection. Rapidly detected targets were associated with pretarget intrusion errors, and slower target detection was associated with posttarget intrusion errors.

The results of single-task RSVP tasks clearly indicate that (a) target identification requires the conjoining of the target-defining characteristic with the to-be-reported feature, (b) feature conjunction in this task takes approximately 100 ms, and (c) the processing of such information requires attention. One might assume that once a target is identified, the perceptual and attentional mechanisms would be free to begin analyzing subsequent stimuli. Multiple-task RSVP research, however, strongly suggests that this is not the case. Rather, it appears that after target identification is presumably complete, large deficits in the processing of subsequent stimuli are found for up to 700 ms later.

Through the use of a multiple-task RSVP procedure, D. E. Broadbent and M. H. P. Broadbent (1987) asked subjects to identify two different target words (defined by uppercase letters or flanking hyphens) that were embedded at different serial positions within a stream of lowercase words. The number of items between the target words was varied. They found that when the two targets were temporally adjacent (with an SOA of 80 ms), subjects could produce a correct response to either the first or the second target but not both. As SOA was increased and other items were presented between the two targets, the probability of correctly identifying the second word when the first word was correct remained at a minimum of .1 for SOAs up to 400 ms, rising again to an asymptote of .7 with SOAs of 720 ms. Not only were subjects unable to correctly identify the second target during the 400-ms interval after the first target, they frequently reported being unaware that it had been embedded in the stimulus stream.

A similar observation that uses a multiple-task RSVP procedure, called *repetition blindness (RB)*, has been reported. Subjects viewed a stream of words that form a sentence or a stream of letters that form a word. On half the trials, one of the items in the stream was presented twice. Subjects were asked to report the sentence or word. It was found that when an item had been repeated, the subjects tended to omit the second repetition of the item in their response (Kanwisher & Potter, 1989, 1990). In other studies, a stream of unrelated words was presented and subjects were required to indicate the word they thought had occurred twice in the list (Kanwisher, 1987). Kanwisher reported that for word-presentation rates between 5.4 and 8.5 words/s, subjects showed a low probability of reporting word repetitions if 1–4 intervening words were presented between the first and second presentation of the repeated item (i.e., with SOAs of 185–741 ms). The RB effect was also found when the repeated item differed in case from the first instance (Kanwisher, 1987), when omission of the second occurrence of the repetition greatly reduced the grammaticality of the sentence to be reported (Kanwisher, 1987), and when the repeated word shared orthographic identity but had a different meaning or pronunciation than that of the first instance (Kanwisher & Potter, 1990). The effect was not found when items were presented auditorily at the same rate in compressed speech (Kanwisher & Potter, 1989) or for visually presented synonym pairs (Kanwisher & Potter, 1990). RB was found at the level of letter groups when words were the perceptual unit in a given task and at the level of letters when letters were presented one at a time in RSVP to spell words (Kanwisher & Potter, 1990).

Through another variant on the multiple-task RSVP procedure, Reeves and Sperling (1986) and Weichselgartner and Sperling (1987) observed large deficits in the processing of posttarget items. In Weichselgartner and Sperling's experiments, highly practiced subjects were presented with an RSVP stream of digits and asked to identify a highlighted or boxed digit (target) and to name the first three posttarget digits. They found that subjects' reports generally consisted of the target, the first posttarget item, and items presented about 300 and 400 ms after the target. The item presented in the interval between 100 and 300 ms posttarget was rarely reported. With this complex response requirement, it is not clear whether subjects were unable to process the item perceptually during this interval or whether they were unable to store or retrieve its memory for later recall.

In either event, a deficit in the ability to process posttarget items to an output stage was reported.

The three types of multiple-task RSVP studies outlined all indicate that the allocation of visual attention to an item in an RSVP stream produces a temporary but relatively long-lasting suppression of visual processing. These data suggest that the mechanisms involved in target identification are temporally shut down after use. It is as if the perceptual and attentional mechanisms blink. Eyeblinks produce a dramatic brief reduction in pattern vision and are only initiated after important stimuli are viewed. The results of multiple-task RSVP studies suggest that sensory and attentional mechanisms may undergo a covert analog to this overt ocular process.

Is this suppression due to attentional or sensory factors? Although the data from the RB studies suggest an attentional basis, the tasks in the RB studies are substantially different from those in the other two multiple-task RSVP studies described here. In the studies that involve identification of a visually distinct target, the posttarget processing deficit could result from sensory processes, such as visual masking of the probe by adjacent stimuli regardless of the subject's attentional state, rather than from attentional factors related to target identification. In the present study, we explore the basis for the posttarget processing deficit, either attentional or sensory. To anticipate, the present data indicate that the posttarget processing deficit does result from attentional factors.

The first experiment reported here attempts to replicate one of the experiments reported by Weichselgartner and Sperling (1987). This study was conducted to determine if our stimuli and temporal parameters are able to produce a posttarget processing deficit. In the second experiment we used a simplified multiple-task RSVP procedure somewhat similar to that of D. E. Broadbent and M. H. P. Broadbent (1987) so that visual processing following target identification could be probed systematically. In one condition, subjects were asked to identify a target letter in a letter stream; in a control condition with identical stimuli, subjects were told to ignore the target color and that identification was not required. In both conditions, subjects were also asked to detect the presence or absence of a fully specified letter presented at various intervals after the target. This experiment was per-formed to determine whether passive sensory versus active attentional processing of the target produced the posttarget processing deficit and whether this effect could be obtained with a simple posttarget detection task as opposed to the more complex identification tasks used by D. E. Broadbent and M. H. P. Broadbent (1987), Weichselgartner and Sperling (1987), and in the RB studies. In the third and fourth experiments, we used a procedure similar to that of the second experiment to investigate the role of immediate posttarget stimulation on the production of the posttarget processing deficit.

EXPERIMENT 1

The purpose of the present experiment was to replicate one of the experiments reported by Weichselgartner and Sperling (1987) with different stimuli (letters rather than digits) and slightly faster presentation rates (11 items/s rather than 10 items/s) to determine whether such stimuli could indeed produce a posttarget processing deficit. The subject's tasks were to identify a white target letter embedded in a stream of black letters and to identify the three letters presented immediately after the target letter.

Method

Subjects.   Five University of Calgary (Alberta, Canada) students and staff members (3 women, 2 men) ranging from 22 to 39 years of age volunteered to participate in the experiment. All subjects had from 90 to 180 trials of practice prior to participation. All subjects had normal or corrected-to-normal visual acuity. Informed consent was obtained prior to participation for subjects in all of the experiments reported in this article.

Apparatus.   The stimuli for this and all subsequent experiments were generated by an Apple Macintosh II computer with custom software and displayed on an Apple 13-in. (32.5-cm) color monitor. Subjects viewed the display in this and all other experiments binocularly from a distance of 35 cm and stabilized their head position with the aid of a chinrest. Responses were reported verbally and were recorded by an experimenter with the aid of a second computer.

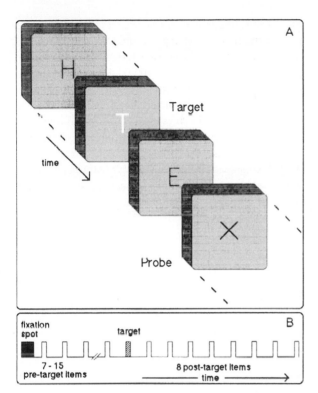

FIGURE 1.1 Panel A depicts an illustration of the rapid serial visual presentation stimuli presentation used in all of the experiments. (The target, embedded in the stimulus stream, was a white letter that subjects were required to identify in some experiments. The probe was used in Experiments 2–4. It was always a black X presented at a variable serial position after the target [except in Experiment 2, where it was also presented as the target on some trials].) Panel B depicts a diagram of the temporal arrangement used in stimulus presentation. (See text for details.)

The experimenter was unaware of the correct responses for all trials in this and all experiments.

Procedure. Each subject participated in one experimental session that consisted of 90 RSVP trials. In this and all experiments, each trial consisted of a series of successively presented simple, block-style uppercase letters, as shown in Figure 1.1. The computer randomly chose the letters to be presented from the 26 letters in the alphabet with the condition that no letter be presented twice within a trial. Each letter was presented for 15 ms with an interstimulus interval (ISI) of

75 ms, producing a presentation rate of 11.11 letters/s. Each letter was displayed singly at the same location in the center of a uniform gray field (9.1 cd/m^2) that subtended 16.3" × 12.5". Letters were 0.82" in height and approximately the same width. All letters appeared black with the exception of the target letter, which was white (32.9 cd/m^2). The number of pretarget letters was randomly chosen by the computer on each trial and varied between 7 and 15. Eight letters always succeeded the target. The uniform gray field was viewed during the ISI. Each trial began with a 180-ms presentation of a small white fixation dot. The subject initiated a trial when ready by depressing the mouse button. In this experiment, the subject was instructed to report the name of the white letter and the name of the next three letters in the stream as in the procedure used by Weichselgartner and Sperling (1987).

Results and Discussion

The group mean probability of reporting a letter anywhere in the response string is plotted as a function of the serial position of the letter in relation to the target in Figure 1.2. On the horizontal axis in this figure and all others like it, the target was assigned a relative serial position of 0; items preceding the target are given negative values and items succeeding the target were assigned positive values. A repeated measures analysis of variance (ANOVA) on the probability of reporting a letter revealed a significant main effect of relative serial position, $F(10, 40) = 69.53$, $p < .01$. Panel A of Figure 1.2 shows that the target letter and the last letter in the stream were reported with the highest and about equal probability (.8). Items presented at +1, +5, +6, and +7 serial positions were reported with about equal probability (.35), whereas post hoc multiple comparisons through the Scheffé method show that the +2 and +3 items were reported with significantly less probability ($p < .05$) than the former items. Subjects rarely reported items presented prior to the target. These data replicate the posttarget processing deficit reported by Weichselgartner and Sperling (1987), indicating that in this situation the effect is maximal during the interval between 180 and 270 ms posttarget.

Panel B of Figure 1.2 illustrates the probability of reporting an item at a specific location in the response

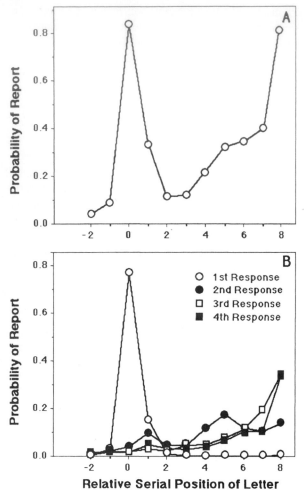

FIGURE 1.2   Panel A depicts the group mean probability of reporting a letter anywhere in the response string as a function of the letter's relative serial position in the stimulus stream. (The target's serial position is denoted as 0. Positive serial position values indicate posttarget stimuli, and negative values indicate pretarget stimuli.) Panel B depicts the group mean probability of reporting a letter at a specific position in the response string as a function of relative serial position in the stimulus stream.

string as a function of its actual serial position in the stimulus stream. Three points are of interest. First, there was a high probability (.77) that the target was reported as the first item in the response string. The +1 item, however, was occasionally reported as such, demonstrating that +1 posttarget intrusion errors were

made on average on 16% of trials. Second, the second item in the response string was most frequently the +5 item and was rarely the +2 or +3 item. Third, items reported as the third and fourth response were drawn predominantly from the last three items in the stream, which indicates that the order of item presentation was not well preserved in the verbal report, a finding consistent with previous research (Reeves & Sperling, 1986; Weichselgartner & Sperling, 1987).

The results demonstrate that a posttarget processing deficit was found with less-practiced subjects than those of the Weichselgartner and Sperling (1987) study and with slightly different stimuli and temporal parameters.

EXPERIMENT 2

The purpose of Experiment 2 was to answer two questions. First, would performance on a simple posttarget probe-detection task, as opposed to the complex posttarget identification task used in Experiment 1, be negatively affected by a prior target-identification task? Second, if so, is the posttarget processing deficit mediated by sensory or attentional factors?

Previous research demonstrating posttarget processing deficits probed the posttarget period by asking subjects to identify words (D. E. Broadbent & M. H. P. Broadbent, 1987; Kanwisher, 1987; Kanwisher & Potter, 1989, 1990) or a string of items in an RSVP stream (Reeves & Sperling, 1986; Weichselgartner & Sperling, 1987) after identifying a partially specified target. From the word-identification studies, it is unclear whether the posttarget processing deficit reported in these studies affects the mechanisms involved in word identification or acts at a lower level interfering in some way with perception of letters. Similarly, in the Weichselgartner and Sperling (1987) study, it is not possible to disentangle the role of memory or attentional or sensory factors in the posttarget processing deficit. In the present experiment, the posttarget period was probed by asking the subjects to detect a fully specified item, that is, a black X. If a posttarget processing deficit is found with this detection task, then the level of operation must be at least as low as a letter-recognition stage and is unlikely to be the result of memory-encoding difficulties or response demands.

Two conditions were conducted in this experiment. The experimental condition required subjects first to identify a white letter (target) embedded in a letter stream of black letters and subsequently to respond whether an X (probe) had been presented in the posttarget letter stream. In the control condition, subjects were told to ignore the target color and that identification was not required and simply to respond whether the X had been presented in the posttarget letter stream. This control condition was conducted to determine whether posttarget processing deficits were due to either the generation of passive sensory transients (as in masking) by the novel white target or the active attentional demand of having to identify the target.

Method

Subjects.   Ten University of Calgary students (7 women, 3 men) ranging from 19 to 37 years of age (M = 25) volunteered to participate in the experiment. All subjects were naive to the purpose of the study and participated in both experimental and control conditions within a single 60-min session. The order of conditions tested was counterbalanced.

Procedure.   For each condition, 180 RSVP letter streams (trials) were presented. The letter streams were generated the same as those for Experiment 1 except as noted in the following. In half of the trials, an X was present at one of Serial Positions 0–+8; in the remaining trials, an X was never presented. An X was never presented prior to the target and never appeared twice within a single stream. When the probe was presented as the target, it appeared to be white. The probe X was presented 10 times at each of the possible serial positions, yielding 90 probe-present trials. In the experimental condition, the subject was asked to name the white letter and to say whether an X was present or absent. In the control condition, the subject was instructed to ignore the white letter and to determine whether an X was present or absent. Subjects received 10 practice trials in each condition prior to data collection. One-minute rest breaks were given every 60 trials, and a longer rest was permitted between conditions.

Results and Discussion

Probe detection.   The group mean percentage of trials in which the probe was correctly detected is plotted as a function of the relative serial position of the probe for both conditions in Panel A of Figure 1.3. We calculated means for the experimental condition by using only those trials in which subjects identified the target correctly. For the control condition, subjects correctly detected the probe on 85% or better of trials for all probe serial positions. For the experimental condition, however, the detection of the percentage correct dropped below 60% for the posttarget interval from 180 to 450 ms.

A two-variable (Condition × Probe Serial Position) repeated measures ANOVA revealed a significant main effect of condition, $F(1, 72) = 35.23$, $p < .01$, a significant main effect of probe serial position, $F(8, 72) = 8.34$, $p < .01$, and a significant Condition × Probe Serial Position interaction, $F(8, 72) = 6.33$, $p < .01$. Multiple post hoc comparisons that used Scheffé's method revealed that the group mean percentage of probe detection for the experimental condition was significantly lower ($p < .05$) than the corresponding point for the control condition for items +2, +3, +4, and +5, indicating a significant posttarget processing deficit for the posttarget interval occurring between 180 and 450 ms. The group mean false-alarm rate for the experimental condition was 12.6% (ranging from 0% to 34%), and for the control condition it was 11.3 (ranging from 1% to 28%).

Target-identification errors.   An analysis of target-identification errors in the experimental condition revealed that the position of the probe influenced the pattern of target errors. Panel B of Figure 1.3 shows the group mean probability of reporting an item as the target as a function of the relative serial position of the reported letter. These probabilities are illustrated separately for trial types in which the probe was presented as the target, the +1 item, the +2 item, or was absent. A two-variable repeated measures ANOVA on the probability of reporting an item as the target for these trial types revealed a significant main effect of relative serial position of the letter identified as the target, $F(4, 96) = 148.53$, $p < .01$, and a significant

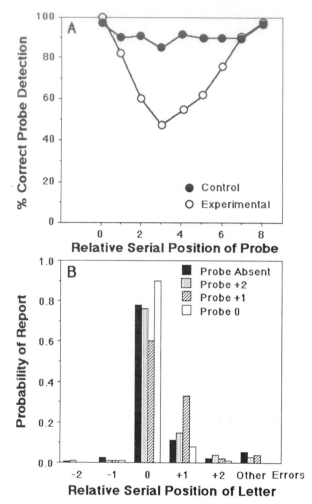

FIGURE 1.3   Panel A depicts the group mean percentage of trials in which the probe was correctly detected, plotted as a function of the relative serial position of the probe. (Closed symbols represent data obtained in the control condition in which subjects were told to ignore the target letter. Open symbols represent data obtained in the experimental condition in which subjects were told to identify the target letter.) Panel B depicts the group mean probability of reporting a letter as the target as a function of the letter's relative serial position. (The solid bars represent data for trials in which the probe was absent from the stimulus stream. The hatched and stippled bars represent data for trials in which the probe was presented as the first and second item after the target, respectively. Open bars indicate the data from trials in which the probe was presented as the target item.)

interaction effect of relative serial position of the letter identified as the target with the relative position of the probe in the stream, $F(9, 81) = 6.63$, $p < .01$.

For probe-absent trials, target-identification errors were made on 22% of trials on average. Subjects made +1 intrusion errors on 50% of these error trials or on 11% of all probe-absent trials. This number is comparable to the 16% +1 intrusion errors found in Experiment 1. The probability of +2 errors was .02, which indicates that the target-identification task was completed in less than 180 ms, because the to-be-reported feature (letter name) from a +2 item was unlikely to be conjoined with the target-defining feature (white color). A similar probability of +2 errors was found for probe-present trials, which indicates that the duration of target-identification processes was not extended because of the probe's presence.

When the probe was presented as the +1 item, +1 intrusion errors were significantly more frequent ($p < .05$) than for any other trial type. When the X was in +1 position, +1 errors accounted for 82% of the 40% total errors. Thus for this condition, +1 intrusions were made on 33% of trials, which is triple the rate of the probe-absent trials. Target-identification errors for trials in which the X was presented as the target were made only 10% of the time, which was significantly lower ($p < .05$) than for any other trial type. Eighty percent of such errors were +1 intrusions. For all other probe-present trials (probe presented at Serial Positions +2–+8), target-identification error rates did not differ significantly from those in the probe-absent trials.

The results of Experiment 2 indicate two important points. First, the probe-detection data from the experimental condition provide evidence that the posttarget processing deficit previously reported to affect the identification of words (D. E. Broadbent & M. H. P. Broadbent, 1987; Kanwisher, 1987; Kanwisher & Potter, 1990) and letter strings (Reeves & Sperling, 1986; Weichselgartner & Sperling, 1987) also affects the detection of a fully specified item. This observation suggests that the deficit operates at a relatively early stage of processing. Second, comparison of probe-detection data obtained in the experimental and control conditions demonstrate that the posttarget processing deficit is attentional. In both control and experimental conditions, the subject's visual system was stimulated with a novel white target midway through the stream of black letters. Because there was no evidence of a posttarget processing deficit in the control condition, the temporary posttarget reduction in probe detection found in the experimental condition cannot be due to low-level visual transients produced by the target. Rather, reduced performance in detecting a posttarget X must stem from attentional processes arising from the target-identification process.

A possible explanation for the effect is that failure to detect the probe in the posttarget interval in the experimental condition was due to subject's neglecting the probe-detection task to enhance accuracy on the target-identification task. Nevertheless, subjects were able to detect the probe when presented at Serial Position 1 on 80% of trials, which indicates that switching tasks could be accomplished in a short period of time. Moreover, identification errors in the experimental condition provide evidence that subjects were more readily prepared to select Xs than any other letter. In the experimental condition, the rate of +1 intrusion errors was three times as great for trials in which the probe was the +1 item than it was for probe-absent trials. Moreover, when the target was an X, +1 intrusion errors were significantly less than for other trial types. If it can be assumed that target identification involves the conjunction of the target-defining feature (white color) with the to-be-reported feature (letter name), then these data strongly suggest a preference to select Xs from the available sensory store. During the critical posttarget interval (180–450 ms), however, it appears that such a top-down selection mechanism fails to operate, possibly because lower level attentive mechanisms are suppressing input.

EXPERIMENT 3

The results from Experiment 2 suggest that the posttarget processing deficit is initiated by events related to target identification, that it is mediated by an attentional mechanism, and that this mechanism acts at a relatively early stage of visual processing. The purpose of this experiment was to investigate whether the action of the attentional suppression mechanism is ballistic once it is initiated, that is, nonadaptive to

posttarget events, or alternately whether it depends on the nature of posttarget stimulation. The experiment was designed so that if a ballistic mechanism were found, it could be determined whether it was time- or event-dependent.

Through the same RSVP procedure with both of the experimental and control conditions as in Experiment 2, posttarget stimulation was manipulated by inserting a uniform field (blank interval) of variable duration between the target and the posttarget letter stream. We reasoned that if the attentional suppression mechanism is ballistic and time-dependent, then the insertion of a blank interval between the target and the posttarget letter stream containing the probe should yield attenuated probe detection for specific posttarget times, as was seen in the experimental condition of Experiment 2. On the other hand, if suppression is ballistic but event-related, then detection of probes presented at the +2, +3, +4, or +5 positions should remain attentuated in spite of the insertion of the blank interval.

In contrast to these two possibilities, the suppression mechanism could be adaptive (i.e., sensitive) to posttarget events. If so, suppression might be initiated and maintained only when posttarget events interfered with target identification. When posttarget events do not interfere with target identification, as might be the case with a blank interval, then activity of the suppressive mechanism is not necessary, and the posttarget processing deficit can be eliminated.

Method

Subjects.   Ten University of Calgary students (9 women, 1 man) ranging from 17 to 19 years of age (M = 18) volunteered to participate in the experiment. All subjects participated in both experimental and control conditions, which were conducted in two separate 60-min sessions. The order of conditions tested was assigned randomly.

Procedure.   For each condition, 440 RSVP letter streams (trials) were presented. Stimuli and procedures were identical to that used in Experiment 2 except that in some trials a blank of variable duration was presented at the offset of the first posttarget ISI

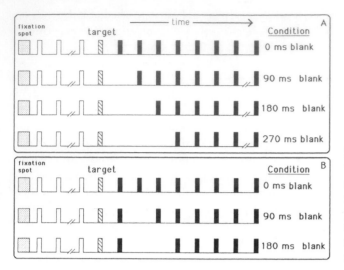

FIGURE 1.4   Diagram describing temporal characteristics of stimulus presentation in Experiment 3 (Panel A) and Experiment 4 (Panel B). (The filled rectangles indicate serial positions in which probes could be presented. There were eight posttarget letters presented in all conditions for Experiment 3 and eight, seven, and six posttarget letters presented in the 0-, 90-, and 180-ms blank conditions, respectively, of Experiment 4.)

period and before the first posttarget stimulus. This is illustrated in Panel A of Figure 1.4. Blank intervals of 0, 90, 180, and 270 ms were used. (Note that for the 0-ms blank conditions, a 75-ms posttarget ISI of blank stimulation was still presented, as in the previous experiments.) One hundred trials that contained each interval type were presented in a random order. Only half of these trials contained a probe in the posttarget letter stream. The probe was either the +1, +2, +3, +4, or +7 posttarget event. Ten trials were presented for each combination of blank duration and probe position. This set of stimulus conditions allows the comparison of probe-detection performance for items presented at either a specific interval after the target or after a specific number of events. In addition to the trial types described earlier, 40 additional trials were presented in random order among the trials described earlier, 20 with blanks of 450 ms and 20 with blanks of 540 ms. When present (on 50% of trials), probes were presented at either the +1 or +2 serial position. These trial types were used to test for probe detection with blank intervals longer than the posttarget processing deficit found in Experiment 2. In the experimental condition, the subject was asked to name the white letter and to say whether an X was present or absent. In the control condition, the subject was instructed to ignore the white letter and to determine whether an X was present or absent. Practice and rest breaks were given as in Experiment 2.

Results and Discussion

Probe detection.   Figure 1.5 shows the group mean percentage of trials in which the probe was correctly detected, plotted as a function of probe presentation time after the target for the four blank durations for the experimental condition (Panel A) and for the control condition (Panel B). We calculated means for the experimental condition by using only those trials in which subjects identified the target correctly. In the control condition, subjects correctly detected the probe on 75% or better of trials for all probe serial positions. In experimental condition trials in which the blank duration was 90 ms or longer, the probe was also detected at least 75% of the time or better for all probe positions. For experimental trials containing no blank interval (replication of Experiment 2), however, probe detection dropped to below 60% for probes presented 360 ms after the target, a result comparable to that of Experiment 2. Probe detection on trials with long blank durations (450 and 540 ms) was 85% or greater for all probe serial positions.

A three-variable (Condition × Blank Duration × Probe Serial Position) repeated measures ANOVA revealed significant main effects for blank duration, $F(3, 108) = 7.40$, $p < .01$, and probe serial position, $F(4, 108) = 3.85$, $p = .01$. The ANOVA also showed a significant Condition × Blank Duration interaction, $F(3, 108) = 12.17$, $p < .01$, a significant Blank Duration × Probe Serial Position interaction, $F(12, 108) =$

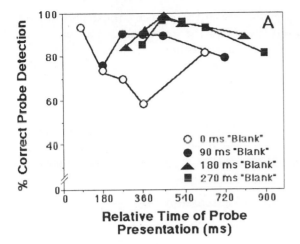

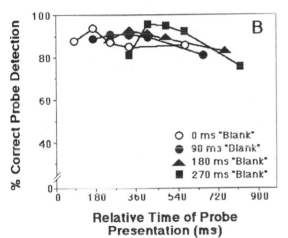

FIGURE 1.5   The group mean percentage of trials in which the probe was correctly detected in the experimental conditions (Panel A) and for the control conditions (Panel B), plotted as a function of the time of probe presentation after the target. (Open circles represent data obtained for the 0-ms blank conditions. Closed symbols represent data obtained for the 90-ms [closed circles], 180-ms [closed triangles], or 270-ms [closed squares] blank conditions.)

5.25, $p < .01$, and a significant three-way Condition × Probe Serial Position × Blank Duration interaction $F(12, 108) = 2.13$, $p < .02$. The mean false-alarm rate for the experimental condition was 5.9% (ranging from 3% to 10%); for the control condition, it was 4.0% (ranging from 1% to 9%) and did not vary as a function of blank interval duration.

Post hoc tests with the Scheffé method compared probe detectability in experimental versus control conditions for probes presented at 360 ms posttarget. Results revealed that differences were significant only for the 0-ms blank condition ($p < .05$). In addition, Scheffé tests that compared probe detectability in experimental versus control conditions for probes presented as the +4 letter regardless of its posttarget presentation time revealed that only the difference for the 0-ms blank condition was significant ($p < .05$).

This pattern of results indicates that the attentional mechanism mediating the suppression of posttarget processing is not ballistically generated by events related to the target-identification task. In accounting for their RSVP results, Weichselgartner and Sperling (1987) proposed that the target initiates both a transient and a sustained attentional response. They proposed that the transient response had a rapid buildup and decay and that the sustained response had a slow buildup. They suggested that the posttarget processing deficit occurred during the interval after the transient attentional response had decayed and before the sustained response was built up, leaving the system without an attentional mechanism. Nakayama and Mackeben (1989) proposed a similar mechanism. The results of our Experiment 3 fail to provide any evidence for this idea. Rather, the data suggest that the suppressive mechanism is sensitive to posttarget stimulation and raise the possibility that attentional suppression occurs only when posttarget stimulation interferes with target identification. Trials with a posttarget blank interval might relieve the visual system of having to process a novel stimulus immediately after the target. This would allow target-identification processes to be completed in an unencumbered fashion, thus eliminating the need to invoke a suppression of subsequent visual input.

Target-identification errors.   For 0-ms blank duration trials, subjects made target-identification errors on 32% of trials. +1 intrusion errors were made on about 15% of trials, a rate consistent with that found in Experiment 2. For trials with longer blank durations, target-identification errors dropped to 4% of trials, which indicates that target identification was significantly eased by reducing stimulation in the immediate posttarget period. Such a finding supports the conjecture that the initiation of attentional suppression results from interference in the target-identification task.

EXPERIMENT 4

Experiment 3 demonstrated that if a blank interval of at least 90 ms was inserted after the first posttarget ISI and before the first posttarget letter, no evidence of a posttarget processing deficit was obtained. These data suggest that an attentional suppressive mechanism is used only when posttarget stimulation interferes with target identification. If so, then presentation of a single posttarget item immediately following the target should be enough to elicit the suppression. In Experiment 4 we tested this possibility by repeating the experimental conditions of Experiment 3 but with blank intervals inserted between the +1 and +2 items rather than between the target and the +1 item as in Experiment 3.

Method

Subjects.   Ten University of Calgary students (7 women, 3 men) ranging from 20 to 37 years of age (M = 26) participated in the experiment to fulfill a course requirement. All subjects were naive to the purpose of the study. Each participated in a single 60-min session.

Procedure.   Each subject viewed 380 RSVP letter streams (trials). Stimuli and procedures were similar to those used in the experimental conditions of Experiment 3 except that when present, the variable-duration blank intervals were presented after the offset of the ISI following the +1 letter and before the onset of the +2 letter, as shown in Panel B of Figure 1.4. Control conditions were not conducted in the experiment. Blank intervals of 0, 90, and 180 ms were presented (the 270-ms interval was not used). One hundred sixty trials were presented with 0-ms blank durations, 120 trials were presented with 90-ms blank durations, and 100 trials were presented with 180-ms blank durations presented in a random order. Half of the trials for each duration contained a probe in the posttarget letter stream; the remaining trials did not. For 0-ms blank duration trials, the probe, when present, appeared in one of the eight posttarget positions. For the remain-

ing probe-present trials (i.e., those with blanks inserted), the probe was presented at one of the postblank letter positions and was never presented either as the target or in the +1 position. For blank durations of 90 and 180 ms, the number of postblank letters presented was five and four, respectively. Ten trials were presented for each combination of blank duration and probe position. For all trials, subjects were instructed to report the identity of the white letter and state whether the probe had been presented.

Results and Discussion

Probe detection.   Figure 1.6 shows the group mean percentage of trials in which the probe was detected correctly, plotted as a function of the time of probe presentation after the target. We calculated means for Figure 1.6 by using only those trials in which the subject identified the target correctly. We conducted a two-variable (Blank Duration × Probe Serial Position) repeated measures ANOVA on the data obtained for

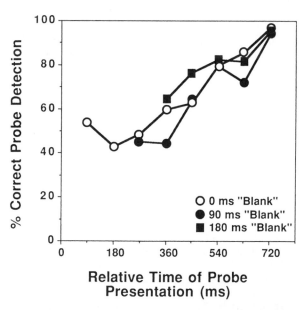

FIGURE 1.6   The group mean percentage of trials in which the probe was correctly detected (experimental conditions), plotted as a function of the time of probe presentation after the target. (Open circles represent data obtained for the 0-ms blank conditions. Closed symbols represent data obtained for the 90-ms [closed circles] and 180-ms [closed squares] blank conditions.)

trials in which probes were presented 360 ms post-target and later, because probes were presented at these times for all blank conditions. This analysis revealed a significant main effect of probe serial position, $F(4, 72) = 17.90$, $p < .01$, a marginally significant main effect of blank duration, $F(2, 72) = 4.76$, $p < .05$, and a nonsignificant interaction effect, which indicates that probe presentation time affected probe detection equally for all blank duration conditions. Scheffé post hoc tests revealed that performance on the probe-detection task averaged across probe presentation time was slightly but significantly greater for the 180-ms blank duration condition than for the 90-ms blank duration condition ($p < .01$). Post hoc tests also revealed that performance on the probe-detection task, averaging across blank duration condition, was significantly worse when probes were presented 360 ms after the target than the average performance for probes presented 540, 630, and 720 ms after the target ($p < .01$). For all three blank durations, probes presented 360 ms after the target were correctly detected on less than 65% of trials. This result is comparable to results shown for the experimental conditions of Experiments 2 and 3 (no blank condition) and constitutes a posttarget processing deficit. When probes were presented 540 ms or more after the target, however, on average they were correctly detected on greater than 85% of trials. The group mean false-alarm rate for all conditions was 11.4% (ranging from 3.2% to 21.6%) and did not vary as a function of blank interval duration.

Target-identification errors. The rates of target-identification errors were similar for the three blank durations, ranging from 17% (no blank condition) to 24% (90-ms blank duration condition). The rate of +1 intrusion errors was also similar for all blank durations, ranging from 7% for the no-blank condition to 10% for the 90-ms blank duration condition. These error rates are consistent with those obtained in Experiment 2 and for the no-blank condition in Experiment 3 and are approximately double the rate found in any of the conditions in Experiment 3 containing a significant blank interval.

Unlike the results of Experiment 3, the results of this experiment demonstrate that a significant posttarget processing deficit can be produced when pro-longed intervals (> 90 ms) lacking in visual input are inserted into the posttarget stimulus stream. In Experiment 3, the blank intervals were presented immediately after the target, whereas in the present experiment, the identical-duration blank intervals were presented after the +1 letter. The difference in the results obtained indicates that the posttarget processing deficit must result from the presentation of a letter stimulus immediately after the target. This finding strongly suggests that the attentional suppression mediating the posttarget processing deficit is only initiated when posttarget stimuli are presented with enough temporal proximity to the target to interfere with its identification.

These data also suggest that once initiated, the attentional suppression acts ballistically and is non-adaptive to levels of stimulation during the posttarget period. If the suppressive mechanism were sensitive to the nature of posttarget stimulation in effect during suppression, then there should have been a significant interaction between blank duration condition and time of probe presentation. Because the magnitude of the deficit for probes presented 360 ms after target presentation did not differ for the short and long blank durations, it can be concluded that the mechanism mediating the posttarget suppression is insensitive to stimulation presented after the +1 item.

GENERAL DISCUSSION

In Experiment 1, which used the RSVP paradigm of Weichselgartner and Sperling (1987), subjects were asked to report a partially specified target letter and the first three items following the target. Letters presented at the +2 and +3 relative serial positions were reported with a very low probability, and letters presented later in the stimulus stream were reported with a significantly greater probability. Experiment 2 explored this selective neglecting of posttarget items by maintaining the same target-identification task but simplifying the task requirement after target identification by asking subjects to detect a single fully specified letter (probe). Three main points should be noted with regard to the data obtained in Experiment 2.

First, target-identification errors (experimental condition) were made in 22% of trials; 50% of these errors were +1 intrusion errors. (The bulk of the remaining target-identification errors were random naming of letters, which suggests an overall lapse of attention during those trials.) Target-identification errors for Experiments 3 (0-ms blank experimental conditions) and 4 (all conditions) were similar both quantitatively and qualitatively. The preponderance of +1 intrusion errors indicate that the to-be-reported feature of the +1 item and the target-defining feature of the target were conjoined incorrectly on a significant proportion of trials. These data suggest that target-identification processes remain somewhat sensitive to incoming stimuli for about 105 ms (the time of offset of the +1 item) and that target-identification processes in this task are complete in less than 180 ms (the time of the onset of the +2 item) in at least 89% of trials.

Second, detection of the probe was significantly and dramatically suppressed for 450 ms after the target had been presented in the experimental (identify target) condition. This suggests that the deficit in posttarget identification and report seen in Experiment 1 results from a suppression in visual processing operating at a relatively early detection stage, as opposed to a later identification stage, as has been suggested by previous research (D. E. Broadbent & M. H. P. Broadbent, 1987).

Third and most important, the posttarget processing deficit was not found in the control (ignore target) condition. This finding clearly shows that the posttarget processing deficit results from attentional factors instead of sensory factors such as masking. In the control condition, the white target letter failed to produce any masking effects of immediately subsequent (+1) probes. Moreover, because probe detection in the control condition was greater than 85% for all probe locations, detection of probes presented later in the posttarget stream was obviously not masked by immediately preceding or succeeding items.

The results reported here provide a dramatic demonstration of an attentional blinklike process. The loose analogy of this effect to an eyeblink is based on its temporal characteristics. First, the lid closure during an eyeblink is accompanied by visual suppression lasting about 150 ms (Volkman, Riggs, & Moore, 1980). The duration of the posttarget processing deficit was 180 ms for Experiment 1, and when found in

Experiments 2–4, was between 180 and 270 ms. Second, an eyeblink is typically initiated after information in a scene is acquired. Similarly, in the RSVP task, the drop in probe detectability seen in Experiment 2 becomes significant for probes presented after target identification is complete.[1] Third, like an eyeblink, the attentional blink appears to be ballistic.

In Experiments 3 and 4, short blank intervals were embedded in the posttarget letter stream to determine whether the attentional blink was initiated by the presentation of the target per se or by the posttarget stimuli interfering with target identification. The explanation offered by Weichselgartner and Sperling (1987) for the posttarget processing deficit was that it does not result from any sort of suppression but rather reflects the interval between a rapid automatically cued attentional response and a slower, more controlled attentional response, both of which occur in response to the target. The results of the present experiments do not support this explanation. Rather, our data show that if visual input is eliminated for 165 ms after target offset (a blank interval is inserted in which the +1 item would have been), a posttarget processing deficit is not produced. If a similar-duration blank interval is inserted in place of the +2 item (Experiment 4), however, a large posttarget processing deficit is produced. These results suggest that an attentional blink is initiated only if novel visual input occurs before target-identification processes are complete.

A Model for the Attentional Blink

On the basis of these data obtained in the four experiments described here, we can postulate that the following sequence of events may lead to an attentional blink. During the presentation of the RSVP stream of letters, the white color of the target is detected preattentively. This information is then used to initiate an attentional response to facilitate target identification. If attention is allocated episodically, as suggested by Sperling and Weichselgartner (1990), then target identification may involve the opening and closing of a gate to regulate the flow of postreceptoral visual information to recognition centers of the brain (Reeves & Sperling, 1986). According to this model, an attentional episode begins (i.e., the gate opens) when the target-defining feature is detected and continues until target identification is complete. The presentation of a new item (+1 item) immediately after the target but before the termination of the attentional episode will result in features of the +1 item being processed along with features of the target item. This possibility is supported by the observation that probes presented in the +1 position were detected on an average of 82% of trials in experiments in which attentional blinks were found. The availability of features from both the target and the +1 item in the sensory store, however, will provide the identification mechanism with confusing information: two letter colors and two letter names. Extrapolating from visual search research, similarity theory (Duncan & Humphreys, 1989) suggests that the greater the similarity between the target and the +1 letter (distractor), the greater the potential for confusion. The serial report data of Weichselgartner and Sperling (1987) and in our own replication of that study show that the temporal order of information is not preserved, which supports this idea. Thus, the target color and the target name may be inappropriately matched on some occasions, resulting in Serial Position 1 intrusions.

This potential confusion is noted by the system and then used to initiate a suppressive mechanism to eliminate further confusion. When confusion is not present (i.e., target identification can reach completion without interference from new stimuli), the attentional gate is merely closed, and the next attentional episode can be initiated rapidly (i.e., probes can be readily detected at any time). When confusion is present, however, the attentional gate is both shut and locked, making the initiation of the next attentional episode a more time-consuming process than if a locking operation had not been conducted. The possibility of a shut-and-lock procedure when interference is present is supported by the finding (reported here) that once initiated, suppression of visual processing lasts for the same amount of time whether there is a steady stream of new stimulation being presented or not (Experiment 4). The extent of interference should depend on the temporal relationship between the target and +1 item (Experiments 3 and 4), the similarity between these two items, and the similarity between the +1 item and the other nontarget items in the stream (Duncan & Humphreys, 1989). Experiments

to test the latter two possibilities are currently underway. In the blink analogy, the locking of the gate is like the closing of an eyelid.

Relationship to Other Multiple-Task RSVP Experiments, Including RB

Can this model be used to account for previous data in which posttarget processing deficits have been found? The RSVP experiments of Reeves and Sperling (1986), Weichselgartner and Sperling (1987), and D. E. Broadbent and M. H. P. Broadbent (1987) all involved the identification of a partially specified target as the initial task and the identification of one or more subsequent items. The shut-and-lock model suggests that the posttarget processing deficits reported in these studies result because the +1 item was presented before identification of the target was complete. The close temporal proximity of the +1 item to the target caused interference in the target-identification task and thus produced an attentional blink. During the blink, items could not be detected easily and thus their identification was impaired. That detection and not identification was impaired in the D. E. Broadbent and M. H. P. Broadbent (1987) study is supported by their comment that subjects in this experiment were often unaware that a second target had been presented.

Application of the shut-and-lock model to the findings in RB experiments (Kanwisher, 1987; Kanwisher & Potter, 1989, 1990) is more problematic. There are two striking similarities between the RB results and those reported in the present article. First, the duration of the RB effect closely parallels the duration of the attentional blink. Kanwisher (1987) found that recall of a repeated word is significantly reduced in relation to nonrepeated words in an RSVP task if the repeated word is presented within about 500 ms of its first presentation. In the present experiments, probe detectability recovered to control levels about 540 ms after the target. Second, no RB was found for repeated items presented during the critical posttarget (first instance) interval if slow presentation rates were used, that is, if the SOA between the first presentation of a word and the next item in the string was 250 ms. Thus, in both the RB paradigm and the probe-detection procedure used in our studies, it appears that if recognition of an item can proceed without the occurrence of immediate novel stimulation, then difficulties in processing subsequent stimuli are eliminated.

Although the results of the RB studies and the present data bear a resemblance on the aforementioned points, there is a distinct difference in the two tasks. In Kanwisher's (1987) RB experiment, subjects were required to indicate which word had been repeated in an RSVP stream of randomly related words. In the later studies, the order of item presentation was constrained so that words constructed sentences or letters constructed words, and the subject's task was to report the sentence or the word (Kanwisher & Potter, 1990). These tasks, especially the latter, required subjects to identify each item in the stream. They may have used their attentional mechanisms in a mode quite different from that in multiple-task RSVP studies in which identification of a clearly demarcated target stimulus is the first task and stimulus items are unrelated to each other.[2]

Kanwisher and Potter (1990) explained their results by suggesting that each word in the stream is recognized as the first instance (token) of a specific stimulus (type). When a word is repeated, it is also recognized (typed), but it is not individualized from the first instance (i.e., it is not tokenized). Support for the idea that the repeated item is typed but not tokenized comes from the finding that subjects can recall the last word in an RSVP string with slightly greater accuracy when the last item is a repeated item (52%) than when it is a nonrepeated item (35%) and both are followed by a mask (Kanwisher, 1987).

Our shut-and-lock model accounts for these data by suggesting that an attentional episode is initiated with the presentation of each item because each must be recognized and therefore attended. The model further suggests that the attentional gate is closed and locked for about 400 ms after the presentation of the next item. How, then, is it that a nonrepeated item is recognized on about 80% of trials? Perhaps when subjects must attend to every item in the stream and are attempting to link items in a meaningful manner, the attentional gate behaves more like an attentional filter, that is, is more effective at locking out stimuli with high visual similarity to items previously processed than other items. When subjects need attend only to a stimulus that is highly localized in the temporal domain (i.e., a target) and do not need to relate information from one item to information in subsequent items, the gate may be less permeable, reducing detectability of all stimuli. Experiments are currently underway to determine the characteristics of stimuli screened out during an attentional blink and the relationship between the target task and the probe task.

The results of the experiments described here demonstrate that if attention has been allocated to a stimulus presented briefly at time $t = 0$, and if a distracting item has been presented while target identification of that stimulus is still underway, attention cannot be consistently reallocated to new stimuli presented during the interval of $t = 180$ ms to $t = 450$ ms. These data suggest that attentional mechanisms "blink," that is, transiently limit visual processing, when the flow of visual information interferes with an attention-demanding task.

AUTHOR NOTES

This research was supported by National Science and Engineering Research Council (NSERC) Operating Grant 0GP0000526 to Jane E. Raymond and NSERC Operating Grant 0GP0001279 to Kimron L. Shapiro. Karen M. Arnell was supported by an NSERC Summer Studentship. Part of this research was presented at the November 1990 annual meeting of the Psychonomic Society in New Orleans.

We thank Cathy Laughlin and Sandra Drake for assistance in testing subjects and contributing to the development of ideas expressed here. We are grateful to Bernie T. Wieser for writing the software used in this study.

Karen M. Arnell is now at the Department of Psychology, University of Waterloo, Waterloo, Ontario, Canada.

Correspondence concerning this article should be addressed to Jane E. Raymond, Department of Psychology, University of Calgary, Calgary, Alberta, Canada T2N 1N4.

ENDNOTES

1. Although not systematically measured in the present experiments, oculomotor measurements of subjects participating in other highly similar experiments were conducted and revealed that subjects do inhibit eyeblinks during the viewing of an RSVP stream.

2. It is interesting to note that Kanwisher and Potter (1990) conducted an RSVP experiment in which subjects were required to recall a stream of seven unrelated letters. They reported that subjects' performance was substantially worse on this task compared with condi-

tions in which the sequence of letters was arranged so that a word was spelled. This indicates that if items are linked in some way, visual processing of RSVP stimuli is facilitated.

REFERENCES

Broadbent, D. E., & Broadbent, M. H. P. (1986). Encoding speed of visual features and the occurrence of illusory conjunctions. *Perception, 15,* 515–524.

Broadbent, D. E., & Broadbent, M. H. P. (1987). From detection to identification: Response to multiple targets in rapid serial visual presentation. *Perception & Psychophysics, 42,* 105–113.

Duncan, J., & Humphreys, G. (1989). Visual search and stimulus similarity. *Psychological Review, 96,* 433–458.

Gathercole, S. E., & Broadbent, D. E. (1984). Combining attributes in specified and categorized target search: Further evidence for strategic differences. *Memory & Cognition, 12,* 329–337.

Intraub, H. (1985). Visual dissociation: An illusory conjunction of pictures and forms. *Journal of Experimental Psychology. Human Perception and Performance, 11,* 431–442.

Kanwisher, N. G. (1987). Repetition blindness: Type recognition without token individuation. *Cognition, 27,* 117–143.

Kanwisher, N. G., & Potter, M. C. (1989). Repetition blindness: The effects of stimulus modality and spatial displacement. *Memory & Cognition, 17,* 117–124.

Kanwisher, N. G., & Potter, M. C. (1990). Repetition blindness: Levels of processing. *Journal of Experimental Psychology: Human Perception and Performance, 16,* 30–47.

Keele, S. W., & Neill, W. T. (1978). Mechanisms of attention. In E. C. Carterette & M. P. Friedman (Eds.), *Handbook of perception IX* (pp. 3–47). New York: Academic Press.

Lawrence, D. H. (1971). Two studies of visual search for word targets with controlled rates of presentation. *Perception & Psychophysics, 10,* 85–89.

McLean, J. P., Broadbent, D. E., & Broadbent, M. H. P. (1982). Combining attributes in rapid serial visual presentation tasks. *Quarterly Journal of Experimental Psychology, 35A,* 171–186.

Nakayama, K., & Mackeben, M. (1989). Sustained and transient components of focal visual attention. *Vision Research, 29,* 1631–1647.

Reeves, A., & Sperling, G. (1986). Attention gating in short term visual memory. *Psychological Review, 93,* 180–206.

Sperling, G., & Weichselgartner, E. (1990, November). *Episodic theory of visual attention.* Paper presented at the meeting of the Psychonomic Society, New Orleans, LA.

Treisman, A. M., & Gelade, G. (1980). A feature-integration theory of attention. *Cognitive Psychology, 12,* 97–136.

Volkmann, F. C. (1986). Human visual suppression. *Vision Research, 26,* 1401–1416.

Volkmann, F. C., Riggs, L. A., & Moore, R. K. (1980). Eyeblinks and visual suppression. *Science, 207,* 900–902.

Weichselgartner, E., & Sperling, G. (1987). Dynamics of automatic and controlled visual attention. *Science, 238,* 778–780.

2 | SIMON EFFECT

This short, unassuming paper describes the results of a single experiment in which observers heard a tone presented to either the left or the right ear and made corresponding left or right movements with a sliding handle. In one condition observers were asked to move the handle away from the source of the sound; thus, a tone played to the right ear should produce a movement to the left, while a tone played to the left ear should produce a movement to the right. In a second condition observers were asked to move the handle toward the source of the sound. Simon found that people could start their movements faster if they moved in the same direction as the source of the sound. As Simon noted, it seemed that people had a natural tendency to respond toward the location of the sound. This is an example of what is now called the Simon effect.

This simple finding has significant application for man–machine interfaces. Good interfaces are ones in which the actions of the human feel natural according to the information provided by the machine. The Simon effect suggests that human responses will tend to be faster and more natural if they are toward the source of a stimulus. Thus, for example, imagine that you are flying a plane, and the left engine has a problem. The controls for that engine should be to the left of a corresponding indicator for the right engine. If it is the other way around, you may adjust the wrong engine. That could be problematic, to say the least!

In addition to its practical applications, the Simon effect has also been used to investigate details of human cognition. Many theories of cognition propose that there are separate stages of information processing. Even in a simple experiment like this one, a person must process a variety of information and make some decisions. First, the observer must identify the stimulus (sensory stage): Was there a tone? Second, the observer must decide what kind of response to make to the tone (response stage): Should the handle be moved to the left or to the right? Third, the observer must execute the response (motor execution): Organize the muscles of the back, arm, and hand to move the joystick.

Although this early paper gave little indication of it, subsequent work suggested that the Simon effect had its influence on the second stage: response selection. This conclusion was made partly by a process of elimination. The stimulus identification task was trivial because the observer was to respond as soon as any stimulus was present. Likewise, Simon's data suggested that motor execution was not influenced by the location of the stimulus. Thus, the Simon effect interferes with the response selection stage of information processing. The Simon effect makes observers faster when its influences tend to agree with the task (respond in the same direction as the source of the sound) and makes observers slower when its influences tend to oppose the task (respond in the opposite direction as the source of the sound).

The interference properties of the Simon effect can be used to study how people make their response selections. In particular, an experimenter can ask people to respond in certain ways to different sets of stimuli, and then observe how the Simon effect interferes with completing the tasks. Simon interference can be used to identify properties of the response selection stage of information processing. Much of cognition involves making responses under various situations, and the Simon effect is widely used to study the details of this key cognitive process.

In the CogLab version of the Simon effect, observers are asked to choose their responses (left or right keys on the keyboard) according to the color of small squares of light that are presented on either the right or the left of the screen. This version of the experiment is more complicated than Simon's because the observer must process the color of the stimulus in order to identify how to respond. However, this increased complexity allows an experimenter, across a variety of studies, to explore the cognitive details of how people establish and maintain mappings between stimuli and responses. Understanding these interactions between perception and action is one of the fundamental issues in cognitive psychology. For a more in-depth discussion of the Simon effect and related perception–action topics, see Proctor and Dutta (1995).

REFERENCE

Proctor, R. W., & Dutta, A. (1995). *Skill acquisition and human performance.* Thousand Oaks, CA: Sage.

QUESTIONS

1. Simon distinguishes between reaction time (RT) and motion time (MT). What are the differences?
2. In summarizing his results, Simon notes that RT was faster for "abductive reactions to the right." What does this mean?
3. Did the sex of the observers have any influence on the RT results?
4. The magnitude of the Simon effect is often measured as the difference between the RT when the movement is away from the stimulus and the RT when the movement is toward the stimulus. Use Table 2.1 to calculate the magnitude of the Simon effect in this study.

Reactions Toward the Source of Stimulation

J. Richard Simon

University of Iowa

ABSTRACT

Sixty-four Ss *used their right hand to move a control handle to the right or left from the midline of the body depending on the ear in which they heard a 1,000-cps tone. The* Ss *moved the handle toward the side of the ear stimulated for one block of 50 trials (25 to each ear in a random sequence) and away from the side of the ear stimulated for another block. Reactions toward the stimulus source were significantly faster than reactions away. Reaction time was faster for reactions to the right, while movement time was faster for movements to the left.*

This research was concerned with determining whether reaction time (RT) is faster when a response is directed toward the source of stimulation than when it is directed away from the stimulus source. In a recent experiment, Simon and Rudell (1967) had Ss press right- or left-hand keys in response to commands of "right" or "left," which were presented to the right or left ear. RT was significantly faster when the content of the command corresponded with the ear stimulated (i.e., "right" in right ear or "left" in left ear) than when it did not (i.e., "right" in left ear or "left" in right ear). In other words, the rate of information processing was affected by a cue irrelevant to the task itself, the ear in which the command was heard. In a subsequent study, Simon (1968) demonstrated that this phenomenon was not caused by a simple isomorphic association between ear stimulated and ipsilateral hand since the response interference also occurred in a unimanual task. Alternatively, it appeared that the irrelevant cue affecting RT was a "natural" tendency to respond toward the source of stimulation. The present study was designed to test this basic notion.

METHOD

Subjects.   The Ss were 32 male and 32 female undergraduates, who ranged in age from 18 to 24. All Ss classified themselves as strongly right-handed and reported using their right hand exclusively to write, turn a screwdriver, throw a ball, hold a toothbrush, and swing a tennis racket. The Ss all passed a standard audiometric screening test in which pure tones of 1,000 and 2,000 cps were presented to each ear separately.

Apparatus.   The apparatus measured choice RT and movement time (MT) to the onset of a 1,000-cps monaural tone, which S heard through one of two Grason-Stadler TDH-39 matched earphones. The S's task was, using his right hand, to move a control handle to either the right or the left from a center position depending on the ear in which he heard the tone. A klockounter which measured RT started when the tone was presented and stopped when S moved the handle from the center position. Another klockounter, which measured MT, started when the handle had been moved from the center position and stopped when the 10-in. lateral movement had been completed.

A random sequence of stimulus tones was recorded on tape, half in the right channel and half in the left, and presented by a Sony TC-500 stereocorder. Each tone was 500 msec. in duration and approximately 85-db. SPL. A 2,000-cps binaural ready signal was presented 2 sec. prior to each tone. There was a 7-sec. interval between trials.

Procedure and experimental design.   Each S performed on two blocks of trials. Each block involved responding to a recorded random sequence of 50 stimulus tones, 25 in the right ear and 25 in the left. The S was told, "This is a test to see how quickly you can react and move in response to a tone which you will hear either in your right ear or left ear." In one block of trials, he was instructed to:

> move the control handle away from the side of the ear stimulated. In other words, when you hear the tone in your left ear, move the control handle to the right as quickly as possible, and when you hear the tone in your right ear, move the control handle to the left as quickly as possible.

In the second block of trials, S heard the same sequence of stimulus tones, but this time was instructed to "move the control handle *toward* the side of the ear stimulated." Each block of test trials was preceded by four practice trials, two in the right ear and two in the left.

Half of the males and half of the females performed the "away" block first and the "toward" block second, while the other half of each group performed in the reverse sequence. For half of the Ss in each Sex × Sequence subgroup, the earphones were reversed to balance out any differences that may have existed between the two stimulus channels.

RESULTS

Table 2.1 summarizes the means of the median RTs and MTs which were computed for each S for each of the four responses; i.e., right responses and left re-

sponses made both toward and away from the ear stimulated. Analysis of variance revealed that RT toward the stimulus source was significantly faster than RT away (292 vs. 351 msec.), $F(1, 60) = 145.12$, $p < .001$, and that RT to the right was significantly faster than RT to the left (312 vs. 330 msec.), $F(1, 60) = 9.03$, $p < .01$. None of the other main effects or interactions were significant. A comparable analysis of the MT data revealed no differences between movements toward and away from the ear stimulated. Movements to the left were, however, significantly faster than movements to the right (177 vs. 199 msec.), $F(1, 60) = 175.92$, $p < .001$, and males moved significantly faster than females (166 vs. 211 msec.), $F(1, 60) = 18.20$, $p < .001$.

DISCUSSION

Results clearly indicated that Ss reacted faster when instructed to move a control handle toward instead of away from the side of the ear stimulated. These data may be explained by postulating a "natural" tendency to react toward the source of stimulation. The necessity for overriding this stereotype before responding to the tones presented in the "away" block of trials would account for the slower information processing during that block. The interference observed here and in previous studies (Simon, 1968; Simon & Rudell, 1967) may be a manifestation of the orienting reflex (OR), which, when fully developed can involve a specific molar reaction of turning toward the source of

TABLE 2.1   Reaction Time and Movement Time (in msec.) to Monaural Tones as a Function of Instructions, Direction of Response, and Sex

Group	Instructions	Reaction time Direction of response			Movement time Direction of response		
		Right	Left	M	Right	Left	M
Males	Toward source	269	301	285	175	152	164
	Away from source	341	362	352	178	157	168
	M	305	332	318	177	155	166
Females	Toward source	291	306	299	223	200	212
	Away from source	347	353	350	221	201	211
	M	319	329	324	222	200	211
All Ss	Toward source	280	304	292	199	176	188
	Away from source	344	357	351	200	179	189
	M	312	330	321	199	177	188

stimulation (Razran, 1961). Ordinarily, however, the OR evoking capacity of a stimulus decreases with repeated presentations, whereas the present findings show no evidence of representing a transient phenomenon. The reaction toward the stimulus source observed in this study has its analogues in other areas of research. For example, Chun, Pawsat, and Forster (1960), in their work on sound localization, found that infants over 26 wk. of age turn their heads and eyes toward the source of a sound and some even reach out for the sound source. The taxes or directed orientation reactions of lower animals (Fraenkel & Gunn, 1961) provide another interesting parallel.

Other aspects of the present results bear mention. Whereas RT was significantly faster for abductive reactions to the right (toward the side of the responding member), MT was significantly faster for movements to the left (toward the opposite arm). These findings confirm results of an earlier study in which the same motor response was employed (Simon, 1968). Brown and Slater-Hammel (1949) have also found that right-to-left lateral movements of the right hand were faster than left-to-right, but they did not find that the direction of the move affected RT.

AUTHOR NOTE

Requests for reprints should be sent to J. Richard Simon, Department of Psychology, University of Iowa, Iowa City, Iowa 52240.

REFERENCES

Brown, J. S., & Slater-Hammel, A. T. (1949). Discrete movements in the horizontal plane as a function of their length and direction. *Journal of Experimental Psychology, 39*, 84–95.

Chun R. W. M., Pawsat, R., & Forster, F. M. (1960). Sound localization in infancy. *Journal of Nervous and Mental Disease, 130*, 472–476.

Fraenkel, G. S., & Gunn, D. L. (1961). *The orientation animals.* New York: Dover.

Razran, G. (1961). The observable unconscious and the inferable conscious in current Soviet psychophysiology: Interoceptive conditioning, semantic conditioning, and the orienting reflex. *Psychological Review, 68*, 81–147.

Simon, J. R. (1968). Effect of ear stimulated on reaction time and movement time. *Journal of Experimental Psychology, 78*, 344–346.

Simon, J. R., & Rudell, A. P. (1967). Auditory S-R compatibility: The effect of an irrelevant cue on information processing. *Journal of Applied Psychology, 51*, 300–304.

3   SPATIAL CUEING

To focus our attention on something, we often stare directly at it. However, it is easy to verify that we can attend to things that we do not stare at directly. Fixate some object across the room and then pay attention to other objects. A significant property of this kind of attentional focus is that it helps determine what object we will look at next. This paper reviews a variety of spatial cueing experiments that investigate how we focus visual attention in space.

The basic experiment is described in Figure 3.1 of this paper. The observer was instructed to respond as quickly as possible when a target appeared, and reaction time (RT) was measured. A cue was presented before the target that biased the observer to direct attention to one side of the visual screen. If the target appeared on the same side as attention was directed, the RT was faster, but if the target appeared on the opposite side, RT was slower (Figure 3.2).

With this simple experimental task, it became possible to investigate many different properties of attention. For example, does attention move in a digital or an analog way? That is, if you have attention focused on one place, and then move it to a second place, does the attention have to move over some path from the first to second place (analog) or can it jump from the first to the second (digital)? With an appropriately constructed spatial cueing task (see text near Figure 3.4), the evidence suggests that spatial attention moves in an analog way.

The data generated by spatial cueing experiments led to the development of a "spotlight" theory of attention. This theory suggests that visual attention can be focused on different regions in space, much like a flashlight can illuminate only parts of a dark room. Spatial attention cannot be divided between two separate regions, although the beam of attention can be made larger or narrower as necessary. To move the attentional beam from one place to another takes time and requires that the beam go over the spaces between the two locations. Although exceptions to this description of spatial attention exist, it remains a fairly good description of the basic properties of spatial attention.

Much of the reading focuses on the relationship between attention and eye movements. In everyday situations we look directly at the things we want to attend, so where your eyes are focused is the same place where attention is focused. This direction of the eyes is sometimes called *overt* attention, because other people can see where you are looking. A key property of spatial attention is that it can be separated from eye movements, thereby allowing for a type of *covert* attention. Even if the observer's eyes are fixed on the middle of the screen, attention can be focused to specific places to the left or right side of the middle.

The discussion on *efference theory* reports tests of a particular theory that hypothesized that covert attention is a sort of preparation for a subsequent eye movement to that location. A series of complicated spatial cueing experiments led to the conclusion that efference theory was not correct because covert attention could be moved in a direction opposite of eye movements.

The CogLab version of the spatial cueing experiment is most similar to the experiment described in Figure 3.1 of this reading. The task is simply to respond as quickly as the target is detected. Your data should be similar to the data generated by the "Simple" task described in Figure 3.2 of the reading.

The spotlight theory of attention is not the only possibility. Other researchers have suggested that attention can be guided at an object level. Moreover, there is much interest in identifying the neurophysiological mechanisms that are responsible for attention effects. See Pei, Pettet, and Norcia (2002) for a recent investigation of these topics.

REFERENCE

Pei, F., Pettet, M. W., & Norcia, A. M. (2002). Neural correlates of object-based attention. *Journal of Vision*, *2*(9), 588–596, http://journalofvision.org/2/9/1/.

QUESTIONS

1. Describe the difference between a valid and an invalid trial in a spatial cueing experiment.
2. Why do you think Posner and others tend to use reaction time instead of percentage correct detections?
3. In the introduction, Posner distinguishes between *orienting* and *detecting*. Which behavior is measured in the basic spatial cueing experiments?
4. Why do you think spatial cueing experiments have the cue be valid on only 80% of the trials? Why not have the trials be 100% valid?
5. Explain how the spotlight theory of attention accounts for the finding that the RT for neutral trials is between that for the invalid and valid trials.

Orienting of Attention[1]

Michael I. Posner

University of Oregon

ABSTRACT

Bartlett viewed thinking as a high level skill exhibiting ballistic properties that he called its "point of no return." This paper explores one aspect of cognition through the use of a simple model task in which human subjects are asked to commit attention to a position in visual space other than fixation. This instruction is executed by orienting a covert (attentional) mechanism that seems sufficiently time locked to external events that its trajectory can be traced across the visual field in terms of momentary changes in the efficiency of detecting stimuli. A comparison of results obtained with alert monkeys, brain injured and normal human subjects shows the relationship of this covert system to saccadic eye movements and to various brain systems controlling perception and motion. In accordance with Bartlett's insight, the possibility is explored that similar principles apply to orienting of attention toward sensory input and orienting to the semantic structures used in thinking.

INTRODUCTION

Sir Frederic Bartlett wrote a book, *Thinking*, during the last part of his life (Bartlett, 1958). It is not as widely known as his earlier work, *Remembering* (Bartlett, 1932), but it had a strong impact on me, perhaps because it was among the first psychology books I read. Bartlett's theme was as simple as it was powerful. Thinking is a skill and should be studied with the techniques that had proved successful in the study of other skilled behaviour. In particular, I was struck with Bartlett's metaphor that thinking, like swinging a bat, has a "point of no return." Once committed in a particular direction, thought is ballistic in that it cannot be altered.

It may be hard to understand why this idea should have been so exciting to someone reading the psychological literature in 1959. In retrospect, what captured the imagination must have been the idea that a hidden psychological process like the formation of a thought might be rendered sufficiently concrete to measure. Twenty years later, when psychologists routinely measure the speed of rotation of visual images (Cooper and Shepard, 1973) or the time needed to scan the next item of an internally stored list (Sternberg, 1969), it is hard to reinstate the excitement that the prospect of such research could have engendered in at least one reader of Bartlett's book.

During the last few years of research on human cognition, there has grown up a number of similar views of how the human nervous system is organized in the performance of species-specific human behaviour such as reading (LaBerge and Samuels, 1974; Posner, 1978). The idea of a limited capacity attentional system has been a central feature of these views. Although some have argued that a skills approach is antithetical to the study of internal attentional mechanisms (Neisser, 1976), most work on skill has also assumed, with Bartlett, the importance of mechanisms of limited capacity (Broadbent, 1977).

Currently, the study of spatial attention in alert monkeys (Mountcastle, 1978; Robinson, Goldberg and Stanton, 1978; Wurtz and Mohler, 1976), brain injured persons (Weiskrantz, Warrington, Sanders and Marshall, 1974) and normal subjects (Posner, 1978, Chapter 7) seems to me to be a most promising model system for relating an important component of

SOURCE: From Posner, M. I. (1980). Orienting of attention. *Quarterly Journal of Experimental Psychology, 32,* 3–25. Reprinted by permission of The Experimental Psychology Society.

complex human cognition to studies of the neural systems underlying performance. While orienting to stimuli in visual space is a restricted sense of attention, I believe that its study is capable of providing us both with important tests of the adequacy of general models of human cognition and with new insights into the role of attention in more complex human activity. Accordingly, this paper will be devoted to a discussion of the results of experiments in human spatial attention and a comparison of them with animal approaches to the same topic. If there should emerge satisfactory convergence between human performance and physiological approaches with this simple model system, I believe that the psychological methods used to explore attention in more complex tasks will receive added support. In addition, studies of human performance may help investigators of neural systems toward the needed integration of their studies of separate anatomical structures.

Orienting

I will use the term *orienting* to mean the aligning of attention with a source of sensory input or an internal semantic structure stored in memory. The term *orienting* has been closely tied to a reflex (Sokolov, 1963), the operation of which is indexed by a variety of autonomic, CNS and overt changes. The idea of an orienting reflex is related to the mental operation of orienting as I use it. However, the orienting reflex does not distinguish between aligning of attention and the resulting perception of a stimulus.

Detecting

I distinguish orienting from another cognitive act that I call *detecting*. By detecting I will mean that a stimulus has reached a level of the nervous system at which it is now possible for the subject to report its presence by arbitrary responses that the experimenter may assign. These may be verbal ("I see it") or manual (pressing a key). Detecting means to be aware or conscious of the stimulus. The distinction between orienting and detecting allows one to explore the proposition that some responses (e.g., saccadic eye movements) may be available to a stimulus before it has been detected in the sense used here. This distinc-

tion makes it reasonable that a normal subject may move his eyes toward a stimulus, but not be able to otherwise report it, or that a brain damaged subject might have impairments in detecting an event to which he can orient (Weiskrantz, Warrington, Sanders and Marshall, 1974).

Locus of Control

It is also important to make a distinction between external and central control over orienting. If orienting to memory and to external stimulus events is to have a common base, it is clear that we must be able to orient attention in the absence of an external stimulus. Similarly, movements of the eyes can either be driven by stimulus input or result from a search plan internal to the organism.

Overt and Covert Orienting

Finally, it is important to distinguish between overt changes in orienting that can be observed in head and eye movements, and the purely covert orienting that may be achieved by the central mechanism alone. In order to make this distinction, one must be able to measure covert orienting by means other than observation of overt head and eye movements. With human subjects it is possible to manipulate the direction of attention by an instruction, by changing the probability of a target event, or by the use of appropriate overt movements. To measure whether orienting occurs, changes in the efficiency of detecting events that occur at various spatial positions are examined. Some variant of mental chronometry (Posner, 1978) such as reaction time (Posner, Nissen and Ogden, 1978), threshold detection (Remington, 1978), evoked potential amplitude (Von Voorhis and Hillyard, 1977) or changes in firing rates of single cells (Mountcastle, 1976) can be used as a dependent measure of processing efficiency.

It is important to keep in mind the definitions of orienting and detecting and the distinction between external and central control as we review experimental evidence. Evidence is examined in four major sections. The first establishes the ability of subjects to shift attention around the visual field in accordance with instructions. By measuring both the facilitatory and inhibitory effects of orienting on the efficiency of detection, it is possible to examine the relationship of the covert attentional mechanism to the fine structure of the retina. The second section supports the idea of analogue movements of attention across the visual field that are measured by time locking of attention shifts to external cues. The third section examines the relationship between movements of attention and overt changes of eye position. In this section it is possible to compare our results with those arising from single cell recording and to distinguish between theories outlining the relationship between perceptual and movement systems. The fourth section deals with the crucial role of peripheral stimuli in controlling attention movements. The concluding portion of the paper examines the implications of our results on spatial attention for more complex performance.

ATTENTION SHIFTS

It is not obvious that shifting spatial attention involves anything more than the movement of the eyes to positions in the visual field. Certainly, no one would dispute the close connection between movements of our eyes and shifts of attention. Nonetheless, there has always been speculation that one can shift attention independent of eye movements. For example, Wundt (1912, p. 20) commented on the ability to separate the line of fixation from the line of attention. Natural language refers to the ability to look out of the corner of our eyes, and athletic coaches instruct their players to do so in order to confuse their opposition.

Many experimental studies using methods of mental chronometry (Grindley and Townsend, 1968; Mertens, 1956; Mowrer, 1941; Shiffrin and Gardner, 1972) were not successful in showing this ability, at least in empty visual fields. More recently, successful reports of attention shifts in the absence of eye movements have been frequent (Eriksen and Hoffman, 1973; Klein, 1979; Posner, Nissen and Ogden, 1978; Shaw, 1978; Von Voorhis and Hillyard, 1977; Wurtz and Mohler, 1976).

We (Posner, Nissen and Ogden, 1978) sought to determine whether responses to clear above threshold luminance increments in dark fields would occur more quickly when subjects knew where the stimulus would occur than when they did not. We used differences in

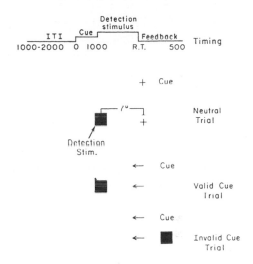

FIGURE 3.1   Organization of individual trials in the central cue experiments.

reaction time to a stimulus at expected and unexpected positions in the visual field as a measure of the efficiency of detection due to turning attention toward the expected position. To insure that the differences in reaction time did not depend upon shifting one's eyes, we monitored eye movements by use of EOG. We used only those trials in which the eyes remained fixated. In order to eliminate overt response preparations as a contributor, we used either a single key (simple RT) which the subject pressed regardless of where the stimulus occurred or made the response choice unrelated to stimulus position. Figure 3.1 illustrates the sequence of events within a trial. The subject was presented with a plus sign or an arrow pointing to the right or left. If the plus sign was presented, the detection stimulus was equally likely to occur to the left or right of fixation. If an arrow was presented, the probability was 0.8 that the detection stimulus would occur on the indicated side (valid) and 0.2 that it would occur on the other side (invalid). One can then examine both the benefits from knowing where in space the stimulus will occur, and the cost when it occurs at a position other than the expected position.

We have now tried this basic design with a variety of tasks. Figure 3.2 shows highly significant benefits from valid information and highly significant costs when the trial is invalid in all these studies. For any one task the costs and benefits are of roughly the same

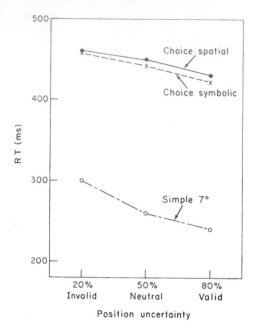

FIGURE 3.2   Reaction time for valid, invalid, and neutral trials for simple RT to luminance increments (Posner, Nissen and Ogden, 1978); choice RT to determine whether the stimulus is above or below the middle of the display and choice RT to letter versus digit judgements (Posner, Snyder and Davidson, 1980).

magnitude. The simple RT conditions involve only a single key that the subject presses irrespective of the location of the signal. The choice spatial task involves a report about whether the stimulus was higher or lower than the cue. As in the simple RT task, the cue provides no information about the response that is most likely. The symbolic task involves a report concerning whether the target is a letter or digit. In the choice tasks there are no more errors in the valid condition than in the invalid condition although the effects of the cue on error rate are always small.

The costs and benefits of a spatial cue are highly regular and it may seem surprising that many previous efforts were not successful in finding improvements in RT or threshold detection in similar experiments. One reason is that the overall effect seems to get smaller as the task is made more difficult. Because our studies were run on separate subjects at different times, no direct comparison is appropriate, but the tendency for the effects of the choice RT tasks to be

smaller than the simple RT tasks is striking. This is especially true because many people expect attentional limitations only when overall task complexity is high (Kahneman, 1973; Norman and Bobrow, 1975). If the effect really is smaller in complex tasks, I believe that this may be because subjects have to reorient attention from visual input to internal structures. If subjects are required to discriminate between a letter and a digit, for example, calling attention to a position in space will not be very useful in an empty field such as used in these experiments. Subjects will have to reorient attention from spatial position to the area in memory that is available for analysis of the discrimination. Indeed, we (Posner, Snyder and Davidson, 1980) found that when given a single key to press whenever they saw a digit, subjects could hardly avoid false alarms when a letter appeared at the correct spatial position. If two keys were given, subjects did benefit from their knowledge of spatial position in RT without compensating increases in error as shown in Figure 3.2, but the benefits were small. These ideas fit with the usual observation that knowledge of spatial position only helps complex tasks when the field is cluttered. In tasks where there are good methods of quickly summoning attention, one might be better off not to know where the stimulus will occur rather than having to reorient from visual position to semantic code.

There is another reason that previous investigations have not always found knowledge of spatial position to aid performance. Our basic method involves cueing on each trial. If, instead, one spatial position is made likely for a whole block of trials, we found no benefits for the frequent position in comparison with conditions in which all positions are equally likely (Posner, Snyder and Davidson, 1980), although there were small costs at the infrequent position. This result fits with the active nature of orienting. Orienting does not seem to involve a passive filter that can easily be set in place and left. Rather, an active process of maintaining the orientation seems important.

Our method can be exploited in an effort to understand the way in which the visual system constrains spatial attention. It is a common conviction that foveal stimuli have a more direct relation to attention than peripheral stimuli. Physiologists sometimes believe the reverse based on the idea that transient (y cells) dominate in the periphery. In fact, costs and benefits from attention did not vary much when we studied stimuli from 0.5 to 25 degrees eccentricity (Posner, 1978, p. 202).

This result led us to examine more completely the costs of an unexpected foveal stimulus when the subject was attending outside the fovea vs. those of an unexpected peripheral stimulus when he was attending to the fovea. We found roughly the same cost for an unexpected event when it is foveal as when it is peripheral (Posner, 1978, p. 202).[2]

What accounts for the strong subjective feeling that the fovea represents the centre of the attentional field? In my view, it is as important for a psychologist to account for this subjective feeling as it is to account for the objective data. Fortunately, it turns out to be possible to study this question. If subjects are given a cue as to which side is more likely, but are not told if the stimulus will be a peripheral or a foveal one, they uniformly prepare for the peripheral stimulus (Posner, 1978, Figure 7.8). Their strategy assumes that the fovea will take care of itself, even though our data say clearly that the costs in RT will be as great as for the periphery. The strategy must arise from the correlation between the fovea and attention brought about by the eye movement system.

When a task demands acuity (upper panel, Figure 3.3), as in the work of Engle (1971), the fovea does play a special role (middle panel, Figure 3.3). This contrasts with the luminance detection results illustrated in the bottom panel of Figure 3.3 in which attention is unrelated to the fovea. Although orientation to the periphery allows detection to occur more quickly, it does not provide an increase in the retinal grain and thus does not produce strong acuity changes. Attention represents a system for routing information and for control of priorities. It does not provide a substitute for the sensory specific wiring intrinsic to the visual system. Ells and I (Note 1) observed that subjects adjust their behaviour differently in luminance detection and in acuity experiments. In a luminance detection experiment, if subjects are told they can move their eyes on each individual trial if they wish, after a few trials they give up doing so. They quickly recognize that it is an effort to move their eyes and that it does not help performance. On the other hand, if free to move in an acuity demanding task, they clearly prefer to do so and the different levels of

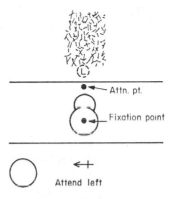

Figure 3.3   Upper panel indicates a high acuity task of searching visual noise for an L shaped figure studied by Engle (1971). As shown in the middle panel the fovea always plays a special role even though attention can expand the area of high conspicuity in the direction of the attention point. Lower panel contrasts our results in which the focus of attention shifts away from the fovea to be centered on the expected position.

performance with foveal and nonfoveal vision confirm the wisdom of their preference.

Overall these results have something to say about the problem of ecological validity in perceptual experiments. It is true that the separation between attention and the fovea that occurs in our experiments is not a normal property of visual perception. It is revealed only under the close experimental control of the laboratory. Nonetheless, it appears that subjects do not adopt a special strategy in our experimental task, but rather carry over their natural tendencies from everyday perception. Under our special conditions we learn that the normal correlation between fovea and attention occurs as a result of the usual demands for high acuity and not as a result of any special wiring that ties attention to foveal stimulation. Only because our luminance detection task does not demand high acuity are we able to observe that the covert mechanisms of attention are not tied intrinsically to the fine structure of the visual system.

ATTENTION MOVEMENTS

The introduction to this paper remarked on the importance of time locking as a way of bringing together physiological and behavioural methods for the investigation of spatial attention. It is important to ask whether the shift in efficiency that we have found when subjects move their attention is sufficiently time locked that measurements of attention movements might be made. One indication of such time locking is found in work by Jonides (Note 2). He varied the time interval between the cue and stimulus in studies otherwise like those I have described. Jonides found quite clearly that he could trace the time course of efficiency changes over a few hundred milliseconds. He also found a rather marked difference between the time course of efficiency when the subject's attention was brought to a position in space by a peripheral cue and when it was so directed by a central cue. The differences between a central and a peripheral cue will become important as we begin to look at the relationship between the time locked attentional movement and time locked movements of the eyes.

For the moment we will consider only the use of a central cue. Shulman, Remington and McLean (1979) asked the question whether movements across the visual field are digital or analogue in form. The eye moves across the visual field continuously, although in one sense the efficiency of its performance is digital since thresholds for taking in stimuli tend to be raised during the saccade. The technique used by these three investigators was to ask whether a visual detection stimulus that occurred on less than 10% of trials at a position between the fixation point and a target would show facilitation in latency at a time intermediate between leaving the home position and reaching the target. If so, one could expect RT for this position first to improve relative to the target as attention moved through it, and then to get worse relative to the target.

Each trial began with an arrow cue which instructed subjects to move attention to a visible target 18° from fixation. At varying intervals following this cue (SOA), detection stimuli were presented. The detection stimuli occurred on 75% of the trials, the remainder serving as catch trials. On trials where there was a detection stimulus it occurred at the designated target 70% of the time. It occurred at the intermediate position on the cued side, at a position opposite the target or at an intermediate point on the side opposite the target, each with probability 0.1.

The result of one experiment is shown in Figure 3.4. The most salient feature in the data is the U-

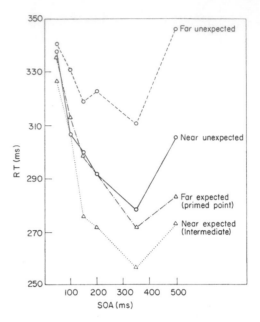

FIGURE 3.4   Reaction time to target stimulus (far expected) and three infrequent probe positions including one on the expected side intermediate between fixation and target (near expected). After Shulman, Remington and McLean (1979). Stimulus onset asynchrony refers to the time between the cue to move attention and the probe detection stimulus.

shaped function relating reaction time to interval following the cue (SOA) for all positions. This alerting effect is well documented in reaction time literature. There is also an advantage to those lights near the fovea. Reaction time to lights near fixation is generally faster than to lights far from fixation.

In these experiments the crucial measure that addresses the question whether movements are analogue or discrete is the difference between reaction time to target (far expected) and intermediate light on the target side (near expected) as a function of SOA. This subtraction is displayed in Figure 3.5, both for the original experiment and its replication.

In both experiments this subtraction shows a divergence followed by a convergence.[3] The maximum difference appears at 150 ms in both experiments. At this point attention appears to give the greatest relative advantage to the intermediate probe. Although these effects are small they are sufficiently consistent

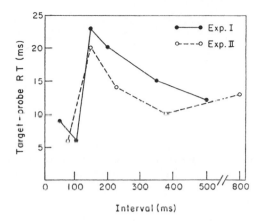

FIGURE 3.5   Subtraction from the target stimulus RT of the RT to the near expected probe as a function of interval following the cue to move attention. Two separate experiments are plotted. After Shulman, Remington and McLean (1979).

to reach statistical significance and to allow us a provisional decision that time locking can occur and that the analogue model is supported by the data.

Relationship Between Attention and Movement

Orienting to positions in space can be obtained covertly through movements of attention or overtly through shifts of the head and eyes. No one would doubt that these two are very closely coupled in daily life. There has been interest in the degree of relationship of the internal mechanisms controlling attention and eye movement. Much of the relevant literature comes from single cell recording in alert monkeys. Goldberg and Wurtz (1972) showed at the level of the superior colliculus enhancement in the firing rate of single cells whose receptive field was to be the target for an eye movement at a latency well before the eyes began to move. At first they were inclined to identify this system with a general attention mechanism because the time course did not seem to couple it closely with eye movements. Later, it was shown (Wurtz and Mohler, 1976) that methods of producing attention to events outside of the fovea other than by inducing eye movements did not produce enhancement of colliculur cells. At the level of the superior colliculus it appeared that selective enhancement was intrinsically

related to eye movements. Work by Mountcastle (1976) could be viewed as suggesting a direct relationship between enhancement of single cells in the parietal lobe and movement of the hands and eyes into the surrounding environmental space. However, Mountcastle (1978) explicitly recognizes the contingent nature of the movements generated in response to parietal activity.

There was reason from our data to deny too close a relationship between attention and overt eye movements. The costs and benefits of attention shifts neither depend upon movements of the eyes nor seem to be closely related to distance from the fovea. Indeed, our finding that attention shifts are symmetric between periphery and fovea suggests a different structure from that of the eye movement system. Subsequent work on single cell recording (Bushnell, Robinson and Goldberg, 1978; Robinson, Goldberg and Stanton, 1978) shows selective enhancement of single cells in parietal lobe (area 7) without eye movements and argues that such cells are more closely related to visual properties of the stimulus than to motor commands.

Logical Possibilities

Figure 3.6 outlines a series of logically possible relationships between overt and covert attentional mechanisms. The behavioural evidence, discussed previously, that attention can be shifted with eyes fixed, together with results showing enhancement of evoked potentials (Eason, Harter and White, 1969; Von Voorhis and Hillyard, 1977) and of the firing rates of single cells (Bushnell et al., 1978), eliminates the idea that attention and eye movements are identical systems.

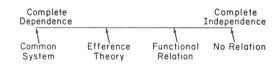

FIGURE 3.6   Logical relationships between overt and covert orienting of attention.

These findings led Wurtz and Mohler (1976) to propose that attention shifts were programmes for the movement of the eyes. This might be called an efference theory. Klein (1979) describes this view as follows: "When attention to a particular location is desired, the observer prepares to make an eye movement to that location; the oculomotor readiness, via as yet unknown feedforward pathways, has the effect of enhancing processing in or from sensory pathways dealing with information from the target location."

A less restrictive notion of the relationships between the two forms of movement would be that attention and eye movements are both summoned by important peripheral events and thus have a close functional but no intrinsic physiological relationship. An even less restrictive view would be to posit complete functional and physiological independence between the two systems.

EFFERENCE

The efference view proposes a restricted relation between our ability to move attention and the eyes. It indicates that whenever one moves attention to a location, eye movements in that direction are facilitated and that the readiness to move the eyes to a target necessarily improves detection there. Klein (1979) examined both of these hypotheses. His technique is shown in Figure 3.7. Each trial begins with a cue. There are two kinds of trials. On eye movement trials an asterisk appears to the left or right of fixation. On detection trials the subjects must respond to a luminance increment by pressing a key.

Experiment I has only a small proportion of eye movement trials. Most trials involve detection to insure that the subject uses the cue to shift attention to the expected position. He found clear costs and benefits on detection trials. There was no effect of the cue on eye movement latencies. When the subject has to move his eyes in the direction he is attending, he is no faster than when he moves opposite to the direction of attention.

In Experiment II eye movements are the primary task and detection trials were used to assess the prediction that detection will be faster for a stimulus presented at the target for the eye movement. One group of subjects was instructed to move their eyes right and

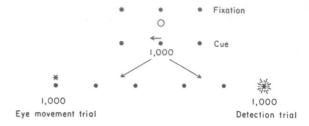

FIGURE 3.7 A paradigm for testing the efference view. Subjects are given a cue as to where to shift attention and then are commanded either to move their eyes or to report a detection stimulus by pressing a key. After Klein, 1979.

a separate group to move them left on each eye movement trial. When the imperative stimulus for the eye movement is in the direction of the actual movement (compatible) eye movements are faster than when it is not (incompatible). However, the detection task is totally unaffected by the direction in which the subject moves his eyes.

These results show clearly that there are conditions under which one gets no relationship between spatial attention shifts and eye movement latencies. Thus they are sufficient to reject an efference theory as a full account of the relationship of eye movement and attention movement. However, Klein's experiments involve difficult conditions for the subjects. The subject first has to determine if he is in a detection or an eye movement trial based on the type of stimulus change. On some trials eye movements are opposite to the direction of the visual input. These conditions produce long RTs. As illustrated in Figure I [in Klein, 1979], complex conditions produce the poorest evidence for spatial attention effect. While the experiments are sufficient to refute the forced conjunction between eye movement and attention, they do not give us a very good handle on how these two might be linked under less difficult conditions. Some recent studies (Nissen, Posner and Snyder, Note 4; Remington, 1978) provide a view of the relationship between eye movement and attention movements under simpler conditions.

Combined Eye and Attention Movements

In our experiments the subject's attention and eye movement are summoned by a 1° unfilled box that occurs 8° to the left or right of a similar fixation box.

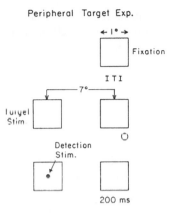

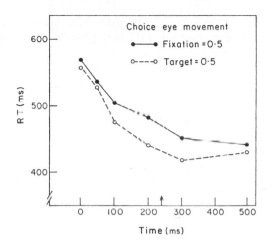

FIGURE 3.8 Organization of a trial to study eye movements and attention movements simultaneously. The target stimulus commands a movement. The detection stimulus is reported by pressing a key. After Nissen, Posner and Snyder, Note 4.

FIGURE 3.9 Reaction time as a function of the time the detection stimulus follows the target stimulus when the location of the detection stimulus is equally likely to be at fixation or at the target. The arrow indicates mean RT for an eye movement (see text).

The detection stimulus is a clear dot well above threshold. The sequence of events in a trial is shown in Figure 3.8. The detection stimulus occurs with equal probability in the fixation box or at the target.

Figure 3.9 shows mean RTs for detection stimuli at fixation and at the target as a function of time following the peripheral eye movement cue. The results show that by 50 to 100 ms after the occurrence of the target stimulus for the eye movement, one gets benefits in reaction time to a detection event that occurs at the target, in comparison to the position at which the subject is currently looking. This time course is roughly consonant with the results obtained by Goldberg and Wurtz (1972) for the latency of collicular unit enhancement. Thus where eye movements and attention are conjoined by the occurrence of a peripheral stimulus, the movement of attention seems to precede the movement of the eyes.

Because of the use of the reaction time technique, it is difficult to be sure that the earliest point at which one gets facilitation is the point at which attention has shifted to the peripheral position. To address this question, Remington (1978) required his subjects to detect a 3 ms luminance increment. Otherwise, the basic paradigm is similar to the one shown in Figure 3.8. Each trial begins with three boxes in the field. At time 0 a plus sign appears over one of the peripheral boxes indicating the eye movement direction. The detection

stimulus occurs with equal probability at the fixation point, the target, or on the side opposite the target.

Prior to the presentation of the eye movement target (plus sign) the subject is most sensitive at the fovea. By 100 ms after the occurrence of the target event and well before the eyes have started to move, the subject shows higher sensitivity at the target position than either at fixation or opposite sides. Shortly before the eyes begin to move there is a reduction in probability of detection that could be due to saccadic suppression. Finally, when the eyes reach the target, the subject is now more sensitive in the position of the target than at the original fixation. The effects are all small but sufficiently consistent to be statistically significant. They show that in the presence of a stimulus which elicits eye movement, the subject's attention tends to move prior to his eyes.[4]

These two experiments show that there is a strong tendency for attention to shift to the target position for an eye movement prior to the eye leaving the fixation point. The time course for this attention shift is in the neighbourhood of 50–100 ms following the peripheral target presentation which is about the same as reported for selective enhancement of collicular units by Goldberg and Wurtz (1972). This result argues for a firmer link between attention and eye movements than was suggested by Klein's result. In both of these experiments detection stimuli were equally likely to occur at the target for the eye movement or at the fixation point. In order to investigate the strength of the link between overt and covert orienting, we wanted to see if subjects would be able to maintain attention at fixation if given incentive to do so. It is very difficult to know introspectively whether attention can be maintained at fixation when generating an eye movement.

To provide an incentive for subjects to attend to the fixation if they could, we increased the probability that the detection stimulus would be presented there to 0.8, with a probability of 0.2 that it would occur at the target. We ran two different conditions. In one condition the subjects were not to make eye movements but were to remain fixated at all times. In the other condition they were to move their eyes as quickly as possible after the target box was presented. In all other respects the two conditions were identical. In our first experiment six subjects were run under each of these conditions.

The results of our experiment are shown in Figure 3.10. In the fixation condition it is clear that a high

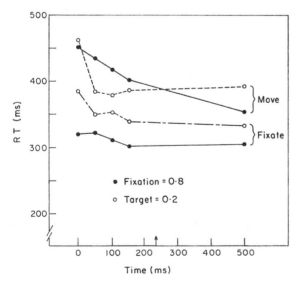

FIGURE 3.10   Reaction time to the detection stimulus for an eye movement condition (move) and a fixation condition (fixate). The detection stimulus occurs at fixation with probability 0.8 and at the target with probability 0.2. Arrow indicates mean RT for an eye movement (see text).

probability stimulus that occurs on the fovea is detected much more rapidly at all intervals than a low probability peripheral event. There is no evidence that the occurrence of the peripheral target event *per se* improves detection in its location relative to fixation. In the movement condition the detection stimulus is responded to more rapidly when it occurs at the target rather than at fixation at about 50 ms following input. These subjects become faster at detecting a peripheral event of low probability than at detecting an event which falls on the fovea and is of much higher probability.[5] There is a reversal after the eyes land on the target stimulus. By 300 ms the subjects are fixating the target, but at our next probe time, which is 500 ms, they show more sensitivity to the original fixation point at which they are no longer looking than at the target. Once they reach the target attention seems clearly under the control of the probabilities.

These results confirm in a different paradigm the idea that the trajectories of attention movements can be traced dynamically over time (Shulman et al., 1979). Attention moves rapidly prior to the eye movement and returns to the original fixation as the fovea settles in at the target. Even with the incentive of a high probability detection stimulus at fixation, subjects do not maintain attention while programming the eye movement. At first this finding may seem to contradict Klein's rejection of efference theory. Certainly it suggests a non-trivial tie between overt and covert orienting that cannot easily be resisted by the subject. However, we had the distinct impression that we were able to return attention to fixation even as the eye was moving toward the target. Since there were no probe events around 300 ms we were not able to confirm the impression in this experiment.

To see if attention could move in a direction opposite to eye movement programming, we instituted blocks in which the subject fixated at the left edge of the cathode ray screen. At time 0 a target occurred 8° to the right of fixation. Four hundred milliseconds later a second target occurred 8° further to the right of fixation. The subject's task was to move his eyes as quickly as possible from the original fixation point to the first target and then, following the occurrence of the second target, to move his eyes again. Detection stimuli occurred at the original fixation with probability 0.8 and at the position of the first target with a 0.2

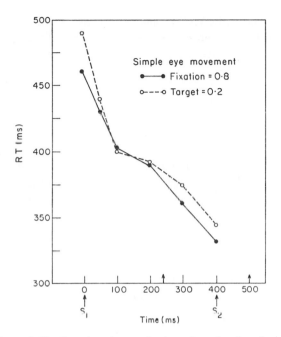

FIGURE 3.11   Reaction time to the detection stimulus when embedded in a double eye movement experiment. Command for the first eye movement occurs at S1 and the second at S2. Arrows indicate mean RT for each movement (see text).

probability. Our interest was in whether the subject would tend to move attention back to the original fixation point, even as his eyes were preparing to move to a target still further away. Thus we were interested in detection events which occurred shortly before and during the reaction time to the second target event. The results are shown in Figure 3.11. Detection stimuli that occur at fixation are initially responded to somewhat faster than those that occur at the target. As the subject begins to prepare to move his eyes to the first target there is an improvement in the efficiency of detecting stimuli at that target by comparison with the fixation point. This replicates the shift found in the previous studies, but here does not actually yield reliably faster reaction times to the target than to the fixation point. However, for the crucial events (300–400 ms following the original target) that occur during the time the subject reaches the first target and is preparing to begin the movement to the second target, reaction times back at the initial fixation are significantly better than at the first target stimulus

at which he is currently fixated. Since reaction times to the second movement are very rapid, it is clear that the programming of the eyes is in the direction opposite to the movement of attention. These results agree with Klein's (1979) conclusion and seem fatal to an efference theory.

Functional Relationships

Overall, our results suggest that the relationship between eye movements and attention is not as close as either a complete dependence or an efference view requires. Our studies showing attention movements with eyes fixed, Klein's finding of no influence on eye movement latencies of shifts of attention, and our result showing attention movements in the opposite direction to eye movement programmes are fatal to these notions.

However, the two orienting systems are not completely independent. The striking tendency of attention to move to the target prior to an eye movement even when detection signals are more probable at fixation shows that the two can be exquisitely related.

We conclude that the relation is a functional one. It often depends more upon the presentation of an important peripheral event than on the eye movement toward that event. If the peripheral event is not important, subjects can clearly avoid moving attention to it, as is shown by the fixation condition of Figure 3.10. Making the stimulus a target for an eye movement is a particularly good way to make it important, but very clearly not the only way. An instruction to attend to the stimulus is also sufficient, as we have shown in the central cue experiments.[6]

In many ways the relationship between eye and attention movements resembles that found to hold between eye and hand movements (Posner and Cohen, 1980). The eye and hand function in close relationship to one another in many tasks, yet the physiological systems for their control are quite distinct. The eye frequently moves to stimuli in anticipation of hand movements, but one can easily move the hand with the eyes fixed. Indeed, even when one is instructed to move the two in synchrony toward a target, they may become erroneously dissociated (Posner, Nissen and Ogden, 1978). If one is instructed to move hand and eye rapidly toward a visual stimulus that is very likely to arise from one position, then on occasions when the expectancy is wrong the hand has a tendency to follow the expectancy while the eye is controlled by the visual input. Comparisons of central cues and peripheral input have proved useful in understanding the functional interconnections of the control systems for hand and eye movements. The next section examines a similar strategy for understanding the control of the overt and covert components of orienting.

CENTRAL AND PERIPHERAL CONTROL OF ORIENTING

Attention can be directed by a central decision, as discussed in section two of this paper, or it can be drawn by a peripheral stimulus, as is done in the experiments discussed in the last section. Comparisons of exogenous (reflexive) and endogenous (central) control of orienting is made difficult because external signals do not operate completely reflexively but will only summon attention and eye movements if they are important to the subject. Moreover, central mechanisms that may control covert orienting, such as the parietal lobe, also receive input from subcortical centres involved in overt orienting. Nonetheless, it would be useful to attempt to compare central and peripheral systems for producing changes in orienting as a model system for the interaction of external and internal control.

Remington (1978) compared peripheral and central cues for eye movements in order to determine their relationship to shifts of attention. When he used a peripheral cue he found improved sensitivity in the vicinity of the peripheral target about 50 ms after the cue and well before the eye movement. When a central arrow was used to cue the movement, there was no evidence of any change in sensitivity in the direction of the target until after the eye movement began. This result is not consistent with as strong a connection between attention and eye movements as an efference theory would require. It is consistent with the idea that both attention and the eyes tend to be drawn to peripheral stimuli, with attention movements occurring somewhat more rapidly. A comparison of the eye movement latency in Remington's two experiments confirms the general advantage of peripheral over central eye movements of about 50 ms.

Recently, Yoav Cohen and I (Posner and Cohen, 1980) have reported behavioural evidence of a qualitative difference between control of eye movements from peripheral and central cues. In these experiments we compared binocular viewing with conditions in which only the left or right eye viewed the stimulus. Subjects were instructed to move their eyes in the direction that seemed most natural. In all trials the stimuli were pairs of dots that occurred 10° to the left or right of fixation. On most trials one of the dots led the other by 150 or 500 ms. Under these conditions subjects got used to moving their eyes to whatever stimulus occurred first. When the two stimuli occurred simultaneously, with binocular viewing there was no movement bias, but with monocular viewing subjects moved their eyes 80% of the time in the direction of the temporal visual field.

This result was not due to a general movement bias. When a central visual or auditory cue was substituted for the lateralized input, the bias of moving toward the temporal visual field was lost.

There were also clear differences between conscious judgement of which stimulus occurred first (temporal order judgements) and eye movements induced by the same stimulus conditions. In these studies pairs of dots with time differences of 0, 10, 30 or 60 ms were used. Conscious judgements were greatly influenced by which stimulus came first (ranging from 80–90% correct when either event led by 60 ms) and were only slightly influenced by the eye that was occluded. Eye movements were influenced much less strongly by the time difference but were markedly affected by the viewing eye. These results suggest that temporal visual field input has more direct access to systems controlling exogenously produced eye movements than does nasal visual field input.

There are also anatomical reasons for supposing that crossed fibres have stronger input to the superior colliculus than do uncrossed fibres (Kaufman, 1974). However, to our knowledge, this is the first exploration of functional asymmetry of external control over eye movements to be reported with normal human adults.[7] It will be interesting to find out whether covert orienting resembles the eye movement system in being more influenced by contralateral input or whether it appears to be more like conscious judgements in being relatively symmetric.

These studies provide potential methods for studying fundamental differences in the external and central control of overt orienting.

CONCLUSIONS

The most important outcome of this research concerns our ability to measure the movements of attention across the visual field. The time locking of shifts of attention, both to central instructional cues and to changes in eye position, provides evidence that covert orientation can be measured with almost as much precision and ease as overt shifts in eye position. The convergence of measurements of sensory thresholds, reaction time and electrical activity on common questions and, to some extent, common results, gives some assurance that the observed change of efficiency is genuine. These findings may do more than add to the catalogue of internal mental activity that has been successfully measured in recent years. The centrality of attention to mental theories and the breadth and precision of methods involved in its measurement suggest a wealth of new issues that may now be ready for analysis.

An alternative language for discussing orienting is in terms of signal detection theory. One could discuss our results as being due to shifts in criterion as probability and momentary expectancy vary. Elsewhere we have discussed some of the disadvantages of this signal detection language as applied to our results (Posner, Snyder and Davidson, 1980). Some of our findings place constraints on the nature of criterion shifts that seem antithetical to the use of that language. These include differences between cued and blocked presentation, reductions in costs and benefits with increases in task difficulty, facilitation of low probability probes that lie between fixation and target, shifts in efficiency toward the target for the eye movement even when fixation stimuli are more probable, and the relative difficulty of dividing attention between non-contiguous spatial positions (Posner, Snyder and Davidson, 1980). While such results may be described as placing gambles at expected spatial positions, they seem to imply a mechanism that severely limits and constrains the possible criteria.

Much work on orienting (Sokolov, 1963) has confounded the alignment of attention to a source of input with the detection of a stimulus event. The orienting reflex does not distinguish between the processes that occur prior to detection and that which occurs subsequently. The relatively slow nature of autonomic changes often precludes such a division. Although our method of measuring orienting is via changes in the efficiency of detecting, the two mental operations must be quite distinct. Since one can move attention to a potential source of signals before any input has occurred it is clear that orienting can occur without detection. For overt orienting this is obvious, but it has not been as obvious that orienting and detection are two quite distinct internal operations of attention.

The ability to dissociate the two in normal subjects fits well with observations that emerge from data on brain injured individuals. In the case of occipital lesions (field cuts) it has been shown that there can be a relative sparing of the ability to do overt orienting combined with a striking deficit in the ability to detect (be aware of) stimuli in the blind field (Gassel and Williams, 1963; Perenin and Jeannerod, 1978; Weiskrantz, Warrington, Sanders and Marshall, 1974). On the other hand, damage in the right parietal region can be described as producing a severe deficit in orienting with a less severe loss in the ability to detect a stimulus once orienting is accomplished (Heilman and Watson, 1977). When only one event is presented, subjects may show good acuity in the neglected field, but when competing events are presented there is a deficit in orienting toward the side opposite the lesion. The view that brain injury may dissociate more completely mental functions that are isolable by chronometric analysis in normals (Posner, 1980) seems one of the general principles that may emerge from sustained interaction of cognitive and neuroscience thinking.

The important effect that parietal lobe damage has for orienting in humans supports the view that some portions of the mechanisms for selective attention to space rely upon this part of the brain. This line of reasoning underlies the effort made in this paper to relate our findings on spatial attention to observations being made in area 7 by single cell investigators.[8] There is a tendency when looking at association areas of the brain to identify their activity with either sensory or motor systems. An important idea emerging from studies of attention suggests that there are unique properties of internal structures that preclude their identification with either sensory or motor systems. Our data show that attention is not intrinsically tied to the foveal structure of the visual system nor slaved to the overt movements of the eye.

Attention movements have properties that are analogous to the skilled movements of the hand and eye. This is the theme that Bartlett proposed as a way toward the objective study of thought. It remains to establish that attention in the sense developed in this paper is related to the attentional system postulated by cognitive theories of internal thought processes. It is one thing to claim that ideas for the study of spatial attention arose from an effort to confirm models of the role of attention in tasks related to language and thought, but it is quite another to show that studies of simple luminance detection will increase our understanding of complex performance. On a very general level it seems that evolution has selected similar principles of movement for the hand, the eye and covert visual attention. It seems reasonable to suppose that orienting in semantic memory will take advantage of these same principles.

There are a number of promising avenues open for linking evidence on spatial orienting to the mechanisms used for orienting to internal mental structures. Let me outline a few places where concepts arising from work in spatial orienting and those from work in orienting to higher level systems seem to be related. Analogue processes have been shown in mental rotation (Cooper and Shepard, 1973) and scanning of images (Kosslyn, 1973). Similarly, the effects of distance in semantic space (Rosch, 1975) on reaction time suggest they are also applicable to verbal concepts. This work suggested the studies on analogue attentional movements. The buildup of benefits and costs with the shift of thought from one idea (e.g., letter or semantic category) to another has been traced in some detail (McLean and Shulman, 1978; Neely, 1977). It remains to be shown if evidence of activation-based orienting found in semantic memory (McLean and Shulman, 1978) will also apply to spatial orientation. When stimulus input controls the shift of attention toward an internal structure it has been found that benefits occur before costs. When a letter primes a pathway there is first a general commitment of atten-

tion followed after time by the specific costs to letters other than the one primed. One might expect that the arrow cues used in spatial orienting will produce a similar structure. Becker and Killion (1977) have shown that the amount of cost to an unexpected word is reduced as the signal to noise ratio increases. One would suppose this to be a reasonable expectation for visual orienting as well, although there is no convincing evidence of it as yet.

Twenty years after Bartlett first suggested that thought exhibits a "point of no return" we seem able to make a genuine commitment to an exploration of his insight. Perhaps we have reached a point on this road where we will not wish to turn back.

AUTHOR NOTE

These experiments were supported by NSF Grant BNS 176-18907-A02 to the University of Oregon. I am grateful to Ray Klein, Gordon Shulman, John McLean and Roger Remington for stimulating discussion of their experiments, which they have allowed me to cite. Mary Jo Nissen was a very close collaborator in the conception and design of these experiments and aided substantially in the development of the ideas outlined here.

ENDNOTES

1. Text of the Seventh Sir Frederick Bartlett Lecture given at a meeting of the Experimental Psychology Society in Oxford, 5 July 1979.
2. This result has implications for some of the theories arising from single cell recording at parietal levels. For example, Yin and Mountcastle (1977) argued that the attention system they were studying did not involve foveal representation. If they had been right, this would be evidence against area 7 being crucial in the kind of spatial orientation reported here. More recently, foveal representation has been found in these cells (Bushnell et al., 1978; Mountcastle, Note 3).
3. It is important to note that no similar pattern of divergence or convergence is found with stimuli that occur on the side opposite the cued target. In unpublished work we found that alerting alone, with no cue as to where to direct attention, produces uniform improvements in RT to detection events at differing places from fixation. The usual advantage of foveal over peripheral events was also present. Thus the pattern of interaction

found for the intermediate and target events on the cued side depends on the instruction to move attention in that direction. The results that we obtained for pure alerting argue that alerting does not introduce a bias in the distribution of attention over the visual field as might be expected from some views of the relationship between arousal and performance.

4. There are a number of other interesting features of the Remington study. There is a small but not significant tendency for the detection of events on the opposite side of the target to be facilitated in the period shortly before and after target presentation. This suggests that subjects may first show increased sensitivity to both sides as they await the cue as to the direction of movement. This ability to split attention has not been found in other luminance detection studies, however (Posner, Snyder and Davidson, 1980). It is also of potential importance that the attention shifts Remington found seem to occur prior to evidence for saccadic suppression.

5. This experiment showed the most striking results favouring the target. Subsequent experiments using similar procedures have not always yielded a striking cross over favouring the target during the period before the eye movement. We have replicated the relative shift in detection RT favouring the target even though many subjects do not reverse the normal advantage in RT favouring foveal stimuli.

6. These conclusions appear to be in accord with recent observations (Kowler and Steinman, 1979) showing oculomotor drifts in the direction of the subject's expectancy when they are induced either by the requirement to move the eyes or by the expectation of a peripheral signal even when fixation is maintained. The extent of voluntary control over the oculomotor drift may be less than for attention movements, however.

7. A very recent abstract (Lewis, Maurer and Milewski, 1979) suggests that newborns have a strong functional asymmetry favouring the temporal visual field that is reduced over the first two months of life. This observation seems to fit closely with our adult data and may provide an opportunity to investigate its neural locus by studies of maturation.

8. There is nothing in our results that can prove that the spatial attentional mechanisms that we study are identical to those under investigation in area 7 of the parietal lobe. Our results are suggestive of this link. Single cell studies will need to be informed by the known properties of spatial attention as they seek to relate their results to attention.

REFERENCES

Bartlett, Sir F. C. (1932). *Remembering*. Cambridge, England: Cambridge University Press.

Bartlett, Sir F. C. (1958). *Thinking*. New York: Basic Books.

Becker, C. A., & Killion, T. H. (1977). Interaction of visual and cognitive effects in word recognition. *Journal of Experimental Psychology: Human Perception and Performance, 3,* 389–401.

Broadbent, D. E. (1977). Levels, hierarchies, and the locus of control. *Quarterly Journal of Experimental Psychology, 29,* 181–201.

Bushnell, M. C., Robinson, D. L., & Goldberg, M. E. (1978). Dissociation of movement and attention: Neuronal correlates in posterior parietal cortex. *Neurosciences Abstracts, 4,* 621.

Cooper, L. A., & Shepard, R. N. (1973). Mental rotation of letters. In W. G. Chase (Ed.), *Visual information processing*. New York: Academic Press.

Eason, R. G., Harter, R., & White, C. T. (1969). Effects of attention and arousal on visually evoked cortical potentials and reaction time in man. *Physiology and Behavior, 4,* 283–289.

Engle, F. L. (1971). Visual conspicuity, directed attention and retinal locus. *Vision Research, 11,* 563–576.

Eriksen, C. W., & Hoffman, J. E. (1973). The extent of processing of noise elements during selective encoding from visual displays. *Perception and Psychophysics, 14,* 155–160.

Gassel, M. M., & Williams, D. (1963). Visual function in patients with homonymous hemianopia. Part II: Oculomotor mechanisms. *Brain, 86,* 1–36.

Goldberg, M. E., & Wurtz, R. H. (1972). Activity of superior colliculus in behaving monkeys. II. Effect of attention on neuronal responses. *Journal of Neurophysiology, 35,* 560–574.

Grindley, C. G., & Townsend, V. (1968). Voluntary attention in peripheral vision and its effects on acuity and differential thresholds. *Quarterly Journal of Experimental Psychology, 20,* 11–19.

Heilman, K. M., & Watson, R. T. (1977). Mechanisms underlying the unilateral neglect syndrome. In E. A. Weinstein & R. P. Friedland (Eds), *Hemi-inattention and hemisphere specialization*. New York: Raven Press.

Kahneman, D. (1973). *Attention and effort*. Englewood Cliffs, N.J.: Prentice-Hall.

Kaufman, L. (1974). *Sight and mind: An introduction to visual perception*. New York: Oxford University Press.

Klein, R. (1979). Does oculomotor readiness mediate cognitive control of visual attention? In *Attention and perfor-*

mance VIII. Hillsdale, N.J.: Lawrence Erlbaum and Associates.

Kosslyn, S. M. (1973). Scanning visual images: Some structural implications. *Perception and Psychophysics, 14,* 90–94.

Kowler, E., & Steinman, R. M. (1979). The effect of expectations on slow oculomotor control—I. Periodic target steps. *Vision Research, 19,* 619–632.

LaBerge, D. H., & Samuels, J. (1974). Toward a theory of automatic information processing in reading. *Cognitive Psychology, 6,* 293–323.

Lewis, T. L., Maurer, D., & Milewski, A. E. (1979, May). The development of nasal detection in young infants. *ARVO Abstracts,* 271.

McLean, J., & Shulman, G. L. (1978). On the construction and maintenance of expectancies. *Quarterly Journal of Experimental Psychology, 30,* 441–454.

Mertens, J. J. (1956). Influence of knowledge of target location upon the probability of observations of peripherally observable test flashes. *Journal of the Optical Society of America, 46,* 1069–1070.

Mountcastle, V. B. (1976). The world around us: Neural command functions for selective attention. The F. O. Schmitt Lecture in Neuroscience for 1975. *Neuroscience Research Progress Bulletin, 14,* Supplement 1–47.

Mountcastle, V. B. (1978). Brain mechanisms for directed attention. *Journal of the Royal Society of Medicine, 71,* 14–27.

Mowrer, O. H. (1941). Preparatory set (expectancy)—further evidence of its "central" locus. *Journal of Experimental Psychology, 28,* 116–133.

Neely, J. H. (1977). Semantic priming and retrieval from lexical memory: Roles of inhibitionless spreading activation and limited-capacity attention. *Journal of Experimental Psychology: General, 106,* 226–254.

Neisser, U. (1976). *Cognition and reality.* San Francisco: Freeman.

Norman, D. A., & Bobrow, D. G. (1975). On data-limited and resource-limited processes. *Cognitive Psychology, 7,* 44–64.

Perenin, M. T., & Jeannerod, M. (1978). Visual function within the hemianopic field following early cerebral hemidecortication in man. I. Spatial localization. *Neuropsychologia, 16,* 1–13.

Posner, M. I. (1980). Mental chronometry and the problem of consciousness. In R. Klein & P. Jusczyk (Eds.), *The nature of thought: Essays in honor of D. O. Hebb.* Hillsdale, N.J.: Lawrence Erlbaum Associates.

Posner, M. I. (1978). *Chronometric explorations of mind.* Hillsdale, N.J.: Lawrence Erlbaum Associates.

Posner, M. I., & Cohen, Y. (1980). Attention and the control of movements. In G. E. Stelmach and J. Requin (Eds.), *Tutorials in motor behavior.* Amsterdam: North-Holland.

Posner, M. I., Nissen, M. J., & Ogden, W. C. (1978). Attended and unattended processing modes: The role of set for spatial location. In H. L. Pick, & E. Saltzman (Eds), *Modes of perceiving and processing information.* Hillsdale, N.J.: Lawrence Erlbaum Associates.

Posner, M. I., Snyder, C. R. R., & Davidson, B. J. (1980). Attention and the detection of signals. *Journal of Experimental Psychology: General, 109,* 160–174.

Remington, R. (1978). *Visual attention, detection and the control of saccadic eye movements.* Unpublished doctoral dissertation, University of Oregon.

Robinson, D. L., Goldberg, M. E., & Stanton, G. B. (1978). Parietal association cortex in the primate: Sensory mechanisms and behavioral modulations. *Journal of Neurophysiology, 41,* 910–932.

Rosch, E. (1975). Cognitive representations of semantic categories. *Journal of Experimental Psychology: General, 104,* 192–233.

Shaw, M. L. (1978). A capacity allocation model for reaction time. *Journal of Experimental Psychology: Human Perception and Performance, 4,* 586–598.

Shiffrin, R. M., & Gardner, G. T. (1972). Visual processing capacity and attentional control. *Journal of Experimental Psychology, 93,* 73–82.

Shulman, G. L., Remington, R. W., & McLean, J. P. (1979). Moving attention through visual space. *Journal of Experimental Psychology: Human Perception and Performance, 5,* 522–526.

Sokolov, E. N. (1963). *Perception and the conditioned reflex.* New York: McMillan.

Sternberg, S. (1969). The discovery of processing stages: Extensions of Donders' method. In W. G. Koster (Ed.), *Attention and performance II.* Amsterdam: North-Holland. (*Acta Psychologica, 30,* 276–315.)

Von Voorhis, S., & Hillyard, S. A. (1977). Visual evoked potentials and selective attention to points in space. *Perception and Psychophysics, 22,* 54–62.

Weiskrantz, L., Warrington, E. K., Sanders, M. D., & Marshall, J. (1974). Visual capacity in the hemianopic field following a restricted occipital ablation. *Brain, 97,* 709–728.

Wundt, W. (1912). *Introduction to psychology* (R. Pinter, trans.). London: George Allen.

Wurtz, R. H., & Mohler, C. W. (1976). Organization of monkey superior colliculus: Enhanced visual response of superficial layer cells. *Journal of Neurophysiology, 39,* 745–765.

Yin, T. C. T., & Mountcastle, V. B. (1977). Visual input to the visuomotor mechanisms of the monkey's parietal lobe. *Science, 197,* 1381–1383.

REFERENCE NOTES

1. Ells, J., & Posner, M. I. (Unpublished). *Studies of attention with high acuity.*
2. Jonides, J. (1976, November). *Voluntary vs. reflexive control of the mind's eye movement.* Paper presented at the Psychonomics Society.
3. Mountcastle, V. B. (1979, April). Lecture to the Harvey Society, New York.
4. Nissen, M. J., Posner, M. I., & Snyder, C. R. R. (1978, November). *Relationship between attention shifts and saccadic eye movement*s. Paper presented at the Psychonomics Society.

STROOP EFFECT

This paper is one of the most highly cited and influential papers in cognitive psychology; and because the effect is so striking and easy to demonstrate, the Stroop effect is reported in nearly every introduction to psychology textbook. At the time Stroop published his paper, psychology was largely investigated by identification of associations. From this perspective, many aspects of cognition were described as the existence or development of associations between different stimuli and responses. The introduction to this reading reflects this interpretation of human behavior by summarizing several studies that investigated interference effects in association. Interference refers to how one association may limit, restrict, inhibit, or change another association. In the 1930s, memory, language, habits, problem solving, and other cognitive capabilities were interpreted as the creation and interference of different associations. These ideas are still central to cognitive psychology today, but there is now a greater emphasis on identifying the mechanisms and systems that process information.

A common technique was to measure or create associations of certain strengths and then study interference as other associations were created or changed. Stroop used a novel approach to study interference. Instead of measuring interference as associations were changed, Stroop measured interference for two already well-learned associations: reading color words and identifying colors by name.

In the first experiment, observers quickly read color words (e.g., words such as *blue* or *red*) from a sheet of paper. In one condition the words were printed in black ink, and in another condition the words were printed in colored ink that was different than the color word itself. Thus, the word *red* might be printed in green ink. The color of the ink had no statistical effect on the time required for observers to read the words. Thus, there was no interference of the color of the ink on the task of reading the color words.

The second experiment used the color ink/color words as in Experiment 1, but switched the task of the subjects. Now observers were to report the color of the ink, and ignore the name of the word. As a comparison, a new page was created that consisted of squares that were the same colors as the ink used for the words. For this page, the task was to identify the colors. Again, the observer was to complete the task as quickly as possible. In contrast to Experiment 1, there was a huge interference effect. Observers took almost twice as long to identify the color ink of color words than to identify the color ink of square patches. Apparently, the presence of the color words interfered with observers' ability to report the ink color. This is what is now called the Stroop effect.

The third experiment included some minor modifications of the stimuli but primarily tested practice across many days. The finding was that practice could substantially decrease the time required to identify ink color with color words; that is, the Stroop effect grew weaker with practice.

A common explanation for the Stroop effect is that observers (especially college undergraduates) are highly practiced at the task of reading. Thus, the color names of the words are always processed very quickly, regardless of the color of the ink. On the other hand, identifying colors is not a task that observers have to report on very often, and because it is not well practiced it is slower. Because observers are asked to respond as quickly as possible, there is a tendency to report the first color that comes into thought. The fast and automatic processing of the color name of the word interferes with the reporting of the ink color when the two responses are in conflict. In many respects this explanation is not much different from Stroop's characterization of association and interference.

One reason this paper has had such a large impact on cognitive psychology is that, with one exception, it is very well written. The exception involves the use of convoluted acronyms in the tables that describe the results. Stroop prepared Appendix A as a quick reference to interpret the acronyms. You might want to bookmark that page before you start reading; otherwise, it is easy to become confused when looking at the data in the tables.

The CogLab version of the Stroop effect measures reaction time to single stimuli instead of measuring the time required to read a whole set of stimuli. The CogLab version also always uses colored fonts, sometimes matching the color word and sometimes different from the color word. The Stroop effect is such a robust phenomenon, however, that these changes make almost no difference in the general effect. You could also replicate Stroop's practice effect by repeating the CogLab experiment many times and tracking your reaction times.

For a modern discussion of the Stroop effect and related topics, see Melara and Algom (2003).

REFERENCE

Melara, R. D., & Algom, D. (2003). Driven by information: A tectonic theory of Stroop effects. *Psychological Review, 110,* 422–471.

QUESTIONS

1. How are interference effects measured in this paper?
2. What do the results of the first experiment indicate about interference and associations?
3. What sex differences were found in Experiment 2?
4. What effect did practice with reporting the ink color of color words have on reading color names?

Studies of Interference in Serial Verbal Reactions

J. Ridley Stroop[1]
George Peabody College

INTRODUCTION

Interference or inhibition (the terms seem to have been used almost indiscriminately) has been given a large place in experimental literature. The investigation was begun by the physiologists prior to 1890 (Bowditch and Warren, J. W., 1890) and has been continued to the present, principally by psychologists (Lester, 1932). Of the numerous studies that have been published during this period only a limited number of the most relevant reports demand our attention here.

Münsterberg (1892) studied the inhibiting effects of changes in common daily habits such as opening the door of his room, dipping his pen in ink, and taking his watch out of his pocket. He concluded that a given association can function automatically even though some effect of a previous contrary association remains.

Müller and Schumann (1894) discovered that more time was necessary to relearn a series of nonsense syllables if the stimulus syllables had been associated with other syllables in the meantime. From their results they deduced the law of associative inhibition which is quoted by Kline (1921, p. 270) as follows: "If *a* is already connected with *b*, then it is difficult to connect it with *k*, *b* gets in the way." Nonsense syllables were also used by Shepard and Fogelsonger (1913) in a series of experiments in association and inhibition. Only three subjects were used in any experiment and the changes introduced to produce the inhibition were so great in many cases as to present novel situations. This latter fact was shown by the introspections. The results showed an increase in time for the response which corresponded roughly to the increase in the complexity of the situation. The only conclusion was stated thus: "We have found then that in ac-

quiring associations there is involved an inhibitory process which is not a mere result of divided paths but has some deeper basis yet unknown" (p. 311).

Kline (1921) used "meaningful" material (states and capitals, counties and county seats, and books and authors) in a study of interference effects of associations. He found that if the first associative bond had a recall power of 10 percent or less it facilitated the second association, if it had a recall power of 15 percent to 40 percent the inhibitory power was small, if it had a recall power of 45 percent to 70 percent the inhibiting strength approached a maximum, if the recall power was 70 percent to 100 percent the inhibition was of medium strength and in some cases might disappear or even facilitate the learning of a new association.

In card sorting Bergström (1893 and 1894), Brown (1914), Bair (1902), and Culler (1912) found that changing the arrangement of compartments into which cards were being sorted produced interference effects. Bergström (1894, p. 441) concluded that "the interference effect of an association bears a constant relation to the practice effect, and is, in fact, equivalent to it." Both Bair and Culler found that the interference of the opposing habits disappeared if the habits were practiced alternately.

Culler (1912), in the paper already referred to, reported two other experiments. In one experiment the subjects associated each of a series of numbers with striking a particular key on the typewriter with a particular finger; then the keys were changed so that four of the numbers had to be written with fingers other than those formerly used to write them. In the other experiment the subjects were trained to react with the right hand to "red" and with the left hand to "blue." Then the stimuli were interchanged. In the former

SOURCE: From Stroop, J. R. (1935). Studies of interference in serial verbal reactions. *Journal of Experimental Psychology, 18*, 643–662.

experiment an interference was found which decreased rapidly with practice. In the latter experiment the interference was overbalanced by the practice effect.

Hunter and Yarbrough (1917), Pearce (1917), and Hunter (1922) in three closely related studies of habit interference in the white rat in a T-shaped discrimination box found that a previous habit interfered with the formation of an "opposite" habit.

Several studies have been published which were not primarily studies of interference, but which employed materials that were similar in nature to those employed in this research, and which are concerned with why it takes more time to name colors than to read color names. Several of these studies have been reviewed by Telford (1930) and by Ligon (1932). Only the vital point of these studies will be mentioned here.

The difference in time for naming colors and reading color names has been variously explained. Cattell (1886) and Lund (1927) have attributed the difference to "practice." Woodworth and Wells (1911, p. 52) have suggested that, "The real mechanism here may very well be the mutual interference of the five names, all of which, from immediately preceding use, are 'on the tip of the tongue,' all are equally ready and likely to get in one another's way." Brown (1915, p. 51) concluded "that the difference in speed between color naming and word reading does not depend upon practice" but that (p. 34) "the association process in naming simple objects like colors is radically different from the association process in reading printed words."

Garrett and Lemmon (1924, p. 438) have accounted for their findings in these words, "Hence it seems reasonable to say that interferences which arise in naming colors are due not so much to an equal readiness of the color names as to an equal readiness of the color recognitive processes. Another factor present in interference is very probably the present strength of the associations between colors and their names, already determined by past use." Peterson (1918 and 1925) has attributed the difference to the fact that, "One particular response habit has become associated with each word while in the case of colors themselves a variety of response tendencies have developed" (1925, p. 281). As pointed out by Telford (1930), the results published by Peterson (1925, p. 281) and also published by Lund (1927, p. 425) confirm Peterson's interpretation.

Ligon (1932) has published results of a "genetic study" of naming colors and reading color names in which he used 638 subjects from school grades 1 to 9 inclusive. In the light of his results he found all former explanations untenable (He included no examination of or reference to Peterson's data and interpretation.) and proceeded to set up a new hypothesis based upon a three factor theory, a common factor which he never definitely describes and special factors of word reading and color naming. He points out that the common factor is learned but the special factors are organic. He promises further evidence from studies now in progress.

The present problem grew out of experimental work in color naming and word reading conducted in Jesup Psychological Laboratory at George Peabody College for Teachers. The time for reading names of colors had been compared with the time for naming colors themselves. This suggested a comparison of the interfering effect of color stimuli upon reading names of colors (the two types of stimuli being presented simultaneously) with the interfering effect of word stimuli upon naming colors themselves. In other words, if the word "red" is printed in blue ink how will the interference of the ink-color "blue" upon reading the printed word "red" compare with the interference of the printed word "red" upon calling the name of the ink-color "blue"? The increase in time for reacting to words caused by the presence of conflicting color stimuli is taken as the measure of the interference of color stimuli upon reading words. The increase in the time for reacting to colors caused by the presence of conflicting word stimuli is taken as the measure of the interference of word stimuli upon naming colors. A second problem grew out of the results of the first. The problem was, What effect would practice in reacting to the color stimuli in the presence of conflicting word stimuli have upon the reaction times in the two situations described in the first problem?

EXPERIMENTAL

The materials employed in these experiments are quite different from any that have been used to study interference.[2] In former studies the subjects were given practice in responding to a set of stimuli until associative bonds were formed between the stimuli and the desired responses, then a change was made in the experimental "set up" which demanded a different set of responses to the same set of stimuli. In the present study pairs of conflicting stimuli, both being inherent aspects of the same symbols, are presented simultaneously (a name of one color printed in the ink of another color—a word stimulus and a color stimulus). These stimuli are varied in such a manner as to maintain the potency of their interference effect. Detailed descriptions of the materials used in each of the three experiments are included in the reports of the respective experiments.

EXPERIMENT 1

The Effect of Interfering Color Stimuli Upon Reading Names of Colors Serially

Materials. When this experiment was contemplated, the first task was to arrange suitable tests. The colors used on the Woodworth Wells color-sheet were considered but two changes were deemed advisable. As the word test to be used in comparison with the color test was to be printed in black it seemed well to substitute another color for black as an interfering stimulus. Also, because of the difficulty of printing words in yellow that would approximate the stimulus intensity of the other colors used, yellow was discarded. After consulting with Dr. Peterson, black and yellow were replaced by brown and purple. Hence, the colors used were red, blue, green, brown, and purple. The colors were arranged so as to avoid any regularity of occurrence and so that each color would appear twice in each column and in each row, and that no color would immediately succeed itself in either column or row. The words were also arranged so that the name of each color would appear twice in each line. No word was printed in the color it named but an equal number of times in each of the other four colors; *i.e.*, the word "red" was printed in blue, green, brown, and purple inks; the word "blue" was printed in red, green, brown, and purple inks; etc. No word immediately succeeded itself in either column or row. The test was printed from fourteen point Franklin lower case type. The word arrangement was duplicated in black print from same type. Each test was also printed in the reverse order which provided a second form. The tests will be known as

"Reading color names where the color of the print and the word are different" (*RCNd*),[3] and "Reading color names printed in black" (*RCNb*).

Subjects and Procedure. Seventy college undergraduates (14 males and 56 females) were used as subjects. Every subject read two whole sheets (the two forms) of each test at one sitting. One half of the subjects of each sex, selected at random, read the tests in the order *RCNb* (form 1), *RCNd* (form 2), *RCNd* (form 1), and *RCNb* (form 2), while the other half reversed the order thus equating for practice and fatigue on each test and form. All subjects were seated so as to have good daylight illumination from the left side only. All subjects were in the experimental room a few minutes before beginning work to allow the eyes to adjust to light conditions. The subjects were volunteers and apparently the motivation was good.

A ten-word sample was read before the first reading of each test. The instructions were to read as quickly as possible and to leave no errors uncorrected. When an error was left the subject's attention was called to that fact as soon as the sheet was finished. On the signal "Ready! Go!" the sheet which the subject held face down was turned by the subject and read aloud. The words were followed on another sheet (in black print) by the experimenter and the time was taken with a stop watch to a fifth of a second. Contrary to instructions 14 subjects left a total of 24 errors uncorrected on the *RCNd* test, 4 was the maximum for any subject, and 4 other subjects left 1 error each on the *RCNb* test. As each subject made 200 reactions on each test this small number of errors was considered negligible. The work was done under good daylight illumination.

Results. Table 4.1 gives the means (*m*), standard deviations (σ), differences (*D*), probable error of the difference (PE_d), and the reliability of the difference (D/PE_d) for the whole group and for each sex.

Observation of the bottom line on the table shows that it took an average of 2.3 seconds longer to read 100 colors names printed in colors different from that named by the word than to read the same names printed in black. This difference is not reliable which is in agreement with Peterson's prediction made when the test was first proposed.

TABLE 4.1   The Mean Time in Seconds for Reading One Hundred Names of Colors Printed in Colors Different From That Named by the Word and for One Hundred Names of Colors Printed in Black

Sex	No. Ss.	RCNd	σ	RCNb	σ	D	PE$_d$	D/PE$_d$
Male	14	43.20	4.98	40.81	4.97	2.41	1.27	1.89
Female	56	43.32	6.42	41.04	4.78	2.28	.72	3.16
Male and Female	70	43.30	6.15	41.00	4.84	2.30	.63	3.64

The means for the sex groups show no particular difference. An examination of the means and standard deviations for the two tests shows that the interference factor caused a slight increase in the variability for the whole group and for the female group, but a slight decrease for the male group.

Table 4.2 presents the same data arranged on the basis of college classification. Only college years one and two contain a sufficient number of cases for comparative purposes. They show no differences that approach reliability.

EXPERIMENT 2

The Effect of Interfering Word Stimuli Upon Naming Colors Serially

Materials.   For this experiment the colors of the words in the *RCNd* test, described in Experiment 1, were printed in the same order but in the form of solid squares (■) from 24 point type instead of words. This sort of problem will be referred to as the "Naming color test" (*NC*). The *RCNd* test was employed also but in a very different manner from that in Experiment 1. In this experiment the colors of the print of the series of names were to be called in succession ignoring the colors named by the words; *e.g.*, where the word "red" was printed in blue it was to be called "blue," where it was printed in green it was to be called "green," where the word "brown" was printed

in red it was to be called "red," etc. Thus color of the print was to be the controlling stimulus and not the name of the color spelled by the word. This is to be known as the "Naming color or word test where the color of the print and the word are different" (*NCWd*). (See Appendix A.)

Subjects and Procedure.   One hundred students (88 college undergraduates, 29 males and 59 females, and 12 graduate students, all females) served as subjects. Every subject read two whole sheets (the two forms) of each test at one sitting. Half of the subjects read in the order *NC, NCWd, NCWd, NC,* and the other half in the order *NCWd, NC, NC, NCWd,* thus equating for practice and fatigue on the two tests. All subjects were seated (in their individual tests) near the window so as to have good daylight illumination from the left side. Every subject seemed to make a real effort.

A ten-word sample of each test was read before reading the test the first time. The instructions were to name the colors as they appeared in regular reading line as quickly as possible and to correct all errors. The methods of starting, checking errors, and timing were the same as those used in Experiment 1. The errors were recorded and for each error not corrected, twice the average time per word for the reading of the sheet on which the error was made was added to the time taken by the stop watch. This plan of correction was arbitrary but seemed to be justified by the situation. There were two kinds of failures to be accounted for:

TABLE 4.2   Showing Data of Table 4.1 Arranged on the Basis of College Classification

College Year	No. Ss.	RCNd	σ	RCNb	σ	D	D/PE$_d$
1st	35	43.9	6.31	41.7	5.58	2.2	.38
2d	20	44.9	6.74	41.8	4.32	3.1	.57
3d	8	39.8	4.62	39.2	3.73	.6	.16
4th	7	40.8	3.60	39.2	2.93	1.6	.51

TABLE 4.3   The Mean Time for Naming One Hundred Colors Presented in Squares and in the Print of Words Which Name Other Colors

Sex	No. Ss.	NCWd	σ	NC	σ	D/NC	D	PE$_d$	D/PE$_d$
Male	29	111.1	21.6	69.2	10.8	.61	42.9	3.00	13.83
Female	71	107.5	17.3	61.0	10.5	.76	46.5	1.62	28.81
Male and Female	100	110.3	18.8	63.3	10.8	.74	47.0	1.50	31.38

first, the failure to see the error, and second, the failure to correct it. Each phase of the situation gave the subject a time advantage which deserved taking note of. Since no accurate objective measure was obtainable and the number of errors was small the arbitrary plan was adopted. Fifty-nine percent of the group left an average of 2.6 errors uncorrected on the NCWd test (200 reactions) and 32 percent of the group left an average of 1.2 errors uncorrected on the NC test (200 reactions). The correction changed the mean on the NCWd test from 108.7 to 110.3 and the mean of the NC test from 63.0 to 63.3.

Results.   The means of the times for the NC and NCWd tests for the whole group and for each sex are presented in Table 4.3 along with the difference, the probable error of the difference, the reliability of the difference, and difference divided by the mean time for the naming color test.

The comparison of the results for the whole group on the NC and NCWd test given in the bottom line of the table indicates the strength of the interference of the habit of calling words upon the activity of naming colors. The mean time for 100 responses is increased from 63.3 seconds to 110.3 seconds or an increase of 74 percent. (The medians on the two tests are 61.9 and 110.4 seconds, respectively.) The standard deviation is increased in approximately the same ratio from 10.8 to 18.8. The coefficient of variability remains the same to

the third decimal place ($\sigma/m = .171$). The difference between means may be better evaluated when expressed in terms of the variability of the group. The difference of 47 seconds is 2.5 standard deviation units in terms of the NCWd test or 4.35 standard deviation units on the NC test. The former shows that 99 percent of the group on the NCWd test was above the mean on the NC test (took more time); and the latter shows that the group as scored on the NC test was well below the mean on the NCWd test. These results are shown graphically in Figure 4.1 where histograms and normal curves (obtained by the Gaussian formula) of the two sets of data are superimposed.

The small area in which the curves overlap and the 74 percent increase in the mean time for naming colors caused by the presence of word stimuli show the marked interference effect of the habitual response of calling words.

The means for the sex groups on the NCWd test show a difference of 3.6 seconds which is only 1.16 times its probable error; but the means on the NC test have a difference of 8.2 seconds which is 5.17 times its probable error. This reliable sex-difference favoring the females in naming colors agrees with the findings of Woodworth-Wells (1911), Brown (1915), Ligon (1932), etc.

The same data are arranged according to college classification in Table 4.4. There is some indication of improvement of the speed factor for both tests as the

TABLE 4.4   Showing the Data of Table 4.3 Arranged on the Basis of College Classification

Class	No. Ss.	NCWd	σ	NC	σ	D	D/NC	D/PE$_d$
1st yr.	17	116.5	24.9	70.9	15.9	45.6	.64	22.7
2d yr.	37	114.4	18.0	66.1	10.6	48.3	.73	32.6
3d yr.	12	106.1	14.0	62.8	7.0	43.3	.69	41.2
4th yr.	22	96.6	16.8	57.8	8.9	38.8	.67	30.3
Graduates	12	111.2	19.4	59.9	11.5	51.3	.86	37.6

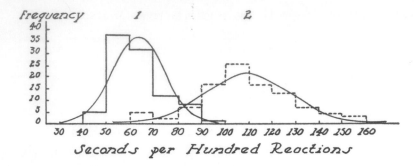

FIGURE 4.1   Showing the effect of interference on naming colors. No interference (1); interference (2).

college rank improves. The relative difference between the two tests, however, remains generally the same except for fluctuations which are probably due to the variation in the number of cases.

EXPERIMENT 3

The Effects of Practice Upon Interference

Materials.   The tests used were the same in character as those described in Experiments 1 and 2 (*RCNb*, *RCNd*, *NC*, and *NCWd*) with some revision. The *NC* test was printed in swastikas (卐) instead of squares (■). Such a modification allowed white to appear in the figure with the color, as is the case when the color is presented in the printed word. This change also made it possible to print the *NC* test in shades which more nearly match those in the *NCWd* test. The order of colors was determined under one restriction other than those given in section 2. Each line contained one color whose two appearances were separated by only one other color. This was done to equate, as much as possible, the difficulty of the different lines of the test so that any section of five lines would approximate the difficulty of any other section of five lines. Two forms of the tests were printed; in one the order was the inverse of that in the other.

Subjects and Procedure.   Thirty-two undergraduates in the University of Arizona (17 males and 15 females), who offered their services, were the subjects. At each day's sitting 4 half-sheets of the same test were read, and the average time (after correction was made for errors according to the plan outlined in Experiment 2) was recorded as the day's score. Only a few errors were left uncorrected. The largest correction

made on the practice test changed the mean from 49.3 to 49.6. The plan of experimentation was as follows:

Day	Test
1	RCNb
2	RCNd
3	NC
4	NCWd
5	NCWd
6	NCWd
7	NCWd
8	NCWd
9	NCWd
10	NCWd
11	NCWd
12	NC
13	RCNd
14	RCNd

On the 1st day the *RCNb* test was used to acquaint the subjects with the experimental procedure and improve the reliability of the 2nd day's test. The *RCNd* test was given the 2nd day and the 13th day to obtain a measure of the interference developed by practice on the *NC* and *NCWd* tests. The *RCNd* test was given the 14th day to get a measure of the effect of a day's practice upon the newly developed interference. The *NC* test was given the 3rd and 12th days, just before and just after the real practice series, so that actual change in interference on the *NCWd* test might be known. The test schedule was followed in regular daily order with two exceptions. There were two days between test days 3 and 4, and also two between test days 8 and 9, in which no work was done. These irregularities were occasioned by week-ends. Each subject was assigned a regular time of day for his work throughout the experiment. All but two subjects followed the schedule with very little irregularity. These two were finally dropped from the group and their data rejected.

All of the tests were given individually by the author. The subject was seated near a window so as to have good daylight illumination from the left side. There was no other source of light. Every subject was in the experimental room a few minutes before beginning work to allow his eyes to adapt to the light conditions. To aid eye-adaptation and also to check for clearness of vision each subject read several lines in a current magazine. Every subject was given Dr. Ishihara's test for color vision. One subject was found to have some trouble with red-green color vision; and her results were discarded though they differed from others of her sex only in the number of errors made and corrected.

Results.   The general results for the whole series of tests are shown in Table 4.5 which presents the means, standard deviations, and coefficients of variability for the whole group and for each sex separately, together with a measure of sex differences in terms of the probable error of the difference. Table 4.6, which is derived from Table 4.5, summarizes the practice effects upon the respective tests. The graphical representation of the results in the practice series gives the learning curve presented in Figure 4.2.

The Effect of Practice on the *NCWd* Test Upon Itself

The data to be considered here are those given in the section of Table 4.5 under the caption "Days of Practice on the *NCWd* Test." They are also presented in summary in the left section of Table 4.6 and graphically in Figure 4.2. From all three presentations it is evident that the time score is lowered considerably by practice.

Reference to Table 4.6 shows a gain of 16.8 seconds or 33.9 percent of the mean of the 1st day's practice. The practice curve is found to resemble very much the "typical" learning curve when constructed on time units.

The coefficient of variability is increased from .14 $\pm$ .012 to .19 $\pm$ .015. This difference divided by its probable error gives 2.60 which indicates that it is not reliable. The probability of a real increase in variability, however, is 24 to 1. Hence, practice on the *NCWd* test serves to increase individual differences.

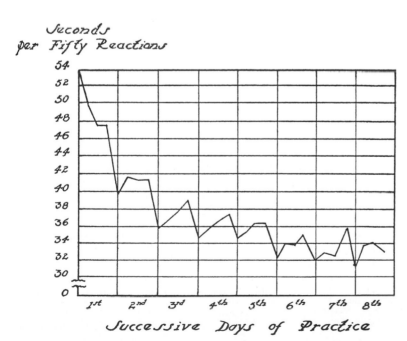

FIGURE 4.2   Mean scores for the group in each of the four half-sheets of the *NCWd* test, which constituted the daily practice.

TABLE 4.5   Showing the Effects of Practice on the *NCWd* Test Upon Itself, Upon the *NC* Test, and Upon the *RCNd* Test in Terms of Mean Score, Standard Deviation (σ), and Coefficients of Variability (σ/m) for Thirty-Two College Students
The score is the average time for four trials of fifty reactions each.

Sex	No. Ss.	Initial Tests						Days of Practice on the NCWd Test							
		RCNb	σ	RCNd	σ	NC	σ	1	σ	2	σ	3	σ	4	σ
Male	17	19.8	1.8	19.6	2.5	30.6	3.6	51.2	8.5	41.6	7.8	38.2	7.6	37.3	8.0
Female	15	18.3	2.9	19.1	3.4	26.5	2.8	47.8	4.2	39.1	4.4	35.8	3.4	33.7	3.7
M & F	32	19.1	2.6	19.4	3.0	28.7	3.5	49.6	7.1	40.5	6.4	37.1	6.1	35.7	6.5

	Sex Differences														
M & F		1.5		.5		4.1		3.4		2.5		2.4		3.6	
PE_d		.49		.70		.76		1.55		1.47		1.36		1.45	
D/PE_d		3.06		.71		5.39		2.19		1.70		1.76		2.48	

Sex	Coefficients of Variability						
Male	.09 ± .011	.13 ± .015	.12 ± .014	.17 ± .020	.19 ± .022	.20 ± .024	.22 ± .026
Female	.16 ± .024	.18 ± .028	.11 ± .016	.09 ± .013	.11 ± .017	.09 ±.14	.11 ± .017
M & F	.14 ± .012	.15 ± .013	.12 ± .010	.14 ± .012	.16 ± .014	.17 ± .014	.18 ± .016

Sex	No. Ss.	Days of Practice on the NCWd Test								Final Tests					
		5	σ	6	σ	7	σ	8	σ	NC	σ	RCNd	σ	RCNd	σ
Male	17	36.3	7.4	33.9	7.3	33.5	6.7	33.4	7.1	25.9	4.2	37.3	13.7	22.2	4.8
Female	15	32.8	4.3	32.3	4.0	31.6	3.3	31.5	3.3	23.6	1.9	32.0	6.2	21.8	6.1
M & F	32	34.9	6.2	33.2	5.4	32.6	5.5	32.8	6.1	24.7	3.2	34.8	11.7	22.0	5.5

	Sex Differences														
M & F		3.5		1.6		1.9		1.9		2.3		5.3		.4	
PE_d		1.41		1.34		1.23		1.30		.77		2.56		1.31	
D/PE_d		2.48		1.19		1.54		1.46		2.99		2.07		.31	

Sex	Coefficients of Variability						
Male	.20 ± .024	.22 ± .026	.20 ± .024	.21 ± .025	.16 ± .019	.37 ± .048	.22 ± .026
Female	.13 ± .020	.12 ± .019	.10 ± .016	.11 ± .016	.08 ± .012	.19 ± .030	.28 ± .045
M & F	.18 ± .016	.16 ± .014	.17 ± .015	.19 ± .015	.13 ± .011	.34 ± .031	.25 ± .022

TABLE 4.6   A Summary of the Means in Table 4.5, Showing the Effect of Practice in the *NCWd* Test Upon the *NCWd*, the *NC*, and the *RCNd* Tests

Test	NCWd			NC			RCNd		
Sex	M	F	M & F	M	F	M & F	M	F	M & F
Initial Score	51.2	47.8	49.6	30.6	26.5	28.7	19.6	19.1	19.4
Final Score	33.4	31.5	32.8	25.9	23.6	24.7	37.3	32.0	34.8
Gain	17.8	16.3	16.8	4.7	2.9	4.0	−17.7	−12.9	−15.4
Percent Gain	34.8	34.1	33.9	15.4	10.9	13.9	−90.3	−67.5	−79.3

Minus signs show loss.

An examination of the data of the sex groups reveals a differences in speed on the *NCWd* test which favors the females. This is to be expected as there is a difference in favor of females in naming colors. Though the difference is not reliable in any one case it exists throughout the practice series; indicating that the relative improvement is approximately the same for the two groups. This latter fact is also shown by the ratio of the difference between the halves of practice series to the first half. It is .185 for the males and .180 for the females.

The Effect of Practice on the *NCWd* Test Upon the *NC* Test

The middle section of Table 4.6 shows a gain on the *NC* test of 4.0 seconds or 13.9 percent of the initial score. This is only 23.7 percent of the gain on the *NCWd* test which means that less than one fourth of the total gain on the *NCWd* test is due to increase in speed in naming colors. The improvement is greater for the males, which is accounted for by the fact that there is more difference between naming colors and reading names of colors for the males than for the females.

The Effects in the RCNd Test of Practice on the *NCWd* and *NC* Tests

The right section of Table 4.6 shows that the practice on the *NCWd* and *NC* tests resulted in heavy loss in speed on the *RCNd* test. A comparison of the right and left sections of the table shows that the loss on the *RCNd* test, when measured in absolute units, is practically equal to the gain on the *NCWd* test; when measured in relative units it is much greater. It is interesting to find that in ten short practice periods the relative values of opposing stimuli can be modified so greatly. There is little relation, however, between the

gain in one case and the loss in the other. The correlation between gain and loss in absolute units is .262 ± .11, while the correlation between percent of gain and percent of loss is .016 ± .17, or zero. This is what one might expect.

From a consideration of the results of the two applications of the *RCNd* test given in the final tests of Table 4.5, it is evident that the newly developed interference disappears very rapidly with practice. From one day to the next the mean decreases from 34.8 to 22.0 seconds. This indicates that renewing the effectiveness of old associations which are being opposed by newly formed ones is easier than strengthening new associations in opposition to old well established ones.

The variability of the group is increased by the increase in interference due to practice on the *NCWd* test. The coefficient of variability increases from .15 ± .013 to .34 ± .031, the difference divided by its probable error being 5.65. This is not surprising as the degree of the interference varies widely from different subjects. Its degree is determined by the learning on the practice series which is shown by the individual results to vary considerably. One day's practice on the *RCNd* test reduced the variability from .34 ± .031 to .25 ± .022. The decrease in variability is 2.3 times its probable error.

The data from this experiment present interesting findings on the effect of practice upon individual differences. The results which have already been discussed separately are presented for comparison in Table 4.7.

These results show that practice increases individual differences where a stimulus to which the subjects have an habitual reaction pattern is interfering with reactions to a stimulus for which the subjects do not have an habitual reaction pattern (the word stimulus interfering with naming colors, *NCWd* test); but decreases individual differences where a stimulus to which the subjects do not have an habitual reaction

TABLE 4.7   The Effects of Practice on the NCWd Test and the RCNd Test Upon the Coefficient of Variability for the Group

| Test | No. Ss. | Coefficents of Variability | | D | PE_d | D/PE_d |
		Initial	Final			
NCW	32	.14	.19	.05	.034	2.60
RCNd	32	.34	.25	.09	.037	2.33

pattern is interfering with reactions to a stimulus for which the subjects have an habitual reaction pattern (the color stimulus interfering with reading words, *RCNd* test). There are two other variables involved, however: initial variability and length of practice. Thus in the *NCWd* test the initial variability was less, the difficulty greater, and the practice greater than in the *RCNd* test. These findings lend some support to Peterson's hypothesis, "Subjects of normal heterogeneity would become more alike with practice on the simpler processes or activities, but more different on the more complex activities" (Peterson and Barlow, 1928, p. 228).

A sex difference in naming colors has been found by all who have studied color naming and has been generally attributed to the greater facility of women in verbal reactions than of men. There is some indication in our data that this sex difference may be due to the difference in the accustomed reaction of the two sexes to colors as stimuli. In other words responding to a color stimulus by naming the color may be more common with females than with males. This difference is probably built up through education. Education in color is much more intense for girls than for boys as observing, naming, and discussing colors relative to dress is much more common among girls than among boys. The practice in naming colors in the *NCWd* test decreased the difference between the sex groups on the *NC* test from a difference 5.38 times its probable error to a difference 2.99 times its probable error. This decrease in the difference due to practice favors the view that the difference has been acquired and is therefore a product of training.

SUMMARY

1. Interference in serial verbal reactions has been studied by means of newly devised experimental materials. The source of the interference is in the materials themselves. The words red, blue, green, brown, and purple are used on the test sheet. No word is printed in the color it names but an equal number of times in each of the other four colors; *i.e.*, the word "red" is printed in blue, green, brown, and purple inks; the word "blue" is printed in red, green, brown, and purple inks; etc. Thus each word presents the name of one color printed in ink of another color. Hence, a word stimulus and a color stimulus both are presented simultaneously. The words of the test are duplicated in black print and the colors of the test are duplicated in squares or swastikas. The difference in the time for reading the words printed in colors and the same words printed in black is the measure of the interference of color stimuli upon reading words. The difference in the time for naming the colors in which the words are printed and the same colors printed in squares (or swastikas) is the measure of the interference of conflicting word stimuli upon naming colors.

2. The interference of conflicting color stimuli upon the time for reading 100 words (each word naming a color unlike the ink-color of its print) caused an increase of only 2.3 seconds or 5.6 percent over the normal time for reading the same words printed in black. This increase is not reliable. But the interference of conflicting word stimuli upon the time for naming 100 colors (each color being the print of a word which names another color) caused an increase of 47.0 seconds or 74.3 percent of the normal time for naming colors printed in squares.

These tests provide a unique basis (the interference value) for comparing the effectiveness of the two types of associations. Since the presence of the color stimuli caused no reliable increase over the normal time for reading words ($D/PEd = 3.64$) and the presence of word stimuli caused a considerable increase over the normal time for naming colors (4.35 standard deviation units) the associations that have been formed between the word stimuli and the reading response are evidently more effective than those that have been formed between the color stimuli and the naming response. Since these associations are products of training, and since the difference in their strength corresponds roughly to the difference in training in reading words and naming colors, it seems reasonable to conclude that the difference in speed in reading names of colors and in naming colors may be satisfactorily accounted for by the difference in training in the two activities. The word stimulus has been associated with the specific response "to read," while the color stimulus has been associated with various responses: "to admire," "to name," "to reach for," "to avoid," etc.

3. As a test of the permanency of the interference of conflicting word stimuli to naming colors eight days practice (200 reactions per day) were given in naming the colors of the print of words (each word naming a color unlike the ink-color of its print). The effects of this practice were as follows: 1. It decreased the interference of conflicting word stimuli to naming colors but did not eliminate it. 2. It produced a practice curve comparable to that obtained in many other learning experiments. 3. It increased the variability of the group. 4. It shortened the reaction time to colors presented in color squares. 5. It increased the interference of conflicting color stimuli upon reading words.

4. Practice was found either to increase or to decrease the variability of the group depending upon the nature of the material used.

5. Some indication was found that the sex difference in naming colors is due to the difference in the training of the two sexes.

ENDNOTES

1. The writer wishes to acknowledge the kind assistance received in the preparation of this thesis. He is indebted to Dr. Joseph Peterson for encouragement, helpful suggestions, and criticism of the manuscript; to Major H. W. Fenker, a graduate student in psychology, for helpful suggestions relative to preparation of the manuscript; to Drs. J. Peterson, S. C. Garrison, M. R. Schneck, J. E. Caster, O. A. Simley, W. F. Smith, and to Miss M. Nichol for aid in securing subjects; to some three hundred college students who served as subjects; and to William Fitzgerald of The Peabody Press for substantial assistance in the printing of the test materials.

2. Descoeudres (1914) and also Goodenough and Brian (1929) presented color and form simultaneously in studying their relative values as stimuli.

3. In Appendix A will be found a key to all symbols and abbreviations used in this paper.

REFERENCES

Bair, J. H., The practice curve: A study of the formation of habits. *Psychol. Rev. Monog. Suppl.*, 1902 (No. 19), 1–70.

Bergström, J. A., Experiments upon physiological memory. *Amer. J. Psychol.*, 1893, 5, 356–359.

Bergström, J. A., The relation of the interference of the practice effect of an association. *Amer. J. Psychol.*, 1894, 6, 433–442.

Bowditch, H. P., and Warren, J. W., The knee-jerk and its physiological modifications. *J. Physiology*, 1890, 11, 25–46.

Brown, Warner, Practice in associating color names with colors. *Psychol. Rev.*, 1915, 22, 45–55.

Brown, Warner, Habit interference in card sorting. *Univ. of Calif. Studies in Psychol.*, 1914, V. i, No. 4.

Cattell, J. McK., The time it takes to see and name objects. *Mind*, 1886, 11, 63–65.

Culler, A. J., Interference and adaptability. *Arch. of Psychol.*, 1912, 3 (No. 24), 1–80.

Descoeudres, A., Couleur, forme, ou nombre. *Arch. de psychol.*, 1914, 14, 305–341.

Garrett, H. E., and Lemmon, V. W., An analysis of several well-known tests. *J. Appld. Psychol.*, 1924, 8, 424–438.

Goodenough, F. L., and Brian, C. R., Certain factors underlying the acquisition of motor skill by pre-school children. *J. Exper. Psychol.*, 1929, 12, 127–155.

Hunter, W. S., and Yarbrough, J. U., The interference of auditory habits in the white rat. *J. Animal Behav.*, 1917, 7, 49–65.

Hunter, W. S., Habit interference in the white rat and in the human subject. *J. Comp. Psychol.*, 1922, 2, 29–59.

Kline, L. W., An experimental study of associative inhibition. *J. Exper. Psychol.*, 1921, 4, 270–299.

Lester, O. P., Mental set in relation to retroactive inhibition. *J. Exper. Psychol.*, 1932, 15, 681–699.

Ligon, E. M. A., Genetic study of color naming and word reading. *Amer. J. Psychol.*, 1932, 44, 103–121.

Lund, F. H., The role of practice in speed of association. *J. Exper. Psychol.*, 1927, 10, 424–433.

Müller, G. E., and Schumann, F., Experimentalle Beiträge zu Untersuchung des Gedächtnisses. *Zsch. f. Psychol.*, 1894, 6, 81–190.

Münsterberg, Hugo, Gedächtnisstudien. *Beiträge zur Experimentellen Psychologie*, 1892, 4, 70.

Pearce, Bennie D., A note on the interference of visual habits in the white rat. *J. Animal Behav.*, 1917, 7, 169–177.

Peterson, J., and Barlow, M. C., *The effects of practice on individual differences.* The 27th Yearbook of Nat. Soc. Study of Educ., Part II, 1928, 211–230.

Peterson, J., Lanier, L. H., and Walker, H. M., Comparisons of white and negro children. *J. Comp. Psychol.*, 1925, 5, 271–283.

Peterson, J., and David, Q. J., *The psychology of handling men in the army.* Minneapolis, Minn. Perine Book Co., 1918, p. 146.

Shepard, J. F., and Fogelsonger, H. M., Association and inhibition. *Psychol. Rev.*, 1913, 20, 291–311.

Telford, C. W., Differences in responses to colors and their names. *J. Genet. Psychol.*, 1930, 37, 151–159.

Woodworth, R. S., and Wells, F. L., Association tests. *Psychol. Rev. Monog. Suppl.*, 1911, 13 (No. 57), p. 85.

APPENDIX A

A Key to Symbols and Abbreviations

NC	Naming Colors.
NCWd	Naming the Colors of the Print of Words Where the Color of the Print and the Word Are Different.
RCNb	Reading Color Names Printed in Black Ink.
RCNd	Reading Color Names Where the Color of the Print and the Word Are Different.
D	Difference.
D/*PE*$_d$	Difference divided by the probable error of the difference.
M & F	Males and Females.
PE$_d$	Probable error of the difference.
σ	Sigma or standard deviation.
σ/*m*	Standard deviation divided by the mean.

CHAPTER TWO
Perception

5 APPARENT MOTION

Motion perception is fundamental to our ability to survive in a rapidly changing world. As we move around in the world, it is critical for us to be able to detect and identify moving objects. Indeed, much of our visual system contributes to the perception of moving objects. Current understanding of the perceptual, neurophysiological, and computational properties of motion perception probably surpasses any other area of cognitive psychology. Thus, it is entirely appropriate to recognize a monograph by Wertheimer (1912) as a classic article that has influenced the study of motion perception for almost 100 years. Nevertheless, a classic article is not always easy to read. Wertheimer's monograph is around 100 pages long, written in German, and written with a style that is foreign to today's culture. As a result, a translation of part of Wertheimer's monograph would likely be difficult for most students. Fortunately, this article by Robert Sekuler acts as a convenient substitute. It discusses Wertheimer's manuscript from a modern perspective. By focusing on those parts that are most relevant to modern studies of perception, this reading provides both an interesting view of a classic document and a summary of important issues in modern studies of motion perception.

Wertheimer's monograph was a study of apparent motion, which is a percept of motion that results when two nonmoving stimuli are presented in different places, one after the other. As Sekuler notes, Wertheimer did *not* discover apparent motion. Indeed, by the time Wertheimer published his study, people around the world were already viewing movies, which are based on apparent motion. Wertheimer's contribution was in the scientific study of apparent motion rather than its discovery. As a result of his study, Wertheimer identified many new properties of apparent motion.

Wertheimer was particularly interested in apparent motion because it seemed to demonstrate a situation in which the visual percept was different from the stimuli that produced it. In the beginning of the 20th century there was a vigorous philosophical debate about the nature of visual percepts. Some researchers believed that visual perception involved detecting and registering properties of the physical world. From this point of view, the study of visual perception should involve manipulating the stimuli and measuring detection. Wertheimer (and others) favored a different view that perception involved a process of perceptual organization that required an understanding of the relationships between stimuli.

In the apparent motion displays used by Wertheimer, the stimuli were simply dots or lines that appeared and disappeared. If perception involved simply detecting the properties of the physical world, one would expect that observers would either be able to detect the stimuli or not, but the percept is quite different: Motion is observed, even though it is not a property of either of the stimuli. Wertheimer later elaborated on these ideas as part of the development of Gestalt psychology.

Wertheimer's monograph reported on many different phenomena regarding apparent motion. Sekular's review of the monograph reports on only a subset of Wertheimer's investigation. Even in that subset, though, one finds a variety of interesting topics: tests of theories, effects of varying the timing of the stimuli, attentional influences, hysteresis, motion paths, and contextual effects. The CogLab demonstration on apparent motion explores only one of those effects: variation of stimulus timing. Wertheimer (and other researchers before him) noted that if two stimuli appear very quickly one after the other any motion percepts were weak, and instead observers tended to see the two stimuli as presented simultaneously. Likewise, if there was a long delay between the offset of the first stimulus and the onset of the second stimulus, observers tended to see the two stimuli as presented one after the other, with only a weak percept of motion. Motion percepts were most strong at some intermediate interstimulus interval (ISI) between the offset of the first stimulus and the onset of the second stimulus.

In the CogLab experiment, the observer is asked to find the ISI that produces the strongest percept of motion. This is done for various spatial separations of the stimuli. One could also use the same demonstration to investigate Wertheimer's reports of partial apparent motion and hysteresis effects.

The references in Sekuler's paper provide an excellent introduction into modern studies of motion perception. The book by Kolers (1972) provides an excellent and readable discussion of earlier work on motion perception.

REFERENCE

Kolers, P. A. (1972). *Aspects of motion perception.* Oxford: Pergamon Press.

QUESTIONS

1. What is the main difference between apparent and real motion?
2. How did Wertheimer use afterimages to allow observers to detect eye movements?

3. What hysteresis effects did Wertheimer report on ISI?
4. In what Sekuler calls studies on "transparency," Wertheimer does report a difference between real and apparent motion. What is this difference?

Motion Perception: A Modern View of Wertheimer's 1912 Monograph

Robert Sekuler

Volen Center for Complex Systems, Brandeis University

ABSTRACT

Max Wertheimer's 1912 monograph on apparent motion is a seminal contribution to the study of visual motion, but its actual contents are not widely known. This article attempts to clarify what the monograph did and did not contribute, emphasizing links between Wertheimer's principal findings and the results of subsequent investigations of motion perception, including currently active lines of research. The topics discussed include Wertheimer's experimental tests of explanations for apparent motion; his work with motion phenomena that lie between succession and optimum motion; his studies of the influence of attention on motion, explorations of various forms of hysteresis and motion transparency; and Wertheimer's work with a motion-blind patient.

1. INTRODUCTION

In 1912 Max Wertheimer published the first of the papers on which his reputation rests, a monograph entitled "Experimentelle Studien über das Sehen von Bewegung." In the course of little more than 100 pages Wertheimer described several dozen experiments and demonstrations, touching upon many issues that now occupy a central position in research on motion perception. Today there can be no doubt that Wertheimer's monograph was a seminal contribution.

My impression, which may be unjustified in its cynicism, is that this important paper is cited far more often than it is actually read. Of course, many papers have high cite-to-read ratios, so why remark on this particular case? There are four reasons. First, significant aspects of the monograph are not only ignored by

secondary sources, they are actually misrepresented or distorted in the retelling. Second, the monograph is of continuing interest because it foreshadows issues in contemporary research on motion perception. Third, the ingenuity behind some of the questions and experiments offers valuable lessons for students of perception. Finally, Wertheimer's monograph illustrates how a thoughtful researcher can wring objective quantitative insights out of subtle phenomena without sliding into uninterpretable subjectivity.

Just as there are several reasons why the monograph should be read, there are also several reasons why this tends not to happen, despite the current high interest in motion perception. First, the field now uses what Teller (1990) terms "special stimuli"— spatiotemporal displays designed specifically to test particular physiological linking hypotheses. In the domain of visual motion, special stimuli include second-order motion displays (Chubb and Sperling 1988; Pantle 1973), isoluminant gratings (Cavanagh et al 1984), plaids (Adelson and Movshon 1982), and displays whose elements follow complex trajectories (Scase et al 1996; Sekuler 1992). Although some of Wertheimer's experiments did use special stimuli for similar purpose, the stimuli in his experiments were inspired by a view of the nervous system that bears little connection to our current understanding. Second, Wertheimer attempted to communicate not only the results of his psychophysical experiments, but also the nuances of his subjects' experiences. As a result of this laudable effort the monograph contains many passages in which the language is opaque or obscure. As one translator put it, "This paper is particularly

SOURCE: From Sekuler, R. (1996) Motion perception: A modern view of Wertheimer's 1912 monograph. *Perception, 25,* 1243–1258. Reprinted with permission of Pion, London.

difficult to translate because of Wertheimer's deliberate use of words and phrases in a novel manner, ie as symbols of the event (eg 'stationary-position-character') rather than as simple names or descriptions" (Shipley 1961, page 1032).[1] Third, to my knowledge no complete English translation of the monograph has been published, though excerpts have been. For example, Shipley (1961) published a translation of about 70 pages; Herrnstein and Boring (1965) offered a fluid rendition of only 7 pages. Finally, although it is not a translation, Paul Kolers's book on visual motion (1972) devotes a full chapter to Wertheimer's monograph, and is also an excellent introduction to the topic.

1.1 Caveat Lector

My goal here is not to provide a complete guide to Wertheimer's monograph; that task belongs rightly to the person who prepares and publishes a full translation into English. Instead, I want to call attention to aspects of the monograph that might benefit and stimulate research on motion perception. I would like to encourage more people to read for themselves what Wertheimer had to say.

The interpretation of history is colored by the interpreter's knowledge and perspective (Butterfield 1931/1950). The most familiar manifestation of such influences may be the "Rashomon effect"[2] in which eyewitness observers diverge in their interpretation and report of some event. But the Rashomon effect does not exhaust the ways in which knowledge and perspective influence historical studies. The interpretation of written historical documents is not immune from the influence of one's background knowledge of events and developments subsequent to the document. When one reads an historical document, one tends to interpret ambiguous remarks in light of knowledge that comes from outside the text. With Wertheimer's monograph a reader is unavoidably mindful of Wertheimer's own later contributions, as well as of other subsequent developments in the field.

One may try to recognize and resist the tendency to re-interpret history, but success is far from assured. This general concern will be familiar to students of perception, and particularly to readers of this journal,

who, as well as anyone, recognize the contribution of top-down influences to perception (Gregory 1969; Gregory 1995). Perhaps this historiographic problem is another reason to read Wertheimer's monograph oneself.

2. WHAT WERTHEIMER DID NOT DO

Some secondary sources credit Wertheimer with discoveries that rightly belong to others. So, before getting to Wertheimer's actual contributions, it might be useful to identify several things he did not contribute. For example, long before Wertheimer people realized that visual motion could be generated by properly sequenced stationary targets. In 1824, Peter Roget, best known today for his thesaurus, presented a paper to the Royal Society describing his idea that visual motion arose from a succession of static images (Boorstin 1992, page 740). And, several decades before Wertheimer's monograph, Exner (1875) recognized that apparent motion could be important for understanding perception more generally. Exner, with whom Wertheimer did some postdoctoral study (Sarris and Wertheimer 1987) demonstrated that motion perception was not a mere parasite on the perception of space or time. In particular, Exner showed that apparent motion could be seen even though the two targets producing that motion were too close, in time or space, to be discriminated from one another.

And, long before Wertheimer's monograph, researchers knew that variation in the timing of stimulus sequences carved out three perceptual domains, which we call "succession," "motion," and "simultaneity." Of course, the best-known application of apparent motion is its use in television and movies. Coincidentally, the word "movie" was coined in the year of Wertheimer's publication. By that time, apparent motion was being exploited to good financial advantage by Thomas Alva Edison and others (Boorstin 1992).

None of these facts diminishes the importance of what Wertheimer did. His depth of understanding and persistent curiosity were extraordinary. He appreciated the rich theoretical implications of the very simple phenomenon he studied. He was equally aware of the phenomenon's experimental possibilities.

3. THE APPARENT MYSTERY OF APPARENT MOTION

In the opening paragraphs of his monograph Wertheimer identified the most intriguing feature of apparent motion: two static objects, presented in succession at different locations, produce motion—a perceptual attribute not owned by either object alone.

> When seeing motion is the result of an "illusion" (that is, if there is actually physically a single, resting position and then another resting position, clearly separated from the first), the two perceptions of static objects somehow produced an associated, subjective completion: The passage through [the space], the assumption of intermediate positions, was somehow completed subjectively. The following investigation deals with the impressions of motion that result from the presentation of two such successive positions, even when the two are widely separated. (Wertheimer 1912, pages 162–163)

From prior work by others, Wertheimer collated several alternative explanations for apparent motion. Taking just two of these alternatives, apparent motion had been attributed to factors such as: (a) processes associated with eye movements; and (b) cognitive inferences of the type "I saw X, I saw Y, therefore X must have moved to Y." Without the benefit of modern tools, such as eye-trackers and computer-generated displays, Wertheimer managed to address these explanations experimentally, usually offering several experiments to test each one of them.

Consider, for instance, some of the five experiments done to determine whether eye movements could explain apparent motion. Wertheimer (page 182) began by confirming that apparent motion could be generated with total exposure times below one-tenth second, comfortably less than the reaction time of the oculomotor system. (Total exposure time is the sum of each object's duration, plus the interval between them.) Wertheimer went on to devise a method that allowed him to detect eye movements that might occur while subjects viewed the display (pages 183–184). At the start of each trial, the subject fixated a small luminous cross [Figure 5.1, panel (a)]. With the afterimage of the cross on his or her fovea, the subject fixated the spot where a small square would appear during the motion sequence. Then the subject was given the sequence whose components are illustrated in panels (b) and (c). The resulting apparent movement is represented in panel (d). Subjects reported that the afterimage remained quietly at locus of fixation, suggesting that eye movements were either small or nonexistent. Just as important, subjects reported that the motion was the same as it had been in a control condition with no afterimage present. Another experiment used displays designed to evoke simultaneous opposite directions of motion. Such movements would rule out a causal role for eye movements, which could take only one direction at a time (pages 184–185). Figure 5.2 illustrates the successive frames of one such display, along with a diagram suggesting what subjects reported. Although scant details are given, Wertheimer commented that he could generate three

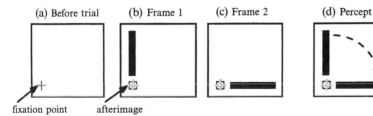

(a) Before trial   (b) Frame 1   (c) Frame 2   (d) Percept

fixation point   afterimage

FIGURE 5.1   Schematic of the method Wertheimer used to detect subjects' eye movements. (a) At the start of each trial the subject fixated a small luminous cross. With the afterimage of the cross on the fovea, the subject fixated the spot where a small square would appear, and saw a (b) vertical bar alternate with (c) a horizontal bar. (d) Despite the stability of the fixation point relative to the small square subjects saw apparent motion.

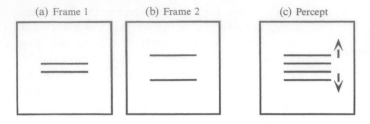

(a) Frame 1   (b) Frame 2   (c) Percept

FIGURE 5.2   Schematic of display used to evoke simultaneous opposite directions of motion. In the movement space, the lines shown in panel (a) alternated with those in panel (b). The result—simultaneous opposite directions of apparent motion—is illustrated in panel (c).

or four disparate simultaneous impressions of motion. For example, he found that good motion was produced when some novel collection of complex objects (a small cage, a plant, and [a] bunch of grapes) were presented for the first time. In such cases, the various objects could be made to move in different directions.

As I indicated above, Wertheimer also tested whether apparent motion depended upon some form of cognitive inference. In one experiment on this issue, Wertheimer presented apparent and real motion side by side. Observers who were ignorant of which stimulus was which attempted to distinguish the two.

> In most cases, real movement and apparent movement were generally indistinguishable, even by observers who had many months' training making precise observations of things seen in brief presentations. In some cases, . . . the stimuli were finally recognized correctly, but not because one was marked as movement and the other as non-movement. Instead, there was a qualitative difference between the movements. . . . [C]omments were made like "one movement differed from the other because one was so intense, so strong, it was the best movement of all," but this comment did not always pertain to the presentation of the real motion, but to that of the two static stimuli. (pages 173–174)

This result—equivalence of real and apparent motion—depends upon careful choice of stimulus parameters. With most parameter sets, including most in the monograph, apparent motion is not likely to be confused with continuous motion, a point considered further in the next section.

4. WHY DO WE SEE MOTION AND WHAT DOES THE MOTION LOOK LIKE?

Wertheimer was intrigued by the fact that nonmoving stimuli produced clear and compelling motion. Almost certainly part of the explanation of apparent

motion lies in the limited spatial and temporal resolution of the visual system. The visual system is blind to spatiotemporal variations falling outside these limits, which Watson et al (1983) designated the "window of visibility." This construct can be used to predict whether some time-sampled stimulus would be perceptually indistinguishable from one in which motion is continuous. Any time-sampled stimulus, like the one schematized in Figure 5.1, can be represented on space-time frequency axes. Spectral components that fall outside the window of visibility would have a diminished effect or no effect on vision. This opens the possibility that two physically different stimuli could generate identical visual responses, and would therefore be perceptually indistinguishable from one another.

However attractive it may be as a simplifying heuristic, as an explanatory construct the window of visibility is deficient. First, the window of visibility ignores directional selectivity, one of the motion system's defining properties. Because it operates on spatiotemporal variations without regard to the directional characteristics of those variations, the window of visibility is silent about perceived direction of motion. It is also silent about subtle phenomena that depend upon the characteristics of directional tuning, for example the efficiency with which directional information is extracted from stimuli comprising many different spatially-intermingled directions (Watamaniuk 1993). Because it ignores directional properties, the window of visibility has nothing to tell us about the actual *appearance* of the sampled motion: [I]t tells us *whether* a sampled stimulus will be distinguishable from a continuous one, but it says nothing about what either one will look like. In addition, predictions from the window of visibility ignore masking effects from spatiotemporal variations that lie just beyond the limits of visibility. Though such components are not visible themselves, they can influence (mask) the appear-

(a) Percept with optimal ISI

(b) ISI slightly below optimal

(c) ISI much below optimal

FIGURE 5.3 One form of partial movement studied by Wertheimer. The dotted line in panel (a) illustrates the complete movement seen with an optimal interval between the two stimulus components, a vertical bar and a horizontal bar. Panel (b) suggests the partial movement seen when the interval between the two display frames is shortened. Panel (c) illustrates the consequence of shortening the interval still further.

ance of motion (Wandell 1995). The window's deficiencies are particularly important in connection to Wertheimer's monograph, which emphasized stimulus-related variations in the strength and clarity of apparent motion.

Exner (1875) was probably first to identify three temporal regimes of apparent motion: long intervals between stimuli yield succession; short intervals yield simultaneity; and appropriate intermediate intervals yield apparent motion. This tripartite scheme now is familiar to even the most casual student of psychology. Wertheimer, however, realized that the visual system did not entirely respect Exner's scheme. In fact, he was intrigued by the percepts that lay between stages. Wertheimer asked (1912, page 166):

> How does the optimal stage of motion arise? How does it develop from simultaneity, from succession? How does it break down into these stages? What is rendered in the transitions from stage to stage? Could there be qualitatively distinct, specifically characterized impressions between stages, which might illuminate the qualitative development and the psychological idiosyncrasy of the impression of optimal motion impression?

With painstaking care Wertheimer explored motion's in-between stages. Changing the interstimulus interval in very small steps,[3] he would present a stimulus and record the observer's report. Typically, two minutes elapsed before the next stimulus presentation. This leisurely pace allowed him to do some necessary calculations and also allowed any residual effects from the preceding trial to dissipate. Among the subtleties revealed by this effort was partial movement (*Teilbewegung*), in which the elements move only part way toward one another, and singular movement (*Singularbewegung*), in which only one of the two elements appears to move (Wertheimer 1912, pages 191–196). Figure 5.3 schematized one form of

partial movement. This stimulus sequence in each panel of that figure was the same as in Figure 5.1, a vertical object followed by a horizontal one. The left panel shows that when the interval between the two frames is optimal the resulting motion seems to cover the entire space between the objects: [T]he vertical object rotates all the way to horizontal. When the interstimulus interval (ISI) is made slightly shorter, though, subjects report that the vertical moved only part way [panel (b)]. If the ISI is shortened further, without reaching the point of simultaneity, partial movements become even shorter (as illustrated in the right panel of Figure 5.3).

Note that these effects do not lend themselves to easy quantification by ordinary psychophysical methods. Subjects can be encouraged to map these variations in the character of motion onto response categories of "motion" and "no motion," but only at the cost of obscuring phenomena that may be significant theoretically, however inconvenient they may be in data analysis. DeSilva articulated this point with particular clarity (1928, pages 553–555).

Wertheimer explored several factors that encouraged partial motion, or promoted partial motion into full blown motion. One particularly potent factor was attention, to which I next turn.

5. ATTENTION INFLUENCES APPARENT MOTION

In several experiments Wertheimer showed how the characteristics of apparent motion are altered by shifts in observers' attention (pages 208–211). Generally, the appearance of motion is favored in a place to which the observer is attending. For example, Wertheimer presented a red horizontal stripe followed by a similar blue (or green or white) stripe located below the red one (page 209). He found an ISI that produced good

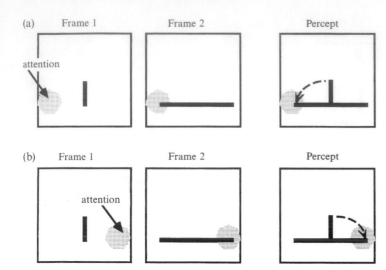

FIGURE 5.4   Schematic result of one of Wertheimer's experiments on attention. A short vertical line was followed by a longer horizontal line. (a) When attention was positioned in the vicinity of the left of the horizontal line, observers saw motion toward the left. (b) Positioning attention at the other side of the horizontal line produced motion toward the right.

(but not optimal) motion from the red stripe to the blue. He then encouraged subjects to concentrate attention on the first stripe, for instance by presenting that stripe alone several times. Now subjects reported that the attended-to stripe moved part way toward the non-attended stripe, which seemed not to have moved at all. When subjects attended to the lower stripe, the upper stripe (presented first) seemed to be stationary, while the blue stripe moved clearly and distinctly into its lower position.

Figure 5.4 illustrates another of Wertheimer's experiments on attention (page 211). A short vertical line was followed by a longer horizontal line. When attention was positioned in the vicinity of the left end of the horizontal line, the observer saw motion toward the left; positioning attention at the other side of the horizontal line produced motion toward the right.

In recent years many researchers have explored the impact of attention on perceived motion, though none seems to have acknowledged Wertheimer's pioneering work in this area. One example of such influence is the motion-induction effect. Here an observer is shown a spatially extended stimulus, such as a horizontal line, and movement is seen within the stimulus in a direction *away* from the end of the stimulus to which the observer attends. For example, Hikosaka et al (1993a, 1993b) found that a briefly flashed horizontal line appeared to be drawn either left to right or right to left, depending upon the side to which the observer attended: [W]hen the subject attended to a spot at the left side of the to-be-drawn line, the line ap-

peared to grow outward from the attended spot. This effect is most likely caused by enhanced processing speed within the attended region (von Grünau et al 1995), which could also describe Wertheimer's original observations. All of these, in turn, are related to the generalization known as the law of prior entry (Reber 1995, page 597): "Of two simultaneously presented stimuli the one upon which one's attention is focused will be perceived as having occurred first."

6. PERCEPTUAL INERTIA: HYSTERESIS

Earlier I commended Wertheimer's caution in allowing two minutes to elapse between trials in some experiments. A similar caution led him to keep subjects uninformed, wherever possible, about the details and purpose of an experiment. This was especially important because his three main subjects (Wolfgang Köhler, Kurt Koffka, and Mira Klein-Koffka) served repeatedly in the studies, and during the course of these experiments Wertheimer, Köhler, and K. Koffka "saw one another daily, and actually discussed everything under the sun" (Koffka, quoted in Sarris and Wertheimer 1987, page 483).

6.1 Hysteresis of Motion

Into some experiments Wertheimer inserted catch trials—a maneuver that kept observers honest and also led to one intriguing result (page 217). A horizontal and a vertical line (as in Figure 5.1) were alternated

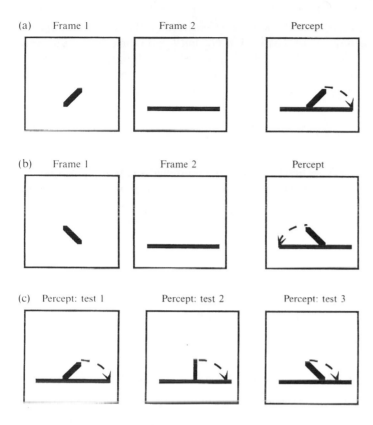

(a) Frame 1   Frame 2   Percept

(b) Frame 1   Frame 2   Percept

(c) Percept: test 1   Percept: test 2   Percept: test 3

FIGURE 5.5 Hysteresis: exposure to a stimulus that produces motion in one direction biases the response to subsequently seen stimulus. The upper two panels, (a) and (b), show the result when a short oblique line is followed by a horizontal line. The resulting apparent motion takes the shorter of the two possible paths, either rightward (a) or leftward (b). After several presentations of the sequence illustrated in the top panel, any of the sequences in panel (c) produced motion to the right, which would not have happened in the absence of the conditioning exposure.

several times at a rate that produced good to-and-fro motion. Then, without the observer's knowledge, Wertheimer omitted the horizontal line, while continuing to present its vertical partner at its own appropriate time (page 218). The result was that for two or three presentations observers reported that they continued to see the motion, although the motion was partial and grew smaller with repeated presentations. By the third or fourth cycle no motion at all was seen. Bear in mind that the observer did not know that one of the lines had been omitted. This intriguing form of perceptual preservation was studied in more detail by DeSilva (1929), who not only omitted an element without warning the observer (page 282), as Wertheimer did, but also examined the effect of suddenly reversing the direction of motion, again without warning the observer (page 287). In both cases DeSilva found that for a short time after the stimulus changed observers continued to see the original direction of motion.

6.2 Hysteresis of Stimulus Orientation

Figure 5.5 illustrates a related effect which Wertheimer examined quantitatively. The upper two panels suggest what happens when a short oblique line is followed by a horizontal line: [T]he resulting apparent motion takes the shorter of the two possible paths, either rightward (top panel) or leftward (middle panel). After establishing these baseline results, Wertheimer gave an observer several successive presentations of the sequence shown in the top panel. As expected, each presentation produced motion to the right. Now, while continuing to present this stimulus, Wertheimer interspersed single presentations like those illustrated in the bottom panel of Figure 5.5. The first test resulted in motion to the right, which is what would have been produced in the absence of the conditioning sequence. The second test produced a similar result—motion toward the right. And the same result even occurred in the third test, which previously would have produced motion to the left. Exposure to a stimulus that produces motion in one direction biases or primes the response to a subsequently seen stimulus. To quantify this phenomenon Wertheimer measured the orientation at which perceived direction reversed. The effects of the biasing motion were very substantial, shifting the critical orientation by as much as 35° or 40°.

6.3 Hysteresis of Stimulus Timing

Wertheimer reported another demonstration of hysteresis, by examining the interstimulus intervals (ISIs) at which good apparent motion could be seen. Far from being a fixed value (even for constant spatial conditions), the range of ISIs for good motion varied with the preceding exposure conditions. For example, exposures to an optimal ISI allowed a subsequently presented non-optimal ISI to evoke good motion. Thus, exposure to "good" ISIs allowed subjects to see good motion at an ISI that ordinarily produced poor motion (pages 194–196). The converse also held: [S]tarting with a "poor" ISI narrowed the range of ISIs that could produce good motion.

In recent years hysteresis in motion perception has become an important theoretical issue because hysteresis is one sign of nonlinear cooperative interactions among visual mechanisms. Similar interactions may contribute to other perceptual domains, but the relatively extended time scale of motion perception makes motion a particularly sensitive index of nonlinear neural interactions. And several researchers have demonstrated hysteresis using random-element cinematograms, comprising spatially intermingled motion vectors in various directions (Chang and Julesz 1984; Nawrot and Sekuler 1990; Williams et al 1986). But random-element cinematograms obviously differ from Wertheimer's stimuli in a number of ways, and results from the two kinds of stimuli may not be completely interchangeable.

Recently Hock et al (1996) quantified the hysteresis that can be generated by stimuli much like those used by Wertheimer. Hock and colleagues devised a display in which the luminance values of two nearby dots were simultaneously exchanged on alternate frames. Under favorable conditions, despite its physical simultaneity, this interchange produced a clear percept that the dots had moved from one position to the other. Hock et al found that the threshold for seeing

such movement depended on the relative luminances of the two dots (L_1 and L_2), on their mean luminance (L_m), and on the background luminance (L_b). These variables were expressed in the ratio $(L_1 - L_2)/(L_m - L_b)$, which Hock et al call background-relative luminance change (BRLC). Note that in this ratio the numerator holds the time-varying properties of the stimulus, and the denominator holds those stimulus properties that do not vary with time. Ordinarily, values of BRLC > 0.5 promoted seeing motion; values < 0.5 promoted seeing the dots stationary (simultaneity).

Hock et al found that once either percept—motion or no motion—was established, it resisted change: [T]he percept persisted despite changes in BRLC that favored the alternative percept. Eventually, when BRLC became sufficiently unfavorable to the current percept, the rival percept emerged. This resistance to change is an index of hysteresis which Hock et al attribute to recurrent facilitatory influences among motion detectors. Note that although these influences show up as "errors" in subjects' perceptions, outside the laboratory such influences would ordinarily benefit their owners by stabilizing perception in the presence of noise.

Hysteretic effects in motion recall Newton's first law of motion: [A] physical object moving at uniform velocity in one direction will persevere in its state of uniform motion unless acted upon by an external force to change that state. Based on their own observations of perceptual inertia, Ramachandran and Anstis (1983) suggested that, because the visual system evolved to process information from a world in which Newton's law holds, it is not surprising that vision exhibits a parallel perceptual version of Newton's law.

7. TRANSPARENCY

In the natural world various circumstances can cause one surface to appear to move across another. For example, as you jog along a country road, your shadow moves across the road's surface, producing perceptual transparency. And, when a speedier runner passes you, her or his shadow moves transparently across your own more slowly moving body. In terms of the flow field of the stimulus, motion transparency arises from a discontinuity in the distribution of local velocities. In recent years, vision researchers have been quite interested in perceptual movement of one object or surface relative to another (Qian and Andersen 1994; Stoner and Albright 1994; Zohary et al 1996). This psychophysical work and its physiological counterparts (Qian et al 1994) seek to understand how the visual system manages to represent multiple motion vectors within a single region of visual space.

Although Wertheimer did not write about "velocity distributions" or about "multiple neural representations" his motivation for studying transparency was not too different from the motivation that drives current research. He wanted to know what actually transpired when a target was seen to move (apparently) from position x to position y. Did the motion trajectory induce some measurable visual perturbation in the surface or objects over which it passed, or was the motion transparent to the surface or objects? He wondered about this, particularly for what he called pure phi, when motion, but no moving object per se, was seen. Because the term "phi" is so often misused, a brief clarifying digression may be in order before proceeding. Today, the terms "phi phenomenon" or "phi movement" are sometimes used to signify apparent motion that is optimal; that is, apparent motion that is perceptually compelling. This usage is certainly not what Wertheimer intended. To him, "φ" meant objectless motion, as can be seen by Wertheimer's description of what happens when the successive presentation of two stimuli, a and b, produces apparent motion:

> Let the psychological state of affairs—with no implication whatever—be designated as a φ b; φ signifies what is present other than the perception of a and b; what takes place between a and b in the interval between a and b; what is added to a and b. (Wertheimer 1912, page 186)

It may help to note that φ has a more familiar counterpart in continuous motion. For example, when a small ribbon snake moved rapidly through the grass in a meadow, my friend Florence Harris remarked that she could "see the slithering, but not the slitherer." This observation vividly communicates that there was a clear sense of motion, but that the moving object itself was not seen.

To study transparency Wertheimer inserted various objects into the path of apparent motion (page 221 and following). In one case the interposed object was consonant with the objects that produced the movement. Would the movement passing across the interposed object summate with that object? Against a black background, a white vertical stripe, a, alternated at an optimal rate with a white horizontal stripe, b. Then, when b was presented, a short white oblique stripe, c, was also presented, in the middle of the two other stripes. Wertheimer wanted to know whether c gave any evidence of the passage of the longer stripe. For example, would the interposed line appear to lengthen or brighten? Subjects saw the motion across the field, but there was no sign that the interposed stripe was affected. The interposed bar did not, for instance, appear to lengthen, as one might expect had the interposed bar summed with the passing stripe.

Five decades after Wertheimer's monograph, Kolers (1963) measured such interactions with greater precision. Kolers briefly flashed a small target in the path of a moving line. He adjusted the intensity of the light flash so that, when it was presented alone, the flash could be detected about nine times of every ten. He then allowed the line to move across the position in which the flash would occur. The motion of the line was either apparent or continuous ("real"). Although motions from the two sources were similar perceptually, they had disparate effects on the threshold for the interposed flashed target. A continuously moving line diminished the target detectability, but a line in apparent motion had no effect. The transparency of apparent motion accords with Wertheimer's original report.

8. PHYSIOLOGY OF MOTION PERCEPTION

Near the end of his monograph Wertheimer turned to the physiological underpinnings of apparent motion. Drawing on the observations of Exner and others, including haploscopic observations, Wertheimer strongly endorsed the proposition that seen motion draws on processes "which lie behind the retina" (page 246). For him the contributions of attention and experience which he had investigated further strengthened this endorsement. Now it is taken for granted that the perception of apparent motion depends upon activity in several centers in the human cerebral cortex, including the middle temporal area (MT). Although many diverse studies have contributed to the development of this hypothesis, the work of Newsome and his colleagues has been especially influential (Newsome et al 1986). One of their studies triangulated on the substrate of apparent motion, with the same stimuli used to study the responses of single cortical neurons in macaque visual cortex, as well as psychophysical responses in both macaque and humans. From careful systematic variation in the temporal and spatial parameters of the stimulus, Newsome et al identified detailed parallels between motion sensitivity at the single neuron level and sensitivity measured psychophysically both in macaque monkeys and in human observers.

8.1 Physiological Short Circuits and Isomorphism

Wertheimer attributed apparent motion to a physiological short circuit, a spread of excitation across adjacent centers of activity in the brain. (These centers of activity were set up by the presentation of the stimuli.) The short-circuit hypothesis is both well-known and wrong, so I will not discuss it here, except to note that it asserts an isomorphism that later was expanded and formalized by Wertheimer's colleague and experimental subject, Wolfgang Köhler (1920).

Note that the assumed isomorphism is not between stimulus and brain activity, but between brain activity and perception. As a result the theory could accommodate non-stimulus influences, including the influence of attention. For example, Wertheimer suggested that attending to one component of a motion stimulus increased the excitability of the cortical representation of the attended locus, thereby enhancing the likelihood of a physiological short circuit (pages 248–249). Although the physiological details were wrong, the overall approach seems to foreshadow contemporary accounts of exogenous influences on motion perception (O'Craven and Savoy 1995; Sekuler 1995).

8.2 An Early Report of Motion Blindness

Wertheimer's monograph contains a long footnote that resonates strongly with current research interests:

> I mention that recently a case of pathology (a case of bilateral occipital damage) appears to say that motion

perception has a central basis: In *Wiener Klinische Wochenschrift*, 1911, volume 24, number 14, page 518, Dr Pötzl[4] described the affected female patient: "If one presents her with a bright light that moves slowly or quickly, she seems not to perceive the motion of the object, but describes what she sees as multiple lights. . . ." As a result, in May of 1911, I applied to Dr P. and had an opportunity to test the patient repeatedly during the summer of that year, both with various real movements, as well as with apparent motion stimuli. Unfortunately, the rigor [of these observations] suffered somewhat because of the subject's diminished intelligence but, over and over, her motion perception proved to be deficient, despite recognizing the [object's] color, and so on, while the subject, if prompted by acoustic impressions (rustling and so on) spoke of a "fluttering back and forth." At the same time, the passing object's color was recognized." (Wertheimer 1912, pages 246–247)

Wertheimer realized that the patient's impaired cognitive state muddied the interpretation of her results. And the absence of anatomical details, such as one would have with autopsy or with modern brain imagery, makes it impossible to know the precise site and extent of the damage, further reducing the scientific value of this case (Zeki 1991). With both these caveats firmly in mind, we should acknowledge Wertheimer's priority among researchers who have made psychophysical measurements in motion-blind patients.

For his part Wertheimer was eager to learn whether Pötzl's patient, who had trouble seeing real motion, would also fail to see apparent motion, which she did. Wertheimer's comment that the patient, despite impaired motion perception, could still recognize the color of the moving object is consistent with what has been seen in recent cases of akinetopsia. The reduced visibility of both real and apparent motion is also consistent with recent findings, including those with patient L. M. (Zihl et al 1991). Like many modern psychophysicists who have studied patients with akinetopsia, Wertheimer's goal was to exploit Nature's experiment to understand motion perception, particularly the physiological basis of various forms of motion perception. Today, of course, researchers use more diverse and sophisticated stimuli to test motion-impaired patients (Nawrot and Rizzo 1995; Zihl et al 1983). Of particular theoretical importance have been demonstrations of selective losses to one type of motion coexisting with preserved responses to other types of motion (Vaina and Cowey, 1996; Vaina et al 1990).

9. GESTALT INFLUENCES ON MOTION

Max Wertheimer is known as one of the founders of Gestalt psychology—a perspective that insisted on the primacy of perceptual organization. In empirical research, such perceptual organization shows itself in two distinct, but related, guises: demonstrations that the perceptual whole is different from the sum of its parts, and demonstrations that configural relationships among stimulus elements shape various perceptual phenomena (Rock 1995). Clearly, many of the phenomena in Wertheimer's 1912 monograph confirm the first of these points. Time and again Wertheimer noted that under optimal conditions subjects saw not alternating static objects, but pure disembodied movement—perceptual wholes different from their constituent parts. But Wertheimer's monograph contains only a few observations that foreshadow his later work on configural factors in perception, such as the Gestalt principles of perceptual organization. Those few observations that do relate to configural factors involve a two-stage experimental approach (section 10, pages 201–204). First, Wertheimer assessed the movement generated by alternation of two elements presented by themselves. Then he reassessed this movement after other elements had been introduced into the display field. Varying the identity and position of these added elements revealed a variety of figural effects, though the monograph does not make much of them.

Figure 5.6 shows some stimuli that Wertheimer devised for this purpose (page 202). Two horizontal stripes, separated by a gap, were presented with timing arranged to produce poor or no movement [panel (a)]. After confirming that this arrangement did indeed reliably produce poor movement, Wertheimer inserted an additional figure into each of the two alternating displays. As panel (b) suggests, these additional elements formed an angle that seems to link the

horizontal lines perceptually. When a frame containing one added element was alternated with a frame containing the other added element, temporal conditions that previously yielded poor motion or no motion at all now produced good movement: the horizontal lines were seen as moving back and forth (based on Figure XXIV, page 265 of the monograph).

Wertheimer suggested (page 202) that the angle altered the effective separation between the horizontal stripes . . . , thereby creating a stimulus that was better suited to produce movement with the existing timing. To test this general idea, Wertheimer devised several variants of . . . the components producing the "angle". Most of these variants, some of which are shown in panels (c) and (d), failed to promote perception of movement. Note that the drawings shown in these panels are based on Wertheimer's scant verbal descriptions of what he did (page 204).

These observations show that the movement between two elements is strongly influenced by the presence and configuration of other, neighboring elements. Recently such phenomena have attracted considerable interest in connection with occlusion, image segmentation, and the integration of motion signals arising from adjacent or spatially separated regions (Braddick 1993; Nakayama and Silverman 1988a, 1988b; Stoner and Albright 1994). Perhaps new research will one day show that Wertheimer's results (Figure 5.6) are determined by factors that promote propagation of motion signals from one region to another or inhibit such propagation.

Whatever their explanation may be, it is natural to wonder how such observations relate to the work that Wertheimer would do later, on Gestalt principles of organization. For example, one wonders whether the observations in the 1912 monograph were inspired by some nascent vision of the importance of figural factors in perception. But, in my opinion, the monograph gives little support for this idea. In fact, Wertheimer's observations on adding a third element to the basic movement sequence were motivated less by an interest in figural effects per se than by an interest in the effects of attention on movement. Several paragraphs in the 1912 monograph allude to Gestalt influences, but such allusions are few and scattered, for example, on page 211 and in footnote 1 on page 251.

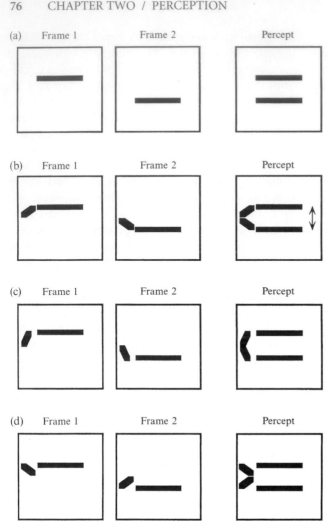

(a)   Frame 1   Frame 2   Percept

(b)   Frame 1   Frame 2   Percept

(c)   Frame 1   Frame 2   Percept

(d)   Frame 1   Frame 2   Percept

FIGURE 5.6   Movement between two elements is influenced by the presence and configuration of other, neighboring elements. In panel (a), two horizontal stripes, separated by a gap, were presented with timing that produced poor movement. As panel (b) suggests, other elements were added to form an angle that seems to link the horizontal lines perceptually. When the frames were alternated. temporal conditions that previously yielded poor motion or no motion at all produced good movement: the horizontal lines were seen as moving back and forth. Panels (c) and (d) illustrate other stimulus sequences in which the extra components stood in different figural relations to the original elements. Many such arrangements failed to produce apparent motion.

As Sarris (1989) points out, over the next two decades Wertheimer's doctoral students, including Wolfgang Metzger (1934) and Josef Ternus (1926), published important work on Gestalt influences on motion. Both these students examined the maintenance or loss of figural identity of moving objects. Of the two, Ternus's work (1926) is better known today, having provoked at least a dozen studies of group and element motion, beginning with Pantle and Picciano (1976). A small section of Ternus's paper is available in English (1938), but not even a partial translation of Metzger's has been published. Despite this lack, one portion of Metzger's work appears to have stimulated a valuable line of modern research (Bertenthal et al

1993; Goldberg and Pomerantz 1982). Even a cursory reading of Metzger's paper reveals several phenomena that will interest and challenge contemporary motion researchers, for example Metzger's work on the perception of multiple targets that traverse irregular or unpredictable trajectories.

10. CONCLUSIONS

This look back at Wertheimer's monograph shows how far we have come in understanding apparent motion. For example, today we have a reasonable picture of the key neural events that probably underlie the basic, early phenomenon of apparent motion (Newsome et al 1986). The monograph reminds us also of how much remains beyond our grasp. Wertheimer posed, or at least hinted at, many significant questions that remain unanswered. He noted the complex interactions between Gestalt (form) factors and the variables that govern motion. Such interactions quite likely reflect neural events in several different regions of the brain. How are these distributed events bound together to generate a unified multidimensional percept?

The transparency phenomena described by Wertheimer comprise another enduring puzzle. Such phenomena imply that multiple contradictory objects can be assigned the same location in visual space, though usually in different depth planes. This possibility seems to conflict with computational rules that have been assumed to operate in other domains, eg the one-to-one matching rules from which the visual system has been assumed to generate element correspondences over successive frames of random-element cinematograms. Obviously, we need to develop a deeper understanding of the coordination of multiple representations.

As I mentioned earlier, in many of Wertheimer's experiments special attention was paid to conditions that produced partial or otherwise sub-optimal movements. These sub-par movements are an interesting challenge to any theory that aspires to be a complete account of apparent motion. These phenomena require that a theory predict not only the existence of perceived motion and its direction, but also variations in the clarity and extent of motion as spatiotemporal parameters change.

A final set of unanswered research questions comes from Wertheimer's experiments on hysteresis. These effects, which seem to be nearly ubiquitous in visual motion, create some obstacles as well as opportunities. Clearly, experiments on visual motion must be designed in a way that takes account of such effects. Wertheimer had the good fortune to allow significant time to elapse between successive trials in his experiments, but most modern researchers do not. Can we say how much experimental noise is added by our (necessary) haste? Finally, we need to understand hysteresis itself, particularly how it relates to the kinds of learning, fast and slow, that are currently being explored in research on visual motion.

ACKNOWLEDGEMENTS

I thank Allison B. Sekuler for helpful comments on a much earlier version of this manuscript. Preparation of the manuscript was supported by the M. R. Bauer Foundation. I thank Viktor Sarris, University of Frankfurt am Main, for inviting me to deliver the Max Wertheimer Memorial Lecture in 1995 which stimulated this article. I am indebted to James R. Lackner who made available to me an unpublished verbatim translation of Wertheimer's monograph, to Howard Hock for allowing me to describe his unpublished data, to Mark Hulliung for pointing me to Butterfield's historiographic work, and to Stuart Anstis, Oliver J Braddick, and Michael Wertheimer for excellent suggestions during the review process.

ENDNOTES

1. Shipley's translation has at least one serious, substantive error. On page 1081, footnote 48, it inverts an experimental result reported by Wertheimer. I first suspected this might be the case when I was unable to replicate the results as Shipley described it. Later, after reading the original, I discovered the reason for my apparent failure to replicate.
2. Named for *Rashomon*, a 1951 film by the distinguished director Akira Kurosawa. In the film, four eyewitnesses to a murder and rape report strikingly different versions of what they all saw.
3. I am not reporting the numerical values given by Wertheimer because those values would vary considerably with actual stimulus conditions. I do not want to encourage misleading overgeneralizations, such as "the boundary between good motion and succession occurs at so-and-so many milliseconds."
4. The paper to which Wertheimer referred was actually published by Pötzl and Redlich, not by Pötzl alone.

REFERENCES

Adelson, E. H., & Movshon J. A. (1982). Phenomenal coherence of moving visual patterns. *Nature (London), 300*, 523–525.

Bertenthal, B. I., Banton, T., & Bradbury A. (1993). Directional bias in the perception of translating patterns. *Perception, 22*, 193–208.

Boorstin, D. J. (1992). *The creators. A history of heroes of the imagination.* New York: Random House.

Braddick, O. J. (1993). Segmentation versus integration in visual motion processing. *Trends in Neurosciences, 16,* 263–268.

Butterfield, H. (1931/1950). *The Whig interpretation of history.* London: Bell and Sons.

Cavanagh, P., Tyler, C., & Favreau, O. (1984). Perceived velocity of moving chromatic gratings. *Journal of the Optical Society of America A, 1,* 893–899.

Chang, J. J., & Julesz, B. (1984). Cooperative phenomena in apparent movement perception. *Vision Research, 24,* 1781–1788.

Chubb, C., & Sperling, G. (1988). Drift-balanced random stimuli: A general basis for studying non-Fourier motion perception. *Journal of the Optical Society of America A, 5,* 1986–2007.

DeSilva, H. R. (1928). Kinematographic movement of parallel lines. *Journal of General Psychology, 1,* 550–557.

DeSilva, H. R. (1929). An analysis of the visual perception of movement. *British Journal of Psychology, 19,* 268–305.

Exner, S. (1875). Über das Sehen von Bewegungen und die Theorie des zusammengesetzen Auges. *Sitzungsberichte der Akademie der Wissenschaften in Wien, Mathematisch-Naturwissenschaftliche Klasse, Abteilung 3, 72,* 156–190.

Goldberg, D. M., & Pomerantz, J. R. (1982). Models of illusory pausing and sticking. *Journal of Experimental Psychology: Human Perception and Performance, 8,* 547–561.

Gregory, R. L. (1969). How so little information controls so much behaviour. In C. H. Waddington (Ed.), *Towards a theoretical biology* (2nd ed.). Edinburgh, United Kingdom: University of Edinburgh Press.

Gregory, R. L. (1995). Black boxes of artful vision. In R. Gregory, J. Harris, P. Heard, & D. Rose (Eds.), *The artful eye* (pp. 5–27). Oxford: Oxford University Press.

Grünau, M. von, Saikali, Z., & Faubert, J. (1995). Processing speed in the motion-induction effect. *Perception, 24,* 477–490.

Herrnstein, R., & Boring, E. G. (1965). Max Wertheimer on the phi phenomenon as an example of nativism in perception, 1912. In *A sourcebook in the history of psychology* (pp. 163–168). Cambridge, MA: Harvard University Press.

Hikosaka, O., Miyauchi, S., & Shimojo, S. (1993a). Focal visual attention produces illusory temporal order and motion sensation. *Vision Research, 33,* 1219–1240.

Hikosaka, O., Miyauchi, S., & Shimojo, S. (1993b). Voluntary and stimulus-induced attention detected as motion sensation. *Perception, 22,* 517–526.

Hock, H. S., Kogan, K., & Espinoza, J. K. (1996). Dynamic thresholds for the perception of elementary apparent motion: Bistability from local cooperativity. *Investigative Ophthalmology, 37,* S745.

Köhler, W. (1920). *Die physische Gestalten in Ruhe und im stationären Zustand.* Brunswick, Nova Scotia, Canada: Vieweg.

Kolers, P. A. (1963). Some differences between real and apparent visual movement. *Vision Research, 3,* 191–206.

Kolers, P. A. (1972). *Aspects of motion perception.* Oxford: Pergamon Press.

Metzger, W. (1934). Beobachtungen über phänomenale Identität. *Psychologische Forschung, 19,* 1–49.

Nakayma, K., & Silverman, G. H. (1988a). The aperture problem. I: Perception of non-rigidity and motion direction in translating sinusoidal lines. *Vision Research, 28,* 739–746.

Nakayama, K., & Silverman, G. H. (1988b). The aperture problem. II: Spatial integration along contours. *Vision Research, 28,* 747–753.

Nawrot, M., & Rizzo, M. (1995). Motion perception deficits from midline cerebellar lesions in human. *Vision Research, 35,* 723–731.

Nawrot, M., & Sekuler, R. (1990). Assimilation and contrast in motion perception: Explorations in cooperativity. *Vision Research, 30,* 1439–1451.

Newsome, W. T., Mikami, A., & Wurtz, R. H. (1986). Motion selectivity in macaque visual cortex. III. Psychophysics and physiology of apparent motion. *Journal of Neurophysiology, 55,* 1340–1351.

O'Craven, K. M., & Savoy, R. L. (1995). Attentional modulation of activation in human MT with functional magnetic resonance imaging (FMRI). *Investigative Ophthalmology and Visual Science, 36,* S856.

Pantle, A. J. (1973). Stroboscopic movement based on global information in successively presented visual patterns. *Journal of the Optical Society of America, 63,* 1280.

Pantle, A. J., & Picciano, L. M. (1976). A multistable movement display: Evidence for two separate motion systems in human vision. *Science, 193,* 500–502.

Qian, N., & Andersen, R. A. (1994). Transparent motion perception as detection of unbalanced motion signals. II. Physiology. *Journal of Neuroscience, 14,* 7367–7380.

Qian, N., Andersen, R. A., & Adelson, E. H. (1994). Transparent motion perception as detection of unbalanced motion signals. I. Psychophysics. *Journal of Neuroscience, 14,* 7357–7366.

Ramachandran, V. S., & Anstis, S. M. (1983). Extrapolation of motion path in human visual perception. *Vision Research, 23,* 83–86.

Reber, A. S. (1995). *The Penguin dictionary of psychology.* London: Penguin Books.

Rock, I. (1995). *Perception.* New York: W H Freeman.

Sarris, V. (1989). Max Wertheimer on seen motion: Theory and evidence. *Psychological Research, 51*, 58–68.

Sarris, V., & Wertheimer, M. (1987). Max Wertheimer (1880–1943) im Bilddokument—ein historiografischer Beitrag. *Psychologische Beitrage, 29*, 469–493.

Scase, M. O., Braddick, O. J., & Raymond, J. E. (1996). What is noise for the motion system? *Vision Research, 16*, 2579–2586.

Sekuler, A. B. (1992). Simple pooling of unidirectional motion predicts speed discrimination for looming stimuli. *Vision Research, 32*, 2277–2288.

Sekuler, R. (1995). Motion perception as a partnership: Exogenous and endogenous contributions. *Current Directions in Psychological Science, 4*, 43–46.

Shipley, T. (Ed.) (1961). *Classics in psychology.* New York: Philosophical Library.

Stoner, G. R., & Albright, T. D. (1994). Visual motion integration: A neurophysiological and psychophysical perspective. In A. T. Smith & R. J. Snowden (Eds.), *Visual detection of motion* (pp. 253–290). London: Academic Press.

Teller, D. Y. (1990). The domain of visual science. In L. Spillmann & J. S. Werner (Eds.), *Visual perception: The neurophysiological foundations* (pp. 11–21). New York: Academic Press.

Ternus, J. (1926). Experimentelle Untersuchungen über phänomenale Identität. *Psychologische Forschung, 7*, 81–136.

Ternus, J. (1938). The problem of phenomenal identity. In W. D. Ellis (Eds.), *A source book of Gestalt psychology* (pp. 149–160). London: Routledge & Kegan Paul.

Vaina. L. M., & Cowey, A. C. (1996). Impairment of the perception of second order motion but not first order motion in a patient with unilateral focal brain damage. *Proceedings of the Royal Society of London—Series B, 263*, 1225–1232.

Vaina, L. M., Lemay, M., Bienfang, D. C., Choi, A. Y., & Nakayama, K. (1990). Intact "biological motion" and "structure from motion" perception in a patient with impaired motion mechanisms: A case study. *Visual Neuroscience, 5*, 353–369.

Wandell, B. A. (1995). *Foundations of vision.* Sunderland, MA: Sinauer Associates.

Watamaniuk, S. N. J. (1993). Ideal observer for the discrimination of the global direction of random-dot stimuli. *Journal of the Optical Society of America A, 10*, 16–28.

Watson, A. B., Ahumada, A., & Farrell, J. E. (1983). *The window of visibility: A psychophysical theory of fidelity in time sampled visual motion displays.* AMES Air Force Base, Ames, CA: NASA.

Wertheimer, M. (1912). Experimentelle Studien über das Sehen von Bewegung. *Zeitschrift für Psychologie und Physiologie der Sinnesorgane, 61*, 161–265.

Williams, D. W., Phillips, G. C., & Sekuler, R. (1986). Hysteresis in the perception of motion direction: Evidence for neural cooperativity. *Nature (London), 324*, 253–255.

Zeki, S. (1991). Cerebral akinetopsia (visual motion blindness). *Brain, 114*, 811–824.

Zihl, J., Cramon, D von., & Mai, N (1983). Selective disturbance of movement vision after bilateral brain damage. *Brain, 106*, 313–340.

Zihl, J., Cramon, D von., Mai, N., & Schmid, C. (1991). Disturbance of movement after bilateral brain damage. Further evidence and follow up observations. *Brain, 114*, 2235–2252.

Zohary, E., Scase, M. O., & Braddick, O. J. (1996). Integration across directions in dynamic random dot displays: Vector summation or winner take all? *Vision Research, 36*, 2321–2332.

The Müller-Lyer illusion is one of the most well known visual illusions in the history of psychology. The stimulus is trivial to create, the existence of the illusion is easy to verify, and the effect is striking for nearly everyone who sees it. The stimulus is shown in Figure 6.6 of this reading. It appears that the vertical line on the left is shorter than the vertical line on the right; however, if you take a ruler and measure both lines, you will discover that they are exactly the same length.

In this reading, Gregory argues that the Müller-Lyer illusion, and many other illusions, can tell us a great deal about how the brain processes visual information. As part of this discussion, Gregory proposes what is now the most popular (but not only) explanation of the Müller-Lyer illusion. His explanation involves two steps: size constancy and what is involved in viewing pictures of 3-D scenes.

Size constancy refers to the fact that our perception of the size of an object does not seem to change with our distance from the object. It is a property of physics that as an object gets farther away, the image of that object in our eye gets smaller. You can verify this by using your finger and thumb to frame the top and bottom of the head of someone nearby. Now keep your finger and thumb in the same position and center them on the head of someone much further away (say, across a room). The head of the person farther away will not fill the separation of your finger and thumb, thus, the image of the person farther away is much smaller than the image of the person close by. What is significant is that we do not see the person who is far away as much smaller than the person who is nearby. We perceive them to be approximately the same size. In a sense, when judging the size of an object, our visual system uses both the size of the image and the distance of the object.

Perceived size depends on perceived depth, so if two objects produce the same sized image in the eye, the one that is perceived to be farther away will also appear to be larger. Gregory's suggestion was that this is exactly what is happening in the Müller-Lyer illusion. He argued that the line with fins pointing in (on the left side of Figure 6.6) corresponded to a closer object than the line with fins pointing out (the right side of Figure 6.6). To support this claim, Gregory noted that lines with fins are quite common in the modern world, as shown in Figure 6.9. The photograph on the top shows a corner of a room; the vertical line in the corner is met by what appears to be outward fins where the corner meets the ceiling and floor. Likewise, the photograph on the bottom shows the exterior corner of a building; the vertical corner meets inward fins where the corner meets the ground and other parts of the building. Thus, Gregory demonstrated that outward fins tend to appear with corners that are further away than for inward fins (where the corner points toward the observer). In the Muller-Lyer illusion the inward fins make the vertical line seem closer (and hence smaller) and the outward fins make the vertical line seem farther away (and hence larger).

However, as Gregory notes, what is lacking in this explanation is the fact that the Müller-Lyer lines do not really seem to be at different depths. Both lines are printed on the same sheet of paper. To address this issue, Gregory notes that viewing a three-dimensional picture on a printed page is a rather odd experience. On the one hand we know it is a picture that is flat, but on the other hand, we clearly see depth arrangements of objects. Gregory argues that for the traditional Müller-Lyer drawing, the percept of the flat paper overwhelms the sense of depth that otherwise would be invoked by the fins. He then ran a series of experiments to show that if the Müller-Lyer illusion is shown without a printed page to enforce the two-dimensional depth percept, the fins *do* introduce depth percepts, and that varying the angle of the fins varies both the depth percept and the size illusion in a similar way.

In much of the rest of the discussion, Gregory examines the kinds of models that must exist to carry out the computations of visual perception. He argues that the computations necessary for the visual system to function properly will inevitably lead to some kinds of illusions.

One part of this discussion may be particularly confusing to psychology students, although it would be quite familiar to engineers. Gregory refers to a Wheatstone bridge, which is an electronic circuit that can be used to identify the resistance of an unknown resistor by its relation to three other known resistors. It works by balancing the resistance of the known resistors until there is zero current. Gregory argues that a process in the brain performs a similar balancing to build a percept, taking image size and depth percepts to produce object size, for example. If some of the information feeding into the circuit is incorrect, an illusion is perceived. As this discussion indicates, Gregory (and many other vision scientists) study visual perception with an engineer's perspective. They want to build working systems. Gregory's book *Eye and Brain*, although somewhat dated, is still recommended reading for anyone interested in visual perception.

The CogLab Müller-Lyer experiment measures the magnitude of the illusion using a psychophysical technique known as the *method of constant stimuli*. A version of the Müller-Lyer stimulus is shown and compared to other stimuli that are not subjected to the illusion. On each trial the observer reports whether the illusion stimulus is longer or shorter than the nonillusion stimulus. The line length that an observer of the illusion stimulus reports as longer about half the time is taken as the perceived length of the Müller-Lyer stimulus.

REFERENCES

Gregory, R. L. (1966). *Eye and brain.* London: Weidenfeld and Nicolson.

Gregory, R. L. (1997). *Eye and brain* (5th ed.). New York: Princeton University Press.

QUESTIONS

1. How does Gregory explain the Ponzo illusion (Figure 6.7) using the same method for explaining the Müller-Lyer illusion?
2. What is the horizontal-vertical illusion?
3. What is so significant about the "impossible object" shown in Figure 6.11?
4. Why did Gregory use glowing wires in a dark room to study the depth of the Müller-Lyer stimuli?

Perceptual Illusions and Brain Models

R. L. Gregory

Department of Machine Intelligence and Perception, University of Edinburgh

This paper develops the notion of perceptual hypotheses and also raises questions concerning the distinction to be made between "analogue" and "digital." This is made in the context of the brain, and seems important if we are to be clear in how we use an engineering distinction. The point is: Should the distinction be regarded as one of engineering convenience (continuous or discontinuous mechanisms, or circuits) or should it be regarded as a deeper logical distinction? I incline to the latter view.

An adequate theory of visual perception must explain how the fleeting patterns of light upon the retinas give knowledge of surrounding objects. The problem of how the brain "reads" reality from images is acute, because images represent directly but few, and biologically unimportant, characteristics of objects. What matters biologically are such things as whether an object is poisonous or food, hard or soft, heavy or light, sharp or blunt, friend or foe. These are not properties of images. The owner of the eye cannot eat or be eaten by its images, and yet his life depends upon interpreting them in terms of quite different characteristics of objects. It follows that eyes are of little biological value unless there is an adequate brain to interpret their images; which raises the evolutionary problem: How did the eye-brain combination arise? (cf. Gregory, 1968a). To read reality from images is to solve a problem: a running set of very difficult problems throughout active life. Errors are illusions. Certain situations present special difficulty, giving rise to systematic errors: Can these serve as clues to how the brain generally solves the problem of what objects are represented by which images?

Illusions can occur in any of the sense modalities, and they can cross the senses. A powerful illusion crosses from the seen size of an object to its apparent weight, as judged by lifting. Small objects feel up to fifty per cent heavier than larger objects of the same scale weight. Thus weight is evidently not judged simply by the input from the arm but also by prior expectation set by the previous handling of weights. When the density is unexpectedly great or small we suffer a corresponding illusion of weight.

There are, however, illusions of quite different types. There are purely *optical* illusions, where light from the object to the eye is bent by reflection (mirrors) or by refraction (the bent-stick-in-water effect, and mirages). There are also what we may call *sensory* illusions. The sense organs, the eyes, ears, touch and heat sensitive nerve endings can all be upset, when they will transmit misleading information to the brain. They are upset by prolonged stimulation and by over-stimulation. For example, the 'waterfall effect' observed by Aristotle, is dramatically demonstrated by watching a rotating spiral (Figure 6.1). If this is rotated on a turntable for ten or twenty seconds while the eyes are held at its centre, it will seem to contract or expand, depending on the direction of rotation. When stopped, there is a marked illusory movement in the opposite direction to the original movement. In the illusion, movement is seen but with no change of position.

Evidently a velocity detecting system has been adapted by prolonged stimulation to movement. As is well known, after-images occur after intense or prolonged stimulation of the retina by light: we see first a positive "picture" which soon changes to a negative "picture" which may persist for many minutes. This is due to local retinal adaptation, the brain receiving retinal signals essentially the same as for the normal image of an object but persisting beyond the physical stimulation of the retina. It is also possible for any

SOURCE: From Gregory, R. L. (1968). "Perceptual illusions and brain models." *Proceedings of the Royal Society, B 171*, 279–296. Reprinted with permission.

FIGURE 6.1   Spiral. When rotating anticlockwise it is seen to contract. If stopped after ten to twenty seconds viewing, a marked apparent expansion is observed. There is however no observed change in size. It seems that a specific velocity-detecting system has been adapted by the real movement.

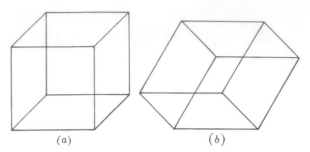

FIGURE 6.2   (a) Necker cube. This is the most famous of many depth-ambiguous, figures. (When presented with no background it changes in shape with each reversal, the apparent back being larger than the apparent front face.) (b) Necker rhomboid. This is the original form, presented by L. A. Necker in 1832.

sense organ to signal a quite wrong kind of stimulus. Pressure on the eye will send signals to the brain which are experienced as light; and electric current through the eye will produce the sensation of light, and through the ear sound. Fortunately, these sensory illusions seldom occur in normal conditions, though they are easily evoked in the laboratory.

The types of illusions which concern us here are, however, entirely different from either optical or sensory illusions. We may call these *perceptual* illusions. They arise from misinterpretation by the brain of sensory information.

Several perceptual illusions were known to the ancient Greeks, but they have only been studied experimentally for just over a century. The first scientific description in modern times was a letter by a Swiss naturalist, L. A. Necker, to Sir David Brewster (Necker, 1832) describing how a rhomboid reverses in depth, sometimes one face appearing the nearer, sometimes another. Necker correctly noted that changes of eye fixation could induce this change in perception, but that it would occur quite spontaneously. This famous effect is generally illustrated with an isometric skeleton cube (Figure 6.2a) rather than Necker's original figure (Figure 6.2b). Perceptual reversals, or alternations (there can be several alternative perceptions) are not limited to vision. Repeated words, presented on an endless tape loop, give analo-

gous auditory reversals (Warren & Gregory 1958); A similar, even more striking effect, was noted by W. J. Sinsteden: that the rotating vanes of a windmill spontaneously reverse direction when it is not clear whether one is seeing the front or the back of the windmill (for references, see: Boring, 1942). This effect is well shown by casting the shadow of a slowly rotating vane upon a screen, thus removing all information of which is the back and which the front. The shadow will also at times appear to expand and contract upon the plane of the screen. It is important to note that these effects are not perceptual distortions of the retinal image: they are alternative interpretations of the image, in terms of possible objects, and only one interpretation is correct.

The most puzzling visual illusions are systematic distortions of size or shape. These distortions occur in many quite simple figures; the distortions occurring in the same directions and to much the same extent in virtually all human observers and probably also in many animals. Their explanation presents a challenge which should be accepted, for a viable theory of normal perception must account for them and they could be important clues to basic perceptual processes.

The simplest distortion illusion was the first to be described: by the father of experimental psychology, Wilhelm Wundt (1832–1920), who was Hermann von Helmholtz's assistant at Heidelburg. Wundt described the "horizontal–vertical" illusion—that a vertical line looks longer than the horizontal line of equal length.

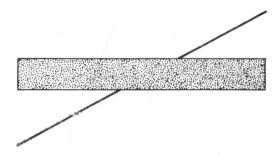

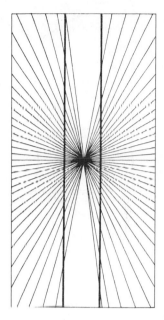

FIGURE 6.3   The Poggendorff illusion figure (1860). The straight line crossing the rectangle appears displaced.

FIGURE 6.4   Hering illusion (1861) The straight parallel lines appear bowed outwards.

He attributed this distortion to asymmetry of the eye movement system. Although this has been invoked many times since to explain distortion illusions it must be ruled out, for the distortions occur in after-images, or in normal retinal images optically stabilized so as to remain stationary on the eye though it moves. In addition, distortions can occur in several directions at the same time, which could hardly be due to eye movements; and in any case it is difficult to see how curvature distortions could be related to eye movements. All the evidence points to the origin of the distortions being not in the eyes but in the brain.

Interest in the illusions became general upon the publication of several figures showing distortions which could produce errors in using optical instruments. This concerned physicists and astronomers a hundred years ago, when photographic and other ways of avoiding visual errors were not available. The first of the special distortion figures was the Poggendorff figure of 1860 (Figure 6.3). This was followed by the Hering illusion (1861); its converse being devised by Wundt much later, in 1896 (Wundt 1898) (Figures 6.4 and 6.5). The most famous illusion of all is the Müller-Lyer arrow figure (Figure 6.6). This was devised by F. C. Müller-Lyer and was first presented in fifteen variants (Müller-Lyer, 1889). This figure is so simple, and the distortion so compelling that it was immediately accepted as the primary target for theory and experiment. All sorts of theories were advanced: Wundt's eye movement theory (in spite of its inadequacy); that the "wings" of the arrow heads drew attention away from the ends of the central line, or "arrow shaft," to make it expand or contract; that the

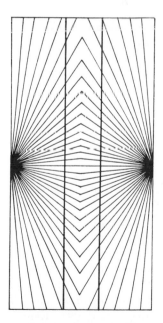

FIGURE 6.5   Wundt's variant of the Hering illusion: the parallel lines appear bowed inwards (1896).

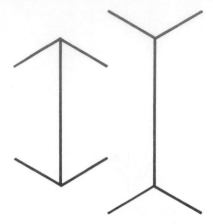

FIGURE 6.6   Müller-Lyer arrows figure (1889). The most famous illusion: the outward-going "arrow heads" produce expansion of the "shaft" and the inward-going heads contraction.

FIGURE 6.7   Ponzo figure. The upper of the parallel lines is expanded with respect to the lower.

heads induced a state of empathy in the observer (though the distortion seems far too constant for such an explanation), that the distortion is a special case of a supposed general principle that acute angles tend to be overestimated and obtuse angles underestimated. This was, however, left unexplained, and it is not clear why it should produce size changes without apparent changes of angle. All these theories had a common feature: they were attempts to explain the distortion in terms of the stimulus pattern without reference to its significance in terms of the perception of objects. There was, however, one quite different suggestion made by A. Thiéry (1896) that the distortions are related to perspective depth features. Thiéry regarded the Müller-Lyer arrows as drawings of such objects as a sawhorse, seen in three dimensions, with the legs going away from the observer in the acute-angled figure and towards him in the obtuse-angled figure.[1] This suggestion has seldom been considered until recently, though the "perspective theory" was described by R. H. Woodworth in 1938: "In the Müller-Lyer figure the obliques readily suggest perspective and if this is followed one of the vertical lines appears farther away and therefore objectively longer than the other." This quotation brings out the immediate difficulties of developing an adequate theory along these lines, for the distortion occurs even when the perspective suggestion is not followed up, for the figure generally appears flat and yet distorted; and there is no hint given

of a *modus operandi*, or brain mechanism responsible for the size changes. An adequate theory following Thiéry's suggestion that perspective is somehow important must show how distortion occurs though the figures appear flat. It should also indicate the kind of brain mechanisms responsible.

The idea that geometrical perspective—the converging of parallel lines with distance—has a bearing is at least borne out by the occurrence of these distortions in actual scenes. A simple example is the Ponzo illusion (Figure 6.7). This is a skeleton drawing of typical perspective convergence of parallel lines with distance, as in the railway lines of Figure 6.8 (cf. Tausch, 1954). The upper superimposed rectangle, which would be more distant, is expanded. Similarly, the inside corner is expanded (Figure 6.9a) and the outside corner shrunk (Figure 6.9b) just as in the Müller-Lyer figures, which are like skeleton corners. In both cases, regions indicated by perspective as *distant* are *expanded*, while near regions are shrunk. The distortions are opposite to the normal shrinkings of the retinal image of objects with increased distance. Is this merely fortuitous, or is it a clue to the origin of the illusions? Before we come to grips with the problem of trying to develop an adequate perspective theory, it will be helpful to consider some curious features of ordinary pictures.

Pictures are the traditional material of perceptual research, but all pictures are highly artificial and

FIGURE 6.8   The Ponzo illusion is seen in this photograph of receding (railway) lines. Here the perspective significance of converging lines is obvious.

(a)

(b)

FIGURE 6.9   (a) The outward-going fins of the Müller-Lyer figure are here seen in flat projection of a photograph of the inside corner of a room. (b) The inward-going arrows are seen in the outside corner of the building. As in the Ponzo example, distance indicated by perspective is associated with illusory expansion.

present special problems to the perceptual brain. In a sense, all pictures are impossible: they have a double reality. They are seen both as patterns of lines, lying on a flat background and also as objects depicted in a quite different, three-dimensional, space. No actual object can be both two- and three-dimensional and yet pictures come close to it. Viewed as patterns they are seen as two-dimensional; viewed as representing objects they are seen in a quasi three-dimensional space. Pictures lying both in two and in three dimensions are paradoxical visual inputs. Pictures are also ambiguous, for the third dimension is never precisely defined. The Necker cube is an example where the depth ambiguity is so great that the brain never settles for one answer. But any perspective projection could represent an infinity of three-dimensional shapes: so one would think that the perceptual system has an impossible task. Fortunately, the world of objects does not have infinite variety; there is usually a best bet, and we generally

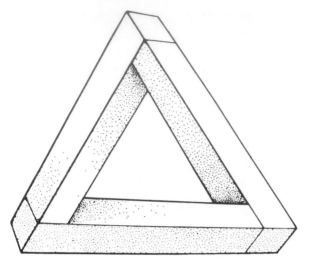

FIGURE 6.10   An "impossible figure." This cannot be seen as a sensible three-dimensional figure—no appropriate "perceptual model" is selected. (After L. S. and R. Penrose 1958.)

interpret our flat images more or less correctly in terms of the world of objects. The sheer difficulty of the problem of seeing the third dimension from the two dimensions of a picture—or the retinal images of normal objects—is brought out by special "impossible pictures" and "impossible objects," as we shall call

them. They show just what happens when clearly incompatible distance information is presented to the eye. The impossible triangle (Figure 6.10) (Penrose & Penrose 1958) cannot be seen as an object lying in normal three-dimensional space. It is, however, perfectly possible to make actual three-dimensional objects—not mere pictures—which give the same perceptual confusion. Figure 6.11a shows an actual wooden object which, when viewed from one critical position, gives the same retinal image as the Penrose triangle (Figure 6.11b). It looks just as impossible—but it really exists. In fact, though one knows all about its true shape, it continues to look impossible from the critical viewing position.

Ordinary pictures are not so very different from obviously "impossible" pictures. All pictures depicting depth are paradoxical, for we both see them as flat (which they really are) and in a kind of suggested depth which is not quite right. We are not tempted to touch objects depicted in a picture through or in front of its surface. What happens, then, if we remove the background—does the depth paradox of pictures remain?

To remove the background, in our experiments, we make the pictures luminous to glow in the dark. They are viewed with one eye in order to remove stereoscopic information that they are truly flat. They

(a)

(b)

FIGURE 6.11   (a) An "impossible object." From this view its true shape is apparent. (b) The same object viewed from the critical position from which it looks impossible. As in the Penroses' figure, but here an actual object appears impossible.

may be wire figures coated in luminous paint, or photographic transparencies back-illuminated with an electro-luminescent panel. In either case there is no visible background, so we can discover how far the background is responsible for the depth paradox of pictures, including the illusion figures. Under these conditions the Müller-Lyer arrows generally look like true corners, according to their perspective. They generally appear indistinguishable from actual (luminous) corners. The figures are, however, not entirely stable; they sometimes reverse spontaneously in depth but generally they appear according to their perspective, and without the paradoxical depth of pictures with a background. The distortions are still present. The outward-going fins figure, looking like an inside corner, is expanded; while the in-going fins figure, looking like an outside corner, is shrunk as before—but now the paradox has disappeared. The figures look like true corners: one can point out their depth as though they were normal three-dimensional objects.

Having removed the paradox it is possible to measure, by quite direct means, the apparent distances of any selected parts of the figures. This we do by using the two eyes to serve as a rangefinder for indicating the apparent depth of the figure as seen by one eye. The back-illuminated picture is placed behind a sheet of polaroid; one eye being prevented from seeing the picture with a crossed polarizing filter. Both eyes are however allowed to see one[2] or more small movable reference lights, which are optically introduced into the picture with a 45° part-reflecting mirror. The distance of these lights is given by stereoscopic vision (convergence angle of the eyes), and so by placing them at the seen distance of selected parts of the picture we can plot the visual space of the observer, in three dimensions. The apparatus is shown in Figure 6.12. Figure 6.13 shows the result of measuring depth (difference between the distance of the central line and the ends of the arrow heads) for various fin angles of the Müller-Lyer illusion figure. For comparison, the measured illusion for each angle for the same (20) subjects is plotted on the same graph. It is important to note that though the depth was measured with luminous figures, the illusion was measured (using an adjustable comparison line set to apparent equality) with the figures drawn on a normally textured background. So they appeared flat when the *illusion* was measured but as a true corner when the background was removed for measuring *depth*. This experiment shows that when the background is removed, depth very closely follows the illusion for the various fin angles. The similarity of these curves provides evi-

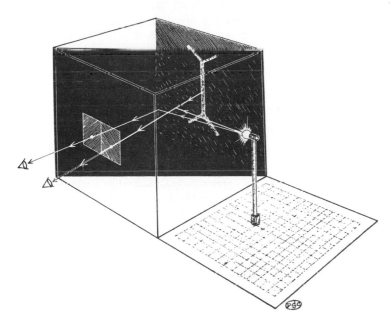

FIGURE **6.12** "Pandora's Box." Apparatus for measuring subjective visual depth in pictures. The picture (in this case, an illusion figure) is back-illuminated with an electro-luminescent panel, to avoid background texture. In front of the picture there is a sheet of polaroid and in front of the eyes two sheets of polaroid at right angles; thus the picture can be seen by only one eye. The image of the reference lamp is reflected off a sheet of neutral density Perspex lying diagonally across the box and can be seen with both eyes. The real distance of the lamp, seen binocularly, is matched with the apparent distance of the picture, seen monocularly; and the positions are marked on the graph paper.

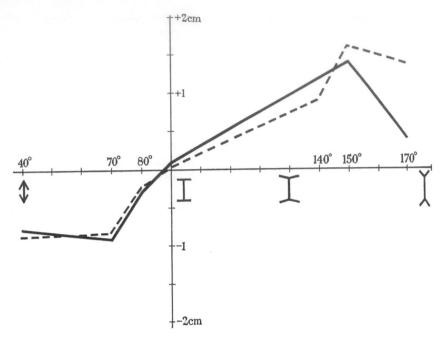

FIGURE 6.13   Müller-Lyer illusion and apparent depth, for various fin angles. The *x* axis represents the angle between the shaft and fins in the Müller-Lyer figure. (With fins at 90° the figure is a capital I, giving zero illusion and zero depth.) For angles greater than 90° the illusion is positive, for smaller angles negative. The illusion is measured by adjusting a line to the same apparent length for each angle of the illusion figure. The *illusion* is shown in the *dotted* line. It was presented on a normally textured background.

The same observers were used to measure apparent depth for the same angles; the illusion being presented without background texture and monocularly to avoid competing depth information. The results in both cases are the means of three readings for each of twenty observers in all conditions. The figure was ten centimeters in length viewed from half a meter. Depth was measured with the "Pandora's Box" technique, the comparison light being set to the apparent distance of the shaft and the ends of the fins. *Depth* shown in the *solid* line.

The correlation between apparent depth and the length distortion is better than 0.9 (experiment by R. L. Gregory and Linda Townes, at M.I.T.).

dence of a remarkably close tie-up between the illusion as it occurs when depth is not seen with the depth which is seen when the background is removed. This suggests that Thiéry was essentially correct: that perspective can somehow produce distortions. But what is odd is that perspective produces the distortion according to *indicated* perspective depth even when depth is not seen, because it is countermanded by the visible background.

The next step is to look for some perceptual mechanism which could produce this relation be-

tween perspective and apparent size. A candidate that should have been obvious many years ago is "size constancy." This was clearly described by René Descartes (1596–1650), in his *Dioptrics* of 1637.

"It is not the absolute size of images (in the eyes) that counts. Clearly they are a hundred times bigger (in area) when objects are very close than when they are ten times further away; but they do not make us see the objects a hundred times bigger; on the contrary, they seem almost the same size, at any rate as we are not deceived by too great a distance."

We know from many experiments that Descartes is quite correct. But what happens when distance information, such as perspective, is present when there is no actual difference in distance to shrink the image in the eye? Could it be that perspective presented on a flat plane sets the brain's compensation for the normal shrinking of the images with distance—though in pictures there is no shrinking to compensate? If this happened, illusions *must* be given by perspective. We would then have the start of a reasonable theory of distortion illusions. Features indicated as distant would be expanded; which is just what we find, at least for the Müller-Lyer and the Ponzo figures.

It is likely that this approach to the problem was not developed until recently because although size constancy was very well known, it has always been assumed that it follows apparent distance in all circumstances. Also, it has not been sufficiently realized how very odd pictures are as visual inputs; but they are highly atypical and should be studied as a very special case, being both paradoxical and ambiguous.

"Size constancy" is traditionally identified with Emmert's Law, as illustrated by the apparent size of after-images. An after-image (preferably from an electronic flash) is "projected" upon screens or walls lying at various distances. The after-image will appear almost twice as large with each doubling of distance, though the size of the retinal image from the flash of course remains constant. It is important to note, however, that there *is* a change in retinal stimulation for each wall or screen lying at a different distance, for *their* images will be different. It is therefore possible that Emmert's Law is due merely to the relative areas covered by the after-image and the screen, and not to visual information of distance changing the size of the after-image by internal scaling. This presents an experimental problem, which it is vital to solve.

There is a simple solution. We can use the ambiguous depth phenomenon of the Necker cube to establish whether Emmert's Law is due to central scaling by the brain, or is merely an effect of relative areas of stimulation of the retina by after-image and background. When we see a Necker cube drawn on paper reverse in depth, there is no appreciable size change. When presented on a textured background it lies in the paradoxical depth of all pictures with backgrounds. It does not change in size when it reverses in

this quasi-depth. What happens, though, if we remove the background? The effect is dramatic, and entirely repeatable: Whichever face appears most *distant* always appears the *larger*. The use of depth-ambiguous figures allows us to distinguish between what happens as a result of central brain size scaling mechanisms from what happens when the pattern of stimulation of the retina is changed. The answer is that at least part of "size constancy," and of Emmert's Law, is due to a central size scaling mechanism following apparent distance, though the retinal stimulation is unchanged. But this is not the whole story.

Size is evidently set in two ways. (1) It can be set purely by apparent distance, but (2) it can also be set directly by visual depth features, such as perspective, even though depth is not seen because it is countermanded by the competing depth information of a visible background. When atypical depth features are present, size scaling is set inappropriately, to give a corresponding distortion illusion (cf. Gregory 1965, 1966a, b, 1967b).

The size scaling set directly by depth features (giving systematic distortions when set inappropriately) we may call "depth cue scaling." It is remarkably consistent, and independent of the observer's perceptual "set." The other system is very different, being but indirectly related to the prevailing retinal information. It is evidently linked to the interpretation of the retinal image in terms of what object it represents. When it appears as a different object, the scaling changes at once to suit the alternative object. If we regard the seeing of an object as a hypothesis suggested (but never strictly proved) by the image, then we may call this system "depth hypothesis scaling." It changes with each change of hypothesis of what object is represented by the image. When the hypothesis is wrong we have an illusion, which may be dramatic.

We started by pointing out that visual perception must involve "reading" from retinal images characteristics of objects not represented directly by the images in the eyes. Non-visual characteristics must already have been associated, by individual learning or through heredity, for objects to be recognized from their images. Illusions associated with misplaced size scaling provide evidence that features are selected for scaling according to early perceptual experience of the individual. This is suggested by anthropological data

(Segall et al. 1966) and perhaps from the almost total absence of these illusions found in a case of adult recovery from infant blindness (Gregory & Wallace 1963).[3]

Perception seems, then, to be a matter of "looking up" stored information of objects, and how they behave in various situations. Such systems have great advantages.

Systems which control their output directly from currently available input information have serious limitations. In biological terms, these would be essentially reflex systems. Some of the advantages of using input information to select stored data for controlling behavior, in situations which are not unique to the system, are as follows:

1. In typical situations they can achieve high performance with limited information transmission rate. It is estimated that human transmission rate is only about 15 bits/second (Miller, Bruner & Postman, 1954). They gain results because perception of objects—which are redundant—requires identification of only certain key features of each object.
2. They are essentially predictive. In typical circumstances, reaction-time is cut to zero.

3. They can continue to function in the temporary absence of input; this increases reliability and allows trial selection of alternative inputs.
4. They can function appropriately to object-characteristics which are not signalled directly to the sensory system. This is generally true of vision, for the image is trivial unless used to "read" non-optical characteristics of objects.
5. They give effective gain in signal/noise ratio, since not all aspects of the model have to be separately selected on the available data, when the model has redundancy. Provided the model is appropriate, very little input information can serve to give adequate perception and control.

There is, however, one disadvantage of "internal model" look-up systems, which appears inevitably when the selected stored data are out of date or otherwise inappropriate. We may with some confidence attribute perceptual illusions to selection of an inappropriate model, or to mis-scaling of the most appropriate available model. [An example of selecting an inappropriate model is the Orbison illusion, which illustrates how radiating lines appear to distort a perfect square; see Figure 6.14.]

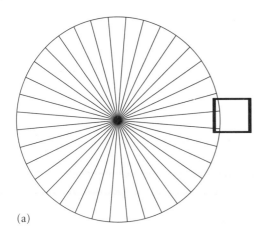

(a)

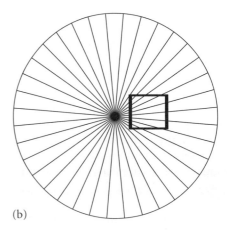

(b)

FIGURE 6.14   (a) Orbison illusion: shown by Perspex sheets with engraved square, on background sheet of engraved radiating lines. By sliding the Perspex sheet, the distortion can be observed during movement, or stationary in any position. (b) Showing the distortion increased when the superimposed figure (a square) is close to the origin of the radiating lines.

SELECTING AND SCALING OF MODELS, AND THE ILLUSIONS

The models must, to be reasonably economical, represent average or typical situations. There could hardly be a separate stored model for every position and orientation an object might occupy in surrounding space. It would be economical to store typical characteristics of objects and use current information to adjust the selected model to fit the prevailing situation. If this idea is correct, we can understand the nature of our "depth cue" scaling—and why perspective features presented on a flat plane give the observed distortions. Inappropriate depth cues will scale the model inappropriately, to give a corresponding size distortion. This, I suggest, is the origin of the distortion illusions. They occur whenever a model is inappropriately scaled.

There will also be errors, possibly gross errors, when a wrong model is selected—mistaking an object for something very different, confusing a shadow with an object, seeing "faces-in-the-fire," or even flying saucers. Each model seems to have a typical size associated with it, so mis-selection can appear as a size error. This occurs in the case of the luminous cubes, which change shape with each reversal though the sensory input is unchanged.

If this general account of perception as a "look-up" system is correct, we should expect illusions to occur in any effective perceptual system faced with the same kind of problems. The illusions, on this theory, are not due to contingent limitations of the brain, but result from the necessarily imperfect solution adopted to the problem of reading from images information not directly present in the image. In considering the significance of experimental data and phenomena for understanding brain function, it seems very important to distinguish between effects which depend on the particular, contingent, characteristics of the brain and the much more general characteristics of any conceivable system faced with the same kinds of problem. Non-contingent characteristics can be regarded in terms of logical and engineering principles, and engineering criteria of efficiency can be employed (cf. Gregory, 1961) to help decide between possible systems.

I have distinguished between: (a) selecting models according to sensory information, and (b) size-scaling models to fit the orientation and distance of external objects. I have also suggested that errors in either selecting or scaling give corresponding illusions. These systematic illusions are regarded as non contingent, resulting from the basic limitations of the system adopted—probably the best available—by brains to solve the perceptual problem of reading reality from images. We should thus expect to find similar illusions in efficiently designed "seeing machines" (Gregory 1967d).

Now let us consider an experimental situation designed to tell us something about the "engineering" nature of brain models. We make use of the size/weight illusion, mentioned above, but we look for a change in discrimination as a function of scale distortion of weight.

Consider the following paradigm experiment. We have two sets of weights, such as tins filled with lead shot. Each set consists of say seven tins all of a certain size, while the other set has seven tins each of which is, say, twice the volume of the first set. Each set has a tin of weight, in grams, 85, 90, 95, 100, 105, 110, 115. The 100 g weight in each set is the standard, and the task is to compare the other weights in the same set with this standard, and try to distinguish them as heavier or lighter. (The tins are fitted with the same-sized handles for lifting, to keep the touch inputs constant except for weight). Is discrimination the same for the set of *apparently* heavier weights, which are in fact the same weights? The answer is that discrimination is *worse* for weights either apparently *heavier* or *lighter* than weights having a specific gravity of about one (Gregory & Ross 1967c). Why should this be so?

Suppose that sensory data are compared with the current internal model—as they must be to be useful. Now if the data are not only *compared* with it, but *balanced against it*, then we derive further advantages of employing internal models. We then have systems like Wheatstone bridges, and these have useful properties. Bridge circuits are especially good (a) over a very large input intensity range and (b) with components subject to drift. Now it is striking how large an intensity range sensory systems cover ($1:10^5$ or even $1:10^6$), and the biological components are subject to far more drift than would be tolerated by engineers in our technology confronted with similar problems. Balanced bridge circuits seem a good engineering choice in the biological situation.

Consider a Wheatstone bridge in which the input signals provide one arm and the prevailing internal model the opposed arms against which the inputs are balanced. Now the internal arms are parts of the model—and will be set inappropriately in a scale-distortion illusion. In the size weight illusion, visual information may be supposed to set a weight arm incorrectly. An engineer's bridge will give impaired discrimination either when the bridge is not balanced or when the ratio arms are not equal. The biological system gives just what a practical engineer's bridge would give—loss of discrimination associated with an error in balancing the bridge. This is perhaps some evidence that internal models form arms of bridge circuits. There is no evidence for suggesting whether scale-distortion illusions result from unequal ratio arms or from imbalance of the supposed bridges. We propose to do further work, experimental and theoretical, to clear up this point.

Are brain models digital or analogue? It is possible to make an informed guess as to which system is adopted by the brain, in terms of speed of operation, types of errors and other characteristics typical of analogue or digital engineering systems (cf. Gregory, 1953). The engineering distinction arises from the fact that in practice analogue systems work continuously but digital systems work in precisely defined discrete steps. This difference is immensely important to the kinds of circuits or mechanical systems used in practical computers. Discontinuous systems have higher reliability in the presence of "noise" disturbance while analogue devices can have faster data transmission rates, though their precision is limited to around 0.1%. There is no limit in principle to the number of significant figures obtainable from a digital computer, if it has space enough and time.

Because of the clear engineering distinction between continuous and discontinuous systems, there is a temptation to define analogue in terms of continuous and digital in terms of discontinuous. But this will not do. We can imagine click stops fitted to a slide rule; this would make it discontinuous, but it would still be an analogue device. We must seek some deeper distinction.

The point is that both "analogue" and "digital" systems represent things by their internal states. The essential difference between them is not *how* they represent things, but rather in *what* they represent. The distinction is between representing events *directly* by the states of the system, and representing *symbolic accounts* of real (or hypothetical) events. Real events always occur in a continuum, but symbolic systems are always discontinuous. The continuous discontinuous computer distinction reflects, we may suggest, this difference between representing the world of objects directly and representing symbolic systems. (Even the continuous functions of differential calculus have to be handled as though they were discretely stepped.)

A continuous computing device can work without going through the steps of an analytical or mathematical procedure. A digital device, on the other hand, has to work through the steps of an appropriate mathematical or logical system. This means that continuous computers functioning directly from input variables necessarily lack power of analysis, but they can work as fast as the changes in their inputs—and so are ideal for real-time computing systems, provided high accuracy is not required. The perceptual brain must work in real time, and it does not need the accuracy or the analytical power of a digital system, following the symbolic steps of a mathematical treatment of the situation.

It is most implausible to suppose that the brain of a child contains mathematical analyses of physical situations. When a child builds a house of toy bricks, balancing them to make walls and towers, we cannot suppose that the structural problems are solved by employing analytical mathematical techniques, involving concepts such as centre of gravity and coefficient of friction of masses. It is far better to make the lesser claim for children and animals: that they behave appropriately to objects by using analogues of sensed object-properties, without involving mathematical analyses of the properties of objects and their interactions. Perceptual learning surely cannot require the learning of mathematics. It is far more plausible to suppose that it involves the building of quite simple analogues of relevant properties of objects: relevant so far as they concern the behavior of the animal or the child.

This and other considerations force us to question the traditional distinction between "analogue" and "digital." The discontinuous continuous distinction will not serve. It is a matter of distinguishing between computing systems which solve problems by going through the steps of a formal argument, or mathematical analysis, from systems which solve problems without "knowing" logic or mathematics—by following the input variables and reading off solutions with a look-up system of internal functions. We need a new terminology for this distinction.

To name the first type of computer, we can go back to Charles Babbage's Analytical Engine, of about 1840. Systems employing formal or mathematical analysis we may call "*Analytical computers.*" In practice these will be discontinuous, the steps representing the steps of the analytical argument, or mathematics. But this is not its defining characteristic, which is that it works by following an analysis of the prevailing problem or situation. A convenient term for computers which arrive at solutions by look-up systems of internal syntheses of past data—"models" reflecting aspects of reality—is more difficult to find. We propose the term: "*Synthetical computers.*" It is hoped that these terms—analytical and synthetical computers—may be helpful.

It is reasonable to suppose that the invention of logic and mathematics has conferred much of the power humans have compared with other animals for many kinds of problem solving. We have *synthetical* brains which use, with the aid of explicit symbols, *analytical* techniques. It is interesting that even the most advanced analytical techniques are useless for some physical problems—predicting the weather, the tides, economic trends, for example—and then we have to rely on inductively derived models and crude synthetical techniques. Almost always simplifications and corrections have to be used when analytical techniques are applied to the real world; so it is not entirely surprising that synthetical brains are so successful. Indeed, we do not know how to program an analytical computer to process optical information for performing tasks that would be simple for a child. Surely the child does not do it this way.

The brain must work in real time, but it need not work according to analytical descriptions of the physical world, if all it requires are quite crude synthetical analogues of input—output functions, selected by distinguishing features of objects. The perceptual brain reflects the redundancy of the external world: When it does so correctly we see aspects of reality without illusion. A wrong model—or the right model wrongly scaled—gives corresponding illusions. These can serve as clues to the way sensory information is handled by the brain, to give perception and behavior.

REFERENCES

Anstis, S. M., Shopland, C. D. and Gregory, R.L. 1961. Measuring visual constancy for stationary or moving objects. *Nature, Lond.* 191, 416–417.

Boring, E. G. 1942. *Sensation and perception in the history of experimental psychology.* Appleton-Century Inc.

Gregory, R. L. 1953. Physical model explanations in psychology. *Br. J. Phil. Sci.,* 4, 192–197.

Gregory, R. L., Wallace, Jean G. and Campbell F. W. 1959. Changes in the size and shape of visual after-images observed in complete darkness during changes of position in space. *Quart. J. Exp. Psychol.* 11, 54–55.

Gregory, R. L. 1961. The brain as an engineering problem, in *Current problems in animal behaviour* (ed. W. H. Thorpe and O. L. Zangwill). Cambridge University Press.

Gregory, R. L. & Wallace, J. G. 1963. *Recovery from early blindness: a case study,* Monogr. Supp. 2, Quart J Exp Psychol. Heffers, Cambridge.

Gregory, R. L. & Ross, Helen. 1964a. Is the Weber fraction a function of physical or perceived input? *Quart. J. Exp. Psychol.* 16, 2.

Gregory, R. L. 1964. Stereoscopic shadow images. *Nature, Lond.* 203, 1407–1408.

Gregory, R. L. 1965. Seeing in depth. *Proc. Roy. Instn.* 40, 311–323.

Gregory, R. L. 1966a. Visual illusions, in *New horizons in psychology* (ed. B. Foss). Penguin Books.

Gregory, R. L. 1966b. *Eye and brain.* London: Weidenfeld and Nicolson.

Gregory, R. L., 1967a. Origin of eyes and brains, *Nature, Lond.* 213, 369–372.

Gregory, R. L. 1967b. Comments on the inappropriate constancy scaling theory of the illusions and its implications, *Quart. J. Exp. Psychol.* 19, 3.

Gregory, R. L. & Ross, Helen E. 1967c. Arm weight, adaptation, and weight discrimination. *Percept. Motor Skills* **24**, 1127–1130.

Gregory, R. L. 1967d. Will seeing machines have illusions? in *Machine intelligence 1* (ed. N. L. Collins and D. Michie). Edinburgh: Oliver and Boyd.

Hering, E. 1861. *Beitrage zur Physiologie*, **1**, 74.

Miller, G. A., Bruner, J. S. & Postman, L. 1954. Familiarity of letter sequences and tachistoscopic identification. *J. Genet. Psychol.* **50**, 129–139.

Müller-Lyer, F. C. 1889. Optische Urtheilstäuschungen, *Arch. Physiol.*, Suppl. Bd. pp. 263–270.

Necker, L. A. 1832. Observations on some remarkable phaenomena seen in Switzerland; and an optical phaenomenon which occurs on viewing of a crystal or geometrical solid. *Phil. Mag.* (3 ser.) **1**, 329–337.

Penrose, L. S. & Penrose, R. 1958. Impossible objects: a special type of illusion. *Br. J. Psychol.* **49**, 31–33.

Poggendorff, J. C. 1860. Poggendorff did not publish his illusion, of this date. He called F. Zöllner's attention to it, and it was named for him by Burmester. (Burmester, E. 1896. Beitrag zur experimentellen. Bestimmung geometrisch-optischer, *Z. Psychol.* **12**, 355–394.)

Segall, M. H., Campbell, D. T. & Melville, J. H. 1966. *The influence of culture on visual perception.* New York: Bobbs-Merrill.

Tausch, R. 1954. Optische Täuschungen als artifizielle Effekte der Gestaltungsprozesse von Grössen und Formenkonstanz in der natürlichen Raumwahrnehmung. *Psychol. Forsch*, **24**, 299–348.

Thiéry, A. 1896. Ueber geometrisch-optische Täuschungen. *Phil. Stud.* **12**, 67–125.

Warren, R. M. & Gregory, R. L. 1958. An auditory analogue of the visual reversible figure. *Amer. J. Psychol.* **71**, 612–613.

Woodworth, R. H. 1938. *Experimental psychology.* New York: Holt Inc.

Wundt, W. 1898. *Die geometrisch-optische Täuschungen*, p. 117. (Previously published by A. Thiéry. 1896. Ueber geometrisch-optische Täuschungen, *Phil. Stud.* **12**, 74.)

ENDNOTES

1. Thiéry's choice of a "saw-horse" (a horizontal beam supported on legs forming triangles at each end) is a poor example for the legs are not at any specific angle, such as a right angle. He may not have seen that for perspective to serve as a depth cue, reliable assumptions about angles must be possible. The legs of a saw-horse can be at almost any angle; so it is not a good example of depth being given by perspective projection (cf. Segall et al. 1966).

2. There is no "physical" reason why a luminous object viewed with a single eye should have any assignable distance. In fact even after-images have an apparent distance viewed in darkness (Gregory et al. 1959). Luminous figures remain at remarkably constant apparent distance, for almost all observers, so that consistent measurements can be made with a single reference light. Presumably a fairly stable "internal model" is called up, and this settles the apparent distance. This is true also for viewing the moon in a clear sky: It remains remarkably constant in size and distance, until near the horizon when it looks larger and nearer. Perspective and other information then seems to scale the "model" and so change the size of the moon.

3. It seems possible that the curvature distortions given by radiating background lines (e.g., Hering's and Wundt's illusions, Figures 6.4 and 6.5 [as well as the Orbison illusion, Figure 6.14]) should be attributed to mis-scaling from the spherical perspective of the images on the hemispherical surface of the retina to the effective linear perspective of perception. The distortions are in the right direction for such an interpretation, but precise experiments remain to be completed.

   Errors in the prevailing model can be established independently of the standard distortion illusions, by introducing systematic movement. Most simply, a point light source is used to cast a shadow of a slowly rotating (1 rev/min) skeleton object. The projected shadow, giving a two-dimensional projection of a rotating three-dimensional object, is observed. It is found that simple familiar objects will generally be correctly identified, as they rotate. The projections of unfamiliar objects, and especially random or irregular shapes will, however, continually change, the angles and lengths of lines of the projection changing as the object rotates, often appearing different each time the object comes round to the same position. By adding stereoscopic information (using a pair of horizontally separated point sources, cross-polarized to the eyes and a silver or ground-glass screen to prevent depolarization) we find that, on this criterion, the correct model is given more readily for unfamiliar or irregular figures: but stereoscopic information does *not* invariably select the correct model (Gregory, 1964b). We also use shadow projections for measuring perceptual constancy, especially during movement, as this allows null measures (Anstis, Shopland & Gregory 1961).

7   SIGNAL DETECTION

This paper marks a significant turning point in the analysis of experimental data. Although the first line of the reading claims that this paper is about detecting light signals on a uniform background, the analysis reported here turns out to be much more general and useful. This paper was the first psychology paper to use what would subsequently be called *signal detection theory.* This theory is now used to analyze data in most, if not all, aspects of cognitive psychology.

Signal detection refers to a task in which the observer must decide if a particular stimulus has appeared. Many everyday cognitive behaviors are essentially variations of this kind of task. For example, suppose you are in the basement of your home doing laundry. You are expecting an important phone call, so while you work on your laundry you listen carefully for the phone to ring. If the phone does ring, you may or may not hear it because of noise from the laundry machines. At the same time, you might think you hear the phone ring, but be incorrect. This could happen if some other sound seems similar to the phone (e.g., the dryer buzzes). Essentially, your task of hearing the phone ring is a signal detection task. You want to be able to discriminate between situations where the phone does ring and where it does not ring.

It is often the case, as with the laundry example, that other factors can interfere with your ability to discriminate the presence or absence of a signal. We can group all those factors into a general term called *noise*, which is essentially anything that is not the signal. If the signal is the phone ringing, then noise from the laundry machines, a radio playing, and ringing in your ears all count as noise. The interesting aspect to measure is how well someone can discriminate the signal embedded in noise (the phone ringing with other background noises) from the noise alone (just background noise).

This description of the situation is rather different than previous views. Since the beginnings of psychology, psychologists have been interested in the thresholds of perception, which identify the limits of human capabilities. Thus, for example, they want to know how faint a light we can detect. It was common to simply present a stimulus (for example, a small spot of light) with different intensities and ask observers whether they saw it or not. A problem with this approach was that sometimes an observer would report that he or she saw the spot, even though the spot was not actually presented. Clearly, on those trials the observer was just guessing, but the same type of guessing could occur for trials where the dot was present but really was too faint to detect. Thus, it is not an easy task to identify the faintest dot that can be reliably detected, because guessing always gets in the way. Everyone realized that the guessing needed to be factored out, but Tanner and Swets realized that previous approaches were flawed.

Tanner and Swets used the newly developed signal detection approach to identify thresholds. They realized that the task was really one of signal discrimination amongst noise. They suggested that the noise was due to the neural representation of visual information. Signal detection theory makes certain (mathematical) assumptions about the properties of that noise and provides a means of calculating how well people can discriminate the signal from the noise, regardless of their tendency to guess. Discrimination capability is calculated as d' (d-prime), which considers both the trials where observers report seeing the stimulus and it is there (a correct detection) and the trials where observers report seeing the stimulus and it is not there (a false alarm).

Tanner and Swets tested the theory by running two different experiments. The expectation was that if d' accurately captured the ability of an observer to see a small spot of light, then the value of d' calculated from one experiment would be able to predict the values produced by the other experiment. The data agree with this expectation. This is best summarized by Figures 7.14–7.16, where all the points lie close to the curve. The points are values computed from an experiment. The curve is a prediction based on d' values computed from a different experiment. The close match of the points to the curve verifies the theory that underlies the d' calculation.

The CogLab experiment on signal detection measures your ability to identify a particular pattern of dots in a field of noise. At the end of the experiment you are given your d' value. Larger values of d' indicate better discrimination. In-depth discussions of signal detection theory and its application to cognitive psychology can be found in Green and Swets (1966) and Macmillan and Creelman (1991). A method of using spreadsheets to compute d' can be found in Sorkin (1999).

REFERENCES

Green, D. M., & Swets, J. A. (1966). *Signal detection theory and psychophysics.* New York: Wiley.

Macmillan, N. A., & Creelman, C. D. (1991). *Detection theory: A user's guide.* Cambridge: Cambridge University Press.

Sorkin, R. D. (1999). Spreadsheet signal detection. *Behavior, Research Methods, Instruments & Computers, 31,* 46–54.

QUESTIONS

1. What is a "false alarm"? Why might someone make a false alarm?
2. Why is the title of the reading appropriate? How is this a decision-making theory?
3. What is a "yes-no" experiment?
4. Generate an example of signal detection that does not involve visual perception.

A Decision-Making Theory of Visual Detection

Wilson P. Tanner, Jr., and John A. Swets

University of Michigan

This paper is concerned with the human observer's behavior in detecting light signals in a uniform light background. Detection of these signals depends on information transmitted to cortical centers by way of the visual pathways. An analysis is made of the form of this information, and the types of decisions which can be based on information of this form. Based on this analysis, the expected form of data collected in "yes-no" and "forced-choice" psychophysical experiments is defined, and experiments demonstrating the internal consistency of the theory are presented.

As the theory at first glance appears to be inconsistent with the large quantity of existing data on this subject, it is wise to review the form of these data. The general procedure is to hold signal size, duration, and certain other physical parameters constant, and to observe the way in which the frequency of detection varies as a function of intensity of the light signal. The way in which data of this form are handled implies certain underlying theoretical viewpoints.

In Figure 7.1 the dotted lines represent the form of the results of hypothetical experiments. Consider first a single dotted line. Any point on the line might represent an experimentally determined point. This point is corrected for chance by application of the usual formula:

$$p = \frac{p' - c}{1 - c}$$

where p' is the observed proportion of positive responses, p is the corrected proportion of positive responses, and c is the intercept of the dotted curve at $\Delta I = 0$.

Justification of this correction depends on the validity of the assumption that a "false alarm" is a guess, independent of any sensory activity upon which a decision might be based. For this to be the case it is necessary to have a mechanism which triggers when seeing occurs and which becomes incapable of discriminating between quantities of neural activity when seeing does not occur. Only under such a system would a guess be equally likely in the absence of seeing for all values of signal intensity. The application of the chance correction to data from both yes-no and forced-choice experiments is consistent with these assumptions.

The solid curve represents a "true" curve onto which each of the dotted, or experimental, curves can be mapped by using the chance correction and proper estimates of "c." The parameters of the solid curve are assumed to be characteristic of the physiology of the individual's sensory system, independent of psychological control. The assumption carries with it the notion that if some threshold of neural activity is exceeded, phenomenal seeing results.

To infer that the form of the curve representing the frequency of seeing as a function of light intensity is the same as the curve representing the frequency of seeing as a function of neural activity is to assume a linear relationship between neural activity and light intensity. Efforts to fit seeing frequency curves by normal probability functions suggest a predisposition toward accepting this assumption.

A NEW THEORY OF VISUAL DETECTION

The theory presented in this paper differs from conventional thinking about these assumptions. First, it is assumed that false-alarm rate and correct detection vary together. Secondly, neural activity is assumed to

---

SOURCE: From Tanner, W. P., & Swets, J. A. (1954). A decision-making theory of visual detection. *Psychological Review, 61,* 401–409.

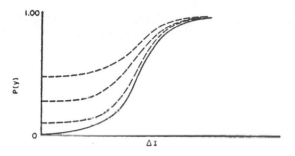

FIGURE 7.1   Conventional seeing frequency or betting curve

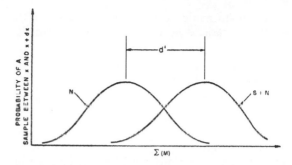

FIGURE 7.3   Hypothetical distributions of noise and signal plus noise

be a monotonically increasing function of light intensity, not necessarily linear. A more specific statement than this is left for experimental determination.

Figure 7.2 is a block diagram of the visual pathways showing the major stages of transmission of visual information. All the stages prior to that labelled "[visual] cortex" are assumed to function only in the transmission of information, presenting to the cortex a representation of the environment. The function of interpreting this information is left to mechanisms at the cortical level.

In this simplified presentation, the displayed information consists of neural impulse activity. In the case under consideration, in which a signal is presented at a specified time in a known spatial location, the same restrictions are assumed to exist for the display. Thus, if the observer is asked to state whether a signal exists in location A at time B, he is assumed to consider only that information in the neural display which refers to location A at time B.

A judgment on the existence of a signal is presumably based on a measure of neural activity. There exists a statistical relationship between the measure and signal intensity. That is, the more intense the signal, the greater is the average of the measures resulting. Thus, for any signal there is a universe distribution which is in fact a sampling distribution. It

includes all measures which might result if the signal were repeated and measured an infinite number of times. The mean of this universe distribution is associated with the intensity level of the signal. The variance may be associated with other parameters of the signal such as duration or size, but this is beyond the scope of this paper.

Figure 7.3 shows two probability distributions: N represents the case where noise alone is sampled—that is, no signal exists—and $S + N$, the case where signal plus noise exists. The mean of N depends on background intensity; the mean of $S + N$ on background plus signal intensity. The variance of N depends on signal parameters, not background parameters in the case considered here; that is, where the observer knows a priori that if a signal exists then it is a particular signal. From the way the diagram is conceptualized, the greater the measure, $\Sigma(M)$, the more likely it is that this sample represents a signal. But one can never be sure. Thus, if an observer is asked if a signal exists, he is assumed to base his judgment on the quantity of neural activity. He makes an observation, and then attempts to decide whether this observation is more representative of N or of $S + N$. His task is, in fact, the task of testing a statistical hypothesis.

The ideal behavior, that which makes optimum use of the information available in this task, is defined mathematically by Peterson and Birdsall (2). The mathematics and symbols used are theirs, unless otherwise stated. The first case considered is the yes-no psychophysical experiment in which a signal is presented at a known location during a well-defined interval in time. This corresponds to Peterson and Birdsall's case of the signal known exactly.

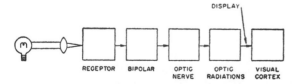

FIGURE 7.2   Block diagram of the visual channel

For mathematical convenience, it is assumed that the distributions shown in Figure 7.3 are Gaussian, with variance equal for N and all values of $S + N$. Experimental results suggest that equal variance is not a true assumption, but that the deviations are not great enough to justify the inconvenience of a more precise assumption for the purpose of this analysis.

It is also assumed that there is a cutoff point such that any measure of neural activity which exceeds that cutoff is in the criterion; that is, any value exceeding cutoff is accepted as representing the existence of a signal, and any value less than the cutoff represents noise alone.

Again, for mathematical convenience, the cutoff point is assumed to be well defined and stable. The justification for accepting this convenience is twofold: first, such behavior is statistically optimum, and second, if absolute stability is physically impossible, any lack of definition or random instability throughout an experiment has the same effect mathematically as additional variance in the sampling distributions.

Now, consider the way in which the placing of the cutoff affects behavior in the case of a given signal. In the lower right-hand corner of Figure 7.4 the distribu-

tions N and $S + N$ are reproduced for a value of $d' = 1$. The parameter d' is the square root of Peterson and Birdsall's d. The square root of d is more convenient here; d' is the difference between the means of N and $S + N$ in terms of the standard deviation of N. The criterion scale is also calibrated in terms of the standard deviation of N. On the abscissa there is $P_N(A)$, the probability that, if no signal exists, the measure will be in the criterion, and on the ordinate, $P_{SN}(A)$, the probability that if a signal exists, the measure will be in the criterion.

If the cutoff is at $-\infty$, all measures are in the criterion: $P_N(A) = P_{SN}(A) = 1$. At -1 standard deviation, $P_N(A) = .84$, and $P_{SN}(A) = .98$. At 0, $P_N(A) = .5$ and $P_{SN}(A) = .84$. At $+1$, $P_N(A) = .16$ and $P_{SN}(A) = .5$; and for $+\infty$ $P_N(A) = P_{SN}(A) = 0$. Thus, for $d' = 1$ this is the curve showing possible detections for each false-alarm rate. The curve represents the best that can be done with the information available, and the mirror image is the curve of worst possible behaviors.

The maximum behavior in any given experiment is a point on this curve at which the slope is β where

$$\beta = \frac{1 - P(SN)}{P(SN)} \frac{\left(V_{N \cdot CA} + K_{N \cdot A} \right)}{\left(V_{SN \cdot A} + K_{SN \cdot CA} \right)}$$

$P(SN)$ is the a priori probability that the signal exists, $V_{N \cdot CA}$ is the value of a correct rejection, $K_{N \cdot A}$ the cost of a false alarm, $V_{SN \cdot A}$ the value of a correct detection, and $K_{SN \cdot CA}$ is the cost of a miss. Thus, as $P(SN)$ or $V_{SN \cdot A}$ increases, or $K_{N \cdot A}$ decreases, β becomes smaller, and it is worthwhile to accept a higher false-alarm rate in the interest of achieving a greater percentage of correct decisions.

Figure 7.5 shows a family of curves of $P_{SN}(A)$ vs. $P_N(A)$ with d' as a parameter. For values of d' greater than 4, detection is very good. This is to be compared with the predictions of the conventional theory shown in Figure 7.6 with $P_N(A)$ assumed to represent guesses. For each value of d' it is assumed that there is a true value of $P_{SN}(A)$ either for $P_N(A) = 0$ or for some very small value. The chance correction should transform each of these to horizontal lines.

Another way of comparing the predictions of this theory with those of conventional theory is to construct the so-called betting curves, or curves showing

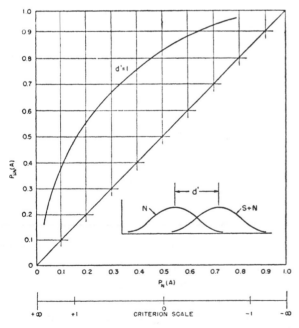

FIGURE 7.4 $P_{SN}(A)$ vs. $P_N(A)$. The criterion scale shows the corresponding criteria expressed in terms of σ_N from M_N.

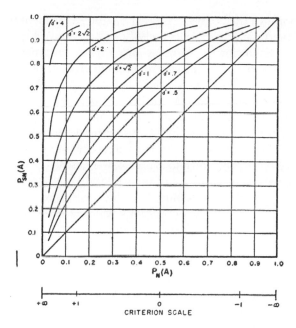

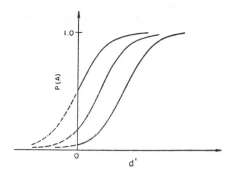

FIGURE 7.7   *P(A)* as a function of *d'* assuming the theory

FIGURE 7.5 $P_{SN}(A)$ vs. $P_N(A)$

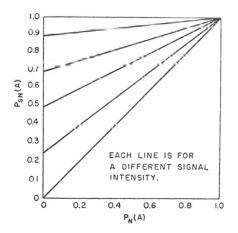

EACH LINE IS FOR
A DIFFERENT SIGNAL
INTENSITY.

FIGURE 7.6 $P_{SN}(A)$ vs. $P_N(A)$ as a function of *d'* assuming the guessing hypothesis

the predicted shape of the psychophysical function. These are shown in Figure 7.7, where *P(A)*, the probability of acceptance, is plotted as a function of *d'*. These curves will not map onto the same curve by the application of the chance correction. The shift is hori-

zontal rather than vertical. The dotted portions of the curve show that we are dealing with only a part of the curve, and thus, in the terms of this theory, it is improper to apply a normalizing procedure such as the chance-correction formula to that part of the curve.

In the forced-choice psychophysical experiment, maximum behavior is defined in a different way. In the general forced choice experiment, the observer knows that the signal will occur in one of *n* intervals, and he is forced to choose in which of these intervals it occurs. The information upon which his decision is based is contained in the same display as in the case of the yes-no experiment, and, presumably, the values of *d'* for any given light intensity must be the same. While the solution of this problem is not contained in their study, Peterson and Birdsall have assisted greatly in determining this solution. The probability that a correct answer *P(C)* will result for a given value of *d'* is the probability that one sample from the *S + N* distribution is greater than the greatest of *n* − 1 samples from the distribution of noise alone. The case in which four intervals are used is the basis for Figure 7.8. This figure shows the probability of one sample from *S + N* being greater than the greatest of three from *N*. For a given value of *d'* this is

$$P(C) = \int_{x=-\infty}^{+\infty} F(x)^3 g(x)dx$$

where *F(x) is* the area of *N* and *g(x)* is the ordinate of *S + N*. In Figure 7.8, *P(C)*, as determined by this integration, is plotted as a function of *d'* for the equal-variance case.

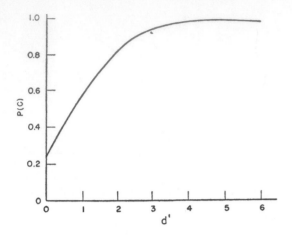

FIGURE 7.8   *P(C)* as a function of *d'*. A theoretical curve.

CRITERION OF INTERNAL CONSISTENCY

These two sets of predictions are for the standard experimental situations. They are based on the same neurological parameters. Thus, if the parameters, that is, *d'*s, are estimated from one of the experiments, these estimates should furnish a basis for predicting the data for the other experiment if the theory is internally consistent. An equivalent criterion of internal consistency is that both experiments yield the same estimates of *d'*.

EXPERIMENTAL DESIGN

Experiments were conducted to test this internal consistency, using three Michigan sophomores as observers. All the experiments employed a circular target 30 minutes in diameter, 1/100 second in duration, on a 10-foot-lambert background. Details of the experimental procedure and the laboratory have been published by Blackwell, Pritchard, and Ohmart (1).

The observers were trained in the temporal forced-choice experiment. The signal appeared in a known location at one of four specified times, and the observers were forced to choose the time at which they thought the signal occurred. Five light intensity increments were used here, with 50 observations per point per experimental session. The last two of these sessions were the test sessions, so that each forced-choice

point in the analysis is based on 100 experimental observations.

Following the forced-choice experiments, there was a series of yes-no experiments under the same experimental conditions, except that only four light intensity increments were used. These were the same as the four greatest intensities used in the forced-choice experiments, reduced by adding a .1 fixed filter. In the first four of these sessions, two values of a priori probabilities, *P(SN)* equal to .8 and .4, were used. The observers were informed of the value of *P(SN)* before each experimental session. No values or costs were incorporated in these four sessions, which were thus excluded from the analysis as practice sessions.

The test experiments consisted of 12 sessions in each of which all of the information necessary for the calculation of a β (the best possible decision level) was furnished [to] the observers. While they did not know the formal calculation of β, that they knew the direction of cutoff change indicated by a change in any of these factors was suggested by the fact that the obtained values of $P_N(A)$ varied approximately with changes in the information given them. The values and costs were made real to the observers, for they were actually paid in cash. It was possible for them to earn as much as two dollars extra in a single experimental session as a result of this payment.

The first four sessions each carried the same value of β as *P(SN)* = .8 and the same payment was maintained. A high value of $P_N(A)$, or false-alarm rate, resulted. In the next four sessions with *P(SN)* held at .8, $K_{N \cdot A}$ and $V_{N \cdot CA}$ were gradually increased from session to session (not within sessions) until $P_N(A)$ dropped to a low value. Then *P(SN)* was dropped to .4, and K_{NA} and $V_{N \cdot CA}$ were reduced so that for the thirteenth session $P_N(A)$ stayed low. The last three sessions successively involved increases in $V_{S \cdot NA}$ and $K_{SN \cdot CA}$, again forcing $P_N(A)$ toward a higher value.

RESULTS

Figures 7.9 and 7.10 show scatter diagrams of $P_{SN}(A)$ vs. $P_N(A)$ for a particular intensity of signal and for a single observer. These scatter diagrams can be used to estimate *d'*. In Figure 7.9 the estimate of *d'* is .7. In Figure 7.10, the estimate of *d'* is 1.3. Each *d'* estimated

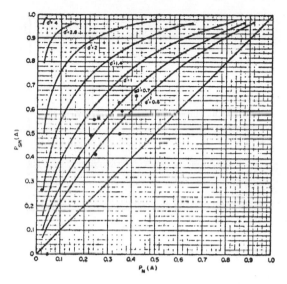

FIGURE 7.9   A scatter diagram of $P_{SN}(A)$ vs. $P_N(A)$

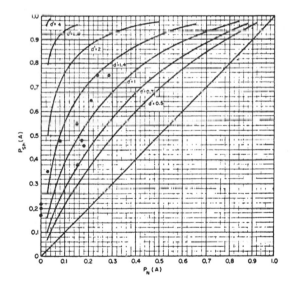

FIGURE 7.10   A scatter diagram of $P_{SN}(A)$ vs. $P_N(A)$

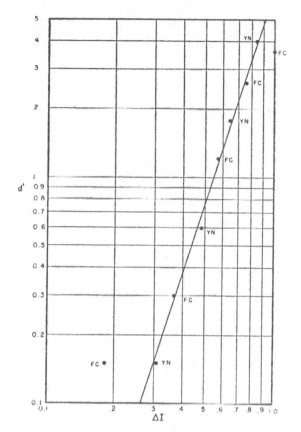

FIGURE 7.11   Log d' vs. Log ΔI for Observer 1

in this way is based on 560 observations. A procedure similar to this was used for the d's for each of four signals for each of the four observers.

In the forced-choice experiment the estimates of d' are made by entering our forced-choice curve (Figure 7.8), using the observed percentage correct as an estimate of $P'(C)$. Figure 7.11 shows log d' as a function of log signal intensity for the first observer, the estimates of d' being from both forced-choice and yes-no experiments. In general the agreement is good. The deviation of the forced-choice point at the top can be explained on the basis of inadequate experimental data for the determination of the high probability involved. The deviation of the low point is unexplained. Figure 7.12 is the same plot for the second observer, showing about the same picture. Figure 7.13 is for the third observer, showing not quite as good a fit, but nevertheless satisfactory for psychological experiments. For this observer, the lowest point for forced choice is off the graph to the right of the line.

Figures 7.14, 7.15, and 7.16 show the predictions for forced-choice data (when yes-no data are used to

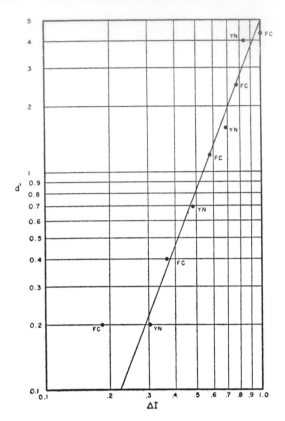

FIGURE 7.12   Log d' vs. Log ΔI for Observer 2

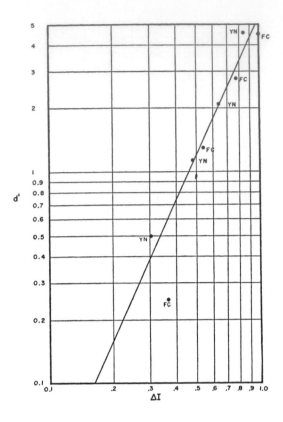

FIGURE 7.13   Log d' vs. Log ΔI for Observer 3

estimate d') for the three observers. Note that the lowest point is on the curve in both of the first two cases, suggesting that the deviation which appeared on the curves in Figures 7.11, 7.12, and 7.13 is not significant.

DISCUSSION

The results satisfy the criterion of internal consistency. The theory also turns out to be consistent with the vast amount of data in the literature, for, when the d' vs. ΔI function for any one of the observers is used to predict probability of detection as a function of ΔI in terms of this theory, the result closely approximates the type of curve frequently reported. Shapes of curves thus furnish no basis for selecting between the two theories, and a decision must rest on the other arguments.

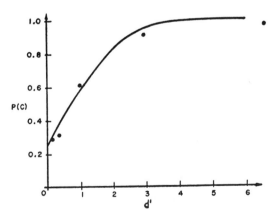

FIGURE 7.14   Prediction of forced-choice data from yes-no data for Observer 1

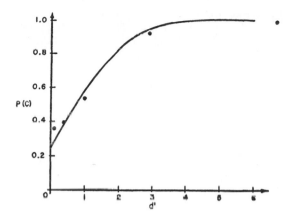

FIGURE 7.15   Prediction of forced-choice data from yes-no data for Observer 2

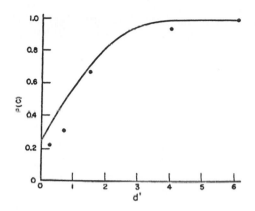

FIGURE 7.16   Prediction of forced-choice data from yes-no data for Observer 3

According to conventional theory, application of the chance correction should yield corrected values of $P_{SN}(A)$ which are independent of $P_N(A)$, or should yield corrected thresholds in the conventional sense which are independent of $P_N(A)$. Rank-order correlations for the three observers between $P_N(A)$ and corrected thresholds (.30, .71, .67) are highly significant; the combined $p \ll .001$. This is a result consistent with theory presented here.

Another method of comparison is to fit the scatter diagrams (Figure 7.9 and 7.10) by straight lines. According to the independence theory, these straight lines should intercept the point (1.00, 1.00). Sampling error would be expected to send some of the lines to either side of this point. There are 12 of these scatter diagrams, and all 12 of these lines intersect the line $P_{SN}(A) = 1.00$ at values of $P_N(A)$ between 0 and 1.00 in an order which would be predicted if these lines were arcs of the curves $P_{SN}(A)$ vs. $P_N(A)$ as defined by the theory of signal detectability.

Two additional sessions were run in which the observers were permitted three categories of response (yes, no, and doubtful), and were told to be sure of being correct if they responded either yes or no. Again, two a priori probabilities (.8 and .4) were employed, and again $P_N(A)$ was correlated with $P(SN)$. The observers, interviewed after these sessions, re-

ported that their "yes" responses were based on "phenomenal" seeing.

This does not mean that the observers were abnormal because they hallucinated. It suggests, on the other hand, that phenomenal seeing develops through experience, and is subject to change with experience. Psychological as well as physiological factors are involved. Psychological "set" is a function of β, and after experience with a given set one begins to see, or not to see, rather automatically. Change the set, and the level of seeing changes. The experiments reported here were such that the observers learned to adjust rapidly to different sets.

CONCLUSIONS

The following conclusions are advanced: (a) The conventional concept of a threshold, or a threshold region, needs re-evaluation in the light of the present theory that the visual detection problem is the problem of detecting signals in noise. (b) The hypothesis that false alarms are guesses is rejected on the basis of statistical tests. (c) Change in neural activity is a power function of change in light intensity. (d) The mathematical model of signal detection is applicable to problems of visual detection. (e) The criterion of seeing depends on psychological as well as physiological factors. In the experiments reported here the observers tended to use optimum criteria. (f) The experimental data support the assumption of a logical connection between forced-choice and yes-no techniques developed by the theory.

AUTHORS' NOTE

This paper is based on work done for the U.S. Army Signal Corps under Contract No. DA-36-039 sc-15358. The experiments reported herein were conducted in the Vision Research Laboratories of the University of Michigan.

REFERENCES

1. Blackwell, H. R., Pritchard, B. S., & Ohmart, T. G. (1954). Automatic apparatus for stimulus presentation and recording in visual threshold experiments. *Journal of the Optical Society of America, 44*, 322–326.
2. Peterson, W. W., & Birdsall, T. G. (1953). The theory of signal detectability. Electronic Defense Group, University of Michigan, *Technical Report*, No. 13 (September).

8 VISUAL SEARCH

This paper summarizes a variety of experiments that investigate visual perception and visual attention. Taken all together, these experiments suggest that identification of stimuli in the world involves two stages: a preattentive stage that automatically computes basic features and an attentive stage that binds together the basic features to form objects.

The visual search experiments in particular have had a lasting impact on cognitive psychology because the experimental task can be easily modified to investigate many different situations, and the task is applicable to a variety of important human behaviors. The basic task is to report the presence or absence of a target amongst a set of distracters. This task is not unlike many everyday situations in which you are searching for a particular item in a cluttered room. The item may be within your line of sight, but it may be easy or difficult to find, depending on what else is also visible.

Treisman suggested that the visual search task could be used for two basic purposes. First, it could be used to identify the basic features of visual perception that are processed preattentively. Second, it could be used to investigate the nature of the attentive stage.

A visual search task identifies basic features of visual perception by varying the number of distracters. On each trial, the observer responds as quickly as possible whether the target is present or absent. If the reaction time does *not* vary with the number of distracters, then this indicates that a characteristic of the target is computed as a basic feature. The percept is typically that the target "pops out" at you, like a green circle amongst distracters of blue circles. It doesn't matter how many blue circles there are, because all you have to do to judge whether the target is there is see if there is anything green.

Across a variety of visual search experiments (see Figure 8.4) Treisman found a small number of features that produce flat reaction times as the number of distracters increases. The features include color, size, contrast, tilt, curvature, line ends, and closure. In a clever set of experiments, Treisman showed that the representation of these features seems to be based exclusively on the *presence* of the feature rather than the absence of the feature. An example of this is in Figure 8.4b, where search for a tilted line amongst vertical line distracters is unaffected by the number of distracters, but search for a vertical line amongst tilted distracters is affected by the number of distracters. It is as if verticalness of a line is the default, and when a line is vertical it does not generate an active representation. Only deviations from the default (tilted) cause an active representation; and only active representations can cause the pop-out effect.

When reaction time increases with the number of distracters, Treisman attributes this to an attentive process that searches the items in the display one at a time. Consistent with this hypothesis, reaction time is linearly related to the number of distracters. Moreover, the reaction time increases twice as fast for trials where the target was absent compared to trials where the target was present. This difference makes sense because if you are searching items one at a time, and the target is not there, you have to search every item to be sure the target is not one of them. On the other hand, if the target is present, sometimes you will find it early in your search and sometimes you will find it later in your search. On average, you will find the target after judging half of the distracters.

The CogLab experiment on visual search demonstrates the basic task. The results are extremely robust. Nearly everyone shows evidence of the pop-out effect when the target is a different color from the distracters. Moreover, nearly everyone shows the expected increases in reaction time when the search requires attentive focus. The generality of these findings has made the visual search task a staple of cognitive psychology.

Treisman's explanation of these results continues to influence thinking on visual attention and visual perception; however, there are alternative interpretations. See Wolfe (1998) for a modern discussion of these issues. The title of Wolfe's article is accurate by the way; Wolfe's lab really has performed more than 1 million visual search trials.

REFERENCE

Wolfe, J. M. (1998). What can 1,000,000 trials tell us about visual search? *Psychological Science, 9,* 33–39.

QUESTIONS

1. What is the dependent variable measured on each trial in a visual search experiment?
2. Which do you think would be more difficult: to search for a *c* among a set of *o*s or to search for an *o* among a set of *c*s?
3. How might you use knowledge of the pop-out effect to improve your ability to search for something like a stapler?

4. When search seems to be unaffected by the number of distracters, the re-action times for trials with the target are the same for trials without the target. Is this consistent with Treisman's idea that the target is processed preattentively?

Features and Objects in Visual Processing

Anne Treisman

INTRODUCTION

Look around the area where you are now located. If you are inside, you are likely to see furniture, windows, walls, and a floor; if you are outside, you are likely to see plants, the sky, and perhaps a road or a sidewalk. Of course, you do not really directly see these objects. You actually detect details like edges, movement, and spatial clues about distances, then these features and properties somehow combine into meaningful wholes. How does simple feature detection become perception of multidimensional, complete objects? This perceptual task, which humans do effortlessly, has turned out to be remarkably difficult for computers to accomplish, much more so than complex tasks such as chess or solving mathematical problems.

Treisman has described some general conclusions about visual perception that are emerging from research done in her lab and elsewhere. The visual perception of an object appears to involve three steps. The first step is coding simple features with reference to maps that preserve spatial (i.e., location) information. The second step requires focused attention (i.e., paying attention to the object being perceived) and results in a temporary representation of the object. The third step is to compare the temporary representation with descriptions of objects stored in memory. If a match is found between the temporary representation and a stored description, the object has been recognized, completing the process of visual perception.

Why should an article on vision written for a general scientific magazine be included in a book of readings in cognitive psychology? For one consideration, its author is one of the foremost contributors in the

world to the field of vision. This article gives readers a chance to learn about her work in a forum that is more accessible than some of the original journal articles that have published the work. For another, this article gives a broader account of vision than would many individual journal articles. In this article, Treisman displays an important skill that many cognitive psychologists lack: the ability to describe complicated concepts and findings from their work and that of others in a way that is accessible to the general reader. Such a task, easy as it sounds, in fact is quite a difficult challenge. One has to make sure that the ideas and findings are presented correctly and clearly and in a way that general readers can understand. One has to know not only what details to include, but what details to omit. Also, one has to know how to relate one's own work to that of others in a way that is informative and not self-serving. Treisman is among the best writers of such articles.

* * *

The seemingly effortless ability to perceive meaningful wholes in the visual world depends on complex processes. The features automatically extracted from a scene are assembled into objects.

If you were magically deposited in an unknown city, your first impression would be of recognizable objects organized coherently in a meaningful framework. You would see buildings, people, cars, and trees. You would not be aware of detecting colors, edges, movements, and distances, and of assembling them into multidimensional wholes for which you could retrieve identities and labels from memory. In short,

SOURCE: From Treisman, A. (1986). Features and objects in visual processing. *Scientific American, 255,* 114–125. This reading is reprinted with permission of Scientific American. Copyright © 1986 by Scientific American, Inc. All rights reserved. Figures are reprinted with permission of Jerome Kuhl. Photos are reprinted with permission of Jon Brennis.

meaningful wholes seem to precede parts and properties, as the Gestalt psychologists emphasized many years ago.

This apparently effortless achievement, which you repeat innumerable times throughout your waking hours, is proving very difficult to understand or to simulate on a computer—much more difficult, in fact, than the understanding and simulation of tasks that most people find quite challenging, such as playing chess or solving problems in logic. The perception of meaningful wholes in the visual world apparently depends on complex operations to which a person has no conscious access, operations that can be inferred only on the basis of indirect evidence.

Nevertheless, some simple generalizations about visual information processing are beginning to emerge. One of them is a distinction between two levels of processing. Certain aspects of visual processing seem to be accomplished simultaneously (that is, for the entire visual field at once) and automatically (that is, without attention being focused on any one part of the visual field). Other aspects of visual processing seem to depend on focused attention and are done serially, or one at a time, as if a mental spotlight were being moved from one location to another.

In 1967, Ulric Neisser, then at the University of Pennsylvania, suggested that a "preattentive" level of visual processing segregates regions of a scene into figures and ground so that a subsequent, attentive level can identify particular objects. More recently, David C. Marr, investigating computer simulation of vision at the Massachusetts Institute of Technology, found it necessary to establish a "primal sketch": a first stage of processing, in which the pattern of light reaching an array of receptors is converted into a coded description of lines, spots, or edges and their locations, orientations, and colors. The representation of surfaces and volumes and finally the identification of objects could begin only after this initial coding.

In brief, a model with two or more stages is gaining acceptance among psychologists, physiologists, and computer scientists working in artificial intelligence. Its first stage might be described as the extraction of features from patterns of light; later stages are concerned with the identification of objects and their settings. The phrase "features and objects" is therefore

a three-word characterization of the emerging hypothesis about the early stages of vision.

I think there are many reasons to agree that vision indeed applies specialized analyzers to decompose stimuli into parts and properties, and that extra operations are needed to specify their recombination into the correct wholes. In part the evidence is physiological and anatomical. In particular, the effort to trace what happens to sensory data suggests that the data are processed in different areas of considerable specialization. One area concerns itself mainly with the orientation of lines and edges, another with color, still another with directions of movement. Only after processing in these areas do data reach areas that appear to discriminate between complex natural objects.

Some further evidence is behavioral. For example, it seems that visual adaptation (the visual system's tendency to become unresponsive to a sustained stimulus) occurs separately for different properties of a scene. If you stare at a waterfall for a few minutes and then look at the bank of the river, the bank will appear to flow in the opposite direction. It is as if the visual detectors had selectively adapted to a particular direction of motion independent of *what* is moving. The bank looks very different from the water, but it nonetheless shows the aftereffects of the adaptation process.

How can the preattentive aspect of visual processing be further subjected to laboratory examination? One strategy is suggested by the obvious fact that in the real world parts that belong to the same object tend to share properties: they have the same color and texture, their boundaries show a continuity of lines or curves, they move together, they are at roughly the same distance from the eye. Accordingly the investigator can ask subjects to locate the boundaries between regions in various visual displays and thus can learn what properties make a boundary immediately salient—make it "pop out" of a scene. These properties are likely to be the ones the visual system normally employs in its initial task of segregating figure from ground.

It turns out that boundaries are salient between elements that differ in simple properties such as color, brightness, and line orientation but not between elements that differ in how their properties are combined or arranged (Figure 8.1). For example, a region of *T*s

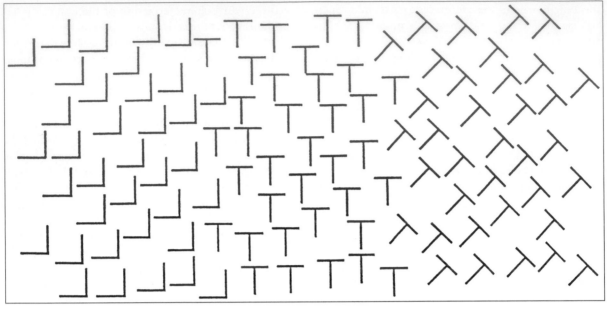

(a)

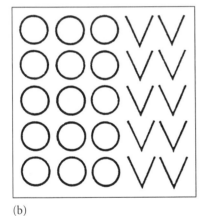

(b)

FIGURE 8.1 Boundaries that "pop out" of a scene are likely to reveal the simple properties, or features, of the visual world that are seized on by the initial stage of visual processing. For example, a boundary between *T*s and tilted *T*s pops out, whereas a boundary between *T*s and *L*s does not (a). The implication is that line orientations are important features in early visual processing but that particular arrangements of conjunctions of lines are not. A boundary between *O*s and *V*s pops out (b). The implication is that simple shape properties (such as line curvature) are important.

segregates well from a region of tilted *T*s but not from a region of *L*s made of the same components as the *T*s (a horizontal line and a vertical line). By the same token, a mixture of blue *V*s and red *O*s does not segregate from a mixture of red *V*s and blue *O*s. It seems that the early "parsing" of the visual field is mediated by separate properties, not by particular combinations of properties. That is, analysis of properties and parts precedes their synthesis. And if parts or properties are identified before they are conjoined with objects, they must have some independent psychological existence.

This leads to a strong prediction, which is that errors of synthesis should sometimes take place. In other words, subjects should sometimes see illusory conjunctions of parts or properties drawn from different areas of the visual field. In certain conditions such illusions take place frequently. In one experiment my colleagues and I flashed three colored letters, say a blue *X*, a green *T*, and a red *O*, for a brief period (200 milliseconds, or a fifth of a second) and diverted our subjects' attention by asking them to report first a digit shown at each side of the display and only then

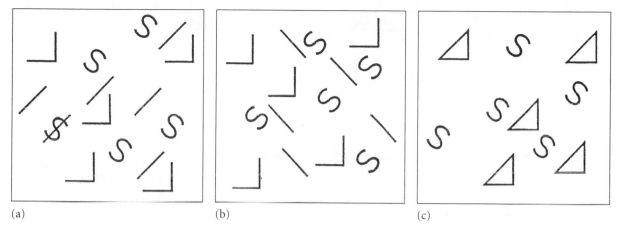

(a)   (b)   (c)

FIGURE 8.2   Illusory dollar signs are an instance of false conjunctions of features. Subjects were asked to look for dollar signs in the midst of Ss and line segments (a). They often reported seeing the signs when the displays to which they were briefly exposed contained none (b). They had the same experience about as often when the line segment needed to complete a sign was embedded in a triangle (c). The experiment suggests that early visual processing can detect the presence of features independent of location.

the colored letters. In about one trial in three, the subjects reported the wrong combinations—perhaps a red *X*, a green *O*, or a blue *T*.

The subjects made these conjunction errors much more often than they reported a color or shape that was not present in the display, which suggests that the errors reflect genuine exchanges of properties rather than simply misperceptions of a single object. Many of these errors appear to be real illusions, so convincing that subjects demand to see the display again to convince themselves that the errors were indeed mistakes.

We have looked for constraints on the occurrence of such illusory conjunctions. For example, we have asked whether objects must be similar for their properties to be exchanged. It seems they do not: Subjects exchanged colors between a small, red outline of a triangle and a large, solid blue circle just as readily as they exchanged colors between two small outline triangles. It is as if the red color of the triangle were represented by an abstract code for red rather than being incorporated into a kind of analogue of the triangle that also encodes the object's size and shape.

We also asked if it would be harder to create illusory conjunctions by detaching a part from a simple unitary shape, such as a triangle, than by moving a loose line. The answer again was no. Our subjects saw

illusory dollar signs in a display of Ss and lines. They also saw the illusory signs in a display of Ss and triangles in which each triangle incorporated the line the illusion required (Figure 8.2). In conscious experience the triangle looks like a cohesive whole. Nevertheless, at the preattentive level, its component lines seem to be detected independently.

To be sure, the triangle may have an additional feature, namely the fact that its constituent lines enclose an area, and this property of closure might be detected preattentively. If so, the perception of a triangle might require the detection of its three component lines in the correct orientations and also the detection of closure. We should then find that subjects do not see illusory triangles when they are given only the triangles' separate lines in the proper orientations (Figure 8.3). They may need a further stimulus, a different closed shape (perhaps a circle), in order to assemble illusory triangles. That is indeed what we found.

Another way to make the early, preattentive level of visual processing the subject of laboratory investigation is to assign visual-search tasks. That is, we ask subjects to find a target item in the midst of other, "distractor" items. The assumption is that if the preattentive processing occurs automatically and across the visual field, a target that is distinct from its

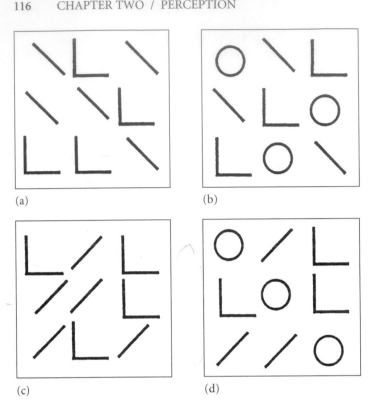

(a)

(b)

(c)

(d)

FIGURE 8.3   Illusory triangles constitute a test of what features must be available to support the perception of triangles. Subjects seldom reported seeing a triangle when they were briefly exposed to displays consisting of the line segments that make up a triangle (a). They saw triangles far more often when the displays also included closed stimuli, that is, shapes that enclose a space, in this case Os (b). Evidently, closure is a feature analyzed in early visual processing. This conclusion was supported by showing displays that lack the diagonal line to make a triangle (c, d). Subjects seldom saw triangles in such displays.

neighbors in its preattentive representation in the brain should "pop out" of the display. The proverbial needle in a haystack is hard to find because it shares properties of length, thickness and orientation with the hay in which it is hidden. A red poppy in a haystack is a much easier target; its unique color and shape are detected automatically.

We find that if a target differs from the distractors in some simple property, such as orientation or color or curvature, the target is detected about equally fast in an array of 30 items and in an array of three items. Such targets pop out of the display, so that the time it takes to find them is independent of the number of distractors. This independence holds true even when subjects are not told what the unique property of the target will be. The subjects take slightly longer overall, but the number of distractors still has little or no effect.

On the other hand, we find that if a target is characterized only by a conjunction of properties (for example, a red O among red Ns and green Os), or if it is defined only by its particular combination of compo-

nents (for example, an R among Ps and Qs that together incorporate all the parts of the R), the time taken to find the target or to decide that the target is not present increases linearly with the number of distractors. It is as if the subjects who are placed in these circumstances are forced to focus attention in turn on each item in the display in order to determine how the item's properties or parts are conjoined. In a positive trial (a trial in which a target is present) the search ends when the target is found; on the average, therefore, it ends after half of the distractors have been examined. In a negative trial (in which no target is present) all the distractors have to be checked. As distractors are added to the displays, the search time in positive trials therefore increases at half the rate of the search time in negative trials.

The difference between a search for simple features and a search for conjunctions of features could have implications in industrial settings. Quality-control inspectors might, for example, take more time to check manufactured items if the possible errors in manufacture are characterized by faulty combinations of properties than they do if the errors always result in a salient change in a single property. Similarly, each of the symbols representing, say, the destinations for baggage handled at airline terminals should be characterized by a unique combination of properties.

In a further series of experiments on visual-search tasks, we explored the effect of exchanging the target and the distractors. That is, we required subjects to find a target distinguished by the fact that it *lacks* a feature present in all the distractors. For example, we employed displays consisting of Os and Qs, so that the difference between the target and the distractors is that one is simply a circle whereas the other is a circle intersected by a line segment (Figure 8.4). We found a remarkable difference in the search time depending on whether the target was the Q and had the line or was the O and lacked the line. When the target had the line, the search time was independent of the number of distractors. Evidently, the target popped out of the display. When the target lacked the line, the search time increased linearly with the number of distractors. Evidently, the items in the display were being subjected to a serial search.

The result goes against one's intuitions. After all, each case involves the same discrimination between the same two stimuli: Os and Qs. The result is consistent, however, with the idea that a pooled neural signal early in visual processing conveys the presence but not the absence of a distinctive feature. In other words, early vision extracts simple properties, and each type of property triggers activity in populations of specialized detectors. A target with a unique property is detected in the midst of distractor items simply by a check on whether the relevant detectors are active. Conversely, a target lacking a property that is present in the distractors arouses only slightly less activity than a display consisting exclusively of distractors. We propose, therefore, that early vision sets up a number of what might be called *feature maps*. They are not necessarily to be equated with the specialized visual areas that are mapped by physiologists, although the correspondence is suggestive.

We have exploited visual-search tasks to test a wide range of candidate features we thought might pop out of displays and so reveal themselves as primitives: basic elements in the language of early vision. The candidates fell into a number of categories: quantitative properties such as length or number; properties of single lines such as orientation or curvature; properties of line arrangements; topological and relational properties such as the connectedness of lines, the presence of the free ends of lines or the ratio of the height to the width of a shape.

Among the quantitative candidates, my colleagues and I found that some targets popped out when their discriminability was great. In particular, the more extreme targets—the longer lines, the darker grays, the pairs of lines (when the distractors were single lines)—were easier to detect. This suggests that the visual system responds positively to "more" in these quantitative properties and that "less" is coded by default. For example, the neural activity signaling line length might increase with increasing length (up to some maximum), so that a longer target is detected against the lower level of background activity produced by short distractors. In contrast, a shorter target, with its concomitant lower rate of firing, is likely to be swamped by the greater activity produced by the longer distractors. Psychophysicists have known for more than a century that the ability to distinguish differences in intensity grows more acute with decreasing background intensity. We suggest that the same phenomenon, which is known as Weber's law, could account for our findings concerning the quantitative features.

Our tests of two simple properties of lines, orientation and curvature, yielded some surprises. In both cases we found pop-out for one target, a tilted line among vertical distractors and a curved line among straight lines, but not for the converse target, a vertical line among tilted distractors and a straight line among curves. These findings suggest that early vision encodes tilt and curvature but not verticality or straightness. That is, the vertical targets and the straight targets appear to lack a feature the distractors possess, as if they represent null values on their respective dimensions. If our interpretation is correct, it implies that in early vision, tilt and curvature are represented relationally, as deviations from a standard or norm that itself is not positively signaled.

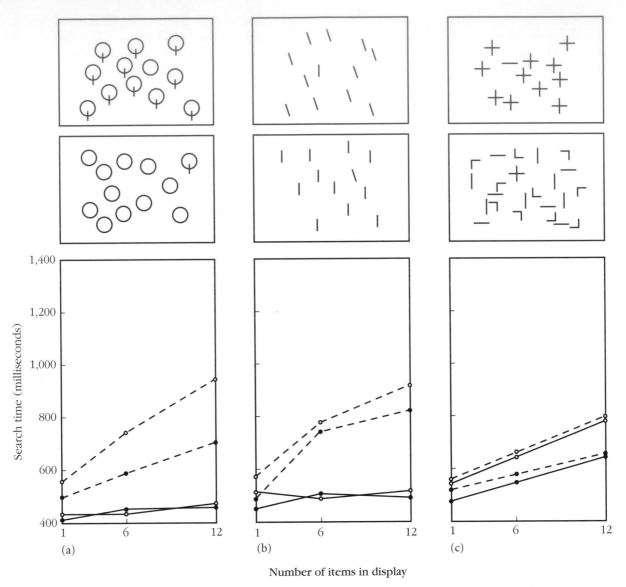

Number of items in display

FIGURE 8.4   Presence or absence of a feature can have remarkably different effects on the time it takes to find a target in the midst of distractors. In one experiment (a) the target was a circle intersected by a vertical line segment or a circle without that feature. The search time for the intersected circle (solid) proved to be largely independent of the number of items in the display, suggesting that the feature popped out. The search time for the plain circle (dashed) increased steeply as distractors were added, suggesting that a serial search of the display was being made. A second experiment (b) required subjects to search for a vertical line (dashed) or a tilted line (solid). The tilted line could be found much faster; evidently only the tilted line popped out of the displays. A third experiment (c) tested an isolated line segment (dashed) or intersecting lines in the form of a plus sign (solid). Evidently neither popped out.

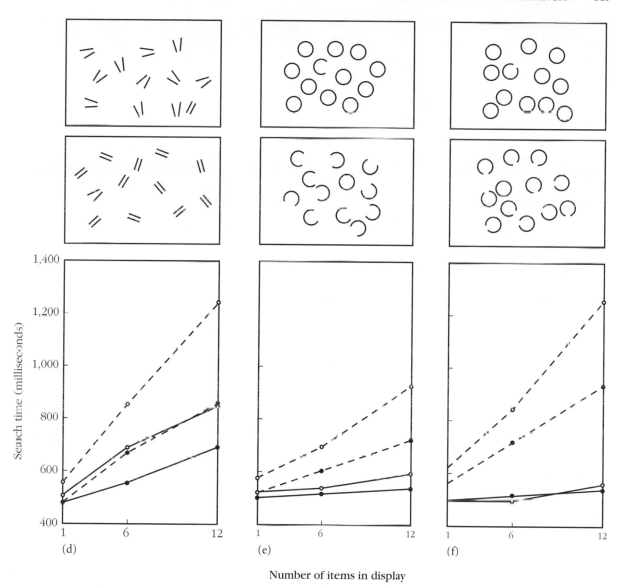

Number of items in display

FIGURE 8.4 (CONTINUED)   A fourth experiment (d) tested parallel lines (dashed) or converging lines (solid). Again neither popped out. A fifth experiment (e) tested closure with complete circles (dashed) or circles with a gap of a fourth of their circumference (solid). A sixth experiment (f), again testing closure, had complete circles (dashed) or circles with smaller gaps (solid). The size of the gap seemed to make no difference: The incomplete circle popped out. On the other hand, a complete circle became harder to find as the size of the gaps in distractors was reduced. Open dots represent data from trials in which the display included only distractors.

A similar conclusion emerged for the property of closure. We asked subjects to search for complete circles in the midst of circles with gaps and for circles with gaps among complete circles. Again we found a striking asymmetry, this time suggesting that the gap is preattentively detectable but that closure is not—or rather that it becomes preattentively detectable only when the distractors have very large gaps (that is, when they are quite open shapes like semicircles). In other words, closure is preattentively detectable, but only when the distractors do not share it to any significant degree. On the other hand, gaps (or the line ends that gaps create) are found equally easily whatever their size (unless they are too small for a subject, employing peripheral vision, to see).

Finally, we found no evidence that any property of line arrangements is preattentively detectable. We tested intersections, junctions, convergent lines and parallel lines. In every case we found that search time increases with an increasing number of distractors. The targets become salient and obvious only when the subject's attention is directed to them; they do not emerge automatically when that attention is disseminated throughout the display.

In sum, it seems that only a small number of features are extracted early in visual processing. They include color, size, contrast, tilt, curvature, and line ends. Research by other investigators shows that movement and differences in stereoscopic depth are also extracted automatically in early vision. In general the building blocks of vision appear to be simple properties that characterize local elements, such as points or lines, but not the relations among them. Closure appears to be the most complex property that pops out preattentively. Finally, our findings suggest that several preattentive properties are coded as values of deviation from a null, or reference, value.

Up to this point I have concentrated on the initial, preattentive stages of vision. I turn now to the later stages. In particular I turn to the evidence that focused attention is required for conjoining the features at a given location in a scene and for establishing structured representations of objects and their relations.

One line of evidence suggesting that conjunctions require attention emerges from experiments in which we asked subjects to identify a target in a display and say where it was positioned. In one type of display only a simple feature distinguished the target from the distractors. For example, the target was a red *H* in the midst of red *O*s and blue *X*s or an orange *X* among red *O*s and blue *X*s. In other displays, the target differed only in the way its features were conjoined. For example, it was a blue *O* or a red *X* among red *O*s and blue *X*s.

We were particularly interested in the cases in which a subject identified the target correctly but gave it the wrong location. As we expected, the subjects could sometimes identify a simple target, say a target distinguished merely by its color, but get its location wrong. Conjunction targets were different: The correct identification was completely dependent on the correct localization. It does indeed seem that attention must be focused on a location in order to combine the features it contains.

In a natural scene, of course, many conjunctions of features are ruled out by prior knowledge. You seldom come across blue bananas or furry eggs. Preattentive visual processing might be called "bottom up," in that it happens automatically, without any recourse to such knowledge. Specifically, it happens without recourse to "top down" constraints. One might hypothesize that conjunction illusions in everyday life are prevented when they conflict with top-down expectations. There are many demonstrations that we do use our knowledge of the world to speed up perception and to make it more accurate. For example, Irving Biederman of the State University of New York at Buffalo asked subjects to find a target object such as a bicycle in a photograph of a natural scene or in a jumbled image in which different areas had been randomly interchanged. The subjects did better when the bicycle could be found in a natural context (see the photo).

In order to explore the role of prior knowledge in the conjoining of properties. Deborah Butler and I did a further study of illusory conjunctions. We showed subjects a set of three colored objects flanked on each side by a digit. Then, some 200 milliseconds later, we showed them a pointer, which was accompanied by a random checkerboard in order to wipe out any visual persistence from the initial display. We asked the subjects to attend to the two digits and report them, and

Prior knowledge as a guide in visual perception is tested by asking subjects to search for a familiar object in a photograph of an unexceptional scene (top) and in a jumbled photograph of the scene (bottom). Here, the task is simply to find the bicycle. It tends to take longer in the jumbled image. The implication is that knowledge of the world (in this case, expectations about the characteristic locations of bicycles in urban landscapes) speeds up perception and makes it less subject to error. Certain early aspects of the information processing that underlies visual perception nonetheless seem to happen automatically: without the influence of prior knowledge. The illustration was modeled after experiments done by Irving Biederman of the State University of New York at Buffalo.

then to say which object the pointer had designated. The sequence was too brief to allow the subjects to focus their attention on all three objects.

The crucial aspect of the experiment lay in the labels we gave the objects. We told one group of subjects that the display would consist of "an orange carrot, a blue lake, and a black tire." Occasional objects (one in four) were shown in the wrong color to ensure that the subjects could not just name the color they would know in advance ought to be associated with a given shape. For another group of subjects the same display was described as "an orange triangle, a blue ellipse, and a black ring."

The results were significant. The group given arbitrary pairings of colors and shapes reported many illusory conjunctions: 29 percent of their responses represented illusory recombinations of colors and shapes from the display, whereas 13 percent were reports of colors or shapes not present in the display. In contrast, the group expecting familiar objects saw rather few illusory conjunctions: They wrongly recombined colors and shapes only 5 percent more often than they reported colors and shapes not present in the display.

We occasionally gave a third group of subjects the wrong combinations when they were expecting most objects to be in their natural colors. To our surprise we found no evidence that subjects generated illusory conjunctions to fit their expectations. For example, they were no more likely to see the triangle (the "carrot") as orange when another object in the display was orange than they were when no orange was present. There seem to be two implications: Prior knowledge and expectations do indeed help one to use attention efficiently in conjoining features, but prior knowledge and expectations seem not to induce illusory exchanges of features to make abnormal objects normal again. Thus illusory conjunctions seem to arise at a stage of visual processing that precedes semantic access to knowledge of familiar objects. The conjunctions seem to be generated preattentively from the sensory data, bottom-up, and not to be influenced by top-down constraints.

How are objects perceived once attention has been focused on them and the correct set of properties has been selected from those present in the scene? In particular, how does one generate and maintain an object's perceptual unity even when objects move and change? Imagine a bird perched on a branch, seen from a particular angle and in a particular illumination. Now watch its shape, its size, and its color all change as it preens itself, opens its wings, and flies away. In spite of these major transformations in virtu-

ally all its properties, the bird retains its perceptual integrity: It remains the same single object.

Daniel Kahneman of the University of California at Berkeley and I have suggested that object perception is mediated not only by recognition, or matching to a stored label or description, but also by the construction of a temporary representation that is specific to the object's current appearance and is constantly updated as the object changes. We have drawn an analogy to a file in which all the perceptual information about a particular object is entered, just as the police might open a file on a particular crime, in which they collect all the information about the crime as the information accrues. The perceptual continuity of an object would then depend on its current manifestation being allocated to the same file as its earlier appearances. Such allocation is possible if the object remains stationary or if it changes location within constraints that allow the perceptual system to keep track of which file it should belong to.

In order to test this idea we joined with Brian Gibbs in devising a letter-naming task (Figure 8.5). Two letters were briefly flashed in the centers of two frames. The empty frames then moved to new locations. Next, another letter appeared in one of the two frames. We devised the display so that the temporal and spatial separations between the priming letter and the final letter were always the same; the only thing that differed was the motion of the frames. The subjects' task was to name the final letter as quickly as possible.

We knew that the prior exposure to a given letter should normally lessen the time it takes to identify the same letter on a subsequent appearance; the effect is known as *priming*. The question that interested us was whether priming would occur only in particular circumstances. We argued that if the final letter is the same as the priming letter and appears in the same frame as the priming letter, the two should be seen as belonging to the same object; in this case, we could think of the perceptual task as simply re-viewing the original object in its shifted position. If, on the other hand, a new letter appears in the same frame, the object file should have to be updated, perhaps increasing the time it takes for subjects to become aware of the letter and name it.

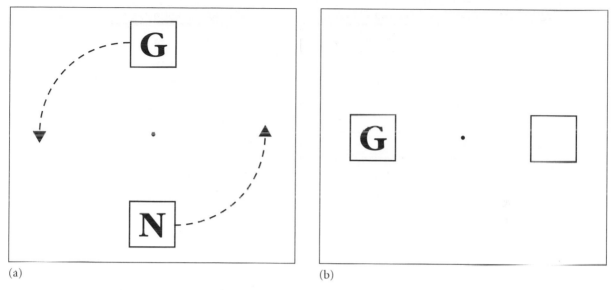

(a)   (b)

FIGURE 8.5   Integration of sensory information into what amounts to a file on each perceptual object was tested by the motion of frames. In each trial, two frames appeared, then two letters were briefly flashed in the frames (a). The frames moved to new locations, and a letter appeared in one of the two (b). The subject's task was to name the final letter as quickly as possible. If the final letter matched the initial letter and appeared in the same frame, the naming was faster than if the letter had appeared in the other frame or differed from the initial letter. The implication is that it takes more time to create or update a file on an object than it does simply to perceive the same object a second time.

Actually the priming was found to be object-specific: Subjects named the final letter some 30 milliseconds faster if the same letter had appeared previously in the same frame. They showed no such benefit if the same letter had appeared previously in the other frame. The result is consistent with the hypothesis that the later stages of visual perception integrate information from the early, feature-sensitive stages in temporary object-specific representations.

The overall scheme I propose for visual processing can be put in the form of a model (Figure 8.6). The visual system begins by coding a certain number of simple and useful properties in what can be considered a stack of maps. In the brain such maps ordinarily preserve the spatial relations of the visual world itself. Nevertheless, the spatial information they contain may not be directly available to the subsequent stages of visual processing. Instead the presence of each feature may be signaled without a specification of *where* it is.

In the subsequent stages, focused attention acts. In particular, focused attention is taken to operate by means of a master map of locations, in which the presence of discontinuities in intensity or color is registered without specification of what the discontinuities are. Attention makes use of this master map, simultaneously selecting, by means of links to the separate feature maps, all the features that currently are present in a selected location. These are entered into a temporary object representation, or file.

Finally, the model posits that the integrated information about the properties and structural relations in each object file is compared with stored descriptions in a "recognition network." The network specifies the critical attributes of cats, trees, bacon and eggs, one's grandmothers, and all other familiar perceptual objects, allowing access to their names, their likely behavior, and their current significance. I assume that conscious awareness depends on the object files and on the information they contain. It depends, in other

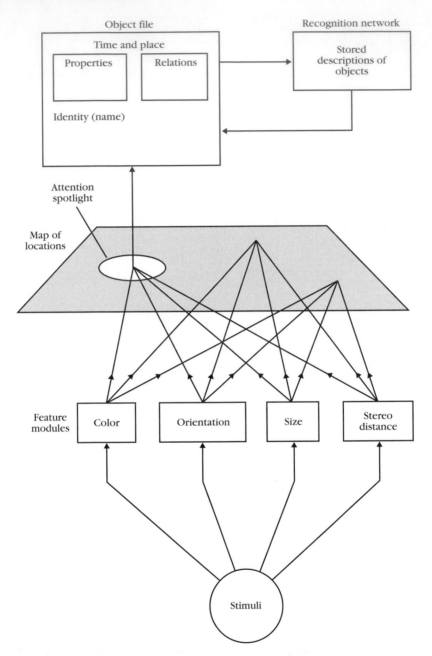

FIGURE 8.6   Hypothetical model of the early stages in visual perception emerges from the author's experiments. The model proposes that early vision encodes some simple and useful properties of a scene in a number of feature maps, which may preserve the spatial relations of the visual world but do not themselves make spatial information available to subsequent processing stages. Instead, focused attention (employing a master map of locations) selects and integrates the features present at particular locations. At later stages, the integrated information serves to create and update files on perceptual objects. In turn, the file contents are compared with descriptions stored in a recognition network. The network incorporates the attributes, behavior, names, and significance of familiar objects.

words, on representations that collect information about particular objects, both from the analyses of sensory features and from the recognition network, and continually update the information. If a significant discontinuity in space or time occurs, the original file on an object may be canceled: it ceases to be a source of perceptual experience. As for the object, it disappears and is replaced by a new object with its own new temporary file, ready to begin a new perceptual history.

CHAPTER THREE
Neurocognition

9 BRAIN ASYMMETRY

This paper is one of a series of papers from the research laboratory of Roger Sperry that described specialization in different hemispheres of the brain. Sperry won a Nobel Prize for his work on this topic. Your brain consists of left and right sides, or hemispheres, that are connected by a mass of neural fibers known as the corpus callosum. This report describes the behavior of a patient who had his corpus callosum (and other similar neural fibers for noncortical brain regions) severed to control the spread of debilitating epileptic seizures. The surgery was successful in controlling the epilepsy, and it offered an opportunity to study the behavioral effects of separating the left and right hemispheres of the brain. People who have had this type of surgery are sometimes called "split-brain" patients.

In order to understand the results of the behavioral tests, it is necessary to know a bit about brain anatomy. It is an interesting characteristic of humans and other animals that, in general, the right hemisphere of the brain controls the left side of the body, and the left hemisphere of the brain controls the right side of the body. Thus, when the reading refers to properties of the left hand, it can be interpreted as tapping the right hemisphere, and properties of the right hand refer to behavior of the left hemisphere. The reading refers to the "dominant left hemisphere," which indicates that the patient was right handed.

Given these anatomical connections, when the main connection between the hemispheres is severed, like it is in the patient discussed in this article, it is not surprising that touches on the left hand cannot be reproduced by the patient's right hand. Different hemispheres control the two hands, and with the corpus callosum severed, information from one hand cannot reach the other hand. As the authors noted, tasks that could be completed by one hand alone were relatively unimpaired, but using both hands together was difficult.

Other behaviors were not predicted based on simple anatomical connections. In general, the right hand (left hemisphere) seemed unimpaired, but the left hand (right hemisphere) seemed particularly debilitated. For example, if a familiar object was placed in the left hand while the patient was blindfolded, the right hemisphere was able to manipulate the object appropriately but was unable to identify the object verbally. More generally, the right hemisphere suffered from agnosia (an inability to recognize objects), anomia (an inability to name objects), and agraphia (an inability to write). The problem with writing was not, however, because the right hemisphere lacked the control to make fine movements. The right hemisphere could copy geometric shapes. Thus, the right hemisphere seemed to suffer from an ability to work with language in general.

The right hemisphere could carry out habitual tasks with the left hand, but had difficulty converting a verbal command into a coordinated movement. This apraxia (an inability to make purposeful movements) was a source of frustration for the patient.

A similar pattern of behavior was found for visual perception. Here too, the anatomical connections of the eye and brain should be reviewed. If you stare straight ahead, images on the left side of where you are fixating are sent to the right hemisphere of your brain, while images on the right side of where you are fixating are sent to the left hemisphere of your brain. It is important to emphasize that it is *not* the case that information from the left eye goes to the right brain. If you close your right eye, you can still use your left eye to see some images on the right side of your field of view. That information goes to the left hemisphere. It is field of view, not eye side, that determines which hemisphere receives information.

This reading was a starting point for many more investigations of split-brain patients. Subsequent work verified that for most people the left hemisphere was specialized for language, while the right hemisphere was specialized for spatial awareness. Much of the early work on these split-brain patients is summarized in Gazzaniga (1970). Work on split-brain patients continues to this day (e.g., O'Shea & Corballis, 2003).

The CogLab experiment on brain asymmetry measures reaction times to shape discrimination and verb tense discrimination when stimuli are presented to the right or left sides of the visual field (left or right hemispheres). It is unlikely that this experiment will actually demonstrate differences in the hemispheres of your brain. Differences do probably exist, but because you probably have an intact corpus callosum, it is quite difficult to measure those differences. Moreover, the biggest hemisphere differences are found for right-handed males; people who are left handed or female tend to show smaller differences. As you complete the CogLab experiment pay attention to the task and try to understand what each part of the experiment measures.

REFERENCES

Gazzaniga, M. (1970). *The bisected brain.* New York: Appleton-Century-Crofts.

O'Shea, R. P., & Corballis, P. M. (2003). Binocular rivalry in split-brain observers. *Journal of Vision, 3*(10), 610–615, http://journalofvision.org/3/10/3/, doi:10.1167/3.10.3.

QUESTIONS

1. Why was the patient blindfolded when asked to name objects placed in the left hand?
2. Why did the right hand seem to do so much better on the tests than the left hand?
3. Why do normal-brained people not generally notice the differences between the hemispheres?
4. Discuss some of the difficulties of using brain-damaged patients to study cognition.

Some Functional Effects of Sectioning the Cerebral Commissures in Man

M. S. Gazzaniga, J. E. Bogen, and R. W. Sperry

California Institute of Technology, Pasadena, and Loma Linda University School of Medicine, Los Angeles

It has been possible in studies of callosum-sectioned cats and monkeys in recent years to obtain consistent demonstration of a variety of interhemispheric integrational functions mediated by the corpus callosum.[1,2] These animal findings stand in marked contrast to the apparent lack of corresponding functional deficits produced by similar surgery in human patients.[3-9] The general picture of callosal functions based on the animal studies tends to be supported in current early testing of a 48-year-old male war veteran with recent complete section of the corpus callosum, anterior and hippocampal commissures.

The patient (W. J.) had been having grand mal convulsions for fifteen years subsequent to war injuries suffered in 1944. The seizures were refractory to medical management with a frequency, at best, of about 1 per week and, at worst, of 7 to 10 per day culminating in status epilepticus every 2–3 months. The subject was right handed, had an I.Q. of 113, and showed no significant sensory, motor, or associative disturbances in a battery of visual, tactile, and motor tests applied prior to surgery, excepting a mild hypesthesia on the left side.

The commissures were sectioned in a single operation by exposure and retraction of right frontal and occipital lobes. The massa intermedia was judged by the surgeons[10] to be absent and some atrophy of the exposed right frontal pole was observed. Generalized weakness, akinesis, and mutism were evident immediately after surgery but had largely cleared when postoperative testing was started. Anticonvulsant medication was reinstated shortly after surgery. There have since been three brief attacks with loss of consciousness but as yet no major convulsions. Occasional brief episodes of clonic-like tremor confined to the distal portions of the right arm or leg have also been noted. The operation appears to have left no gross changes in temperament or intellect, and the patient has repeatedly remarked that he feels better generally than he has in many years

The tests referred to below were carried out from the 6th to 20th weeks after surgery in weekly 3-hour sessions, mostly in the laboratory but on a few occasions in the patient's home, usually with the patient's physician and wife present. The general test repertoire included a considerable carry-over of items from previous clinical studies plus some new and revised test procedures designed on the basis of observed effects of brain bisection in animals.

Tests involving tactual function have revealed no significant impairments in the right side of the body connected to the dominant left hemisphere. Similar testing of the left hand, however, has indicated a severe agnosia, anomia, and agraphia. For example, in blindfold tests, the patient has regularly been able to manipulate and use correctly most familiar objects such as a pencil, cigarette, ring, pistol, hat, glasses, etc., but has been totally unable to name or to describe any of these. Prior to surgery he could write legibly with the left hand, but afterward has produced only a meaningless scribble.

Also, he locates accurately points of tactile stimulation on the fingers of either hand by touching with the thumb of the same hand, immediately or with a 5-sec delay imposed. He is quite unable, however, under similar conditions to cross-locate with either hand

SOURCE: From Gazzaniga, M. S., Bogen, J. E., & Sperry, R. W. (1962). Some functional effects of sectioning the cerebral commissures in man. *Proceedings of the National Academy of Sciences, 48,* 1765–1769. Reprinted with permission.

across to the other. Such cross localization is possible for points on the head, face, and upper neck. Taste and touch are both reported correctly from either side of the tongue. When tapped lightly one to four times on one foot or hand, the subject can accurately tap a corresponding number of times with the hand of the same side but is unable to tap the correct number with the opposite hand. Simple jigsaw cutouts could be put together correctly with either hand separately but not when cooperation between both hands was required. In general, when stimulus and response are confined to the same hemisphere in such tests, the performance goes well, but when cross-integration is required, the activity breaks down.

Visual tests were conducted with tachistoscopic presentation of stimuli at 1/10 and 1/100 sec. The results reveal no marked abnormality in response to stimulation of the right visual half-field, projected to the dominant hemisphere. In the left half-field, however, there is a profound agnosia for all stimuli presented. When very simple geometric designs, or single large numbers or letters are flashed to this half-field, the subject can retrieve the corresponding figure at a level 30 per cent above chance from among a series of five or more patterns on cards placed within easy reach of the left hand. He is unable to perform above chance, however, when colors are used, or when he is obliged to select the same cards with the opposite hand. Also, he has been unable to name, draw a rough semblance, or to otherwise describe the left field figures with either hand or verbally. More complicated written material is read easily in the right half-field but evokes only a blank response from the left field. In visuomotor studies with the right hand working a push button, he responds to the simple on-flash of a small light when it appears in the right half-field only, while with the left hand he is able to respond to the light signal in either field. When a choice between red and green lights was required, the reaction was correct only for responses of the right hand to stimuli in the right half field. In simple visual constructional tests, as in copying a sketch of a Necker cube, the drawings of the left hand were less defective than those of the right.

With respect to motor function no special coordinative difficulty has been observed in tests involving independent use of the right hand. The left hand also is capable of refined individuated finger movements and generally is adept and dextrous enough in the performance of familiar automatic activities such as handling and smoking a cigarette, lifting a coffee cup, putting on glasses, and the like. The left hand also works well along with the right in other habitual tasks such as tying a knot in the belt of his robe, folding towels, putting on and removing clothes. In other respects, however, the use of the left hand is obviously impaired. For example, if the patient is interrupted in any of the foregoing activities and asked to repeat on command with his left hand any of these motor performances or even to make much simpler movements, the left arm and hand may fail to respond at all or the response may be spasmodic and grossly inadequate. Much as in a stammerer's block, the more intense the effort, the more difficult to achieve the movement. In the early tests especially, a profound apraxia was apparent with respect to any independent movements of the left hand in response to a purely verbal command. Beginning with the 3rd month, however, if the test was presented with nonverbal aids, i.e., if the experimenter said, "Do this" and demonstrated the requested movement, then the patient with the left hand was usually able to follow very simple actions like writing a T or an L and lifting individual fingers as in a piano exercise.

Movements like lifting the left hand and placing it behind the head or using it to point to something, i.e., responses that could not be carried out by the left hand alone to a verbal command, were achieved readily when he was directed to use both hands to make the same or symmetrical movements. Frequently, when his left hand had been fumbling ineffectively at some task, he would become exasperated and reach across with the right hand to grab the left and place it in the proper position.

None of these apraxic difficulties was apparent in the use of the dominant right hand during the regular testing sessions. However, transient difficulty with the right hand was reportedly seen on a few occasions by the patient's wife. She has also noted antagonism between the actions of the right and left hands, e.g., the patient would pick up the evening paper with the right hand, but put it down abruptly with the left and then have to pick it up again with the right. Similar contradictory movements were observed occasionally in the course of dressing and undressing, and in other daily activities, at times on a scale sufficient to be distinctly bothersome. It was as if the control of the left hand were strongly centered in the minor hemisphere at such times and hence isolated from the main intent and prevailing directorship of the dominant hemisphere.

There were further indications that the separated hemispheres were each unaware of activity going on in the other in the case of those functions that are highly lateralized, e.g., visual perception within right or left half-field, language functions, or tactile and motor functions of the extremities. For example, the patient often retrieved a correct visual stimulus card with the left hand after exposure to the left visual half-field, but after the card had been turned over he was completely unable, on request, to describe or to otherwise use the major hemisphere to identify the figure he had chosen. Or, after responding intently with the correct count by the left hand to a series of tactile stimuli applied to the left leg or hand, it was often clear from his reply to question that in his literate hemisphere he had been totally unaware of having either felt the stimuli or made the response. In a few tests involving the learning of simple tactile discriminations with right or left hand, the learning did not carry over to the opposite hand.

The severe left apraxia following callosal section may have been exaggerated in this patient by an unnatural potentiation of cerebral dominance and the lateralization of volitional control as a result of the damage to the nondominant cortex incurred in his injuries of 1944. On the other hand, since pre-operative studies suggested a focus in the left parietal lobe, [10] it is also possible that damage to the left hemisphere may have impaired its ipsilateral motor control thus leading to exaggeration of the left apraxia after commissurotomy. The extent to which visual perception is intact in the left half-field still remains something of a problem that it may be possible to settle with further tests that combine half-field presentation with nonverbal responses.

The question of how typical the findings in this case may be is complicated by the unknown amount and nature of the pre-existent cerebral damage. Nevertheless the marked differences between the pre- and post-operative results and most of the other impairments observed seem best ascribed to interruption of the commissural connections, particularly those linking the sensory and motor areas of the right cerebral cortex with the speech and related centers of the dominant left hemisphere. The results are in line with the picture of callosal function obtained from recent animal studies and with certain minority interpretations of callosal lesions in man as reviewed by Sweet[11] and amplified recently by Geschwind. [12] They appear to favor the existence of a genuine callosal or cerebral deconnection syndrome in human adult subjects who have been free of childhood cerebral complications, and have the normal lateralization of language.

With regard to the discrepancy between the foregoing and the apparent absence of similar disconnection impairments in the majority of callosum-sectioned patients previously described, the following are of interest: Visual testing without tachistoscopic control in the present patient failed to demonstrate satisfactorily his left hemiagnosia. His depth perception and stereoscopic vision are preserved. Blindfold learning of part of a stylus maze of the same type used in the earlier studies[8] transferred at a high level in this patient also from either hand to the other. Further, the first author had earlier applied a number of the same visual and tactile tests to a nine-year-old boy of above-average intelligence with reported congenital agenesis of the corpus callosum complicated by postnatal hydrocephalus. This boy performed close to the level of normal control children with almost no indication of the disconnection effects observed in the adult surgical patient. Bilateralization of cortical speech centers and other compensatory developmental effects are presumed to be present in the boy with agenesis. On the other hand, the normal right-handedness of the surgical patient and correlated lateralization of speech, the development of which took a normal course to well beyond 30 years of age is considered important to the observed impairments. By contrast, many of the earlier cases studied had childhood neurological complications. Finally, it is entirely possible that a significant range of variability is normal in the development of callosal functions in different individuals, and that a corresponding spectrum is therefore to be expected in the syndrome of the corpus callosum. Even so, there remain some puzzling inconsistencies not satisfactorily resolved as yet. Testing is still in progress and more thorough detailed reports are contemplated.

AUTHORS' NOTE

The authors wish to express their regard and thanks to the patient and his wife for the invaluable cooperation throughout. Aided by the F. P. Hixon Fund of the California Institute of Technology and by grants to the Institute, No. M3372 and No. 2G86, from the U.S. Public Health Service.

ENDNOTES

1. Sperry, R. W., *Fed. Proc.*, 20, 609 (1961).
2. Sperry, R. W., *Science,* 133, 1749 (1961).
3. Akelaitis, A. J., *Arch. Neurol. Psychiat.,* 45, 788 (1941).
4. Akelaitis, A. J., *J. Neuropath. Exp. Neurol.,* 2, 226 (1943).
5. Akelaitis, A. J., *J. Neurosurg.,* 1, 94 (1944).
6. Bremer, F., J. Brihaye, and G. Andre-Balisaux, *Schweiz. Arch. Neurol. Psychiat.,* 78, 31–87 (1956).
7. Bridgman, C. S., and K. U. Smith, *J. Comp. Neurol.,* 83, 57–68 (1945).
8. Smith, K. U., *Science,* 114, 117 (1951).
9. Smith, K. U., and A. J. Akelaitis, *Arch. Neurol. Psychiat.,* 47, 519–543 (1942).
10. Bogen, J. E., and P. J. Vogel, *Bull. Los Angeles Neurol. Soc.* (in press).
11. Sweet, W. H., *Arch. Neurol. Psychiat.,* 45, 86–104 (1941).
12. Geschwind, N., *New Engl. J. Med.* (in press).

10 MAPPING THE BLIND SPOT

The back of each of your eyes contains a dense set of receptors that are sensitive to light energy. These receptors convert light energy into electrical energy, which eventually is transferred to your nervous system and your brain. These receptors, however, are not distributed evenly across your eye. There is a central location, called the fovea, where the receptors are very densely packed. Generally, when you stare at an object you are arranging your eyes so that the object's image falls on the foveae of your eyes. Outside the fovea there are fewer receptors. In fact, in some places there are no receptors at all.

There is a place in each eye where the optic nerve exits the back of the eye to send information to the brain. This "hole" is called the optic disk. It contains no light sensitive receptors. As a result, any light that falls on this part of the eye is undetected and invisible to you. Functionally, this location on the eye is called the blind spot.

You have probably never noticed your blind spots (one in each eye). This is for several reasons. First, each blind spot is far away from its eye's fovea. Because the fovea is typically where you are "looking," you would not generally notice that something has disappeared into a blind spot. Second, when you view the world with two eyes, one eye can compensate for the other eye's blind spot. Light that falls into the blind spot of one eye generally does not fall on the blind spot of the other eye. Third, your brain processes only the presence of information, not the absence. Your brain does not notice a "hole" in the information it receives from the eye. It simply works with the information it receives. In a similar way, the brain does not observe that we are unable to view ultraviolet light. It has no knowledge about "missing" information.

An interesting characteristic of the blind spot is that you actually see visual properties that appear to cover the regions of visual space that correspond to the blind spot. What is seen is determined by what is visible in the regions around the blind spot. Thus, a line that goes through the blind spot does not appear broken, but seems to have a visible color and size. This kind of demonstration is found in many introduction to psychology textbooks. This completion of information across the blind spot is sometimes referred to as "filling-in" of the blind spot.

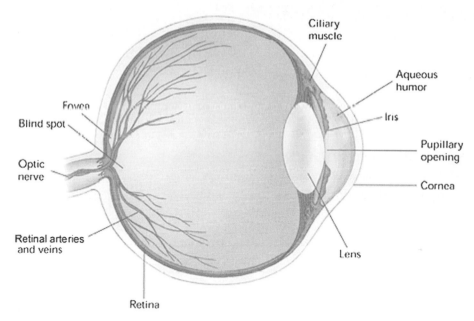

FIGURE 10.A   The structure of the eye.

This reading by Durgin, Tripathy, and Levi is part of a discussion on several interesting demonstrations involving the blind spot that were described by V. S. Ramachandran (1992). They argue that what is seen in the blind spot is quite similar to the percepts that result from an object being partly occluded by another object. In addition to explaining a number of percepts in the blind spot, this reading touches on the importance of this issue for philosophical understandings of perception and for computational models of perception.

The CogLab experiment measures the spatial extent of your blind spot. Throughout the experiment you are asked to fixate a small spot on the left side of the screen with your left eye closed. Then dots are presented at various positions on the screen and you are asked to report whether the dot is seen or not. When the dot is presented in the blind spot, it will not be seen. At the end of the experiment you are shown which dots were seen and which were not. You should find a relatively large patch of dots that were not seen. This corresponds to your blind spot. As you do this experiment, it is very important that you keep your left eye closed and your right eye focused on the fixation spot. If your left eye opens or your right eye moves, your blind spot will also move and this will contaminate the experiment.

The references in this reading provide an excellent starting point for further discussion of the blind spot and its significance. Especially recommended are the papers by Ramachandran (1992, 1995). The latter is a reply to this reading.

REFERENCE

Ramachandran, V. S. (1992). Blind spots. *Scientific American, 266*(5), 86–91.
Ramachandran, V. S. (1995). Filling in gaps in logic: Reply to Durgin et al. *Perception, 24*, 841–845.

QUESTIONS

1. What is "amodal" completion, as discussed in section 2?
2. Why is the title of this reading consistent with the main thesis?
3. Why does the blind spot not matter very much in everyday viewing?
4. What percept is supposed to be seen when viewing Figure 10.2?

On the Filling in of the Visual Blind Spot: Some Rules of Thumb

Frank H. Durgin

Swarthmore College

Srimant P. Tripathy and Dennis M. Levi

College of Optometry, University of Houston

ABSTRACT

In monocular viewing there is a region in the peripheral visual field that is blind owing to the absence of photoreceptors at the site where the optic nerve exits the eye. This region, like certain other blind spots, nonetheless appears filled in. Several novel demonstrations of filling in at the blind spot have recently been reported. Here the implications of many of these effects are critically reevaluated. Specifically, it is argued that many blind-spot phenomena taken to support early filling in (e.g. pop out and alteration in apparent motion) are actually consistent with the thesis that the visual blind spot is treated by early perceptual processing as a region of reduced or absent information. In support of this, it is shown that many perceptual effects observed in blind-spot completion are similar in detail to the amodally perceived completion of partly occluded objects viewed somewhat peripherally. The goals were to point out striking similarities between blind-spot completion and the amodal completion of occluded parts of surfaces, and to provide a common theoretical framework for understanding these phenomena in the context of surface segregation and perceptual interpolation.

1. INTRODUCTION

The blind spot of each eye corresponds to the region of the retina where the optic nerve exits the eye. Because there are no photoreceptors associated with that region, objects obscured entirely by the blind spot remain, of course, unseen in monocular vision. However, the region of the visual field corresponding to the blind spot is never perceived as a gap in perception, even in the case of monocular viewing. The apparent filling in of the blind spot may be considered a case of perceptual surface interpolation which would presumably take place as part of the segregation of surfaces. In the present paper many of the interesting blind-spot demonstrations of Ramachandran and his colleagues and others will be reevaluated and shown to be similar in detail to the completion of occluded objects. In addition, we will discuss findings of axial asymmetry and size distortion in blind-spot interpolation.

The goal in this paper is to make explicit comparisons between blind-spot interpolation and other kinds of normal perceptual interpolation. After demonstrating that a number of important blind-spot phenomena are consistent with normal interpolation, we will describe how comparisons with normal interpolation may help illuminate an interesting axial asymmetry of blind-spot interpolation. Our intention is to argue that many of the intriguing phenomena associated with completion in the blind spot (e.g. Ramachandran 1992a) are entirely consistent with the following principle and its corollary:

> The blind spot is a region of no information and is treated by early image processing as such: it is an "occluded" region of vision, without an occluder.

> Corollary: The edges of the blind spot are not treated as real edges in the visual array.

SOURCE: From Durgin, F. H., Tripathy, S. P., & Levi, D. M. (1995). On the filling in of the visual blind spot: Some rules of thumb. *Perception, 24*, 827–840. Reprinted with permission of Pion, London.

How does the blind spot get filled in? We will argue that "filling in" may be a rather general phenomenon that occurs under a variety of conditions (Walls 1954; see also Ramachandran 1992a, 1992b) and that the "filling in" of objects that pass through the blind spot results from perceptual constructions which are accomplished in ways similar to the modally and amodally perceived completion of objects presented away from the blind spot (von der Heydt et al. 1984; Kanizsa 1979; Kellman and Shipley 1991, 1992; Shimojo and Nakayama 1990). We will show that (i) the content of our perceptual experience of surfaces passing through the blind spot is functionally similar to the amodal completion of parts of surfaces occluded by other means (e.g., by a thumb), when the surfaces are viewed peripherally; (ii) several demonstrations of blind-spot phenomenology (e.g., by Ramachandran) require reevaluation (in particular, these demonstrations do not in themselves provide evidence that filling in precedes the detection of motion or the preattentive processing that produces pop-out); (iii) axial asymmetries in the perception of alignment across the blind spot may suggest a polar, rather than a Cartesian coordinate system for visual perception. We will present some novel amodal-completion phenomena that support this viewpoint.

To accomplish these goals we will briefly review some background information on visual interpolation and edge extraction outside the blind spot and then consider in detail several rather interesting demonstrations of blind-spot effects.

2. PERCEPTUAL INTERPOLATION

Two perceptual phenomena that are structurally similar to blind-spot interpolation are subjective or illusory contours and amodal completion. The most familiar cases of subjective contours are variants of the Kanizsa triangle such as is shown in Figure 10.1a. In this figure, the "subjective" triangle appears to be brighter than the background white of the paper and a luminance edge is seen around its entire perimeter, where in reality no physical luminance edge exists. Von der Heydt et al. (1984) have demonstrated the physiological "reality" of certain kinds of subjective contours in neurons in visual area V2. A unit that responds to edges of a certain orientation may also respond when (i) moving stimuli are presented outside of its receptive field so as to specify an appropriately oriented illusory bar passing through the receptive field (Figure 10.1b) or (ii) when an edge specified by orthogonal line discontinuities is presented (Figure

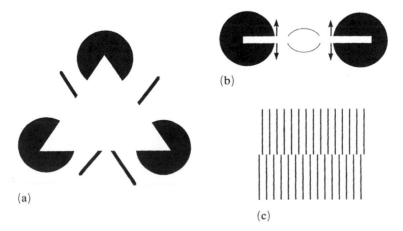

FIGURE 10.1   Three stimuli which illustrate subjective contours. (a) A Kanizsa triangle. The triangle appears to be whiter than the rest of the page. (b) Common motion of two "ends" of a bar results in the perceptual completion of the bar. (c) Collinear line terminations produce a continuous illusory edge.

10.1c). Such findings indicate that early vision is indeed working efficiently to extract surface edges that might be specified by occlusion and that there is cooperativity across space in this effort.

Amodal completion refers to the perceptual completion of an object behind an occluder, while modal contours refer to contours seen in the foreground. The "pacmen" of Figure 10.1a are perceived (amodally represented) as circles which are occluded by the triangle. Sekuler and Palmer (1992) have demonstrated that partly occluded shapes like these will prime the perceptual discrimination of their unoccluded counterparts. Moreover, perceived occlusion and amodal completion have been shown to have important influences on many basic visual phenomena, such as motion perception (Shimojo and Nakayama 1990) and visual search (He and Nakayama 1992). While tradition and common sense would suggest that blind-spot interpolation is based upon "modal" completion, because the completed contours are *experienced* as seen, the distinction between amodal and modal completion may be irrelevant for purposes of early visual processing. The blind spot represents an unusual situation in which, for monocular viewing, a portion of the visual field is occluded, although there is nothing out there in the world that is doing the occluding.

To make the converse point, although there is clear evidence that certain illusory contours may be "physiologically real" in area V2 (von der Heydt et al. 1984) and perhaps as early as V1 (Lamme et al. 1993), it should also be noted that these representations of edges may not always constitute a perceived *image*. Thus, although Sekuler and Palmer (1992) have demonstrated that partly occluded shapes can prime perceptual discrimination, there is no illusion of "seeing" these shapes as physically completed. Rather, one is aware "amodally" of the shape. To individuals who entertain a cathode-ray-tube model of perceptual representation, this distinction may seem odd. However, there are ample demonstrations available that the contents of conscious perception, though usually *consistent* with the visually extracted information, can, in Bruner's words (e.g., 1957), go "beyond the information given." For example, we normally walk about with the illusion that the entire visual field is of equal perceptual resolution, even when we may have learned that foveal acuity (present in only the central 1 deg of vision) is of a different order of magnitude from what is available in the periphery.

3. A ROUGH SKETCH OF THE TRADITIONAL MODEL

In most computational theories of early vision (e.g., Marr 1982) it is supposed that vision entails the extraction of surfaces largely by means of the processing of visually available information. Without a need to agree about the particulars, in most models it is assumed that important initial processes include the rough location of contrast boundaries (known as zero crossings, because of the mathematics of their derivation), a crude local-spatial-frequency analysis to assess the lay of the luminance, and other specialized processes, such as motion detection and the analysis of binocular disparity—all of which aid in the segregation of surfaces. In addition to these kinds of visually available information, the evidence reviewed above suggests that the interpolation of surface contours may also occur. However, the final description of surfaces probably is not settled by any single early mechanism, because information about edges may be specified in many forms including disparity, motion, and texture.

In some cases, blind-spot effects result from the *absence* of information necessary for interpolation. We will use zero crossings and edge extraction for the analysis of some blind-spot effects, although an analysis of local spatial frequencies would come to an equivalent conclusion. The important thing about traditional theories is that, as is consistent with the relevant neurophysiology, they tend to work with contrast information rather than luminance information per se. For example, a zero-crossing map of an image represents the places in the image where there are sharp changes in luminance. The second important distinction about these theories is that their major goal is the segregation of surfaces from one another, which requires a refinement of the contrast and luminance information available.

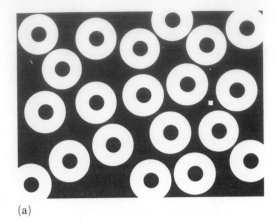

(a)

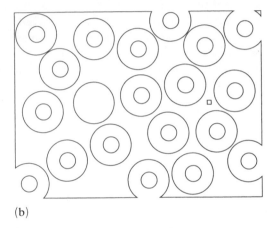

(b)

FIGURE 10.2   (a) A donut texture (after Ramachandran 1992a), and (b) a map of the zero crossings in the image when the blind spot occludes one of the donut holes.

4. THE HOLE IN THE DONUT DEMONSTRATION

To understand how this model of the representation of object boundaries might interpret perception in the blind spot, consider Ramachandran's demonstration of "pop out" which was originally (1992a, 1992b) offered as evidence of how early in the visual pathway filling in must occur.[1] This display consists of a texture of donuts, as in Figure 10.2a. When the blind spot "occludes" the "hole" in one of the donuts, the donut appears as a disk and seems to pop out from the rest of the texture elements.

Although no experimental evidence of true pop out has been offered (e.g., apparent pop out for sub-

jects not initially attending to their blind spots) the phenomenon appears subjectively compelling. However, as shown in Figure 10.2b, a zero-crossing analysis of the information available when the hole is "occluded" offers a clear picture of why perceptual pop out could occur. The contrast boundary that would correspond to the hole is not represented because no information is available to specify it. Nothing special needs to be "filled in" for an apparent difference in texture to arise. Note that the filling in of surface color could occur much later than the texture differences that might produce the subjective pop-out effect.

5. THE GAP IN THE MOTION ARGUMENT

Similar interpretations may be applied to experiments on the temporal relationship between filling in and the detection of motion (Ramachandran 1992a). Figure 10.3 shows a schematic diagram of the relevant apparent motion displays. In each condition, a black horizontal bar (ours was 36 deg × 2 deg, 99.7% contrast on a background of 80 cd m^{-2}) stepped vertically between two locations, separated by 10 deg, every 250 ms. A 1.7 deg gap was always present in the bar when in the upper position, 12 deg from the righthand end. When the gap appeared in the lower position, it was displaced by 10 deg to the left. In Figure 10.3a, the displacement of the gap within the lines produces the impression of diagonal motion when viewed outside of the blind spot, but at a comparable eccentricity. When there is no gap in the lower line, vertical motion is perceived (Figure 10.3b). The critical display occurs when the blind spot is positioned to "occlude" the gap in the lower line of Figure 10.3a: a display like that of Figure 10.3b is perceived. Ramachandran reasons that this perception of vertical motion requires that the line be filled in across the blind spot *prior* to the detection of motion. However, if the gap is occluded with a gray spot (4 deg in diameter, 16 cd m^{-2}) as in Figure 10.3c, vertical motion is perceived. Using a thumb to cover the gap works too. In all of these cases, one simply cannot see a correspondence between the gap in the upper line and the occluded region of the lower line. The gap in visual information produced by the blind spot is not represented as a gap in the image. The contrast edges which would specify a gap in the

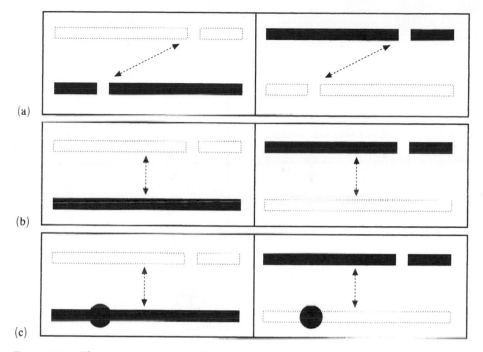

FIGURE 10.3   Three apparent-motion displays represented schematically. (a) Occlusion of the lower gap produces a perception like that seen in (b); (c) represents a control condition. For details see text.

line are simply not seen when they are "occluded" by the blind spot. We suggest the following rule of thumb: [I]f the same perception arises whether the thumb or the blind spot is used to occlude a portion of an image, then the results at the blind spot are probably not special.

Ramachandran (1992b) attempted to reject the "no-edges-are-there-to-see" interpretation of the situation by modifying the motion paradigm so that the blind spot occludes the end of a line, thus shortening it perceptually, as depicted in Figure 10.4. In this case diagonal motion is seen. But this trick works with the thumb, too. To make the demonstration convincing, we covered the end of the (black) line with a black circle so that there would be no luminance edge where the line was cut off. Diagonal motion of the line is still seen.

6. PERSISTENT NOISE

Ramachandran (1992a, 1993; see also Ramachandran et al. 1993) has argued that filling in involves the activation of spatially appropriate neurons, and in support he refers to the demonstration of Ramachandran and Gregory (1991). They found that a small square of gray light that was stabilized by fixation would "fill in" with surrounding dynamic visual noise. They further reported that once the gray region had been subjectively filled in, the perception of dynamic noise in that square region persisted for several seconds even after the surrounding visual noise has been replaced with a matching gray. Recent evidence suggests that this "persistence" may be misleading, however. It has since been demonstrated that a similar aftereffect of induced visual noise can be generated even when the region has not been perceptually filled in, and indeed, that the af-

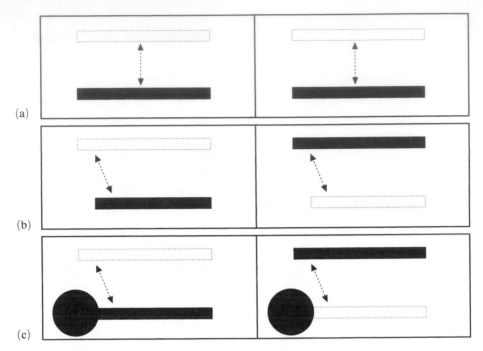

FIGURE 10.4   An apparent-motion display in which (a) a single bar moves vertically can be altered by occluding the end of the bar with either (b) the blind spot, a thumb, or (c) simply a black disk. The resulting perceived motion includes a diagonal component.

tereffect and the perceived filling in have very different spatial characteristics (Hardage and Tyler 1995). Thus, it appears that the aftereffect is not a consequence of perceptual filling in, but rather of differential adaptation, a possibility also recognized by Ramachandran (e.g., Ramachandran and Gregory 1991).

Last, we note that there are important differences between the filling in of artificial scotomata and of (retinal) blind spots. With regard to the dynamic-noise effect, we observe that if the blind spot is used instead of the grey square, the filling in of dynamic noise is instantaneous but there is no aftereffect.

7. COMPLETING THE PICTURE

In general, the blind spot may be regarded as a physical occluder. Both with the blind spot and with occluded objects, only the surrounding information is available for visual analysis. As discussed above, it is a striking fact about the perceptual experience of partly occluded objects that we typically have a definite per-

ceptual sense of how these objects are completed (Kanizsa 1979; Kanizsa and Gerbino 1982; Kellman and Shipley 1991; Michotte et al. 1964). Figure 10.5 shows several examples of shapes that are amodally completed behind other figures. In each case, one "sees" how the occluded shapes are completed despite not representing the completed part as "seen." Interestingly, most demonstrations of things that get filled in (e.g., Ramachandran 1992a) produce the same (amodal) perceptual content when a thumb or a coin is placed over the region to be occluded instead of the blind spot.

Using Figure 10.6, a thumb, and a blind spot, the reader may make the following observations. (i) As with the blind spot, the lines of Figure 10.6a appear to continue behind one's thumb. Even when a luminance change without a clear border produces a mild paradox, one does not (amodally or with the blind spot) perceive a border. (ii) Viewed either in the blind spot or behind the thumb, the crossed lines of Figure 10.6b produce a pair of surfaces of which the larger is

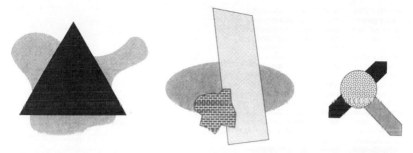

FIGURE 10.5   Three examples of amodal completion. Note that the boundaries of the apparently occluded regions seem well defined despite the lack of unambiguous information.

usually perceived as occluding the smaller (perhaps owing to an interpretation of depth from relative size). (iii) Similarly in Figure 10.6c, the spokes appear to continue to the center whether a thumb or the blind spot is placed over the gray disk.

The effects of thumb and blind spot are similar in detail. Note, for example, that for Figure 10.6c, neither completion through the blind spot nor amodal completion behind a thumb produce[s] any impression of the central blob that is seen when the spokes are actually completed. The occluded T-shape in Figure 10.5 represents a novel demonstration of a blind-spot phenomenon consistent with amodal completion: [T]he gray bar appears to terminate in a rectangular edge at the black bar both amodally and in the blind spot.

In cases where there appears to be some difference between amodal completion and the percepts reported around the blind spot (e.g., Ramachandran 1992a), the difference disappears when the display is viewed somewhat peripherally (as displays in the blind spot must be). For example, foveal presentation of Figure 10.7a suggests completion of the horizontal lines beneath the occluding disk, but peripheral presentation by 10–15 deg (where receptive field sizes are larger) results in perceiving the continuity of the vertical white bar behind the occluder. This same perception occurs when the disk is "occluded" by the blind spot, which is at a similar eccentricity. Note that it is probably more appropriate to describe this as the completion of a luminance bar rather than a "subjective contour" (Churchland and Ramachandran 1993; Ramachandran 1992a, 1992b).[2]

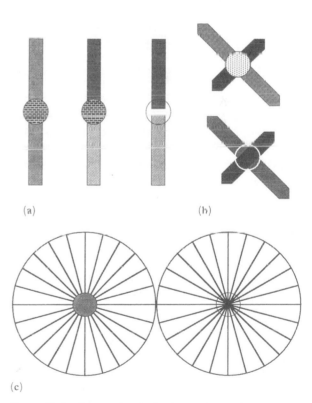

(a)   (b)

(c)

FIGURE 10.6   Structurally similar impressions of completion occur for these displays (after blind-spot demonstrations of Ramachandran 1992a) whether the areas enclosed by the small circles are occluded by the blind spot, or by a coin, or by a thumb.

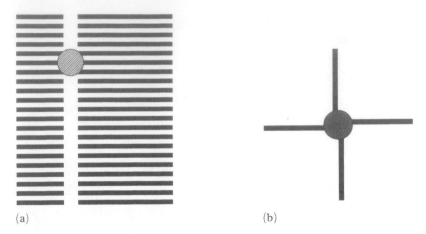

(a)   (b)

FIGURE **10.7**   Patterns (after blind-spot demonstrations of Ramachandran 1992a) for which amodal completion is different foveally from in the periphery. Blind-spot completion resembles peripheral amodal completion.

8. REVEALING ASYMMETRIES

Though it may be obvious to the skeptical viewer, it is probably worth noting that perceptual observations around the blindspot are often "indistinct" as described by Lettvin (1976). This is a general property of spatial vision in the periphery, and it raises difficulties for relying on phenomenological observations regarding percepts in the blind spot. To make stronger claims about structural similarities or differences in performance will require more-rigorous methods. Nonetheless, in some cases, the comparison with amodal completion can help to discriminate between hypotheses concerning completion in the blind spot.

For example, when the misaligned cross of Figure 10.7b is presented in the blind spot, Lettvin (1976; also see Ramachandran 1992a) has noted that the vertical lines appear (incorrectly) to be aligned, while the horizontals do not. The reader may observe that the same phenomenon occurs for this figure when it is simply presented in the left or right periphery in an amodal-completion condition.[3] Thus, it is not a blind-spot property, but a periphery property. Is this evidence of greater sensitivity to the horizontal axis of Cartesian space? It is possible instead that it is the result of a polar visual geometry in which we are more sensitive to position in terms of orientation relative to the fovea

than to eccentricity. White et al. (1992) have shown that there are marked asymmetries in sensitivity to absolute eccentric position in the periphery, which is consistent with isoeccentric thresholds being markedly superior to radial thresholds (see also Yap et al. 1987). This asymmetry in positional sensitivity might account for the asymmetrical sensitivity to misalignment. Cartesian and polar axes are difficult to dissociate with the retinal blind spot, because it cannot easily be moved to a new location. However, by presenting the cross in the upper or lower periphery and observing the resulting amodal completion, it is easy to tell that the polar hypothesis is the correct one: [I]n the upper or lower periphery the horizontals appear aligned and the misalignment of the verticals becomes evident. In other words, this spatial asymmetry is not merely a blind-spot phenomenon and it seems to depend, at least in part, on a spatial representation of position which is effectively polar, rather than Cartesian.

9. SOMETHING IS MISSING

Several researchers in the early part of this century examined size distortions for objects presented across the blind spot (e.g., Ferree and Rand 1912; Helson 1929), but their results have always remained contro-

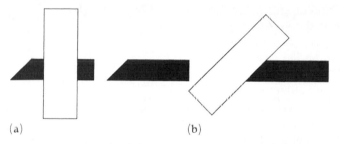

FIGURE 10.8   Demonstrations of size distortion of occluded objects (after Kanizsa and Gerbino 1982). (a) An amodally completed object appears smaller than an unoccluded version; (b) implied occlusion expands the apparent size of the visible portion of the object.

versial. A number of recent investigations have reexamined size distortions associated with lines completed monocularly through the blind spot (Andrews and Campbell 1991; Sears and Mikaelian 1989). The general finding is that lines or bars completed through the blind spot may sometimes appear shorter than their geometrical length. Tripathy et al. (1995) examined this phenomenon by using several careful quantitative methods and found only slight (if any) size distortions, once they had controlled for eye movements. These distortions, when present, were very much smaller (< 1 deg) than the size of the blind spot.

Gatass et al. (1992) have shown fascinating evidence of "interpolative" neural response in the nominally monocular regions in area V1 associated with the blind spots. They discuss these responses in terms of interpolative receptive fields extending beyond the classical receptive field. We suggest that the interpretation of these findings should be tempered by the recognition that slight size distortions may remain even when a bar crossing the blind spot appears complete.

Interestingly, analogous size distortions are found in normal situations involving partial occlusion. Kanizsa and Gerbino (1982) have demonstrated that amodally completed objects appear slightly smaller than their unoccluded counterparts. Conversely, they have also shown that a shape that abuts a second region in a manner suggestive of occlusion will seem larger than it is, as if the implied occlusion produces a perceptual extension of the occluded surface. These two phe-

nomena (shrinkage of the whole and expansion of the parts) are illustrated in Figure 10.8. Although we do not wish to argue that these effects are identical to blind-spot size distortions, we would like to note the extent of the apparent analogy between the two situations.

10. CONCLUSION

Unlike objects that are occluded by other surfaces, objects in the blind spot are occluded by nothing real in the environment. Because we typically have two eyes open and would in any case not normally be likely to keep the blind spot directed at some specific stimulus (so far as we know!), this anomaly of the blind spot is of little consequence. We often experience objects as completed when they are partially occluded. The completion is called "amodal" when the content of our perception is [this surface (completed), behind x (e.g., a thumb)]. Completion through the blind spot may have the same perceptual content as amodal completion except that there is no "x." Although there may be important differences between blind-spot interpolation and amodal completion,[4] several demonstrations offered by Ramachandran to support the thesis that the filling in of the blind spot occurs prior to motion and preattentive processing have been found to be interpretable within this framework. In all of the cases that we have examined the results are consistent with the null hypothesis that the blind spot is treated visually as a region of little or no information.

Our findings are consistent with an "evidentiary" view of perception in which the content of perception is informed by, but not limited to, the transduction of various kinds of information indicative of size, motion, form, continuity, orientation, and the like. Thus, we do not consider that the content of perception in the blind spot must directly reflect the activity of "filled in"[5] visual maps. We emphasize that the utility of this analysis of the blind spot is indicated by comparisons between blind-spot interpolation and amodal completion in other parts of the periphery, for example. This is not to say that the blind spot is not interesting in its own right. The gaps in retinal afferents to the cortical region corresponding to the blind spot present a special challenge for the topographical mapping of binocular visual space and the representation of binocular information which has been investigated both at a neural level (Fiorani et al. 1992) and psychophysically (Tripathy and Levi 1994). What we have demonstrated here is that the present evidence concerning the perceptual filling in of the blind spot does not require that this perceptual filling in be completed at any particularly early level of visual analysis.

11. POSTSCRIPT

Part of the philosophical dispute over the nature of perceptual "filling in" has been over whether filled-in images are "really" filled in. Dennett (1991) has criticized this view as a return to the Cartesian Theater in which some homunculus (or soul) is assumed to be presented with images (or three-dimensional sketches) upon an inner stage. In fact, the visual cortex is laid out spatially so as to map onto the retinally recorded visual world, and there are indeed processes that take place in the visual cortex that can be best described as the interpolation of edges. In this sense, perception really is "filled in," though our perceptual experience may frequently go even farther "beyond the information given." The demonstrations presented above are consistent with a number of philosophical interpretations. However, we feel it may be argued from our observations that perceptual interpolation in the periphery does not take place in a Cartesian Theater. If an internal perceptual theater for the soul does exist, its coordinate system is, with respect to position, polar.

12. CODICIL

It is proper that Dr. Ramachandran should have final reply to the points made above regarding his interpretations of many of his blind-spot demonstrations, and we leave it to the reader to compare the arguments made in each article on these points. Indeed, we are pleased that Dr. Ramachandran (see Ramachandran 1995) feels he is in such substantial agreement with our principal observations. However, we believe some further clarification is appropriate in order to complete the gaps.

The point of dispute can be brought to a single issue: [C]an the process underlying blind-spot filling in be distinguished in essence from processes underlying amodal completion on the grounds that they result in modal rather than amodal percepts?[6] We were at pains in the introduction to our article to note that this distinction was less critical than it might first appear. It should be noted that we believe that the content of perception has at least 2.5 dimensions so that it makes sense to talk of perceiving (not *believing*!) things as extending behind other things.[7]

Ramachandran (1995) says that what he means by filling in is that one literally sees the area filled in. This is a sensible operational definition of blind-spot completion ("Did you see it filled in?"), but not of the filling-in process. For if filling in is equivalent to literally seeing then questions of whether filling in precedes or follows the perception of motion, for example, can only be a question for an odd sort of introspection, for it amounts to asking, which qualia happened first?[8]

An alternative gloss would have it that "seeing" can be translated directly into the neural activity underlying the corresponding mental state. We believe, with Dr. Ramachandran, that every mental state corresponds to a neural state, but doubt that every local neural state has a single corresponding mental content. We therefore think it may be safer to speak of neural processes when trying to do psychoanatomy (though one must not forget that the feedback channels in vision are quite as dense as the feedforward channels, so even this tactic is not foolproof for studying temporal precedence). To come back to the main issue, we do not think it necessary that the neural processes responsible for filling in be identical to those responsible for "literally seeing." Indeed, it was our thesis, and appears to be Dr. Ramachandran's as well, that an interpolation process might precede (or occur in parallel with) the final decision about what to perceive as "seen."

Perception, in our view, is not of the contents of the retina, but of the world (see Gibson 1966). Although our eyes move about many times each second, the world is not jumpy. Although retinotopic visual maps may signal the possible existence of a contour, our visual system need not treat that contour as "in front" of all others, merely by virtue of recording its possible existence. These points seem hardly controversial in principle, but it remains to be seen, as Dr. Ramachandran notes, what the fact of the matter is with regard to the filling-in process.

Our principal argument has it that the structural similarities between modal blind-spot completion and amodal completion are striking and that apparent differences in the structure of the resulting perceptions can, in the cases we examined, be attributed to peripheral vs. central observation of the test patterns. Dr. Ramachandran (1995) has suggested a counterexample (see his point number 2), but the crucial experiments controlling for peripheral presentation do not seem to have been done.[9] We are pleased that Dr. Ramachandran feels positively about the contributions we have made following upon his and hope that these papers together will serve to clarify rather than obscure these important issues.

ACKNOWLEDGEMENTS

Preparation of the manuscript was supported in part by a grant from the National Eye Institute (RO1EY01728). We thank V. S. Ramachandran and Alex Mussap for their helpful suggestions on an earlier version of the manuscript.

ENDNOTES

1. In addition to psychoanatomy, Ramachandran (1992a, 1992b) argues for at least one other implication of this demonstration: that perceptual "filling in" in the region corresponding to the blind spot "must involve the generation of a perceptual representation" (1992a, page 89) or "must involve creating a sensory representation" (1992b, page 201). We agree that filling in, like all perceptual interpolation, involves perceptual representation of some sort! Indeed, following Kanizsa and

Gerbino (1982), we regard amodal completion as perceptual rather than as, say, a thought process. However, if Ramachandran intended to suggest that the donut demonstration of pop out substantiates this claim, the principal issue with respect to the display is, what processes must be complete for pop out to occur? We believe the filling in of surface color, for example, may be a red herring.

2. Another case where peripheral completion may appear to differ dramatically from completion near central vision is that of partly occluded (geometrical) forms. Ramachandran (1992a, 1992b) reports that occluded portions of circles and squares may appear bitten off in the blind spot, but appear to become completed across scotomata that are "*near the center* of [the patient's] field of view" (1992a, page 91, emphasis added). Even in situations supportive of amodal completion, the perception of a "mosaic" produced by the subtraction of the occluded portion of a surface may sometimes arise. Lettvin (1976) has argued that perception in the periphery is more like texture perception than form perception (see also Ramachandran and Gregory 1991). "Mosaic" perception in the periphery is consistent with this insight. It would therefore be interesting to determine experimentally whether the perceptual representation of partly occluded geometric forms is, in general, modulated by eccentricity of regard.

3. Ramachandran has noted similar phenomena, though with different temporal properties: [H]e reports that misaligned vertical line elements may appear to *become* aligned after 10–15 s in the periphery in normal vision (1993) or, after several seconds, across a scotoma (1992a).

4. For example, the blind spot is fixed, whereas extrinsic occluders must be identified as such. On the other hand, the "blind spot" of the optic disk does not exist in normal binocular vision, and so may be (effectively or metaphorically) ignored most of the time. Last, it has also been suggested that retinal scotomata (such as the optic disk) tend to fill in instantaneously whereas cortical scotomata take time (e.g., Gerrits and Vendrik 1970). Amodal completion may be subjectively instantaneous, yet have a time course that is not perceived (e.g., Sekuler and Palmer 1992).

5. With regard to color assignment in scotomata, Ramachandran (1993) has clearly stated that he believes the term "filling in" is metaphorical in the sense that the actual process is not one that "begins from the outside and invades" a filled-in region (page 60). Such a description had been proposed by Gerrits and Vendrik (1970), for example, for the filling in of brightness in

artificial scotomata. However, Ramachandran does argue that filling in involves "creating a neural representation of the surround in the region of the scotoma," (1993, page 59) which seems rather like literal filling in.

6. This issue is the crux of points numbers 1, 5, and 6 of Ramachandran (1995). Ramachandran's point number 3 suggests that subjectively modal completion of a line and non-completion of a blind-spot–occluded moving dot are distinct from a peripheral amodal-completion case. We disagree: [E]ven if the line was composed of lots of little dots and was "completed" behind an occluder that wouldn't mean that one was "really" seeing the dots. Imagine trying to count them. On the other hand, the purported sense of a "smudged" occluder to account for the disappearance of a large (and individually resolvable) spot is consistent with just the kind of evidentiary view we are advocating.

7. Titchener would of course accuse us of something amounting to the "stimulus-error" (see Boring 1950, pages 417ff) in reporting our introspection of amodally perceived forms as "seen," but he is no longer quite as influential as he once was.

8. This strategy can actually work if the qualia arise at measurably distinct times, but does not appear to have been the strategy employed by Ramachandran (e.g., 1992a, 1992b).

9. Indeed, Gibson has reported a different view of the matter altogether: "My observations suggest that the slant of a surface, or the curvature, or an edge or *a corner* is also continued within the area [of the blind spot]" (1966, page 263, emphasis added).

REFERENCES

Andrews, P. R., & Campbell, F. W. (1991). Images at the blind spot. *Nature (London), 353,* 308.

Boring, E. G. (1950). *A history of experimental psychology (Second edition).* New York: Appleton-Century-Crofts.

Bruner, J. S. (1957). Going beyond the information given. In *Contemporary Approaches to Cognition: A symposium held at the University of Colorado* (pp. 41–69). Cambridge, MA: Harvard University Press.

Churchland, P. S., & Ramachandran, V. S. (1993). Filling in: Why Dennett is wrong. In B. Dahlbom (Ed.), *Dennett and his critics: Demystifying mind* (pp. 28–52). Oxford: Blackwell Scientific.

Dennett, D. C. (1991). *Consciousness explained.* Boston: Little, Brown.

Ferree, C. E., & Rand, G. (1912). The spatial values of the visual field immediately surrounding the blind spot and the question of the associative filling in of the blind spot. *American Journal of Physiology, 29,* 398–412.

Fiorani, M., Rosa, M. G. P., Gatass, R., & Rocha-Miranda, C. E. (1992). Changes in receptive field size in V 1 and its relation to perceptual completion. *Proceedings of the National Academy of Sciences of the United States of America, 89,* 8547–8551.

Gatass, R., Fiorani, M., Rosa, M. G. P., Pinon, M. C. F., Sousa, A. P. B., & Soares, J. G. M. (1992). Visual responses outside the "classical" receptive field RF in primate striate cortex: A possible correlate of perceptual completion. In R. Lent (Ed.), *The visual system from genesis to maturity* (pp. 233–244). Boston: Birkhauser.

Gerrits, H. J. M., & Vendrik, A. J. H. (1970). Simultaneous contrast, filling-in process and information processing in man's visual system. *Experimental Brain Research, 11,* 411–430.

Gibson, J. J. (1966). *The senses considered as perceptual systems.* Boston: Houghton Mifflin.

Hardage, L., & Tyler, C. (1995). Induced twinkle aftereffect as a probe of dynamic visual processing mechanisms. *Vision Research, 35,* 757–766.

He, J. Z., & Nakayama, K. (1992). Surfaces vs. features in visual search. *Nature (London), 359,* 231–233.

Helson, H. (1929). The effects of direct simulation of the blind-spot. *American Journal of Psychology, 61,* 345–397.

Heydt, R. von der, Peterhans, E., & Baumgartner, G. (1984). Illusory contours and cortical neuron responses. *Science, 224,* 1260–1262.

Kanizsa, G. (1979). *Organization in vision.* New York: Praeger.

Kanizsa, G., & Gerbino, W. (1982). Amodal completion: Seeing or thinking? In J. Beck (Ed.), *Organization and representation in perception* (pp. 167–190). Hillsdale, NJ: Lawrence Erlbaum Associates.

Kellman, P. J., & Shipley, T. F. (1991). A theory of visual interpolation in object perception. *Cognitive Psychology, 23,* 141–221.

Kellman, P. J., & Shipley, T. F. (1992). Perceiving objects across gaps in space and time. *Current Directions in Psychological Science, 1,* 193–199.

Lamme, V. A. F., Dijk, B. W. van, & Spekreijse, H. (1993). Contour from motion processing occurs in primary visual cortex. *Nature (London), 363,* 541–543.

Lettvin, J. Y. (1976). On seeing sidelong. *The Sciences, 16,* 10–20.

Marr, D. (1982). *Vision.* San Francisco: W. H. Freeman.

Michotte, A., Thines, G., & Crabbe, G. (1964). Les complementes amodaux des structure perceptives. In *Studia psychologica.* Louvain: Publications Universitaires.

Ramachandran, V. S. (1992a). Blind spots. *Scientific American, 266,* 86–91.

Ramachandran, V. S. (1992b). Filling in gaps in perception: Part I. *Current Directions in Psychological Science, 1,* 199–205.

Ramachandran, V. S. (1993). Filling in gaps in perception: Part II. Scotomas and phantom limbs. *Current Directions in Psychological Science, 2,* 56–65.

Ramachandran, V. S. (1995). Filling in gaps in logic: Reply to Durgin et al. *Perception, 24,* 841–845.

Ramachandran, V. S., & Gregory, R. L. (1991). Perceptual filling in of artificially induced scotomas in human vision. *Nature (London), 350,* 699–702.

Ramachandran, V. S., Gregory, R. L., & Aiken, W. (1993). Perceptual fading of visual texture borders. *Vision Research, 33,* 717–721.

Sears, C. R., & Mikaelian, H. H. (1989). Exploration of perceptual functioning surrounding the optic disk. *Canadian Psychology, 30,* 408.

Sekuler, A. B., & Palmer, S. E. (1992). Perception of partly occluded objects: A microgenetic analysis. *Journal of Experimental Psychology: General, 121,* 95–111.

Shimojo, S., & Nakayama, K. (1990). Amodal representation of occluded surfaces: The role of invisible stimuli in apparent motion correspondence. *Perception, 19,* 285–289.

Tripathy, S. P., & Levi, D. M. (1994). Long-range dichoptic interactions in the human visual cortex in the region corresponding to the blind spot. *Vision Research, 34,* 1127–1138.

Tripathy, S. P., Levi, D. M., Ogmen, H., & Harden, C. (1995). Perceived length across the physiological blind spot. *Visual Neuroscience, 12,* 385–402.

Walls, G. L. (1954). The filling-in process. *American Journal of Optometry, 31,* 329–341.

White, J. M., Levi, D. M., & Aitsebaomo, A. P. (1992). Spatial localization without visual references. *Vision Research, 32,* 513–526.

Yap, Y. L., Levi, D. M., & Klein, S. A. (1987). Scaling peripheral positional acuity: Isoeccentric bisection is better than radial bisection. *Journal of the Optical Society of America, 4,* 1562–1567.

CHAPTER FOUR
Sensory Memory

11   METACONTRAST MASKING

It may be premature to refer to this reading as a "classic," but it is a well-written paper that both reviews classic effects of visual masking and identifies areas that are ripe for future research. Many masking studies deal with stimuli that are presented for only fractions of a second. The idea is to test the limits of the visual system by using stimuli that are difficult to see. It is difficult to find such limits, however. If you are paying careful attention, a target stimulus that is presented for only one millisecond (a thousandth of a second) can be perceived, provided the stimulus intensity is high enough. However, the same target stimulus (or even one presented for much longer) can be made virtually invisible if a mask stimulus is also presented.

As the introduction of the reading discusses, this masking effect can be used to study the development of visual percepts. It seems that if the mask arrives at just the right time, it can weaken the visual representation of the target. By varying the timing of the target and the mask, vision scientists can explore the fine temporal structure of visual percepts of the target stimulus.

Masking is also useful as a tool for studying other aspects of cognition, by controlling the duration of information processing. If you see a word for 50 milliseconds, you cannot fully process the word and its meaning during the presentation of the word itself. However, even after the word has physically disappeared, your visual system will maintain a representation of the word for nearly a hundred milliseconds, a phenomenon known as visual persistence. In addition, as information about the word is processed, that information passes on to higher-level cognitive systems, so that even when the visual representation of the word has faded away, processing of word meaning can continue. A mask, however, can curtail that extended processing. If a target word is followed by a mask of other letters (e.g., XXXX), the mask seems to limit both visual persistence and higher-level processing of the word. By varying the timing between the target and the mask and observing when the word can just be identified, a cognitive psychologist can estimate how long it takes to process a word. Masks of this type are very common in cognitive psychology (see Reading 27, "Word Superiority Effect").

As this paper describes, many details of the target, the mask, and the timing between them influence masking effects. Masks with different spatial properties seem to have quite different masking effects. One of the most interesting effects is found with a mask that surrounds a target stimulus (Figure 11.1b). This kind of mask is called a metacontrast mask, and it has a surprising effect as the timing between the target and mask is varied. It is often the case that a metacontrast mask has its strongest masking effect when it follows the target by around 80 milliseconds (see Figure 11.3). If the target and mask are presented at the same time, the target is easy to identify. Likewise, if the mask follows the target by around 200 milliseconds, the target is easy to identify. This masking effect has always struck researchers as odd because it seemed that if the mask could interfere with the target when the mask appears 80 milliseconds later, then the mask should also be able to interfere with the target when they are presented together. The data consistently show that this is not the case. The CogLab experiment demonstrates this unusual masking effect.

This reading also discusses a variety of other masking situations, and considers theories of what kinds of mechanisms are involved in masking. They show that interesting new effects can be found by combining visual masking with the visual search task to investigate attention effects on masking.

QUESTIONS

1. Visual perception is often considered similar to a camera taking a picture. How do the effects of metacontrast masking argue against that analogy?
2. What does the acronym SOA stand for?
3. What are the characteristics of "integration masking"?
4. What is the effect of introducing distracters in the common onset masking display?

What's New in Visual Masking?

James T. Enns and Vincent Di Lollo

University of British Columbia

A brief display that is clearly visible when shown alone can be rendered invisible by the subsequent presentation of a second visual stimulus. Several recently described backward masking effects are not predicted by current theories of visual masking, including masking by four small dots that surround (but do not touch) a target object and masking by a surrounding object that remains on display after the target object has been turned off. A crucial factor in both of these effects is attention: [A]lmost no masking occurs if attention can be rapidly focused on the target, whereas powerful masking ensues if attention directed at the target is delayed. A new theory of visual masking, inspired by developments in neuroscience, can account for these effects, as well as more traditional masking effects. In addition, the new theory sheds light on related research, such as the attentional blink, inattentional blindness and change blindness.

Masking is a widely used and powerful way of studying visual processes. At the most general level, masking refers to a reduction in the visibility of an object (the target) caused by the presentation of a second object (the mask) nearby in space or time. In the spatial domain, merely surrounding the target with non-target items (an effect that is termed "crowding"[1]) can reduce the visibility of a target. Inserting a temporal interval between the target and mask leads to more complex effects. For example, a target that is highly visible when presented briefly by itself can be rendered completely invisible by the subsequent presentation of a non-target object in the same (or nearby) spatial location. "Backward masking" of this kind has its strongest influence not when target and mask objects are presented simultaneously, as intuition might suggest, but rather when a brief temporal gap is inserted between the presentation of the target and the mask. Such spatio-temporal interactions provide valuable insights into the mechanics of the visual system and provide information about the time required to form a percept,[2] the spatial range of influence between objects[3] and visual processes that are beyond conscious awareness.[4,5]

In this article, we summarize insights that have been gained in recent studies of visual masking. However, we first distinguish between two ways in which masking is used to study vision. On the one hand, masking is a convenient tool used by many researchers to regulate the difficulty of a task, so that accuracy falls into a measurable range. An informal survey of a recent volume of *Perception and Psychophysics* (Vol. 61, 1999) indicated that 14/93 (15%) of articles on vision used backward masking for the practical purpose of limiting visual access to the target over a controlled period of time. A second, smaller group of articles (5/93 or 5%) was concerned with the fine-grained spatial and temporal aspects of masking itself. It is important to note that although the present article might seem to be concerned primarily with the latter concept, our theory has equally important implications when masking is used as a tool of convenience.

THE STANDARD VIEW

Visual masking is typically divided into two types, based on the spatial relationships that exist between the contours of the target and mask patterns. Masking that involves spatial superimposition of contours is commonly referred to as "pattern masking," while masking that involves closely adjacent but nonoverlapping contours is called "metacontrast." Typical examples of stimuli used in each of these types of masking are shown in Figure 11.1a [and] 11.1b.

Pattern masking presents the visual system with two kinds of spatio-temporal conflict. One occurs when the target and mask are perceived as part of the same pattern as a consequence of imprecise temporal resolution by the visual system. In this case, masking is akin to the addition of spatial noise (the mask) to the signal (the target) at early levels of visual representation and is therefore referred to as "integration masking."[3,6–8] The temporal signature of this form of masking is approximate symmetry around a peak at a stimulus onset asynchrony (SOA, the interval between the presentation of the target and mask) of 0 ms, with a complete absence of masking beyond an SOA of about 100 ms in either direction.

A second conflict arises when processing of a first pattern (the target) is interrupted by a second pattern (the mask) that appears in the same spatial location before the target has been fully processed. This conflict does not involve the early stages of processing, where contours are defined, but instead involves a competition for higher-level mechanisms that are engaged in object recognition. It is referred to as "interruption masking."[9] The amount of time spent processing the target is sharply curtailed if a mask follows in rapid succession. The temporal characteristics of masking by interruption are very different from those of masking by integration. Interruption masking can occur only when the mask appears after the target. The masking function is referred to as U- or J-shaped, because target accuracy is often lowest at SOAs that are greater than zero and improve at longer SOAs (Refs 10,11).

In addition to their temporal characteristics, pattern-masking processes are distinguishable on the basis of physical attributes (which influence integration masking) and informational attributes (which influence interruption masking). For example, integration masking increases with the luminance contrast of the mask, whereas contrast has little (if any) effect on interruption masking.[3,7,12] Conversely, varying the number of potential targets between trials (i.e. manipulating set size) has little effect on integration masking, but markedly increases masking by interruption (see Figure 11.2).[12]

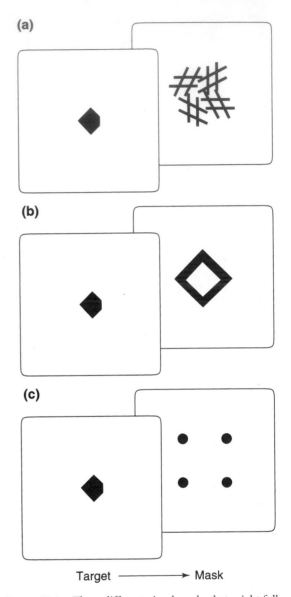

(a)

(b)

(c)

Target ⟶ Mask

FIGURE 11.1   Three different visual masks that might follow a briefly presented target shape in studies of visual backward masking. For the target depicted, observers attempt to identify which corner of a diamond has been erased. (a) Pattern mask: contours of the mask are spatially superimposed on the contours of the target. (b) Metacontrast: mask contours closely fit (but do not overlap) the target contours. (c) Four-dot mask: four small dots surround the target. There are no standard theories that predict that masking will occur with the four-dot mask.

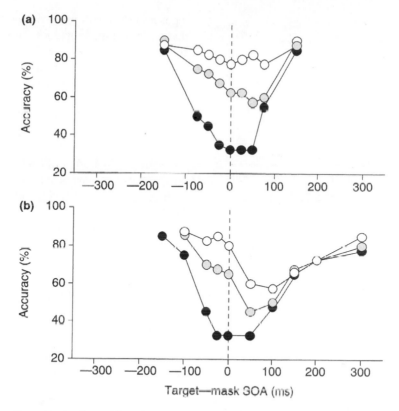

FIGURE 11.2 Letter identification accuracy in a pattern masking experiment. A letter is flashed briefly at one of 12 possible locations in a clock-face configuration. Three different levels of mask intensity (black symbols = high; gray symbols = medium; white symbols = low) were tested over a range of target–mask SOAs. Negative SOAs represent forward masking and positive SOAs backward masking. (a) Set of one letter. (b) Set of 12 letters. Mask intensity is most effective when mask and target are presented simultaneously (SOA = 0), whereas set size is most effective when SOA > 0 (backward masking). Abbreviation: SOA, stimulus onset asynchrony. (Adapted from Ref. 12.)

Metacontrast masking occurs when masking shapes closely fit the contours of a target shape but do not touch them.[3,13] Importantly, when the interval between the presentation of the target and mask is either very short or very long, the target is clearly visible. At intermediate SOAs, however, perception of the target is impaired and leads to a U-shaped function of accuracy versus SOA. The mechanisms thought to be at work are inhibitory interactions between neurons that represent the contours of the target and the mask.[3,14] The main idea in such "two-channel" theories is that the onset of each shape initiates neural activity in two channels; one fast-acting but short-lived, the other slower acting but longer lasting. The fast-acting channel transmits transient events that signal the stimulus onset and offset, whereas the slower channel transmits sustained signals regarding the stimulus shape and color. Metacontrast masking occurs when fast-acting signals in response to the mask inhibit the sustained activity generated by the earlier target. Figure 11.3 shows the typical time course of metacontrast masking.[15]

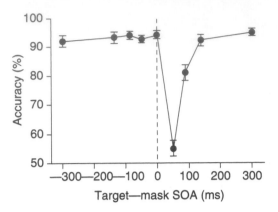

FIGURE 11.3   Shape identification accuracy in a meta-contrast masking experiment. A diamond shape was flashed briefly at the center of gaze while a surrounding mask appeared briefly over a range of target–mask SOAs. No forward (SOA < 0) or simultaneous (SOA = 0) masking occurred and backward masking was greatest at SOAs of 50–100 ms. Abbreviation: SOA, stimulus onset asynchrony. (Adapted from Ref. 15.)

A key piece of evidence consistent with meta-contrast masking theories based on inhibitory contour interactions is the relationship between masking strength and contour proximity.[3,16] Masking is sharply reduced as the separation between target and masking contours is increased even by a fraction of a degree.

NAGGING PROBLEMS FOR THE STANDARD VIEW

Although these standard views account for a large portion of the data on visual masking, there are several persistent findings that complicate the picture. First, consider the perceptual fate of masked targets. In the standard view, backward masking terminates the processing of the target at a precategorical level.[7–9] However, a phenomenon known as "masked priming" suggests that processing of masked targets continues to lexical and even semantic levels. In conventional priming, where the prime word is not masked, a target is identified more easily if it is preceded by a semantically-related prime word.[5,17] In masked priming, the prime word is followed by a mask that prevents the observer from being able to report the target. However, the facilitation that is found in visible prim-

ing is also seen with masked priming.[4,5] This suggests that backward masking does not interrupt target processing at an early level, which is contrary to current theories. It is not the analysis of the target that is disrupted, but access to this analysis by conscious visual processes.

A second finding that is difficult to reconcile with the standard view is that there is little neurophysiological evidence that a backward mask suppresses the target signal. In studies of backward masking by pattern, visual components of the neural signal associated with the target (e.g. P1, N1, N400 components of the ERP) are indistinguishable under conditions in which behavioral masking does and does not occur.[18,19] A similar effect occurs with metacontrast masking.[20–22] These outcomes cast serious doubt on standard inhibition theories. The apparent inconsistency between behavioural and neurophysiological measures of masking can be resolved by replacing the idea of inhibitory interactions with that of cortical "multiplexing,"[20,23] with the same neurons participating in different computations at various stages in the processing of a visual display.

Finally, current theories do not accommodate the notion that attention plays a crucial role in visual masking. We mentioned earlier that one characteristic of integration masking that distinguishes it from interruption masking is differential sensitivity to attentional manipulations such as set size.[12] However, no interruption masking theories predict that increments in set size should result in larger masking effects. The same is true for metacontrast masking, the strength of which is modulated by: (1) the way in which observers subjectively organize an ambiguous display;[24] (2) the extent of practice;[25] (3) speed-accuracy criteria;[26] and (4) semantic relationships.[27] Clearly, all forms of masking await an account in which spatial attention plays an integral role in masking.

In our laboratory, we have been exploring two new forms of masking that are difficult to reconcile with current theories. Here, we provide only a brief introduction to give the reader a flavor of the phenomena that require explanation. These masking effects can be experienced first hand on the internet (http://www.interchange.ubc.ca/enzo/osdescr.htm) and can be read about elsewhere.[15,28,29]

The first form of masking (Figure 11.1c) occurs when a briefly presented target is followed by four dots that surround (but do not touch) the target shape.[15] Standard theories predict that no masking will occur in this case because the four dots constitute neither a superimposed pattern nor a surrounding contour. Nonetheless, strong masking does occur. Furthermore, four-dot masking is crucially dependent on the target not being the focus of attention. When attention can be focused on the target location before the target-mask sequence, no masking occurs.

The second form of masking is called "common onset" because the target and mask come into view simultaneously.[28] No masking occurs if the target and mask disappear simultaneously, which indicates that the duration and contrast of the display items are sufficient to support perception. Masking does occur, however, if those parts of the initial configuration that belong to the target are deleted and only the mask continues to be displayed. Even a short postponement of mask deletion causes masking, the strength of which increases with the duration of visibility of the mask. This is a form of masking that is not predicted by the previously described mechanisms of integration (which incorrectly predicts maximum masking at a mask duration of 0 ms), interruption or metacontrast (which require the onset of a second pattern to interrupt processing of the first). Instead, the key factor appears to be that the mask remains visible following deletion of the target.

These two new forms of masking were recently combined in a series of experiments in which an initial, brief display, consisting of several potential targets with four small dots surrounding one of them, was followed by a second display that contained only the four dots.[29] The observer's task was to report the target item highlighted by the four dots, as shown in Figure 11.4. Little or no masking was observed when: (1) there was only one potential target; (2) the target differed from all other non-target items by a distinctive feature; or (3) the four dots preceded the target display by 90 ms. By contrast, pronounced masking occurred when: (1) many potential targets were displayed; (2) targets and non-targets were not easily distinguishable; and (3) no prior spatial cue was provided. These results suggest that common-onset masking by four dots is crucially dependent on the focus of spatial attention.

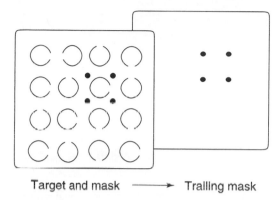

Target and mask ⟶ Trailing mask

FIGURE 11.4   Illustration of the display sequence in a common-onset masking experiment involving a four-dot mask. The observer is required to indicate the orientation of the gap in a broken ring that is highlighted by four dots. The other broken rings served as distractors. In any given display, the number of broken rings varied from 1 (target with no distractors) to 16 (target with 15 distractors, illustrated). The sequence began with a combined display of the target, mask and distractors for 10 ms and continued with a display of the mask alone for a variable amount of time. (Adapted from Ref. 29.)

MASKING BASED ON CORTICAL RE-ENTRANT PROCESSING

Our novel view of masking is based on recent advances in neuroscience and psychophysics. Our starting point was the principle that communication between two brain areas is never unidirectional: [I]f a source area sends signals to a target area, then the target area sends signals back to the source area through re-entrant pathways.[30–32] It has been suggested that the architecture of cortical re-entry might be used to test for the presence of specific patterns in the incoming signals.[33,34] Specifically, it is thought that the circuit actively searches for a match between a descending code, representing a perceptual hypothesis, and an ongoing pattern of low-level activity. When such a match occurs, the neural ensemble is "locked" onto the stimulus.

We incorporated these findings into a computational model of masking.[29] The central assumption in the model is that perception is based on the activity of modules, similar to that illustrated in Figure 11.5, which are arrayed over the visual field. Each module is

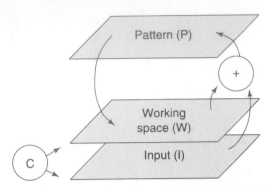

FIGURE 11.5   One module in the computational model for object substitution. The onset of a new visual event initiates activity in all layers on the first cycle. The activity in the pattern layer (P) is then fed back to the working space (W) by means of a simple overwriting operation. In this transfer, pattern information is translated back to the codes of the input layer (I), permitting a direct comparison (C). If the code in the pattern layer is to be successfully bound to its actual display location, the re-entrant signals need to be placed in spatial registration with the active signals in the input layer. Most important for masking is that the contents of the input layer change dynamically with new visual input. The contents of the pattern layer, by contrast, change more slowly because its input is a weighted sum of what is currently in the input layer and what was in the working space on the previous iteration. This produces a degree of inertia in the system's response to changes in input, which is an unavoidable consequence of re-entrant processing. If the visual input changes during this crucial period of inertia, masking will ensue. (Reproduced, with permission, from Ref. 29.)

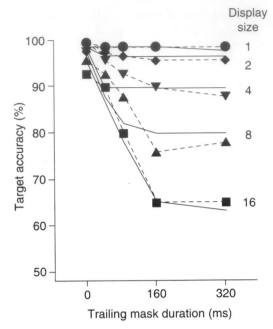

FIGURE 11.6   Target identification accuracy in a common-onset masking experiment involving a four-dot mask. Symbols and dashed lines represent psychophysical data and the solid lines represent the quantitative predictions of the computational model for object substitution. No masking occurs when attention can be rapidly deployed to the target location, such as when set size is one. Accuracy is also not greatly affected by increments in set size, provided that the four-dot mask terminates with the target display (mask duration equal to zero). However, masking occurs when set size and mask duration increase. According to object-substitution theory, this is the result of the representation of the unattended target being replaced by the mask representation before target identification is complete. (Reproduced, with permission, from Ref. 29.)

conceived as a circuit comprising connections between cortical area V1 and a topographically related region in an extrastriate visual area. The output of each module is a representation of the spatial pattern within its receptive field.

Based on the model in Figure 11.5, perception of the input pattern emerges from iterative comparisons between the high-level codes and the ongoing low-level activity generated by the initial stimulus. For example, given a brief display in which the target and the mask are displayed simultaneously, target processing can be based on the visible persistence that follows the brief display. The fact that all parts of the display decay uniformly means that there is no imbalance in activity between mask and target pattern representations

and observers are consequently able to identify the target accurately. Indeed, target identification accuracy was found to be high in this case, as shown in Figure 11.6.

By contrast, masking occurs when there is a mismatch between the re-entrant signal and ongoing activity at a lower level. This occurs when the target items are deleted, leaving only the four-dot mask in the target location. The ongoing activity at the lower level would then consist of an image of the mask, maintained by continued sensory input, and a decaying image of the target. This creates a mismatch with the re-entrant perceptual hypothesis, which includes the target as well as the mask. Given this kind of conflict, what is perceived will depend on the number of iterations required to identify the target. If only a few iterations are required, conscious target identification might be completed before the target signal has faded completely. However, if more iterations are needed, a new perceptual hypothesis is formed that is consistent with the currently predominant low-level activity and the "mask alone" percept replaces the "target plus mask" percept. As shown in Figure 11.6 and in the internet demonstrations, masking by four dots becomes stronger as a joint function of set size (delaying attention to the target location) and mask duration (increasing the likelihood of seeing the mask alone percept).

Two alternative interpretations should be considered and dismissed. It might be argued that the masking seen in Figure 11.6 is caused by the abrupt termination of the mask. Such offset transients are known to influence the degree of meta-contrast masking.[35] However, offset transients are not the primary influence in common-onset masking for two reasons. First, masking is very much in evidence at a mask duration of 320 ms, which is too long after the target presentation to be effective. Second, the offset-transient hypothesis predicts progressively weaker masking with increasing mask duration.[35] Instead, masking becomes progressively stronger and as such cannot be explained by offset transients alone.

It could also be argued that re-entrant processes are not really needed to explain common-onset masking. Perhaps it is the relatively long duration of the mask that causes attention to be drawn to it rather than to the shorter-lived target item at the same location. This hypothesis was ruled out by experiments in which the mask was shown for an even longer period, beginning before the onset of the target display and outlasting it.[29] Although this modification had the effects of both increasing the overall duration of the mask and focusing attention directly on it, masking was still sharply reduced. This indicates that it is the presence of the mask *after* the target that is critical, not its absolute duration relative to the target. We regard this as strong support for the important role played by re-entrant processes in perception.

The object-substitution model accounts naturally for the relationship between masking and spatial attention. Because the main mechanism involves successive iterations of re-entrant processing, every variable that increases the number of iterations required to identify a target will also increase the strength and the temporal course of backward masking. It is well established in the attention literature that conscious target identification is delayed by a wide spatial distribution or misdirection of attention.[36,37] This proposed role for attention in masking phenomena is also consistent with what is known about masked priming.[4,5,18,19] Although items outside the focus of attention might not be experienced consciously, they nonetheless are processed sufficiently to influence ongoing cognitive processes.

The object-substitution model also accounts for standard masking effects. Indeed, there is no difference in principle between masking with common onset and the broad characteristics of metacontrast and pattern masking. From this perspective, all forms of backward masking involve the perceptual substitution of a temporally leading target by a trailing mask, if the mask appears before target identification is complete. We might expect there to be minor differences that would be unique to each form of masking, especially at very short temporal intervals, where contour integration and interactions are most likely. For example, we have distinguished between classical meta-contrast masking, which occurs early in processing and depends critically on the proximity of target and masking contours, and object-substitution masking, which occurs later and is unaffected by proximity of contours.[29] However, the crucial ingredient of object substitution that is shared by all forms of backward masking is that the mask is visible during the period in which the iterations between higher-level pattern and lower-level contour representations are likely to occur.

An important feature of object substitution is that it makes sense of several puzzling findings that cannot be resolved with the standard view of masking. First, it is now easier to understand why both pattern masking[12] and metacontrast,[2] which were believed to be distinctly different mechanisms, produce similar effects when set size is varied. Specifically, very little masking occurs when the target is the only item on display, while pronounced masking of the same target occurs when it is only one of several items on display. The same is true for common-onset masking by four dots.

A second result that is readily explained by object substitution is the finding that a backward mask is more effective as the duration of the mask increases.[29,38] Neither the standard view of interruption masking (based on the termination of target processing) nor that of metacontrast (based on channel inhibition) predicts that the influence of a mask will increase with its duration. Object substitution, however, makes precisely this prediction, because a mask of longer duration will be more likely to complete and reinforce the iterative pattern-confirmation process.

Third, object substitution predicts that a mask will not simply terminate target processing, but that the mask itself will become the new focus of object identification mechanisms. This prediction has been observed in studies of visual masking in rapid serial visual presentations (Ref. 39, and J. Martin *et al.*, unpublished; see also Box 11.1, Figure 11.7). When observers fail to report the identity of a masked target, they usually report the item that has followed (and therefore masked) the target. This effect is seldom seen in traditional studies of masking because observers are rarely asked to report directly on their perception of the mask. Nevertheless, shape priming in a study of metacontrast masking suggests that this phenomenon also occurs in traditional studies of masking.[40]

Finally, object substitution can explain the large imbalance between forward and backward effects, both in standard masking[3,12] and masking by common onset.[29] As stated above, forward masking has a very narrow temporal window and is fully accounted for by the inherent temporal "smearing" of the visual system, which reduces it to the mechanisms of masking by spatial crowding and noise integration. Backward masking, by contrast, has a much wider temporal window and is often much larger in magnitude. As we noted above, both of these characteristics can be exaggerated easily by manipulating the set size and similarity of the target and mask. The large bias that favors the effectiveness of backward masking is exactly what is predicted if the primary mechanism involves the replacement of an emerging object representation with another, because the initial representation has been contradicted by subsequent input.

OBJECT SUBSTITUTION AND THE ROLE OF ATTENTION IN PERCEPTION

One of the most important practical implications to arise from our understanding of object substitution is that backward masking does not simply terminate the processing of a target. Rather, the perceptual mechanisms of conscious perception appear to be actively engaged in perceiving the mask. An example of this principle is illustrated in Box 11.1 for a phenomenon known as "the attentional blink."

We believe that masking by object substitution also has direct relevance to the recently popularized phenomena of "inattentional blindness" and "change blindness." Inattentional blindness refers to the phenomenon wherein objects that are presented to the visual system are not seen because the observer is attending to something else.[41] One of the key details of the induction procedure that is rarely given much consideration is the role played by a pattern mask, which is presented immediately following the display. Usually, the mask is used to prevent additional processing of the display after it is removed from the screen. However, object substitution predicts that perception of the mask directly interferes with access to briefly presented and unattended targets. More specifically, object substitution predicts that inattentional blindness will increase directly with mask duration, even if the mask consists of four surrounding dots that would otherwise not interfere with target perception.

Change blindness refers to the finding that large changes to the visual world go undetected if attention is not already focused on the objects or area in which the change occurs.[42–46] There have been few systematic studies of the role played by the visual image that replaces the retinal (or environmental) location of the original image. Yet, from the perspective of object substitution, such an image would seem to play an important role because it prevents access to the fading representation of the original image and replaces it in consciousness.

In conclusion, it is important to emphasize the distinction between masking as a tool of convenience and as a tool for probing underlying perceptual mechanisms. For example, in the attentional blink, inattentional blindness and change blindness, we have

Box 11.1   Visual Masks Influence Perceptual Processes

A good example of how the choice of mask alters the perceptual processes under investigation can be seen in recent research into the attentional blink. In these studies, the perception of the second of two briefly displayed targets is impaired if it is presented with a temporal lag (up to 500 ms) after the first target (Ref. a). For example, observers could be asked to report the identity of two letters inserted into a visual stream of digits, as shown in Fig. 11.7a. Although accuracy of reporting the first letter is nearly perfect, accuracy in identifying the second letter is substantially lower, as shown in Fig. 11.7b. This deficit has been attributed to the second target being unattended while processing resources are devoted to the first target. However, it has long been recognized that the second target must be masked for the attentional blink to occur. Ostensibly, the purpose of masking was to increase the difficulty of processing the second target, thereby bringing accuracy within a measurable range. However, if this is the principal function served by masking, masking by integration and interruption should be the same, with the second target deficit occurring in both procedures.

In fact, the lag-dependent second target accuracy deficit occurs in this task only if backward masking is used (Refs b,c). If a simultaneous mask is used, identification of the second target is impaired equally across all time lags (Fig. 11.7c). This suggests that object substitution is the mechanism that accounts for masking in the attentional blink. That is, while unattended, the second target is vulnerable to replacement by the trailing mask. As a consequence of this replacement, the mask is substituted for the second target as the object for eventual conscious registration. This clearly demonstrates that backward masking of the second target is not simply a methodological convenience, but in fact reveals the functional mechanisms that are involved in masking, which would have gone undetected had masking been used merely as a tool.

References

a. Shapiro, K. L. (1994) The attentional blink: the brain's eyeblink. *Curr. Direct. Psychol. Sci.* 3, 86–89

b. Brehaut, J. C. *et al.* (1999) Visual masking plays two roles in the attentional blink. *Percept. Psychophys.* 61, 1436–1448

c. Giesbrecht, B. L. and Di Lollo, V. (1998) Beyond the attentional blink: visual masking by object substitution. *J. Exp. Psychol. Hum. Percept. Perform.* 24, 1454–1466

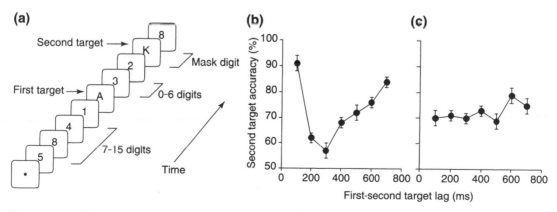

FIGURE 11.7   Illustration of the display sequence in the attentional blink paradigm (a). Second-target accuracy is shown as a function of lag from the first target when (b) a pattern mask follows the second target and (c) a pattern mask is presented simultaneously with the second target.

established that a backward visual mask is a crucial factor in the failure to "see" objects that are clearly registered on the retina. Nevertheless, it is important to note that the mechanisms under investigation are not inherently tied to backward masking; masking simply makes them more readily apparent. In support of this view, recent reports in each of the above-mentioned areas have showed that failures of perception can be induced in the absence of a mask. Specifically, (1) an attentional blink occurs without masking if the nature of the task is sufficiently different for the first and second targets;[47] (2) inattentional blindness occurs when no mask follows the target, although the rate is much reduced;[41] and (3) change blindness can be induced simply by splashing "mud" unexpectedly onto parts of a picture other than the target.[48] Importantly, in accordance with object-substitution theory, each of these manipulations involves directing attention away from the visual target, which will then go undetected. Specifically, while attention is either focused on the task of identifying an initial target or "captured" by unexpected events (such as mud-splashes), before attention can be redeployed to the visual target, the iterative processes of conscious perception would have lost trace of the crucial target or any changes that might have occurred.

ACKNOWLEDGEMENT

The research described in this article was supported by grants from the Natural Sciences and Engineering Research Council of Canada to each author.

REFERENCES

1. Bouma, H. (1970) Interaction effects in parafoveal letter recognition. *Nature* 226, 177–178
2. Averbach, E. and Coriel, A.S. (1961) Short-term memory in vision. *Bell Sys. Tech. J.* 40, 309–328
3. Breitmeyer, B.G. (1984) *Visual Masking: An Integrative Approach*, Oxford University Press
4. Debner, J.A. and Jacoby, L.L. (1994) Unconscious perception: attention, awareness, and control. *J. Exp. Psychol. Learn. Mem. Cognit.* 20, 304–317
5. Cheesman, J. and Merikle, P.M. (1986) Distinguishing conscious from unconscious perceptual processes. *Can. J. Psychol.* 40, 343–367
6. Kahneman, D. (1968) Method, findings, and theory in studies of visual masking. *Psychol. Bull.* 70, 404–425
7. Scheerer, E. (1973) Integration, interruption and processing rate in visual backward masking. *Psychologische Forschung* 36, 71–93
8. Turvey, M.T. (1973) On peripheral and central processes in vision: inferences from an information-processing analysis of masking with patterned stimuli. *Psychol. Rev.* 81, 1–52
9. Kolers, P.A. (1968) Some psychological aspects of pattern recognition. In *Recognizing Patterns* (Kolers, P.A. and Eden, M., eds), pp. 4–61, MIT Press
10. Bachmann, T. and Allik, J. (1976) Integration and interruption in the masking of form by form. *Perception* 5, 79–97
11. Michaels, C.F. and Turvey, M.T. (1979) Central sources of visual masking: indexing structures supporting seeing at a single, brief glance. *Psychol. Res.* 41, 1–61
12. Spencer, T.J. and Shuntich, R. (1970) Evidence for an interruption theory of backward masking. *J. Exp. Psychol.* 85, 198–203
13. Alpern, M. (1953) Metacontrast. *J. Opt. Soc. Am.* 43, 648–657
14. Weisstein, N. *et al.* (1975) A comparison and elaboration of two models of metacontrast. *Psychol. Rev.* 82, 325–343
15. Enns, J.T. and Di Lollo, V. (1997) Object substitution: a new form of masking in unattended visual locations. *Psychol. Sci.* 8, 135–139
16. Growney, R. *et al.* (1977) Metacontrast as a function of spatial separation with narrow line targets and masks. *Vis. Res.* 17, 1205–1210
17. Meyer, D.E. *et al.* (1975) Loci of contextual effects on visual word recognition. In *Attention and Performance* (5th edn) (Rabbitt, P.M.A. and Dornic, S., eds), pp. 98–118, Academic Press
18. Luck, S.J. *et al.* (1996) Word meanings can be accessed but not reported during the attentional blink. *Nature* 383, 616–618
19. Vogel, E.K. *et al.* (1998) Electrophysiological evidence for a postperceptual locus of suppression during the attentional blink. *J. Exp. Psychol. Hum. Percept. Perform.* 24, 1656–1674
20. Bridgeman, B. (1980) Temporal response characteristics of cells in monkey striate cortex measured with metacontrast masking and brightness discrimination. *Brain Res.* 196, 347–364
21. von der Heydt, R. *et al.* (1997) Neuronal responses in monkey V1 and V2 unaffected by metacontrast. *Invest. Ophthalmol. Vis. Sci.* 38, S459

22. Jeffreys, D.A. and Musselwhite, M.J. (1986) A visual evoked potential study of metacontrast masking. *Vis. Res.* 26, 631–642

23. Mumford, D. (1992) On the computational architecture of the neocortex: II. The role of cortico-cortical loops. *Biol. Cybern.* 66, 241–251

24. Ramachandran, V.I. and Cobb, S. (1995) Visual attention modulates metacontrast masking. *Nature* 373, 66–68

25. Hogben, J.H. and Di Lollo, V. (1985) Practice reduces suppression in metacontrast and in apparent motion. *Percept. Psychophys.* 35, 441–445

26. Lachter, J. and Durgin, F.H. (1999) Metacontrast masking functions: a question of speed? *J. Exp. Psychol. Hum. Percept. Perform.* 25, 936–947

27. Shelley-Tremblay, J. and Mack, A. (2000) Metacontrast masking and attention. *Psychol. Sci.* 10, 508–515

28. Di Lollo, V. *et al.* (1993) Stimulus-onset asynchrony is not necessary for motion perception or metacontrast masking. *Psychol. Sci.* 4, 260–263

29. Di Lollo, V. *et al.* Competition for consciousness among visual events: the psychophysics of re-entrant pathways. *J. Exp. Psychol. Gen.* (in press)

30. Felleman, D.J. and Van Essen, D.C. (1991) Distributed hierarchical processing in primate visual cortex. *Cereb. Cortex* 1, 1–47

31. Zeki, S. (1993) *A Vision of the Brain*, Blackwell Science

32. Bullier, J. *et al.* (1988) Physiological studies on the feedback connection to the striate cortex from cortical areas 18 and 19 of the cat. *Exp. Brain Res.* 70, 90–98

33. Sillito, A.M. *et al.* (1994) Feature-linked synchronization of thalamic relay cell firing induced by feedback from the visual cortex. *Nature* 369, 479–482

34. Hupe, J.M. *et al.* (1998) Cortical feedback improves discrimination between figure and ground by V1, V2, and V3 neurons. *Nature* 394, 784–787

35. Breitmeyer, B.G. and Kersey, M. (1981) Backward masking by pattern stimulus offset. *J. Exp. Psychol. Hum. Percept. Perform.* 7, 972–977

36. Posner, M.I. (1980) Orienting of attention. *Q. J. Exp. Psychol.* 32, 3–25

37. Treisman, A. and Gelade, G. (1980) A feature integration theory of attention. *Cognit. Psychol.* 12, 97–136

38. Dixon, P. and Di Lollo, V. (1994) Beyond visible persistence: an alternative account of temporal integration and segregation in visual processing. *Cognit. Psychol.* 26, 33–63

39. Chun, M.M. (1997) Temporal binding errors are redistributed in the attentional blink. *Percept. Psychophys.* 59, 1191–1199

40. Klotz, W. and Wolff, P. (1995) The effect of a masked stimulus of the response to the masking stimulus. *Psychol. Res.* 58, 92–101

41. Mack, A. and Rock, I. (1998) *Inattentional Blindness*, MIT Press

42. Rensink, R.A. *et al.* (1997) To see or not to see: the need for attention to perceive changes in scenes. *Psychol. Sci.* 8, 368–373

43. Levin, D.T. and Simons, D.J. (1997) Failure to detect changes to attended objects in motion pictures. *Psychonomic Bull. Rev.* 4, 501–506

44. Simons, D.J. (1996) In sight, out of mind: when object representations fail. *Psychol. Sci.* 7, 301–305

45. Simons, D.J. and Levin, D.T. (1998) Failure to detect changes to people during a real-world interaction. *Psychonomic Bull. Rev.* 5, 644–649

46. Scholl, B.J. Attenuated change blindness for exogenously attended items in a flicker paradigm. *Vis. Cognit.* (in press)

47. Enns, J.T. *et al.* Visual masking and task switching in the attentional blink. In *The Limits of Attention: Temporal Constraints on Human Information Processing* (Shapiro, K., ed.), Oxford University Press (in press)

48. O'Regan J.K. *et al.* (1999) Change-blindness as a result of "mudsplashes." *Nature* 398, 34

49. Raymond, J.E. (2000) Attentional modulation of visual motion perception. *Trends Cognit. Sci.* 4, 42–50

12 PARTIAL REPORT

In the early beginnings of psychology, researchers were interested in something called the "span of apprehension." This quest was to determine how much information could be gathered in a single glance. For example, when you read text, how many letters can you interpret in a glimpse? Or, how many coins can you distinguish if you take a quick look at them? A variety of ingenious studies seemed to draw similar conclusions that people could accurately report about four and a half items from a brief percept; thus, the so-called span of apprehension was a little more than four objects. This fact was built into many theories of cognition until the current paper suggested this estimate was wrong.

This paper describes a series of experiments conducted by George Sperling (1960) with the purpose of investigating how much information is seen when a visual stimulus array is presented briefly. The goals of the experiments were to examine the different characteristics of visual sensory memory—how much information could be held, how long that information lasts, and how forgetting occurs.

In Experiment 1, Sperling flashed a variable number of letters and numbers for a very brief period (50 ms). An example of a typical stimulus array is shown in Figure 12.2 of the paper. The stimuli were letters or numbers arranged in rows and columns. What he found was that the average number of letters reported was slightly greater than four, regardless of the size of the display—just like the number that had been found previously. However, as he noted in the paper, this number might more correctly reflect a person's memory span (the number of things that can be recalled from memory) instead of the number of objects actually *seen* in the display. Sperling's subjects claimed that they could "see" more than the four items reported; they just could not report all of them. The array seemed to fade away as time passed.

In order to investigate this possibility, Sperling developed a technique, called the "partial report" technique, in which subjects were required to report only particular parts of the display. Importantly, the subjects did not know ahead of time which letters would be tested. He used these partial results to infer how much information is available in the total display.

The logic is as follows: When you take any kind of test, you are almost never tested for everything that you know. For example, when you take a test in cognitive psychology, you may get 20 questions about various theories and experiments discussed in the book or in class. If you get 15 out of 20 correct, the instructor infers that you know approximately 75% of the material. Rather than examining you on every possible topic, most exams test only a portion of your knowledge and then estimate what you know about the untested information from the partial sample. It is important that you do not know ahead of time which pieces of information will be on the test or this logic no longer follows.

In Experiment 3 Sperling implemented this idea and cued his subjects as to which row of the array to report by playing one of three tones. If a high-pitched tone were played, the subject knew to recall just the top row; a medium-pitched tone indicated that the middle row should be recalled; and a low-pitched tone meant that the bottom row should be recalled. A trial would go as follows: The display would be presented briefly, for perhaps 50 ms. Then, immediately following, a tone would be played, signaling which row to recall. The results from Experiments 1 and 3 are shown in Figure 12.3 both as an average across subjects (top left) and as individual subjects (all the rest). Each figure contains three lines; The lowest one is the result from the whole report conditions, the second line is the inferred number of letters available immediately after the display was turned off, and the diagonal line indicates what perfect performance would be. Note that the performance in the partial report conditions is much higher than the whole report, in some cases almost approaching perfect performance.

In Experiment 4 Sperling systematically varied the duration of the interval between the offset of the display and the onset of the tone from 0 to 1 s in order to examine the duration of the sensory trace or how long it lasted. There was also a condition in which the delay was -0.1 s, which means the tone was actually played 100 ms before the offset of the display. Because there were three possible rows to recall and the subjects did not know until after they had heard the tone which row was the correct one, Sperling reasoned that the subjects had to attend to all of the items in all three rows. Thus, he multiplied the number of items the subjects recalled by 3 to estimate the total amount of information available. For example, if a subject heard the high-pitched tone and recalled three of the four items in the top row correctly, Sperling would estimate a total knowledge of nine items. When the tone was played 100 ms after the offset of the matrix, the estimated number of items available was about 7.2. When the tone was played 1 second after the offset of the matrix, the estimated number of letters available to the subject was equal to the actual number of letters recalled in the whole report procedure. The results are shown in Figures 12.4 (for 9-letter displays) and 12.5 (for 12-letter displays). The bar indicates performance on the whole report condition. There was an advantage for partial report only if the cue to recall occurred within about 500 ms of the offset of the stimulus. If the tone was delayed much further, the number of estimated items available using the partial report technique was the same as the number of items recalled using whole report.

The CogLab demonstration follows the procedure in Experiment 4 for nine-letter displays quite closely. The only difference is that, instead of a tone, the to-be-reported line is indicated by an arrow. The delay between the offset of the display and the arrow varies between 20 ms (one-fifth of a second) and 1000 ms (one second). If the data replicate Sperling's results, they should show a decrease in the number of letters reported as the delay increases, with the number being close to 4.5 after one second.

Sperling concluded from these and other results that information is briefly registered in a sensory memory system (later called "iconic memory") and is almost totally available if accessed quickly enough. If the information is not soon attended to, however, it is rapidly lost. Current conceptions of iconic memory have refined Sperling's original formulation. The persistence of information in iconic memory proper has been separated into two distinct phenomena, stimulus persistence and information persistence. The former lasts for much less time than originally thought, perhaps as little as one–fifth of the original estimate, and the latter is more properly conceived of as the same form of memory responsible for maintaining information over the short term (Loftus & Irwin, 1998).

REFERENCE

Loftus, G. R., & Irwin, D. E. (1998). On the relations among different measures of visible and informational persistence. *Cognitive Psychology, 35,* 135–199.

QUESTIONS

1. What is a real-world example of the partial report technique?
2. How is the "number of letters available" calculated in Experiment 4?
3. Using the partial report technique, approximately how long after the presentation of the stimulus array is the information still available in the visual sensory store?

The Information Available in Brief Visual Presentations

George Sperling
Harvard University

How much can be seen in a single brief exposure? This is an important problem because our normal mode of seeing greatly resembles a sequence of brief exposures. Erdmann and Dodge (1898) showed that in reading, for example, the eye assimilates information only in the brief pauses between its quick saccadic movements. The problem of what can be seen in one brief exposure, however, remains unsolved. The difficulty is that the simple expedient of instructing the observer of a single brief exposure to report what he has just seen is inadequate. When complex stimuli consisting of a number of letters are tachistoscopically presented, observers enigmatically insist that they have seen more than they can remember afterwards, that is, report afterwards.[1] The apparently simple question: "What did you see?" requires the observer to report both what he remembers and what he has forgotten.

The statement that *more is seen than can be remembered* implies two things. First, it implies a memory limit, that is, a limit on the (memory) report. Such a limit on the number of items which can be given in the report following any brief stimulation has, in fact, been generally observed; it is called the span of attention, apprehension, or immediate-memory (cf. Miller, 1956b). Second, *to see more than is remembered* implies that more information is available during, and perhaps for a short time after, the stimulus than can be reported. . . .

In order to circumvent the memory limitation in determining the information that becomes available following a brief exposure, it is obvious that the observer must not be required to give a report which exceeds his memory span. If the number of letters in the stimulus exceeds his memory span, then he cannot give a whole report of all the letters. Therefore, the observer must be required to give only a partial report of the stimulus contents. Partial reporting of available information is, of course, just what is required by ordinary schoolroom examinations and by other methods of sampling available information.

An examiner can determine, even in a short test, approximately how much the student knows. The length of the test is not so important as that the student not be told the test questions too far in advance. Similarly, an observer may be "tested" on what he has seen in a brief exposure of a complex visual stimulus. Such a test requires only a partial report. The specific instruction which indicates which part of the stimulus is to be reported is then given only after termination of the stimulus. On each trial the instruction, which calls for a specified part of the stimulus, is randomly chosen from a set of possible instructions which cover the whole stimulus. By repeating the interrogation (sampling) procedure many times, many different random samples can be obtained of an observer's performance on each of the various parts of the stimulus. The data obtained thereby make feasible the estimate of the total information that was available to the observer from which to draw his report on the average trial.

The time at which the instruction is given determines the time at which available information is sampled. By suitable coding, the instruction may be given at any time: before, during, or after the stimulus presentation. Not only the available information immediately following the termination of the stimulus, but a continuous function relating the amount of information available to the time of instruction may be obtained by such a procedure.

SOURCE: From Sperling, G. (1960). The information available in brief visual presentations. *Psychological Monographs,* 74, (Whole No. 498).

Many studies have been conducted in which observers were required to give partial reports, that is, to report only on one aspect or one location of the stimulus. In prior experiments, however, the instructions were often not randomly chosen, and the set of possible instructions did not systematically cover the stimulus. The notions of testing or sampling were not applied.[2] It is not surprising, therefore, that estimates have not been made of the total information available to the observer following a brief exposure of a complex stimulus. Furthermore, instructions have generally not been coded in such a way as to make it possible to control the precise time at which they were presented. Consequently, the temporal course of available information could not have been quantitatively studied. In the absence of precise data, experimenters have all too frequently assumed that the time for which information is available to the observer corresponds exactly to the physical stimulus duration. Wundt (1899) understood this problem and convincingly argued that, for extremely short stimulus durations, the assumption that stimulus duration corresponded to the duration for which stimulus information was available was blatantly false, but he made no measurements of available information.

The following experiments were conducted to study quantitatively the information that becomes available to an observer following a brief exposure. Lettered stimuli were chosen because these contain a relatively large amount of information per item and because these are the kind of stimuli that have been used by most previous investigators. The first two experiments are essentially control experiments; they attempt to confirm that immediate-memory for letters is independent of the parameters of stimulation, that it is an individual characteristic. In the third experiment the number of letters available immediately after the extinction of the stimulus is determined by means of the sampling (partial report) procedure described above. The fourth experiment explores decay of available information with time. The fifth experiment examines some exposure parameters. In the sixth experiment a technique which fails to demonstrate a large amount of available information is investigated. The seventh experiment deals with the role of the historically important variable: order of report.

GENERAL METHOD

Apparatus.   The experiments utilized a Gerbrands tachistoscope.[3] This is a two-field, mirror tachistoscope (Dodge, 1907b), with a mechanical timer. Viewing is binocular, at a distance of about 24 inches. Throughout the experiment, a dimly illuminated fixation field was always present.

The light source in the Gerbrands tachistoscope is a 4-watt fluorescent (daylight) bulb. Two such lamps operated in parallel light each field. The operation of the lamps is controlled by the microswitches, the steady-state light output of the lamp being directly proportional to the current. However, the phosphors used in coating the lamp continue to emit light for some time after the cessation of the current. This afterglow in the lamp follows an exponential decay function consisting of two parts: the first, a blue component, which accounts for about 40% of the energy, decays with a time constant which is a small fraction of a millisecond; the decay constant of the second, yellow, component was about 15 msec. in the lamp tested. Figure 12.1 illustrates a 50-msec. light impulse on a linear intensity scale. The exposure time of 50 msec. was used in all experiments unless exposure time was itself a parameter. Preliminary experiments indicated that, with the presentations used, exposure duration was an unimportant parameter. Fifty msec. was sufficiently short so that eye movements during the exposure were rare, and it could conveniently be set with accuracy.

Stimulus materials.   The stimuli used in this experiment were lettered 5 × 8 cards viewed at a distance of 22 inches. The lettering was done with a Leroy No. 5 pen, producing capital letters about 0.45 inch high. Only the 21 consonants were used, to minimize the possibility of Ss interpreting the arrays as words. In a few sets of cards the letter Y was also omitted. In all, over 500 different stimulus cards were used.

There was very little learning of the stimulus materials either by the Ss or by the E. The only learning that was readily apparent was on several stimuli that had especially striking letter combinations. Except for the stimuli used for training, no S ever was required to report the same part of any stimulus more than two or three times, and never in the same session.

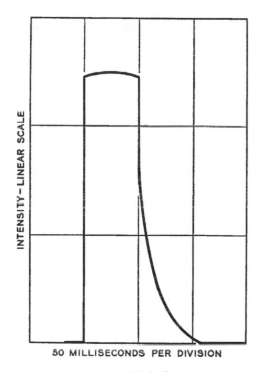

INTENSITY—LINEAR SCALE

50 MILLISECONDS PER DIVISION

FIGURE 12.1   A 50-millisecond light flash, such as was used in most of the experiments. (Redrawn from a photograph of an oscilloscope trace)

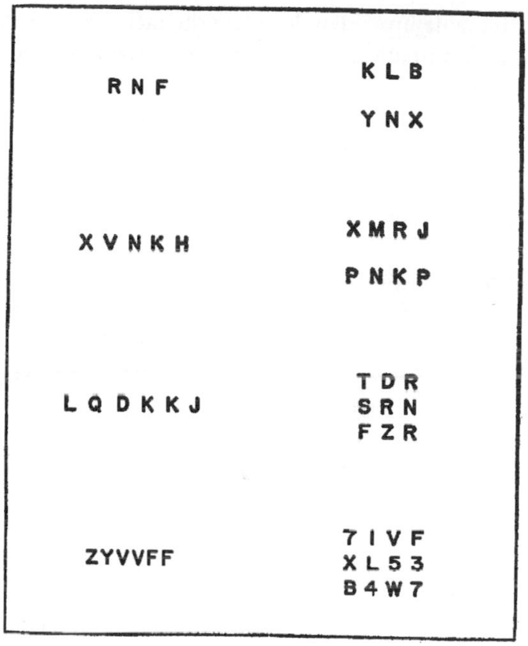

```
RNF                    KLB
                       YNX


XVNKH                  XMRJ
                       PNKP


LQDKKJ                 TDR
                       SRN
                       FZR


                       7IVF
ZYVVFF                 XL53
                       B4W7
```

FIGURE 12.2   Typical stimulus materials. Col. 1: 3, 5, 6, 6-massed. Col. 2: 3/3, 4/4, 3/3/3, 4/4/4 L&N.

Figure 12.2 illustrates some typical arrays of letters. These arrays may be divided into several categories: (*a*) stimuli with 3, 4, 5, 6, or 7 letters normally spaced on a single line, (*b*) stimuli with six letters closely spaced on a single line (6-massed); (*c*) stimuli having two rows of letters with three letters in each row (3/3), or two rows of four letters each (4/4); (*d*) stimuli having three rows of letters with three letters in each row (3/3/3). . . .

In addition to stimuli that contained only letters, some stimuli that contained both letters and numbers were used. These had eight (4/4 L&N . . .) and twelve symbols (4/4/4 L&N . . .) respectively, four in each row. Each row had two letters and two numbers—the positions being randomly chosen. The *S* was always given a sample stimulus before L&N stimuli were used and told of the constraint above. He was also told that O when it occurred was the number "zero" and was not considered a letter. . . .

Subjects.   The nature of the experiments made it more economical to use small numbers of trained *S*s rather than several large groups of untrained *S*s. Four of the five *S*s in the experiment were obtained through the student employment service. The fifth *S* (RNS) was a member of the faculty who was interested in the research. Twelve sessions were regularly scheduled for each *S*, three times weekly.

Instructions and trial procedures.   *S* was instructed to look at the fixation cross until it was clearly in focus; then he pressed a button which initiated the presentation after a 0.5-sec. delay. This procedure constituted an approximate behavioral criterion of the degree of dark adaptation prior to the exposure, namely, the ability to focus on the dimly illuminated fixation cross.

Responses were recorded on a specially prepared response grid. A response grid appropriate to each stimulus was supplied. The response grid was placed on the table immediately below the tachistoscope, the room illumination being sufficient to write by. The Ss were instructed to fill in all the required squares on the response grid and to guess when they were not certain. The Ss were not permitted to fill in consecutive X's, but were required to guess "different letters." After a response, S slid the paper forward under a cover which covered his last response, leaving the next part of the response grid fully in view.

Series of 5 to 20 trials were grouped together without a change in conditions. Whenever conditions or stimulus types were changed, S was given two or three sample presentations with the new conditions or stimuli. Within a sequence of trials, S set his own rate of responding. The Ss (except ND) preferred rapid rates. In some conditions, the limiting rate was set by the E's limitations in changing stimuli and instruction tones. This was about three to four stimuli per minute.

Each of the first four and last two sessions began with and/or ended with a simple task: the reporting of all the letters in stimuli of 3, 4, 5, and 6 letters. This procedure was undertaken in addition to the usual runs with these stimuli to determine if there were appreciable learning effects in these tasks during the course of the experiment and if there was an accuracy decrement (fatigue) within individual sessions. Very little improvement was noted after the second session. This observation agrees with previous reports (Whipple, 1914). There was little difference between the beginning and end of sessions.

Scoring and tabulation of results.   Every report of all Ss was scored both for total number of letters in the report which agreed with letters in the stimulus and for the number of letters reported in their correct positions. Since none of the procedures of the experiments had an effect on either of these scores independently of the other, only the second of these, *letters in the correct position,* is tabulated in the results. This score, which takes position into account, is less subject to guessing error,[4] and in some cases it is more readily interpreted than a score which does not take position into account. As the maximum correction for guessing would be about 0.4 letter for the 4/4/4 (12-letter) material—and considerably less for all other materials—no such correction is made in the

treatment of the data. In general, data were not tabulated more accurately than 0.1 letter.

Data from the first and second sessions were not used if they fell below an S's average performance on these tasks in subsequent sessions. This occurred for reports of five and of eight (4/4) letters for some Ss. A similar criterion applied in later sessions for tasks that were initiated later. In this case, the results of the first "training" session(s) are not incorporated in the total tabulation if they lie more than 0.5 letter from S's average in subsequent sessions.

EXPERIMENT 1: IMMEDIATE-MEMORY

When an S is required to give a complete (whole) report of all the letters on a briefly exposed stimulus, he will generally not report all the letters correctly. The average number of letters which he does report correctly is usually called his *immediate-memory span* or *span of apprehension for that particular stimulus material under the stated observation conditions.* An expression such as immediate-memory span (Miller, 1956a) implies that the number of items reported by S remains invariant with changes in stimulating conditions. The present experiment seeks to determine to what extent the span of immediate-memory is independent of the number and spatial arrangement of letters, and of letters and numbers on stimulus cards. If this independence is demonstrated, then the qualification "for that particular stimulus material" may be dropped from the term immediate-memory span when it is used in these experiments.

Procedure. Ss were instructed to write all the letters in the stimulus, guessing when they were not certain. All 12 types of stimulus materials were used. At least 15 trials were conducted with each kind of stimulus with each S. Each S was given at least 50 trials with the 3/3 (6-letter) stimuli which had yielded the highest memory span in preliminary experiments. The final run made with any kind of stimulus was always a test of immediate-memory. This procedure insured that Ss were tested for memory when they were maximally experienced with a stimulus.

Results.   The lower curves in Figure 12.3 represent the average number of letters correctly reported by

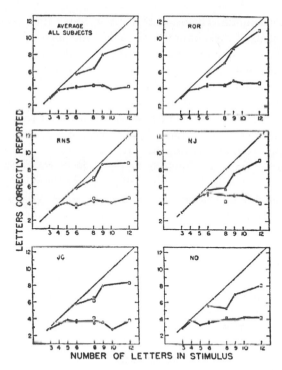

FIGURE 12.3   "Channel capacity curves." Immediate-memory and letters available (output information) as functions of the number of stimulus letters (input information). Lower curves = immediate-memory (Exp. 1); upper curves = letters available immediately after termination of the stimulus; diagonal lines = maximum possible score (i.e., input = output). Code: × = letters on one line; + = 6-massed; o = 3/3, 4/4, 5/5; △ = 3/3/3, □ = 4/4 L&N, 4/4/4 L&N.

each S for each material.[5] The most striking result is that immediate-memory is constant for each S, being nearly independent of the kind of stimulus used. The immediate-memory span for individual Ss ranges from approximately 3.8 for JC to approximately 5.2 for NJ with an average immediate-memory span for all Ss of about 4.3 letters. (The upper curves are discussed later.)

The constancy which is characteristic of individual immediate-memory curves of Figure 12.3 also appears in the average curve for all Ss. For example, three kinds of stimuli were used that had six letters each: six letters normally spaced on one line, 6-massed, and 3/3-letters (see Figure 12.2). When the data for all Ss are pooled, the scores for each of these

three types of materials are practically the same: the range is 4.1–4.3 letters. The same constancy holds for stimuli containing eight symbols. The average number of letters correctly reported for each of the two different kinds of eight letter stimuli, 4/4, 4/4 L&N, is nearly the same: 4.4, 4.3, respectively.

Most Ss felt that stimuli containing both letters and numbers were more difficult than those containing letters only. Nevertheless, only NJ showed an objective deficit for the mixed material.

In conclusion, the average number of correct letters contained in an S's whole report of the stimulus is approximately equal to the smaller of (*a*) the number of letters in the stimulus or (*b*) a numerical constant—the span of immediate-memory—which is different for each S. The use of the term immediate-memory span is therefore justified within the range of materials studied. This limit on the number of letters that can be correctly reported is an individual characteristic, but it is relatively similar for each of the five Ss of the study....

[In Experiment 1, Sperling presents the stimuli for .05 sec (500 msec.). In Experiment 2, he shows that the number of letters that subjects report correctly does not change with exposure durations ranging from .015 to .5 secs (150 to 500 msecs.).]

EXPERIMENT 3: PARTIAL REPORT

Experiments 1 and 2 have demonstrated the span of immediate-memory as an invariant characteristic of each S. In Experiment 3 the principles of testing in a perceptual situation that were advanced in the introduction are applied in order to determine whether S has more information available than he can indicate in his limited immediate-memory report.

The S is presented with the stimulus as before, but he is required only to make a partial report. The length of this report is four letters or less, so as to lie within S's immediate-memory span. The instruction that indicates which row of the stimulus is to be reported is coded in the form of a tone. The instruction tone is given after the visual presentation. The S does not know until he hears the tone which row is called for. This is therefore a procedure which samples the information that S has available after the termination of the visual stimulus.

Procedure.   Initially, stimulus materials having only two lines were used, that is, 3/3 and 4/4. The *S* was told that a tone would be sounded, that this tone would come approximately simultaneously with the exposure, and that it would be either a high tone (2500 cps) or a low tone (250 cps). If it were a high tone, he was to write only the upper row of the stimulus; if a low tone, only the lower row. He was then shown a sample card of 3/3 letters and given several high and low tones. It was suggested that he keep his eyes fixated on the fixation point and be equally prepared for either tone. It would not be possible to outguess the *E* who would be using a random sequence of tones.

The tone duration was approximately 0.5 sec. The onset of the tone was controlled through the same microswitch that controlled the off-go of the light, with the completion of a connection from an audio-oscillator to the speaker. Intensity of the tone was adjusted so that the high (louder) tone was "loud but not uncomfortable."

In each of the first two sessions, each *S* received 30 training trials with each of the materials 3/3, 4/4. In subsequent sessions *S*s were given series of 10 or more "test" trials. Later, a third, middle (650 cps) tone was introduced to correspond to the middle row of the 3/3/3 and 4/4/4 stimuli. The instructions and procedure were essentially the same as before.

In any given session, each tone might not occur with equal frequency for each type of stimulus. Over several sessions, usually two, this unequal frequency was balanced out so that an *S* had an exactly equal number of high, medium, and low tones for each material. If an *S* "misinterpreted" the tone and wrote the wrong row, he was asked to write what he could remember of the correct row. Only those letters which corresponded to the row indicated by the tone were considered.

Treatment of the data.   In the experiments considered in this section, *S* is never required to report the whole stimulus but only one line of a possible two or three lines. The simplest treatment is to plot the percentage of letters correct. This in fact, will be done for all later comparisons. The present problem is to find a reasonable measure to enable comparison between the partial report and the immediate-memory data for the same stimuli. The measure, *percent correct,* does not describe the results of the immediate-memory experiments parsimoniously. In Experiment 1 it was shown that *S*s report a constant number of letters, rather than a constant percentage of letters in the stimulus. The measure, *number of letters correct,* is inappropriate to the partial report data because the number of letters which *S* reports is limited by the *E* to at most three or four. The most reasonable procedure is to treat the partial report as a random sample of the letters which the *S* has available. Each partial report represents a typical sample of the number of letters *S* has available for report. For example, if an *S* is correct about 90% of the time when he is reporting three out of nine letters, then he is said to have 90% of the nine letters—about eight letters—available for partial report at the time the instruction tone is given.

In order to calculate the number of available letters, the average number of letters correct in the partial report is multiplied by the number of equiprobable (nonoverlapping), partial reports. If there are two tones and two rows, multiplication is by 2.0; if three, by 3.0. As before, only the number of correct letters in the correct position is considered.

Results.   The development of the final, stable form of the behavior is relatively rapid for *S*s giving partial reports. The average for all *S*s after 30 trials (first session) with the 3/3 stimuli was 4.5; on the second day the average of 30 more trials was 5.1. On the third day *S*s averaged 5.6 out of a possible six letters. Most of the improvement was due to just one *S*: ND who improved from 2.9 to 5.8 letters available. In the 3/3/3 stimulus training, all *S*s reached their final value after the initial 40 trials on the first day of training. The considerable experience *S*s had acquired with the partial reporting procedure at this time may account for the quick stabilization. NJ, whose score was 7.7 letters available on the first 20 trials, was given almost 150 additional trials in an unsuccessful attempt to raise this initial score.

In Figure 12.3 the number of letters available as a function of the number of letters in the stimulus are graphed as the upper curves. For all stimuli and for all *S*s, the available information calculated from the partial report is greater than that contained in the immediate-memory report. Moreover, from the divergence of the two curves it seems certain that, if still more complex stimuli were available, the amount of available information would continue to increase.

The estimate above is only a lower bound on the number of letters that Ss have available for report after the termination of the stimulus. An upper bound cannot be obtained from experiments utilizing partial reports, since it may always be argued that, with slightly changed conditions, an improved performance might result. Even the lower-bound measurement of the average available information, however, is twice as great as the immediate-memory span. The immediate-memory span for the 4/4/4 (12-letters and numbers) stimuli ranges from 3.9 to 4.7 symbols for the Ss, with an average of 4.3. Immediately after an exposure of the 4/4/4 stimulus material, the number of letters available to the Ss ranged from 8.1 (ND) to 11.0 (ROR), with an average of 9.1 letters available. . . .

EXPERIMENT 4: DECAY OF AVAILABLE INFORMATION

. . . It was established in Experiment 3 that more information is available to the Ss immediately after termination of the stimulus than they could report. It remains to determine the fate of this surplus information, that is, the "forgetting curve." The partial report technique makes possible the sampling of the available information at the time the instruction signal is given. By delaying the instruction, therefore, decay of the available information as a function of time will be reflected as a corresponding decrease in the accuracy of the report.

Procedure. The principal modification from the preceding experiment is that the signal tone, which indicates to the S which row is to be reported, is given at various other times than merely "zero delay" following the stimulus off-go. The following times of indicator tone onset relative to the stimulus were explored: 0.05 sec. before stimulus onset (−0.10 sec.), ±0.0-, +0.15-, +0.30-, +0.50-, +1.0-sec. delays after stimulus off-go. The stimuli used were 3/3, 4/4.

The Ss were given five or more consecutive trials in each of the above conditions. These trials were always preceded by at least two samples in order to familiarize S with the exact time of onset. The particular

delay of the instruction tone on any trial was thus fixed rather than chosen randomly. The advantages of this procedure are (*a*) optimal performance is most likely in each delay condition, if S is prepared for that precise condition (cf. Klemmer, 1957), (*b*) minimizing delay changes makes possible a higher rate of stimulus presentations. On the other hand, a random sequence of instruction tone delays would make it more likely that S was "doing the same thing" in each of the different delay conditions.

The sequence in which the different delay conditions followed each other was chosen either as that given above (ascending series of delay conditions) or in the reverse order (descending series). Within a session, a descending series always followed an ascending series and vice versa, irrespective of the stimulus materials used. At least two ascending and two descending series of delay conditions were run with each S and with each material after the initial training (Experiment 3) with that material. This number of trials insures that for each S there are at least 20 trials at each delay of the indicator tone. . . .

[In the first series of analyses of Experiment 4, Sperling analyzes how subjects' strategies change with more practice and with different stimulus conditions, focusing first on one subject, ROR.]

ROR's performance is analyzable in terms of two kinds of observing behavior (strategies) which the situation suggests. He may follow the instruction, given by E prior to training, that he pay equal attention to each row. In this case, errors are evenly distributed between rows. Or, he may try to anticipate the signal by guessing which instruction tone will be presented. In this case, S is differentially prepared to report one row. If the signal and S's guess coincide, S reports accurately; if not, poorly. . . .

. . . The accuracy of report resulting from the first of these behaviors (equal attention) is correlated with the delay of the instruction tone; it is associated with the Ss initially giving equal attention to all parts of the stimulus. The accuracy of the other kind of report (guessing) is uncorrelated with the delay of the instruction; it is characterized by Ss' differential preparedness for some part of the stimulus (guessing). Equal attention observing is selected for further study here. The preceding experiment suggests three modifications that would tend to make equal attention observing more likely to occur, with a corresponding exclusion of guessing.

1. The use of stimuli with a larger number of letters, that is, 3/3/3 and 4/4/4. Differential attention to a constant small part of the stimulus is less likely to be reinforced, the larger the stimulus. The use of three tones instead of two diminishes the probability of guessing the correct tone.

2. Training with instruction tones that begin slightly before the onset of the stimulus. It is not necessary for S to guess in this situation since he can succeed by depending upon the instruction tone alone. This situation not only makes equal attention likely to occur, but differentially reinforces it when it does occur. . . .

3. The E may be able to gain *verbal* control over Ss' modes of responding. Initially, however, even S cannot control his own behavior exactly. This suggests a limit to what E can do. For example, frequently Ss reported that, although they had tried to be equally prepared for each row, after some tones they realized that they had been selectively prepared for a particular row. This comment was made both when the tone and the row coincided and (more frequently) when they differed.

Some verbal control is, of course, possible. An instruction that was well understood was:

You will see letters illuminated by a flash that quickly fades out. This is a visual test of your ability to read letters under these conditions, not a test of your memory. You will hear a tone during the flash or while it is fading which will indicate which letters you are to attempt to read. Do not read the card until you hear the tone [etc.].

The instruction was changed at the midway point in the experiment. The S was no longer to do as well as he could by any means, but was limited to the procedure described above. Part 2 of this experiment, utilizing 9- and 12-letter stimuli, was carried out with the three modifications suggested above.

Results. The results for 3/3/3 and 4/4/4 letters and numbers are shown for each individual S in Figures 12.4 and 12.5. The two ordinates are linearly related by the equation:

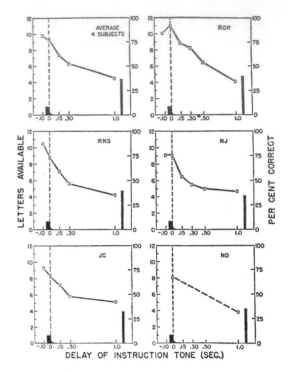

FIGURE 12.4   Decay of available information: nine (3/3/3) letters. Light flash is shown on same time scale at lower left. Bar at right indicates immediate-memory for this material.

$$\frac{\text{percent correct}}{100} \times \text{no. letters in stimulus}$$

$$= \text{letters available}$$

Each point is based on all the test trials in the delay condition. The points at zero delay of instructions for NJ and JC also include the training trials, as these Ss showed no subsequent improvement.

The data indicate that, for all Ss, the period of about one sec. is a critical one for the presentation of the instruction to report. If Ss receive the instruction 0.05 sec. before the exposure, then they give accurate reports: 91% and 82% of the letters given in the report are correct for the 9- and 12-letter materials, respectively. These partial reports may be interpreted to indicate that the Ss have, on the average, 8.2 of 9 and 9.8 of 12 letters available. However, if the instruction is delayed until one sec. after the exposure, then the accu-

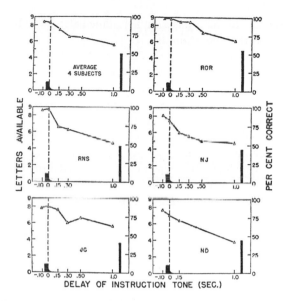

FIGURE 12.5   Decay of available information: twelve (4/4/4) letters and numbers. Light flash is shown on same time scale at lower left. Bar at right indicates immediate-memory for this material.

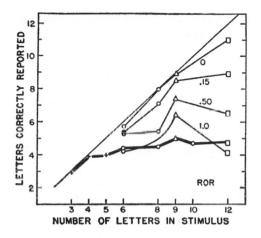

FIGURE 12.6   Immediate-memory and available information. The parameter is the time at which available information is sampled (delay of instruction). Heavy line indicates immediate-memory for the same materials. One subject (ROR).

racy of the report drops 32% (to 69%) for the 9-letter stimuli, and 44% (to 38%) for the 12-letter stimuli. This substantial decline in accuracy brings the number of *letters available* very near to the number of letters that Ss give in immediate-memory (whole) reports.

The decay curves are similar and regular for each S and for the average of all Ss. Although individual differences are readily apparent, they are small relative to the effects of the delay of the instruction. For example, when an instruction was given with zero delay after the termination of the stimulus, the *least* accurate reports by any Ss are given by ND, who has 8.1 letters available immediately after the termination of the stimulus. With a one-sec. delay of instructions, the *most* accurate reports were given by JC, who has only 5.1 letters available at this time.

In Figure 12.3, in which whole reports and partial reports were compared, only that particular partial report was considered in which the instruction tone followed the stimulus with zero delay. It is evident from this experiment that the zero delay instruction is unique only in that it is the earliest possible "after" instruction, but not because of any functional difference.

In Figure 12.6, therefore, the 0.15-, 0.50-, and 1.00-sec. instruction delays are also plotted for one S, ROR. . . . Figure 12.6 clearly highlights the significance of a precisely controlled coded instruction, given within a second of the stimulus off-go, for the comparison of partial and immediate-memory reports. One second after termination of the stimulus, the accuracy of ROR's partial reports is no longer very different from the accuracy of his whole reports. . . .

[In Experiment 5, Sperling compares subjects' performance when presentation of the stimulus is followed by a bright light (a procedure now called masking; see Introduction to Reading 11) and when stimulus presentation is followed by a dark (post-exposure) field. He finds that performance suffered overall, and it didn't matter whether stimuli were exposed for 150 or for 500 msecs.]

SUMMARY AND CONCLUSIONS

When stimuli consisting of a number of items are shown briefly to an observer, only a limited number of the items can be correctly reported. This number defines the so-called "span of immediate-memory." The fact that observers commonly assert that they can *see* more than they can *report* suggests that memory sets a limit on a process that is otherwise rich in available information. In the present studies, a sampling procedure (partial report) was used to circumvent the limitation imposed by immediate-memory and thereby to show that at the time of exposure, and for a few tenths of a second thereafter, observers have two or three times as much information available as they can later report. The availability of this information declines rapidly, and within one second after the exposure the available information no longer exceeds the memory span.

Short-term information storage has been tentatively identified with the persistence of sensation that generally follows any brief, intense stimulation. In this case, the persistence is that of a rapidly fading, visual image of the stimulus. Evidence in support of this hypothesis of visual information storage was found in introspective accounts, in the type of dependence of the accuracy of partial reports upon the visual stimulation, and in an analysis of certain response characteristics. These and related problems were explored in a series of seven experiments.

An attempt was first made to show that the span of immediate-memory remains relatively invariant under a wide range of conditions. Five practiced observers were shown stimuli consisting of arrays of symbols that varied in number, arrangement, and composition (letters alone, or letters and numbers together). It was found (Experiments 1 and 2) that each observer was able to report only a limited number of symbols (for example, letters) correctly. For exposure durations from 15 to 500 msec., the average was slightly over four letters; stimuli having four or fewer letters were reported correctly nearly 100% of the time.

In order to circumvent the immediate-memory limit on the (whole) report of what has been seen, observers were required to report only a part—designated by location—of stimuli exposed for 50 msec. (partial report). The part to be reported, usually one out of three rows of letters, was small enough (three to four letters) to lie within the memory span. A tonal signal (high, middle, or low frequency) was used to indicate which of the rows was to be reported. The S did not know which signal to expect, and the indicator signal was not given until after the visual stimulus had been turned off. In this manner, the information

available to the S was sampled immediately after termination of the stimulus.

Each observer, for each material tested (6, 8, 9, 12 symbols), gave partial reports that were more accurate than whole reports for the same material. For example, following the exposure of stimuli consisting of 12 symbols, 76% of the letters called for in the partial report were given correctly by the observers. This accuracy indicates that the total information available from which an observer can draw his partial report is about 9.1 letters (76% of 12 letters). This number of randomly chosen letters is equivalent to 40.6 bits of information, which is considerably more information than previous experimental estimates have suggested can become available in a brief exposure. Furthermore, it seems probable that the 40-bit information capacity observed in these experiments was limited by the small amount of information in the stimuli rather than by a capacity of the observers.

In order to determine how the available information decreases with time, the instruction signal, which indicated the row of the stimulus to be reported, was delayed by various amounts, up to 1.0 sec. (Experiment 4). The accuracy of the partial report was shown to be a sharply decreasing function of the delay in the instruction signal. Since, at a delay of 1.0 sec., the accuracy of the partial reports approached that of the whole reports, it follows that the information in excess of the immediate-memory span is available for less than a second. In contrast to the partial report, the accuracy of the whole report is not a function of the time at which the signal to report is given (Experiment 7).

The large amount of information in excess of the immediate-memory span, and the short time during which this information is available, suggests that it may be stored as a persistence of the sensation resulting from the visual stimulus. In order to explore further this possibility of visual information storage, some parameters of visual stimulation were studied. A decrease of the exposure duration from 50 to 15 msec. did not substantially affect the accuracy of partial reports (Experiment 5). On the other hand, the substitution of a white post-exposure field for the dark field ordinarily used greatly reduced the accuracy of both partial and whole reports. The ability of a homogeneous visual stimulus to affect the available information is evidence that the process depends on a persisting visual image of the stimulus.

Whether other kinds of partial reports give similar estimates of the amount of available information was examined by asking observers to report by category rather than by location. The observer reported numbers only (or the letters only) from stimuli consisting of both letters and numbers (Experiment 6). These partial reports were no more accurate than (whole) reports of all the letters and numbers. The ability of observers to give highly accurate partial reports of letters designated by location (Experiment 3), and their inability to give partial reports of comparable accuracy when the symbols to be reported are designated as either letters or numbers, clearly indicates that all kinds of partial reports are not equally suitable for demonstrating the ability of observers to retain large amounts of information for short time periods.

In the final study (Experiment 7), the order of report was systematically varied. Observers were instructed to get as many letters correct as possible, but the order in which they were to report the letters was not indicated until after the exposure. An instruction tone, following the exposure, indicated which of the two rows of letters on the stimulus was to be reported first. This interference with the normal order of report reduced only slightly the total number of letters that were reported correctly. As might be expected, the first row—the row indicated by the instruction tone—was reported more accurately than the second row (order effect). There was, however, a strong tendency for the top row to be reported more accurately than the bottom row (position effect). Although, as a group, the observers showed both effects, some failed to show either the order or the position effect, or both. The fact that, for some observers, order and position are not correlated with response accuracy suggests that order of report, and position, are not the major *causes* of, nor the necessary conditions for, response accuracy. The high accuracy of partial report observed in the experiments does not depend on the order of report or on the position of letters of the stimulus, but rather it is shown to depend on the ability of the observer to read a visual image that persists for a fraction of a second after the stimulus has been turned off.

REFERENCES

Adams, J. S. The relative effectiveness of pre- and post-stimulus setting as a function of stimulus uncertainty. Unpublished master's dissertation, Department of Psychology, University of North Carolina, 1955.

Alpern, M. Metacontrast. *J. Opt. Soc. Amer.*, 1953, 43, 648-657.

Baxt, N. Uber die Zeit welche nötig ist damit ein Gesichtseindruck zum Bewusstsein kommt und über die Grösse (Extension) der bewussten Wahrnehmung bei einem Gesichtseindrucke von gegebener Dauer. *Pflüger's Arch. ges. Physiol.*, 1871, 4, 325–336.

Berry, W., & Imus, H. Quantitative aspects of the flight of colors. *Amer. J. Psychol.*, 1935, 47, 449–457.

Bidwell, S. On the negative after-images following brief retinal excitation. *Proc. Roy. Soc. Lond.*, 1897, 61, 268–271.

Bridgin, R. L. A tachistoscopic study of the differentiation of perception. *Psychol. Monogr.*, 1933, 44(1, Whole No. 197), 153–166.

Broadbent, D. E. Immediate memory and simultaneous stimuli. *Quart. J. exp. Psychol.*, 1957, 9, 1–11 (a)

Broadbent, D. E. A mechanical model for human attention and memory. *Psychol. Rev.*, 1957, 64, 205–215. (b)

Broadbent, D. E. *Perception and communication.* New York: Pergamon, 1958.

Cattell, J. McK. Über die Trägheit der Netzhaut und des Sehcentrums. *Phil. Stud.*, 1883, 3, 94–127.

Chapman, D. W. The comparative effects of determinate and indeterminate aufgaben. Unpublished doctor's dissertation, Harvard University, 1930.

Chapman, D. W. Relative effects of determinate and indeterminate "Aufgaben." *Amer. J. Psychol.*, 1932, 44, 163–174.

Cohen, L. D., & Thomas, D. R. Decision and motor components of reaction time as a function of anxiety level and task complexity. *Amer. Psychologist*, 1957, 12, 420. (Abstract).

Dallenbach, K. M. Attributive vs. cognitive clearness. *J. exp. Psychol.*, 1920, 3, 183–230.

Diefendorf, A. R., & Dodge, R. An experimental study of the ocular reactions of the insane from photographic records. *Brain*, 1908, 31, 451–489.

Dodge, R. An experimental study of visual fixation. *Psychol. Monogr.*, 1907, 8 (4, Whole No. 35). (a)

Dodge, R. An improved exposure apparatus. *Psychol. Bull.*, 1907, 4, 10–13. (b)

Erdmann, B., & Dodge, R. *Psychologische Untersuchungen über das Lesen auf experimenteller Grundlage.* Halle: Niemeyer, 1898.

Glanville, A. D., & Dallenbach, K. M. The range of attention. *Amer. J. Psychol.*, 1929, 41, 207–236.

Goldiamond, I. Operant analysis of perceptual behavior. Paper read at Symposium on Experimental Analysis of Behavior, APA Annual Convention, 1957.

James, W. *The principles of psychology.* New York: Holt, 1890.

Klemmer, E. T. Simple reaction time as a function of time uncertainty. *J. exp. Psychol.*, 1957, 54, 195–200.

Klemmer, E T., & Loftus, J. P. *Numerals, nonsense forms, and information.* USAF Cambridge Research Center, Operational Applications Laboratory, Bolling Air Force Base, 1958. (Astia Doc. No. AD110063)

Külpe, O. Versuche über Abstraktion. In *Bericht über den erste Kongress für experimentelle Psychologie.* Leipzig: Barth, 1904. Pp. 56–68.

Ladd, G. T. *Elements of physiological psychology: A treatise of the activities and nature of the mind.* New York: Scribner, 1889.

Lawrence, D. H., & Coles, G. R. Accuracy of recognition with alternatives before and after the stimulus. *J. exp. Psychol.*, 1954, 47, 208–214.

Lawrence, D. H., & Laberge, D. L. Relationship between accuracy and order of reporting stimulus dimensions. *J. exp. Psychol.*, 1956, 51, 12–18.

Lindsley, D. B., & Emmons, W. H. Perception time and evoked potentials. *Science,* 1958, 127, 1061.

Long, E. R., Henneman, R. H., & Reid, L. S. Theoretical considerations and exploratory investigation of "set" as response restriction: The first of a series of reports on "set" as a determiner of perceptual responses. *USAF WADC tech. Rep.,* 1953, No. 53–311.

Long, E. R., & Lee, W. A. The influence of specific stimulus cuing on location responses: The third of a series of reports on "set" as a determiner of perceptual responses. *USAF WADC tech. Rep.,* 1953, No. 53–314. (a)

Long, E. R., & Lee, W. A. The role of spatial cuing as a response-limiter for location responses: The second of a series of reports on "set" as a determiner of perceptual responses. *USAF WADC tech. Rep.,* 1953, No. 53–312. (b)

Long, E. R., Reid, L. D., & Garvey, W. D. The role of stimulus ambiguity and degree of response restriction in the recognition of distorted letter patterns: The fourth of a series of reports on "set" as a determiner of perceptual responses. *USAF WADC tech. Rep.,* 1954, No. 54–147.

Luce, D. R. *A survey of the theory of selective information and some of its behavioral applications.* New York: Bureau of Applied Social Research, 1956.

McDougall, W. The sensations excited by a single momentary stimulation of the eye. *Brit. J. Psychol.,* 1904, 1, 78–113.

Miller, G. A. Human memory and the storage of information. *IRE Trans. Information Theory,* 1956, IT-2, No. 3, 129–137. (a)

Miller, G. A. The magic number seven, plus or minus two: Some limits on our capacity for processing information. *Psychol. Rev.,* 1956, 63, 81–97. (b)

Miller, G. A., & Nicely, P E. An analysis of perceptual confusions among some English consonants. *J. Acoust. Soc. Amer.,* 1955, 27, 338–352.

Pieron, H. L'évanouissement de la sensation lumineuse: Persistance indifferenciable et persistance totale. *Ann. Psychol.,* 1934, 35, 1–49.

Pollack, I. The assimilation of sequentially-encoded information. *Hum. Resources Res. Lab. memo Rep.,* 1952, No. 25.

Pritchard, R. M. Visual illusions viewed as stabilized retinal images. *Quart. J. exp. Psychol.,* 1958, 10, 77–81.

Quastler, H. Studies of human channel capacity. In H. Quastler, *Three survey papers.* Urbana, Ill.: Control Systems Laboratory, Univer. Illinois, 1956. Pp. 13–33.

Schumann, F. Die Erkennung von Buchstaben und Worten bei momentaner Beleuchtigung. In *Bericht über den erste Kongress für experimentelle Psychologie.* Leipzig: Barth, 1904. Pp. 34–40.

Schumann, F. The Erkennungsurteil. *Z. Psychol.* 1922, 88, 205–224.

Sperling, G. Information available in a brief visual presentation. Unpublished doctor's dissertation, Department of Psychology, Harvard University, 1959.

Sperling, G. Afterimage without prior image. *Science,* 1960, 131, 1613–1614.

Von Helmholtz, H. *Treatise on Physiological optics.* Vol. II. *The sensations of vision* (Transl. from 3rd German ed.) Rochester, New York: Optical Society of America, 1924–25.

Wagner, J. Experimentelle Beitrage zur Psychologie des Lesens. *Z. Psychol.,* 1918, 80, 1–75.

Weyer, E. M. The Zeitschwellen gleichartiger und disparater Sinneseindrucke. *Phil. Stud.,* 1899, 15, 68–138.

Whipple, G. M. *Manual of physical and mental tests.* Vol. I. *Simpler processes.* Baltimore: Warwick & York, 1914.

Wilcocks, R. W. An examination of Külpe's experiments on abstraction. *Amer. J. Psychol.* 1925, 36, 324–340.

Woodworth, R. S. *Experimental psychology.* New York: Holt, 1938.

Wundt, W. Zur Kritik tachistosckopischer Versuche. *Phil. Stud.* 1899, 15, 287–317.

Wundt, W. *An introduction to psychology.* London: Allen & Unwin, 1912.

NOTES

This paper is a condensation of a doctoral thesis (Sperling, 1959). For further details, especially on methodology, and for individual data, the reader is referred to the original thesis. It is a pleasure to acknowledge my gratitude to George A. Miller and Roger N. Shepard whose support made this research possible and to E. B. Newman, J. Schwartzbaum and S. S. Stevens for their many helpful suggestions. Thanks are also due to Jerome S. Bruner for the use of his laboratory and his tachistoscope during his absence in the summer of 1957. This research was carried out under Contract AF 33 (038) 14343 between Harvard University and the Operational Applications Laboratory, Air Force Cambridge Research Center, Air Research Development Command.

[Author] now at Bell Telephone Laboratories, Murray Hill, New Jersey.

1. Some representative examples are: Bridgin (1933), Cattell (1883), Chapman (1930), Dallenbach (1920), Erdmann and Dodge (1898), Glanville and Dallenbach (1929), Külpe (1904), Schumann (1922), Wagner (1918), Whipple (1914), Wilcocks (1925), Woodworth (1938).

2. The experiments referred to are (cf. Sperling, 1959): Külpe (1904), Wilcocks (1925), Chapman (1932), Long, Henneman, and Reid (1953), Long and Lee (1953a), Long and Lee (1953b), Long, Reid, and Garvey (1954), Lawrence and Coles (1954), Adams (1955), Lawrence and Laberge (1956), Broadbent (1957a).

3. Ralph Gerbrands Company, 96 Ronald Road, Arlington 74, Massachusetts.

4. If there are a large number of letters in the stimulus, the probability that these same letters will appear somewhere on the response grid, irrespective of position, becomes very high whether or not S has much information about the stimulus. In the limit, the correspondence approaches 100% provided only that the relative frequency of each letter in the response matches its relative frequency of occurrence in the stimulus pack. If the response is scored for both letter *and* position, then the percent guessing correction is independent of changes in stimulus size.

5. See Sperling (1959) for tables giving the numerical values of all points appearing in this and in all other figures.

The suffix effect (sometimes called the "stimulus suffix effect") is the finding that when an irrelevant spoken item (the "suffix") is appended to a spoken list, memory for the final item on the list is significantly reduced. This occurs even though subjects are told to expect the suffix and even when it is the same item on every trial (usually the word "zero" or "go"). The relationship between the physical form of the list items and the suffix has been shown to be critical: The potency of the suffix is dramatically lessened when the suffix is spoken in a different voice than that of the list, when it comes from a different direction, or when it is not speech but is an environmental sound. This paper describes six experiments examining why it is so difficult to ignore the irrelevant item.

When we hear a new sound in the world, it initially grabs our attention but we quickly begin to ignore it, or adapt to it if it repeats over and over again. This is called habituation, and it is very useful evolutionarily: We have only a limited amount of attention and it is better to focus it on new things in the environment and ignore repeating things if they have not hurt us. Watkins and Sechler were interested in discovering what it would take to make subjects ignore the suffix so that it no longer caused disruption of memory for the final item on a list. If the suffix is merely due to attentional factors, there should be habituation with repeated presentation. However, if it is truly a memory phenomenon, and the suffix actually overwrites the memory trace in memory, we may not see a change in performance with repeated presentation of the suffix.

The task used in the suffix effect experiments is immediate serial recall in which a list of words (or digits in this case) is presented one at a time and the subject is asked to recall the items in the order in which they were presented. In general, this method results in a U-shaped curve with good performance at the beginning of the list ("primacy effect") and good performance at the end of the list ("recency effect") when the items are presented out loud but not when they are presented silently. (This can be contrasted with free recall discussed in Reading 19 on the serial position effect where the subjects can recall the items in any order they choose [hence, "free"]. Using that method, the U-shaped curve appears with both auditory [out loud] and visual [silent] presentation.)

In the suffix effect experiments, a spoken item (usually the same item on every trial) is presented after the list. Usually there is a control condition with either no suffix or a nonspeech irrelevant item (recall that a nonspeech stimulus does not cause a suffix effect). This basic method results in robust suffix effects (Crowder & Morton, 1969) and is the one used in the CogLab demonstration.

In Experiment 1 of the present reading, Watkins and Sechler were attempting to discover whether the suffix caused less and less disruption over the course of the experiment. The question they were asking was whether subjects can habituate to the suffix. They found that there was a decrease in the amount of disruption with repeated presentation of the suffix, but only a very small amount. In the second and third experiments Watkins and Sechler played the suffix after every list item. Still, they found no great reduction in the effectiveness of the suffix. So, in Experiments 4–6 they decided to do their best to get the subjects to habituate to the suffix by presenting it in an unbroken stream throughout the presentation and recall of the list. The authors were finally able to obtain an attenuation of the suffix effect, but performance on the suffix trials never reached that of the no suffix trials.

This paper illustrates a thorough and systematic exploration of an effect and the robustness of the suffix effect. It is difficult to ignore even when it is presented continuously throughout an experiment. The best explanation of the underlying cause of the suffix effect is that when the suffix is perceptually grouped with the list items, it functionally increases the list length. So, rather than trying to recall a 9-item list, you are in effect recalling a 10-item list (Neath & Surprenant, 2003).

Although this seems to be a purely laboratory result, there is a real-world application: in an interaction between a directory assistance operator and a telephone customer. As predicted by the laboratory experiments, when the telephone numbers were followed by the phrase "Have a nice day," there were reliable reductions in the subjects' ability to recall the telephone number accurately (Schilling & Weaver, 1983).

REFERENCES

Crowder, R. G., & Morton, J. (1969). Precategorical acoustic storage (PAS). *Perception & Psychophysics. 5*, 365–373.

Neath, I., & Surprenant, A. M. (2003). *Human memory,* 2nd ed. Belmont, CA: Wadsworth.

Schilling, R. F., & Weaver, G. E. (1983). Effect of extraneous verbal information on memory for telephone numbers. *Journal of Applied Psychology, 68,* 559–564.

QUESTIONS

1. Describe the serial recall task used in these experiments.
2. Describe the basic suffix effect.
3. What are the two methods used to calculate the size of the suffix effect?
4. What was the effect of practice over successive lists in the size of the suffix effect (Experiment 1)?
5. What was the effect of continuous presentation of the suffix throughout the presentation and recall periods?

Adapting to an Irrelevant Item in an Immediate Recall Task

Michael J. Watkins and Elizabeth S. Sechler

Rice University

ABSTRACT

Recall of the last one or two items of a spoken list is impaired when the list is followed by a nominally irrelevant item. At issue here was whether this suffix effect is reduced with repeated exposure to the irrelevant item. The effect was found to decline over successive blocks of trials, but only slightly (Experiment 1). No decisive evidence for adaptation to the irrelevant item was found when it was spoken after each of the list items rather than after the last one only (Experiments 2 and 3). The strongest evidence for adaptation was obtained when the irrelevant item was repeated in an unbroken stream that extended through the presentations and recall periods of successive lists: The recency effect and the level of recall at the last position within a list were greater under these conditions than when the irrelevant item was presented only once after each list (Experiments 4, 5, and 6).

Postbehaviorist conceptions of memory tend to neglect the stimulus as a source of control over the remembering process. For perceivable stimuli, our powers of attention and organization and rehearsal are seen as overshadowing any effects of the physical aspects of the stimuli. We are therefore considered to have more or less complete control over what is and what is not remembered.

As has been argued elsewhere (M. J. Watkins, 1989), there are problems with this perspective. A particularly striking problem arises in experimental procedures in which a to-be-recalled list of spoken items is followed by a spoken item that is nominally irrelevant to the subjects' task: The subjects appear unable to ignore this item, for it sharply reduces the probability of recall for the last one or two items of the to-be-recalled list (Crowder & Morton, 1969). Indeed, some studies have found that the suffix item impairs recall of the preceding items just about as much as does an additional to-be-remembered item (Crowder, 1967, Experiment 3; Dallett, 1965). To be sure, the effect of the suffix item is lessened if it occurs in a voice (Greenberg & Engle, 1983; Morton, Crowder, & Prussin, 1971, Experiments 14 and 15, O. C. Watkins & M. J. Watkins, 1980, Experiment 3) or comes from a direction (Morton et al., 1971, Experiments 2, 7, and 8) that is different from that of the to-be-remembered list items, but by and large it is remarkably robust.

Why should we have so much trouble ignoring a suffix item when we are capable of functioning in a world that bombards us with a vast array of irrelevant stimuli? The purpose of this article is to explore the possibility of resolving this paradox by invoking the concept of adaptation—by appealing to the commonplace that even if a stimulus commands our attention on initial exposure, it may relinquish its hold as exposure increases. The ticking of a clock or the hum of a fan engages us initially, but soon frees us to concentrate on something else. In a more formal vein, research shows that stimuli having nominally irrelevant features tend to be classified faster if the irrelevant features are exposed beforehand (Lorch, Anderson, & Well, 1984). Adaptation to irrelevant information might similarly be inferred from findings that performance on the Stroop task improves with practice (Reisberg, Baron, & Kemler, 1980; Stroop, 1935). Particularly relevant to the present purpose is evidence that adaptation can occur to irrelevant spoken infor-

SOURCE: From Watkins, M. J., & Sechler, E. S. (1989). Adapting to an irrelevant item in an immediate recall task. *Memory & Cognition, 17,* 682–692. Reprinted by permission of Psychonomic Society, Inc.

mation: The ability to solve arithmetic problems presented in a male voice while nominally irrelevant information is heard in a female voice has been found to be enhanced by prior exposure to the female voice (Waters, McDonald, & Koresko, 1977).

In the present study we sought evidence for adaptation to the suffix item. In each of six experiments we inquired whether exposure to the suffix item would diminish its effect. The idea behind Experiment 1 was simply to see whether the magnitude of the suffix effect would decrease over the course of a sequence of lists. In Experiments 2 and 3 we examined the effect of presenting the suffix item not only in its regular suffix position at the end of the list, but after each list item. In Experiments 4, 5, and 6 we further intensified exposure to the suffix item by presenting it throughout both list presentations and the recall intervals between the lists.

THE SUFFIX EFFECT OVER THE COURSE OF A SEQUENCE OF LISTS

Experiment 1

If adaptation can occur to a suffix item, then the suffix effect might be expected to diminish over the successive list presentations of a typical testing session; however, evidence on this point is sparse and inconclusive. Crowder (1969) found no significant evidence for a decline in the suffix effect even after extensive practice, whereas Balota and Engle (1981) found that practice reduced the effect of a suffix item on preterminal items (specifically, items presented in Positions 3–6 of a 7-item list) but not on the last item. Penney (1985, Experiment 1), by contrast, found that practice reduced the effect of the suffix at the last position, although she failed to replicate this result in a second experiment (her Experiment 2); for preterminal positions, she found an influence of practice on the suffix effect only in the form of higher order interactions.

The present experiment was intended to shed a little more light on this confusing situation. The subjects were required to reproduce 9-digit lists. They were tested on both a sequence of suffix lists and a control sequence of no-suffix lists, the order of these sequences being counterbalanced. At issue was whether recall of the last one or two digits of the lists would gain more over the course of the suffix sequence than over the course of the control sequence.

Method

Stimulus lists. The stimulus lists consisted of the digits 1 through 9 in an order that was random within the constraint that consecutive digits (e.g., 6, 7) not occupy adjacent list positions either in forward (6, 7) or in backward (7, 6) order. The suffix item was "zero." In all, there were 56 such lists, 54 for the experiment proper and 2 for practice. The lists were presented in a synthetic male voice (the "bass" voice of "Smoothtalker," distributed by First Byte, Inc.) on an Apple Macintosh 512 microcomputer. The digits occurred at 1-sec onset-to-onset intervals with, in the case of the suffix condition, the zero occurring 1 sec after the onset of the last to-beremembered digit.

Design. Aside from the practice lists, 27 lists were presented in the control condition and 27 in the suffix condition. Half of the subjects received the control lists before the suffix lists, and half received the suffix lists before the control lists. Within each of these groups of subjects, the ordering of the individual lists was counterbalanced across three subgroups of 16 subjects according to a Latin square so that each block of nine lists occurred equally often as the first, second, and third block within each of the two conditions. For the purposes of analysis, there were two withinsubjects factors, namely list condition (no-suffix or suffix) and position within the testing sequence (first, second, or third block within a condition).

Subjects. The subjects were 96 Rice University undergraduates.

Procedure. Some subjects were tested individually, others in small groups. To familiarize the subjects with the synthetic speech used to present the lists, we first required them simply to copy four lists while they were being presented. These lists consisted of random permutations of the digits 0 through 9, and they were presented at a rate of one digit every second. Two subjects each made one error on the first of these lists, but otherwise the responses were correct.

The experiment itself involved the presentation of a long sequence of digit lists, with the lists of either the first or second half of the sequence being followed by a nominally irrelevant zero. Successive lists were separated by a 21-sec recall interval, after 15 sec of which the experimenter signaled the upcoming list by saying "Ready." The subjects wrote their responses on sheets that had been ruled with rows of nine short lines. They were required to record the digits in presentation order, beginning with the first digit in the leftmost space and ending with the last digit in the rightmost space; when they could not recall a digit, they were to respond with a dash. Responding was monitored to ensure compliance with the instructions. Each half of the sequence was preceded by a control or suffix practice list, as appropriate, and by an invitation for questions.

Results and Discussion

Before presenting the results of this experiment we need to comment on the way in which, for the entire series of experiments, the effect the suffix item had on recall of the last few list items was operationalized for the purpose of data analysis. To capture recency recall we used two measures, the first pertaining to the trend in recall across the last part of the serial position curve and the second to level of recall at just the last serial position.

For the first, or recency-trend, measure, we defined the effect of the suffix item as the magnitude of the recency trend in the no-suffix control condition minus the magnitude of the recency trend in the suffix (or other irrelevant-item) condition. All of the experiments we report here involved nine-item lists, and for this list length the results of published studies more often than not show the low point of the serial position curve for the no-suffix control condition to be at the seventh position (e.g., Crowder, 1967, Experiment 3; Crowder & Morton, 1969, Experiment 2; Morton et al., 1971, Experiments 3, 13, and 14; Routh & Frosdick, 1978, Experiment 5; Salame & Baddeley, 1982, Experiments 3, 4, and 5). Consequently, we defined the magnitude of the recency trend as the proportion of items recalled at the ninth serial position minus the proportion recalled at the seventh position.

Our second measure was simply the probability of recall at the ninth position of the no-suffix condition minus the corresponding probability for the suffix (or other irrelevant-item) condition. This last-position measure complements the recency-trend measure in two important respects. First, it is in keeping with the growing conviction (e.g., Baddeley & Hull, 1979; Balota & Engle, 1981; Morton, Marcus, & Ottley, 1981; Penney, 1985) that the effect of the suffix item on the last position is of particular theoretical significance. Second, it deals with absolute levels of performance rather than with position-to-position differences in levels of performance. The inferential analyses based on these two measures should be interpreted in the context of the serial position functions, which are displayed graphically for each experiment; the numerical values of the two measures are given in the Appendix.

The results of the first experiment are summarized in Figure 13.1. Each panel refers to a block of lists within the no-suffix and suffix conditions, and it shows for these conditions the mean proportion of items recalled at each serial position. Clearly, there was a marked suffix effect for all three list blocks, but it is not so clear whether the suffix effect declined from the first list block to the third.

An analysis of the recency-trend data showed no reliable change across list blocks. It revealed a difference between conditions $[F(1,95) = 150.49, MS_e = .063, p < .001]$, indicating the presence of a suffix effect, but no difference among blocks $[F(2,190) = 0.54, MS_e = .016]$. Most importantly, it showed no reliable interaction between condition and block $[F(2,190) = 0.50, MS_e = .036]$.

Analyses based on the last-position measure were a bit more supportive of the adaptation hypothesis. Thus, whereas in the control condition the proportion of items recalled at the last position remained fairly constant across blocks, in the suffix condition it increased (see Appendix). An analysis of variance indicated reliable effects of condition $[F(1,95) = 401.99, MS_e = .057, p < .001]$ and block $[F(2,190) = 4.64, MS_e = .046, p < .02]$, and, importantly, a reliable interaction between condition and block $[F(2,190) - 7.57, MS_e = .018, p < .001]$. This interaction was substantially accounted for by a difference between the

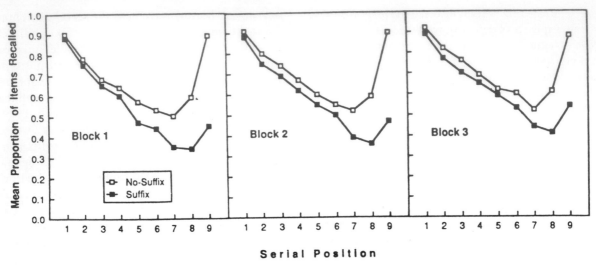

FIGURE 13.1   Mean proportion of items recalled in correct position as a function of serial position, suffix condition, and list block (Experiment 1).

conditions in the linear component of trend across blocks [$t(95) = 3.47$, $p < .001$].[1] Of course, even in the third block, there remained an appreciable and statistically significant advantage for the no-suffix condition [$t(95) = 13.79$, $p < .001$].

The evidence this experiment provides for the notion that one can adapt to the suffix item is at best modest. The recency-trend measure provided no evidence at all for adaptation: [I]ncreasing exposure to the suffix item resulted in no significant gain in recency trend in the suffix condition over that which occurred in the no-suffix condition. The last-position measure did show that performance in the suffix condition gained on that in the no-suffix condition across successive blocks of lists. However, the gain was rather small, and it conflicted with previous findings (Balota & Engle, 1981; Penney, 1985, Experiment 2). Clearly, a convincing demonstration of adaptation to the suffix items requires a different approach.

THROUGH-LIST PRESENTATION OF THE NOMINALLY IRRELEVANT ITEM

Perhaps Experiment 1 failed to produce more impressive evidence for adaptation because the presentation schedule of the nominally irrelevant item was unsuitable. The irrelevant item occurred only once with each list presentation, for a rate of one occurrence approximately every 30 sec. Adaptation to a clock that ticked at such a rate might also be difficult. In the following two experiments the irrelevant item was presented not just in the regular suffix position, but after each item of the list. Of interest was whether this more intensive exposure schedule would enhance recency recall.

We should note that this procedure is formally similar to one known as the through-list (or continual) distractor procedure, in which subjects study a list of words for recall and engage in a distractor task after the presentation of each word (or each pair of words). The distractor task typically involves counting backward by threes for several seconds. It has long been known that if given after only the last item of the list, this task has the effect of virtually eliminating the recency effect (Glanzer & Cunitz, 1966; Postman & Phillips, 1965). When, however, it is given throughout list presentation as well as at the end of the list, the recency effect reemerges (Bjork & Whitten, 1974; Tzeng, 1973). In other words, the damaging effect of postlist distractor activity on recall of the last few items can be avoided, or at least sharply attenuated, by requiring that the distractor activity also be performed throughout list presentation. Such a procedure differs from the procedure of the following two experiments in its explicit requirement that the interpolated material be attended to. Nevertheless, the data it generates are certainly consistent with the notion of adaptation to distractor material.

A search of the literature turned up two experiments specifically relevant to the question of whether presentation of a to-be-ignored item throughout the list as well as immediately following the list helps bring back the recency effect. The findings from these two experiments are somewhat inconsistent. In one, reported by Hitch (1975, Experiment 2), subjects were tested on serial recall of digit lists in three conditions pertinent to the present purposes: a standard suffix condition, a no-suffix control condition, and a through-list condition in which the item serving as the suffix was presented after each of the preterminal list items as well as in the regular suffix position. The critical comparison, namely that between the through-list and standard suffix conditions, was not formally made by Hitch, but it can be made in a qualitative way by superimposing serial position functions from two of the panels of his Figure 13.2. As near as can be discerned, neither the recency-trend nor the last-position recall differed to any marked extent between the two conditions. On the other hand, the results of an experiment briefly reported by Kahneman and Henik (1981, Experiment 9) suggest that through-list presentation of a nominally irrelevant item may have enhanced last-position recall. The experiment included the same three conditions used in the Hitch experiment, although this time the irrelevant item was heard from a different speaker from the one used for the to-be-remembered items. Kahneman and Henik reported recall performance only for the last position, and although they reported no statistical analysis, the proportion of items recalled at this position was higher in the through-list suffix condition (.94) than in the standard suffix condition (.87).

More complete evidence on the effect of through-list exposure to the irrelevant item was sought in the following two experiments.

Experiment 2

In essence, subjects engaged in a serial recall task under each of three conditions: a no-suffix control condition, in which only to-be-remembered digits were presented; a standard suffix condition, in which a nominally irrelevant zero was presented after just the last to-be-remembered digit; and a through-list condition, in which the irrelevant zero was presented after each of the to-be-remembered digits. The question of interest was whether recall of the last one or two digits would be enhanced by presenting the irrelevant item after each digit rather than just the last one.

Method

Stimulus lists. The stimulus lists consisted of the digits 1 through 9 arranged in the quasi-random order described under Experiment 1. A total of 51 lists were prepared, 45 for the experiment proper and 6 for practice.

The lists were recorded on audio tape in a female voice, with a separate recording being made for each of the three subject groups used to counterbalance order and condition. For all conditions the to-be-remembered digits occurred at a rate of one per second. For the standard suffix condition the onset of the irrelevant zero occurred 0.5 sec after the onset of the last digit of each list, and for the through-list condition it occurred 0.5 sec after the onset of each digit, including the last.

Design. For the experiment proper, all subjects were presented with the same sequence of 45 to-be-remembered lists. The condition was changed after 15 lists and then again after another 15 lists, so that the same number of lists were recalled under each of the three conditions. The order of the conditions was varied among three equal-sized groups of subjects according to a Latin square, so that across all subjects each set of 15 lists occurred equally often in each condition, and each condition was represented equally often in the beginning, middle, and end portions of the testing sequence.

Subjects. The subjects were 21 Rice University undergraduates.

Procedure. The subjects were tested in small groups. They were presented with a long sequence of digit lists played on a tape recorder, and were told to ignore all presentations of the item zero and to concentrate on recalling the digits 1 through 9 in their order of presentation. Details of the recall instructions were as in Experiment 1. The list sequence was blocked by condition and, prior to each block, the condition of the upcoming lists was described and two practice lists were presented.

Results and Discussion

The results are summarized in Figure 13.2. A comparison of the standard suffix and no-suffix control curves shows a typical suffix effect, with level of performance being lower in the standard suffix condition, especially near the end of the list. The no-suffix control condition showed a reliable advantage with both the recency-trend measure [$t(20) = 4.06$, $p < .001$] and the last-position measure [$t(20) = 8.76$, $p < .001$], these measures being defined as in Experiment 1.

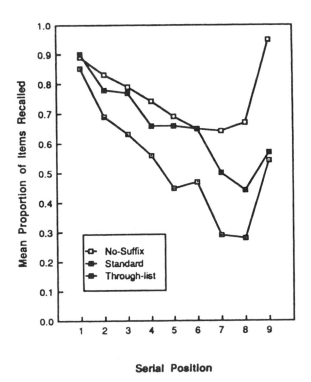

FIGURE 13.2   Mean proportion of items recalled in correct position as a function of serial position and suffix condition (Experiment 2).

Of more concern here is how performance in the through-list condition fitted into the picture. As Figure 13.2 makes plain, performance in this condition was not only lower than in the no-suffix control condition, but also lower than in the standard suffix condition. The impairment relative to the standard suffix condition was not evenly distributed across the serial positions, for the recency trend was sharper in the through-list condition [$t(20) = 4.07$, $p < .01$]. Indeed, the recency trend was only slightly and not reliably smaller in the through-list condition than in the no-suffix control condition [$t(20) = .92$]. Nevertheless, absolute level of recall in the through-list condition was no higher than in the standard suffix condition even at the last serial position; in fact, it was slightly—though not reliably [$t(20) = .74$, $p > .10$]—lower. Of course, last-position recall was reliably lower in the through-list condition than in the no-suffix control condition [$t(20) = 10.54$, $p < .001$].

It would appear, then, that presenting the irrelevant item after each list item rather than after only the last one enhances the recency trend but does not give rise to a greater absolute level of recency recall.

Experiment 3

In the preceding experiment we assumed that the nominally irrelevant item was the same for the through-list condition as for the standard suffix condition. Certainly, it was zero in both cases, but it is conceivable that its repeated presentation in the through-list condition resulted in its utterance in the critical suffix position being subtly different from its utterance in the standard suffix condition. The procedure was replicated in the present experiment in a way that precluded the possibility of such a confound: The stimuli were all presented in synthetic speech, thereby ensuring that all utterances of the irrelevant item were physically identical.

Method

The method was the same as that of Experiment 2 with the exception that the stimuli, both the to-be-remembered list items and the nominally irrelevant zero, were presented in synthetic speech. The details of the stimuli and their recording are as described in Experiment 1.

The subjects were 18 Rice University undergraduates.

Results and Discussion

The data are summarized in Figure 13.3. Note that overall level of recall was somewhat lower than in the previous experiment. Presumably, this reduction was the result of switching from natural to synthetic speech, for although each item was clear enough to be identified, synthetically presented lists do seem to require more attention.

In other respects, the results closely resemble those of Experiment 2. There was a regular suffix effect, with level of recall toward the end of the list being sharply lower in the standard suffix condition than in the no-suffix control condition: Statistical analyses

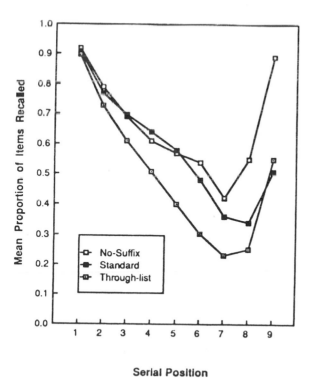

FIGURE 13.3   Mean proportion of items recalled in correct position as a function of serial position and suffix condition (Experiment 3).

confirmed the advantage of the no-suffix control condition for both the recency trend measure [$t(17) = 5.03$, $p < .001$] and the last-position measure [$t(17) = 7.75$, $p < .001$].

Performance in the through-list condition revealed a recency trend that was more pronounced than in the standard suffix condition [$t(17) = 2.96$, $p < .01$], although less pronounced than in the no-suffix control condition [$t(17) = 2.65$, $p < .02$]. Even by the last position, however, probability of recall in the through-list condition was only trivially, and certainly not reliably [$t(17) = .63$, $p > .10$], higher than in the standard suffix condition, and it was, of course, substantially lower than in the no-suffix control condition [$t(17) = 7.75$, $p < .001$].

In both this experiment and the previous one, presenting an irrelevant item after every list item proved to be less detrimental to the recency trend than did presenting it after only the last item. On the other hand, it appreciably impaired overall level of recall, so that probability of recall was no greater than in the standard suffix condition even at the last position. Consequently, the sharper recency effect in the through-list condition could be attributed just as readily to an impairment in recall for items prior to the last one as to adaptation to the suffix item. The case for adaptation to an irrelevant item would clearly be stronger if the most intensive schedule of exposure to the irrelevant item resulted in not only a more pronounced recency trend but also a higher absolute level of recency recall. It was in search of such a result that we conducted the remaining three experiments.

CONTINUOUS PRESENTATION OF THE NOMINALLY IRRELEVANT ITEM

In Experiment 1, the nominally irrelevant item was presented only once every 30 sec or so. In Experiments 2 and 3, it occurred more frequently, but in all likelihood this presentation schedule was still not as conducive to adaptation as it might be: The clock ticked more quickly, but it kept stopping. In the remaining three experiments, the clock was made to run at the same comparatively fast rate but without stopping. In other words, a regular and unbroken sequence of zeros extended through both the presentation and recall intervals of successive lists, beginning before the first item of the first list and ending at the conclusion of the recall period of the last list. Recall in this condition was compared with that in both a no-suffix condition and a standard suffix condition.

In addition to these three conditions, a triple suffix condition was included. This condition was like the standard suffix condition except that the suffix item was presented three times in succession rather than just once. Its inclusion was prompted by findings that a triple suffix impairs the recency effect less than does a conventional single suffix (Crowder, 1978, Experiments 1 and 1a; Morton, 1976, Experiments 3 and 4). Thus, we added the triple suffix condition to check that whatever enhancement in recency recall occurred with the continuous presentation procedure was not attributable solely to the first two additional presentations of the suffix item at the beginning of the recall period.

Experiment 4

In the previous three experiments, the nominally irrelevant item, whether presented in the suffix position or among the list items, was always in the same voice as the list items. This was not the case in the present experiment: [A]ll list items were presented in a female voice and all presentations of the nominally irrelevant zero were in a male voice. Because such physical characteristics as voice quality can be used in directing attention (Broadbent, 1952; Treisman, 1964), we had a hunch—probably ill-founded, as it turned out—that a physical distinction between the suffix item and the list items would enhance adaptation.

Method

Stimulus lists.   The stimulus lists were as in the previous experiments. This time, however, there were four sets of 21 lists, with the first list of each set being used for practice. For each of the 84 lists, four versions (no-suffix control, standard suffix, triple suffix, and continuous presentation) were prepared in such a way that the same physical recording of each list was used for each version, and all presentations of the zero were from the same utterance. This was accomplished with the aid of a Tascam Ministudio cassette recorder, a de-

vice that allows merging of independently recorded tracks. The to-be-remembered digits occurred at a rate of one every second. Successive lists were separated by a recall interval of 15 sec, with the warning "Ready" being spoken 10 sec into the interval. Hence the onset of each of the list items and of the warning signal were all separated from one another by multiples of 1 sec. Any given presentation of the zero, whether located within or between list presentations, was displaced from any given list item or from the warning signal by $(n + 0.5)$ sec. In particular, for the standard suffix condition the zero began 0.5 sec after the onset of the last list item; for the triple suffix condition it was added three times at 1-sec intervals, with the first beginning 0.5 sec after the onset of the last list item; and for the continuous presentation condition it occurred at a 1-sec rate in an uninterrupted sequence that began 9.5 sec before the first item of the first list and continued in exact alternation with the to-be-remembered items of each list until the end of the recall interval of the last list.

Design.   All subjects heard the same sequence of 84 lists, with each successive block of 21 lists occurring in a different condition. The assignment of blocks to conditions was varied among four equal-sized groups of subjects according to a Latin square, so that each list occurred equally often in each condition and each condition occurred equally often in each quarter of the testing sequence.

Subjects.   The subjects were 20 Rice University undergraduates.

Procedure.   Some subjects were tested in small groups, others by themselves. The instructions and general testing procedures were the same as in the previous experiments, with the subjects being told to ignore any zeros and to recall the list items in their presentation order.

Results and Discussion

The results of main concern, namely those of the no-suffix control condition, the standard suffix condition, and the continuous presentation condition, are summarized in Figure 13.4. Those for the triple suffix

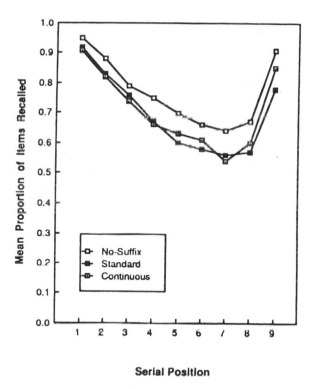

FIGURE 13.4 Mean proportion of items recalled in correct position as a function of serial position and suffix condition (Experiment 4).

condition turned out to be unimportant for the present purposes, and their summary will be deferred until after consideration of the results of the other conditions.

It is clear from Figure 13.4 that overall level of recall is rather high. Also, a comparison of the no-suffix control condition and the standard suffix condition reveals little by way of a regular suffix effect. To be sure, level of recall was lower in the standard suffix condition, and reliably so at the final list position $[t(19) = 3.91, p < .001]$. The distribution of the effect of the suffix across list positions was surprisingly uniform, however, and the recency trend was only slightly, and not reliably, smaller in the standard suffix condition than in the no-suffix control condition $[t(19) = 1.14, p > .10]$.

Of more interest is the comparison between the results of the standard suffix condition and those of the continuous presentation condition. In the first

place, overall level of recall in the continuous presentation condition (.71) was no lower than that in the standard suffix condition (.69). Thus, compared to recall in the no-suffix control condition (.77), recall was appreciably reduced by a single utterance of the irrelevant item, but adding 23 more utterances of the same item resulted in no further reduction. Remember, too, that in Experiments 2 and 3, overall level of recall was appreciably lower in the through-list condition than in the standard suffix condition. That there was no comparable impairment in the present experiment is consistent with the notion that repeating the irrelevant item throughout the recall interval as well as throughout list presentation serves to foster adaptation.

Also consistent with the notion of adaptation to the irrelevant item, the recency trend (defined as in Experiment 1) was greater in the continuous presentation condition than in the standard suffix condition. Given the uncharacteristically sharp recency trend in the standard suffix condition, however, this trend advantage was small and not statistically significant $[t(19) = 1.70, p < .05]$. Firmer support for the adaptation hypothesis was obtained with the last-position measure, by which the continuous presentation condition held a significant advantage over the standard suffix condition $[t(19) = 2.19, p = .03]$, even though it fared less well than the no-suffix control condition $[t(19) = 2.44, p = .02]$.

Performance in the triple suffix condition was virtually indistinguishable from performance in the standard suffix condition. The mean overall level of recall was .71 in the former condition and .70 in the latter. For list positions 1 through 9, the mean proportions of items recalled in the triple suffix condition were .94, .84, .80, .69, .64, .60, .55, .58, and .78, respectively, and the corresponding means for the standard suffix conditions were .92, .83, .76, .67, .60, .57, .56, .56, and .78. Both the recency trend measure and the last-position measure showed virtually no difference between the two conditions. Thus, as has happened in previous research (O. C. Watkins & M. J. Watkins, 1982), we failed to replicate findings of a reduction in the suffix effect with the triple suffix procedure. In any event, the higher level of last-position recall obtained with the continuous presentation procedure was clearly not a consequence merely of the second and third postlist utterances of the irrelevant item.

Experiment 5

The results of Experiment 4 provide stronger evidence for the adaptation hypothesis than do those of the first three experiments. The purpose of the present experiment was to see whether even stronger evidence could be obtained by lowering the level of performance in the critical standard suffix and continuous presentation conditions. To this end, we replicated the procedure of Experiment 4 with the exception that the zero was presented in the same voice as the list items. By eliminating voice as a feature for discriminating the list items, the magnitude of the regular suffix effect should be increased (e.g., Morton et al., 1971, Experiments 14 and 15) and, perhaps as a result, any effects of adaptation would be more apparent.

Method

The method was identical to that of Experiment 4, except for the manner in which the stimuli were recorded for presentation. The lists were as before, but this time the list items (1 through 9) and the irrelevant item (zero) were uttered in the same male voice. Each utterance lasted no longer than 450 msec and was digitized and stored in a separate file on an Apple Macintosh 512 microcomputer; the digitizing apparatus and software were distributed by MacNifty (see Gibson, 1987, for a description). The timing of the item and list presentations was as in Experiment 4. Four versions of each list, one for each condition, were compiled and transferred to audio cassette tape. A separate tape was made for each of the four subject groups.

The subjects were 20 Rice University undergraduates.

Results and Discussion

The main results are summarized in Figure 13.5. The overall level of recall was not as high as it was in Experiment 4. Also, a comparison of the no-suffix control condition and the standard suffix condition shows a somewhat more typical suffix effect in that, although it appeared to extend well back into the list,

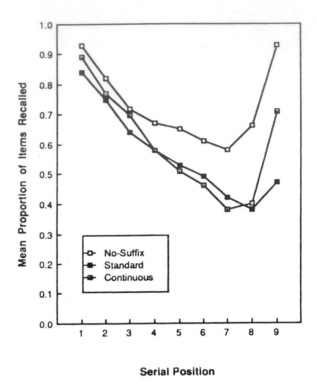

FIGURE 13.5   Mean proportion of items recalled in correct position as a function of serial position and suffix condition (Experiment 5).

the effect was most pronounced toward the end of the list. The effect was indicated by both the recency-trend measure [$t(19) = 4.79$, $p < .001$] and the last-position measure [$t(19) = 7.77$, $p < .001$].

Consider now the results for the continuous presentation condition. The recency trend in this condition was only trivially, and not reliably, smaller than in the no-suffix control condition [$t(19) = .56$, $p > .10$], and was greater than in the standard suffix condition [$t(19) = 5.13$, $p < .001$]. Moreover, probability of last-item recall in the continuous presentation condition was greater than in the standard suffix condition [$t(19) = 3.71$, $p < .001$], even though it was lower than in the no-suffix control condition [$t(19) = 5.39$, $p < .001$]. The results for both measures of recency recall are therefore in accord with the notion that the irrelevant item is subject to adaptation.

Finally, the results for the triple suffix condition were again similar to those for the standard suffix condition. The mean level of overall recall for the triple suffix was .61, and for the single suffix it was .57; the difference was not reliable [$t(19) = 1.09, p > .10$]. The recall probabilities for Positions 1 through 9 were .91, .80, .70, .62, .57, .55, .45, .41, and .50 for the triple suffix condition, and .84, .75, .64, .58, .53, .49, .42, .38, and .47 for the standard suffix condition. Neither the recency-trend measure nor the last-position measure showed a reliable difference between these conditions [$ts(19) = .05$ and .50, respectively, $p > .10$ in both cases]. Moreover, the triple suffix condition yielded a recency trend that was smaller than in either the continuous presentation condition or the no-suffix control condition [$ts(19) = 4.38$ and 4.90, respectively, $p < .001$ in both cases], and the level of last-position recall was lower than in either of the latter conditions [$t(19) = 3.50, p < .01$, and $t(19) = 7.58, p < .001$, respectively].

Experiment 6

In the concluding experiment of the series we sought to check whether the findings of Experiments 4 and 5 would hold up with a between-subjects design. In light of the findings of the first experiment, we had assumed in designing Experiments 2 through 5 that performance in a given condition would change only modestly over the course of the experimental session. We therefore thought a within-subjects design would increase our chances of discerning differences between conditions. It is possible, however, that there was transfer, even differential transfer, between conditions in the previous experiments. The between-subjects design of the present experiment precludes the possibility of such confounds.

A more particular question addressed in this experiment was whether the adaptation observed in the continuous presentation condition would persist beyond the point at which the stream of zeros ceased. In other words, we wanted to know whether adaptation would carry over from the continuous suffix condition to a standard suffix condition given immediately afterward. To the extent that our measures of recency recall in such a condition resemble those for the con-

tinuous presentation condition, adaptation could be said to persist beyond the duration of the continuous presentation condition; to the extent that these measures resemble those obtained for subjects in the standard suffix group, which had not experienced continuous presentation of the suffix, adaptation could be said to be confined to the duration of the continuous presentation condition.

Method

The subjects were 60 Rice University undergraduates. Some were tested 2 or 3 at a time, others individually. They were assigned to three groups in a way that was random within the constraints that each group include 20 subjects and that those tested be assigned to the same group. The groups may be referred to as the control, or no-suffix, group; the standard suffix group; and the continuous presentation/standard suffix group. Subjects in the no-suffix and standard suffix groups each received one set of 21 lists, the first of which was considered a practice list. Those in the continuous presentation/standard suffix group received two sets of 21 lists, one of which was used in the continuous presentation condition and the other in the standard suffix condition.

The lists were random permutations of the digits 1 to 9, spoken at the rate of one every second, exactly as in the previous five experiments. In fact, the recordings of the two sets of lists were taken directly from those used in Experiment 5. Within both the no-suffix group and the standard group, half of the subjects received one set and half received the other set. Within the continuous presentation/standard suffix group, half of the subjects received one set of lists in the continuous presentation condition and the other set in the standard suffix condition; for the other half of the subjects, these sets were reversed. Thus, the data for each of the four conditions (no-suffix, standard suffix, continuous presentation, and standard suffix after continuous presentation) were based on one set of 20 lists presented to 10 subjects and another set of 20 lists presented to 10 other subjects. We should note that we did not feel justified in presenting more than 20 lists (plus 1 practice list) in each condition because the continuous presentation condition is extraordinarily stressful.

Results

The results are summarized in Figure 13.6. The first point to note is that, relative to the no-suffix control condition, the standard suffix procedure reduced recall for the last few serial positions. This suffix effect was shown to be statistically reliable with each of our measures of recency recall [for the recency-trend measure, $t(38) = 4.30$, $p < .001$; for the last-position measure, $t(38) = 7.90$, $p < .001$].

More importantly, we replicated the findings of the previous two experiments of adaptation to the suffix item. Thus, both measures showed recency recall to be more pronounced in the continuous presentation condition than in the standard suffix condition [for the recency-trend measure, $t(38) = 6.24$, $p < .001$; for the last-position measure, $t(38) = 3.51$, $p = .001$]. Compared to the no-suffix control condition, the continuous presentation condition showed a trivially stronger recency effect [$t(38) = 0.86$, $p > .10$], but a lower level of recall at the final position [$t(38) = 3.57$, $p < .001$]. Clearly, the evidence obtained in Experiments 4 and 5 for adaptation to the suffix item was not an artifact of the within-subjects design.

We consider now whether the adaptation shown in the continuous presentation condition was critically dependent on the continuous stream of suffix items having occurred during the presentation of the to-be-remembered lists, or whether it would also have arisen if the continuous stream had been presented immediately beforehand. The question turns on whether the recency recall in the suffix condition that was given directly following the continuous presentation condition more closely resembles recency recall in the standard suffix condition than recency recall in the continuous presentation condition. As is evident from Figure 13.6, it closely resembled recency recall in the standard suffix condition. The recency trend was very slightly more pronounced and the level of recall at the last position was slightly higher following continuous presentation of the suffix item, but by neither measure was the difference statistically significant [$ts(38) = 0.31$ and 0.82, respectively, $p > .10$ in both cases]. On the other hand, within-subject comparisons showed that recency was significantly less pronounced in the suffix condition following the continuous presentation condition than in the continuous presentation condition itself [for the

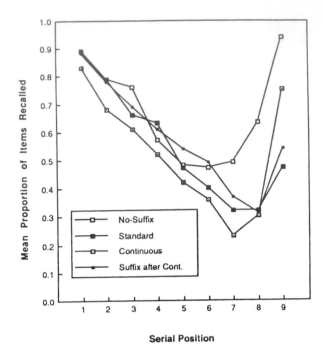

Figure 13.6 Mean proportion of items recalled in correct position as a function of serial position and suffix condition (Experiment 6).

recency-trend measure, $t(19) = 4.92$, $p < .001$; for the last-position measure, $t(19) = 4.94$, $p < .001$]. This experiment therefore provides no evidence that the adaptation caused by the continuous stream of suffix-item presentations persists once the stream stops.

Finally, we should mention that level of recall in the prerecency positions (i.e., through the first seven serial positions) was somewhat lower in the continuous presentation condition than in the other conditions. We cannot draw firm conclusions about this finding because the inferential analyses were inconclusive. In particular, prerecency recall in the continuous presentation condition was not reliably different from that in the standard suffix condition [$t(38) = 1.20$, $p = .24$]. It was reliably different from that in the suffix condition following the continuous presentation condition [$t(19) = 3.06$, $p < .01$], but this result could be due merely to improvement with practice rather than to the suspension of the continuous presentation schedule. In any event, whatever impairment in prerecency recall occurs in the continuous presentation condition throws into bolder relief the superiority of this condition over the standard suffix condition in last-position recall.

Taken together, the results of Experiments 4–6 show comparatively clear evidence of adaptation to a nominally irrelevant item. Specifically, they show that when lists of verbal items are read aloud for serial recall, an irrelevant item tends to be more detrimental to the recall of the recency portions of the lists when uttered once immediately after each list presentation than when repeated in an unbroken stream extending through the list presentations and the recall intervals between them. This result holds whether recency recall is indexed by the trend in recall over the last three positions within a list or by level of recall at only the last position. By keeping the clock ticking, as it were, we seem to have achieved partial adaptation to the suffix item.

GENERAL DISCUSSION

The experiments reported here lend some support to the notion that the detrimental effect that a nominally irrelevant suffix item has on the recall of the last one or two items of a to-be-remembered list can be attenuated with repeated exposure to the irrelevant item. Experiment 1 showed a decline in the suffix effect across the course of a sequence of lists. Although slight, the decline took the form of an increment in recall in the suffix condition rather than a decrement in recall in the control condition, which is consistent with the hypothesis that subjects adapted to some degree to the suffix item. In Experiments 2 and 3 the irrelevant item was presented after each list item, rather than after just the last one. Compared with the standard suffix condition, this through-list condition yielded a stronger recency trend, although overall level of recall was depressed and absolute level of recall was nowhere higher than in the standard suffix condition. In the remaining three experiments we pursued the strategy of massing the suffix presentations a step further by presenting the irrelevant item in a steady stream that continued uninterrupted throughout the presentation and test phases alike. The result was a noticeably enhanced recency trend and a higher probability of recall for the last item within a list.

From some perspectives, the results of our experiments are surprising. For one thing, reducing the detrimental effect of an irrelevant item by intensifying its schedule of presentation is in some sense paradoxical. Also, previous research has clearly shown the detrimental effect of an irrelevant item presented in the suffix position to be robust and not easily modified. And in contrast to previous exceptions to this rule, the attenuation of the effect found in the present experiments was not the result of a physical distinction between the suffix item and the list items.

From another perspective, our evidence for adaptation is unsurprising. If a stimulus occurs over and over in regular and rapid succession, then any given occurrence carries minimal information and so, from a functional standpoint, does not justify control of our attention. In the real world beyond the laboratory, not only are we able to ignore repeating stimuli when we wish to, but it is difficult to keep our attention on them even when we try (see Davies & Parasuraman, 1982). Hence, we might have expected an even greater enhancement of recency from intensive exposure to the irrelevant item than we did in fact obtain. After all, even our unrelenting continuous presentation procedure did not fully restore recency recall to the level observed in the absence of any irrelevant stimuli.

AUTHOR NOTE

The research was supported by National Institute of Mental Health Grant MH35873. We thank Michael Gemar for testing some of the subjects in Experiment 1 and Ian Neath for writing the computer programs for list presentation in Experiments 5 and 6. Elizabeth Sechler is now at Belmont Abbey College. Correspondence concerning this article should be addressed to Michael J. Watkins at the Department of Psychology, Rice University, P.O. Box 1892, Houston, TX 77251.

REFERENCES

Baddeley, A., & Hull, A. (1979). Prefix and suffix effects: Do they have a common basis? *Journal of Verbal Learning & Verbal Behavior, 18,* 129–140.

Balota, D. A., & Engle, R. W. (1981). Structural and strategic factors in the stimulus suffix effect. *Journal of Verbal Learning & Verbal Behavior, 20,* 346–357.

Bjork, R. A., & Whitten, W. B. (1974). Recency-sensitive retrieval processes in long-term free recall. *Cognitive Psychology, 6*, 173–189.

Broadbent, D. E. (1952). Listening to one of two synchronous messages. *Quarterly Journal of Experimental Psychology, 4*, 51–55.

Crowder, R. G. (1967). Prefix effects in immediate memory. *Canadian Journal of Psychology, 21*, 450–461.

Crowder, R. G. (1969). Improved recall for digits with delayed recall cues. *Journal of Experimental Psychology, 82*, 258–262.

Crowder, R. G. (1978). Mechanisms of auditory backward masking in the stimulus suffix effect. *Psychological Review, 85*, 502–524.

Crowder, R. G., & Morton, J. (1969). Precategorical acoustic storage (PAS). *Perception & Psychophysics, 5*, 365–373.

Dallett, K. M. (1965). "Primary memory": The effects of redundancy upon digit repetition. *Psychonomic Science, 3*, 237–238.

Davies, D. R., & Parasuraman, R. (1982). *The psychology of vigilance.* London: Academic Press.

Gibson, J. M. (1987). Using digitized auditory stimuli on the Macintosh computer. *Behavior Research Methods, Instruments, & Computers, 19*, 257–259.

Glanzer, M., & Cunitz, A. R. (1966). Two storage mechanisms in free recall. *Journal of Verbal Learning & Verbal Behavior, 5*, 351–360.

Greenberg, S. N., & Engle, R. W. (1983). Voice changes in the stimulus suffix effect: Are the effects structural or strategic? *Memory & Cognition, 11*, 551–556.

Hitch, G. J. (1975). The role of attention in visual and auditory suffix effects. *Memory & Cognition, 3*, 501–505.

Kahneman, D., & Henik, A. (1981). Perceptual organization and attention. In M. Kubovy & J. R. Pomeranz (Eds.), *Perceptual organization* (pp. 181–212). Hillsdale, NJ: Erlbaum.

Lorch, E. P., Anderson, D. R., & Well, A. D. (1984). Effects of irrelevant information on speeded classification tasks: Interference is reduced by habituation. *Journal of Experimental Psychology: Human Perception & Performance, 10*, 850–864.

Morton, J. M. (1976). Two mechanisms in the stimulus suffix effect. *Memory & Cognition, 4*, 144–149.

Morton, J., Crowder, R. G., & Prussin, H. A. (1971). Experiments with the stimulus suffix effect. *Journal of Experimental Psychology, 91*, 169–190.

Morton, J., Marcus, S. M., & Ottley, P. (1981). The acoustic correlate of "speechlike": A use of the suffix effect. *Journal of Experimental Psychology: General, 10*, 568–593.

Penney, C. G. (1985). Elimination of the suffix effect on preterminal list items with unpredictable list length: Evidence for a dual model of suffix effects. *Journal of Experimental Psychology: Learning, Memory, & Cognition, 11*, 229–247.

Postman, L., & Phillips, L. W. (1965). Short-term temporal changes in free recall. *Quarterly Journal of Experimental Psychology, 17*, 132–138.

Reisberg, D., Baron, J., & Kemler, D. G. (1980). Overcoming Stroop interference: The effects of practice on distractor potency. *Journal of Experimental Psychology: Human Perception & Performance, 6*, 140–150.

Routh, D. A., & Frosdick, R. M. (1978). The basis and implications of the restoration of a recency effect in immediate serial recall. *Quarterly Journal of Experimental Psychology, 30*, 201–220.

Salame, P., & Baddeley, A. D. (1982). Disruption of short-term memory by unattended speech: Implications for the structure of working memory. *Journal of Verbal Learning & Verbal Behavior, 21*, 150–164.

Stroop, J. R. (1935). Studies of interference in serial verbal reaction. *Journal of Experimental Psychology, 18*, 643–662.

Treisman, A. M. (1964). Verbal cues, language, and meaning in selective attention. *American Journal of Psychology, 77*, 206–219.

Tzeng, O. J. L. (1973). Positive recency effect in a delayed free recall. *Journal of Verbal Learning & Verbal Behavior, 12*, 436–439.

Waters, W. F., McDonald, D. G., & Koresko, R. L. (1977). Habituation of the orienting response: A gating mechanism subserving selective attention. *Psychophysiology, 14*, 228–236.

Watkins, M. J. (1989). Willful and nonwillful determinants of memory. In H. L. Roediger, III & F. I. M. Craik (Eds.), *Varieties of memory and consciousness: Essays in honour of Endel Tulving* (pp. 59–72). Hillsdale, NJ: Erlbaum.

Watkins, O. C., & Watkins, M. J. (1980). Echoic memory and voice quality: Recency recall is not enhanced by varying presentation voice. *Memory & Cognition, 8*, 26–30.

Watkins, O. C., & Watkins, M. J. (1982). Lateral inhibition and echoic memory: Some comments on Crowder's (1978) theory. *Memory & Cognition, 10*, 279–286.

ENDNOTE

1. To ensure that this interaction was not the product of a ceiling effect, the 864 list recalls (9 lists from each of 96

subjects) within each condition-block combination were assigned to two sets, one for low-scoring recalls (0–4 items correctly recalled) and one for high-scoring recalls (5–9 items correctly recalled). The linear compo-

nent of trend for the condition-block interaction turned out to be similar for the two sets of data, which suggests that this effect for the combined data was not the result of a ceiling effect.

APPENDIX

Mean Recency-Trend and Last-Position Scores for Each Condition of Experiments 1-6

Condition	Recency-Trend	Last-Position
Experiment 1		
Suffix		
Block 1	.11	.45
Block 2	.09	.47
Block 3	.10	.54
Control		
Block 1	.39	.89
Block 2	.38	.90
Block 3	.36	.88
Experiment 2		
Through-list	.25	.54
Standard suffix	.08	.57
Control	.31	.95
Experiment 3		
Through-list	.32	.55
Standard suffix	.15	.51
Control	.47	.89
Experiment 4		
Continuous suffix	.31	.85
Triple suffix	.23	.78
Standard suffix	.22	.78
Control	.27	.91
Experiment 5		
Continuous suffix	.33	.71
Triple suffix	.05	.50
Standard suffix	.05	.47
Control	.35	.93
Experiment 6		
Continuous	.51	.75
Suffix after continuous	.17	.54
Standard suffix	.15	.47
Control	.45	.94

Note: Last-position score is defined as the proportion of items recalled from Serial Position 9, and the recency-trend score as the proportion of items recalled from Serial Position 9 minus the proportion recalled from Serial Position 7.

CHAPTER FIVE

Short-Term Memory

14 BROWN-PETERSON TASK

Prior to the 1940s, memory loss was widely considered to be the result of new information interfering with previously learned information. In the late 1950s, two groups of researchers (one named Brown and a husband and wife team named Peterson) published data that forced a new interpretation of human memory. They found that the passage of time, in the absence of any interfering material, caused a decrease in memory performance. Because the two teams of researchers published almost identical methods simultaneously, the task has been named the "Brown-Peterson task."

In the method described by Peterson and Peterson (1959), the participant viewed a trigram of consonants (e.g., GKT, WCH, . . .) and then performed a number of algebraic computations (e.g., counting backwards by threes) for different amounts of time. Performing this distractor task prevented the participant from actively rehearsing the trigram. The researchers assumed that the materials in the counting task (numbers) were different enough from those in the memory task (consonants) that they would not cause any interference.

The data (displayed in Figure 14.3) showed that recall of the trigram was worse as the participant worked on the algebraic computations for longer durations. In addition, the decay of memory as a function of time was regular and could be accounted for by an exponential equation. Peterson and Peterson concluded that a short-term memory (STM) system exists that holds information for several seconds. Without an active effort by the participant, information in STM fades away or decays in a regular manner. This hypothesized STM is now a fundamental part of most theories of cognitive psychology.

The language and the abbreviations used in this paper are somewhat unfamiliar to modern eyes. For example, the exact instructions that were given to the participants were reproduced, something we do not usually do today. Parenthetically, it is interesting to note the instructions that Peterson and Peterson (1959, p. 194) gave to their subjects: "Please sit against the back of your chair so that you are comfortable. You will not be shocked during this experiment." Finally, most of the theoretical development is in terms of what was called "verbal behavior," the precursor to current-day cognitive psychology. The terms and interpretation, such as conditioned stimulus and response, are those used in the behaviorist era.

Nonetheless, this paper is still relevant to the issue of whether the main source of forgetting in STM is due to the mere passage of time (decay) or whether interfering information is the root cause of memory loss. Although the conclusion reached by Peterson and Peterson is no longer widely accepted, this paper (and others) stimulated a great deal of debate over the cause of forgetting in STM: passive decay (as suggested by Peterson and Peterson) or interference (Keppel & Underwood, 1962). More recent reviews of the debate between decay and interference in short-term memory can be found in Crowder (1982), Cowan, Saults, and Nugent (2001), and Neath and Surprenant (2003).

The Brown-Peterson demonstration on CogLab uses almost exactly the same method as Experiment 1 described in this reading. As in Peterson and Peterson's study, the independent variable (the variable manipulated by the experimenter) is the duration of the distractor task and the dependent variable (the outcome variable) is percent correct recall of consonant trigrams. The experiment is a bit simplified in that only three distractor intervals are used (1, 11, and 21 seconds). In addition, because it is impossible to monitor a vocal distractor task on CogLab, the distractor task in the demonstration involves classifying numbers that appear on the screen as odd or even in a very short period of time. This task is sufficiently difficult that it should not allow for rehearsal of the consonant trigrams.

REFERENCES

Cowan, N., Saults, S., & Nugent, L. (2001). Origin of autonoesis in episodic memory. In H. L. Roediger, III, J. S. Nairne, I. Neath, & A. M. Surprenant (Eds.), *The nature of remembering: Essays in honor of Robert G. Crowder*. Science conference series (pp. 315-330). Washington, DC: American Psychological Association.

Crowder, R. G. (1993). Short-term memory: Where do we stand? *Memory & Cognition, 21*, 142–145.

Keppel, G., & Underwood, B. J. (1962). Proactive inhibition in short-term retention of single items. *Journal of Verbal Learning and Verbal Behavior, 1*, 153–161.

Neath, I., & Surprenant, A. M. (2003). *Human memory: An introduction to research, data, and theory* (2nd ed.). Belmont, CA: Wadsworth.

QUESTIONS

1. Why is a distractor task used in these types of experiments?
2. What were the results of Experiment 1?
3. What was the explanation of the cause of forgetting in this paper?
4. What is the effect of repetition on memory reported in Experiment 2?

Short-Term Retention of Individual Verbal Items

Lloyd R. Peterson and Margaret J. Peterson
Indiana University

It is apparent that the acquisition of verbal habits depends on the effects of a given occasion being carried over into later repetitions of the situation. Nevertheless, textbooks separate acquisition and retention into distinct categories. The limitation of discussions of retention to long-term characteristics is necessary in large part by the scarcity of data on the course of retention over intervals of the order of magnitude of the time elapsing between successive repetitions in an acquisition study. The presence of a retentive function within the acquisition process was postulated by Hull [et al.] (1940) in his use of the stimulus trace to explain serial phenomena. Again, Underwood (1949) has suggested that forgetting occurs during the acquisition process. But these theoretical considerations have not led to empirical investigation. Hull (1952) quantified the stimulus trace on data concerned with the CS-UCS interval in eyelid conditioning and it is not obvious that the construct so quantified can be readily transferred to verbal learning. One objection is that a verbal stimulus produces a strong predictable response prior to the experimental session and this is not true of the originally neutral stimulus in eyelid conditioning.

Two studies have shown that the effects of verbal stimulation can decrease over intervals measured in seconds. Pillsbury and Sylvester (1940) found marked decrement with a list of items tested for recall 10 sec. after a single presentation. However, it seems unlikely that this traditional presentation of a list and later testing for recall of the list will be useful in studying intervals near or shorter than the time necessary to present the list. Of more interest is a recent study by Brown (1958) in which among other conditions a single pair of consonants was tested after a 5-sec. interval. Decrement was found at the one recall interval, but no systematic study of the course of retention over a variety of intervals was attempted.

EXPERIMENT I

The present investigation tests recall for individual items after several short intervals. An item is presented and tested without related items intervening. The initial study examines the course of retention after one brief presentation of the item.

Method

Subjects.   The Ss were 24 students from introductory psychology courses at Indiana University. Participation in experiments was a course requirement.

Materials.   The verbal items tested for recall were 48 consonant syllables with Witmer association value no greater than 33% (Hilgard, 1951). Other materials were 48 three-digit numbers obtained from a table of random numbers. One of these was given to S after each presentation under instructions to count backward from the number. It was considered that continuous verbal activity during the time between presentation and signal for recall was desirable in order to minimize rehearsal behavior. The materials were selected to be categorically dissimilar and hence involve a minimum of interference.

Procedure.   The S was seated at a table with E seated facing in the same direction on S's right. A black plywood screen shielded E from S. On the table in front of S were two small lights mounted on a black box.

SOURCE: From Peterson, L. R., & Peterson, M. J. (1959). Short-term retention of individual verbal items. *Journal of Experimental Psychology, 58*, 193–198.

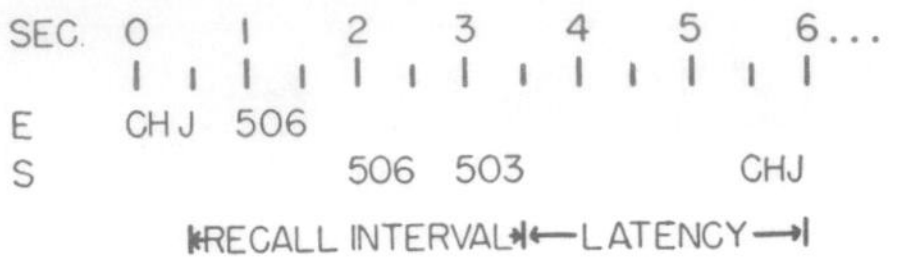

```
SEC.  0    1    2    3    4    5    6...
      |  |  |  |  |  |  |  |  |  |  |  |
E     CHJ  506
S               506  503         CHJ
      |◄RECALL INTERVAL►|◄─LATENCY─►|
```

FIGURE 14.1   Sequence of events for a recall interval of 3 sec.

The general procedure was for *E* to spell a consonant syllable and immediately speak a three-digit number. The *S* then counted backward by three or four from this number. On flashing of a signal light *S* attempted to recall the consonant syllable. The *E* spoke in rhythm with a metronome clicking twice per second and *S* was instructed to do likewise. The timing of these events is diagrammed in Figure 14.1. As *E* spoke the third digit, he pressed a button activating a Hunter interval timer. At the end of a preset interval the timer activated a red light and an electric clock. The light was the signal for recall. The clock ran until *E* heard *S* speak three letters, when *E* stopped the clock by depressing a key. This time between onset of the light and completion of a response will be referred to as a latency. It is to be distinguished from the interval from completion of the syllable by *E* to onset of the light, which will be referred to as the recall interval.

The instructions read to *S* were as follows: "Please sit against the back of your chair so that you are comfortable. You will not be shocked during this experiment. In front of you is a little black box. The top or green light is on now. This green light means that we are ready to begin a trial. I will speak some letters and then a number. You are to repeat the number immediately after I say it and begin counting backwards by 3's (4's) from that number in time with the ticking that you hear. I might say, ABC 309. Then you say, 309, 306, 303, etc., until the bottom or red light comes on. When you see this red light come on, stop counting immediately and say the letters that were given at the beginning of the trial. Remember to keep your eyes on the black box at all times. There will be a short rest period and then the green light will come on again and we will start a new trial." The *E* summarized what he had already said and then gave *S* two practice trials. During this practice *S* was corrected if he hesitated before starting to count, or if he failed to stop counting on signal, or if he in any other way deviated from the instructions.

Each *S* was tested eight times at each of the recall intervals, 3, 6, 9, 12, 15, and 18 sec. A given consonant syllable was used only once with each *S*. Each syllable occurred equally often over the group at each recall interval. A specific recall interval was represented once in each successive block of six presentations. The *S* counted backward by three on half of the trials and by four on the remaining trials. No two successive items contained letters in common. The time between signal for recall and the start of the next presentation was 15 sec.

Results and Discussion

Responses occurring any time during the 15-sec. interval following signal for recall were recorded. In Figure 14.2 are plotted the proportions of correct recalls as cumulative functions of latency for each of the recall intervals. Sign tests were used to evaluate differences among the curves (Walker & Lev, 1953). At each latency differences among the 3-, 6-, 9-, and 18-sec. recall interval curves are significant at the .05 level. For latencies of 6 sec. and longer these differences are all significant at the .01 level. Note that the number correct with latency less than 2 sec. does not constitute a majority of the total correct. These responses would not seem appropriately described as identification of the gradually weakening trace of a stimulus. There is a suggestion of an oscillatory characteristic in the events determining them.

The feasibility of an interpretation by a statistical model was explored by fitting to the data the exponential curve of Figure 14.3. The empirical points plotted here are proportions of correct responses with latencies shorter than 2.83 sec. Partition of the correct responses on the basis of latency is required by considerations developed in detail by Estes (1950). A given probability of response applies to an interval of time equal in length to the average time required for the response under consideration to occur. The mean latency of correct responses in the present experiment was 2.83 sec. Differences among the proportions of correct responses with latencies shorter than 2.83 sec. were evaluated by sign tests. The difference between the 3- and 18-sec. conditions was found to be significant at the .01 level. All differences among the 3-, 6-,

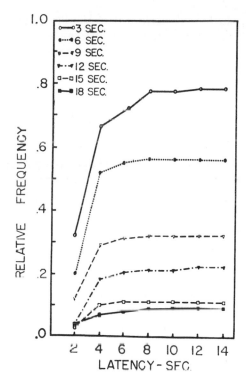

FIGURE 14.2   Correct recalls as cumulative functions of latency.

9-, 12-, and 18-sec. conditions were significant at the .05 level.

The general equation of which the expression for the curve of Figure 14.3 is a specific instance is derived from the stimulus fluctuation model developed by Estes (1955). In applying the model to the present experiment it is assumed that the verbal stimulus produces a response in *S* which is conditioned to a set of elements contiguous with the response. The elements thus conditioned are a sample of a larger population of elements into which the conditioned elements disperse as time passes. The proportion of conditioned elements in the sample determining *S's* behavior thus decreases and with it the probability of the response. Since the fitted curve appears to do justice to the data, the observed decrement could arise from stimulus fluctuation.

The independence of successive presentations might be questioned in the light of findings that performance deteriorates as a function of previous learn-

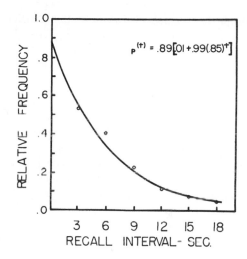

FIGURE 14.3   Correct recalls with latencies below 2.88 sec. as a function of recall interval.

ing (Underwood, 1957). The presence of proactive interference was tested by noting the correct responses within each successive block of 12 presentations. The short recall intervals were analyzed separately from the long recall intervals in view of the possibility that facilitation might occur with the one and interference with the other. The proportions of correct responses for the combined 3- and 6-sec. recall intervals were in order of occurrence .57, .66, .70, and .74. A sign test showed the difference between the first and last blocks to be significant at the .02 level. The proportions correct for the 15- and 18-sec. recall intervals were .08, .15, .09, and .12. The gain from first to last blocks is not significant in this case. There is no evidence for proactive interference. There is an indication of improvement with practice.

EXPERIMENT II

The findings in Exp. I are compatible with the proposition that the aftereffects of a single, brief, verbal stimulation can be interpreted as those of a trial of learning. It would be predicted from such an interpretation that probability of recall at a given recall interval should increase as a function of repetitions of the stimulation. Forgetting should proceed at differential rates for items with differing numbers of repetitions.

Although this seems to be a reasonable prediction, there are those who would predict otherwise. Brown (1958), for instance, questions whether repetitions, as such, strengthen the "memory trace." He suggests that the effect of repetitions of a stimulus, or rehearsal, may be merely to postpone the onset of decay of the trace. If time is measured from the moment that the last stimulation ceased, then the forgetting curves should coincide in all cases, no matter how many occurrences of the stimulation have preceded the final occurrence. The second experiment was designed to obtain empirical evidence relevant to this problem.

Method

The Ss were 48 students from the source previously described. Half of the Ss were instructed to repeat the stimulus aloud in time with the metronome until stopped by E giving them a number from which S counted backward. The remaining Ss were not given instructions concerning use of the interval between E's presentation of the stimulus and his speaking the number from which to count backward. Both the "vocal" group and the "silent" group had equated intervals of time during which rehearsal inevitably occurred in the one case and could occur in the other case. Differences in frequency of recalls between the groups would indicate a failure of the uninstructed Ss to rehearse. The zero point marking the beginning of the recall interval for the silent group was set at the point at which E spoke the number from which S counted backward. This was also true for the vocal group.

The length of the rehearsal period was varied for Ss of both groups over three conditions. On a third of the presentations S was not given time for any repetitions. This condition was thus comparable to Exp. I, save that the only recall intervals used were 3, 9, and 18 sec. On another third of the presentations 1 sec. elapsed during which S could repeat the stimulus. On another third of the presentations 3 sec. elapsed, or sufficient time for three repetitions. Consonant syllables were varied as to the rehearsal interval in which they were used, so that each syllable occurred equally often in each condition over the group. However, a given syllable was never presented more than once to

any S. The Ss were assigned in order of appearance to a randomized list of conditions. Six practice presentations were given during which corrections were made of departures from instructions. Other details follow the procedures of Exp. I.

Results and Discussion

Table 14.1 shows the proportion of items recalled correctly. In the vocal group recall improved with repetition at each of the recall intervals tested. Conditions in the silent group were not consistently ordered. For purposes of statistical analysis the recall intervals were combined within each group. A sign test between numbers correct in the 0- and 3-repetition conditions of the vocal group showed the difference to be significant at the .01 level. The difference between the corresponding conditions of the silent group was not significant at the .05 level. Only under conditions where repetition of the stimulus was controlled by instructions did retention improve.

The obtained differences among the zero conditions of Exp. II and the 3-, 9-, and 18-sec. recall intervals of Exp. I require some comment, since procedures were essentially the same. Since these are between-S comparisons, some differences would be predicted because of sampling variability. But another factor is probably involved. There were 48 presentations in Exp. I and only 36 in Exp. II. Since recall was found to improve over successive blocks of trials, a superiority in recall for Ss of Exp. I is reasonable. In the case of differences between the vocal and silent groups of Exp. II a statistical test is permissable, for Ss were

TABLE 14.1   Proportions of Items Correctly Recalled in Exp. II

Group	Repetition Time (Sec.)	Recall Interval (Sec.)		
		3	9	18
Vocal	3	.80	.48	.34
	1	.68	.34	.21
	0	.60	.25	.14
Silent	3	.70	.39	.30
	1	.74	.35	.22
	0	.72	.38	.15

assigned randomly to the two groups. Wilcoxon's (1949) test for unpaired replicates, as well as a *t* test, was used. Neither showed significance at the .05 level.

The 1- and 3-repetition conditions of the vocal group afforded an opportunity to obtain a measure of what recall would be at the zero interval in time. It was noted whether a syllable had been correctly repeated by *S*. Proportions correctly repeated were .90 for the 1-repetition condition and .88 for the 3-repetition condition. The chief source of error lay in the confusion of the letters "m" and "n." This source of error is not confounded with the repetition variable, for it is *S* who repeats and thus perpetuates his error. Further, individual items were balanced over the three conditions. There is no suggestion of any difference in responding among the repetition conditions at the beginning of the recall interval. These differences developed during the time that *S* was engaged in counting backward. A differential rate of forgetting seems indisputable.

The factors underlying the improvement in retention with repetition were investigated by means of an analysis of the status of elements within the individual items. The individual consonant syllable, like the nonsense syllable, may be regarded as presenting *S* with a serial learning task. Through repetitions unrelated components may develop serial dependencies until in the manner of familiar words they have become single units. The improved retention might then be attributed to increases in these serial dependencies. The analysis proceeded by ascertaining the dependent probabilities that letters would be correct given the event that the previous letter was correct. These dependent probabilities are listed in Table 14.2. It is clear that with increasing repetitions the serial dependencies increase. Again combining recall intervals, a

TABLE 14.2 Dependent Probabilities of a Letter Being Correctly Recalled in the Vocal Group When the Preceding Letter Was Correct

Repetition Time (Sec.)	Recall Interval (Sec.)		
	3	9	18
3	.96	.85	.72
1	.90	.72	.57
0	.86	.64	.56

sign test between the zero condition and the three repetition condition is significant at the .01 level.

Learning is seen to take place within the items. But this finding does not eliminate the possibility that another kind of learning is proceeding concurrently. If only the correct occurrences of the first letters of syllables are considered, changes in retention apart from the serial dependencies can be assessed. The proportions of first letters recalled correctly for the 0-, 1-, and 3-repetition conditions were .60, .65, and .72, respectively. A sign test between the 0- and 3-repetition conditions was significant at the .05 level. It may tentatively be concluded that learning of a second kind took place.

The course of short-term verbal retention is seen to be related to learning processes. It would not appear to be strictly accurate to refer to retention after a brief presentation as a stimulus trace. Rather, it would seem appropriate to refer to it as the result of a trial of learning. However, in spite of possible objections to Hull's terminology the present investigation supports his general position that a short-term retentive factor is important for the analysis of verbal learning. The details of the role of retention in the acquisition process remain to be worked out.

SUMMARY

The investigation differed from traditional verbal retention studies in concerning itself with individual items instead of lists. Forgetting over intervals measured in seconds was found. The course of retention after a single presentation was related to a statistical model. Forgetting was found to progress at differential rates dependent on the amount of controlled rehearsal of the stimulus. A portion of the improvement in recall with repetitions was assigned to serial learning within the item, but a second kind of learning was also found. It was concluded that short-term retention is an important, though neglected, aspect of the acquisition process.

NOTE

The initial stages of this investigation were facilitated by National Science Foundation Grant G-2596.

REFERENCES

Brown, J. (1958). Some tests of the decay theory of immediate memory. *Quarterly Journal of Experimental Psychology, 10,* 12–21.

Estes, W. K. (1950). Toward a statistical theory of learning. *Psychological Review, 57,* 94–107.

Estes, W. K. (1955). Statistical theory of spontaneous recovery and regression. *Psychological Review, 62,* 145–154.

Hilgard, E. R. (1951). Methods and procedures in the study of learning. In S. S. Stevens (Ed.), *Handbook of experimental psychology.* New York: Wiley.

Hull, C. L., Hovland, C. I., Ross, R. T., Hall, M., Perkins, D. T., & Fitch, F. B. (1940). *Mathematico-deductive theory of rote learning: A study in scientific methodology.* New Haven, CT: Yale University Press.

Hull, C. L. (1952). *A behavior system.* New Haven, CT: Yale University Press.

Pillsbury, W. B., & Sylvester, A. (1940). Retroactive and proactive inhibition in immediate memory. *Journal of Experimental Psychology, 27,* 532–545.

Underwood, B. J. (1949). *Experimental psychology.* New York: Appleton-Century-Crofts.

Underwood, B. J. (1957). Interference and forgetting. *Psychological Review, 64,* 49–60.

Walker, H., & Lev, J. (1953). *Statistical inference.* New York: Holt.

Wilcoxon, F. (1949). *Some rapid approximate statistical procedures.* New York: American Cyanamid Co.

15 STERNBERG SEARCH

Many theories of short-term memory say nothing about how information is retrieved from short-term memory. As Sternberg (1966) pointed out, there is often an implicit assumption that information in short-term or working memory is automatically available without having to be retrieved. Rather than just assuming that information does not have to be retrieved, Sternberg devised a task that would allow an empirical test.

The Sternberg task is based on the idea that the amount of time it takes a person to give a response about information in short-term memory can allow inferences to be made about retrieval from short-term memory. Because the only memory process of interest was retrieval, the task was set up to minimize the role of other factors. A well-known set of items—the digits 0–9—were used so that the subjects would be highly familiar with the stimuli. Moreover, no more than six items were used because Sternberg wanted to make sure the stimuli were not beyond the subject's memory span. Subjects saw one to six digits and then, following a 2 s delay, were shown a test digit. They were asked to press a button as quickly as they could to indicate whether the test item was in the list they had just seen. Half the time the test digit was in the sequence just shown (called a positive trial); half the time the test digit was not in the list (a negative trial).

The mean response times come from trials on which the subjects made correct responses, and are shown in Figure 15.1. There are two important results to note. First, it takes the same amount of time to respond that the target was in the list (a yes response, black circles) as to respond that the target was not in the list (a no response, white circles). Second, adding an item to the memory set increases the response time by approximately 40 ms. The increase in response time is the same whether going from two to three items or from five to six items.

In Experiment 1, the to-be-remembered items changed on each trial, what Sternberg calls a varied set procedure. Experiment 2 used a fixed set procedure in which the subjects were told which items to remember. The subjects then received 60 practice trials followed by 120 test trials on the same set of stimuli. In this way, there could be no doubt on the part of the subject as to what the items were. The results from Experiment 2 are shown in Figure 15.2 and replicate the results of Experiment 1. Importantly, the data again form a straight line.

At least three possible search processes could have been used. Subjects could use a *parallel* search, in which all items are examined simultaneously. This type of search would show no increase in response time as the number of items in the search increases, and both yes and no responses should take the same amount of time. A second possibility is that subjects could use a *self-terminating serial* search. With this type of search, the test item is compared to the first item in the search set and if a match is found, then the subject responds yes and the search stops. If no match is made, then the test item is compared to the next item in the search set. Response times will increase as the number of items in the search set increases, and yes responses should be faster than no responses.

Sternberg interpreted these data as supporting the third type of search, an *exhaustive serial scanning* search. The memory set is scanned one by one, just as in the self-terminating search; however, the search continues even after a match is found. The entire search set is scanned on every trial. This predicts an increase in response time as the number of items in the search set increases, and also predicts that yes and no responses will take the same amount of time. For a negative trial, this type of search makes sense. The target is compared with each item in memory, one at a time (hence, serial). Because the target did not occur, the search must involve comparisons with every list item (hence exhaustive). This would produce the linear functions seen in Figures 15.1 and 15.2 for negative responses. Evidence for the serial part includes the observation that the addition of one item to the search set increases the response time by a fixed amount.

An exhaustive search on a positive trial means that subjects will continue the search after they have found the item they were searching for. Although this may not sound very plausible at first—why would subjects keep comparing the target to the remaining items in memory if they have already found a match?—Sternberg offered a convincing rationale. The basic idea is that the process that determines whether a match has been made requires more resources (i.e., it is slower and interferes with other processes) than the one that does the scanning. The subject initiates a (perhaps automatic) scanning process, which runs to completion. After this process terminates, the subject then evaluates the results of the comparisons. Sternberg's argument is that it would take far longer on average to scan the first item, then evaluate the comparison, then scan the second item, then evaluate that comparison, and so on, than to do the scanning first and the evaluation only once. Sternberg argues that a parallel model, one in which multiple comparisons are made simultaneously, cannot account for the data. Subsequent research has found the situation to be far more complex, however, and the simple serial exhaustive search interpretation is no longer tenable (see Van Zandt & Townsend, 1993).

This paper is famous because of the (initially) counterintuitive explanation of the data and for the elegant methodology. The CogLab demo is very similar to the original experiment; the most notable differences are that only set sizes of 1, 3, and 5 are tested, and, unlike most traditional Sternberg-paradigm experiments, there is no practice before the experimental trials begin.

REFERENCE

Van Zandt, T., & Townsend, J. T. (1993). Self-terminating versus exhaustive processes in rapid visual and memory search: An evaluative review. *Perception & Psychophysics, 53*, 563–480.

QUESTIONS

1. In Sternberg's terms, what is the difference between a parallel search process and a serial search process?
2. How would Figure 15.1 have looked if the search on positive trials was not exhaustive (i.e., terminated as soon as a match was found)?
3. What is the significance of Sternberg's finding that the rate of scanning (approximately 25 to 30 items per second) is substantially faster than the maximum rate of subvocal speech?

High-Speed Scanning in Human Memory

Saul Sternberg

INTRODUCTION

How do people scan information that they are holding in their short-term memory? For example, if you read the digits 6–0–1–9–7, and commit them to memory, how would you then go about identifying whether the number 1, or the number 5 for that matter, was among the set of numbers you committed to memory?

In a paradigm-setting series of studies, Saul Sternberg compared alternative models of how people might scan such information. The models differed in serial or parallel, and self-terminating or exhaustive, methods.

According to a serial model, people would scan each of the successive digits in turn, one after another. According to a parallel model, however, people would scan the digits simultaneously—all at once. A serial model would predict, Sternberg believed, a variable scanning time—scanning more digits would take longer to scan. A parallel model would predict a constant scanning time regardless of the number of symbols in the string. For example, a parallel model would expect the same amount of time to scan three digits (8–2–4) or six (8–2–4–1–6–3).

According to a self-terminating information-scanning model, someone will scan until encountering the desired digit and respond "yes" as soon as it appears. A person scans to the end of the list only if the digit is the last one or is not in the set to be remembered. According to an exhaustive model, in contrast, someone always scans to the end of the list, regardless of the number of items to be scanned. The self-terminating model predicts faster responses for items early in the stimulus set (such as the 8 in 8–2–4), and slower responses for items later in the stimulus set (such as the 4 in 8–2–4).

Sternberg found that the number of items in the stimulus set affected response time, but serial position did not. He therefore concluded that people were using a serial, exhaustive scanning process. Scanning can take anywhere from 10 to 30 milliseconds per stimulus item.

The Sternberg studies are among the most famous in cognitive psychology for several reasons. First, they were exceedingly elegant, showing in a way that seemed compelling at the time that individuals use a serial, exhaustive scan when searching for items in short-term memory. Later study revealed that the demonstration was nowhere nearly as compelling as it had first appeared, thus reinforcing the impossibility of so-called "critical" experiments that decide something once and for all, at least in psychology. Second, the work introduced a task to psychology, short-term memory scanning, that became widely used and is still fairly widely used today, three decades later. Third, the work introduced a method, called the additive-factor method, for isolating stages of processing in cognition. Sternberg argued that one could infer independent stages of processing by showing that variables that affect one stage of processing have no effect on other stages. For all these reasons, Saul Sternberg's work became a classic in the study of cognition.

*   *   *

When subjects judge whether a test symbol is contained in a short memorized sequence of symbols, their mean reaction-time increases linearly with the length of the sequence. The linearity and slope of the function imply the existence of an internal serial-comparison process whose average rate is between 25 and 30 symbols per sec.

SOURCE: Reprinted with permission from Sternberg, S. (1966). High-speed scanning in human memory. *Science, 153,* 652–654. Copyright © 1966, American Association for the Advancement of Science.

How is symbolic information retrieved from recent memory? The study of short-term memory[1] has revealed some of the determinants of failures to remember, but has provided little insight into error-free performance and the retrieval processes that underlie it. One reason for the neglect of retrieval mechanisms may be the implicit assumption that a short time after several items have been memorized, they can be immediately and simultaneously available for expression in recall or in other responses, rather than having to be retrieved first. In another vocabulary,[2] this is to assume the equivalence of the "span of immediate memory" (the number of items that can be recalled without error) and the "momentary capacity of consciousness" (the number of items immediately available). The experiments reported here[3] show that the assumption is unwarranted.

Underlying the paradigm of these experiments is the supposition that if the selection of a response requires the use of information that is in memory, the latency of the response will reveal something about the process by which the information is retrieved. Of particular interest in the study of retrieval is the effect of the number of elements in memory on the response latency. The subject first memorizes a short series of symbols. He is then shown a test stimulus, and is required to decide whether or not it is one of the symbols in memory. If the subject decides affirmatively, he pulls one lever, making a positive response; otherwise he makes a negative response by pulling the other lever. In this paradigm, it is the identity of the symbols in the series, but not their order, that is relevant to the binary response. The response latency is defined as the time from the onset of the test stimulus to the occurrence of the response.

Because they are well learned and highly discriminable, the ten digits were used as stimuli. On each trial of experiment 1, the subject[4] saw a random series of from one to six different digits displayed singly at a fixed locus for 1.2 seconds each. The length, s, of the series varied at random from trial to trial. There followed a 2.0-second delay, a warning signal, and then the test digit. As soon as one of the levers was pulled, a feedback light informed the subject whether his response had been correct. The trial ended with his attempt to recall the series in order. For every value of s, positive and negative responses

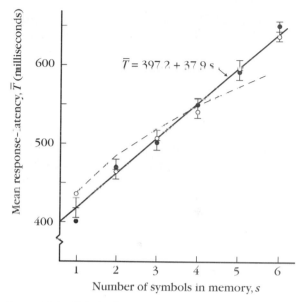

FIGURE 15.1 Relation between response latency and the number of symbols in memory, s, in experiment 1. Mean latencies, over eight subjects, of positive responses (filled circles) and negative responses (open circles). About 95 observations per point. For each s, overall mean (heavy bar) and estimates of ±s are indicated.[6] Solid line was fitted by least squares to overall means. Upper bound for parallel process (broken curve).

were required with equal frequency. Each digit in the series occurred as a test stimulus with probability $(2s)^{-1}$, and each of the remaining digits occurred with probability $[2(10 - s)]^{-1}$.

Each subject had 24 practice trials and 144 test trials. Feedback and payoffs were designed to encourage subjects to respond as rapidly as possible, while maintaining a low error rate. The eight subjects whose data are presented pulled the wrong lever on 1.3 percent of the test trials.[5] Recall was imperfect on 1.4 percent of the trials. The low error-rates justify the assumption that on a typical trial the series of symbols in memory was the same as the series of symbols presented.

Results are shown in Figure 15.1. Linear regression accounts for 99.4 percent of the variance of the overall mean response-latencies.[6] The slope of the fitted line is 37.9 ± 3.8 msec per symbol[7]; its zero intercept is 397.2 ± 19.3 msec. Lines fitted separately to the mean latencies of positive and negative responses differ in slope by 9.6 ± 2.3 msec per symbol. The difference is attributable primarily to the fact that for $s = 1$, positive responses were 50.0 ± 20.1 msec faster than negative responses. Lines fitted to the data for $2 \leq s \leq 6$ differ in slope by an insignificant 3.1 ± 3.2 msec per symbol.

The latency of a response depends, in part, on the relative frequency with which it is required.[8] For this reason the frequencies of positive and negative responses and, more generally, the response entropy,[8] were held constant for all values of s in experiment 1. However, the test-stimulus entropy (predictability) was permitted to co-vary with s.

Both response and test-stimulus entropies were controlled in experiment 2, in which the retrieval process was studied by an alternative method similar to that used in more conventional experiments on choice-reaction time. In experiment 1, the set of symbols associated with the positive response changed from trial to trial. In contrast to this varied-set procedure, a fixed-set procedure was used in experiment 2. In each of three parts of a session, a set of digits for which a positive response was required (the positive set) was announced to the subject[4]; there followed 60 practice trials and 120 test trials based on this set.

The subject knew that on each trial, any of the ten digits could appear as the test stimulus, and that for all the digits not in the positive set (the negative set) the negative response was required. Each subject worked with nonintersecting positive sets of size $s = 1$, 2, and 4, whose composition was varied from subject to subject.

Stimulus and response entropies were both held constant while s was varied, by means of specially constructed populations of test stimuli. Let $x_1, y_1, y_2, z_1, \ldots, z_4$ and $w_1, \ldots, w_3$ represent the ten digits. Their relative frequencies in the population were x_1, 4/15; each y, 2/15; each z, 1/15; and each w, 1/15. The three sequences of test stimuli presented to a subject were obtained by random permutation of the fixed population and assignment of x_1, the y_1, or the z_1 to the positive response. Thus, the population of test stimuli, their sequential properties, and the relative frequency of positive responses (4/15) were the same in all conditions.[9]

A trial consisted of a warning signal, the test digit, the subject's response, and a feedback light. Between a

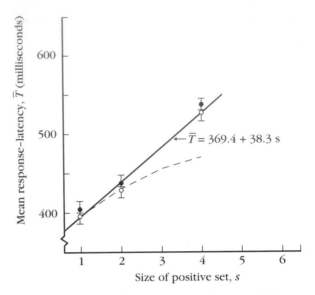

FIGURE 15.2 Relation between response latency and the size of the positive set, s, in experiment 2. Mean latencies, over six subjects, of positive responses (filled circles) and negative responses (open circles). About 200 (positive) or 500 (negative) observations per point. For each s, overall mean (heavy bar) and estimates of $\pm s$ are indicated.[6] Solid line was fitted by least squares to overall means. Upper bound for parallel process (broken curve).

response and the next test digit, 3.7 seconds elapsed. As in experiment 1, feedback and payoffs were designed to encourage speed without sacrifice of accuracy. The six subjects whose data are presented pulled the wrong lever on 1.0 percent of the test trials.[5]

The results, shown in Figure 15.2, closely resemble those of experiment 1. A positive set in experiment 2 apparently played the same role as a series of symbols presented in experiment 1, both corresponding to a set of symbols stored in memory and used in the selection of a response. As in experiment 1, linear regression accounts for 99.4 percent of the variance of the overall mean response-latencies.[6] The slope of 38.3 ± 6.1 msec per symbol is indistinguishable from that in experiment 1; the zero intercept is 369.4 ± 10.1 msec. In experiment 2, the relation between latencies of positive and negative responses when $s = 1$ is not exceptional. Lines fitted separately to latencies of the two kinds of response differ in slope by an insignificant 1.6 ± 3.0 msec per symbol.

The linearity of the latency functions suggests that the time between test stimulus and response is occupied, in part, by a serial-comparison (scanning) process. An internal representation of the test stimulus is compared successively to the symbols in memory, each comparison resulting in either a match or a mismatch. The time from the beginning of one comparison to the beginning of the next (the comparison time) has the same mean value for successive comparisons. A positive response is made if there has been a match, and a negative response otherwise.

On trials requiring negative responses, s comparisons must be made. If positive responses were initiated as soon as a match had occurred (as in a self-terminating search), the mean number of comparisons on positive trials would be $(s + 1)/2$ rather than s. The latency function for positive responses would then have half the slope of the function for negative responses. The equality of the observed slopes shows, instead, that the scanning process is exhaustive: [E]ven when a match has occurred, scanning continues through the entire series. This may appear surprising, as it suggests nonoptimality. One can, however, conceive of systems in which a self-terminating search would be inefficient. For example, if the determination of whether or not a match had occurred were a slow operation that could not occur concurrently with scanning, self-termination would entail a long interruption in the scan after each comparison.

On the basis of the exhaustive-scanning theory, the zero intercept of the latency function is interpreted as the sum of the times taken by motor response, formation of the test stimulus representation, and other unknown processes whose durations are independent of the number of symbols in memory. The slope of the latency function represents the mean comparison-time. The two experiments, then, provide a measure of the speed of purely internal events, independent of the times taken by sensory and motor operations. The average rate of between 25 and 30 symbols per second is about four times as high as the maximum rate of "subvocal speech" when the words are the names of digits.[11] This difference suggests that the silent rehearsal[12] reported by subjects in both experiments should probably not be identified with high-speed scanning, but should be thought of as a separate process whose function is to maintain the memory that is to be scanned.

In view of the substantial agreement in results of the two experiments, one difference in procedure merits particular emphasis. A response in experiment 1 was the first and only response based on a particular series, made about 3 sec after the series had been presented. In contrast, the positive set on which a response was based in experiment 2 had been used on an average of 120 previous trials. Evidently, neither practice in scanning a particular series nor lengthening of the time it has been stored in memory need increase the rate at which it is scanned.

In accounting for human performance in other tasks that appear to involve multiple comparisons, theorists have occasionally proposed that the comparisons are carried out in parallel rather than serially.[13,14] This perhaps corresponds to the assumption mentioned earlier that the momentary capacity of consciousness is several items rather than only one. Are the present data inconsistent with such a proposal? Parallel comparisons that begin and also end simultaneously[14] are excluded because the mean latency has been shown to increase with s. A process in which multiple comparisons begin simultaneously is more difficult to exclude if the comparison times are independent, their distribution has nonzero variance, and the response is initiated when the slowest comparison ends. A linear increase in mean latency cannot alone be taken as conclusive evidence against such a process. The magnitude of the latency increase that would result from a parallel process is bounded above, however[15]; it is possible to apply the bound to these data.[16] This was done for the negative responses in both experiments, with the results shown by the broken curves in Figures 15.1 and 15.2. Evidently, the increase in response latency with s is too great to be attributed to a parallel process with independent comparison times.[17]

Other experiments provide added support for the scanning theory.[16] Two of the findings are noted here: (i) variation in the size, n, of the negative set ($n \geq s$) had no effect on the mean latency, indicating that stimulus confusability[10,18] cannot account for the results of experiments 1 and 2; (ii) variation in the size of a response-irrelevant memory load had no effect on the latency function, implying that the increase in latency reflects the duration of retrieval and not merely the exigencies of retention.

The generality of the high-speed scanning process has yet to be determined, but there are several features of experiments 1 and 2 that should be taken into account in any comparison with other binary classification tasks:[14,19] (i) at least one of the classes is small; (ii) class members are assigned arbitrarily; (iii) relatively little practice is provided; (iv) high accuracy is required and errors cannot be corrected; and (v) until the response to one stimulus is completed the next stimulus cannot be viewed.

REFERENCES AND NOTES

1. A. W. Melton, *J. Verbal Learning Verbal Behavior 2*, 1 (1963).

2. G. A. Miller, *Psychology, the science of mental life* (Harper and Row, New York, 1962), p. 47.

3. These experiments were first reported by S. Sternberg, "Retrieval from recent memory: Some reaction-time experiments and a search theory," paper presented at a meeting of the Psychonomic Society, Bryn Mawr, August 1963.

4. Subjects were undergraduates at the University of Pennsylvania.

5. These trials were excluded from the analysis. Three other subjects in experiment 1 (two in experiment 2) were rejected because they exceeded an error criterion. Their latency data, which are not presented, resembled those of the other subjects.

6. For both experiments the data subjected to analysis of variance were, for each subject, the mean latency for each value of *s*. So that inferences might be drawn about the population of subjects, individual differences in mean and in linear-regression slope were treated as "random effects." Where quantities are stated in the form $a \pm b$, b is an estimate of the standard error of *a*.

Such estimates were usually calculated by using variance components derived from the analysis of variance.

7. The analyses of variance for both experiments provided a means of testing the significance of differences among individual slopes. Significance levels are .07 (experiment 1) and .09 (experiment 2), suggesting true intersubject differences in slope; the population distribution of slopes has an estimated standard deviation of 8.0 msec per symbol.

8. W. R. Garner, *Uncertainty and structure as psychological concepts* (Wiley, New York 1962).

9. A result of this procedure is that other factors in choice-reaction time were also controlled: stimulus discriminability[10]; information transmitted[8]; and information reduced, M. I. Posner, *Psychol. Rev. 71*, 49 (1964); P. M. Fitts and I. Biederman, *J. Exp. Psychol. 69*, 408 (1965).

10. R. N. Shepard and J. J. Chang, *J. Exp. Psychol. 65*, 94 (1963); M. Stone, *Psychometrika 25*, 251 (1960).

11. T. K. Landauer, *Percept. Mot. Skills 15*, 64 (1962).

12. D. E. Broadbent, *Perception and communication* (Pergamon, New York, 1958), p. 225.

13. L. S. Christie and R. D. Luce, *Bull. Math. Biophys. 18*, 89 (1956); A. Rapoport, *Behavioral Sci. 4*, 299 (1959).

14. U. Neisser, *Amer. J. Psychol. 76*, 376 (1963); *Sci. Amer. 210*, 94 (1964).

15. H. O. Hartley and H. A. David, *Ann. Math. Stat. 25*, 85 (1954).

16. S. Sternberg, in preparation.

17. Exponentially distributed parallel comparison[13] and other interesting theories of multiple comparisons[18] lead to a latency function that is approximately linear in log. Deviations of the overall means from such function are significant ($p < .03$) in both experiments.

18. A. T. Welford, *Ergonomics 3*, 189 (1960).

19. I. Pollack, *J. Verbal Learning Verbal Behavior 2*, 159 (1963); D. E. Broadbent and M. Gregory, *Nature 193*, 1315 (1962).

CHAPTER SIX
Working Memory

16 WORKING MEMORY: IRRELEVANT SPEECH, MEMORY SPAN, PHONOLOGICAL SIMILARITY

The term *working memory* was originally introduced by Miller, Galanter, and Pribram (1960, p. 65), and it captured the idea that information often has to be retained briefly in a highly accessible state while performing cognitive tasks. Today, the term is synonymous with a particular account of memory and attention developed by Alan Baddeley and his colleagues (Baddeley, 1986; Baddeley & Hitch, 1974; Baddeley & Logie, 1999).

Unlike the traditional models of memory from the 1960s, working memory divides short-term memory into three components: The central executive is involved with planning and attention, the visuospatial sketchpad processes visual and spatial information, and the phonological loop processes and maintains speech-based information.

The Baddeley (1992) article presents an overview of the working memory model, including a brief description of the three major components and some of the evidence that the model explains. It is also particularly useful in pointing out how researchers have used the basic ideas in different areas, including individual differences in working memory capacity (see Reading 17, "Operation Span"), neuropsychological case studies, and the development of reading and language in children.

By far the most studied component is the phonological loop, which has two main components: the phonological store and the articulatory control process. The phonological store is a memory store that can retain speech-based information for a short period of time. Unless rehearsed, the traces within the store are assumed to fade and decay within about 2 seconds, after which they are no longer usable. The second component is the articulatory control process, which is responsible for two different functions: It translates visual information into a speech-based code and deposits it in the phonological store, and it refreshes a trace in the phonological store, offsetting the decay process.

The visuospatial sketchpad is analogous to the phonological store, and the visual scribe is analogous to the articulatory control process. Baddeley and Logie (1999) describe how this part of working memory is involved with imagery and processing and maintaining spatial information.

The phonological loop component of working memory was designed to explain four basic phenomena (Baddeley, 1986):

- The *phonological similarity effect* refers to the finding that memory is worse for items that sound alike than for items that differ. The CogLab demo tests your ability to recall lists made up of similar-sounding letters (B, C, D, G, P, T, V) and dissimilar sounding letters (F, K, L, M, Q, R, X). This effect arises, according to the working memory theory, because the phonological store retains information in a speech-based format, and things that sound alike are more difficult to distinguish. Crucially, this effect holds whether you hear the items or you read the items silently. In the latter case, the articulatory control process converts the visual information into the appropriate speech-based code.

- The *irrelevant speech effect* refers to the impairment in the ability to recall a list of items if presentation is accompanied by irrelevant background speech compared to when there is no background speech. The most curious aspect is that an auditory item interferes with a visual item. Because the presentation modalities differ, this cannot be a perceptual effect. The CogLab demo tests your memory for the letters F, K, L, M, Q, R, X, and uses a passage in German from a book by Franz Kafka. Working memory explains the irrelevant speech effect by stating that speech information has obligatory access to the phonological store, where it interferes with the to-be-remembered information.

- The *word-length effect* has to do with memory span—the number of items that you can immediately recall in order. Span depends critically on the type of items you are trying to remember. The CogLab demo Memory Span measures your span for digits, dissimilar sounding letters, similar sounding letters, short (monosyllable) words, and long (three- to five-syllable words). Your span should be slightly higher for digits than letters, should be substantially higher for the dissimilar sounding than the similar sounding letters (due to the phonological similarity effect), and should be higher for the short than the long words. According to working memory, the number of items that can be immediately recalled depends on how often each item can be subvocally rehearsed by the articulatory control process. This process is used to refresh the decaying traces in the phonological store, and the shorter the items (in terms of pronunciation time), the more items can be rehearsed before a particular trace decays. An analogy is to imagine you had 2 s worth of tape to record some words; you can fit more short words (e.g., Maine) than long words (e.g., Louisiana).

- When subjects engage in *articulatory suppression*, they repeatedly say a word, such as *the*, over and over out loud. The original idea was to prevent subvocal rehearsal by occupying the articulatory control process. According to working memory, subjects who engage in articulatory suppression cannot translate visually presented information into a speech-based code because the articulatory control process is busy saying "the, the, the, . . .". Working memory thus accounts for the finding that the phonological similarity effect for visually presented items disappears if subjects engage in articulatory suppression. The CogLab demo for the phonological similarity effect illustrates this by asking you to engage in articulatory suppression for half of the lists.

Thus, working memory explains many short-term memory phenomena in terms of decay of speech-based information that can be (partially) offset by subvocal rehearsal. Although approaches based on working memory are currently the most popular, there have been numerous challenges to them (e.g., Nairne, 2002).

REFERENCES

Baddeley, A. D. (1986). *Working memory.* New York: Oxford University Press.

Baddeley, A. D. (2000). The episodic buffer: A new component of working memory? *Trends in Cognitive Sciences, 4,* 417–423..

Baddeley, A. D., & Hitch, G. J. (1974). Working memory. In G. H. Bower (Ed.), *The psychology of learning and motivation* (Vol. 8). New York: Academic Press.

Baddeley, A. D., & Logie, R. L. (1999). Working memory: The multi-component model. In A. Miyake & P. Shah (Eds.), *Models of working memory: Mechanisms of active maintenance and executive control* (pp. 28–61). New York: Cambridge University Press.

Miller, G. A., Galanter, E., & Pribram, K. (1960). *Plans and the structure of behavior.* New York: Holt, Rinehart & Winston.

Nairne, J. S. (2002). Remembering over the short-term: The case against the standard model. *Annual Review of Psychology, 53,* 53–81.

QUESTIONS

1. How does working memory explain the observation that memory span for short (one syllable) words is larger than memory span for long (three- to five-syllable) words?
2. According to working memory, what should happen if you measured your memory span for short (one syllable) and long (three- to five-syllable) words while you engaged in articulatory suppression?
3. According to working memory, what should happen if you ran an irrelevant speech experiment but used tones (i.e., nonspeech sounds) rather than speech as the irrelevant auditory information?

Working Memory

Alan Baddeley

INTRODUCTION

A model of memory has gained increasing favor during recent years with the suggestion that temporary storage and manipulation of memory may occur through a far more active and complex system than was originally proposed by Richard Atkinson and Richard Shiffrin as the short-term store. According to Alan Baddeley's model, temporary storage and manipulation of information occur in a temporarily activated portion of long-term memory called *working memory*. According to Baddeley, with whom the notion is most strongly associated, working memory comprises three main systems, which work together.

Baddeley calls the first system the *central executive*. This system controls and monitors a person's attention according to needs current at a given time. This central executive is particularly important in activities that require one to attend to and manipulate large amounts of information in brief periods of time, as when one plays chess or mentally solves a difficult arithmetic problem.

Two *slave systems* also operate under the control of the central executive. A *visuospatial sketch pad* manipulates visual images, and a *phonological loop* stores and rehearses speech-based information.

The popularity of the working memory model stems from its theoretical elegance, its empirical support, and its usefulness not only in the study of memory but in the study of other aspects of cognition, as well. For example, recent research suggests that differences in working-memory abilities may largely account for individual differences in complex processes as diverse as reading comprehension and inductive reasoning (as when one completes a series of numbers such as 3,8,13,?). Today, Baddeley's model is probably the one that most strongly competes with the early Atkinson–Shiffrin model. Its widespread usage in cognitive research has earned it a place as one of the key seminal contributions to the study, not only of memory, but of cognition in general.

* * *

The term working memory *refers to a brain system that provides temporary storage and manipulation of the information necessary for such complex cognitive tasks as language comprehension, learning, and reasoning. This definition has evolved from the concept of a unitary short-term memory system. Working memory has been found to require the simultaneous storage and processing of information. It can be divided into the following three subcomponents: (i) the central executive, which is assumed to be an attentional-controlling system, is important in skills such as chess playing, and is particularly susceptible to the effects of Alzheimer's disease; and two slave systems, namely (ii) the visuospatial sketch pad, which manipulates visual images, and (iii) the phonological loop, which stores and rehearses speech-based information and is necessary for the acquisition of both native and second-language vocabulary.*

The question of whether memory should be regarded as a single unitary system or whether it should be fractionated into two or more subsystems formed one of the major controversies within cognitive psychology during the mid-1960s. During that time, evidence began to accumulate in favor of a dichotomy.[1] Some of the most convincing evidence came from the study of brain-damaged patients; those suffering from the classic amnesic syndrome appeared to have gross disruption of the capacity to form new lasting memories but showed preserved performance on a range of tasks that were assumed to test short-term memory.[2]

SOURCE: Reprinted with permission from Baddeley, A. (1992). Working memory. *Science, 255*, 556–559. Copyright © 1992 American Association for the Advancement of Science.

Conversely, a second type of patient was identified who appeared to show normal long-term learning but had a short-term memory span limited to one or two items.[3] It was suggested that such patients had a deficit in short-term storage, in contrast to the long-term storage deficit that occurs in the amnesic syndrome. This finding, together with considerable evidence from the study of normal subjects, appeared by the late 1960s to argue for a dichotomous view of memory, such as that proposed by Atkinson and Shiffrin.[4]

By the early 1970s, it was becoming clear that the two-component model was running into difficulties. One of its problems was inherent in the neuropsychological evidence that initially appeared to support it so strongly. Atkinson and Shiffrin[4] suggested that the short-term store within their model acted as a working memory, being necessary for learning, for the retrieval of old material, and for the performance of many other cognitive tasks. If that were the case, one would expect patients with a grossly defective short-term store to show many other cognitive problems, including impaired long-term learning. In fact, such patients appeared to have a normal long-term learning capacity and surprisingly few cognitive handicaps.

Pursuing this issue was difficult because patients with a pure short-term memory deficit are rare. We therefore attempted to simulate this condition in unimpaired subjects by using a dual-task technique.[5] We argued as follows: If the digit-span procedure depends on the short-term store, with the number of digits retained determined by the capacity of the store, then it should be possible to interfere systematically with the operation of the working memory system by requiring the subject to remember digits while performing other cognitive tasks. As the concurrent digit load is increased, the remaining short-term capacity would decrease and the interference would increase, with performance presumably breaking down as the digit load reached the capacity of the system.

Reasoning, comprehension, and learning tasks all showed a similar pattern. As concurrent digit load increased, performance declined, but the degree of disruption fell far short of that predicted. Subjects whose digit memory was at full capacity could reason and learn quite effectively.

These results, together with others, encouraged the abandonment of the idea of a single, unitary short-term store that also functions as a working memory. Instead, we proposed the tripartite system shown in Figure 16.1, which comprises an attentional controller and the central executive, supplemented by two subsidiary slave systems. The articulatory or phonological loop was assumed to be responsible for maintaining speech-based information, including digits in the digit-span test, whereas the visuospatial sketch pad was assumed to perform a similar function in setting up and manipulating visuospatial imagery.

The concept of working memory has increasingly replaced the older concept of short-term memory.[6] Research has subsequently tended to concentrate on one of two complementary but somewhat different approaches. One of these defines working memory as the system that is necessary for the concurrent storage and manipulation of information; tasks are devised that combine processing and storage, and the capacity of such tasks to predict a range of other cognitive skills, such as reading, comprehension, and reasoning, is tested. This psychometric approach, which has flourished most strongly in North America, frequently focuses on the extent to which performance on working memory tasks can predict individual differences in the relevant cognitive skills.

An alternative approach, which has been more favored in Europe, uses both dual-task methodology and the study of neuropsychological cases in an attempt to analyze the structure of the working memory system. Most effort has been devoted to the two slave systems, on the grounds that these offer more tractable problems than the more complex central-executive system.

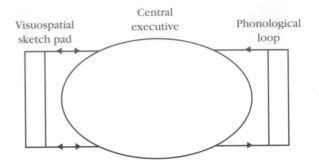

FIGURE 16.1   A simplified representation of the Baddeley and Hitch working memory model.[5]

The two approaches are complementary, and both have strengths and weaknesses; the psychometric correlational approach has the advantage that it can tackle what is probably the most crucial component of the system, the central executive, and can furthermore work directly on problems of practical significance, such as reading comprehension or the reasoning tasks used in tests of intelligence. The weakness of this approach lies in the reliance on complex working memory tasks that have a somewhat arbitrary construction and that do not readily lend themselves to a more detailed analysis of the component processes. The dual-task and neuropsychological approach can be utilized to successfully analyze the constituent processes of the slave systems but has made less headway in teasing apart the complexities of the executive controller.

INDIVIDUAL DIFFERENCES IN WORKING MEMORY

The essence of the psychometric approach is to develop tasks that require the combined storage and manipulation of information and to correlate performance on these tasks with the performance of practically and theoretically important cognitive skills. One influential study in this area was carried out by Daneman and Carpenter,[7] who examined the processes involved in reading comprehension. They devised a series of working memory tasks, one of which required subjects to read aloud or listen to a series of short sentences while retaining the last word from each sentence for subsequent immediate recall. Hence, subjects might read or hear: "The sailor sold the parrot. The vicar opened the book." They should then respond "parrot, book." The test typically starts with two sentences and increases to a point at which subjects are no longer able to recall all the terminal words. This point is designated the subject's working memory span.

Daneman and Carpenter, and others using similar techniques, typically found a correlation coefficient of about 0.5 or 0.6 between working memory span and reading comprehension, as measured by standardized tests.[8] The span task does not have to involve language processing because similar correlations are found when simple arithmetic, combined with word recall, is substituted for sentence processing.[9]

Subsequent studies have indicated that students with high working memory span were better at coping with "garden path sentences," which contain misleading context, and that they are better at drawing inferences from text, suggesting that they have a better grasp of its meaning.[10]

A second area in which the individual differences approach has been applied to the analysis of working memory is concerned with the study of reasoning and concentrates particularly on tasks that have traditionally been used to measure intelligence. One example of this is the working memory analysis by Carpenter, Just, and Shell[11] of performance on the Raven's matrices task, a test in which one sector is missing from a complex pattern and the subject is required to choose which of six possible options offers the best completion. Christal[12] has also shown that working memory tests provide improved prediction of technical learning capacity in U.S. Air Force recruits, when compared with more scholastic measures.

Kyllonen and Christal[13] have carried out a series of studies, each involving several hundred subjects who were required to perform a number of standardized tests of reasoning of the type used to assess intelligence as well as a range of tasks that had been devised to estimate working memory capacity. For each study, their results suggested a very high correlation between working memory capacity and reasoning skill. They concluded, however, that the two concepts, although closely related, were not synonymous; reasoning performance was more dependent on previous knowledge than was working memory, which in contrast appeared to be more dependent on sheer speed of processing.

COMPONENTS OF WORKING MEMORY

Although concurrent storage and processing may be one aspect of working memory, it is almost certainly not the only feature; indeed, Baddeley, Barnard, and Schneider and Detweiler[14] all suggest that the coordination of resources is the prime function of working memory, with memory storage being only one of many potential demands that are likely to be made on the system.

One proposed role for the central executive is that of coordinating information from two or more slave

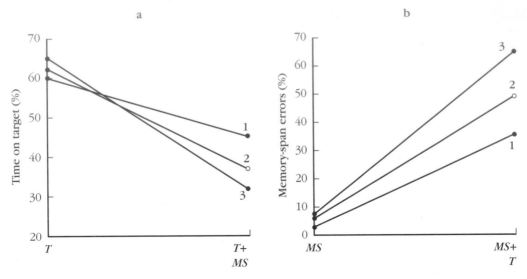

FIGURE 16.2   Dual-task performance of patients with Alzheimer's disease in a series of three sequential tests (1, 2, and 3) 6 months apart. *T*, tracking task; *MS*, memory span task. Normal subjects did not show a difference between single and dual-task conditions. Data from Baddeley et al.[17]

systems. This feature of the central executive was used in an attempt to test the proposal that Alzheimer's disease is associated with a particularly marked deficit in central executive functioning.[15] Patients with Alzheimer's disease, and both young and elderly normal subjects, were required to perform two tasks concurrently, one visual and one verbal. The difficulty of each task was adjusted so that the Alzheimer patients were making the same proportion of errors as the control subjects, and subjects were then required to perform both tasks at the same time. Normal elderly subjects were no more impaired than young controls by this requirement to coordinate, whereas the Alzheimer patients showed a marked impairment in performance on both the memory and tracking tasks when required to combine them.[16] As the disease progressed, performance on the individual tracking and memory span tasks held up very well (Figure 16.2), whereas performance on the combined tasks deteriorated markedly, as would be predicted by the hypothesis of a central executive deficit in Alzheimer's disease.[17]

THE SLAVE SYSTEMS OF WORKING MEMORY

Although an analytic approach to the central executive is beginning to bear fruit, there is no doubt that con-

siderably more progress has been made with the simpler task of understanding the peripheral slave systems of working memory. The dual-task paradigm has been used to demonstrate the separability of the memory systems responsible for learning by means of visuospatial imagery and of learning by rote repetition. Imagery is disrupted by the requirement of performing a visuospatial task, such as tracking a spot of light moving on a screen, by certain types of eye movement, or by the presentation of irrelevant visual material during learning.[18]

There are separable spatial and visual components, with different tasks differentially recruiting the two. Farah[19] distinguishes one imagery component that is principally concerned with the representation of pattern information and that involves the occipital lobes from a second more spatial component that seems to be dependent on parietal lobe functioning. Neuropsychological evidence supports this dichotomy, with some patients having great difficulty in imaging and recalling such visual features as the shape of the ears of a spaniel dog or the color of a pumpkin but having no difficulty in spatial tasks such as describing routes or locating towns on maps; other patients show exactly the reverse pattern of deficits.[20]

Having found ways of separately disrupting spatial and verbal processing, one can explore the relative contribution of different subsystems to complex tasks. One example of this application concerns the nature of the cognitive processes involved in playing chess. The literature reviewed by Holding[21] indicates that both visual and verbal coding have been claimed to be crucial by different studies that principally rely on subjective report. We have sought more objective evidence through a series of experiments that utilize the secondary-task technique to disrupt either the phonological loop, the sketch pad system, or the central executive. Our first study involved memory for complex chess positions and tested subjects ranging from the modest club player to the international grand master. As expected, expertise correlated highly with memory performance, but all subjects showed the same basic pattern: no disruption from the concurrent verbal task but clear impairment from the tasks occupying the visuospatial sketch pad or the central executive. A second study required subjects to choose the optimum next move from a complex middle-game position and found exactly the same pattern. Disruption of verbal activity had no effect, whereas visuospatial disruption was clear, and this problem-solving task was even more susceptible to central executive disruption than the task in the first study.[21]

ANALYZING THE PHONOLOGICAL LOOP

The phonological loop is probably the simplest and most extensively investigated component of working memory. It lies closest to the earlier concept of short-term memory and has been investigated most extensively with the memory-span procedure. It is assumed to comprise two components, a phonological store that can hold acoustic or speech-based information for 1 to 2 sec, coupled with an articulatory control process, somewhat analogous to inner speech. This system serves two functions; it can maintain material within the phonological store by subvocal repetition, and it can take visually presented material such as words or nameable pictures and register them in the phonological store by subvocalization.

This simple model is able to give a good account of a rich range of laboratory-based findings. These include the following:

1. *The acoustic similarity effect.* This is the observation that the immediate ordered recall of items is poorer when they are similar rather than dissimilar in sound.[23] Hence, hearing and repeating dissimilar words such as "pit, day, cow, pen, rig," is easier than a phonologically similar sequence such as "man, cap, can, map, mad." This phenomenon is assumed to occur because the basic code involved in the store is phonological; similar items have fewer distinguishing cues than dissimilar items and are therefore more susceptible to being forgotten. Similarity of meaning does not have this effect, suggesting that this subsystem does not reflect semantic coding.

2. *The irrelevant speech effect.* This refers to a reduction in recall of lists of visually presented items brought about by the presence of irrelevant spoken material.[24] Once again, the semantic characteristics of the material are not important, with a language that is unfamiliar to the subject being just as disruptive as words in his or her native tongue and nonsense syllables being as disruptive as meaningful words. The effect is not due to simple distraction, because loud bursts of noise have little or no effect.[25] These results are interpreted under the assumption that disruptive spoken material gains obligatory access to the phonological memory store.

3. *The word-length effect.* This provides evidence on the nature of the subvocal rehearsal process. Memory span for words is inversely related to spoken duration of the words. Subjects can generally remember about as many words as they can say in 2 sec.[26] This phenomenon accounts for differences in digit span when subjects are tested in different languages; languages in which digits tend to have long vowel sounds or more than one syllable take longer to rehearse and lead to shorter memory spans.[27] The model can also explain the marked tendency for digit span in children to increase with age; as children get older, they are able to rehearse faster.[28]

4. *Articulatory suppression.* It is possible to disrupt the use of subvocal rehearsal by requiring subjects to utter some repeated irrelevant sound, such as the word "the." This process, known as articulatory suppression, prevents the subjects from rehearsing the material they are trying to remember and thus removes the effect of word length. Suppression also prevents subjects from registering

visually presented material in the phonological store. Recall of such visual material is reduced, and the acoustic similarity effect is abolished.[29]

The performance of neuropsychological patients with impaired short-term memory can also be explained as a deficit in the phonological store. They typically show no evidence of phonological coding in memory tasks when presentation is visual, no word length effect, and no influence of articulatory suppression, suggesting that these patients make little or no use of their defective phonological short-term store.[30]

THE FUNCTION OF THE PHONOLOGICAL LOOP

Patients with a specific phonological loop deficit seem to have remarkably few signs of general cognitive impairment. Although they typically have difficulty in comprehending certain types of complex sentences, interpretation of results in this area remains controversial.[31] The most commonly held view is that the phonological store serves as a backup system for comprehension of speech under taxing conditions but may be less important with simple, clearly presented material.

In recent years, we have been exploring another possible function of this system, namely, its role in long-term phonological learning, such as acquiring the vocabulary of one's native, or even a foreign, language. In one study, we asked a patient with a very specific short-term phonological memory deficit to learn eight items of Russian vocabulary, a language with which the patient was unfamiliar; we compared the results with the patient's capacity to learn to associate arbitrary pairs of words in the patient's native language.[32] People tend to learn pairs of familiar words in terms of their meaning, and, as expected, the patient's performance on this task was entirely normal. In contrast, the patient failed to learn the Russian words with auditory presentation and was severely impaired relative to control subjects even when presentation was visual. This result suggests that short-term phonological storage is important for new long-term phonological learning. Subsequent studies with normal adults have shown that factors that influence the phonological loop, such as articulatory suppression, word length, and phonological similarity, strongly influence foreign vocabulary acquisition yet show no effect on learning to associate pairs of familiar words.[33]

Evidence for the importance of the phonological loop in native-language learning comes from a number of sources. Gathercole and Baddeley[34] studied a group of children with a specific language disorder and found that their most striking cognitive deficits occurred in a task involving hearing and repeating back unfamiliar nonwords; on this nonword repetition task, 8-year-old children with the language development of 6-year-olds functioned like 4-year-olds. Further investigation suggested that this was due neither to perceptual difficulties nor to difficulties in speech production but probably resided in the operation of the phonological short-term store.

A subsequent study assessed the role of the phonological short-term store in the development of vocabulary across the normal range.[35] A sample of 118 children was tested after starting school between the ages of 4 and 5 years. Their capacity for nonword repetition was measured, as was their nonverbal intelligence and their vocabulary, which was tested by speaking a series of words to the children and requiring them to point to appropriate pictures. Nonword repetition proved to be highly correlated with vocabulary and to be a powerful predictor of vocabulary 1 year later.

In an experimental simulation of new word learning,[36] we taught children new names for toy monsters. Two groups were tested that were matched for nonverbal intelligence but that differed in nonword repetition capacity. Those with low capacity showed poor learning, particularly in the case of unfamiliar invented names.

Service[37] has studied the acquisition of English as a second language by young Finnish children. Service took a number of measures of cognitive skill before the course began, including measures of nonverbal intelligence and of nonword repetition capacity. Two years later, the children's performances on a range of tests of English language were correlated with these earlier measures. Once again, nonword repetition capacity, which is assumed to depend on short-term phonological storage, was clearly the best predictor of subsequent success. Thus, the evidence supports the view that short-term phonological memory is crucial in the acquisition of vocabulary.

CONCLUSION

The concept of a working memory system that temporarily stores information as part of the performance of complex cognitive tasks is proving to be productive. Studies that have utilized the individual difference approach have linked working memory to performance on a range of important tasks, including language comprehension and reasoning. The more analytic approach has shown that the concept forms a useful conceptual tool in understanding a range of neuropsychological deficits, which in turn have thrown light on normal cognitive functioning.

Working memory stands at the crossroads between memory, attention, and perception. In the case of the slave systems, the phonological loop, for example, probably represents an evolution of the basic speech perception and production systems to the point at which they can be used for active memory. Any adequate model of the phonological loop is thus likely to overlap substantially with an adequate model of speech perception and speech production. The visuospatial sketch pad is probably intimately related to the processes of visual perception and action. The central executive clearly reflects a system concerned with the attentional control of behavior, with subsequent developments almost certainly depending on parallel developments in the study of attention and of the control of action. If these links can be sustained and developed, the concept of working memory is likely to continue to be a fruitful one.

REFERENCES

1. See A. D. Baddeley [*Human memory: Theory and practice* (Allyn and Bacon, Needham Heights, MA, 1990), pp. 39–66] for a review.
2. ——— and E. K. Warrington, *J. Verb. Learn. Verb. Behav. 9,* 176 (1970); B. Milner, in *Amnesia,* C. W. M. Whitty and O. L. Zangwill, Eds. (Butterworths, London, 1966), pp. 109–133.
3. T. Shallice and E. K. Warrington, *Q. J. Exp. Psychol. 22,* 261 (1970); A. Basso, H. Spinnler, G. Vallar, E. Zanobio, *Neuropsychologia 20,* 263 (1982); G. Vallar and T. Shallice, *Neuropsychological impairments of short-term memory* (Cambridge Univ. Press, Cambridge, 1990).
4. R. C. Atkinson and R. M. Shiffrin, in *The psychology of learning and motivation: Advances in research and theory,* K. W. Spence, Ed. (Academic Press, New York, 1968), vol. 2, pp. 89–195.
5. A. D. Baddeley and G. J. Hitch, in *The psychology of learning and motivation,* G. A. Bower, Ed. (Academic Press, New York, 1974), vol. 8, pp. 47–89.
6. R. G. Crowder, *Acta. Psychol. 50,* 291 (1982).
7. M. Daneman and P. A. Carpenter, *J. Verb. Learn. Verb. Behav. 19,* 450 (1980).
8. A. D. Baddeley, R. Logie, I. Nimmo-Smith, N. Brereton, *J. Mem. Lang. 24,* 119 (1985); M. E. J. Masson and G. A. Miller, *J. Educ. Psychol. 75,* 314 (1983).
9. J. V. Oakhill, N. Yuill, A. J. Parkin, *J. Res. Read. 9,* 80 (1986); M. L. Turner and R. W. Engle, *J. Mem. Lang. 28,* 127 (1989).
10. M. Daneman and P. A. Carpenter, *J. Exp. Psychol. Learn. Mem. Cogn. 9,* 561 (1983); J. V. Oakhill, *Br. J. Educ. Psychol. 54,* 31 (1984).
11. P. A. Carpenter, M. A. Just, P. Shell, *Psychol. Rev. 97,* 404 (1990).
12. R. E. Christal, *Armstrong Laboratory Human Resources Directorate Technical Report AL TP 1991 0031* (Brooks Air Force Base, TX, 1991).
13. P. C. Kyllonen and R. E. Christal, *Intelligence 14,* 389 (1990).
14. A. D. Baddeley, *Working memory* (Oxford Univ. Press, Oxford, 1986); P. Barnard, in *Progress in the psychology of language,* A. Ellis, Ed. (Erlbaum, London, 1985), vol. 2, pp. 197–258; W. Schneider and M. Detweiler, in *The psychology of learning and motivation,* G. H. Bower, Ed. (Academic Press, New York, 1987), vol. 21, pp. 54–119.
15. J. T. Becker, in *Alzheimer's disease: Advances in basic research and therapies,* R. J. Wurtman, S. H. Corkin, J. H. Growdon, Eds. (Center for Brain Sciences and Metabolism Charitable Trust, Cambridge, 1987), pp. 343–348; H. Spinnler, S. Della Sala, R. Bandera, A. D. Baddeley, *Cogn. Neuropsychol. 5,* 193 (1988).
16. A. D. Baddeley, R. Logie, S. Bressi, S. Della Sala, H. Spinnler, *Q. J. Exp. Psychol. 38A,* 603 (1986).
17. A. D. Baddeley, S. Bressi, S. Della Sala, R. Logie, H. Spinnler, *Brain,* in press.
18. L. R. Brooks, *Q. J. Exp. Psychol. 19,* 289 (1967); A. D. Baddeley, S. Grant, E. Wight, N. Thomson, in *Attention and performance,* P. M. A. Rabbitt and S. Dornic, Eds. (Academic Press, London, 1973), vol. 5, pp. 205–217 {see R. H. Logie and A. D. Baddeley in *Imagery: Current developments,* J. Richardson, D. Marks, P. Hampson, Eds. (Routledge and Kegan Paul, London, 1990), pp. 103–128 for a review}; A. D. Baddeley and K. Lieberman, in *Attention and performance,* R. S. Nickerson, Ed. (Erlbaum, Hillsdale, NJ, 1980), vol. 8, pp. 521–539.

19. M. J. Farah, *Psychol. Rev. 95*, 307 (1988).

20. ———, K. M. Hammond, D. N. Levine, R. Calvanio, *Cogn. Psychol. 20*, 439 (1988).

21. D. H. Holding, *The psychology of chess skill* (Erlbaum, Hillsdale, NJ, 1985); A. D. Baddeley, in *Attention: Selection, awareness, and control*, A. D. Baddeley and L. Weiskrantz, Eds. (Oxford Univ. Press, Oxford, in press).

22. T. W. Robbins et al., in preparation.

23. R. Conrad, *Br. J. Psychol. 55*, 75 (1964); A. D. Baddeley, *Q. J. Exp. Psychol. 18*, 302 (1966).

24. H. A. Colle and A. Welsh, *J. Verb. Learn. Verb. Behav. 15*, 17 (1976); P. Salamé and A. D. Baddeley, *ibid. 21*, 150 (1982).

25. H. A. Colle, *ibid. 19*, 722 (1980); P. Salamé and A. D. Baddeley, *Ergonomics 30*, 1185 (1987).

26. A. D. Baddeley et al., *J. Verb. Learn. Verb. Behav. 14*, 575 (1975).

27. N. C. Ellis and R. A. Hennelley, *Br. J. Psychol. 71*, 43 (1980); M. Naveh-Benjamin and T. J. Ayres, *Q. J. Exp. Psychol. 38*, 739 (1986).

28. R. Nicolson, in *Intelligence and learning*, M. P. Friedman, J. P. Das, N. O'Connor, Eds. (Plenum, London, 1981), pp. 179–184; G. J. Hitch and M. S. Halliday, *Philos. Trans. R. Soc. London B 302*, 325 (1983); C. Hulme, N. Thomson, C. Muir, A. Lawrence, *J. Exp. Child Psychol. 38*, 241 (1984).

29. A. D. Baddeley, V. J. Lewis, G. Vallar, *Q. J. Exp. Psychol. 36*, 233 (1984); D. J. Murray, *J. Exp. Psychol. 78*, 679 (1968).

30. G. Vallar and A. D. Baddeley, *J. Verb. Learn. Verb. Behav. 23*, 151 (1984).

31. G. Vallar and T. Shallice, Eds., *Neuropsychological impairments of short-term memory* (Cambridge Univ. Press, Cambridge, 1990).

32. A. D. Baddeley, C. Papagno, G. Vallar, *J. Mem. Lang. 27*, 586 (1988).

33. C. Papagno, T. Valentine, A. D. Baddeley, *ibid.*, in press; C. Papagno and G. Vallar, *Q. J. Exp. Psychol. 44A*, 47 (1992).

34. S. Gathercole and A. D. Baddeley, *J. Mem. Lang. 29*, 336 (1990).

35. ———, *ibid. 28*, 200 (1989).

36. ———, *Br. J. Psychol. 81*, 439 (1990).

37. E. Service, *University of Helsinki general psychology monograph* (Univ. of Helsinki Press, Helsinki, Finland, 1989), no. B9.

17 OPERATION SPAN

Psychologists have long been concerned with limits on the ability to process information, and the capacity of memory has been measured in many different ways. Thirty years ago, the limit for short-term memory was said to be seven (plus or minus two) items. This means that for most people, the largest number of unrelated words that they can immediately recall is seven. When more items have to be remembered, accuracy decreases. This measure is often known as memory span.

More recently, the capacity limit for working memory is said to be what you can say in approximately 2 seconds. An analogy is that you have a tape that can store 2 seconds' worth of sound. If you store items that take a long time to say (e.g., hippopotamus), then the tape will fill up quickly and very few items will fit. If you store items that take much less time to say (e.g., ant), then more items will fit.

The term *working memory capacity* refers to something a little different. Rather than focusing on the number of items that can be recalled immediately, working memory capacity examines the ability to retain information "over a period in which there is distraction or shift of attention away from the stored information" (Engle, 2001, p. 301). It can be measured by a variety of tasks, including operation span.

Operation span gets its name from the fact that subjects are asked to perform numerous "operations" instead of only remembering items. First, the subject sees a math problem, such as "Does 10/2 + 2 = 7?" They read this out loud, and then answer the question. A word is then shown, which is also read out loud. Math problems and words alternate until two, three, four, five, or six words have been shown. The subject is then asked to recall the words in order. Conway and Engle (1996) used written recall, whereas the CogLab demo uses reconstruction of order (you are asked to click on buttons labeled with the words to indicate the order). The first three trials are considered practice and do not contribute to the score. Operation span is defined as the sum of the sequence lengths that were recalled correctly given an accuracy level of 85% or better on the math problems. Thus, if the subject recalled a list of three words correctly, three would be added to the operation span score. If the subject recalled a list of six items correctly, six would be added to the operation span.

Measures of working memory capacity correlate highly with many higher-level cognitive tasks, including reading comprehension, language comprehension, spelling, vocabulary learning, writing, and reasoning (Engle et al., 1999). This means that people with high spans generally do better on these tasks than people with low spans. One key question is why.

Conway and Engle (1996) evaluate three hypotheses. The *general processing hypothesis* began as an explanation of changes in performance as children grew older. The central idea is that as various cognitive operations become more automatic, they occur faster. Moreover, automatized processes free up resources that can be used on other tasks or other parts of the task. In contrast, the *task specific hypothesis* attributes the correlation between working memory capacity and higher-level cognition to a shared component. This view says that there will be a correlation only when both tasks share a process. The third view, the *general capacity hypothesis*, argues that individuals differ in their attentional capacity. Those people with larger capacities will perform better on a variety of tasks even if there is no shared component.

To test these three explanations, Conway and Engle (1996) measured performance on two very dissimilar tasks—operation span and verbal SAT (VSAT) score. Importantly, they attempted to equate processing demands for each subject by varying the difficulty of the math component.

They found that all versions of the span task (the original, easy, moderate, and difficult versions) correlated with the VSAT (see Table 17.3). The finding that operation span scores correlate with VSAT measures is problematic for the task specific hypothesis because there is no obvious shared component between the two tasks. The results are also problematic for the general processing hypothesis because it attributes differences in performance to differences in the processing ability, but Conway and Engle equated the processing demands across subjects. In contrast, the general capacity hypothesis says that individuals differ in the total amount of attentional resources available. Therefore, even if the processing component is equated, the other factors may not be.

REFERENCES

Engle, R. W. (2001). What is working memory capacity? In H. L. Roediger III, J. S. Nairne, I. Neath, & A. M. Surprenant (Eds.), *The nature of remembering: Essays in honor of Robert G. Crowder* (pp. 297–314). Washington, DC: APA, .

Engle, R. W., Tuholski, S. W., Laughlin, J. E., & Conway, A. R. A. (1999). Working memory, short-term memory, and general fluid intelligence: A latent variable approach. *Journal of Experimental Psychology: General, 128*, 309–331.

QUESTIONS

1. What is the main difference between memory span and measures of working memory capacity?

2. Why is the computed operation span ignored if accuracy on the math problems is less than 85%?

3. If you have a high operation span, it suggests that you are better at controlling your attention. Why would this make it less likely that you would be easily distracted?

4. What is the major difference between the general processing hypothesis and the general capacity hypothesis?

Individual Differences in Working Memory Capacity: More Evidence for a General Capacity Theory

Andrew R. A. Conway

University of South Carolina

Randall W. Engle

Georgia Institute of Technology, USA

The causes of the positive relationship between comprehension and measures of working memory capacity remain unclear. This study tests three hypotheses for the relationship by equating the difficulty, for 48 individual subjects, of processing demands in complex working memory tasks. Even with difficulty of processing equated, the relationship between number of words recalled in the working memory measure and comprehension remained high and significant. The results favour a general capacity view. We suggest that high working memory span subjects have more limited capacity attentional resources available to them than low span subjects and that individual differences in working memory capacity will have implications for any task that requires controlled effortful processing.

INTRODUCTION

In the two decades that have followed the seminal work of Baddeley and Hitch (1974), evidence supporting the relationship between working memory capacity and cognitive performance has steadily accumulated (for a review, see Engle, 1995). However, it remains unclear exactly why this relationship occurs. The purpose of the current study is to test three competing hypotheses that have been proposed to account for the relationship between working memory capacity and reading comprehension. As such, this introduction will proceed with a brief review of the three competing hypotheses.

Pascual-Leone (1970) argued that keeping schemes active requires attentional control or mental energy and that the amount of mental power or M-space increases developmentally as a result of biological or epigenetic factors. Case (1974) extended the ideas of Pascual-Leone to suggest that differences in M-space are responsible for individual as well as developmental differences in cognition. However, he argued that increases in measured M-space do not result from an increase in attentional resources but as a result of a speed-up in mental operations as they become more automatic. The attentional resources freed by the automatisation of mental operations can be used to keep other schemes in the active portion of memory. Although the NeoPiagetian approach has been primarily used to understand the development of cognition, the ideas may also be helpful in efforts to explain individual differences at a given stage of development. We have referred to this approach to the relationship between working memory capacity and higher-level cognition as the *general processing hypothesis* because Case (1985) viewed the operations that become automatised as general to a wide variety of tasks (Engle, Cantor, & Carullo, 1992).

Baddeley and Hitch (1974) argued that working memory is a complex system used both for the storage of information and for the computational processing of that information. They proposed the central executive as a flexible but limited-capacity work space. The central executive is used for both storage and process-

SOURCE: From Conway, A. R. A., & Engle, R. W. (1996). Individual differences in working memory capacity: More evidence for a general capacity theory. *Memory, 4,* 577–590. Reprinted by permission of Psychology Press Ltd., Hove, UK.

ing—consequently, when greater effort is required to process information, less capacity remains for the storage of that information. They also proposed a variety of data representation systems including one for speech information called the articulatory loop and one for visual and spatial information called the visuospatial sketchpad. Both Case's theory and Baddeley and Hitch's theory propose a moment-to-moment trade-off between resources allocated for storage and resources allocated for processing.

Following the logic of Baddeley and Hitch (1974) and Case (1974), Daneman and Carpenter (1980, 1983) hypothesised that the correlation between working memory capacity and higher-level tasks like reading comprehension will only occur if the processing component of the working memory task is of the same type as is required by the higher-level task. This would lead to the same type of trade-off in the higher-level task as would occur in the working memory task. They used a measure of working memory that required both processing and storage of information. Subjects read aloud sets of sentences and, at the end of a 3–7 sentence set, they were required to recall the last word of each sentence. Daneman and Carpenter (1980) hypothesised that the processing or mental operations required to read the sentences would vary in efficiency across individuals and that a reader with more efficient processes would have more working memory capacity available for storage than would a reader with less efficient processes. Thus, good readers should recall more of the last words than poor readers because they have more automatised reading operations. We therefore call this idea the *task specific hypothesis*. Daneman and Carpenter (1980) found that the number of words recalled in the reading span measure of working memory correlated quite well with global measures of reading such as the Verbal Scholastic Aptitude Test (VSAT) as well as with more molecular measures such as the ability to correctly attribute a delayed pronominal reference.

Another possible explanation for the relationship between working memory capacity and comprehension is that high span subjects simply have more attentional resources to draw on than low span subjects, independent of the task involved. According to this view, which we call the *general capacity hypothesis*, high working memory capacity individuals will have more attentional resources to perform a task regardless of the specific nature of the task. Of course, individuals will also vary in efficiency of their mental operations in a specific task, but, other things being equal, high working memory capacity individuals will still have more attentional resources available to them than low working memory capacity individuals. Thus, there should be a relationship between working memory capacity and reading comprehension regardless of the specific processing component of the span task. All that is necessary is that the processing component place some demand on attentional resources. Turner and Engle (1989) tested this hypothesis by varying the processing component of the reading span task. Instead of having subjects read sentences, they had subjects perform mathematical operations. In this "operation span task," the subject performs simple mathematical operations while maintaining words for later recall. Each operation is presented with a word and after each set of operation–word strings, the subject recalls the words. This task bears much surface similarity to the reading span task except that, instead of reading, the subject performs mathematical operations. Working memory capacity or operation span is defined as the number of words the subject can recall while successfully performing the mathematical problems. Turner and Engle (1989) found that operation span correlated with VSAT as well as reading span. Furthermore, operation span and reading span accounted for about the same variance in comprehension. Engle, Cantor, and Carullo (1992) provided further support for the general capacity hypothesis in a study in which they examined performance on a moving window version of the operation and reading span tasks.

The task specific hypothesis, the general processing hypothesis, and the general capacity hypothesis all predict a correlation between reading span and VSAT. However, the hypotheses differ on two other predictions. First, the general capacity and the general processing hypotheses predict that operation span will also correlate with VSAT (Turner & Engle, 1989). The task specific hypothesis would not predict this correlation. Second, when viewing time on the processing component of the span tasks is partialled out of the correlation between span and VSAT, the general capacity view predicts that the correlation will remain significant. The task specific and general processing hypotheses both predict that partialling out viewing time would eliminate or diminish the correlation between span and VSAT.

The results of Engle, Cantor, and Carullo (1992) clearly supported the general capacity hypothesis. Significant correlations were found between reading span, operation span, and VSAT. Furthermore, when viewing time was partialled out of the correlation between span and VSAT, the correlation remained significant. Therefore, while statistically controlling for the time spent on the processing component of the span tasks, the storage component of the span tasks still predicted comprehension ability. This clearly does not support either the task specific hypothesis or the general processing hypothesis.

Our approach in the current study is similar to that of Engle, Cantor, and Carullo (1992). However, instead of statistically controlling for processing efficiency, we hoped to equate, across subjects, the processing demands of an operation span task. The logic for the experiment is simple. If the relationship between working memory span and comprehension is driven by the trade-off between processing and storage, then equating the difficulty of the span task should eliminate the relationship. In contrast, if the relationship between working memory span and comprehension is driven by attentional resources above and beyond the trade-off between processing and storage, then equating the difficulty of the span task should not affect the relationship.

In order to equate processing across subjects, we first determined each subject's capability on operations exactly like those used in the operation span task. Therefore, we had subjects perform mathematical operations of varying difficulty. From their performance on these operations, we designed three operation span tasks in which the mathematical operations were "tailored" to the mathematical ability of the subject.

The three hypotheses outlined earlier make different predictions regarding the correlations between our new operation span tasks and VSAT. The task specific hypothesis would not predict a correlation between VSAT and our operation span tasks with processing demand equated. This is because the view argues that individuals differ in span because of their differing ability to perform the processing component of the task. Therefore, if each subject is at the same point on the performance function for the processing component, the individual differences in the span score should disappear and the relationship between the span score and reading comprehension should disappear. Similarly, the general processing hypothesis would predict the absence of significant correlations between VSAT and our new operation span tasks with processing demand equated. This is because individual differences in span are argued to result from individual differences in the amount of operation space required by the processing portion of the task. Therefore, if each subject uses the same amount of operation space, they will each have the same amount of residual storage space for remembering words. Unlike the other two views, the general capacity hypothesis would still predict significant correlations between VSAT and our new operation span tasks with processing demand equated. This is because the view argues that individuals differ in the total amount of attentional resources available to them. Therefore, regardless of the demand of the processing component of the task, individual differences in span will remain.

METHOD

Subjects

Forty-eight undergraduates from the University of South Carolina participated in the study. All were tested individually in each of the three sessions, received course credit for participation, and signed permission for access to their Scholastic Aptitude Test (SAT) scores from university files. To ensure a wide range of comprehension skill, we chose subjects based on their Verbal SAT score. We specified five VSAT intervals: 200–340, 350–440, 450–540, 550–640, and 650–800; and chose 6, 12, 12, 12, and 6 subjects from each interval, respectively.

Materials

All the tasks reported here were conducted using an IBM PS/2 computer and a VGA monitor. The original operation span task was programmed using Turbo Pascal software. The mathematical operations and the new operation span tasks were programmed using Micro-Experimental Laboratory (MEL) software (Schneider, 1988).

Procedure

Each subject participated in three experimental sessions. In the first session the subject performed the original operation span task and a backward letter task, both of which are normally administered to hundreds of subjects each semester in our lab. The backward letter task is not totally germane to the current problem but the results are presented for completeness. In the second session the subject performed a series of mathematical operations to determine the points at which they would achieve approximately 75%, 85%, and 95% accuracy. The series of operations was designed as a hierarchy in terms of difficulty. In the third session the subject performed three new operation span tasks in which the difficulty of the mathematical operations was manipulated to conform to the levels of difficulty ascertained in the second session.

Original Operation Span Task.   This task was the same operation span task previously used in our lab (Conway & Engle, 1994). For each subject, a pool of 66 mathematical operations was randomly paired with a pool of 66 to-be-remembered words (taken from LaPointe & Engle, 1990). During the task, subjects were presented with operation–word strings, e.g. (8/4) + 2 − 4? BIRD. Each operation required the subject to multiply or divide two integers and then add or subtract a third integer, i.e. (8/4) + 2= 4. The integers ranged from 1 to 10.

The subject was to read the operation aloud, say "yes" or "no," to indicate if the number to the right of the equal sign was the correct answer, and then say the word aloud. After the subject said the word, the experimenter immediately pressed a key, and another operation–word string was presented. This process continued until a question mark cued the subject to write the to-be-remembered words, in order, on a response sheet. The number of operation–word strings per series varied from two to six. Three series of each length were performed, and the order of series length was randomised. The first three series, each of length

2, served as practice. A subject's span score was the sum of the correctly recalled words for trials that were perfectly recalled in correct order. For example, if a subject recalled all the series of length 2 in correct order and one of the series of length 3 in correct order, their span score would be 9 (2 + 2 + 2 + 3). This score was originally reported by Turner and Engle (1989), and consistently correlates with VSAT (Cantor & Engle, 1993; Cantor, Engle, & Hamilton, 1991; Engle, Cantor, & Carullo, 1992; Engle, Nations, & Cantor, 1990; LaPointe & Engle, 1990). Each subject's accuracy on the operations was also recorded. If accuracy was below 85%, the subject was not used in the experiment.

Backward Letter Task.   The backward letter task consisted of auditory presentation of strings of random letters, chosen from the pool of all consonants except w. The letters were recorded in a female voice at a rate of one letter per second and the word "recall" was spoken in the same voice after the last letter. The lists of letters varied in length from two to eight, with three trials at each length. The subject was required to write the list in the reverse order on an answer sheet. If a subject could not recall a letter, they were to leave a blank space for that letter. The same scoring procedure was used as with the operation span tasks.

Mathematical Operations.   The purpose of this session was to determine each subject's performance on mathematical operations of varying difficulty (see Table 17.1). The subject's performance during this session determined the operations to be used in the subsequent operation span tasks. Before performing the mathematical operations, the subject was given "number recognition" trials to familiarise them with the keyboard. A number was presented in the centre of the computer screen and the subject pressed the corresponding key on the numeric keypad on the right-hand side of the keyboard. Each subject performed 20 of these trials.

Each subject then performed 375 operations in 25 blocks of 15 trials. Each block contained one operation from each of the 15 types of mathematical operations selected in a pilot study.[1] The order of presentation of the 15 types within a block was random.

TABLE 17.1   Types of Mathematical Operations Used

Form	a	b	c
(a + b)	R(1, 9)	R(1, 9)	—
(a − b)	R(1, 9)	R(1, 9)	—
(a + b + c)	R(1, 9)	R(1, 9)	R (1, 9)
(a − b − c)	R(1, 20)	R(1, 20)	R (1, 20)
(a − b − c)	R(20, 50)	R(1, 50)	R (1, 50)
(a − b)	R(51, 99)	R(a /10 *10, a /10 *10+ 8)	
(a − b)	R(50, 99)	R((a /10)*10+ 1, (a /10 − 1) *10+ 9)	
(a/b)	b *R (2, 9)	R(2, 9)	—
(a + b − c)	R(1, 9)	R(1, 9)	R (1, 17)
(a/b)	b *R (2, 9)	R(11, 19)	—
(a + b − c)	R(11, 19)	R(11, 19)	R (13, 37)
(a* b)− c	R(2, 6)	R(2, 6)	R (3, 35)
(a* b)− c	R(7, 11)	R(7, 11)	R (48, 120)
(a/b)− c	b *R (2, 9)	R(2, 9)	R (1, 8)
(a + b)/c	temp-b	R(2, a)	R (2, 9)
	where temp = c *R(2, 9)		

The form of the operation is followed by the range of possible integer values for a, b, and c. The values for a, b, and c were chosen such that the answer of the operation would be an integer between 1 and 9. Formation of the last operation type listed in the table, (a + b) /c, required an algorithm that first assigned a value to c [R (2, 9)], then a temporary value to a [c * R(2,9)], then a value to b [R (2, a)], and then a final value for a (a − b), based on the value of b.

An operation appeared on the computer screen (e.g. 2 + 3 = ?) and the subject's task was to enter the answer using the numeric keypad on the right-hand side of the keyboard within three seconds of the onset of the operation. If the subject did not respond in three seconds, the trial was scored as an error and the next trial began.

Response accuracy was recorded by the computer. If the subject made fewer than three errors (92% accuracy or better) on an operation type, that operation type was designated as the operation type to be used in the "easy" span task for that subject. If the subject made three, four, or five errors (between 80% and 88% accuracy) on an operation type, that operation type was designated as the operation type to be used in the "moderate" span task for that subject. If the subject made six, seven, or eight errors (between 68% and 76% accuracy) on an operation type, that operation type was designated as the operation type to be used in the "difficult" span task for that subject. If more than one operation type qualified for use in the span tasks (i.e. the subject responded at 100% accuracy on more than one operation type) then the op-

eration type defined as more difficult by the pilot study was chosen as the operation type to be used in the span task. If no operation type qualified for either the easy, moderate, or difficult span task then the subject did not participate in the study.

Operation Span Tasks with Maths Difficulty Manipulated and Controlled for Each Subject.   Each subject performed three operation span tasks: easy, moderate, and difficult. The procedure for each span task was exactly the same as the procedure for the original operation span task (described earlier). The only difference between the tasks was the type of mathematical operations used. For the "easy" span task, the subject received the operation type on which he or she made fewer than three errors in the previous session. For the "moderate" span task, the subject received the operation type on which he or she made three, four, or five errors in the previous session. For the "difficult" span task, the subject received the operation type on which he or she made six, seven, or eight errors in the previous session. The order of the three tasks was counterbalanced across subjects within each VSAT range.

TABLE 17.2   Descriptive Statistics

	Span	Viewing Time	Error Rate
Easy	19.65 (10.25)	5077 (966)	1.06 (2.21)
Moderate	18.58 (11.34)	5546 (1121)	1.31 (2.34)
Difficult	18.10 (12.49)	6002 (948)	2.02 (2.25)
Original	13.21 (7.02)		
Backward Letter	35.02 (14.02)		
VSAT	507.90 (116.40)		

Mean and (standard deviation). The span and backward letter measures are the sum of the correctly recalled items for trials that were perfectly recalled in correct order. The viewing time data are in milliseconds and the error rate data are proportions.

Three pools of 66 high-frequency concrete nouns (taken from Carrol, Davies, & Richman, 1971) were randomised for the easy, moderate, and difficult span tasks. Therefore, an individual subject received different words for the easy, moderate, and difficult span tasks, but the same words and the same order of words were used for each subject.

In addition to obtaining each subject's span score, we recorded the time the subject spent reading the operation and word. This "viewing time" began when the experimenter pressed a key to present the operation–word pair and ended when the experimenter pressed a key indicating the subject had finished reading the operation–word pair, which led to the presentation of the next operation–word pair. During this time, the subject was to read the mathematical operation aloud, say "yes" or "no" to indicate whether the given answer was correct or incorrect, and say the word.

RESULTS

Descriptive statistics for the dependent measures of greatest interest are reported in Table 17.2. As can be seen, error rates were relatively low and varied only slightly as a function of difficulty. This was supported by a one-way repeated measures ANOVA on error rate. The main effect for difficulty was marginally significant, $F(2,90) = 2.87$, $P = 0.06$, $MSe = 4.31$. Simple comparisons showed that significantly fewer errors were made in the easy span task ($M = 1.06$) than in the difficult span task, ($M = 2.02$) $F(1,45) = 8.02$, $P < 0.01$. No other simple comparisons were significant.

Our manipulation of difficulty was successful because subjects were slower in the difficult span task than in the moderate span task, and faster in the easy span task than in the moderate span task. This was supported by a one-way repeated measures ANOVA on viewing time.[2] The main effect for difficulty was significant, $F(2,90) = 19.36$, $P < 0.01$, $MSe = 507,472$ and pair-wise comparisons showed that all levels of difficulty significantly differed from one another (for all, $P < 0.01$).

The number of words recalled in the operation span task did not vary as a function of difficulty. This was supported by a one-way repeated measures ANOVA on operation span. The main effect for difficulty was not significant, $F(2,90)<1$, $MSe= 27.85$.

We calculated reliability measures for our operation span tasks with mathematical difficulty manipulated. In each of our operation span tasks, the subject was presented with 15 series of operation–word pairs. These series varied in length from two to six operation–word pairs per series and there were three series of each length, 2, 3, 4, 5, and 6. Therefore, for each operation span task, we calculated three submeasures, each derived from five operation–word pair series of length 2, 3, 4, 5, and 6. We calculated Cronbach's alpha for the easy, moderate, and difficult span tasks based on these submeasures. Cronbach's alpha for the easy, moderate, and difficult tasks is 0.80, 0.84, and 0.84 respectively.

Intercorrelations among the span measures and VSAT are reported in Table 17.3. All of the correlations in the table are significant (for all, $P < 0.01$). Performance on the original operation span task correlates highly with performance on the span tasks in which we manipulated mathematical difficulty. Also, we found the intercorrelations between the new span

TABLE 17.3   Intercorrelations Between Span Tasks and VSAT

	VSAT	Original	Easy	Moderate	Difficult
Original	0.59				
Easy	0.62	0.54			
Moderate	0.49	0.68	0.69		
Difficult	0.54	0.68	0.72	0.82	
Backward Letter	0.44	0.41	0.33	0.43	0.37

tasks to be highly significant. Most importantly, *all* of the span tasks—original, easy, moderate, and difficult—significantly correlate with VSAT. This suggests that individual differences in span are not accounted for by differing ability on the processing component of complex span tasks, such as operation span. These results support the general capacity hypothesis and fail to support both the task specific hypothesis and the general processing hypothesis.

Regression Analyses

Although the intercorrelations among the various span measures are all considerable and significant, we can ask whether the measures account for common variance in VSAT. There are several ways we can converge on an answer to this question. One way is to use a forward selection procedure to determine the amount of new variance the measures account for in VSAT. Table 17.4 shows the results of the forward selection procedure. The easy operation span task accounted for 33% of the variance in VSAT, the original operation span accounted for an additional 10%, backward letter accounted for an additional 3%, and the moderate and difficult accounted for 1% additional each but the latter two were not significant. All

of the measures combined accounted for 48% of the variance in VSAT but the bulk of that was contributed by a single measure, the easy operation span.

Viewing Time

To determine whether the efficiency of processing for an individual in mathematical operations played any role in the relationship between the number of words recalled and the Verbal SAT, we calculated partial correlations between VSAT and our span measures while statistically controlling for viewing time. If the general processing hypothesis is correct, these correlations should become non-significant. The partial correlations are reported in Table 17.5. The correlations between the span tasks and VSAT remain virtually unchanged and, obviously, significant when viewing time is partialled out (for all, $P < 0.01$). Therefore, the significant correlations between the span tasks and VSAT are not due to the amount of time required to process the operation–word pair.

DISCUSSION

The purpose of this study was to investigate the relationship between working memory capacity and read-

TABLE 17.4   Results of Regression Analyses of Variance in VSAT

Variable	Partial R^2	Model R^2	F	P
Forward Selection Results				
Easy	0.33	0.33	21.24	0.0001
Original	0.10	0.43	7.60	0.009
Backward letter	0.03	0.46	2.30	0.14
Moderate	0.01	0.47	1.10	0.30
Difficult	0.01	0.48	0.59	0.45

TABLE 17.5   Correlations Between VSAT and Span Tasks Before and After Partialling Out Viewing Time

	Original	Easy	Moderate	Difficult
VSAT (before)	0.59	0.62	0.49	0.54
VSAT (after)	—	0.60	0.48	0.52

ing comprehension, and to provide a test of three competing hypotheses proposed to account for this relationship. We used the operation span task because it was possible to systematically vary the difficulty of the processing component of the task. We equated the processing demand of the operation span task across subjects and systematically manipulated the level of difficulty across three conditions. The correlations between these three conditions and reading comprehension, as operationalised by VSAT, ranged from 0.49 to 0.62 and did not differ statistically from the original version of the operation span which correlated 0.59 with VSAT   for all pair-wise comparisons, $t(45) <$ 1.43, $P > 0.10$. Further, these correlations were undiminished when we partialled out the time that subjects spent viewing the operation–word string.

The general capacity hypothesis can explain these results but the task specific and general processing hypotheses cannot. The general capacity model of working memory was first proposed by Engle, Cantor, and Carullo (1992). The model assumed that working memory consists of knowledge units in long-term declarative memory which are currently active beyond some critical threshold. The model also assumed that knowledge units vary in their level of activation and that the total amount of activation available to the system is limited. The total amount of activation available to each individual varies, and it is this variance that causes individual differences in working memory capacity. Cantor and Engle (1993) provided support for the general capacity model by reporting that the amount of activation available to long-term memory, as measured by the fact retrieval task (Anderson, 1974), statistically accounted for the correlation between operation span and VSAT.

A recent study conducted in our lab (Conway & Engle, 1994), however, has convinced us that it is not sufficient to simply say that high- and low-span subjects differ in the total amount of activation available

to them. A further qualification for the general capacity model is that individual differences will only reveal themselves in tasks that force the subject to engage in controlled effortful processing. If the task allows for automatic processing, then the limited-capacity resource we call working memory will not be taxed. Indeed, Conway and Engle (1994) found that individual differences in working memory capacity were important in a memory search task that required controlled processing, but were not important in a memory search task that allowed for automatic processing. Thus, we now believe that individual differences on the complex WM measures correspond to differences in general, controlled, effortful, attentional resources.

The question remains, why do we find that operation span predicts VSAT, even when the processing demand of the task is equated for each subject? The operation span task, regardless of the demand of the processing component, requires the subject to switch attention constantly from one aspect of the task to another. Subjects must perform a mathematical operation and then encode a word, perform a mathematical operation, and encode a word, and so on, until they are asked to recall the words. This type of attention switching requires the subject to engage in controlled effortful processing. We agree with Baddeley and Hitch (1974) and Daneman and Carpenter (1980), that tapping both processing and storage is necessary for a span task to be a good measure of a central executive or working memory capacity. However, we argue that it is not the demand of the processing component that is critical. We argue that the simple existence of a processing component beyond the storage component is what is required for a span task to be a good measure of working memory and a good predictor of more complex cognitive behaviour, such as reading comprehension. Of course, the processing component has to be demanding enough that it forces the subject to shift attention away from the storage component of the task and to engage in controlled effortful processing. Support for this argument comes from our finding that viewing time was a function of level of difficulty but the number of words recalled was not. Subjects spent nearly one second longer processing the operation–word pair in the difficult span task than in the easy span task, yet the number of words recalled in each task was not statistically different. If the demand of the processing component of the task was the critical determinant of span, then we should have found the number of words recalled to be a function of the level of difficulty of the operations. However, if attention switching is the critical determinant of span, as we argue, then level of difficulty will not have an effect on the number of words recalled, as we found.

Towse and Hitch (1995) recently reported evidence in support of an attention switching interpretation of developmental differences in performance on the counting span task. They independently manipulated counting difficulty and counting time in the counting span task and found that difficulty did not have an effect on span when time of counting was controlled. They argue, as we have, that performance on span tasks such as reading span, operation–word span, and counting span is not driven by a trade-off between resources allocated to processing and storage. Their view differs from ours however, in that they argue that the timing of the processing component of the task is critical to span performance. Thus, according to their view, span performance is driven by the time spent away from the storage component. The attention switch itself is not critical; the time between successive switches is.

Our data do not support their view. We found that viewing time was a function of level of difficulty, but the number of words recalled was not. That is, subjects spent longer on the processing component in the difficult span task than in the easy span task, yet the number of words recalled in the two tasks was not statistically different. Furthermore, when we partialled viewing time out of the correlations between span and VSAT, the correlations remained virtually unchanged. Thus, we argue that the critical component of the task is the attention switch itself, not the trade-off in resources, and not the time spent processing.

One potential problem with our procedure is that the mathematical ability of each subject was tested under strict time constraint whereas the operation span task is subjectpaced. In the mathematical operations session, the subject was only allowed three seconds to answer each mathematical operation. In the subsequent operation span tasks, the subject read the operation aloud at his or her own pace. One may argue that the nature of the processing underlying these two tasks is quite different due to the differing time constraints. However, before the operation span tasks, we encouraged our subjects to perform the operations as quickly as possible without sacrificing accuracy. Also, if the subject appeared to be performing the operations slowly in the operation span tasks, the experimenter encouraged them to perform the operations more quickly. Therefore, we do not feel that this difference in procedure contaminated the outcome of the experiment.

In conclusion, we argue that working memory is a very general resource which plays a role in a wide variety of cognitive tasks. Furthermore, we hope the current article makes the point that it is not sufficient simply to identify a relationship between working memory and some aspect of cognition. We must go beyond the identification of the relationship and investigate exactly why the relationship occurs. Only then will we be able to understand fully the role of working memory in normal human information processing.

ENDNOTES

This work was supported by Grant RO1-HD27490-01A1 from the National Institute of Child Health and Human Development and Grant F49620-93-1-0336 from the Air Force Office of Scientific Research. We would like to thank Stephen Tuholski for assistance with designing the materials for the study.

1. A pilot study with approximately 100 subjects was conducted to select the mathematical operations used in sessions 2 and 3. A series of 20 types of operations that we intuited to range in difficulty from very easy to very difficult were used. Each subject received 15 operations of each of the 20 types at a rate of three seconds per operation. The subject was to type the correct digit solution to the operation within the three-second period or

the item was counted as an error. The pilot study verified the intuitive order of difficulty of the operations but found that five of the types of operations were either too difficult for our subjects to solve in three seconds or were indiscriminable from other types of operations. This left a series of 15 types of mathematical operations that ranged in difficulty from "2 + 5 = ?" to "(22 + 34)/7 = ?" These types of operations were used in the study reported here and are shown in Table 17.1.

2. The viewing time data for two subjects were not recorded because of a computer error. One subject was from the 650–800 VSAT range and the other was from the 550–640 VSAT range.

REFERENCES

Anderson, J.R. (1974). Retrieval of propositional information from long-term memory. *Cognitive Psychology, 6,* 451–474.

Baddeley, A.D., & Hitch, G. (1974). Working memory. In G.H. Bower (Ed.), *The psychology of learning and motivation* (Vol. 8). New York: Academic Press.

Cantor, J., & Engle, R.W. (1993). Working memory capacity as long-term memory activation: An individual differences approach. *Journal of Experimental Psychology: Learning, Memory, and Cognition, 5,* 1101–1114.

Cantor, J., Engle, R.W., & Hamilton, G. (1991). Short-term memory, working memory, and verbal abilities. How do they relate? *Intelligence, 15,* 229–246.

Carroll, J.B., Davies, P., & Richman, B. (1971). *Word frequency book.* New York: American Heritage.

Case, R. (1974). Structures and strictures, some functional limitations on the course of cognitive growth. *Cognitive Psychology, 6,* 544–573.

Case, R. (1985). *Intellectual development: Birth to adulthood.* New York: Academic Press.

Case, R., Kurland, M.D., & Goldberg, J. (1982). Operational efficiency and the growth of short-term memory span. *Journal of Experimental Child Psychology, 33,* 386–404.

Conway, A.R.A., & Engle, R.W. (1994). Working memory and retrieval: A resource-dependent inhibition model. *Journal of Experimental Psychology: General, 123,* 354–373.

Daneman, M., & Carpenter, P.A. (1980). Individual differences in working memory and reading. *Journal of Verbal Learning and Verbal Behavior, 19,* 450–466.

Daneman, M., & Carpenter, P.A. (1983). Individual differences in integrating information between and within sentences. *Journal of Experimental Psychology: Learning, Memory, and Cognition, 9,* 561–583.

Engle, R.W. (1995). Individual differences in memory and their implications for learning. In R. Sternberg (Ed.), *Encyclopedia of intelligence.* New York: Macmillan .

Engle, R.W., Cantor, J., & Carullo, J.J. (1992). Individual differences in working memory and comprehension: A test of four hypotheses. *Journal of Experimental Psychology: Learning, Memory, & Cognition, 18,* 972–992.

Engle, R.W., Nations, J.K., & Cantor, J. (1990). Is working memory capacity just another name for word knowledge? *Journal of Educational Psychology, 82,* 799–804.

LaPointe, L.B., & Engle, R.W. (1990). Simple and complex word spans as measures of working memory capacity. *Journal of Experimental Psychology: Learning, Memory, and Cognition, 16,* 1118–1133.

Pascual-Leone, J. (1970). A mathematical model for the transition rule in Piaget's developmental stages. *Acta Psychologica, 63,* 301–345.

Schneider, W. (1988). Micro-Experimental Laboratory: An integrated system for IBM PC compatibles. *Behavior Research Methods, Instruments, and Computers, 20,* 206–217.

Towse, J.N., & Hitch, G.J. (1995). Is there a relationship between task demand and storage space in tests of working memory capacity? *The Quarterly Journal of Experimental Psychology, 48,* 108–124.

Turner, M.L., & Engle, R.W. (1989). Is working memory capacity task dependent? *Journal of Memory and Language, 28,* 127–154.

CHAPTER SEVEN
Memory Processes

240

18 ENCODING SPECIFICITY

According to the encoding specificity principle (Tulving, 1983), the recollection of an event depends on the interaction between the properties of the encoded event and the properties of the encoded retrieval information. In other words, how you study a piece of information will determine how you can retrieve the information. You might remember the information easily with some kinds of tests, but you might have no recollection of the information at all with other kinds of tests.

The encoding specificity principle is important because it places limits on what you can say about memory. Because it is the interaction of both encoding and retrieval that is important, the principle prohibits all statements about the mnemonic properties of an item, a type of processing, or a cue unless both the encoding and the retrieval conditions are specified. For example, statements such as "recognition is easier than recall" and "deep processing is better than shallow processing" are meaningless because they do not specify the encoding and retrieval conditions. By varying the conditions at encoding and retrieval, deep processing can lead to worse performance than shallow processing (Morris, Bransford, & Franks, 1977) and recognition can be more difficult than recall (Watkins & Tulving, 1975).

The paper by Thomson and Tulving (1970) played a pivotal role in the development of the encoding specificity principle by showing that even strong, well-established cues might not be useful depending on the retrieval conditions. The encoding specificity hypothesis states that the usefulness of a cue to elicit a particular item depends on the encoding and retrieval conditions. In contrast, the associative continuity hypothesis states that if a strong pre-experimental association exists between two items, the one will serve as an effective retrieval cue for the other. The difference between these two theories is that the association continuity hypothesis claims that a pre-existing association will always be a good cue whereas the encoding specificity principle states that whether a cue will be effective depends on the interaction between the study and test conditions.

A "strong cue" is one that routinely elicits a particular target; for example, if you were asked to respond with the first word that popped into your head when you heard CAT, you are very likely to respond with DOG. In contrast, a "weak cue" is one that rarely elicits the cue; for example, you are unlikely to respond with FLOWER given the cue EYE.

The first experiment contained two encoding conditions (no cue or a weak cue) and four retrieval conditions (no cue, a weak cue, a strong cue, and a free recall condition). The target was presented in uppercase, and the task at test was to write down all of the uppercase words. Strong cues facilitated recall, as predicted by the associative continuity hypothesis. Weak cues also facilitated recall if they were present at both study and test, as predicted by the encoding specificity hypothesis. Unfortunately, the key data are equivocal: The associative continuity hypothesis predicted that Condition Weak-Strong should have been as good as Condition Alone-Strong, but this was not the case (13.9 out of 24 words recalled vs. 19.0). The encoding specificity hypothesis predicted that Condition Weak-Strong should not have been higher than Condition Weak-Alone, but it was (13.9 vs. 10.7).

There are several potential reasons why the experiment might not have yielded clear results. One possibility is that some of the subjects might have been ignoring the weak cues; failing to process the weak cues would lead to the observed ambiguous pattern. The second experiment was designed to strengthen the manipulation of context by presenting several lists. The idea is that by the time of the critical list, the subject will be used to processing weak cues. (The CogLab demo is based on Experiment 2, but omits the first two trials.) The data most often shown come from the third list. Best performance occurs when there is a weak cue at study and a weak cue at test (19.8 correctly recalled out of 24, or 82.5% correct). When there was a weak cue at study and a strong cue at test, performance was substantially worse (5.5, or 22.9% correct). This outcome is exactly what encoding specificity predicts. When there was no cue at study and a strong cue at test, performance was quite good (16.3, or 67.9% correct) but not as good as when there were weak cues at both study and test. The presence of two earlier lists presumably helped the subjects encode the targets specifically with respect to the accompanying cues.

The third study tests two closely related alternative explanations. The idea is that a change from weak to strong cues could have caused confusion or disrupted processing. However, performance on the first list with a weak cue at study and a strong cue at test was just as poor (32.6%) as in Experiment 2. In contrast, performance on a second list with a weak cue at study and a weak cue at test—and thus a potentially disruptive change—was substantially better (75.0%) and again comparable to performance in Experiment 2. As Thomson and Tulving (1970, p. 261) conclude, "When Ss were induced to encode TBR [to-be-remembered] words with respect to weak cues at input, preexperimentally defined strong cues introduced at output failed to facilitate recall."

Subsequent work (reviewed in Tulving, 1983) has refined the basic idea and offered substantial empirical support. When studying, students should be mindful of the encoding specificity principle. Think of the processing that will be required at test (e.g., picking one answer out of four alternatives on a multiple choice test vs. writing a short essay), and choose appropriate processing for studying. Process information in a variety of different ways in a variety of different settings to maximize the number of useful retrieval cues.

The paper is also interesting in that it sheds light on the peer review process and on why certain experiments are run.

REFERENCES

Morris, C. D., Bransford, J. D., & Franks, J. J. (1977). Levels of processing versus transfer appropriate processing. *Journal of Verbal Learning and Verbal Behavior, 16*, 519–533.

Nairne, J. S. (2002). The myth of the encoding-retrieval match. *Memory, 10*, 389–395.

Tulving, E. (1983). *Elements of episodic memory*. New York: Oxford.

Watkins, M. J., & Tulving, E. (1975). Episodic memory: When recognition fails. *Journal of Experimental Psychology: General, 104*, 5–29.

QUESTIONS

1. Define exactly what the encoding specificity principle states.
2. This series of experiments focused on changing how the target was encoded by altering the cue. What other experimental manipulations could achieve the same result?
3. While in the grocery store, you see someone who looks very familiar, but you can't come up with a name. The next time you go to the vets with Poochy, your vet asks why you didn't say hello to her in the store. How would you explain your behavior?

Associative Encoding and Retrieval: Weak and Strong Cues

Donald M. Thomson and Endel Tulving

University of Toronto

ABSTRACT

Data from three experiments are reported in support of the encoding specificity hypothesis of retrieval: the effectiveness of retrieval cues depends upon the specific format of encoding of the to-be-remembered (TBR) words at the time of their storage, regardless of how strongly the cues are associated with the TBR words in other situations. In the critical experimental conditions, TBR words were presented for study in presence of weakly associated cue words. Recall of the TBR words in the presence of these cues was greatly facilitated in comparison with noncued recall; recall of the TBR words in presence of their strongest normative associates, which had not been seen at input, did not differ from noncued recall.

This paper is concerned with the problem of the relation between storage and retrieval of information in a simple event-memory experiment. It follows two earlier papers in the series. The first (Tulving & Pearlstone, 1966) demonstrated that many items available in the memory store that cannot be recalled under noncued recall conditions do become accessible in presence of appropriate retrieval cues. The second (Tulving & Osler, 1968) provided experimental evidence in support of the inference that a retrieval cue is effective if, and only if, the information about its relation to the to-be-remembered (TBR) item is stored at the same time as the TBR item itself. Thus, a specific encoding format of the TBR item seems to constitute a prerequisite for the effectiveness of any particular retrieval cue. The point of view reflected in this inference from the data can be referred to as the encoding specificity hypothesis.

The encoding specificity hypothesis, among other things, clearly implies that no cue, however strongly associated with the TBR item or otherwise related to it, can be effective unless the TBR item is specifically encoded with respect to that cue at the time of its storage. This inference contrasts starkly with comparable derivations from what we refer to as the associative continuity hypothesis. This hypothesis forms the core of the explanation of effectiveness of retrieval cues offered by Bilodeau and his associates (Bilodeau & Blick, 1965; Fox, Blick, & Bilodeau, 1964), as well as by Bahrick (1969, 1970). According to the associative continuity hypothesis, if a strong preexperimental association exists between Verbal Units A and B, then A can serve as an effective retrieval cue for B, and vice versa, simply by virtue of the existence of such an association and regardless of the specific nature of encoding events occurring at the time of the storage of the TBR unit.

An anonymous reviewer of the Tulving and Osler (1968) paper had, as the Editor of the *Journal of Experimental Psychology* put it in correspondence, "vehement objections to the conclusions drawn from the experiment," probably because of his own faith in the transsituational associations between nominally identical verbal units. In addition to finding several of the conclusions trivial, the reviewer was especially critical of Tulving and Osler's suggestion that strong preexperimental associates of TBR words are effective retrieval cues only to the extent that these cues overlap with the subjective encoding pattern into which the TBR item is embedded at input. He concluded his long and detailed criticism of the manuscript with the

SOURCE: From Thomson, D. M., & Tulving, E. (1970). Associative encoding and retrieval: Weak and strong cues. *Journal of Experimental Psychology, 86,* 255–262. Copyright © 1970 by the American Psychological Association. Reprinted with permission.

following query: "Do the authors really wish to say that the *S's* pre-experimental history cannot be effectively utilized by *E* in controlling recall and that prior experiments have really in effect capitalized upon chance correspondences between the word employed as cue and the differential and idiosyncratic responses made by the *S* while he is in training?"[1]

The three experiments reported in this paper provide an answer to our unknown colleague and critic. The answer, in the form of interpretation of data from three new experiments, consists of three parts: (a) *S's* preexperimental history is indeed important, but only insofar as it determines the encoding of a given TBR item at input; (b) effectiveness of cueing at recall is strongly determined by specific encoding of the TBR item at input, and, therefore, (c) *S's* preexperimental history has little effect on recall of an event, such as the occurrence of an otherwise very familiar word in an unfamiliar list, unless this history has influenced the encoding of that event.

In Exp. I, the critical experimental condition—in which the TBR words were accompanied by weakly related associative cues at input and were tested in presence of strongly associated cues at output—constituted one part of an overall design that rather closely followed that used by Tulving and Osler (1968).

EXPERIMENT 1

Method

Design.   Lists of 24 TBR words were presented to *Ss* for study and subsequent recall on a single trial. Three input conditions were combined factorially with four output conditions to yield 12 different experimental treatment conditions. The input conditions were: (a) the TBR words were presented alone (Input Cond. O), (b) each TBR word was accompanied by a weakly associated cue word (Input Cond. W), and (c) each TBR word was accompanied by a strongly associated cue word (Input Cond. S). The output conditions were (a) noncued recall of TBR words (Output Cond. O), (b) recall of TBR words in presence of weakly associated cue words (Output Cond. W), (c) recall of TBR words in presence of strongly associated cue words (Output Cond. S), and (d) free recall of both TBR and cue

words (Output Cond. FR). Each of the resulting 12 treatment combinations can be designated in terms of its input and output conditions. Thus, for instance, Cond. O-O was a standard free recall condition, as was Cond. O-FR; in Cond. W-W, TBR words were accompanied by weakly associated cue words at input, and their recall tested in presence of the same cues; in Cond. S-O, each TBR word was accompanied by a strong cue at input, but recall of TBR words was tested in absence of any cues; in Cond. S-FR, *Ss* studied TBR words in presence of strongly associated cues and recalled as many cues and TBR words as possible under standard free recall conditions, etc.

Independent groups of 15 *Ss* served in each of the 12 treatment combinations. Thus, there were 180 *Ss*, first-year female students at the University of Toronto, meeting the service requirement of their introductory psychology course. The assignment of *Ss* to treatment conditions was free from any known systematic bias, occurring on a haphazard basis subject to certain restrictions mentioned subsequently.

Materials.   To construct lists of TBR words, 48 response words were selected from the Bilodeau and Howell (1965) free association norms. Each selected TBR word occurred in the norms twice: once as a high-frequency response to a strong-cue stimulus word, and once as a low frequency response to a different weak-cue stimulus word. The two stimulus words eliciting each TBR word in the norms constituted the input and output cues in the experiment. The selection of cues and TBR words was further constrained by the important requirement that the weak and the strong cue of each TBR word be associatively and semantically unrelated to each other on the basis of the two authors' judgment.

Two lists of 24 TBR words (A and B), together with the corresponding sets of weak and strong cue words, were used in order to provide a basis for the generalization of the results over a wider selection of materials. Each list was used with approximately one half of the *Ss* in each treatment condition. The mean normative strength of associations between cues and TBR words, in both lists, was 42% for strong cues and 1% for weak cues. Some examples of weak and strong cues and their corresponding TBR words, listed in this order for each triplet, were as follows: train, white,

BLACK; knife, meat, STEAK; lamb, dumb, stupid; hand, woman, MAN; blow, ice, cold; head, dark, LIGHT.

A practice list, given to all *Ss* prior to the experimental list, consisted of 24 proper nouns—names of oceans, rivers, countries, cities, politicians, and monarchs.

Procedure.   Usually four *Ss* were tested at a time, although some variations from this procedure occurred owing to differential availability of *Ss*. In a given session all *Ss* saw the same input list, but they were tested under different output conditions, with the restriction that all output conditions contain an equal number of *Ss* in the whole experiment.

All *Ss* were first given the practice list under free recall conditions. The 24 names were shown on a TV screen in front of the room, at the rate of 2 sec/word, and *Ss* recorded their recall in recall booklets that had been distributed at the beginning of the session.

Instructions given to *Ss* for the experimental list varied according to input and output conditions. The instructions prior to the presentation of the list were read by *E*. Briefly, all *Ss* were told they would next see another list on the TV screen, consisting of words typed in capital letters, and that later on they would have to recall as many of these words as they could. The *Ss* in Input Cond. W and S were also told that each capitalized word would be accompanied by a related word which should be studied as a possible aid in recalling the capitalized word.

Each TBR word, and each cue-TBR word pair, was presented for 3 sec., for a total time of 72 sec/list. Each TBR word was printed in capital letters, with the cue word, if present at input, appearing to the left of it in lowercase letters. Recall instructions, printed at the top of the appropriate page in the recall booklet, varied according to output conditions. The instructions for all *Ss* were: "Now write down all the capitalized WORDS you remember." For *Ss* being tested under Output Cond. W and S, the instructions continued: "The words you see typed on the sheet may help you to remember the WORDS, since each of them is related to one of the capitalized WORDS. If you can, put each of the WORDS opposite the word to which it is related. If you find this too difficult, however, put down the words you remember anyhow, anywhere on the sheet. The most important thing is to get as many WORDS correct as possible."

The *Ss* turned to the recall page only after the list had been presented. Thus, *Ss* did not know how their recall would be tested. It can be assumed, therefore, that the availability of TBR words—the amount and organization of the appropriate information in the store—was constant, within limits of random variation, in each group of *Ss* studying the material under a given input condition.

The recall sheets in recall booklets contained 24 consecutively numbered lines on two successive pages. In Output Cond. W and S, 12 cue words were typed on a page, with space beside each cue for the appropriate TBR word. In Output Cond. FR, two consecutive pages contained two columns of lines, one for recording cue words and the other for TBR words.

The *Ss* were given 5 min. for recording the recall.

Results and Discussion

Lenient scoring was used throughout: *S* was given credit for recall of a TBR word regardless of whether or not the word was paired with its appropriate cue when output cues were provided.

The mean number of TBR words recalled, with the data pooled for treatment conditions, was 14.03 for List A and 13.03 for List B. Analysis of variance showed this to be a significant difference at the .05 level, but since all interactions involving lists yielded *F* ratios smaller than unity, the data to be described were pooled for both lists.

The mean numbers of words recalled in the 12 conditions of Exp. I, and their corresponding standard deviations, are shown in Table 18.1. The important features of these results, all statistically reliable at least at the .05 level, can be summarized as follows:

1. The presence of strong cues at output facilitated retrieval of TBR words, both under the condition where TBR words alone were shown in the input list (mean of 19.0 words for Cond. O-S, compared with the mean of 14.1 words for Cond. O-O) and the condition where the cues accompanied TBR words at input (20.2 for Cond. S-S, compared with 12.2 for Cond. S-O). These data confirm earlier similar results (Bilodeau & Blick, 1965; Fox, Blick, & Bilodeau, 1964; Wood, 1967).

TABLE 18.1   Mean Number of Words Recalled in Twelve Conditions of Experiment I

Input Condition		Output condition			
		O	W	S	FR
O					
	M	14.1	11.1	19.0	14.5
	SD	2.9	3.2	3.1	3.2
W					
	M	10.7	15.7	13.9	9.8 + 6.9*
	SD	2.4	4.0	3.6	2.1
S					
	M	12.2	9.2	20.2	11.1 + 9.4*
	SD	3.6	3.0	3.4	2.3

*Refers to number of cue words recalled.

2. Weak cues presented at output facilitated retrieval of TBR words, provided that the same cues had accompanied TBR words at input (19.7 for Cond. W-W vs. 10.7 for Cond. W-O). This finding corroborates that of Tulving and Osler (1968).
3. Weak cues presented at output did not facilitate recall of TBR words when they had not been present at input (11.1 for Cond. O-W vs. 14.1 for Cond. O-O, and 9.2 for Cond. S-W vs. 12.2 for Cond. S-O). These data, too, confirm and extend the generality of Tulving and Osler's (1968) results.
4. Finally, the results of Exp. I showed that strong associative cues, present at output, facilitated recall of TBR words even when the TBR words had been accompanied by different, weak cues at input (mean of 13.9 for Cond. W-S vs. 10.7 for Cond. W-O), but that this facilitative effect was smaller than the facilitative effect of strong cues at output following no cues or strong cues at input (mean of 13.9 vs. 19.0 and 20.2, respectively).

It is this fourth finding that is critical for the evaluation of the respective merits of the encoding specificity and associative continuity hypotheses. The strict interpretation of the former says that recall under Cond. W-S should not have been higher than under Cond. W-O; the strict interpretation of the latter would have to be that recall under Cond. W-S should have been as high as in Cond. O-S. The actual pattern of results clearly vindicates neither of these

positions. As frequently happens in crucial experiments, the critical datum fell somewhere between the two extremes predicted from the two points of view.

The encoding specificity hypothesis claims that no cue, regardless of how strongly it might be associated with the TBR item in other situations, can facilitate retrieval of the TBR item in absence of appropriate prior encoding of that item. The W-S condition in Exp. I was meant to bring about specific encoding of TBR words in relation to weak cues and to preclude subjective encoding of TBR words with respect to strong cues. The ambiguous outcome in this critical W-S condition may mean that the encoding specificity hypothesis, or at least its strict interpretation, is not tenable. But it may also mean that the attempt to manipulate the encoding pattern of TBR words under weak-cue input conditions was not quite successful. Suppose that some Ss ignored all weak input cues in Cond. W-S, or that all Ss ignored these cues for some of the TBR words. The encoding of such TBR words would then be functionally equivalent to encoding of these words under Input Cond. O, with the consequence that strong cues at output would facilitate their recall. Before rejecting or revising the encoding specificity hypothesis, therefore, it seemed desirable to make a more incisive attempt at experimental manipulation of encoding of TBR items.

Experiment II describes such an attempt. Here the critical condition—the switch from weak cues at input to strong cues at output—was introduced only after Ss had been tested in several lists with output

TABLE 18.2   Design of Experiment II and Summary of the Recall Data

Group		Successive lists			
		1	2	3	4
1	Input condition	0	0	0	0
	Output condition	0	0	0	S
	mean TBR recalled	10.6	9.6	11.7	16.8
	SD	1.6	3.5	1.8	3.8
2	Input condition	0	0	0	0
	Output condition	0	0	W	0
	mean TBR recalled	12.6	10.9	10.3	13.4
	SD	4.5	3.0	2.8	5.1
3	Input condition	0	0	0	0
	Output condition	0	0	S	0
	mean TBR recalled	11.5	10.5	16.3	10.7
	SD	2.0	3.1	3.7	4.0
4	Input condition	W	W	W	W
	Output condition	W	W	0	W
	mean TBR recalled	17.2	19.4	7.1	16.5
	SD	3.7	3.1	3.4	5.3
5	Input condition	W	W	W	W
	Output condition	W	W	W	S
	mean TBR recalled	17.1	19.5	19.8	5.4
	SD	3.4	2.9	3.1	4.7
6	Input condition	W	W	W	W
	Output condition	W	W	S	W
	X TBR recalled	18.0	18.4	5.5	15.6
	SD	3.0	2.8	4.1	2.5

Note: Input and output conditions are abbreviated as follows: O, no cues; W, weak cues; and S, strong cues.

cues that completely matched the input cues. It was hoped that repeated testing of Ss under one and the same set of cue conditions would encourage them to pay close attention to the cues present at input, and discourage them from encoding TBR items in the normal manner characteristic of Input Cond. O and S.

EXPERIMENT II

Method

Design.   The design of Exp. II is schematically shown in Table 18.2. Each of six independent groups of Ss was tested with four successive lists, each containing 24 TBR words. Each list was presented once, each TBR word either occurring alone (Input Cond. O) or accompanied by a weakly associated cue word (Input Cond. W). Recall of TBR words was tested in absence of any cues, in presence of weakly associated cues, or in presence of strongly associated cue words. These three output conditions are labeled O, W, and S, respectively. Each experimental treatment condition can again be described by the combination of input and output cueing conditions, as in Exp. I.

Table 18.2 shows that Groups 1, 2, and 3 studied and recalled the first two lists under the O-O treatment condition, while Groups 4, 5, and 6 did the same under the W-W condition. With respect to the treatment given to the groups on the third list, the experiment can be thought of as a 2 × 3 factorial, in which 2 input-cue conditions, O and W, perfectly confounded with input and output conditions in the first two lists, were orthogonally combined with 3 output-cue conditions (O, W, and S).

The critical conditions were created by List 3 in Group 6 and List 4 in Group 5. In these conditions, *Ss* studied TBR words in presence of weak cues and recalled them in presence of strong cues.

Materials and procedure.   The two lists of 24 TBR words and their corresponding cue words constructed for Exp. I were used as Lists 3 and 4 in this experiment. Two additional lists of 24 words and weak cues were constructed from two sets of free association norms (Bilodeau & Howell, 1965; Riegel, 1965) to serve as Lists 1 and 2 in this experiment.

The procedure was identical with that of Exp. I with respect to all important features, with the exception that (a) no practice list was given in Exp. II, and (b) each *S* was now tested with four successive lists. Words were presented visually on a closed-circuit TV screen, each TBR word and each cue-TBR word pair appearing for 3 sec. The TBR words were again printed in capital letters, cue words on their left in lowercase letters. Three minutes were provided for a written recall test on each list, *Ss* recording their responses in booklets containing, depending upon output conditions, 24 numbered lines, 24 weak cues, or 24 strong cues. The *Ss* were not explicitly told how their recall was going to be tested on any particular list. Instructions before and after the presentation of a list were essentially the same as those used in Exp. I.

Results and Discussion

Again, lenient scoring was employed. The mean numbers of TBR words recalled by all six groups on each of the four lists, together with standard deviations, are recorded in Table 18.2.

The important facts summarized in Table 18.2 are the following:

1. The *Ss* in Groups 1, 2, and 3 recalled, on the average, 11.0 TBR words from Lists 1 and 2. These lists were studied and tested under noncued conditions. The unexpected switch to testing of TBR words in presence of strong cues (List 4 in Group

1, and List 3 in Group 3) produced a sizable facilitation in recall, the means being 16.8 and 16.3. Similar switch to testing of TBR words in presence of weak cues, however, produced no facilitation: the mean number of words recalled from List 3 by Group 2 was 10.3. The pattern of these data is identical with Exp. I.

2. The *Ss* in Groups 4, 5, and 6 recalled, on the average, 18.3 TBR words from Lists 1 and 2. The TBR words in these lists were studied and tested in presence of weak cues. The unexpected switch to noncued recall condition on List 3 for Group 4 produced a striking reduction in performance, the mean number of words recalled being 7.1. The unexpected switch to testing of TBR words in presence of strong cues (List 4 in Group 5, and List 3 in Group 6) produced an equally striking loss in recall, the two means being reduced to 5.4 and 5.5, respectively. These two means were not significantly different from the mean number of words recalled by Group 4 on List 3 under noncued conditions.

The critical finding here again has to do with the effects of strong cues on recall. Strong cues clearly facilitated recall under conditions where *Ss* were left free to subjectively encode the TBR words with a view to expected noncued recall test. Identical strong cues, however, completely failed to augment recall when the TBR words were presumably encoded specifically with respect to their accompanying weak cues.

The outcome of Exp. II thus seems consistent with the implications of the encoding specificity hypothesis, and inconsistent with the associative continuity hypothesis. It seems reasonable to assume, therefore, that the failure to completely demonstrate the highly critical role of encoding processes in Exp. I may have reflected the failure of intended manipulation of these processes in Cond. W-S. However, it might be argued that strong retrieval cues failed to facilitate recall in the W-S conditions in Exp. II for reasons other than encoding specificity. It could be assumed, for instance, that *Ss* in the W-W conditions, in the course of studying and recalling the first two or three lists, developed a set to respond to retrieval cues with weak associates. If this set persisted when strong cues were provided in the critical W-S conditions, *Ss* could not have responded with strong associates of these cues as correct TBR words. It could also be assumed that the sudden unannounced switch to the strong cues in the W-S conditions in some other way confused Ss and that this confusion prevented them from taking maximum advantage of stored information about TBR words at the time of the recall test.

Experiment III represented an attempt to test the reality of this set or confusion notion, using a mixed-list paradigm.

EXPERIMENT III

Method

Design.   Each of 24 Ss was treated exactly alike, being tested with three successive lists. Each list contained 24 TBR words, one half of them accompanied by weak cues and the other half by strong cues, both at input and test. In Lists 1 and 2, the output cue of a given TBR word always matched its input cue. Thus, Lists 1 and 2 contained two experimental conditions, W-W and S-S, each represented by 12 TBR words. In the third list, half of the weak input cues were changed to appropriate strong cues at output, and half of the strong input cues were changed to appropriate weak cues, The remaining TBR words were cued at the recall test with their input cues. Thus, List 3 generated data for four different intralist experimental conditions, W-W, W-S, S-S, and S-W, each represented by 6 TBR words. Two different sets of three lists were used, each set with one half of the Ss. In addition, there were four alternative versions of List 3 in both sets, such that each TBR word occurred in each of the four treatment conditions equally often. The order of presenting TBR words in the study list and the cues in the recall booklets was determined randomly.

Materials and procedure.   The two lists of 24 TBR words and their associated cue words constructed for Exp. I constituted the two sets of List 3 words in this experiment. Four other lists of 24 TBR words and cues were constructed from the association norms (Bilodeau & Howell, 1965; Riegel, 1965) to serve as the first two lists.

In most aspects the procedure was identical to that of Exp. I and II. Usually two or three Ss were tested at a time.

The Ss were first shown a short practice list of four TBR words, the names of famous people and places, together with related cue words, before the three experimental lists were presented. Prior to the presentation of the first experimental list, instructions given in Exp. I and II for Input Cond. W were read to Ss. Each cue-TBR word was presented on the closed-circuit TV screen for 3 sec. Recall instructions, typed at the top of a page in the recall booklets, were essentially the same as Output Cond. W instructions in Exp. I and II. In addition, for List 3, the recall instructions stated that half of the cues had appeared with the TBR words in the input list and half were new but related words. The two types of cues were identified for Ss by being presented in columns headed "old" and "new." The Ss were given as much time as they wanted for the written recall test. They hardly ever took more than 3 min. for recall.

Results and Discussion

The mean proportion of TBR words recalled (lenient scoring) for the different input and output conditions in the three lists, together with standard deviations of these proportions, are presented in Table 18.3.

The main features of the data were as follows:

1. In Lists 1 and 2, recall of TBR words was higher in Cond. S-S than in Cond. W-W. The same tendency in List 3 was not quite statistically significant.
2. Recall in presence of strong output cues was much lower in Cond. W-S than in Cond. W-W—proportions of .33 vs. .73, respectively. The proportion of .33 in Cond. W-S, equivalent to 8 words out of 24, is clearly of the same order of magnitude as noncued recall in Exp. I and II.
3. Recall in Cond. S-W was practically zero. Only 5 Ss out of 24 recalled one word each in this condition, for a mean proportion of .03.

Since the important fact—that strong associative cues do not facilitate recall if specific encoding of TBR items is not appropriate to these cues—was again clearly suggested by the overall pattern of the data, there is no support for the set or the confusion notion as a plausible explanation for the critical results of Exp. II. Strong cues presented at recall in Cond. W-S

TABLE 18.3   Proportion of Words Correctly Recalled in Experiment III

	Output Cue					
	Strong			Weak		
	List					
Input	1	2	3	1	2	3
Strong						
Proportion	.840	.840	.833	—	—	.035
SD	.143	.195	.170			.085
Weak						
Proportion	—	—	.326	.750	.753	.729
SD			.297	.207	.235	.234

were not effective in augmenting access to stored TBR words, despite the fact that in Exp. III no set to respond only with weak associates of retrieval cues could have developed, and despite the fact that any confusion Ss may have experienced as a consequence of switching cues was presumably minimized by recall instructions in List 3.

The striking finding that recall failed almost completely in the S-W condition in Exp. 3 is at variance with a much higher level of recall under the same condition in Exp. 1. The reasons for Ss' failure to recall any words in presence of weak cues after they had been shown in the company of strong cues at input are not clear.

DISCUSSION

The purpose of these experiments was to evaluate two theoretical views from which explanations of the operation of retrieval cues in event memory can be derived: the associative continuity and encoding specificity hypotheses. While in many experimental situations the two hypotheses make identical predictions about cued recall, in certain cases the predictions are different. In all three experiments reported in this paper, the critical conditions were those in which Ss studied TBR words in presence of their weak normative associates and then recalled these words (a) in a noncued recall test, (b) in presence of the previously seen weak input cues, or (c) in presence of strong normative associates not seen in the input list. The associative continuity hypothesis would predict that recall

in the c condition should be considerably higher than in the a condition, while the encoding specificity hypothesis predicts no difference.

The overall pattern of results favored the encoding specificity hypothesis: when Ss were induced to encode TBR words with respect to weak cues at input, preexperimentally defined strong cues introduced at output failed to facilitate recall. According to the encoding specificity hypothesis, retrieval of event information can only be effected by retrieval cues corresponding to a part of the total encoding pattern representing the perceptual cognitive registration of the occurrence of the event. Thus, the cue "white" cannot provide access to stored information about the occurrence of BLACK as a TBR word, if BLACK has been encoded as part of the "train-BLACK" complex, or as part of a unique event in a series of unique events. The two lexical units, BLACK and BLACK, are identical, but the encoded engram of the unique event BLACK, in the context of "train," and in the context of a specific set of TBR events, may be as different from the pattern of neural excitation corresponding to the generalized concept of BLACK as a beautiful and talented actress receiving an Oscar is different from any one of millions of stars twinkling in the endless night.

To the extent that our data support the encoding specificity hypothesis, they rule out the associative continuity hypothesis. We will have to leave it to the proponents of that hypothesis to explain how it might be brought into line with the overall pattern of these data, because we cannot think of any reasonably simple way of doing it. This does not mean that the encoding specificity point of view can readily account for all details of the data. It cannot. For instance, the asymmetry in recall scores between the W-S and S-W conditions in Exp. III appears to be somewhat more compatible with associative continuity than with encoding specificity, suggesting that further thought on the distinction between the two views is needed. It is only on balance that the encoding hypothesis appears to emerge less ruffled from this contact with the experimental data than does the associative continuity hypothesis.

It is not immediately clear why our data are apparently at variance with, and how the encoding specificity hypothesis could explain, Bahrick's (1969, 1970) findings revealing considerable facilitation of recall by prompts (cues) of various strengths presented only at output. It is possible that Bahrick's data reflect the influence of overlap between the encoding patterns of some weak and strong cues, such as "child" and "boy," "weather" and "hot," "parade" and "banner," "small" and "long," and "hospital" and "physician" (Bahrick, 1969). In our present experiments, as we noted earlier, weak and strong cues were selected so as to be semantically unrelated. It is also possible that the specific instructions given to Bahrick's Ss—that, if necessary, they should guess in response to all prompts—are partly responsible for the increased correspondence, under conditions of prompting, between Ss' responses and E's tally sheet. But the evaluation of these and other possible reasons for the apparent discrepancies between Bahrick's findings and ours is difficult at the present time. Further experimental and theoretical analysis suggested by these and other gaps in our knowledge and understanding of effectiveness of retrieval cues should also include a critical appraisal of appropriateness of different methods of measuring this effectiveness, another source of as yet unresolved disagreement between associative continuity and encoding specificity positions.

ENDNOTES

This research was supported by the National Research Council of Canada, Grant No. APA-39, and the National Science Foundation, Grant No. GB-3710 and GB-24171X.

Requests for reprints should be sent to E. Tulving, Department of Psychology, Yale University, 333 Cedar Street, New Haven, Connecticut 06510.

1. D. A. Grant, personal communication, August 28, 1967.

REFERENCES

Bahrick, H. P. (1969). Measurement of memory by prompted recall. *Journal of Experimental Psychology, 79,* 213–219.

Bahrick, H. P. (1970). Two-phase model for prompted recall. *Psychological Review, 77,* 215–222.

Bilodeau, E. A., & Blick, K. A. (1965). Courses of misrecall over long-term retention intervals as related to strength of preexperimental habits of word association. *Psychological Reports, 16* (Monogr. Suppl. No. 6-V16), 1173–1192.

Bilodeau, E. A., & Howell, D. C. (1965). *Free association norms.* (Catalog No. D210.2:F87) Washington, D.C.: United States Government Printing Office.

Fox, P. W., Blick, K. A., & Bilodeau, E. A. (1964). Stimulation and prediction of verbal recall and misrecall. *Journal of Experimental Psychology, 68,* 321–322.

Riegel, K. F. (1965). *Free associative responses to the 200 stimuli of the Michigan restricted association norms.* (USPHS Rep. No. 8) Ann Arbor, Mich.: University of Michigan. (United States Public Health Service Grant MH 07619.)

Tulving, E., & Osler, S. (1968). Effectiveness of retrieval cues in memory for words. *Journal of Experimental Psychology, 77,* 593–601.

Tulving, E., & Pearlstone, Z. (1966). Availability versus accessibility of information in memory for words. *Journal of Verbal Learning and Verbal Behavior, 5,* 381–391.

Wood, G. (1967). Category names as cues for the recall of category instances. *Psychonomic Science, 9,* 323–324.

19 SERIAL POSITION EFFECT

This paper illustrates a number of important factors underlying the serial po
sition curve. Although the language is somewhat old-fashioned, the method is
serial learning (instead of free recall), and the graphs are plotted upside down
(the general practice today is to plot percent correct as opposed to percent errors), the lessons illustrated here are still the ones we use today.

First, the serial position curve is U-shaped with fewer recall errors occurring at the first and last positions compared to the middle positions. Second,
although different types of materials (syllables, meaningful names, etc.), different presentation variables (massed vs. distributed rehearsal; fast vs. slow
presentation), or different subject variables (fast vs. slow learners) result in
different overall levels of recall, the curve itself still follows that same basic U
shape. In order to illustrate this point more clearly, McCrary and Hunter
(1952) plotted the percent of the total errors at each position. This is called
"normalizing," and it allows us to look at the curves in terms of the probability of an error occurring at each serial position. The result is that, even when
overall level of recall is very different, most errors will occur in the same part
of the curve (the middle positions).

This is an important finding because it suggests that there is a great deal of
regularity in the way in which unrelated lists of items are recalled, regardless of
how easy or difficult it is to learn them. Although there are ways of changing
the shape of the curve (see Reading 20, "Von Restorff Effect"), the basic result
is one of the most common findings in the memory literature and has been
the basis for many (if not most) models of immediate memory. In addition,
this basic pattern of recall can be found in a large number of real-world situations, including the day of the week in which a person participated in a telephone survey (Huttenlocher, Hedges, & Prohaska, 1992) and where they
parked their car (da Costa Pinto & Baddeley, 1991).

So what is the answer to why the serial position curve takes the shape that
it does? Originally, it was argued that the items at the beginning of the list (the
primacy effect) were well-recalled because they were rehearsed enough to
transfer them into long-term memory. Items at the end of the list were well-
recalled because they remained in short-term memory. Those in the middle of
the list suffered because they were not rehearsed enough to transfer them to

long-term memory, but they were "bumped" out of short-term memory by the more recent items. Although this is still the explanation given in most textbooks, more recent experiments have indicated that ideas of distinctiveness and rehearsal may give a more complete answer as to why the serial position effect takes the shape that it does (Tan & Ward, 2000).

The CogLab demonstration uses a method called *free recognition*, in which subjects are asked to recall the items that were presented on a list in any order. The serial position effect is so robust that it is found almost regardless of the method, be it serial learning (like in the reading), free recall, or free recognition. Your results are plotted in terms of proportion correct, however, instead of errors.

REFERENCES

da Costa Pinto, A., & Baddeley, A. D. (1991). Where did you park your car? Analysis of a naturalistic long-term recency effect. *European Journal of Cognitive Psychology, 3*, 297–313.

Huttenlocher, J., Hedges, L. V., & Prohaska, V. (1992). Memory for day of the week: A 5+2 day cycle. *Journal of Experimental Psychology: General, 121*, 313–326.

Tan, L. & Ward, G. (2000). A recency-based account of the primacy effect in free recall. *Journal of Experimental Psychology: Learning, Memory, & Cognition, 26*, 1589–1625.

QUESTIONS

1. What variables were examined by McCrary and Hunter in their analysis of the serial position curve?
2. Which variables resulted in better overall performance?
3. Do these different variables result in different shapes of the serial position curve?
4. Why do the authors say that it is not surprising that "when one changes from a less to a more efficient method of learning, the greatest reduction of errors will occur in the central serial positions"?
5. Why is it surprising that "the gains under a more efficient learning method [are] as proportionately distributed as the percentage curves indicate"?

Serial Position Curves in Verbal Learning

John W. McCrary, Jr., and Walter S. Hunter

Psychology Department, Brown University

When a list of nonsense syllables is learned by a subject under conditions that require him to recall the following syllable as each one of the series is presented, it is found that the syllables in the middle of the list are learned more slowly than are those at the two ends, and that in general the initial syllables are learned more rapidly than are the final ones. When the results are plotted in terms of mean number of errors made at each serial position during learning, the graph has the form shown in Figure 19.1.

Of the various theories proposed in explanation of the relatively slow rate at which the middle of the series is learned, that of Lepley[1] and Hull[2] has been the most ingenious and perhaps the best substantiated. The Lepley-Hull theory is that the bow-shaped serial position curve results from the large number of inhibitory processes present in the middle of a series of responses. It is known that during learning each syllable becomes associated not only with adjacent but also with remote syllables, so that both near and remote excitatory tendencies are set up. Progress toward mastery of the list involves a strengthening of the near excitatory tendencies and the weakening (or control) of the remote ones to the point where, when a given syllable is presented, the subject will report the next following syllable and not one farther along in the list, or none at all. A simple diagram can be constructed to show that remote excitatory tendencies pile up in the middle of the list. Proceeding from this point, an analogy is drawn between serial learning and conditioning. It is held that each succeeding syllable in the series becomes conditioned to the traces of preceding syllables so that remote associations are viewed essentially as trace-

conditioned responses. Final mastery is attained as a result both of the building up of internal inhibitions of the trace responses and of the strengthening of near

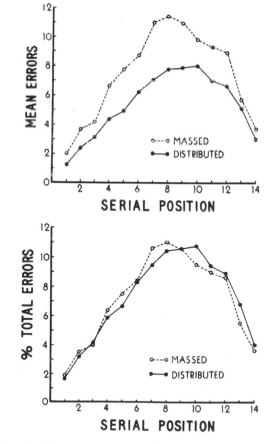

FIGURE 19.1

excitatory tendencies. Inasmuch as the trace response tendencies are most, numerous in the middle of the series, the inhibitory tendencies must be concentrated in the same location, to the relative neglect of the two ends. Many observations, particularly on the spontaneous recovery of extinguished responses, support the view that inhibitory tendencies dissipate more rapidly with the lapse of time than do excitatory tendencies. One can therefore make experimental tests of the effects of various manipulations of the time variable upon the serial position curve, looking for results that may or may not support the inhibition theory.

The most significant data on the serial position curve with respect to this theory come from experiments on massed vs. distributed practice and on changes in the rate of presentation of the syllables. In massed learning, practice periods follow one another with little or no rest between the periods, whereas in distributed learning there are rest periods of varying lengths at the close of each practice period. Within limits, distributed practice results in quicker learning than does massed practice. The inhibition theory predicts that the lapse of time involved in the rest periods of distributed practice will result in a relative loss of inhibitory tendencies and that, therefore, the serial position curve for distributed learning when compared with the massed learning curve will show a decrease in errors at each position, but with the largest decrease in the middle portions of the curve, where the inhibitory effects have been greatest. Similar predictions are made for the effects of varying the rate at which syllables are presented, since, with a slow rate, inhibitory tendencies may be expected to dissipate more rapidly than with a faster rate of presentation.

Patten[3] and Hovland[4,5] have conducted experiments of the above type. The upper half of Figure 19.1 shows the essential results secured by Hovland (One of many experiments) when subjects learned a list of 14 syllables presented at a rate of 1 syllable each 2 sec. In the distributed practice series, there was a rest interval of 2 min 6 sec between successive presentations of the list, whereas in the massed practice series the rest period was only 6 sec. The decrease in mean errors brought about by distributed practice shows up at all serial positions, but it is greatest in the middle of the series, as predicted by the inhibition theory. In another experiment, Hovland compared the serial posi-

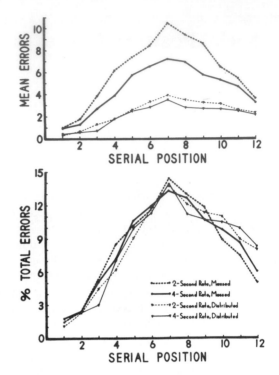

FIGURE 19.2

tion curves for the learning of 12-syllable lists under conditions of massed vs. distributed practice, using 2-sec and 4-sec rates of presentation per syllable. The mean number of errors per serial position under these various conditions is shown in the upper half of Figure 19.2. Again there is evident a marked decrease in mean errors when distributed practice is compared with massed practice, with the greatest decrease in the central portion of the curve. The change from a 2-sec to a 4-sec rate of presentation has little effect under conditions of distributed practice, but a significant effect in massed practice.

The curves in the lower halves of Figures 19.1 and 19.2 show the serial position curves of the upper halves of the figures plotted in percentages, with the mean errors at each position expressed as a percentage of the total mean errors made under a given practice condition. (Since we did not have access to Hovland's original data, the values are computed either from his curves or from his tables. In either case any errors in the calculations would be small.) The striking feature of the percentage plots is that there is essentially no difference in the curves for the different conditions of learning. This is also true for the percentage plots we have made of the data in eight other investigations by various authors. In all cases there was practically complete identity of the percentage serial position curves for the greater and lesser conditions of efficiency within a given experiment, with a rare maximum difference of 3.5% for a given serial position.

The reason for plotting percentage mean error curves is as follows, stated in terms of the experiment on massed vs. distributed practice: Since distributed practice is more efficient than massed practice, fewer errors are made during learning under the former than under the latter condition. Graphs of mean errors per syllable position, therefore, must give two curves which differ in their ordinate values much as is the case in Figure 19.1, irrespective of the explanatory theory being investigated. When the absolute mean error curves are equated for area by plotting them in percentage terms, any essential differences in form are observable. The percentage curves of Figures 19.1 and 19.2 show that the several serial positions have the same order of relative difficulty under the more and the less efficient methods of learning. From the standpoint of the Lepley-Hull inhibition theory, the percentage curves are more significant than the mean error curves, since they show that the reduction of errors brought about by the introduction of elapsed time intervals occurs throughout the series in proportion to the total errors made and in the same overall manner as where no elapsed time is introduced. This does not prove the inhibition theory, but it is consistent with it.

In a further attempt to throw light on the serial position curve and on the relevancy of the inhibition theory, we have conducted an experiment on the serial learning of 14 nonsense syllables vs. 14 familiar names (an initial cue item was added to each list) by the conventional anticipation method counterbalancing the two series. In order to balance out any unevenness in difficulty of the specific items, each subject entered the list at a different point so that, for example, the syllable or name in serial positions 3 and 4 for one subject would be in positions 4 and 5 for another subject. The items were presented at a 2-sec rate, with the intertrial interval set at 8 sec. Learning was completed in one session, massed practice, to a criterion of one

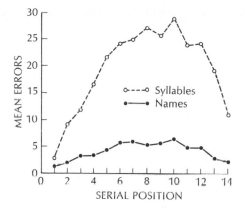

FIGURE 19.3

correct anticipation of each syllable in the course of one trial. The association values of the syllables were from 0 to 3% according to Hull's calibration[6]. The names were the family names of the 16 graduate students who served as subjects and who, at this time, were well acquainted with each other. The mean number of trials required for learning the syllables was 39 and for learning the names, 11.

Figure 19.3 gives the serial position curves for syllables and names plotted in terms of mean errors, and Figure 19.4 replots the same data in terms of the percentage of total errors made at each serial position.

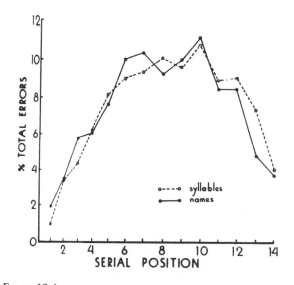

FIGURE 19.4

Again it is to be noted that (1) the curves are the familiar bow-shaped ones current in the literature, (2) the greatest gain in efficiency occurs in the middle of the series or just past the middle, and (3) the percentage plots are essentially identical. Items 2 and 3 above were brought about by the use of familiar names vs. nonsense materials as the material to be learned and not by the introduction of elapsed time, which might allow for a decrease of inhibitory tendencies as predicted by the Lepley-Hull theory.

The 16 subjects of the above experiment were classified as quick or slow learners on the basis of being in the upper or lower half of the group in total errors made during learning. The upper half of Figure 19.5 presents the serial position curves for these two groups in learning familiar names as described above, and the lower half gives the curves on a percentage basis. Similar curves were found for quick vs. slow learners in the nonsense syllable learning of these 16 subjects, as well as in the experiment (not here reported) with 48 subjects in the learning of familiar and unfamiliar nonsense syllables.

The general conclusions from the above experiments and analyses are as follows: (1) Any experimental condition which increases the efficiency of serial verbal learning and which thereby decreases the total number of errors made will result in a serial position curve of mean errors which lies below the curve for a less efficient method of learning. (2) The reduction in mean errors per serial position, although greatest in the middle or just past the middle of the series, will be closely proportional at each position to the total number of errors made. It is in no sense surprising that, when one changes from a less to a more efficient method of learning, the greatest reduction of errors will occur in the central serial positions. This is not a confirmation of the inhibition theory but merely an evidence of the fact that significant gains in efficiency can only occur where serious errors have been made—namely, in the central part of the series. It is surprising, however, that the gains under a more efficient learning method should be as proportionately distributed as the percentage curves indicate.

The theoretical problem still remains of explaining why the serial position curves for verbal learning are bow-shaped. We can offer no solution ourselves, although we believe that a multiple- rather than a

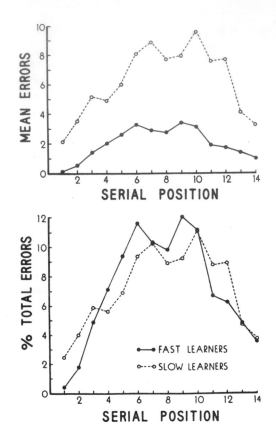

FIGURE 19.5

single-factor theory will finally be indicated. The Lepley-Hull inhibition theory is plausible only under the conditions discussed above, where lapses of time were introduced into the learning process. In order to rank as an adequate general theory it would need to be shown that any condition which increased the efficiency of serial verbal learning (including meaning, familiarity, and quick learning ability) decreased proportionately the inhibitory tendencies postulated in connection with the various serial positions.

REFERENCES

1. Lepley, W. M. *Psychol. Monographs,* 46, (205), (1934).
2. Hull, C. L. *Psychol. Rev.,* 42, 491 (1935).
3. Patten, E. F. *J. Psychol.,* 5, 359 (1938).
4. Hovland, C. I. *J. Exptl. Psychol.,* 23, 172 (1938).
5. *Ibid.,* 27, 271 (1940).
6. Hull, C. L. *Am. J. Psychol.,* 45, 730 (1933).

20 VON RESTORFF EFFECT

When psychologists refer to the von Restorff effect (or, as it is sometimes called, the isolation effect), they are usually referring to the finding that if one item in a list differs from the others, it is better recalled. For example, say you are given a list of words to remember, and all are breeds of dogs except for the sixth word, which is a type of car (e.g., "Ford"). The car term will be remembered much better than if the sixth word had been yet another dog breed. The explanation is that the unusual item is more distinctive than the other items in the list: It stands out from the other items and thus attracts more attention.

Many psychologists describe this scenario and then cite, as evidence, a paper published by Hedwig von Restorff in 1933. The problem is that the experiments, data, and interpretation reported by von Restorff (1933) bear little resemblance to what most psychologists attribute to her. Hunt (1995) describes what von Restorff actually did, clarifies what "distinctiveness" actually refers to, and suggests that many current accounts of the von Restorff effect are invalidated by von Restorff's own data.

Hunt begins by describing some of the background of von Restorff's work, including the important fact that she worked in the lab of one of the leading Gestalt psychologists, Wolfgang Köhler. One of the key ideas of the Gestalt movement was that percepts have characteristics that cannot be derived from the characteristics of their components, or, as it is often described, the whole is different than the sum of its parts.

Hunt, in accord with the Gestalt principles, distinguishes between *difference*, the objective property of being different, and *distinctiveness*, the psychological result of dissimilarity. One can measure how items differ from each other, but this need not correspond to how distinctive a particular item appears to a particular person. The distinction between difference and distinctiveness is similar to the one between intensity and loudness: The former is an objective property of sounds (you measure the physical intensity of a sound), the latter is a subjective experience of a listener (you ask a person how loud a sound seems). The distinction is important because under some circumstances, a less intense sound can appear to be louder than a more intense sound. Hunt is correct that many theorists have failed to distinguish between difference and distinctiveness.

Most current explanations of the von Restorff effect, Hunt argues, are incorrect because they assume that differential attention plays a role. For example, a typical explanation might argue that the unique or distinctive item attracts more attention and so is processed more than a control item. Data in von Restorff's own experiment suggest this explanation is not viable. The problem is easily illustrated by considering what happens to recall of a digit in several types of lists. In list one, the first item might be a nonsense syllable, the second might be a digit, and so on; each item differs from all the others. In list two, the first item is a nonsense syllable, the second is a digit, but now all the rest are also nonsense syllables. In both lists there is an identical change from one type of item (a nonsense syllable) to a different type of item (a digit) so attention should be equally attracted in both cases. However, only list two exhibits a von Restorff effect for the digit; list one does not. The digit differs from all items in list one, but is not distinctive.

One omission in Hunt's paper is the lack of discussion of any of the well-established mathematical models based on distinctiveness. Beginning with Murdock's (1960) seminal model, these accounts provide a precise mathematical description of distinctiveness that refers to the psychological effect, and they all give an account that is quite compatible with von Restorff's original ideas (see, for example, Murray, 1995).

Hunt's (1995) paper is important because it corrects a widespread mistake: von Restorff did not do what is commonly attributed to her, and she included a control condition that refutes many current explanations of the effect. The von Restorff effect itself is important for a variety of reasons. First, it is an empirical confirmation that unusual events can be better remembered than more usual events. Second, the distinction between difference and distinctiveness emphasizes that a memory representation, like a percept, need not be a veridical copy of the original object. Third, the basic idea has led to the development of a number of successful computational models of memory.

The CogLab demo is based on a classic experiment reported by Pillsbury and Raush (1943). Like von Restorff's and Hunt's procedures, it minimizes the possibility that recall of the isolated item is due to increased attention by presenting eight-item lists made up of varying numbers of digits and letters. Following Pillsbury and Raush, the data from the demo are presented as a difference score. The "proportion difference" is the proportion of digits recalled minus the proportion of letters recalled. If the digits and letters are recalled equally well, this value will be zero. If digits are recalled better, this value will be positive; if letters are recalled better, this value will be negative.

REFERENCES

Murdock, B. B., Jr. (1960). The distinctiveness of stimuli. *Psychological Review, 67,* 16–31.

Murray, D. J. (1995). *Gestalt psychology and the cognitive revolution.* New York: Harvester Wheatsheaf.

Pillsbury, W. B., & Raush, H. L. (1943). An extension of the Köhler-Restorff inhibition phenomenon. *American Journal of Psychology, 56,* 293–298.

QUESTIONS

1. Compare and contrast *difference* and *distinctiveness* as Hunt uses the terms.
2. How does the prototypical von Restorff experiment differ from the experiment she actually ran?
3. Why is the unrelated list an excellent control condition?
4. Why does Hunt conclude that perceptual salience is not necessary for obtaining an isolation effect?

The Subtlety of Distinctiveness: What von Restorff Really Did

R. Reed Hunt

University of North Carolina, Greensboro, North Carolina

ABSTRACT

The isolation effect is a well-known memory phenomenon whose discovery is frequently attributed to von Restorff (1933). If all but one item of a list are similar on some dimension, memory for the different item will be enhanced. Modern theory of the isolation effect emphasizes perceptual salience and accompanying differential attention to the isolated item as necessary for enhanced memory. In fact, von Restorff, whose paper is not available in English, presented evidence that perceptual salience is not necessary for the isolation effect. She further argued that the difference between the isolated and surrounding items is not sufficient to produce isolation effects but must be considered in the context of similarity. Von Restorff's reasoning and data have implications for the use of distinctiveness in contemporary memory research, where distinctiveness is sometimes defined as perceptual salience and sometimes as a theoretical process of discrimination. As a theoretical construct, distinctiveness is a useful description of the effects of differences even in the absence of perceptual salience, but distinctiveness must be used in conjunction with constructs referring to similarity to provide an adequate account of the isolation effect and probably any other memory phenomena.

Hedwig von Restorff is remembered for her contributions to research on memory, and especially for the effect that bears her name—a rather remarkable accomplishment, given the unfortunate brevity of her career. She worked as a postdoctoral assistant to Wolfgang Köhler at the Psychological Institute of the University of Berlin up to the time that Köhler resigned in protest against Nazi interference with the Institute. The inci-

dent that precipitated Köhler's resignation in 1935 was the dismissal of the postdoctoral assistants, who included not only von Restorff but also Karl Duncker (Henle, 1986).

During her time in Köhler's laboratory, von Restorff published two papers, the second of which she coauthored with Köhler (Köhler & von Restorff, 1935). This paper, on the topic of spontaneous reminding, included a prescient discussion of the role of intentionality in the memory test. In the first paper, she presented her dissertation research (von Restorff, 1933) and reported the phenomenon named for her. My discussion will be focused on this widely cited but little read piece.

The classic 1933 paper has never been published in English and is likely to surprise the contemporary reader on several dimensions. For example, the first page is devoted to defending studies of memory that use lists of nonsense materials against charges of ecological invalidity. Even though Titchener (1915) had proclaimed Ebbinghaus's innovation of nonsense syllables as the most important advance in the study of memory since Aristotle, criticism of the technique had gained momentum by 1933 on the grounds that memorization of lists was a meaningless activity and consequently would yield no useful information about real-world memory (see, e.g., Bartlett, 1932). Von Restorff's rejoinder is unique: "After all, we do not want to fool ourselves: Millions of people remain in the same work situations day after day, even though their tasks are no more meaningful than the experimental tasks. One would hardly criticize the classical psychology of memory for being too far removed

SOURCE: From Hunt, R. R. (1995). The subtlety of distinctiveness: What von Restorff really did. *Psychonomic Bulletin & Review, 2,* 105–112. Reprinted by permission of Psychonomic Society, Inc.

from everyday experience, just because the subjects were engaged in meaningless tasks" (von Restorff, 1933, p. 300). Her substantive points related to distinctiveness are equally crisp.

THE VON RESTORFF EFFECT AND DISTINCTIVENESS

The von Restorff effect is known to most psychologists as the generic label for the effects of distinctiveness on memory. This attribution stems from the fact that all the experiments in the 1933 paper used the isolation paradigm, the essential feature of which is that one item in a list differs from the remaining items on one or more dimensions. For example, subjects might be asked to remember the two lists depicted in Table 20.1. Each list consists of 10 items, but the isolation list has a syllable embedded in the numbers. The homogeneous list serves as a control in that the same syllable appears in the same serial position. Results from this paradigm show better memory for the syllable in the isolation list than for the same item in the homogenous list. This is the effect that has come to be associated with von Restorff and that is generally ascribed to distinctiveness. Indeed, most instances of distinctiveness effects on memory have come to be categorized as von Restorff effects: "The unusual, bizarre, or distinctive event seems inherently more memorable than common everyday occurrences. Psychologists often refer to this phenomenon as the von Restorff effect" (Schmidt, 1991, p. 523).

TABLE 20.1   An Example of Isolated and Homogeneous Lists

Isolated	Homogeneous
9	TOZ
12	DUQ
3	HOL
16	COS
QXK	QXK
5	DRF
14	TXP
11	XMS
2	FTH
7	HZL

Distinctiveness as an Independent Variable

Distinctiveness, as used in the foregoing, is a descriptive term for events that violate the prevailing context—that is, for events that are perceptually salient. In this sense, distinctiveness is an independent variable whose effects on memory must be explained. The isolation paradigm is one method for manipulating the variable of distinctiveness, and the isolation effect thus comes to be viewed as an instance of distinctiveness effects in memory. The intuitive explanation of the isolation effect in particular and distinctiveness effects in general is that the perceptual salience of the distinctive event attracts additional processing. This intuition is most readily realized through the mechanism of selective attention. Jenkins and Postman (1948) were the first to propose that differential attention could be a necessary condition for the isolation effect, and most prominent theories have since followed suit.

Green (1956) argued that the isolation effect resulted from surprise induced by the change from preceding items: "Surprise increases the attention paid to the item and hence the likelihood of recall" (p. 340). Surprise, the emotional response to perceptual salience, explicitly elicits attention to the item in Green's theory. But why should attention enhance memory? Rundus (1971) suggested that the function of attention was to engage rehearsal in such a way that an isolated item is remembered better because it receives more rehearsal than other items.

More recently, Schmidt (1991) proposed his incongruity hypothesis as an explanation of distinctiveness effects in memory, including isolation effects: "According to this definition, distinctive events are those that are inconsistent with active conceptual frameworks, or that contain salient features not present in active memory. These events lead to increased attention in direct proportion to the degree of incongruity" (p. 537). Thus, Schmidt's hypothesis continues the emphasis on differential attention resulting from salience at presentation of the item, although his idea is considerably more sophisticated than its predecessors. In particular, Schmidt explicitly says that differential attention is not sufficient for enhanced memory, because the retrieval context must be taken into account. Nonetheless, it is clear that differential attention at the time of item presentation is a necessary condition for the incongruity hypothesis.

In these accounts, distinctiveness is treated as an independent variable. The effects of distinctiveness are then explained by the postulation of additional processes, beginning with differential attention to the distinctive event and followed by more elaborative encoding processes. In essence, distinctiveness causes more elaborative processing that in turn facilitates retrieval. Von Restorff's isolation effect is always cited as the progenitor of this view of distinctiveness.

Distinctiveness as a Theoretical Construct

Distinctiveness has recently come to be used in a very different sense. During the theoretical refinement of levels of processing (Craik & Lockhart, 1972), the concept of depth of processing evolved into the concept of distinctive processing. The empirical foundation of levels of processing was the superiority of semantic, as opposed to nonsemantic, encoding tasks. Craik and Tulving (1975) suggested that semantic orienting tasks produced more elaborate memory traces than did nonsemantic tasks, but this raised the question of why elaborative processing facilitated retrieval. Subsequently, theorists invoked the concept of distinctiveness as the answer.

For example, Lockhart, Craik, and Jacoby (1976), suggested that "the beneficial effects of depth of encoding is that deeper, richer encodings are also more distinctive and unique" (p. 86). Craik and Jacoby (1979) proposed that "the notion that greater depth and greater degrees of elaboration of the stimulus allow formation of a more distinctive, discriminable trace" (p. 19). The idea essentially is that the more one knows about something, the less like other things it becomes. The same idea was advocated by others in the context of research on levels of processing (e.g., Eysenck, 1979; Hunt & Elliott, 1980; Nelson, 1979). Distinctiveness in this sense is a theoretical construct describing characteristics of the encoding that supports discriminative processes at retrieval.

The two definitions of distinctiveness as a theoretical construct and as an independent variable cannot be employed in the same explanation. To do so results in a tautology. In one case, distinctiveness causes elaborative processing, and in the other case, elabora-

tive processing results in distinctiveness. Conflating the two usages produces a circular explanation. For example, one might say that an isolated item is distinctive, but to attribute the memorial advantage of isolation to distinctiveness would then be blatantly circular. We can describe the isolated item as distinctive and then go on to postulate psychological processes that mediate the effects of distinctiveness, or we can say that isolation affects psychological processes responsible for discrimination at retrieval which we call theoretical distinctiveness, but we should not do both.

The distinction is clear but subtle, and the subtlety can create confusion. For example, Schmidt (1991) correctly observes that distinctiveness has been used to explain a vast array of phenomena, but then goes on to advocate limiting its use to situations with common operational definitions. On Schmidt's definition of distinctiveness ("distinctive events are those incongruent with active conceptual frameworks" p. 537), the meaning of distinctiveness is limited to that of an independent variable. The theoretical sense of the term that evolved from levels of processing would be proscribed.

There is reason to resist this advice, and ironically, the reason can be found in von Restorff's (1933) original report. The irony is that while the von Restorff effect is taken to be the mother of all distinctiveness effects, she explicitly argued against such an interpretation. In what follows, her reasoning and results will be described along with their implication for contemporary views of distinctiveness.

WHAT VON RESTORFF REALLY DID

As it happened, von Restorff neither pioneered the isolation paradigm nor championed distinctiveness interpretations of the isolation effect. Numerous experiments using the isolation paradigm were reported prior to von Restorff's (1933) paper (e.g., Calkins, 1894, 1896; Jersild, 1929; van Buskirk, 1932—just to mention a few of the papers written in English). Most of these earlier experiments were designed in order to study the effect of vividness on memory. Vividness was taken to be an independent variable and was manipulated in a variety of ways, all of which amounted to isolating an item from other items on some dimension. This early work established the beneficial effects of vividness on memory; that is, the isolated item was remembered better than nonisolated items. Von Restorff, however, was not interested in demonstrating the effects of vividness further and ultimately argued that vividness was not a necessary condition for the isolation effect.

The details of von Restorff's research have been leveled in secondary sources over the years. Her paper has never appeared in English, and the last detailed secondary descriptions of her work appear in Koffka (1935) and Woodworth (1938). By the time of the 1954 revision of Woodworth (Woodworth & Schlosberg, 1954), all reference to von Restorff had disappeared. Although many subsequent texts have mentioned the von Restorff effect (e.g., Crowder, 1976; Hall, 1971; Hilgard & Bower, 1975; Kausler, 1974), none describe the experiments to be discussed here. Osgood (1953) does provide a discussion of an important subsidiary issue that will be mentioned below, but not even Wallace's (1965) excellent review of research on isolation effects describes von Restorff's concern with isolation effects and perceptual salience.

The context for this concern lies in von Restorff's principal interest in interference effects. She used the isolation paradigm as a tool to investigate interference effects (see Bower, Thompson-Schill, & Tulving, 1994, for an account of von Restorff's contribution to this issue), and along with Koffka (1935), she offered the Gestalt interpretation of retroactive interference as instantiated by the isolation effect. Similarity among the massed items of either a homogeneous list or the nonisolated items of the isolated list resulted in agglutination of those items. The isolated item was not aggregated to the homogeneous items because of its lack of similarity. Thus, the isolated item stood out as figure against the ground of the homogeneous items. Using the metaphor of perception, the isolation effect in memory was thus explained essentially in terms of the discriminablity of the isolate.

This general explanation was intended as a model of memory processes derived from perception, but von Restorff was sensitive to the possibility that the effects could be due to perception, not memory. What she meant by this distinction between perception and memory was that the isolation effect could result from either the perceptual salience of the isolated item at presentation or to factors subsequent to the presentation of the item. Her resolution of this issue is what has been lost from secondary accounts and is critical to the difference between the two usages of distinctiveness.

The reason why perceptual salience intuitively appears to be necessary for the isolation effect is that most studies place the isolate around the middle serial position of the list. If the goal is to study distinctiveness or vividness as an independent variable, this methodology makes perfect sense. Preceding the isolate with some number of homogeneous items maximizes the probability that the isolate will be perceptually salient. However, von Restorff actually employed this procedure in only one of the numerous experiments that she reported.

In the first experiments in her paper, von Restorff used paired associate lists consisting of five different types of materials. The members of each pair were of the same type of material, and eight pairs constituted a list. Here is an example taken from her paper:

    laf – rig
    # – !
    dok – pir
    89 – 46
    red square – green square
    zul – dap
    S – B
    tog – fern

Four pairs were of the same type (the nonsense syllables in this example), and the four remaining pairs represented each of the four other types of material. Thus, four of the pairs were homogeneous and four of the pairs were isolated in the sense that they were the only pair from that type of material. She obtained better recall for the isolated pairs than for the homogeneous pairs, but she does not report data relating recall of the isolated pair to its serial position in the list.

In a subsequent recognition experiment, von Restorff isolated a single item in the middle of the serial list for the only time in all of her experiments. The list consisted of 20 items—either 19 syllables and 1 number or 19 numbers and 1 syllable. She moved to this more extreme isolation because her studies of recognition that used several isolated items in a list produced smaller differences between isolated and homogeneous material than she had found in recall. The more stringent manipulation was successful in enhancing the difference between recognition of iso-lated and homogeneous items beyond that even of the recall data. However, the issue of perceptual salience now occurred to von Restorff, because, unlike the method used in her earlier experiments, the presenta-tion of a different item following 10 homogeneous items might induce perceptual salience.

She explicitly addressed the issue with simple, el-egant reasoning, arguing that perceptual salience should not accrue to an item isolated early in the list. Introducing the next experiment, she wrote, "In Lists 1 and 2, the syllable and number were presented at the beginning of the list, namely at the second and third positions, at which point the subjects could not know anything about the contents of the whole list. Thus, the isolated item was not perceived as unusual and was not particularly salient to the subject" (von Restorff, 1933, p. 319). The explicit motivation for this experiment was to separate the effects of isolation on memory from the well-established effects of isolation on perception. "We wanted to avoid the situation where the critical item would stand out as perceptu-ally unique" (von Restorff, 1933, p. 319).

In addition to the issue of perceptual salience, von Restorff raised a second question that is central to the theoretical construct of distinctiveness. Is the iso-lation effect due exclusively to differences between the isolated item and surrounding items? Von Restorff's point here is at once obvious and widely appreciated and at the same time quite subtle. The obvious com-ponent of her discussion is that the isolation effect de-pends on a strong similarity relationship among the nonisolated items of the list. That is, the isolate must be obviously different from the other items of the list. The more subtle point that is pertinent to our discus-sion of distinctiveness is that difference between the isolate and the remaining items is not sufficient to produce an isolation effect.

Von Restorff illustrates this argument in the fol-lowing fashion. Suppose we begin with a standard isolation list consisting of 9 numbers and 1 syllable. The difference between the syllable and numbers is substantial, and this difference should produce an isolation effect for the syllable. But now suppose we substitute a line drawing for one of the numbers; we then would have 2 isolated items (the drawing and

the syllable) and 8 numbers. The drawing and the syllable are different from the numbers, but they also are different from each other. We continue to substi-tute items of different materials (e.g., a symbol, a word, an object) for the numbers in the original list. Ultimately, we have a list of 10 unrelated items, but the difference between the syllable (the original iso-late) and the other items is just as great as the differ-ence between the syllable and the numbers. "In the end, the difference between all other items among themselves and the syllable is equivalent to the initial difference between syllable and numbers" (von Restorff, 1933, p. 313). Thus, if the isolate were re-membered better than the same item in the same serial position of an unrelated list, "then one could argue that other factors besides the difference be-tween one item and other items are important" (von Restorff, 1933, p. 314).

The reasoning, in brief, is that the transition from an isolation list to an unrelated list is a change in the similarity of the homogenous items, not in the differ-ence between the isolate and the remaining items. The isolate remains as different from the other items in the unrelated list as it does in the isolated list. If, then, an isolation effect occurs in relation to an unrelated con-trol list, the effect cannot be due exclusively to the dif-ference between the isolated and homogeneous items.

In describing this reasoning, Osgood (1953) sug-gested that the experiment would determine whether the superiority of the isolated item was due to the dis-tinctiveness (his word) of the isolate or to the aggluti-nation of the nonisolated items: "Since the critical item was equally unique in both cases (isolated and unrelated lists), any difference must be due to the ag-glutination (indiscriminability) of the 'massed' items" (p. 567). The critical aspect of Osgood's recounting is his recognition of von Restorff's point that the item would be "equally unique" in either an isolation list or an unrelated list.

Von Restorff's reasoning about similarity and dif-ference converges with her primary point about per-ceptual salience. Not only is perceptual salience un-necessary for the isolation effect, difference alone is insufficient to account for the effect. We shall find this reasoning instructive in using the contemporary con-cept of distinctiveness.

Experimental Method and Results

The remaining details of von Restorff's experiment are straightforward, but will be briefly described. Subjects saw three separate lists, one on each of 3 succeeding days. All subjects saw the unrelated list on the 1st day and separate isolation lists on the 2nd and 3rd days. The unrelated list was shown first in order to enhance the camouflage of the isolation lists—so that the isolate in the isolation list would not be perceptually salient. Each list consisted of 10 items. The unrelated items were a number, a syllable, a color patch, a single letter, a word, a photograph, a symbol, an actual button, a punctuation mark, and the name of a chemical compound. The subjects recalled the names of each item—for example, the color name, or "button," or the contents of the picture. The critical lists were 9 nonsense syllables and 1 number or 9 numbers and 1 nonsense syllable, with the isolated item located in either the second or the third serial position. Von Restorff does not say how frequently the item appeared in the second or the third position.

The subjects were given intentional memory instructions, following which the items were shown successively for 1.5 sec each. After list presentation, a distractor task required subjects to read a prose passage for a subsequent memory test. Ten minutes were devoted to reading the passage. Then a verbal free recall test of the list was administered, followed by recall for the passage. This procedure was repeated on each of the 3 days of testing. A total of 15 subjects participated in the experiment.

We replicated von Restorff's original procedure with two important changes. The first was to present the lists between subjects rather than within subjects, so that a given subject saw only the unrelated or the isolation list. Two lists were constructed for the isolation condition, one consisting of nine nonsense syllables and one digit and the other of nine digits and one nonsense syllable. The isolated item always appeared in the second serial position, which was the second major change from von Restorff's method. The unrelated lists contained either a digit or a syllable in the second serial position. A total of 40 subjects, all undergraduate volunteers, participated, with 20 subjects in each of the isolation and control conditions.

Each list was presented to half the subjects in the appropriate condition. Thus, our subjects experienced one list and, following a 10-min distraction of reading prose, were asked to free recall the list.

Correct recall of the isolated item as a function of list type is the important measure from these experiments. Von Restorff reported average correct recall of .70 for the isolation list and .40 for the control list. In our replication, the proportion correct for the isolation list was .70 for an isolated syllable and .80 for an isolated digit. The corresponding recall from the unrelated control lists was .40 for syllables and .30 for digits. Thus, our results provide a close replication of von Restorff's data in spite of our procedural changes.

IMPLICATIONS

Von Restorff's results clearly show an isolation effect when the isolate occurred early in the list—in either the second or the third serial position—and she concluded that perceptual salience was not a necessary condition for the isolation effect. Unfortunately, von Restorff did not report how often the isolate appeared in the second as opposed to the third position. With the isolate in the third serial position, one might worry that the first two items provided sufficient context to render the isolate perceptually salient. Two considerations argue against this conclusion. First, von Restorff went to some lengths to camouflage the isolate by presenting the unrelated list first. Second, our replication placed the isolate exclusively in the second serial position, and the data are remarkably consistent with von Restorff's. Even more convincing is an experiment by Pillsbury and Raush (1943), who reported a substantial isolation effect even when the isolate appeared in the first serial position. Perceptual salience apparently is not necessary for obtaining an isolation effect.

This conclusion is inconsistent with all recent theories of the isolation effect (see, e.g., Green, 1956; Rundus, 1971; Schmidt, 1991). These theories share the premise that differential attention to the isolate is necessary for the isolation effect, and that the source of differential attention is the perceptual salience or contextual incongruity of the isolate. On these assumptions, an isolation effect would not be expected if the isolated item were presented prior to some consistent context. In fairness, these theories were all designed to explain data from paradigms in which the isolate occurred after context had been established. Under these circumstances, it is reasonable to assume that the isolate was perceptually salient and attracted additional processing. It may even be the case that this additional processing contributes to enhanced memory for the isolate. If so, the isolation effect would result from a manipulation of distinctiveness.

The mistake is to assume that perceptual salience is necessary for the isolation effect, particularly if the attribution is to von Restorff's research. The important cost of this mistake is not so much in the interpretation of the isolation effect, although it is interesting to realize that this simple effect may require further theoretical work; rather, the cost comes in the confusion about distinctiveness. If one assumes that the isolation effect requires perceptual salience and that the isolation effect is the paradigm case of distinctiveness, any subsequent use of distinctiveness should be traceable to operations producing perceptual salience.

Equating perceptual salience with distinctiveness blurs a fundamental distinction between distinctiveness and difference. *Difference* refers to the objective condition of being dissimilar, whereas *distinctiveness* refers to the psychological effect of dissimilarity. Difference is a description of the characteristics of events or items or the relationship among them, whereas distinctiveness is a psychological construct describing cognition of the differences. Technically, difference is the independent variable that gives rise to the psychological process of distinctiveness. Thus it is the effect of difference that requires explanation.

The typical isolation paradigm is a seductive scaffold on which to mount the explanation because the incongruity between the isolate and context is obvious and extreme. The extremity misleads us into the assumption that perceptual salience is the psychological process arising from difference and that perceptual salience is necessary for a difference in materials to affect memory. Although perceptual salience may be one consequence of difference, the data from von Restorff and others showing an isolation effect when the isolate occurs early in the list argue against the necessity of perceptual salience for effects on memory.

Difference need not produce perceptual salience to affect memory; it is only necessary that sufficient item information be encoded to represent the differences among the items. This essentially is the idea that evolved from levels-of-processing research as the theoretical construct of distinctiveness. Difference, induced by manipulations of materials and orienting tasks, produces a distinctive trace—that is, a trace that includes features unique in relation to those of other items from the episode. Distinctiveness enhances memory by facilitating discriminative processes at retrieval. As a theoretical construct, distinctiveness encompasses not only the effects of perceptual salience and conceptual incongruity but, more generally, any effect of difference.

Thus, the difference between distinctiveness as an independent variable and as a theoretical construct is really the same as von Restorff's distinction between perceptual salience and memorial salience. No one doubts the reality of perceptual salience as a psychological phenomenon, and perceptual salience probably enhances memory for the salient item. It is also the case, however, that differences among items affect memory even if those differences are not operationally salient at the time of perception. That is, processes subsequent to initial perception and comprehension are influenced by difference. Distinctiveness has been used to describe both perceptual and memorial salience, but, as argued above, the two definitions of distinctiveness cannot be employed in the same explanation. Indiscriminate mixing of the meanings invariably results in circular explanations.

The concern about the circularity of distinctiveness (e.g., Schmidt, 1991) is legitimate, but it can be managed easily. Operations that draw attention to differences among items are the antecedents to distinctiveness, and a given experiment can provide indices of distinctiveness that are independent of memory, providing converging operations on the validity of the manipulations (see, e.g., Hunt & Einstein, 1981). In short, distinctiveness is a useful theoretical construct to explain the effects of differences on memory.

Even so, distinctiveness alone is insufficient to account for the isolation effect and probably any other memory phenomenon. Von Restorff argued, largely on empirical grounds, that the isolation effect could not be explained solely as a matter of differences. The argument was that if difference alone caused distinctiveness, the isolation effect should not occur relative to performance on an unrelated control list in which the differences were maximized. In Schmidt's (1991) terminology, each item of an unrelated list should be incongruent with the active conceptual framework established by the preceding item, and hence distinctive. Nonetheless, the isolate was remembered better in the isolation list than in the unrelated list.

The obvious difference between the isolation list and an unrelated list lies in the similarity among the nonisolated items of the isolation list, and von Restorff appealed to this factor to explain the results. Her argument may appear trivial, in that no one is surprised that the similarity of the nonisolated items is critical for the isolation effect; but we must keep in mind the fact that perceptual salience is not necessary. Therefore, the importance of similarity among the nonisolated items cannot be to establish an encoding context in which the isolate is incongruent. Rather, in her terms, the nonisolated items are agglutinated in memory (the differences among the items are lost to the dimension of similarity) while the isolate remains distinct.

There is some parallel between the Gestalt interpretation of the isolation effect and the contemporary principle of cue overload (Watkins & Watkins, 1975), an empirical principle stating that cue effectiveness is inversely related to the number of items sharing a cue. In accord with cue overload, the nonisolated items may all share a single cue—for example, the label for the dimension of similarity. The isolated item has a unique cue and thus has an advantage at retrieval. However, if we extend this analysis to the complete pattern of results from the isolation experiments, an important point about the effects of similarity and difference on memory is revealed along with the insufficiency of cue overload as even an empirical summary of the data.

Unadorned, the principle of cue overload cannot describe the advantage of an isolation list in comparison with an unrelated control list. In both lists, the critical item is different from the other items and presumably then would not share cues with the other items. Recall of the critical item from an unrelated list should be equivalent to recall of the same item in an isolation list. That this does not happen is an indication of the importance of similarity's establishing a context within which difference functions (Hunt & Kelly, in press). In other words, the effects of difference are relative to the effects of similarity.

The relativity of difference has been appreciated by advocates of distinctiveness as a theoretical construct (Craik & Jacoby, 1979). The attributes of individual items that are encoded for memory will be affected by the context of the event, affected in such a way that the perceived differences are aligned with the context. In their recent theory of similarity, Medin, Goldstone, and Gentner (1993) suggest that functional encoded differences are relative to the dominant dimension of similarity. They propose a process of alignment by which the properties of items are brought into correspondence; that is, a dominant dimension of similarity is extracted on the basis of relations among the items and contextual factors such as current intent. The same process of alignment yields attributes that differ among these items. For example, the words *robin, eagle, ostrich* will be aligned along the dimension of *bird*, but the encoding may also include different attributes, such as *song, predator, large*. In contrast, unrelated items (e.g., *robin, gasoline, computer*) will be represented by attributes that differ, but the differences will not be aligned to any dominant dimension of similarity.

When extended to memory, one might suggest that the different attributes function distinctively in retrieval, and thus, for both related and unrelated items, distinctiveness is present. However, the effects of distinctive processing are relative to similarity in that distinctiveness in the context of similarity facilitates performance more than does distinctiveness unaligned to similarity. Indeed, Markman and Gentner (1993) have shown that aligned differences come to mind more readily and more frequently than unaligned differences. Subjects were asked to list the differences between two words that varied in similarity. Highly similar pairs elicited more differences than did less similar pairs. Furthermore, the differences for the similar pairs were much more likely to be aligned to some relation between the items (e.g., cars have four wheels and motorcycles have two wheels) than were the differences between less similar pairs (e.g., cars use gasoline, computers do not).

Medin et al.'s (1993) analysis provides a conceptual footing to von Restorff's empirical argument that difference alone is insufficient to account for the isolation effect. Unaligned differences (e.g., an object that does not use gasoline) are of little diagnostic value at retrieval, and it is in this sense that Medin et al.'s theory provides a basis for von Restorff's argument. Distinctiveness must work in concert with some concept that characterizes similarities and their effects on memory. A reasonable candidate for this role is organization. Thus one would attempt to explain the simultaneous effect of similarity and differences on memory by developing a theory of the concurrent operation of organization and distinctiveness, an exercise in which we and others have been engaged (Hunt & McDaniel, 1993). Regardless, the point is that the concept of distinctiveness is not useful as an absolute explanation of memory phenomena. Von Restorff could have taught us this.

AUTHOR NOTE

This paper was presented to the meeting of the Psychonomic Society in Washington, D.C., November 1993, and the work was supported by a grant from NICHHD (HD 256587). Mark McDaniel, Steve Schmidt, and Endel Tulving provided helpful criticism of the manuscript. Special thanks to Henry L. Roediger for his encouragement on this project. Elizabeth Denny, Mary Henle, Cheryl Logan, Rebekah Kelly, and Christine Pivetta provided helpful comments on the work. The translation of von Restorff's paper was done by Andrea Dorsch. Requests for reprints may be addressed to the author at Department of Psychology, University of North Carolina. Greensboro, NC 27412-5002 (e-mail: huntrr@iris.uncg.edu). The English translation of von Restorff's paper can be accessed on the World Wide Web at http://www.uncg.edu/~huntrr/vonrestorff.

REFERENCES

Bartlett, F. C. (1932). *Remembering.* Cambridge: Cambridge University Press.

Bower, G. H., Thompson-Schill S., & Tulving, E. (1994). Reducing retroactive interference: An interference analysis. *Journal of Experimental Psychology: Learning, Memory, & Cognition, 20,* 51–66.

Calkins, M. W. (1894). Association. *Psychological Review, l,* 476–483.

Calkins, M. W. (1896). Association: An essay analytic and experimental. *Psychological Review Monograph Supplements, 2.*

Craik, F. I. M., & Jacoby, L. L. (1979). Elaboration and distinctiveness in episodic memory. In L. Nilsson (Ed.), *Perspectives on memory research: Essays in honor of Uppsala University's 500th anniversary* (pp. 145–166). Hillsdale, NJ: Erlbaum.

Craik, F. I. M., & Lockhart, R. S. (1972). Levels of processing: A framework for memory research. *Journal of Verbal Learning & Verbal Behavior, 11,* 671–684.

Craik, F. I. M., & Tulving, E. (1975). Depth of processing and retention of words in episodic memory. *Journal of Experimental Psychology: General, 104,* 288–294.

Crowder, R. G. (1976). *Principles of learning and memory.* Hillsdale, NJ: Erlbaum.

Eysenck, M. W. (1979). Depth, elaboration, and distinctiveness. In L. S. Cermak & F. I. M. Craik (Eds.), *Levels of processing in human memory* (pp. 89–118). Hillsdale, NJ: Erlbaum.

Green, R. T. (1956). Surprise as a factor in the von Restorff effect. *Journal of Experimental Psychology, 52,* 340–344.

Hall, J. F (1971). *Verbal learning and retention.* New York: Lippincott.

Henle, M. (1986). *1879 and all that: Essays in the history of psychology.* New York: Columbia University Press.

Hilgard, E. R., & Bower, G. H. (1975). *Theories of learning.* Englewood Cliffs, NJ: Prentice-Hall.

Hunt, R. R., & Einstein, G. O. (1981). Relational and item-specific information in memory. *Journal of Verbal Learning & Verbal Behavior, 20,* 497–514.

Hunt, R. R., & Elliott, J. M. (1980). The role of nonsemantic information in memory: Orthographic distinctiveness effects on retention. *Journal of Experimental Psychology: General, 109,* 49–74.

Hunt, R. R., & Kelly, R. E. S. (in press). Accessing the particular from the general: The power of distinctiveness in the context of organization. *Memory & Cognition.*

Hunt, R. R., & McDaniel, M. A. (1993). The enigma of organization and distinctiveness. *Journal of Memory & Language, 32,* 421–445.

Hunt, R. R., & Mitchell, D. B. (1982). Independent effects of semantic and nonsemantic distinctiveness. *Journal of Experimental Psychology: Human Learning & Memory, 8,* 81–87.

Jenkins. W. O., & Postman, L. (1948). Isolation and spread of effect in serial learning. *American Journal of Psychology. 61,* 214–221.

Jersild, A. (1929). Primacy, recency, frequency, and vividness. *Journal of Experimental Psychology, 12*, 58–70.

Kausler. D. II. (1974). *Psychology of verbal learning and memory.* New York: Academic Press.

Koffka, K. (1935). *Principles of Gestalt psychology.* New York: Harcourt. Brace, & World.

Köhler, W., & von Restorff, H. (1935). Analyse von Vorgängen im Spurenfeld: Zur theorie der reproduktion. *Psychologische Forschung, 19*, 56–112.

Lockhart, R. S., Craik, F. I. M., & Jacoby, L. L. (1976). Depth of processing, recognition, and recall. In J. Brown (Ed.), *Recall and recognition* (pp. 75–102). New York: Wiley.

Markman, A. B., & Gentner, D. (1993). Splitting the differences: A structural alignment view of similarity. *Journal of Memory & Language. 32*, 517–535.

Medin, D. L., Goldstone, R. L., & Gentner, D. (1993). Respects for similarity. *Psychological Review, 100*, 254–278.

Nelson, D. L. (1979). Remembering pictures and words: Appearance. significance, and name. In L. S. Cermak & F. I. M. Craik (Eds.), *Levels or processing in human memory* (pp. 45 76). Hillsdale. NJ: Erlbaum.

Osgood, C. E. (1953). *Method and theory in experimental psychology.* New York: Oxford University Press.

Pillsbury, W. B., & Raush, H. L. (1943). An extension of the Köhler-Restorff inhibition phenomenon. *American Journal of Psychology, 56*, 293–298.

Rundus, D. (1971). Analysis of rehearsal processes in free recall. *Journal of Experimental Psychology, 89*, 63-77.

Schmidt, S. R. (1991). Can we have a distinctive theory of memory? *Memory & Cognition, 19*, 523–542.

Titchener, E. B. (1915). *A textbook of psychology.* New York: Macmillan.

Van Buskirk, W. L. (1932). An experimental study of vividness in learning and retention. *Journal of Experimental Psychology, 15*, 563 573.

von Restorff, H. (1933). Über die Wirkung von Bereichsbildungen im Spurenfeld. *Psychologische Forschung, 18*, 299–342.

Wallace, W. P (1965). Review of the historical, empirical, and theoretical status of the von Restorff phenomenon. *Psychological Bulletin, 63*, 410–424.

Watkins, O. C., & Watkins, M. J. (1975). Build up of proactive inhibition as a cue-overload effect. *Journal of Experimental Psychology: Human Learning & Memory, 1*, 442–452.

Woodworth. R. S. (1938). *Experimental psychology.* New York: Holt.

Woodworth. R. S., & Schlosberg, H. (1954). *Experimental psychology.* New York: Holt, Rinehart & Winston.

CHAPTER EIGHT

Metamemory

21 FALSE MEMORY

One of the most interesting properties of memory is that it is constructive: Our previous knowledge and experience help us interpret each episode in our lives and sometimes lead us to remember things that did not happen or to remember an episode very differently from the actual event. For example, if misleading information is given to an eyewitness after an event (for example in a news report), the eyewitness may recall that information as if it really happened (e.g., Loftus & Ketchum, 1991). In the recent past, investigation of this sort of reconstructive aspect of memory has been restricted to materials that form a meaningful story. However, Roediger and McDermott (1995) demonstrated that reconstructive aspects of memory are active in all memory tasks, including list learning.

Their experiments replicated and extended those reported in a largely ignored manuscript published by Deese in 1959. In the first experiment Roediger and McDermott (1995) gave subjects lists of words presented either auditorily or visually. Memory was tested using two different memory tasks: immediate recall (after every list) and yes-no recognition (after all the lists were presented). In addition, in the recognition segment, the subjects were asked to rate how confident they were that they had heard the word in the encoding phase. In the second experiment the experimenters utilized a procedure called "remember/know" (see Reading 23, "Remember/Know") in which the subjects are asked whether they consciously "remember" the item being presented or whether they just "know" that the item was on the list.

In both experiments there was a very high false recognition rate (i.e., subjects incorrectly recognized words that were not on the list) for items that were not presented but were highly associated to all the members of the list (a "critical lure"). For example, subjects heard a list of words related to the idea of sleeping and then remembered hearing the word "sleep" even though it was never presented. In Experiment 1 the subjects were very confident that the critical lure had actually been presented. Similarly, in Experiment 2 the subjects reported that they vividly recalled hearing the word, so their memory was very strong, despite its inaccuracy.

This paper by Roediger and McDermott was presented at the beginning of a resurgence of interest in reconstructive memories by basic memory theorists. The real-world implications of this result (such as with eyewitness testimony) and the replicability of it in the laboratory have sparked the interest of a great many researchers, resulting in a large number of studies since 1995 investigating the factors that influence this memory illusion (e.g., Roediger, Watson, McDermott, & Gallo, 2001).

Why do we remember a word being on the list when it never was presented? Roediger and McDermott favor an associative explanation: Each of the words on the list is highly associated with the critical lure. So, seeing a word such as *pin* on the list might make us think of *needle*. Then, when we see the word *sew* we might also think of *needle*. On the recognition task, if we encounter the word *needle* we might think it was presented because it *was* actually present (in our minds at least) during list presentation. Extending this idea to everyday events can help us understand the causes of errors in eyewitness testimony and other situations where what we remember is not exactly the way an event occurred.

The CogLab demonstration is very similar to Experiment 2 in this paper except that immediate recognition of the list of items is used, instead of immediate recall and final recognition. In the demonstration, we also do not collect confidence ratings. However, even with these simplifications this is a very powerful effect: Most of the time the critical lure is falsely recognized at the same level as the actually presented items.

REFERENCES

Loftus, E. F., & Ketchum, K. (1991). *Witness for the defense.* New York: St. Martin's Press.

Roediger, H. L., III., Watson, J. M., McDermott, K. B., & Gallo, D. A. (2001). Factors that determine false recall: A multiple regression analysis. *Psychonomic Bulletin & Review, 8,* 385–407.

QUESTIONS

1. In Roediger and McDermott's experiments, what is a "critical lure"?
2. What is the most common error made by the subjects in these experiments?
3. Does the associative response (i.e., thinking of the critical lure) have to occur consciously to the subject in order for this illusion to occur?
4. Are the results of these experiments directly related to the false memory debate induced in the course of therapy?

Creating False Memories: Remembering Words Not Presented in Lists

Henry L. Roediger, III, and Kathleen B. McDermott

Rice University

ABSTRACT

Two experiments (modeled after J. Deese's 1959 study) revealed remarkable levels of false recall and false recognition in a list learning paradigm. In Experiment 1, subjects studied lists of 12 words (e.g., bed, rest, awake); each list was composed of associates of 1 nonpresented word (e.g., sleep). On immediate free recall tests, the nonpresented associates were recalled 40% of the time and were later recognized with high confidence. In Experiment 2, a false recall rate of 55% was obtained with an expanded set of lists, and on a later recognition test, subjects produced false alarms to these items at a rate comparable to the hit rate. The act of recall enhanced later remembering of both studied and nonstudied material. The results reveal a powerful illusion of memory: People remember events that never happened.

False memories—either remembering events that never happened, or remembering them quite differently from the way they happened—have recently captured the attention of both psychologists and the public at large. The primary impetus for this recent surge of interest is the increase in the number of cases in which memories of previously unrecognized abuse are reported during the course of therapy. Some researchers have argued that certain therapeutic practices can cause the creation of false memories, and therefore, the apparent "recovery" of memories during the course of therapy may actually represent the creation of memories (Lindsay & Read, 1994; Loftus, 1993). Although the concept of false memories is currently enjoying an increase in publicity, it is not new;

psychologists have been studying false memories in several laboratory paradigms for years. Schacter (in press) provides an historical overview of the study of memory distortions.

Bartlett (1932) is usually credited with conducting the first experimental investigation of false memories; he had subjects read an Indian folk tale, "The War of the Ghosts," and recall it repeatedly. Although he reported no aggregate data, but only sample protocols, his results seemed to show distortions in subjects' memories over repeated attempts to recall the story. Interestingly, Bartlett's repeated reproduction results never have been successfully replicated by later researchers (see Gauld & Stephenson, 1967; Roediger, Wheeler, & Rajaram, 1993); indeed, Wheeler and Roediger (1992) showed that recall of prose passages (including "The War of the Ghosts") actually improved over repeated tests (with very few errors) if short delays occurred between study and test.[1]

Nonetheless, Bartlett's (1932) contribution was an enduring one because he distinguished between *reproductive* and *reconstructive* memory. Reproductive memory refers to accurate, rote production of material from memory, whereas reconstructive memory emphasizes the active process of filling in missing elements while remembering, with errors frequently occurring. It generally has been assumed that the act of remembering materials rich in meaning (e.g., stories and real-life events) gives rise to reconstructive processes (and therefore errors), whereas the act of remembering more simplified materials (e.g., nonsense syllables, word lists) gives rise to reproductive (and

SOURCE: From Roediger, H. L., III, & McDermott, K. B. (1995). Creating false memories: Remembering words not presented in lists. *Journal of Experimental Psychology: Learning, Memory, and Cognition, 21*, 803–814. Copyright © 1995 by the American Psychological Association. Reprinted with permission.

thus accurate) memory. Bartlett (1932) wrote that "I discarded nonsense materials because, among other difficulties, its use almost always weights the evidence in favour of mere rote recapitulation" (p. 204).

The investigators of false memories have generally followed Bartlett's (1932) lead. Most evidence has been collected in paradigms that use sentences (Bransford & Franks, 1971; Brewer, 1977), prose passages (Sulin & Dooling, 1974), slide sequences (Loftus, Miller, & Burns, 1978), or videotapes (Loftus & Palmer, 1974). In all these paradigms, evidence of false memories has been obtained, although the magnitude of the effect depends on the method of testing (McCloskey & Zaragoza, 1985; Payne, Toglia, & Anastasi, 1994). The predominance of materials that tell a story (or can be represented by a script or schema) can probably be attributed to the belief that only such materials will cause false memories to occur.

There is one well-known case of false memories being produced in a list learning paradigm: Underwood (1965) introduced a technique to study false recognition of words in lists. He gave subjects a continuous recognition task in which they decided if each presented word had been given previously in the list. Later words bore various relations to previously studied words. Underwood showed that words associatively related to previously presented words were falsely recognized. Anisfeld and Knapp (1968), among others, replicated the phenomenon. Although there have been a few reports of robust false recognition effects (Hintzman, 1988), in many experiments the false recognition effect was either rather small or did not occur at all. For example, in a study by L. M. Paul (1979), in which synonyms were presented at various lags along with other, unrelated lures, the false recognition effect was only 3% (a 20% false-alarm rate for synonyms and a 17% rate for unrelated lures). Gillund and Shiffrin (1984) failed to find any false recognition effect for semantically related lures in a similar paradigm. In general, most research on the false recognition effect in list learning does little to discourage the belief that more natural, coherent materials are needed to demonstrate powerful false memory effects. Interestingly, most research revealing false memory effects has used recognition measures; this is true both of the prose memory literature (e.g.,

Bransford & Franks, 1971; Sulin & Dooling, 1974) and the eyewitness memory paradigm (Loftus et al., 1978; McCloskey & Zaragoza, 1985). Reports of robust levels of false recall are rarer.

We have discovered a potentially important exception to these claims, one that reveals false recall in a standard list learning paradigm. It is represented in an experimental report published by Deese in 1959 that has been largely overlooked for the intervening 36 years, despite the fact that his observations would seem to bear importantly on the study of false memories, Deese's procedure was remarkably straightforward; he tested memory for word lists in a single-trial, free-recall paradigm. Because this paradigm was just gaining favor among experimental psychologists at that time and was the focus of much attention during the 1960s, the neglect of Deese's report is even more surprising. However, since the Social Science Citation Index began publication in 1969, the article has been cited only 14 times, and only once since 1983. Most authors mentioned it only in passing, several authors apparently cited it by mistake, and no one has followed up Deese's interesting observations until now, although Cramer (1965) reported similar observations and did appropriately cite Deese's (1959) article. (While working on this article, we learned that Don Read was conducting similar research, which is described briefly in Lindsay & Read, 1994, p. 291.)[2]

Deese (1959) was interested in predicting the occurrence of extralist intrusions in single-trial free recall. To this end, he developed 36 lists, with 12 words per list. Each list was composed of the 12 primary associates of a critical (nonpresented) word. For example, for the critical word *needle*, the list words were *thread, pin, eye, sewing, sharp, point, pricked, thimble, haystack, pain, hurt,* and *injection.* He found that some of the lists reliably induced subjects to produce the critical nonpresented word as an intrusion on the immediate free recall test. Deese's interest was in determining why some lists gave rise to this effect, whereas others did not. His general conclusion was that the lists for which the associations went in a backward (as well as forward) direction tended to elicit false recall. That is, he measured the average probability with which people produced the critical word from which the list was generated when they were asked to associate to the individual words in the list. For example, subjects were given *sewing, point, thimble,* and so on, and the average probability of producing needle as an associate was measured. Deese obtained a correlation of .87 between the probability of an intrusion in recall (from one group of subjects) and the probability of occurrence of the word as an associate to members of the list (from a different group). Our interest in Deese's materials was in using his best lists and developing his paradigm as a way to examine false memory phenomena.

Our first goal was to try to replicate Deese's (1959) finding of reliable, predictable extralist intrusions in a single-trial, free-recall paradigm. We found his result to be surprising in light of the literature showing that subjects are often extremely accurate in recalling lists after a single trial, making few intrusions unless instructed to guess (see Cofer, 1967; Roediger & Payne, 1985). As previously noted, most prior research on false memory phenomena has employed measures of recognition memory or cued recall, Deese's paradigm potentially offers a method to study false recollections in free recall. However, we also extended Deese's paradigm to recognition tests. In Experiment 1, we examined false recall and false recognition of the critical nonpresented words and the confidence with which subjects accepted or rejected the critical nonpresented words as having been in the study lists. In Experiment 2, we tested other lists constructed to produce extralist intrusions in single-trial free recall, to generalize the finding across a wider set of materials. In addition, we examined the extent to which the initial false recall of items led to later false recognition of those same items. Finally, we employed the remember-know procedure developed by Tulving (1985) to examine subjects' phenomenological experience during false recognition of the critical nonpresented items. We describe this procedure more fully below.

EXPERIMENT 1

The purpose of Experiment 1 was to replicate Deese's (1959) observations of false recall by using six lists that produced among the highest levels of erroneous recall in his experiments. Students heard and recalled the lists and then received a recognition test over both studied and nonstudied items, including the critical nonpresented words.

Method

Subjects.   Subjects were 36 Rice University undergraduates who participated as part of a course project during a regular meeting of the class, Psychology 308, Human Memory.

Materials.   We developed six lists from the materials listed in Deese's (1959) article. With one exception, we chose the six targets that produced the highest intrusion rates in Deese's experiment: *chair, mountain, needle, rough, sleep,* and *sweet.* As in Deese's experiment, for each critical word, we constructed the corresponding list by obtaining the first 12 associates listed in Russell and Jenkins's (1954) word association norms. For example, the list corresponding to *chair* was *table, sit, legs, seat, soft, desk, arm, sofa, wood, cushion, rest,* and *stool.* In a few instances, we replaced 1 of the first 12 associates with a word that seemed, in our judgment, more likely to elicit the critical word. (The lists for Experiment 1 are included in the expanded set of lists for Experiment 2 reported in the Appendix.)

The 42-item recognition test included 12 studied and 30 nonstudied items. There were three types of nonstudied items, or lures: (a) the 6 critical words, from which the lists were generated (e.g., *chair*), (b) 12 words generally unrelated to any items on the six lists, and (c) 12 words weakly related to the lists (2 per list). We drew the weakly related words from Positions 13 and below in the association norms; for example, we chose *couch* and *floor* for the *chair* list. We constructed the test sequence in blocks; there were 7 items per block, and each block corresponded to a studied list (2 studied words, 2 related words, 2 unrelated words and the critical nonstudied lure). The order of the blocks corresponded to the order in which lists had been studied. Each block of test items always began with a studied word and ended with the critical lure; the other items were arranged haphazardly in between. One of the two studied words that were tested occurred in the first position of the study list (and therefore was the strongest associate to the critical item);

the other occurred somewhere in the first 6 positions of the study list.

Procedure. Subjects were tested in a group during a regular class meeting. They were instructed that they would hear lists of words and that they would be tested immediately after each list by writing the words on successive pages of examination booklets. They were told to write the last few items first (a standard instruction for this task) and then to recall the rest of the words in any order. They were also told to write down all the words they could remember but to be reasonably confident that each word they wrote down did in fact occur in the list (i.e., they were told not to guess). The lists were read aloud by the first author at the approximate rate of 1 word per 1.5 s. Before reading each list, the experimenter said "List 1, List 2," and so on, and he said "recall" at the end of the list. Subjects were given 2.5 min to recall each list.

After the sixth list, there was brief conversation lasting 2–3 min prior to instructions for the recognition test. At this point, subjects were told that they would receive another test in which they would see words on a sheet and that they were to rate each as to their confidence that it had occurred on the list. The 4-point rating scale was 4 for *sure that the item was old* (or studied), 3 for *probably old*, 2 for *probably new*, and 1 for *sure it was new*. Subjects worked through the recognition test at their own pace.

At the end of the experiment, subjects were asked to raise their hands if they had recognized six particular items on the test, and the critical lures were read aloud. Most subjects raised their hands for several items. The experimenter then informed them that none of the words just read had actually been on the list and the subjects were debriefed about the purpose of the experiment, which was a central topic in the course.

Results

Recall. The mean probability of recall of the studied words was .65, and the serial position curve is shown in Figure 21.1. The curve was smoothed by averaging data from three adjacent points for each position because the raw data were noisy with only six lists. For example, data from the third, fourth, and fifth points

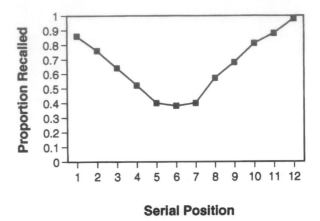

FIGURE 21.1   Probability of correct recall in Experiment 1 as a function of serial position. Probability of recall of the studied words was .65, and probability of recall of the critical nonpresented item was .40.

contributed to the fourth position in the graph. The first and the last positions, however, were based only on the raw data. The serial position curve shows marked recency, indicating that subjects followed directions in recalling the last items first. A strong primary effect is also apparent, probably because the strongest associates to the critical target words occurred early in the list. The critical omitted word was recalled with a probability of .40, or with about the same probability as items that had been presented in the middle of the list (see Figure 21.1). Therefore, items that were not presented were recalled at about the same rate as those that were presented, albeit those in the least favorable serial positions.

The average output position for recall of the critical nonpresented word was 6.9 (out of 8.6 words written down in lists in which there was a critical intrusion). The cumulative production levels of the critical intrusion for those trials on which they occurred is shown in Figure 21.2 across quintiles of subjects' responses. The critical intrusion appeared only 2% of the time in the first fifth of subjects' output but 63% of the time in the last quintile. Thus, on average, subjects recalled the critical nonstudied item in the last fifth of their output, at the 80th percentile of recalled words (6.9 ÷ 8.6 × 100).

Other intrusions also occurred in recall, albeit at a rather low rate. Subjects intruded the critical lure on

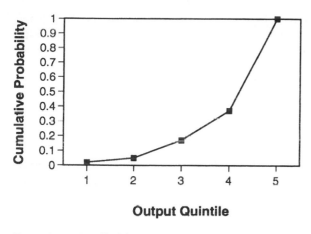

FIGURE 21.2   Recall of the critical intrusion as a function of output position in recall. Quintiles refer to the first 20% of responses, the second 20%, and so on.

40% of the lists, but any other word in the English language was intruded on only 14% of the lists. Therefore, subjects were not guessing wildly in the experiment; as usual in single-trial free recall, the general intrusion rate was quite low. Nonetheless, subjects falsely recalled the critical items at a high rate.

Recognition.   The recognition test was given following study and recall of all six lists, and thus the results were likely affected by prior recall. (We consider this issue in Experiment 2.) The proportion of responses for each of the four confidence ratings are presented in Table 21.1 for studied (old) items and for the three different types of lures: unrelated words, weakly related words, and the critical words from which the lists were derived. Consider first the proportion of

items subjects called old by assigning a rating of 3 (*probably old*) or 4 (*sure old*). The hit rate was 86% and the false-alarm rate for the standard type of unrelated lures was only 2%, so by usual criteria subjects showed high accuracy. The rate of false alarms was higher for the weakly related lures (.21) than for the unrelated lures, $t(35) = 7.40$, $SEM = .026$, $p < .001$. This outcome replicates the standard false-recognition effect first reported by Underwood (1965). The false-recognition rate for weakly related lures was greater than obtained in many prior studies (e.g., L. M. Paul, 1979), and the rate for the critical nonpresented words was dramatically larger than the rate for the weakly related words. As shown in Table 21.1, the false-alarm rate for the critical nonstudied lures (.84) approached the hit rate (.86), $t(35) < 1$, $SEM = .036$, *ns*.

Consider next the results based on subjects' high-confidence responses (i.e., when they were sure the item had appeared in the study list and rated it a "4"). The proportion of unrelated and weakly related lures falling into this category approached zero. However, subjects were still sure that the critical nonstudied items had been studied over half the time (.58). The hit rate for the studied items remained quite high (.75) and was reliably greater than the false-alarm rate for the critical lures, $t(35) = 3.85$, $SEM = .044$, $p < .001$. It is also interesting to look at the rates at which subjects classified items as *sure new*. Unrelated lures were correctly rejected with high confidence 80% of the time. Related lures received this classification only 44% of the time, and critical lures were confidently rejected at an even lower rate, 8%, which is similar to the rate for studied words (5%).

Table 21.1 also presents the mean ratings for the four types of items on the 4-point scale. This measure

TABLE 21.1   Recognition Results for Experiment 1: The Proportion of Items Classified as Sure Old (a Rating of 4), Probably Old (3), Probably New (2), or Sure New (1) and the Mean Ratings of Items as a Function of Study Status

Study Status	Old		New		Mean Rating
	4	3	2	1	
Studied	.75	.11	.09	.05	3.6
Nonstudied					
Unrelated lure	.00	.02	.18	.80	1.2
Weakly related lure	.04	.17	.35	.44	1.8
Critical lure	.58	.26	.08	.08	3.3

seems to tell the same story as the other two: The mean rating of the critical lures (3.3) approached that of studied items (3.6); the difference did reach significance, $t(35) = 2.52$, $SEM = .09$, $p < .05$. In general, the judgments subjects provided for the critical lures appeared much more similar to those of studied items than to the other types of lures.

Discussion

The results of Experiment 1 confirmed Deese's (1959) observation of high levels of false recall in a single-trial free-recall task, albeit with six lists that were among his best. We found that the critical nonpresented items were recalled at about the same level as items actually presented in the middle of the lists. This high rate of false recall was not due to subjects guessing wildly. Other intrusions occurred at a very low rate. In addition, we extended Deese's results to a recognition test and showed that the critical nonpresented items were called old at almost the same level as studied items (i.e., the false-alarm rate for the critical nonpresented items approximated the hit rate for the studied items). The false-alarm rate for the critical nonpresented items was much higher than for other related words that had not been presented. Finally, more than half the time subjects reported that they were sure that the critical nonstudied item had appeared on the list. Given these results, this paradigm seems a promising method to study false memories. Experiment 2 was designed to further explore these false memories.

EXPERIMENT 2

We had four aims in designing Experiment 2. First, we wanted to replicate and extend the recall and recognition results of Experiment 1 to a wider set of materials. Therefore, we developed twenty-four 15-item lists similar to those used in Experiment 1 and in Deese's (1959) experiment. (We included expanded versions of the six lists used in Experiment 1.) Second, we wanted to examine the effect of recall on the subsequent recognition test. In Experiment 1 we obtained a high level of false recognition for the critical nonpresented words, but the lists had been recalled prior to the recognition test, and in 40% of the cases the

critical item had been falsely recalled, too. In Experiment 2, we examined false recognition both for lists that had been previously recalled and for those that had not been recalled. Third, we wanted to determine the false-alarm rates for the critical nonpresented items when the relevant list had not been presented previously (e.g., to determine the false-alarm rate for *chair* when related words had not been presented in the list). Although we considered it remote, the possibility existed that the critical nonpresented items simply elicit a high number of false alarms whether or not the related words had been previously presented.

The fourth reason—and actually the most important one—for conducting the second experiment was to obtain subjects' judgments about their phenomenological experience while recognizing nonpresented items. We applied the procedure developed by Tulving (1985) in which subjects are asked to distinguish between two states of awareness about the past: remembering and knowing. When this procedure is applied in conjunction with a recognition test, subjects are told (a) to judge each item to be old (studied) or new (nonstudied) and (b) to make an additional judgment for each item judged to be old: whether they remember or know that the item occurred in the study list. A *remember* experience is defined as one in which the subject can mentally relive the experience (perhaps by recalling its neighbors, what it made them think of, what they were doing when they heard the word, or physical characteristics associated with its presentation). A *know* judgment is made when subjects are confident that the item occurred on the list but are unable to re-experience (i.e., remember) its occurrence. In short, remember judgments reflect a mental reliving of the experience, whereas know judgments do not. There is now a sizable literature on remember and know judgments (see Gardiner & Java, 1993; Rajaram & Roediger, in press), but we will not review it here except to say that evidence exists that remember-know judgments do not simply reflect two states of confidence (high and low) because variables can affect remember-know and confidence (sure-unsure) judgments differently (e.g., Rajaram, 1993).

Our purpose in using remember-know judgments in Experiment 2 was to see if subjects who falsely recognized the critical nonpresented words would report accompanying remember experiences, showing that they were mentally reexperiencing events that never occurred. In virtually all prior work on false memories, it has been assumed that subjects' incorrect responses indicated false remembering, However, if Tulving's (1985) distinction is accepted, then responding on a memory test should not be equated with remembering. Further metamemorial judgments such as those obtained with the remember know procedure are required to determine if subjects are remembering the events. In fact, in most experiments using the remember-know procedure, false alarms predominantly have been judged as know responses (e.g., Gardiner, 1988; Jones & Roediger, 1995). This outcome would be predicted in our experiment, too, if one attributes false recognition to a high sense of familiarity that arises (perhaps) through spreading activation in an associative network. Therefore, in Experiment 2 we examined subjects' metamemorial judgments with respect to their false memories to see whether they would classify these memories as being remembered or known to have occurred.

In Experiment 2, subjects were presented with 16 lists; after half they received an immediate free recall test, and after the other half they did math problems. After all lists had been presented, subjects received a recognition test containing items from the 16 studied lists and 8 comparable lists that had not been studied. During the recognition test, subjects made old-new judgments, followed by remember-know judgments for items judged to be old.

Method

Subjects. Thirty Rice University undergraduates participated in a one hour session as part of a course requirement.

Materials. We developed 24 lists from Russell and Jenkins's (1954) norms in a manner similar to that used for Experiment 1. For each of 24 target words, 15 associates were selected for the list. These were usually the 15 words appearing first in the norms, but occasionally we substituted other related words when these seemed more appropriate (i.e., more likely to elicit the nonpresented target as an associate). The ordering of words within lists was held constant; the strongest associates generally occurred first. An example of a list

for the target word *sleep* is: *bed, rest, awake, tired, dream, wake, night, blanket, doze, slumber, snore, pillow, peace, yawn, drowsy.* All the lists, corrected for a problem noted in the next paragraph, appear in the Appendix.

The 24 lists were arbitrarily divided into three sets for counterbalancing purposes. Each set served equally often in the three experimental conditions, as described below. The reported results are based on only 7 of the 8 lists in each set because the critical items in 2 of the lists inadvertently appeared as studied items in other lists; dropping 1 list in each of two sets eliminated this problem and another randomly picked list from the third set was also dropped, so that each scored set was based on 7 lists. With these exceptions, none of the critical items occurred in any of the lists.

Design. The three conditions were tested in a within-subjects design. Subjects studied 16 lists; 8 lists were followed by an immediate free recall test, and 8 others were not followed by an initial test. The remaining 8 lists were not studied. Items from all 24 lists appeared on the later recognition test. On the recognition test, subjects judged items as old (studied) or new (nonstudied) and, when old, they also judged if they remembered the item from the list or rather knew that it had occurred.

Procedure. Subjects were told that they would be participating in a memory experiment in which they would hear lists of words presented by means of a tape player. They were told that after each list they would hear a sound (either a tone or a knock, with examples given) that would indicate whether they should recall items from the list or do math problems. For half of the subjects, the tone indicated that they should recall the list, and the knock meant they should perform math problems; for the other half of the subjects, the signals were reversed. They were told to listen carefully to each list and that the signal would occur after the list had been presented; therefore, subjects never knew during list presentation whether the list would be recalled. Words were recorded in a male voice and presented approximately at a 1.5-s rate. Subjects were given 2 min after each list to recall the words or to perform multiplication and division problems. Recall occurred on 4 inch by 11 inch sheets of paper, and subjects turned over each sheet after the recall period, so the recalled items were no longer in view. The first part of the experiment took about 45 min.

The recognition test occurred about 5 min after the test or math period for the 16th list. During this time, subjects were given instructions about making old-new and remember-know judgments. They were told that they would see a long list of words, some of which they had heard during the earlier phase of the experiment. They were to circle either the word *old* or *new* next to each test item to indicate whether the item had been presented by means of the tape player. If an item was judged old, subjects were instructed that they should further distinguish between remembering and knowing by writing an *R* or *K* in the space beside the item. Detailed instructions on the remember-know distinction were given, modeled after those of Rajaram (1993). Essentially, subjects were told that a remember judgment should be made for items for which they had a vivid memory of the actual presentation; know judgments were reserved for items that they were sure had been presented but for which they lacked the feeling of remembering the actual occurrence of the words. They were told that a remember judgment would be made in cases in which they remembered something distinctive in the speaker's voice when he said the word, or perhaps they remembered the item presented before or after it, or what they were thinking when they heard the word. They were always told to make the remember-know judgment about a word with respect to its presentation on the tape recorder, not whether they remembered or knew they had written it down on the free recall test. In addition, they were instructed to make remember-know judgments immediately after judging the item to be old, before they considered the next test item.

The recognition test was composed of 96 items, 48 of which had been studied and 48 of which had not. The 48 studied items were obtained by selecting 3 items from each of the 16 presented lists (always those in Serial Positions 1, 8, and 10). The lures, or nonstudied items, on the recognition test were 24 critical lures from all 24 lists (16 studied, 8 not) and the 24 items from the 8 nonstudied lists (again, from Serial Positions 1, 8, and 10). The 96 items were randomly arranged on the test sheet and beside each item were

the words *old* and *new*; if subjects circled old, they made the remember-know judgment by writing *R* or *K* in the space next to the word. All subjects received exactly the same test sheet; counterbalancing of lists was achieved by having lists rotated through the three conditions (study + recall, study + arithmetic, and nonstudied) across subsets of 10 subjects.

After the recognition test, the experimenter asked subjects an open-ended question: whether they "knew what the experiment was about." Most subjects just said something similar to "memory for lists of words," but 1 subject said that she noticed that the lists seemed designed to make her think of a nonpresented word. She was the only subject who had no false recalls of the critical nonpresented words; her results were excluded from those reported below and replaced by the results obtained from a new subject. After the experiment, subjects were debriefed.

Results

Recall.   Subjects recalled the critical nonpresented word on 55% of the lists, which is a rate even higher than for the 6 lists used in Experiment 1. The higher rate of false recall in Experiment 2 may have been due to the longer lists, to their slightly different construction, to the fact that 16 lists were presented rather than only 6, or to different signals used to recall the lists. In addition, in Experiment 1 the lists were read aloud by the experimenter, whereas in Experiment 2 they were presented by means of a tape player. Regardless of the reason or reasons for the difference, the false-recall effect was quite robust and seems even stronger under the conditions of Experiment 2.

The smoothed serial position curve for studied words is shown in Figure 21.3, where marked primacy and recency effects are again seen. As in Experiment 1, subjects recalled the critical nonpresented items at about the rate of studied items presented in the middle of the lists. Subjects recalled items in Positions 4–11 an average of 47% of the time, compared with 55% recall of nonpresented items, Therefore, recall of the critical missing word was actually greater than recall for studied words in the middle of the list; this difference was marginally significant, $t(29) = 1.80$, *SEM* $= .042$, $p = .08$, two-tailed.

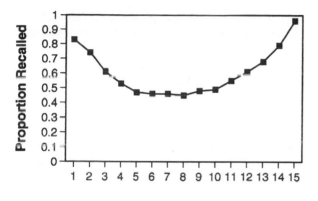

Serial Position

FIGURE 21.3 Probability of correct recall in Experiment 2 as a function of serial position. Probability of recall of the studied words was .62, and probability of recall of the critical nonpresented item was .55.

TABLE 21.2 Recognition Results for Studied Items and Critical Lures in Experiment 2

Item Type and Condition	Proportion of Old Responses		
	Overall	R	K
Studied			
Study + recall	.79	.57	.22
Study + arithmetic	.65	.41	.24
Nonstudied	.11	.02	.09
Critical lure			
Study + recall	.81	.58	.23
Study + arithmetic	.72	.38	.34
Nonstudied	.16	.03	.13

Note: R = remember judgment; K = know judgment.

Recognition. After subjects had heard all 16 lists, they received the recognition test and provided remember-know judgments for items that were called old on the test. We first consider results for studied words and then turn to the data for the critical nonpresented lures.

Table 21.2 presents the recognition results for items studied in the list. (Keep in mind that we tested only three items from each list [i.e., those in Positions 1, 8, and 10].) It is apparent that the hit rate in the study + recall condition (.79) was greater than in the study + arithmetic condition (.65), $t(29) = 5.20$, $SEM = .027$, $p < .001$, indicating that the act of recall enhanced later recognition, Further, the boost in recognition from prior recall was reflected in a greater proportion of remember responses, which differed reliably, $t(29) = 4.87$, $SEM = .033$, $p < .001$. Know responses did not differ between conditions, $t(29) < 1$. The false-alarm rate for items from the nonstudied lists was .11, with most false positives judged as know responses.

Recognition results for the critical nonpresented lures are also shown in Table 21.2. The first striking impression is that the results for false-alarm rates appear practically identical to the results for hit rates. Therefore, to an even greater extent than in Experiment 1, subjects were unable to distinguish items actually presented from the critical lures that were not

presented. Table 21.2 also shows that the act of (false) recall in the study + recall condition enhanced later false recognition relative to the study + arithmetic condition, in which the lists were not recalled. In addition, after recalling the lists subjects were much more likely to say that they remembered the items from the list, with remember judgments being made 72% of the time (i.e., $.58 \div .81 \times 100$) for words that had never been presented. When the lists were presented but not recalled, the rate of remember judgments dropped to 53%, although this figure is still quite high. Interestingly, the corresponding percentages for items actually studied were about the same: 72% for remember judgments for lists that were recalled and 63% for lists that were not recalled.

One point that vitiates the correspondence between the results for studied and nonstudied items in Table 21.2 is that the false-alarm rates for the types of items differed when the relevant lists had not been studied. The rate for the regular list words was .11, whereas the rate for the critical lures (when the relevant prior list had not been studied) was .16, $t(29) = 2.27$, $SEM = .022$, $p = .03$, two-tailed. However, the difference was not great, and in both cases false alarms gave rise to more know responses than remember responses.

One further analysis is of interest. In the study + recall condition, we can consider recognition results for items that were produced in the recall phase (whether representing correct responding or false recall) relative to those that were not produced. Although correlational, such results provide an interesting pattern in comparing the effects of prior correct recall to prior false recall on later recognition. Table 21.3 shows the results of this analysis, including the means for studied items and for the critical items. For the studied items, recognition of items that had been correctly recalled was essentially perfect, and most old responses were judged to be remembered. Items not produced on the recall test were recognized half the time, and responses were evenly divided between remember and know judgments. These effects could have been due to the act of recall, to item selection effects, or to some combination. Nonetheless, they provide a useful point of comparison for the more interesting results about the fate of falsely recalled items, as shown in Table 21.3.

The recognition results for the falsely recalled critical items closely resemble those for correctly recalled studied items. The probability of recognizing falsely recalled items was quite high (.93), and most of these items were judged to be remembered (.73) rather than known (.20). More remarkably, the critical items that were not produced were later (falsely) recognized at a higher rate (.65) than were items actually studied but not produced (.50); this difference was marginally significant, $t(29) = 1.81$, $SEM = .083$, $p = .08$, two-tailed. In addition, these falsely recognized items were judged to be remembered in 58% of the cases (i.e., .38 ÷ .65 × 100), or at about the same rate as for words

that were studied but not produced (52%). These analyses reveal again the powerful false memory effects at work in this paradigm, with people falsely remembering the critical nonstudied words at about the same levels (or even greater levels) as presented words.

GENERAL DISCUSSION

The primary results from our experiments can be summarized as follows: First, the paradigm we developed from Deese's (1959) work produced high levels of false recall in single-trial free recall. In Experiment 1, with 12-word lists, subjects recalled the critical nonstudied word after 40% of the lists. In Experiment 2, with 15-word lists, false recall increased, occurring on 55% of the occasions. Second, this paradigm also produced remarkably high levels of false recognition for the critical items; the rate of false recognition actually approached the hit rate. Third, the false recognition responses were frequently made with high confidence (Experiment 1) or were frequently accompanied by remember judgments (Experiment 2). Fourth, the act of recall increased both accurate recognition of studied items and the false recognition of the critical nonstudied items. The highest rates of false recognition and the highest proportion of remember responses to the critical nonstudied items occurred for those items that had been falsely recalled.

We discuss our results (a) in relation to prior work and (b) in terms of theories that might explain the basic effects. We then discuss (c) how the phe-

TABLE 21.3   Proportion of Items Judged to Be Old on the Recognition Test in the Study + Recall Condition of Experiment 2 as a Function of Whether the Items Were Produced on the Immediate Free Recall Test

		Recognition		
Condition	Production Rate of Free Recall	Overall	R	K
Studied				
Produced	.62	.98	.79	.19
Not produced	.38	.50	.26	.24
Critical lure				
Produced	.55	.93	.73	.20
Not produced	.45	.65	.38	.27

Note: R = remember judgment; K = know judgment.

nomenological experience of remembering events that never happened might occur, and (d) what implications our findings might have for the wider debates on false memories.

Relation to Prior Work

Prior work by Underwood (1965) has shown false recognition for lures semantically related to studied words, but as we noted in the introduction, these effects were often rather small in magnitude. In our experiments, we found very high levels of false recall and false recognition. Our recognition results are similar to those obtained by investigators in the 1960s and 1970s who used prose materials and found erroneous recognition of related material. For example, Bransford and Franks (1971) presented subjects with sentences that were related and created a coherent scene (e.g., The rock rolled down the mountain and crushed the hut. The hut was tiny). Later, they confidently recognized sentences that were congruent with the meaning of the complex idea, although the sentences had not actually been presented (e.g., The rock rolled down the mountain and crushed the tiny hut). Similarly, Posner and Keele (1970) showed subjects dot patterns that were distortions from a prototypic pattern. Later, they recognized the prototype (that had never been presented) at a high rate, and forgetting of the prototype showed less decline over a week than did dot patterns actually presented. Jenkins, Wald, and Pittenger (1986) reported similar observations with pictorial stimuli.

In each of the experiments just described, and in other related experiments (see Alba & Hasher, 1983, for a review), subjects recognized events that never happened if the events fit some general schema derived from the study experiences. A similar interpretation is possible for our results, too, although most researchers have assumed that schema-driven processes occur only in prose materials. Yet the lists for our experiments were generated as associates to a single word and therefore had a coherent form (e.g., words related to sleep or to other similar concepts). The word *sleep*, for example, may never have been presented in the list, but was the "prototype" from which the list was generated, and therefore our lists arguably encouraged schematic processing.

Although our results are similar to those of other research revealing errors in memory, several features distinguish our findings. First, we showed powerful false memory effects in both recall and recognition within the same paradigm. The findings just cited, and others described below, all used recognition paradigms. Although some prior studies have reported false recall (e.g., Brewer, 1977; Hasher & Griffin, 1979; Spiro, 1980), these researchers used prose materials. Second, we showed that subjects actually claimed to remember most of the falsely recognized events as having occurred on the list. The items did not just evoke a feeling of familiarity but were consciously recollected as having occurred. Third, we showed that the effect of prior recall increased both accurate and false memories and that this effect of recall was reflected in remember responses.

Explanations of False Recall and False Recognition

How might false recall and false recognition arise in our paradigm? Actually, the earliest idea about false recognition—the implicit associative response—still seems workable in helping to understand these phenomena, although today we can elaborate on the idea with new models now available. Underwood (1965) proposed that false recognition responses originated during encoding when subjects, seeing a word such as *hot*, might think of an associate (*cold*). Later, if *cold* were presented as a lure, they might claim to recognize its occurrence in the list because of the earlier implicit associative response.

Some writers at the time assumed that the associative response had to occur consciously to the subject during study, so it was implicit only in the sense that it was not overtly produced. Another possible interpretation is that the subject never even becomes aware of the associative response during study of the lists, so that its activation may be implicit in this additional sense, too. Activation may spread through an associative network (e.g., Anderson & Bower, 1973; Collins & Loftus, 1975), with false-recognition errors arising through residual activation. That is, it may not be necessary for subjects to consciously think of the associate while studying the list for false recall and false recognition to occur. On the other hand, the predominance of remember responses for the critical lures on the later recognition test may indicate that the critical nonpresented words do occur to subjects during study of the list. That may be why subjects claim to remember them, through a failure of reality monitoring (Johnson & Raye, 1981).

In further support of the idea that associative processes are critically important in producing false recall, Deese (1959) showed that the likelihood of false recall in this paradigm was predicted well by the probability that items presented in the list elicited the critical nonpresented word in free association tests. In other words, the greater the likelihood that list members produced the critical nonpresented target word as an associate, the greater the level of false recall (see also Nelson, Bajo, McEvoy, & Schreiber, 1989). It is worth noting that some of Deese's lists that contained strong forward associations—including the famous "butterfly" list used in later research—did not lead to false recall. The particular characteristics of the lists that lead to false memories await systematic experimental study, but in general Deese reported that the lists that did not lead to false recall contained words that did not produce the critical targets as associates. The butterfly list did not elicit even one false recall in Deese's experiment.

If false recall and false recognition are produced by means of activation of implicit associative responses, then the reason our false-recognition results were more robust than those usually reported may be that we used lists of related words rather than single related words. Underwood (1965) and others had subjects study single words related to later lures on some dimension, and they showed only modest levels of false recognition, or in some cases none at all (Gillund & Shiffrin, 1984). In the present experiments, subjects studied lists of 12–15 items and the false-recognition effect was quite large. Hall and Kozloff (1973), Hintzman (1988), and Shiffrin, Huber, and Marinelli (1995) have shown that false recognition is directly related to the number of related words in a list. For example, Hintzman (1988, Experiment 1) presented from 0 to 5 items from a category in a list and showed that both accurate recognition of studied category members, as well as false recognition of lures from that category, increased as a function of category size. False recognition increased from about 8% when no category members were included in the list to around 35% when five category members occurred in the list. (These percentages were estimated from Hintzman's Figure 11.) Our lists were not categorized, strictly speaking, but the words were generally related. For our 15-item lists in Experiment 2 that did not receive recall tests, false recognition was 72%; the corresponding figure for recalled lists was 81%. It will be interesting to see if longer versions of standard categorized lists will produce false recognition at the same levels as the lists we have used and whether the average probability that items in the list evoke the lure as an associate will predict the level of false recognition. We are now conducting experiments to evaluate these hypotheses.

If the errors in memory occurring on both recall and recognition tests arise from associative processes, then formal models of associative processing might be expected to predict them. At least at a general level, they would seem to do so. For example, the search of associative memory (SAM) model, first proposed by Raaijmakers and Shiffrin (1980) and later extended to recognition by Gillund and Shiffrin (1984), provides for the opportunity of false recognition (and presumably recall) by means of associative processes. Although it was not the main thrust of their paper, Shiffrin et al. (1995) demonstrated that the SAM model did fit their observation of an increased tendency to produce false alarms to category members with increases in the number of category exemplars presented.

Recently, McClelland (in press) has extended the parallel distributed processing (PDP) approach to explaining constructive memory processes and memory distortions. This model assumes that encoding and retrieval occur in a parallel distributed processing system in which there are many simple but massively interconnected processing units. Encoding an event involves the activation of selected units within the system. Retrieval entails patterns of reactivation of the same processing units. However, because activation in the model can arise from many sources, a great difficulty (for the model and for humans) lies in the failure to differentiate between possible sources of prior activation (McClelland, in press). Therefore, because what is encoded and stored is a particular pattern of activity, subjects may not be able to reconstruct the actual event that gave rise to this activity. For example, if presenting the words associated with *sleep* mimics the activity in the system as occurs during actual presentation of the word *sleep*, then the PDP system will be unable to distinguish whether or not the word actually occurred. Consequently, the PDP system would give rise to false memory phenomena, as McClelland (in press) describes.

As the examples above show, associative models can account for false-recall and false-recognition results, although we have not tried fitting specific models to our data. To mention two other models based on different assumptions, Hintzman's (1988) MINERVA 2 model, which assumes independent traces of events, modeled well the effect of increasing category size on the probability of identifying an item from the category as old; this was true both for correct recognition and false recognition. In addition, Reyna and Brainerd (1995) have also applied their fuzzy-trace theory to the problem of false memories.

Although most theorists have assumed that the false memory effects arise during encoding, all remembering is a product of information both from encoding and storage processes (the memory trace) and from information in the retrieval environment (Tulving, 1974). Indeed, false remembering may arise from repeated attempts at retrieval, as shown in Experiment 2 and elsewhere (e.g., Ceci, Huffman, Smith, & Loftus, 1994; Hyman, Husband, & Billings, 1995; Roediger et al., 1993). Retrieval processes may contribute significantly to the false recall and false recognition phenomena we have observed. Subjects usually recalled the critical word toward the end of the set of recalled items, so prior recall may trigger false recall, in part. Also, in the recognition test, presentation of words related to a critical lure often occurred prior to its appearance on the test; therefore, activation from these related words on the test may have enhanced the false recognition effect by priming the lure (Neely, Schmidt, & Roediger, 1983). The illusion of memory produced by this mechanism, if it exists, may be similar to illusions of recognition produced by enhanced perceptual fluency (Whittlesea, 1993; Whittlesea, Jacoby, & Girard, 1990). Indeed, one aspect of our results on which the theories outlined above remain mute is the phenomenological experience of the subjects: They did not just claim that

the nonpresented items were familiar; rather, they claimed to remember their occurrence. We turn next to this aspect of the data.

Phenomenological Experience

In virtually all previous experiments using the remember-know procedure, false alarms have been predominantly labeled as know experiences (e.g., Gardiner & Java, 1993; Jones & Roediger, 1995; Rajaram, 1993). The typical assumption is that know responses arise through fluent processing, when information comes to mind easily, but the source of the information is not readily apparent (Rajaram, 1993). In addition, Johnson and Raye (1981) have noted that memories for events that actually occurred typically provide more spatial and temporal details than do memories for events that were only imagined. For these reasons, when we conducted Experiment 2 we expected that the false alarms in our recognition tests would, like other recognition errors, be judged by subjects to be known but not remembered. Yet our results showed that, in our paradigm, this was not so. Subjects frequently reported remembering events that never happened. Clearly, false memories can be the result of conscious recollection and not only of general familiarity.

Furthermore, in our current experiments we found that the act of recall increased both overall recognition and remembering of presented items and of the critical nonpresented items. We assume that generation of an item during a free recall test solidifies the subject's belief that memory for that item is accurate and increases the likelihood of later recognition of the item; why, however, should recall enhance the phenomenological experience of remembering the item's presentation? The enhanced remember responses may be due to subjects' actually remembering the experience of recalling the item, rather than studying it, and confusing the source of their remembrance; similarly, it could be that subjects remember thinking about the item during the study phase and confuse this with having heard it. Each of these mistakes would represent a source monitoring error (Johnson, Hashtroudi, & Lindsay, 1993). Note that our instructions to subjects about their remember-know responses specified that they were to provide remember judgments only when they remembered the item's actual presentation in the list (i.e., not simply when they remembered producing it on the recall test). Nonetheless, despite this instruction, subjects provided more remember responses for items from lists that had been recalled in Experiment 2.

The most promising approach to explaining such false remembering comes from an attributional analysis of memory, as advocated by Jacoby, Kelley, and Dywan (1989). They considered cases in which the aftereffects of past events were misattributed to other sources, but more importantly for present concerns, they considered cases in which subjects falsely attributed current cognitive experience to a concrete past event when that event did not occur. They hypothesized that the ease with which a person is able to bring events to mind increases the probability that the person will attribute the experience to being a memory. They also argued that the greater the vividness and distinctiveness of the generated event, the greater the likelihood of believing that it represents a memory (Johnson & Raye, 1981). Thus, in our paradigm, if subjects fluently generate (in recall) or process (in recognition) the word *sleep* (on the basis of recent activation of the concept) and if this fluency allows them to construct a clear mental image of how the word would have sounded if presented in the speaker's voice, then they would likely claim to remember the word's presentation. The act of recall increases the ease of producing an event and may thereby increase the experience of remembering. Jacoby et al.'s (1989) analysis offers promising leads for further research.

Implications

The results reported in this article identify a striking memory illusion. Just as perceptual illusions can be compelling even when people are aware of the factors giving rise to the illusion, we suspect that the same is true in our case of remembering events that never happened. Indeed, informal demonstration experiments with groups of sophisticated subjects, such as wily graduate students who knew we were trying to induce false memories, also showed the effect quite strongly.

Bartlett (1932) proposed a distinction between reproductive and reconstructive memory processes. Since then, the common assumption has been that list learning paradigms encourage rote reproduction of material with relatively few errors, whereas paradigms using more coherent (schematic) material (e.g., sentences, paragraphs, stories, or scenes) are necessary to observe constructive processes in memory retrieval. Yet we obtained robust false memory effects with word lists, albeit with ones that contain related words. We conclude that any contrast between reproductive and reconstructive memory is ill-founded; all remembering is constructive in nature. Materials may differ in how readily they lead to error and false memories, but these are differences of a quantitative, not qualitative, nature.

Do our results have any bearing on the current controversies raging over the issue of allegedly false memories induced in therapy? Not directly, of course. However, we do show that the illusion of remembering events that never happened can occur quite readily. Therefore, as others have also pointed out, the fact that people may say they vividly remember details surrounding an event cannot, by itself, be taken as convincing evidence that the event actually occurred (Johnson & Suengas, 1989; Schooler, Gerhard, & Loftus, 1986; Zaragoza & Lane, 1994). Our subjects confidently recalled and recognized words that were not presented and also reported that they remembered the occurrence of these events. A critic might contend that because these experiments occurred in a laboratory setting, using word lists, with college student subjects, they hold questionable relevance to issues surrounding more spectacular occurrences of false memories outside the lab. However, we believe that these are all reasons to be more impressed with the relevance of our results to these issues. After all, we tested people under conditions of intentional learning, with very short retention intervals, in a standard laboratory procedure that usually produces few errors, and we used college students—professional memorizers—as subjects. In short, despite conditions much more conducive to veridical remembering than those that typically exist outside the lab, we found dramatic evidence of false memories. When less of a premium is placed on accurate remembering, and when people know that their accuracy in recollecting cannot be verified, they may even be more easily led to remember events that never happened than they are in the lab.

AUTHOR NOTES

This research was supported by Grant F49620-92-J-0437 from the Air Force Office of Scientific Research. We thank Ron Haas and Lubna Manal for aid in conducting this research. Also, we thank Endel Tulving for bringing the Deese (1959) report to our attention. The manuscript benefited from comments by Doug Hintzman, Steve Lindsay, Suparna Rajaram, and Endel Tulving.

Correspondence concerning this article should be addressed to Henry L Roediger, III or Kathleen B. McDermott, Department of Psychology, MS 25, Rice University, 6100 S. Main Street, Houston, Texas 77005-1892. Electronic mail may be sent via Internet to roddy@rice.edu or mcdermo@ricevml.rice.edu.

ENDNOTES

1. Bartlett's (1932) results from the serial reproduction paradigm—in which one subject recalls an event, the next subject reads and then recalls the first subject's report, and so on—replicates quite well (e.g., I. H. Paul, 1959). However, the repeated reproduction research, in which a subject is tested repeatedly on the same material, is more germane to the study of false memories in an individual over time. To our knowledge, no one has successfully replicated Bartlett's observations in this paradigm with instructions that emphasize remembering (see Gauld & Stevenson, 1967).

2. Some people know of Deese's (1959) paper indirectly because Appleby (1986) used it as the basis of a suggested classroom demonstration of deja vu.

REFERENCES

Alba, J. W., & Hasher, L. (1983). Is memory schematic? *Psychological Bulletin, 93*, 203–231.

Anderson, J. R., & Bower, G. H. (1973). *Human associative memory*. Washington: V. H. Winston.

Anisfeld, M., & Knapp, M. (1968). Association, synonymity, and directionality in false recognition. *Journal of Experimental Psychology, 77*, 171–179.

Appleby, D. (1986). Déjà vu in the classroom. *Network, 4*, 8.

Bartlett, F. C. (1932). *Remembering: A study in experimental and social psychology*. Cambridge, England: Cambridge University Press.

Bransford, J. D., & Franks, J. J. (1971). The abstraction of linguistic ideas. *Cognitive Psychology, 2*, 331–350.

Brewer, W. F. (1977). Memory for the pragmatic implications of sentences. *Memory & Cognition, 5*, 673–678.

Ceci, S. J., Huffman. M. L. C., Smith, E., & Loftus, E. F. (1994). Repeatedly thinking about non-events. *Consciousness and Cognition, 3*, 388–407.

Cofer, C. N. (1967). Does conceptual organization influence the amount retained in free recall? In B. Kleinmuntz (Ed.), *Concepts and the structure of memory* (pp. 181–214). New York: Wiley.

Collins, A. M., & Loftus, E. F. (1975). A spreading-activation theory of semantic processing, *Psychological Review, 82*, 407–428.

Cramer, P. (1965). Recovery of a discrete memory. *Journal of Personality and Social Psychology, 1*, 326–332.

Deese, J. (1959). On the prediction of occurrence of particular verbal intrusions in immediate recall. *Journal of Experimental Psychology, 58*, 17–22.

Gardiner, J. M. (1988), Functional aspects of recollective experience. *Memory & Cognition, 16*, 309–313.

Gardiner, J. M., & Java, R. I. (1993). Recognizing and remembering. In A. Collins, S. Gathercole, & P. Morris (Eds.), *Theories of memory* (pp. 168–188). Hillsdale, NJ: Erlbaum.

Gauld, A., & Stephenson, G. M. (1967). Some experiments related to Bartlett's theory of remembering. *British Journal of Psychology, 58*, 39–49.

Gillund, G., & Shiffrin, R. M. (1984). A retrieval model for both recognition and recall. *Psychological Review, 91*, 1–67.

Hall, J. F., & Kozloff, E. E. (1973). False recognitions of associates of converging versus repeated words. *American Journal of Psychology, 86*, 133–139.

Hasher, L., & Griffin, M. (1979). Reconstructive and reproductive processes in memory. *Journal of Experimental Psychology: Human Learning and Memory, 4*, 318–330.

Hintzman, D. L. (1988). Judgments of frequency and recognition memory in a multiple-trace memory model. *Psychological Review, 95*, 528–551.

Hyman, I. E., Husband, T. H., & Billings, F. J. (1995). False memories of childhood experiences. *Applied Cognitive Psychology, 9*, 181–197.

Jacoby, L. L. Kelley, C. M., & Dywan, J. (1989). Memory attributions. In H. L. Roediger, III & F. I. M. Craik (Eds.), *Varieties of memory and consciousness: Essays in honour of Endel Tulving* (pp. 391–422). Hillsdale, NJ: Erlbaum.

Jenkins, J. J., Wald, J., & Pittenger, J. B. (1986). Apprehending pictorial events: An instance of psychological cohesion. In V. McCabe & G. J. Balzano (Eds.), *Event cognition: An ecological perspective* (pp. 117–133). Hillsdale, NJ: Erlbaum.

Johnson, M. K., Hashtroudi, S., & Lindsay, D. S. (1993). Source monitoring. *Psychological Bulletin, 114*, 3–28.

Johnson, M. K., & Raye, C. L. (1981). Reality monitoring. *Psychological Review, 88*, 67–85.

Johnson, M. K., & Suengas, A. G. (1989). Reality monitoring judgments of other people's memories. *Bulletin of the Psychonomic Society, 27*, 107–110.

Jones, T. C., & Roediger, H. L., III. (1995). The experiential basis of serial position effects. *European Journal of Cognitive Psychology, 7*, 65–80.

Lindsay, D. S., & Read, J. D. (1994). Psychotherapy and memories of childhood sexual abuse: A cognitive perspective. *Applied Cognitive Psychology, 8*, 281–338.

Loftus, E. F. (1993). The reality of repressed memories. *American Psychologist, 48*, 518–537.

Loftus, E. F., Miller, D. G., & Burns, H. J. (1978). Semantic integration of verbal information into a visual memory. *Journal of Experimental Psychology: Human Learning and Memory, 4*, 19–31.

Loftus, E. F., & Palmer, J. C. (1974). Reconstruction of automobile destruction: An example of the interaction between language and memory. *Journal of Verbal Learning and Verbal Behavior, 13*, 585–589.

McClelland, J. L. (in press). Constructive memory and memory distortions: A parallel-distributed processing approach. In D. L. Schacter, J. T. Coyle, G. D. Fischbach, M. M. Mesulam, & L. E. Sullivan (Eds.), *Memory distortion*. Cambridge, MA: Harvard University Press.

McCloskey, M., & Zaragoza, M. (1985). Misleading post-event information and memory for events: Arguments and evidence against memory impairment hypotheses. *Journal of Experimental Psychology: General, 114*, 1–16.

Neely, J. H., Schmidt, S. R., & Roediger, H. L., III. (1983). Inhibition from related primes in recognition memory. *Journal of Experimental Psychology: Learning, Memory, and Cognition, 9*, 196–211.

Nelson, D. L., Bajo, M., McEvoy, C. L., & Schreiber, T. A. (1989). Prior knowledge: The effects of natural category size on memory for implicitly encoded concepts. *Journal of Experimental Psychology: Learning, Memory, and Cognition, 15*, 957–967.

Paul, I. H. (1959). Studies in remembering: The reproduction of connected and extended verbal material. *Psychological Issues, 1* (Monograph 2), 1–152.

Paul, L. M. (1979). Two models of recognition memory: A test. *Journal of Experimental Psychology: Human Learning and Memory, 5*, 45–51.

Payne, D. G., Toglia, M. P., & Anastasi, J. S. (1994). Recognition performance level and the magnitude of the misinformation effect in eyewitness memory. *Psychonomic Bulletin & Review, 1*, 376–382.

Posner, M. I., & Keele, S. W. (1970). Retention of abstract ideas. *Journal of Experimental Psychology, 83*, 304–308.

Raaijmakers, J. G. W., & Shiffrin, R. M. (1980). SAM: A theory of probabilistic search of associative memory. In G. H. Bower (Ed.), *The psychology of learning and motivation* (Vol. 14, pp. 207–262). New York: Academic Press.

Rajaram, S. (1993). Remembering and knowing: Two means of access to the personal past. *Memory & Cognition, 21*, 89–102.

Rajaram, S., & Roediger, H. L., III. (in press). Remembering and knowing as states of consciousness during recollection. In J. D. Cohen & J. W. Schooler (Eds.), *Scientific approaches to the question of consciousnes*s. Hillsdale. NJ: Erlbaum.

Reyna, V. F., & Brainerd, C. J. (1995). Fuzzy-trace theory: An interim synthesis. *Learning and Individual Differences, 7*, 1–75.

Roediger, H. L., III, & Payne, D. G. (1985). Recall criterion does not affect recall level or hypermnesia: A puzzle for generate/ recognize theories. *Memory & Cognition, 13*, 1–7.

Roediger, H. L., III, Wheeler, M. A., & Rajaram, S. (1993). Remembering, knowing, and reconstructing the past. In D. L. Medin (Ed.), *The psychology of learning and motivation: Advances in research and theory* (pp. 97–134). San Diego, CA: Academic Press.

Russell, W. A., & Jenkins, J. J. (1954). *The complete Minnesota norms for responses to 100 words from the Kent-Rosanoff Word Association Test*. (Tech. Rep. No. 11, Contract N8 ONR 66216, Office of Naval Research). University of Minnesota.

Schacter, D. L. (in press). Memory distortion: History and current status. In D. L. Schacter, J. T. Coyle, G. D. Fischbach, M. M. Mesulam, & L. E. Sullivan (Eds.), *Memory distortion*. Cambridge, MA: Harvard University Press.

Schooler, J. W., Gerhard, D., & Loftus, E. F. (1986). Qualities of the unreal. *Journal of Experimental Psychology: Learning, Memory, and Cognition, 12*, 171–181.

Shiffrin, R. M., Huber, D. E., & Marinelli, K. (1995). Effects of category length and strength on familiarity in recognition. *Journal of Experimental Psychology: Learning, Memory, and Cognition, 21*, 267–287.

Spiro, R. J. (1980). Accommodative reconstruction in prose recall. *Journal of Verbal Learning and Verbal Behavior, 19*, 84–95.

Sulin, R. A., & Dooling, D. J. (1974). Intrusion of a thematic idea in retention of prose. *Journal of Experimental Psychology, 103*, 255–262.

Tulving, E. (1974). Cue-dependent forgetting. *American Scientist, 62*, 74–82.

Tulving, E. (1985). Memory and consciousness. *Canadian Psychologist, 26*, 1–12.

Underwood, B. J. (1965). False recognition produced by implicit verbal responses. *Journal of Experimental Psychology, 70*, 122–129.

Wheeler, M. A., & Roediger, H. L., III. (1992). Disparate effects of repeated testing: Reconciling Ballard's (1913) and Bartlett's (1932) results. *Psychological Science, 3*, 240–245.

Whittlesea, B. W. A. (1993). Illusions of familiarity. *Journal of Experimental Psychology: Learning, Memory, and Cognition, 19*, 1235–1253.

Whittlesea, B. W. A., Jacoby, L. L., & Girard, K. (1990). Illusions of immediate memory: Evidence of an attributional basis for feelings of familiarity and perceptual quality. *Journal of Memory and Language, 29*, 716–732.

Zaragoza, M. S., & Lane, S. M. (1994). Source misattributions and the suggestibility of eyewitness memory. *Journal of Experimental Psychology: Learning, Memory, and Cognition, 20*, 934–945.

APPENDIX: THE TWENTY-FOUR 15-WORD LISTS USED IN EXPERIMENT 2

Within-lists words were presented in this order, which generally follows the association norms. (We replaced two words here for reasons described in the Method section of Experiment 2.)

Anger	Black	Bread	Chair	Cold	Doctor	Foot	Fruit
mad	white	butter	table	hot	nurse	shoe	apple
fear	dark	food	sit	snow	sick	hand	vegetable
hate	cat	eat	legs	warm	lawyer	toe	orange
rage	charred	sandwich	seat	winter	medicine	kick	kiwi
temper	night	rye	couch	ice	health	sandals	citrus
fury	funeral	jam	desk	wet	hospital	soccer	ripe
ire	color	milk	recliner	frigid	dentist	yard	pear
wrath	grief	flour	sofa	chilly	physician	walk	banana
happy	blue	jelly	wood	heat	ill	ankle	berry
fight	death	dough	cushion	weather	patient	arm	cherry
hatred	ink	crust	swivel	freeze	office	boot	basket
mean	bottom	slice	stool	air	stethoscope	inch	juice
calm	coal	wine	sitting	shiver	surgeon	sock	salad
emotion	brown	loaf	rocking	Arctic	clinic	smell	bowl
enrage	gray	toast	bench	frost	cure	mouth	cocktail

Girl	High	King	Man	Mountain	Music	Needle	River
boy	low	queen	woman	hill	note	thread	water
dolls	clouds	England	husband	valley	sound	pin	stream
female	up	crown	uncle	climb	piano	eye	lake
young	tall	prince	lady	summit	sing	sewing	Mississippi
dress	tower	George	mouse	top	radio	sharp	boat
pretty	jump	dictator	male	molehill	band	point	tide
hair	above	palace	father	peak	melody	prick	swim
niece	building	throne	strong	plain	horn	thimble	flow
dance	noon	chess	friend	glacier	concert	haystack	run
beautiful	cliff	rule	beard	goat	instrument	thorn	barge
cute	sky	subjects	person	bike	symphony	hurt	creek
date	over	monarch	handsome	climber	jazz	injection	brook
aunt	airplane	royal	muscle	range	orchestra	syringe	fish
daughter	dive	leader	suit	steep	art	cloth	bridge
sister	elevate	reign	old	ski	rhythm	knitting	winding

Rough	Sleep	Slow	Soft	Spider	Sweet	Thief	Window
smooth	bed	fast	hard	web	sour	steal	door
bumpy	rest	lethargic	light	insect	candy	robber	glass
road	awake	stop	pillow	bug	sugar	crook	pane
tough	tired	listless	plush	fright	bitter	burglar	shade
sandpaper	dream	snail	loud	fly	good	money	ledge
jagged	wake	cautious	cotton	arachnid	taste	cop	sill
ready	snooze	delay	fur	crawl	tooth	bad	house
coarse	blanket	traffic	touch	tarantula	nice	rob	open
uneven	doze	turtle	fluffy	poison	honey	jail	curtain
riders	slumber	hesitant	feather	bite	soda	gun	frame
rugged	snore	speed	furry	creepy	chocolate	villain	view
sand	nap	quick	downy	animal	heart	crime	breeze
boards	peace	sluggish	kitten	ugly	cake	bank	sash
ground	yawn	wait	skin	feelers	tart	bandit	screen
gravel	drowsy	molasses	tender	small	pie	criminal	shutter

22 FORGOT IT ALL ALONG

It is very common for people to confabulate, to include additional information and details in their recollection of what happened that were not part of the original episode. People are also quite poor at distinguishing between memories of events that happened and memories of events that were imagined (Mitchell & Johnson, 2000). The ease with which people can be led to recall events that did not occur and believe that these memories are of real events has led to a controversy that has become known as the recovered memory debate (chapters representing many sides of the debate can be found in Conway, 1997).

One objection to the term *recovered* is that it automatically implies that the memory is of a real event. A better term, which will be used throughout the rest of this discussion, is Schooler, Bendiksen, and Ambadar's (1997) *discovered* memories, which is neutral on whether the memory is of a real event or not. The idea is that when a person discovers a memory and no other information is available, the status of the memory is unknown. In order to demonstrate that a discovered memory is of a real event, three things must be established. First, the reality of the original event must be demonstrated. Second, it must be shown that there was a period of time during which the person did not remember the event. Third, there is the discovery experience, during which the person becomes aware of remembering the event. Schooler et al. point out that these three elements are independent.

Studying discovered memories in the real world can be very time consuming and fraught with interpretative problems because the various aspects of the situation cannot be tightly controlled. Arnold and Lindsay's (2002) paper presents a laboratory analogue of the forgot-it-all-along effect, the finding that a person remembered a particular item at a particular time but then, at a later time, had forgotten that the item had ever been remembered.

In Phase I, subjects saw homographic target words paired with disambiguating context words. For example, some subjects might see the word PALM presented with the word HAND. This biases subjects to think of PALM in the sense of part of the hand rather than as a type of tree. This is followed by the presentation of a sentence that reinforces the meaning of the homograph, such as "He collected coconuts from the **** tree on the beach" or "He used the **** of his hand to swat the fly." The subjects were asked to read the sentence out loud, filling in the missing word. (The CogLab demo differs in that word pairs rather than sentences are used.)

In Phase II, subjects were given two tests. The first test was a cued-recall test in which the cue was either the same disambiguating context item they had seen or a different context item. For example, they might see HAND - P _ _ M or TREE - P _ _ M. The second test was slightly different in two ways. First, the context word was always the one used in the original study phase. Second, after the subjects had tried to recall the target word, they were asked to judge whether they remembered recalling the target in Test 1. (The CogLab demo differs in that only the memory judgment task occurs on Test 2, whereas Arnold and Lindsay had the subjects try to recall the target prior to making the judgment.)

The key data are shown in Table 22.1. The first column of data shows the number of items that subjects said they remembered recalling on Test 1 and the second column shows the proportion of items that subjects said they remembered recalling on Test 1. The top third of the data are for when the cue at Test 1 was the same as in the study cue; the bottom third of the data are for when the cue at Test 1 was different from the study cue. Two numbers are in bold face: When the cue on Test 1 was the same as the cue on Test 2 and the study phase, the proportion of items that were actually recalled on Test 1 that were judged to be recalled was 0.81. When the cue was different, this number decreases to 0.54. This shows that the subjects were more likely to remember recalling a particular item if the cue at test was the same as the cue at study.

Experiment 2 manipulated context on both Test 1 and Test 2. This makes the design more complex, but results similar to those in Experiment 1 were found. Experiment 3 addressed a potential criticism of the first two studies. The word PALM as in tree is technically a different word than PALM as in hand, so in one sense a subject would be correct to say that PALM (hand) was not recalled if the current item was PALM (tree). Experiment 3 manipulated context but kept the meaning of the target word constant by embedding the target words in two different sentences, such as "He swatted the fly with the palm of his hand" or "The fortune teller traced the lifeline on the palm of his hand" Table 22.4 shows that this did not change the basic pattern of results: Subjects are more likely to remember recalling something if the context remains constant.

The final experiment used a remember/know judgment (see Reading 23, "Remember/Know"). After indicating whether the target was recalled, the subjects indicated whether they actually remembered recalling the item, or whether they just "knew" that the item was recalled. The difference between the judgments is that a "remember" judgment means that the subject is consciously aware of some other aspect of the episode, such as they can remember a particular thought that the word triggered, or they can remember thinking it was a coincidence that this particular word followed the previous one. The basic forgot-it-all-along effect was still seen with words that were judged as "recalled" and which were then given the rating "remember."

In all four experiments, the subjects in Arnold and Lindsay's (2002) study were failing to remember that they had remembered the information at an earlier time because of a change in how they were thinking about the target item. Arnold and Lindsay are not claiming that this is exactly the same effect as when people say they have discovered a memory of being abused that they had not remembered earlier. Rather, they are demonstrating that people can forget that they had remembered something. It remains an empirical question whether the explanation of the laboratory forgot-it-all-along effect will be applicable to the discovered memory phenomenon. If it does, it will have the advantage of explaining discovered memories using well-understood general principles of memory.

REFERENCES

Conway, M. A. (Ed.). (1997). *Recovered memories and false memories.* Oxford: Oxford University Press.

Fischhoff, B. (1977). Perceived informativeness of facts. *Journal of Experimental Psychology: Human Perception and Performance, 3,* 349–358.

Mitchell, K. J., & Johnson, M. K. (2000). Source monitoring. In E. Tulving & F. I. M. Craik (Eds.), *The Oxford handbook of memory* (pp. 179–195). New York: Oxford University Press.

Schooler, J. W., Bendiksen, M., & Ambadar, A. (1997). Taking the middle line: Can we accommodate both fabricated and recovered memories of sexual abuse? In M. A. Conway (Ed.), *Recovered memories and false memories* (pp. 251–292). Oxford: Oxford University Press.

QUESTIONS

1. How does the idea of encoding specificity explain the results?
2. Why was it necessary to use the remember/know judgment and show that the forgot-it-all-along effect occurred for words judged as "remember"?
3. How might these results explain why anecdotes you tell people about experiences you have had change from one telling to the next?

Remembering Remembering

Michelle M. Arnold and D. Stephen Lindsay

University of Victoria

ABSTRACT

We developed a laboratory analogue of the "forgot-it-all-along" effect that J. W. Schooler, M. Bendiksen and Z. Ambadar (1997) proposed for cases of "recovered memories" in which individuals had forgotten episodes of talking about the abuse when they were supposedly amnestic for it. In Experiment 1, participants studied homographs with disambiguating context words; in Test 1 they received studied- or other-context words as cues; and in Test 2 they received studied-context cues and judged whether they had recalled each item during Test 1. In Experiment 2 retrieval cues were manipulated on both tests. In Experiment 3, both the studied- and other-context cues corresponded to the same meaning of each homograph. In Experiment 4, Test 1 was free recall, and studied- versus other-context cues were presented in Test 2. Participants more often forgot that they had previously recalled an item if they were cued to think of it differently on the two tests.

The controversy regarding reported "recovered memories" of childhood sexual abuse has highlighted a number of questions of interest to memory researchers (see Lindsay & Read, 2001, for a recent enumeration of some of these). Among these is the question of how people make judgments about whether they had previously recollected a particular episode that they currently recollect.

Schooler and his coworkers (Schooler, 1999, 2001; Schooler, Ambadar, & Bendiksen, 1997; Schooler, Bendiksen, & Ambadar, 1997) described two fascinating cases in which women reported full-blown recovered-memory experiences. What makes these two cases particularly interesting is that in each, a close confidant of the woman involved reported that the woman had talked about the abuse during the period of supposed amnesia. Schooler and his coauthors speculated that during the recovered-memory experience, the women remembered the abuse in a different way than they had previously (e.g., more completely, more episodically, or with a qualitatively different interpretation), such that the experience of remembering was very emotionally intense and qualitatively different from their previous recollections of the abuse, and that this in turn gave rise to what they termed a "forgot-it-all-along effect" (in reference to Fischhoff's, 1977, knew-it-all-along effect). That is, recollecting an event in manner X may cause one to forget having previously recollected it in manner Y.

To the best of our knowledge the only published research on remembering prior instances of recollection is a study by Parks (1999), in which undergraduate participants were first asked to describe various events from their pasts and shortly thereafter asked how recently they had recollected those and other events. Parks found that participants often failed to report their Phase 1 reminiscences a few minutes later, when making the Phase 2 judgments. Relatedly, in a recent study by Padilla-Walker and Poole (in press), participants first studied a list of sentences, then in Test 1 they free recalled the sentences, and in Test 2 they were given either a recognition test, cued-recall test, or free-recall test and were asked to judge whether they had recalled each sentence in Test 1. Participants more often failed to remember their Test 1 recall if Test 2 involved a recognition or cued-recall task than if Test 2 was free recall. Although there are other potential explanations, this pattern is consistent with the notion that a change in the way individuals think about a past event across different episodes of

SOURCE: From Arnold, M. M., & Lindsay, D. S. (2002). Remembering remembering. *Journal of Experimental Psychology: Learning, Memory, and Cognition, 28,* 521–529. Copyright © 2002 by the American Psychological Association. Reprinted with permission.

remembering (in this case, from free to cued recall or recognition) increases the likelihood that individuals will forget a prior instance of remembering (see also Joslyn, Loftus, McNoughton, & Powers, 2001).

We developed a laboratory analogue of the reinterpretation process that Schooler (2001) proposed contributes to the forgot-it-all-along (FIA) effect. The cognitive processes involved in recollecting childhood abuse may differ from those involved in recalling laboratory events. However, if a change in the way a past event is thought about on different occasions can lead to forgetting of previous episodes of recalling abuse, then a change in the way neutral laboratory events are thought about on different tests should also result in the forgetting of previous recollection. In our paradigm, participants first study some verbal materials, then attempt to recall those materials on two occasions; during the second recall occasion, participants are also asked whether they had recalled each item during the first recall attempt. Three of the experiments reported in this article (Experiments 1, 2, and 4) tested for the FIA effect by using context words to manipulate the meaning of studied homographs between the two recall attempts. The other experiment (Experiment 3) tested for the FIA effect by manipulating the context (but not the meaning) of studied words across the two recall attempts. We predicted that participants would more often fail to remember at Test 2, that they had recalled a word on Test 1 if they were led to think of the recalled words differently on the two tests.

Prior research on memory for events supports the prediction that a change across tests in the way a past event is thought about will contribute to the FIA effect. For instance, recognition failure occurs when participants fail to recognize studied target words paired at test with context words different from those with which targets had been studied, yet recall the target words when cued with the studied-context words (Tulving & Thomson, 1973). Recognition failure has been demonstrated both for high-frequency words with multiple meanings (Tulving & Thomson, 1973) and for single-meaning words (Tulving & Watkins, 1977). More generally, memory for past events is usually (although not always) better when study and test occur in the same context, mood, or state (see Bouton, Nelson, & Rosas, 1999; Eich, 1995; Light & Carter-

Soboll, 1970; cf. Franks, Bilbrey, Lien, & McNamara, 2000). The predominant explanation for such effects centers around Tulving's (1984) concept of encoding specificity: [T]he closer the match between the encoding and retrieval conditions, the more likely it is that the event will be successfully retrieved. Recalling prior episodes of recollection is likely similar to recalling other types of past episodes. Therefore, as in the case of recognition failure, it is reasonable to hypothesize that participants in our studies would more often forget prior remembering when they had been cued to think of the items differently on the two tests.

EXPERIMENT 1

Participants studied a list of homographic target words paired with disambiguating context words. On the first cued-recall test, participants were tested on two thirds of the target words, of which half were cued with the studied-context words and half were cued with other context words. For example, a participant who studied the target word *palm* with the context word *hand* could be cued for this target word with the context word *hand* (studied-context condition) or with the context word *tree* (other-context condition). Another third of the items were not tested for on Test 1 (not-tested condition). In a second cued-recall test, participants were tested on all of the target words, and the target words were always cued with the studied-context words. Additionally, the second test required participants to judge whether they remembered having recalled each item in Test 1.

Method

Participants.   Twenty-six University of Victoria undergraduates participated in exchange for optional extra credit in an introductory psychology course. Two participants failed to follow the directions for the judgment task and their data were excluded from the analyses.

Materials.   A set of 113 homographs with two dominant meanings (e.g., *palm* in the type-of-tree sense and in the part-of-hand sense) was constructed from various pools of homograph norms (e.g., Azuma, 1996; Gawlick-Grendell & Woltz, 1994; Twilley,

Dixon, Taylor, & Clark, 1994). Four of the items were used as primacy buffers and four were used as recency buffers. The target words were randomly divided into three lists of 35 words (*test-list* factor), with each list appearing equally often across participants in the studied-context, other-context, and not-tested within-subject conditions of Test 1. A context word was assigned to each of the two different meanings of the target words (e.g., *tree* and *hand* for the target *palm*). Two study lists were constructed (*study-list* factor) to counterbalance the meanings of the target words between subjects (e.g., *palm* studied with *tree* for half of the participants and studied with *hand* for the other half of the participants). A sentence was constructed for each context-target word pair for the study phase, containing the context word and a row of asterisks for the target word (e.g., *He collected coconuts from the *** tree on the beach* and *He used the *** of his hand to swat the fly*).

Procedure.   Participants were tested individually on an IBM-compatible personal computer using Schneider's Micro-Experimental Laboratory Professional software package (Schneider, 1988). Participants were seated in front of the computer monitor, with the experimenter sitting off to one side. The experimenter read the instructions aloud as they appeared on the screen for each phase. Participants were told that for each study trial, a context word and target word would be displayed on the screen for approximately 2 s, and their task was to repeat the words aloud in preparation for a subsequent memory test. The two words were then removed from the screen and a sentence containing the context word and a row of asterisks for the target word was presented for 3.5 s. Participants were instructed to read the sentence aloud, filling in the row of asterisks with the target word. After the 3.5 s elapsed, the target word appeared above the sentence for 1 s, after which the computer screen went blank for 1 s before the next trial began.

The first cued-recall test immediately followed the study phase, with the items presented in random order. Participants were informed that they would be tested on half of the target words (they were actually tested on two thirds of the items, but it was easier to explain the task in terms of half of the items) and that this would be done by presenting a context word along with the first and last letters of a target word (e.g., *hand—p _ _m* or *tree—p _ _m*). Further, participants were instructed that for half of the trials the context words would correspond to the context words presented with the targets during the study phase, and for the remaining trials the context words would not be the same as at study, but nonetheless the context words would be related to the target words, and they were given an example. The test instructions also warned participants only to respond with answers they *remembered* seeing during the study phase: Participants were instructed to say "pass" if they did not remember the answer or if the answer they came up with was a guess (e.g., filling in the blanks instead of remembering the word from the study phase). The computer gave participants item-by-item feedback in the form of a tone for incorrect answers or responses of "pass," and the phrase "correct response" for correct answers. After completing the first test, participants were given a 5-min break during which they conversed with the experimenter before moving on to the second cued-recall test.

All 105 critical target words were tested in random order on the second cued-recall task. The second test was similar in format to the first test. For each trial, participants were given a context word with the first and last letters of a target word separated by dashes and asked to recall the target word from the study phase. Participants were informed that all of the context words on Test 2 corresponded with the context words presented with the target words during the study phase. As in Test 1, participants were told to respond with an answer only if they remembered seeing the target word during the study phase. After each recall attempt, the screen went blank, and whenever a participant gave an incorrect answer or said "pass," the experimenter supplied the correct target word. Participants were then required to judge if they remembered recalling the target word during Test 1. Participants were explicitly instructed that their judgments should not be based on whether or not they had seen the Test 2 context word during Test 1 but rather on whether or not they remembered recalling the target word on Test 1. Participants were also reminded that many of the study items had not been tested for (and hence could not have been recalled) on Test 1. The experimenter emphasized that the task was not to judge if the context word had changed between the two tests, nor whether the target word had merely been tested on Test 1 (e.g., "If you remember that the computer beeped at you for a particular trial during the first test because you said 'pass' or gave the wrong answer, then you should say 'no' "). During the test, participants were stopped two or three times and reminded of the instructions for the judgment task.

Results and Discussion

Our interest focused on participants' judgments about prior remembering. Nonetheless, in this and the subsequent Results and Discussion sections, we first report analyses of recall performance on Test 1 and Test 2 (collapsed across the counterbalancing factors of study list and test list[1]) before turning to analyses of the prior-remembering judgment data.

Recall performance.   Proportion correctly recalled on Test 1 was significantly higher for items cued with studied-context words ($M = .91$) than for items cued with the other-context words ($M = .77$), $t(23) = 9.62$, $p < .01$. A within-subjects analysis of variance (ANOVA) was performed on the proportion correctly

recalled on Test 2 with context on Test 1 (studied, other, or not-tested) as the within-subjects factor. Performance was near ceiling (as intended), and there was no significant difference in proportion of items recalled for the studied-context ($M = .94$), other-context ($M = .92$), and not-tested ($M = .92$) conditions, $F(2, 46) = 1.36$, $MSE - 0.002$, $p > .27$.

Judgment of previous recollection.   The proportion of items judged on Test 2 as recalled on Test 1 is shown in Table 22.1. The analyses reported here were performed on the judgment data for items correctly recalled on both Test 1 and Test 2 (shown in bold in Table 22.1), although the same pattern of results was found when analyses were contingent only on correct recall on Test 1. In an initial omnibus ANOVA, no reliable effects of the counterbalancing factors of study list or test list were found (all $Fs < 1$), and therefore the data were collapsed across these variables. A within-subjects ANOVA was performed on the proportion of correct "yes" judgments, with context on Test 1 (studied vs. other) as the within-subjects factor. Participants were significantly more likely to forget that they had recalled an item on Test 1 if it had been cued with the other-context word on Test 1 than if it

TABLE 22.1   Mean Number of Items and Mean Proportion of Items Judged as "Recalled" as a Function of Recall Status on Test 1 and Test 2 for Experiment 1

Test 1/Test 2 Recall Status	No. of Items	Proportion Judged as "Recalled" on Test 1
Studied-context[a]		
Not recalled/not recalled	1.79	.09 (.06)
Not recalled/recalled	1.37	.04 (.02)
Recalled/recalled	**31.42**	**.81 (.02)**
Recalled/not recalled	.42	.57 (.17)
Other-context[a]		
Not recalled/not recalled	1.62	0 (—)
Not recalled/recalled	6.38	.11 (.03)
Recalled/recalled	**25.83**	**.54 (.04)**
Recalled/not recalled	1.17	.10 (.05)
Not-tested[a]		
NA/not recalled	2.79	.14 (.06)
NA/recalled	32.21	.10 (.03)

Note: Lines in bold are those for which statistical analyses are reported in the article. There were 35 items per condition. Standard errors of the mean are shown in parentheses. Dash indicates that the standard error of the mean could not be calculated. NA = not applicable.

[a]Test 1 cue.

had been cued with the studied-context word, F (1, 23) = 51.09, MSE = 0.02, $p < .01$. Participants rarely erred on not-tested items by saying that they had remembered those items on Test 1.

As predicted, participants were dramatically more likely to forget that they had recalled a word on Test 1 if Test 1 recall of that word had been cued with the other-context word than if it had been cued with the studied-context word. This finding is consistent with the hypothesis that changes in the way an event is remembered can produce a FIA effect. The results of Experiment 1 are also amenable, however, to a slightly different interpretation: It may be that cuing with the other-context word on Test 1 produced weaker or less complete recollection of the target word than did cuing with the studied-context word.[2] If so, then the experience of remembering during Test 1 might be less memorable for words in the other-context condition than for words in the studied-context condition. This mechanism could play a role in real-world cases like those described by Schooler (2001); that is, the women's prememory-recovery recollections of the abuse may have been vague or incomplete and hence, simply not memorable.

EXPERIMENT 2

Experiment 2 was designed to assess the two accounts of the results of Experiment 1 mentioned above by manipulating context on both Test 1 and Test 2. If the tendency to forget prior remembering of words in the other-context condition of Experiment 1 was due only to weaker Test 1 recollections of those words, then in Experiment 2 that effect should be obtained only for items cued with other-context words during Test 1 and studied-context words during Test 2. If, however, shifts in how participants think about the target words on the two tests contribute to the effect, then it should also be observed for words cued on Test 1 with studied-context words but cued on Test 2 with other-context words.

In Experiment 2, we used the same basic procedure as in Experiment 1, but context was manipulated on both the first and the second recall tests. Six within-subject conditions were created, with target items: (a) tested with the studied-context word on Test 1 and Test 2 (*studied/studied* condition), (b) tested with the

other-context word on Test 1 but with the studied-context word on Test 2 (*other/studied* condition), (c) not tested on Test 1, and tested with the studied-context word on Test 2 (*not-tested/studied* condition), (d) tested with the studied-context word on Test 1 but with the other-context word on Test 2 (*studied/other* condition), (e) tested with the other-context word on Test 1 and Test 2 (*other/other* condition), and (f) not tested on Test 1, and tested with the other-context word on Test 2 (*not-tested/other* condition).

Method

Subjects.   Twenty-seven University of Victoria undergraduates participated in exchange for optional extra credit in an introductory psychology course or a $10 payment. Three participants recalled fewer than 50% of the items in at least one of the conditions on Test 1 and/or Test 2, and their data were excluded from the analyses.

Materials.   Three additional homographs were added to the set of homographs used in Experiment 1, resulting in a set of 116 target words. Four of the items were used as primacy buffers and four were used as recency buffers. The target words were randomly divided into six lists of 18 words (test-list factor), with each list appearing equally often across participants in the studied/studied, other/studied, not-tested/studied, studied/other, other/other, and not-tested/other within-subject conditions of Test 1 and Test 2. Two study lists were constructed (study-list factor) to counterbalance the meanings of the target words between subjects.

Procedure.   The basic procedure of Experiment 1 was used, with four modifications. First, instead of viewing the context-target word pairs and sentences during the study phase, participants heard the study materials read aloud. Participants were told that for each study trial, the experimenter would read aloud a context word and a target word, followed by a sentence containing those two words. Participants were instructed to repeat the sentence aloud and then write down the target word on a sheet provided by the experimenter. This change to the way the study list was presented was intended to make it easier for participants, during

Test 2, to differentiate between memories of studying a target word (hearing the context word and target word) and memories of recalling it on Test 1 (seeing a context word with the first and last letters of the target. and responding with the target word).

A second modification involved replacing the dashes between the first and last letters of the target word on Test 2 with asterisks (e.g., *tree p**m*). This difference was incorporated to assist participants in differentiating between Test 1 and Test 2.

As a third modification, participants were instructed on Test 2 that, as in Test 1, half of the context words would be the same as those presented with the target words during the study phase, and half of them would be different. Participants were also warned that the Test 2 context words presented with the items that had been tested on Test 1 could be the same as or different from the context words used to test for those items on Test 1.

The fourth change to the procedure was established to ensure that participants understood the difference between (a) remembering only being *tested* on a target word in Test 1 (being cued for a target word, but not necessarily recalling that target), and (b) remembering *recalling* the target word. On Test 1, participants were given a hand-held microphone and informed that their responses would be tape-recorded. The tape recorder was set so that participants could hear their voices come through the speakers. The instructions for the judgment task in Test 2 were the same as in Experiment 1, with an additional sentence that stated "Another way to think of the judgment task is, if the tape recording from Test 1 was played back, would you hear your voice saying the target word?" Participants were instructed to say "yes" only if they remembered recalling and saying the target word on Test 1.

Results and Discussion

Recall performance. The proportion correctly recalled for each condition of Test 1 and Test 2 is shown in Table 22.2. Proportion correctly recalled on Test 1 was higher for items cued with the studied-context words ($M = .88$) than cued with other-context words ($M = .77$), $F(1, 23) = 57.76$. $MSE = 0.003$. $p < .01$. The proportions of items correctly recalled on Test 2 were

analyzed in a 3 (Test 1: studied-context. other-context. and not-tested) × 2 (Test 2: studied-context vs. other-context) within-subjects ANOVA. Correct recall on Test 2 was higher for items cued with the studied-context words ($M = .90$) than cued with the other-context words ($M = .80$), $F(1, 23) = 26.29$, $MSE = 0.01$, $p < .01$. Correct recall on Test 2 was also influenced by context on Test 1, $F(2, 46) = 3.34$, $MSE = 0.01$, $p = .04$: Test 2 recall performance was slightly poorer for items not tested on Test 1 ($M = .83$) than for items tested in the studied-context condition ($M = .87$), $t(23) = 2.19$, $p = .04$, or other-context condition ($M = .86$), $t(23) = 2.53$, $p = .02$. There was no interaction between context on Test 1 and Test 2, $F < 1$.

Judgment of previous recollection. The proportions of items on Test 2 judged as recalled on Test 1 are shown in Table 22.3. The subsequent analyses were performed on the judgment data for items correctly recalled on both Test 1 and Test 2 (shown in bold in Table 22.3), although the same pattern of results was found when analyses were contingent only on correct recall on Test 1. No reliable effect of the test-list counterbalancing factor for the judgment task was found in an initial omnibus ANOVA (all Fs < 1.73, ps > .20), and therefore analyses collapsed across this manipulation.

The proportions of correct "yes" judgments were analyzed in a 2 (Test 1: studied-context vs. other-context) × 2 (Test 2: studied-context vs. other-context) × 2 (Study list: Study List 1 vs. Study List 2) mixed-factorial ANOVA. As expected, there was a significant interaction between context on Test 1 and context on Test 2, $F(1, 22) = 53.99$, $MSE = 0.01$, $p < .01$. This effect was moderated by a Test 1 Context × Test 2 Context × Study List interaction, $F(1, 22) =$

TABLE 22.2 Mean Proportion of Items Correctly Recalled in Experiment 2

Test 1/Test 2 Cues	Test 1	Test 2
Studied/studied	.89 (.02)	.91 (.02)
Other/studied	.77 (.02)	.91 (.02)
Not-tested/studied		.89 (.02)
Studied/other	.88 (.02)	.82 (.03)
Other/other	.77 (.03)	.82 (.02)
Not-tested/other		.77 (.03)

Note: Standard errors of the mean are shown in parentheses.

TABLE 22.3   Mean Number of Items and Mean Proportion of Items Judged as "Recalled" as a Function of Recall Status on Test 1 and Test 2 for Experiment 2

Test 1/Test 2 Recall Status	No. of Items	Proportion Judged as "Recalled" on Test 1
Studied-context[a]		
Not recalled/not recalled	1.33	.07 (.06)
Not recalled/recalled	.71	.25 (.13)
Recalled/recalled	**15.75**	**.83 (.03)**
Recalled/not recalled	.21	.38 (.24)
Other/studied[a]		
Not recalled/not recalled	.71	.03 (.03)
Not recalled/recalled	3.42	.03 (.01)
Recalled/recalled	**12.92**	**.60 (.03)**
Recalled/not recalled	.96	.27 (.11)
Not-tested/studied[a]		
NA/not recalled	2.04	.02 (.02)
NA/recalled	15.96	.08 (.02)
Studied/other[a]		
Not recalled/not recalled	.83	.21 (.11)
Not recalled/recalled	1.42	.03 (.03)
Recalled/recalled	**13.46**	**.70 (.03)**
Recalled/not recalled	2.29	.57 (.10)
Other/other[a]		
Not recalled/not recalled	2.67	.02 (.01)
Not recalled/recalled	1.54	.07 (.04)
Recalled/recalled	**13.25**	**.79 (.03)**
Recalled/not recalled	.54	.45 (.16)
Not-tested/other[a]		
NA/not recalled	4.17	.05 (.03)
NA/recalled	13.83	.08 (.02)

Note: Lines in bold are those for which statistical analyses are reported in the article. There were 18 items per condition. Standard errors of the mean are shown in parentheses. NA = not applicable.

[a]Test 1/Test2 cue.

10.07, $MSE = 0.01$, $p = .01$. Despite the fact that there was an effect of study list (i.e., the sense with which the target words were studied did influence the judgment task), the pattern of judgments for both Study List 1 and Study List 2 was the same: A significant interaction between context on Test 1 and context on Test 2 was found for participants in the Study List 1 group, $F(1, 11) = 6.98$, $MSE = 0.01$, $p = .02$, and for participants in the Study List 2 group, $F(1, 11) = 73.65$, $MSE = 0.01$, $p < .01$. Planned comparisons (collapsing across study list) showed that for items that had been cued with studied-context words on Test 1, participants less often remembered their previous recall when they were cued with the other-context words on Test 2 (studied/other) than when they were cued with studied-context words on Test 2 (studied/studied), $t(23) = 4.33$, $p < .01$. Conversely, for items that had been cued with other-context words on Test 1, participants less often remembered their prior recall when they were cued with studied-context words on Test 2 (other/studied) than when they were cued with other-context words on Test 2 (other/other), $t(23) = 4.65$, $p < .01$.[3] Additionally, there was a significant main effect of Test 1 context,

$F(1,22) = 11.43$, $MSE = 0.010$, $p = .01$ with correct memory for prior recall being faster for items that had been cued with studied-context words on Test 1 ($M = .76$) than for items that had been cued with other-context words on Test 1 ($M = .70$). This result is consistent with the possibility that correct recall during Test 1 was more complete for items cued with studied-context words than for those cued with other-context words. There was not a reliable main effect of context on Test 2 for correct "yes" judgments, $F < 1$. Finally, as in Experiment 1, participants rarely falsely reported they had remembered items that had not been tested on Test 1.

EXPERIMENT 3

In Experiments 1 and 2, the context words were intended to cue distinctly different meanings of each target word. A participant who recalled *palm* on Test 1, and thought of it as part of a hand, and who later recalled *palm* on Test 2, and thought of it as a tree, would be correct, in a sense, to deny having previously recalled *palm* (tree; see Martin, 1975, for an analogous argument regarding recognition-failure paradigms that use homographs). Of course, it may be that real-world cases of the FIA effect, such as those described by Schooler (2001), also involve fundamental changes in the meaning of the remembered event (e.g., from fondling to rape). Does the FIA effect occur only when a past event is thought about in a dramatically different way, or can more subtle shifts also lead to forgetting of prior remembering? Experiment 3 was designed to explore this possibility.[4]

We designed Experiment 3 to test for the FIA effect by manipulating the context of the target items but not their sense or meaning (e.g., *palm* always studied and tested as part of a hand, but in different contexts). For comparability across studies, we used the same target words as in Experiment 2, with two context sentences prepared for each target word. The design was otherwise similar to that used in Experiment 1.

Method

Subjects.   Twelve University of Victoria undergraduates participated in exchange for optional extra credit in an introductory psychology course.

Materials.   The materials used in Experiment 2 were adapted by creating two context sentences for each target (e.g., *He swatted the fly with the palm of his hand* and *The fortune teller traced the lifeline on the palm of his hand*). Four of the items were used as primacy buffers and four were used as recency buffers, on both Test 1 and Test 2. The cues used to test for the target words were the context sentences. For Test 1, participants were cued with a studied- or other-context sentence containing a row of asterisks for the target word, and the first letter of the target word (e.g., *He swatted the fly with the* ***** *of his hand—p*). On Test 2, participants were cued with studied-context sentences containing the first letter of the target word (e.g., *He swatted the fly with the p of his hand*). The target words were randomly divided into three lists of 36 words (test-list factor), with each list appearing equally often across participants in the studied-context, other-context, and not-tested within-subject conditions of Test 1. Two study lists were constructed (study-list factor) to counterbalance the contexts of studied words between subjects.

Procedure.   The procedure was basically the same as in Experiment 1, but it was adjusted to include three of the modifications from Experiment 2: (a) auditory study, (b) tape recording of Test 1 responses, and (c) changing the symbols of the to-be-recalled target word from an asterisk on Test 1 to a question mark on Test 2.

Results and Discussion

Recall performance.   Proportion correctly recalled on Test 1 was significantly higher for items in the studied-context condition ($M = .94$) than for items in the other-context condition ($M = .81$), $t(11) = 5.02$, $p < .01$. A within-subjects ANOVA was performed on the proportion correctly recalled on Test 2, with context on Test 1 (studied, other, or not-tested) as the within-subjects factor. There was no significant difference in proportion of items recalled for the studied-context ($M = .96$), other-context ($M = .94$), and not-tested ($M = .93$) conditions, $F < 1$.

Judgment of previous recollection.   The proportions of items on Test 2 judged as recalled on Test 1 are shown

TABLE 22.4 Mean Number of Items and Mean Proportion of Items Judged as "Recalled" as a Function of Recall Status on Test 1 and Test 2 for Experiment 3

Test 1/Test 2 Recall Status	No. of Items	Proportion Judged as "Recalled" on Test 1
	Studied-context[a]	
Not recalled/not recalled	1.42	0 (—)
Not recalled/recalled	.83	.05 (.05)
Recalled/recalled	**33.58**	**.93 (.01)**
Recalled/not recalled	.17	.50 (—)
	Other-context[a]	
Not recalled/not recalled	.75	0 (—)
Not recalled/recalled	6.25	.06 (.03)
Recalled/recalled	**27.67**	**.63 (.05)**
Recalled/not recalled	1.33	.18 (.12)
	Not-tested[a]	
NA/not recalled	2.58	0 (—)
NA/recalled	33.42	.03 (.01)

Note: Lines in bold are those for which statistical analyses are reported in the article. There were 36 items per condition. Standard errors of the mean are shown in parentheses. Dash indicates that the standard error of the mean could not be calculated. NA = not applicable.
[a]Test 1 cue.

in Table 22.4. The analyses reported here were performed on the judgment data for target items correctly recalled on both Test 1 and Test 2 (shown in bold in Table 22.4), although the same pattern of results was found when analyses were contingent only on correct recall on Test 1. No reliable effects of the study-list or test-list factors for the judgment task were found in an initial omnibus ANOVA (all $Fs < 2.17$, $ps \geq .20$), and therefore the data were collapsed across these variables. A within-subjects ANOVA was performed on the proportion of "yes" judgments. with context on Test 1 (studied vs. other) as the within-subjects factor. Participants were significantly more likely to forget that they had recalled an item on Test 1 if it had been cued with the other-context sentence on Test 1 than if it had been cued with the studied-context sentence, $F(1, 11) = 48.54$, $MSE = 0.01$, $p < .01$. Participants rarely erred on not-tested items by saying that they had remembered those items on Test 1.

EXPERIMENT 4

The results of Experiments 1–3 support the hypothesis that changes in the way an individual thinks about an event when it is recalled on different occasions can

lead to forgetting of the prior recollections. A critic might argue, however, that participants in our experiments based their judgments of prior recollection not on whether they remembered recalling a target item on Test 1 but rather on whether they remembered encountering the Test 2 retrieval cue on Test 1. We explicitly and emphatically instructed participants that their judgments should be based on whether they remembered recalling the target rather than on whether they remembered encountering the cue, but it is possible that participants did not always follow this instruction. We eliminated this alternative explanation in Experiment 4 by changing Test 1 from cued recall to free recall (with the assumption that during free recall, participants would tend to think about the words in the way they had been biased to do during study). As in Experiments 1–3, Test 2 was cued recall, with some items cued by studied-context words and others cued by other-context words. Because the context cues were not encountered until Test 2, participants could not possibly base their judgments of prior recollection on whether or not they remembered encountering those cues on Test 1. We expected that the FIA effect would be smaller in this procedure than in Experiments 1–3, because free recall is relatively memorable (e.g., the items successfully recalled are the ones that participants are able to bring to mind on their own) and because the familiarity of the cues themselves could not contribute to the FIA effect.

Participants studied five lists of 16 homographic target words presented in disambiguating context sentences. After each study list was presented, participants attempted free recall for the target words (Test 1). To explore the relationship between the phenomenology of Test 1 recall and subsequent judgments of prior remembering, participants were asked to make a "Remember-Know" judgment for each recalled word (e.g., Gardiner & Java, 1990). Later, participants were given a cue to recall each of the target words (Test 2): [H]alf of the items were cued with context words relating to the studied sense of the targets (studied-context condition) and half were cued with context words that did not relate in sense to the sentences presented with the target items at study (other-context condition). Additionally, the second test required participants to judge whether they remembered recalling the word on the free-recall test.

Method

Subjects. Twenty-seven University of Victoria undergraduates participated in exchange for optional extra credit in an introductory psychology course. Three participants recalled fewer than eight items in either the studied-context or other-context conditions on the cued-recall test that they had also previously recalled in free recall; their data were dropped from the analyses.

Materials. A list of 90 target words was constructed from the set of homographic target words used in Experiments 1–3. Ten of the items were used as a practice list. Two study lists were constructed to counterbalance the meanings of the target words between subjects (study-list factor). For each participant, the computer randomly divided the 80 target words into five lists of 16 items. The target words were randomly partitioned into two lists of 40 words (test-list factor), with each list appearing equally often across participants in the studied-context and other-context within-subject conditions of Test 2. The two context words associated with each target word were the same

as those used in Experiments 1 and 2, but the sentences in which the target items were presented during study were modified. In Experiments 1 and 2, the sentences in which the target words were presented during the study phase always included both the target word and one of its two context words. In Experiment 4, the senses of the study sentences were not changed from those used in the first two experiments, but the context words themselves were dropped from the sentences. For example, in Experiments 1 and 2, the target word *palm* was sometimes studied with the sentence *He used the palm of his hand to swat the fly,* and recall of *palm* was sometimes cued with the context word *hand.* In this experiment, some participants studied *palm* with the sentence *He used his palm to swat the fly,* and in Test 2, *palm* was cued with either *hand* or *tree.* Therefore, in both the studied-context and other-context conditions, participants never encountered the context words until the final cued-recall test.

Procedure. Participants were told that on each study trial they would be read a sentence, and that one of the words would be verbally emphasized as a target word. Their task was to repeat the sentence aloud, verbally emphasizing the target word. In the event that a participant did not repeat a sentence or failed to emphasize the target word, the experimenter repeated the sentence (although participants were told it was important to pay close attention to each sentence so that it would not need to be repeated, and participants almost always succeeded). Participants were informed that after each list of 16 sentences was presented, they would be required to recall the target words. The experimenter stressed to participants that they should write down a word only if they were confident that they heard that item as a target word in the study list. Participants were also required to make a Remember-Know judgment for each target word they recalled. Participants were instructed to write an *R* beside the target word if they could actually recollect something about the experience of having studied that target word, and to place a *K* beside the target word if they knew the item was in the study list but could not recollect any specific details of their encounter with it (as in Gardiner & Java, 1990). For each list, participants were given 1.5 min to write down the target words and corresponding Remember-Know judgments. Participants were given the practice list and performed the free-recall task for that list to ensure that they understood the instructions and were comfortable with the tasks. They then completed the five study/recall cycles. Thereafter, participants were given a 10-min break during which they conversed with the experimenter before moving on to the final cued-recall test.

All 80 of the critical target words were tested for in random order with cued recall on Test 2. On each trial, a context word and the first and last letters of a target word were presented on the computer screen, and participants were asked to recall the corresponding studied target word. Participants were told that for half of the trials, the context word would be closely related to the sentence in which the to-be-recalled word had been studied and that for the other half of the trials, the context word would be different from the sentence presented with the target during study but that the context word would nonetheless be related to the target word. To clarify these instructions, participants were shown an example of a studied- and other-context word that could be used to test for a target word; for example: "You studied *palm* with *He used his palm to swat the fly*. We could test you for this target word by presenting the related context word *hand* or by presenting the context word *tree*, which is not related to the sentence with which you studied *palm* but is related to the target *palm*." Participants were instructed to respond with an answer only if they remembered hearing that target word during study. After each item was recalled (or, if recall failed, the experimenter announced the target word) participants judged whether they remembered having recalled the target word during Test 1. Participants were told that they should respond with a "yes" only if they remembered recalling and writing down the target word during the first phase of the experiment.

Results and Discussion

Recall performance. Participants sometimes recalled a word from a list other than that on which they were being tested (across participants, an average of .92 items were recalled from a list other than the one being tested), and these items were scored as correct so

long as they were not items that had been recalled on an earlier test. Overall, participants recalled an average of 36.75 target words in free recall (45.94%). On average, participants classified 71.54% of recalled words as "remember." On the final test, proportion correct cued recall was significantly higher for items in the studied-context condition ($M = .88$) than for items in the other-context condition ($M = .81$), $t(23) = 3.75$, $p = .01$.

Judgment of previous recollection. The proportions of items judged following cued recall (Test 2) as having also been recalled during free recall (Test 1) are shown in Table 22.5. The analyses reported here were performed on the judgment data for target items correctly recalled in both free and cued recall (shown in bold in Table 22.5), although the same pattern of results was found when analyses were contingent only on correct recall on Test 1. No reliable effects of the study-list or test-list factors for the judgment task were found in an initial omnibus ANOVA (all $Fs < 1.49$, $ps \geq .24$), and therefore the data were collapsed across these variables. A within-subjects ANOVA was performed on the proportion of correct "yes" judgments, with context in cued recall (studied vs. other) as the within-subjects factor. Participants were significantly more likely to fail to remember that they had freely recalled an item on Test 1 if it had been cued with the other-context word on Test 2 than if it had been cued with the studied-context word, $F(1, 23) = 8.08$, $MSE = 0.01$, $p < .01$. Participants rarely erred on items that they had not freely recalled on Test 1.

We conducted a subanalysis restricted to items on which participants had made a "remember" (as opposed to "know") response during Test 1. The data from 7 participants were excluded because they claimed to remember fewer than eight items per condition. Among the remaining participants, the effect of context cues on judgments of prior recall was the same as in the overall analysis reported above: Participants more often forgot that they had recalled "remembered" items if the items were cued with the other-context word on Test 2 ($M = .81$) than if they were cued with the studied-context word ($M = .91$), $F(1, 16) = 7.66$, $MSE = 0.01$, $p = .01$.

TABLE 22.5   Mean Number of Items and Mean Proportion of Items Judged as "Recalled" as a Function of Recall Status on Test 1 and Test 2 for Experiment 4

Test 1/Test 2 Recall Status	No. of Items	Proportion Judged as "Recalled" on Test 1
	Studied-context[a]	
Not recalled/not recalled	3.33	.08 (.05)
Not recalled/recalled	17.87	.07 (.01)
Recalled/recalled	**17.29**	**.86 (.03)**
Recalled/not recalled	1.50	.63 (.10)
	Other-context[a]	
Not recalled/not recalled	5.25	.03 (.02)
Not recalled/recalled	16.79	.06 (.01)
Recalled/recalled	**15.42**	**.77 (.03)**
Recalled/not recalled	2.54	.56 (.07)

Note: Lines in bold are those for which statistical analyses are reported in the article. There were 40 items per condition in Test 2. Standard errors of the mean are shown in parentheses.

[a]Test 2 cue.

GENERAL DISCUSSION

As predicted, participants more often forgot that they had previously recalled a studied word if they were led to think about that word differently on the two recall episodes. Thus, our results support the existence of a FIA effect.

Remembering prior remembering is likely similar to remembering other sorts of past experiences. That is, an episode of recollection may be remembered (or forgotten) just as other sorts of episodes are. Similarly, judgments of prior recollection are likely based on the same mechanisms as judgments of other sorts of prior occurrences. In general terms, when attempting to judge whether they have previously recollected a particular event, individuals cue memory and assess its output (a la Tulving's, 1984, concept of synergistic ecphory; cf. Anderson & Bower, 1972; Johnson, Hashtroudi, & Lindsay, 1993; Whittlesea & Williams, 1998).

Memories of episodes of recollection likely have two special (although not unique) characteristics. One is that they share content with memories of the remembered event itself. The more vividly, completely, and veridically a past experience was recollected on a particular occasion, the more the memories of that episode of recollection will share content with memories of the initial experience itself. This may pose a variety of problems for the cognitive system. For example, instances of prior recollection may be difficult to recall as distinct episodes because cues for those prior recollections will also be cues (and perhaps better cues) for memories of the initial event itself; this may limit revival of the memory information for the prior recollection through cue overload (Watkins & Watkins, 1976), or produce blended ecphoric products in which the information from prior recollections is experienced as part of the recollection of the event itself (indeed, this may be an important part of the way rehearsal works). If cuing conditions selectively favor revival of one or more prior instances of recollection over revival of the event itself, that memory information may be mistaken as a memory of a perceptual experience (i.e., the individual thinks she or he is remembering an actual experience but is really reviving memories of prior recollections of that experience rather than memories of the event itself); in other cases in which cuing conditions selectively favor revival of memories of prior instances of recollection, the individual may mistakenly judge that she or he never experienced the event in question but rather had only thought about or imagined experiencing it (cf. Johnson et al., 1993).

The mechanisms governing forgetting prior episodes of word recall are not, of course, necessarily the same as those involved in forgetting prior episodes of recalling childhood abuse. For example, when participants in our experiments recalled a word on Test 2 and failed to remember that they had also previously recalled that word, they probably did not have emotionally charged "recovered-memory experiences" akin to those reported by Schooler (2001). That is, with our materials, participants would rarely spontaneously think something like "Wow, this is amazing—I had totally forgotten about the word *palm* until now!" Principles of memory developed in the laboratory have, for the most part, fared well in terms of generalizing to more naturalistic settings (e.g., Banaji & Crowder, 1989), but the question of generalizability is an empirical one. At minimum, it is likely that forgetting of prior instances of recalling abuse is a more complex and multifaceted phenomenon than is forgetting of prior instances of recalling study-list words. Nonetheless, the fact that in all four experiments a substantial FIA effect was obtained is consistent with the hypothesis that changes in the way an event is thought about on different occasions can contribute to forgetting of prior episodes of recollection.

Although the idea for the present experiments grew out of the recovered memory arena, our findings also have implications for other domains within cognitive psychology. Research on a variety of memory phenomena (e.g., flashbulb memories, permastore) often uses retrospective self-report measures of the number of times a person previously remembered or thought about an event (e.g., to assess the effects of rehearsal). The results presented here suggest that such measures should not be taken at face value and that, like memory for an event itself, memory for previous recollection is subject to systematic biases.

AUTHOR NOTES

Portions of this research were reported at the annual meeting, of the Northwest Cognition and Memory Society, Bellingham, Washington, June 2000. This research was supported by the Natural Sciences and Engineering Research Council (NSERC) of Canada through a postgraduate scholarship to Michelle M. Arnold and by NSERC Grant OGPO121316-95 awarded to D. Stephen Lindsay. We thank Michael E. J. Masson and J. Don Read for their suggestions on an earlier version of this article.

Correspondence concerning this article should be addressed to Michelle M. Arnold, Department of Psychology, University of Victoria, P.O. Box 3050 STN CSC, Victoria, British Columbia V8W 3P5, Canada. E-mail: arnoldm @uvic.ca

ENDNOTES

1. The analyses of recall performance for all four experiments were initially performed using omnibus ANOVAs that included the study-list and test-list counterbalancing factors. In Experiments 2–4 there were sometimes significant effects of the study-list and/or test-list factors (although the pattern was not consistent across experiments). The assignment of the meanings of the target words to either of the two study lists, as well as the assignment of the items to a test list, was random; it appears that flukes of random assignment sometimes led more memorable senses of the target words to be assigned to one study list than the other, and sometimes led one version of the test list to be easier than the other. It is also possible that some of these effects were Type I errors. In any case, differences in recall performance because of the counterbalancing of the study and tests lists are irrelevant to our hypotheses regarding judgments of prior recollection, so we do not report these analyses here; they may be requested from either author.

2. We thank Michael E. J. Masson for bringing this alternative explanation to our attention.

3. It could be argued that because of the reliable three-way interaction of Test 1 Context × Test 2 Context × Study List, these planned comparisons should be carried out separately for the two study lists. Separate directional analyses demonstrated that the same overall patterns for the judgment task were also found for both study-list groups. That is, for Study List 1, participants less often remembered their previous recall of items cued with studied-context words on Test 1 when they were cued with other-context words on Test 2 (studied/other; $M = .69$) than when they were cued with studied-context words on Test 2 (studied/studied; $M = .78$), $t(11) = 1.92$, $p < .05$. Conversely, for Study List l, the items cued with other-context words on Test 1 were less often correctly judged as previously recalled when they were cued with studied-context words on Test 2 (other/studied; $M = .63$) than when they were cued with other-context words on Test 2 (other/other; $M = .72$), $t(11) = 2.03$, $p < .05$. For Study List 2, participants were also less likely to remember their previous recall of target items cued with studied-context words on Test 1 if they were tested with other-context words on Test 2 (studied/other; $M = .70$) than if they were cued with studied-context words on

Test 2 (studied/studied; $M = .89$), $t(11) = 4.55$, $p = .01$. For items that had been cued with other-context words on Test 1, Study List 2 participants less often remembered their previous recall when they were cued with studied-context words on Test 2 (other/studied; $M = .58$) than when they were cued with other-context words on Test 2 (other/other; $M - .85$), $t(11) - 5.04$, $p < .01$.

4. We thank Bruce W. A. Whittlesea for raising this issue.

REFERENCES

Anderson, J. R., & Bower, G. H. (1972). Recognition and retrieval processes in free recall. *Psychological Review, 79*, 97–123.

Azuma, T. (1996). Familiarity and relatedness of word meanings: Ratings for 110 homographs. *Behavior Research Methods, Instruments and Computers, 28*, 109–124.

Banaji, M. R., & Crowder, R. G. (1989). The bankruptcy of everyday memory. *American Psychologist, 44*, 1185–1193.

Bouton, M. E., Nelson, J. B., & Rosas, J. M. (1999). Stimulus generation, context change, and forgetting. *Psychological Bulletin, 125*, 171–186.

Eich, E. (1995). Searching for mood dependent memory. *Psychological Science, 6*, 67–75.

Fischhoff, B. (1977). Perceived informativeness of facts. *Journal of Experimental Psychology: Human Perception and Performance, 3*, 349–358.

Franks, J. L., Bilbrey, C. W., Lien, K. G., & McNamara, T. P. (2000). Transfer-appropriate processing (TAP) and repetition priming. *Memory & Cognition, 28*, 1140–1151.

Gardiner, J. M., & Java, R. I. (1990). Recollective experience in word and nonword recognition. *Memory & Cognition, 18*, 23–30.

Gawlick-Grendell, L. A., & Woltz, D. J. (1994). Meaning dominance norms for 120 homographs. *Behavior Research Methods, Instruments, & Computers, 26*, 5–25.

Johnson, M. K., Hashtroudi; S., & Lindsay, D. S. (1993), Source monitoring. *Psychological Bulletin, 114*, 1–28.

Joslyn, S., Loftus, E. F., McNoughton, A., & Powers, J. (2001). Memory for memory. *Memory & Cognition, 29*, 789–797.

Light, L. L., & Carter-Soboll, L. (1970). Effects of changed semantic context on recognition memory. *Journal of Verbal Learning and Verbal Behavior, 9*, 1–11.

Lindsay, D. S., & Read, J. D. (2001). The recovered memories controversy: Where do we go from here? In G. M. Davies & T. Dalgleish (Eds.), *Recovered memories: Seeking the middle ground* (pp. 71–94). Chichester, England: Wiley.

Martin, E. (1975). Generation-recognition theory and the encoding specificity principle. *Psychological Review, 82*, 150–153.

Padilla-Walker, L. M., & Poole, D. A. (in press). Memory for previous recall: A comparison of free and cued recall. *Applied Cognitive Psychology.*

Parks, T. E. (1999). On one aspect of the evidence for recovered memories. *American Journal of Psychology, 112*, 365–370.

Schneider, W. (1988). Micro-Experimental Laboratory: An integrated system for IBM PC Compatibles. *Behavior Research Methods, Instruments, & Computers, 20*, 206–217.

Schooler, J. W. (1999). Seeking the core: The issues and evidence surrounding recovered accounts of sexual trauma. In L. M. Williams (Ed.), *Trauma and memory* (pp. 203–216). Thousand Oaks, CA: Sage.

Schooler, J. W. (2001). Discovering memories in light of meta-awareness. *The Journal of Aggression, Maltreatment and Trauma, 4*, 105–136.

Schooler, J. W., Ambadar, Z., & Bendiksen. M. (1997). A cognitive corroborative case study approach for investigating discovered memories of sexual abuse. In J. D. Read & D. S. Lindsay (Eds.), *Recollections of trauma: Scientific evidence and clinical practice* (pp. 379–387). New York: Plenum.

Schooler, J. W., Bendiksen, M., & Ambadar, Z. (1997). Taking the middle line: Can we accommodate both fabricated and recovered memories of sexual abuse? In M. A. Conway (Ed.), *Recovered memories and false memories* (pp. 251–92). New York: Oxford University Press.

Tulving, E. (1984). Precis of elements of episodic memory. *Behavioral and Brain Sciences, 7*, 223–268.

Tulving, E., & Thomson, D. M. (1973). Encoding specificity and retrieval processes in episodic memory. *Psychological Review, 80*, 352–373.

Tulving, E., & Watkins, O. C. (1977). Recognition failure of words with a single meaning. *Memory & Cognition, 5*, 513–522.

Twilley, L. C., Dixon, P., Taylor, D., & Clark, K. (1994). University of Alberta norms of relative meaning frequency for 566 homographs. *Memory & Cognition, 22*, 111–126.

Watkins, M. J., & Watkins, O. C. (1976). Cue-overload theory and the method of interpolated attributes. *Bulletin of the Psychonomics Society, 7*, 289–291.

Whittlesea, B. W. A., & Williams, L. D. (1998). Why do strangers feel familiar, but friends don't? A discrepancy-attribution account of feelings of familiarity. *Acta Psychologica, 98*, 141–165.

The "remember/know" procedure has become a very popular assessment of memory. At its most simple level, it is really just one way of asking people to characterize their particular memory experience. Typically, subjects are given a recognition test in which they decide whether an item is old (was on the study list) or new (was not on the study list). For each item judged "old," the subjects are asked to distinguish between whether they actually "remember" the item or whether they just "know" that the item was on the study list. The difference between the judgments is that a "remember" judgment means that the subject is consciously aware of some other aspect of the episode, such as they can remember a particular thought that the word triggered, or they can remember thinking it was a coincidence that this particular word followed the previous one. A "know" judgment means that they lack this other information.

The remember/know methodology was introduced by Tulving (1985) in an article in which he discusses the relation between memory and consciousness. His purpose is to link different kinds of consciousness with different kinds of memory systems. He begins by pointing out that there has been very little research on consciousness *per se* within experimental psychology. For there to be progress, Tulving argues, scientists must not only identify different kinds of consciousness, but also come up with a way of measuring them.

Tulving distinguishes between consciousness, which is seen as a general capability of living things, and awareness, which is the internally experienced event that is caused by being conscious in a particular situation. He ties three types of consciousness to three different memory systems. The lowest level memory system is the procedural system, which has to do with the acquisition and retention of perceptual and motor skills. This type of memory is tied to anoetic consciousness, nonknowing. For example, you may be able to ride a bicycle but you are not aware of how you actually do this.

The middle level is semantic memory, which is the system that stores permanent knowledge. A better term is generic memory, because this type of information need not be semantic. Your knowledge that George Washington was the first president of the United States is retained in semantic memory. The type of consciousness associated with semantic memory is noetic or knowing. The idea is that you are aware that you know this information, but you have no awareness of how or when you acquired it.

The final level is episodic memory, which is the system that handles personally experienced events or episodes. The difference between episodic memory and semantic memory is that the former implies awareness of not just the bare fact, but also other aspects. For example, consider the following (purposefully obscure) statement: "Abraham Lincoln's first vice president was Hannibal Hamlin." If, later on, someone asks you, "Who was Abraham Lincoln's first vice president?", you might answer with Hannibal Hamlin. If you were consciously aware that you first learned this fact while reading a page in the *CogLab Reader*, then you would be aware of additional information about the learning episode. You would have autonoetic consciousness: You would be aware of your relation to the actual event. Note that it is not the type of information that distinguishes between semantic and episodic memory (i.e., facts about political figures can be in either system), but rather the type of awareness.

After discussing a compelling case study, Tulving considers how various levels of autonoetic consciousness could arise from information recalled from a mix of episodic and semantic memory. An unusual term here is *ecphory*, which refers to the process that combines the information in the retrieval cue with the information from the study phase.

Tulving introduces what has become known as the remember/know test and presents two experiments in which different types or amounts of consciousness are associated with different conditions. In general, the prediction is that as the richness of episodic information decreases, the proportion of remember judgments should also decrease.

In the first experiment, subjects studied pairs of words in which the second word was a member of the category indicated by the first word, such as musical instrument–viola. The subjects then received a standard free recall test, followed by a cued-recall test with the category name as a cue, and finally a cued-recall test with the category name as a cue plus the first letter of the target item. The tests differ in the amount of retrieval information provided and in the richness of the episodic information. The proportion of remember judgments decreased as the amount of episodic information decreased. Experiment 2 used only a recognition test, but manipulated the delay between study and test. The idea is that the longer the delay, the worse the episodic information. The proportion of remember judgments decreased with increasing retention interval, relative to overall recognition performance.

The CogLab demo is based on experiments reported by Gardiner (1988) and Rajaram (1993). You are asked to process half of the items deeply, by coming up with a synonym, and half of the items in a more shallow way, by coming up with a rhyme. The prediction is that there will be more remember than know judgments for the deep, semantic task because that process provides a richer episodic experience. In contrast, there will be either no difference or slightly more know than remember judgments for the shallow condition.

It is important to keep in mind that a decrease in remember judgments does not necessarily mean that there is a decrease in overall memory performance. As the proportion of remember judgments decreases, the proportion of know judgments can increase. It is also important to note that confidence is not necessarily related to remember/know judgments. Rajaram, for example, found that subjects could be just as confident that an item had been on the list regardless of whether they subsequently gave the item a remember judgment or a know judgment.

REFERENCES

Gardiner, J. M. (1988). Functional aspects of recollective experience. *Memory & Cognition, 16,* 309–313.

Rajaram, S. (1993). Remembering and knowing: Two means of access to the personal past. *Memory & Cognition, 21,* 89–102.

Yonelinas, A. P. (2002). The nature of recollection and familiarity: A review of 30 years of research. *Journal of Memory and Language, 46,* 441–517.

QUESTIONS

1. What differentiates procedural memory, semantic memory, and episodic memory?
2. What distinguishes autonoetic, noetic, and anoetic consciousness?
3. Why is it important that in Rajaram's (1993) study, subjects were equally confident for items given a remember judgment as items given a know judgment?
4. What other experimental manipulation should produce differences in the proportion of remember/know judgments?

Memory and Consciousness

Endel Tulving
University of Toronto

ABSTRACT

Speculations supported by empirical observations are offered concerning different memory systems (procedural, semantic, and episodic) and corresponding varieties of consciousness (anoetic, noetic, and autonoetic), with special emphasis on episodic memory and autonoetic consciousness as its necessary correlate. Evidence relevant to these speculations is derived from a case study of an amnesic patient who is conscious in some ways but not in others, as well as from simple experiments on recall and recognition by normal subjects. Autonoetic (self-knowing) consciousness is the name given to the kind of consciousness that mediates an individual's awareness of his or her existence and identity in subjective time extending from the personal past through the present to the personal future. It provides the characteristic phenomenal flavour of the experience of remembering. The extent to which autonoetic consciousness is engaged in recall and recognition of word-events was measured in two demonstration experiments whose results were systematically related to the conditions under which the recovery of knowledge about the events was observed.

Of all the mysteries of nature, none is greater than that of human consciousness. Intimately familiar to all of us, our capacity to contemplate the universe and to apprehend the infinity of space and time, and our knowledge that we can do so, have continued to resist analysis and elude understanding.

After its banishment as an epiphenomenon by behaviouristic psychology, consciousness has recently again been declared to be the central problem of psychology (Hilgard, 1980; Miller, 1980; Neisser, 1979). A few psychologists have taken up the challenge posed by the many problems of consciousness, but contemporary psychology at large has continued to overlook this uniquely human property of the human mind.

Nowhere is the benign neglect of consciousness more conspicuous than in the study of human memory. One can read article after article on memory, or consult book after book, without encountering the term "consciousness." Such a state of affairs must be regarded as rather curious. One might think that memory should have something to do with remembering, and remembering *is* a conscious experience. To remember an event means to be consciously aware now of something that happened on an earlier occasion. Nevertheless, through most of its history, including the current heyday of cognitive psychology, the psychological study of memory has largely proceeded without reference to the existence of conscious awareness in remembering.

The literature on consciousness is rich, with many contributions by philosophers (e.g., Dennett, 1969), psychologists (e.g., Gray, 1971; Mandler, 1975; Natsoulas, 1978, 1981; Posner & Klein, 1973; Shallice, 1972; Underwood, 1982; Underwood & Stevens, 1979, 1981), neuroscientists (e.g., Eccles, 1977; Sperry, 1969), and others (e.g., Globus, Maxwell, & Savodnik, 1976; Griffin, 1976, 1984; Josephson & Ramachandran, 1980). But much of it consists of "epistemological, metaphysical, and existential" theorizing—to borrow the apt phrase from Peter Dodwell (1975)—without corresponding empirical facts. Even when attempts are made to relate consciousness to the activity of the brain, the situation is not much better, as observed by Gazzaniga and LeDoux: "When the inevitable topic of consciousness is approached in the light of modern brain research, the experienced student has come to brace himself for the mellifluous intonations of someone's personal experience and ideas on the matter, as opposed to data" (1978, p. 141).

The psychological literature relevant to the problem of the relation between memory and consciousness differs from the larger literature on consciousness by the dearth of both ideas and facts. There has been little apart from the idea that primary memory can be identified with consciousness (e.g., Craik & Jacoby, 1975; James, 1890), the idea that rehearsal of information in primary memory is a conscious process (e.g., Atkinson & Shiffrin, 1971; Wickelgren, 1977), and the idea that latent memory traces are unconscious, whereas activated ones are conscious (e.g., Underwood, 1979). And just about the only facts concerning memory and consciousness come from shadowing experiments in which the level of conscious awareness of to-be-tested materials has been manipulated (e.g., Eich, 1984; Moray, 1959; Norman, 1969).

The present paper describes an attempt to relate memory to consciousness in terms of data obtained through clinical observation and laboratory experiment. Its basic pre-theoretical assumption is that progress in the scientific understanding of consciousness—as against its epistemological, metaphysical, or experiential understanding—requires not only the postulation and identification of different *kinds* of consciousness but also their *measurement* as an aspect of experience, or as a dependent variable.

The paper consists of six parts. First, a hypothetical scheme is described in which different varieties of memory are related to different varieties of consciousness. Second, clinical observations from a case study, together with relevant evidence and ideas from other sources, are used to describe and characterize a particular kind of consciousness and conscious awareness, referred to as autonoetic (self-knowing) consciousness. Third, the concept of autonoetic conscious awareness is further elaborated. In the fourth part, autonoetic consciousness is related to the synergistic ecphory model of recall and recognition (Tulving, 1982, 1983). In the fifth part, two demonstration experiments are described in which autonoetic awareness was measured and shown to vary systematically with conditions under which recall and recognition

were observed. Finally, the question of the biological utility of episodic memory and autonoetic consciousness is briefly discussed.[1]

VARIETIES OF MEMORY AND CONSCIOUSNESS

Let us assume that there are three different kinds of memory, or three memory systems: procedural, semantic, and episodic (Tulving, 1983). They are alike in that they all make possible the utilization of acquired and retained knowledge. But they differ in the kind of knowledge that they handle, and in the ways in which different kinds of knowledge are acquired or used.

Procedural memory (Anderson, 1976; Tulving, 1983; Winograd, 1975) is concerned with how things are done—with the acquisition, retention, and utilization of perceptual, cognitive, and motor skills. Semantic memory—also called generic (Hintzman, 1978) or categorical memory (Estes, 1976)—has to do with the symbolically representable knowledge that organisms possess about the world. Episodic memory mediates the *remembering* of personally experienced events (Tulving, 1972, 1983).

Ideas about the relations between the three systems have varied. Not too long ago (Tulving, 1983), I thought of the three systems as representing two different levels in a hierarchy: memory as a whole subdivided into two general types, procedural and propositional, with episodic and semantic constituting two *parallel*, albeit interacting and overlapping, subsystems of propositional memory. Recently, however, I was led by a number of critics to the view that a more reasonable assumption concerning the relation between the episodic and semantic system is one according to which episodic memory constitutes a single distinct subsystem of semantic memory (Tulving, 1984).

It seems reasonable to extend this idea to cover all three systems and to assume that they constitute a class-inclusion hierarchy in which procedural memory entails semantic memory as a *specialized* subcategory, and in which semantic memory, in turn, entails episodic memory as a specialized subcategory. According to this scheme, it is impossible for an organism to possess episodic memory without the corresponding semantic memory, and impossible for it to possess semantic memory without the corresponding proce-

TABLE 23.1 A Schematic Diagram of the Relations between Memory Systems and Varieties of Consciousness

Memory System		Consciousness
Episodic	↔	Autonoetic
↓		↓
Semantic	⟨⟩	Noetic
↓		↓
Procedural	⟨⟩	Anoetic

dural memory, although semantic memory systems can exist independently of episodic systems, and procedural systems independently of semantic systems.

Each of the three memory systems, in addition to other ways in which it differs from others, is characterized by a different kind of consciousness. I will refer to the three kinds of consciousness as anoetic (non-knowing), noetic (knowing), and autonoetic (self-knowing). Their relation to each other and to the three memory systems is schematically depicted in Table 23.1.[2]

The procedural memory system is characterized by anoetic consciousness. Anoetic consciousness is temporally and spatially bound to the current situation. Organisms possessing only anoetic consciousness are conscious in the sense that they are capable of perceptually registering, internally representing, and behaviourally responding to aspects of the present environment, both external and internal. Anoetic consciousness does not include any reference to non-present extraorganismic stimuli and states of the world.

Semantic memory is characterized by noetic consciousness. Noetic consciousness allows an organism to be aware of, and to cognitively operate on, objects and events, and relations among objects and events, in the absence of these objects and events. The organism can flexibly act upon such symbolic knowledge of the world. Entering information into, and retrieval of information from, semantic memory is accompanied by noetic consciousness.

Of special interest in the present paper is autonoetic consciousness, correlated with episodic memory. It is necessary for the remembering of personally experienced events. When a person remembers such an event, he is aware of the event as a veridical part of his own past existence. It is autonoetic consciousness that confers the special phenomenal flavour to the remem-

bering of past events, the flavour that distinguishes remembering from other kinds of awareness, such as those characterizing perceiving, thinking, imagining, or dreaming.

Evidence for autonoetic consciousness will be drawn from clinical observations of an amnesic patient, to be described presently. The distinction between the other two kinds of consciousness is based on conjecture. But it is not without precedent. Consider, for instance, a classification of different kinds of memory proposed by Hermann Ebbinghaus, who is usually thought of as the inventor of the nonsense syllable and as responsible for psychology's long preoccupation with rote learning. Ebbinghaus distinguished between three kinds of effects of "mental states which were at one time present in consciousness and then have disappeared from it" (1885, p. 1). In the first place, he suggested, we call back into consciousness a seemingly lost state that is then "immediately recognised as something formerly experienced" (1885, p. 1). that is, we *remember*. In the second case—Ebbinghaus said it occurs when we reproduce a mental state "involuntarily"—this accompanying consciousness may be lacking and "we know only indirectly that the 'now' is identical with the 'then'" (1885, p. 2). In the third case, earlier processes leave consequences or effects that facilitate "the occurrence and progress of similar processes," though these effects "remain concealed from consciousness" (1885, p. 2). Ebbinghaus's first case can be thought to correspond to autonoetic, the second to noetic, and the third to anoetic consciousness.

A MAN WITHOUT AUTONOETIC CONSCIOUSNESS: A CASE STUDY

Evidence pertinent to autonoetic consciousness comes from a case study of an amnesic patient whom I and my colleague, Daniel Schacter, have been observing at our Unit for Memory Disorders in Toronto. This young man, here referred to as N.N., suffered a closed head injury a few years ago as a result of a traffic accident.

N.N.'s amnesia for personal events is profound. It covers the time both before and after his accident. When he is distracted, he forgets something said to him almost immediately. Although his immediate memory span is eight digits, on a picture-memory recognition test on which normal subjects score 60 to 70% correct, his score is zero. On a cued-recall test of categorized words, he does not distinguish between correct responses and category intrusions. Although he knows a few things about his past—for instance, what year the family moved into the house where they live now, the names of the schools he went to, or where he spent his summers in his teens—he cannot recall a single event or incident from the past. Like the patient S.S. described by Cermak and O'Connor (1983), N.N.'s knowledge of his own past seems to have the same impersonal experiential quality as his knowledge of the rest of the world.

His language skills and general knowledge are relatively intact. He can define words such as "evasive," "perimeter," and "tangible"; he can provide a reasonably good verbal description of the "script" of going to a restaurant or making a long-distance telephone call; he can describe the typical daily activities of a university student; he knows what the North American continent and the Statue of Liberty look like, and can draw their outlines. He also knows the meaning of the term "consciousness." When asked what consciousness is, he says, "It's being aware of who we are and what we are, and where we are."

N.N. has no difficulty with the concept of chronological time. He knows the units of time and their relations perfectly well and he can accurately represent chronological time graphically. But in stark contrast to his abstract knowledge of time, his awareness of subjective time seems to be severely impaired. When asked what he did before coming to where he is now, or what he did the day before, he says that he does not know. When asked what he will be doing when he leaves "here," or what he will be doing "tomorrow," he says he does not know.

Here is part of the transcript of an interview, with me as the interviewer:

E.T: "Let's try the question again about the future. What will you be doing tomorrow?"

(There is a 15-second pause.)

N.N. smiles faintly, then says, "I don't know."

E.T: "Do you remember the question?"

N.N.: "About what I'll be doing tomorrow?"

E.T: "Yes. How would you describe your state of mind when you try to think about it?"

(A 5-second pause.)

N.N.: "Blank, I guess."

When asked, on different occasions, to describe the "blankness" that characterizes his state of mind when he tries to think about "tomorrow," he says that it is "like being asleep" or that "it's a big blankness sort of thing." When asked to give an analogy, to describe what it is like, he says, "It's like being in a room with nothing there and having a guy tell you to go find a chair, and there's nothing there." On another occasion he says, "It's like swimming in the middle of a lake. There's nothing there to hold you up or do anything with." When asked to compare his state of mind when he is trying to think about what he will be doing tomorrow with his state of mind when he thinks about what he did yesterday, he says it is the *same kind of blankness.* N.N. makes all these observations calmly and serenely, without showing any emotion. Only when he is asked whether he is not surprised that there is "nothing there" when he tries to think about yesterday or tomorrow, does he display slight agitation for a moment and utter a soft exclamation of "Wow!"

N.N. clearly is conscious and he clearly has a good deal of preserved memory capability. At the same time his consciousness and memory are severely impaired, and impaired highly selectively. He knows many things about the world, he is aware of this knowledge, and he can express it relatively flexibly. In this sense he is not greatly different from a normal adult. But he seems to have no capability of experiencing extended subjective time, or chronognosia (Bouman & Grunbaum, 1929): [E]ven if he feels that he has a personal identity, it does not include the past or the future, he cannot remember any particular episodes from his life, nor can he imagine anything that he is likely to do on a subsequent occasion. He seems to be living in a "permanent present." In terms of the threefold classification of consciousness proposed here, we could say that N.N. possesses both anoetic and noetic consciousness but not autonoetic consciousness, and that his procedural and semantic memory systems are relatively unimpaired whereas his episodic memory is severely damaged.

We must obviously be very cautious when we generalize from observations of individual cases, particularly since no two amnesic patients are ever exactly alike. Nevertheless, it is reasonable to believe that N.N.

does not represent an isolated occurrence of a severe impairment in the ability to apprehend and contemplate extended subjective time. His case tells us that amnesia can be characterized as a derangement of consciousness and not just a derangement of memory for past events.

AUTONOETIC CONSCIOUSNESS, SUBJECTIVE TIME, AND EPISODIC MEMORY

Students of amnesia have noted before that some amnesic patients live in a "permanent present" (e.g., Barbizet, 1970, p. 33). The context of the discussion of relevant cases usually implies that such patients are unaware of their *past*. But writers on amnesia have sometimes pointed out that because the patients cannot utilize the past, their future too must remain hazy, vague, and confused, leaving them "marooned in the moment" (e.g., Lidz, 1942, p. 596). Our observations of N.N. corroborate the idea that the lack of conscious awareness of personal time encompasses both the past and the future. A normal healthy person who possesses autonoetic consciousness is capable of becoming aware of her own past as well as her own future; she is capable of mental time travel, roaming at will over what has happened as readily as over what might happen, independently of physical laws that govern the universe. N.N. seems to be completely incapable of doing so. It is this fact that provides the basis for the conclusion that he is severely or completely lacking in autonoetic consciousness.

David Ingvar has measured regional cerebral blood flow in normal people in a resting state, and has observed a "hyperfrontal" pattern of cortical activation (Ingvar, 1979). He has interpreted such hyperfrontality as reflecting properties of a consciousness that embraces the past, the present, and the future: "On the basis of previous experiences, represented in memories, the brain—one's mind—is automatically busy with extrapolation of future events and, as it appears, constructing alternative hypothetical behaviour patterns in order to be ready for what may happen" (Ingvar, 1979, p. 21). Ingvar has also suggested that the frontal lobes constitute the anatomical basis for people's "memory for the future" (Ingvar, personal communication; see also Ingvar, 1983). It seems reasonable to assume, however, that the kind of consciousness that Ingvar is concerned with is more like autonoetic consciousness than consciousness at large.

The lessons learned from N.N. and the ideas suggested by Ingvar make it possible to speculate about the general nature of autonoetic consciousness and to make up a tentative list of its properties. A summary of these properties is as follows:

1. Encompasses personal time: past and future
2. Necessary component of remembering of events
3. Appears late in development
4. Selectively impaired or lost in brain damage
5. Varies across individuals and situations
6. Can be measured

We have already discussed the first idea: [A]utonoetic consciousness encompasses extended subjective time, an individual's ability to apprehend her personal past and future. Although N.N. is conscious in many ways, he does not perceive the present moment as a continuation of his own past and as a prelude to his future. N.N. is like one of Jaynes's bicameral men, who did not have feelings of personal identity in our sense and "who could not reminisce because they were not fully conscious" (Jaynes, 1976, p. 371).

The second suggestion is that autonoetic consciousness is a *necessary correlate* of episodic memory. According to the scheme I am describing, there is no such thing as "remembering without awareness" (cf. Eich, 1984; Jacoby & Witherspoon, 1982; Masson, 1984). Organisms can behave and learn without (autonoetic) awareness, but they cannot *remember* without awareness. Nor can nonliving matter remember anything, even if it can act upon previously stored information (e.g., Robinson, 1976). Like many other amnesic patients described in the literature who can acquire a variety of new skills (Cohen & Squire, 1980; Moscovitch, 1982; Parkin, 1982), N.N. shows normal learning of the kind referred to as priming effects in word-fragment completion (Schacter, 1984; Tulving, Schacter, & Stark, 1982). He can also learn new words, and new meanings of old words, although at a rather slow rate, as shown in ongoing research conducted by Elizabeth Glisky at the Unit for Memory Disorders. But he does not seem to be able to remember anything.

Third, autonoetic consciousness appears later in an individual's development than do other forms of consciousness (e.g., Knapp, 1976). Many writers have suggested that very young children have neither episodic memory nor (autonoetic) consciousness (e.g., MacCurdy, 1928; Neisser, 1978; Nelson & Gruendel, 1981). Nelson and Gruendel's observations are representative: "There is no evidence that the young child who remembers an episode remembers it as having taken place at a particular time in a particular temporal context—that is, that it constitutes an autobiographical memory of the type that older children and adults can draw on" (1981, p. 149). And Neisser has suggested that a young child may be conscious of an object when he perceives it, but "he is not aware that he, a person with a particular history and character and probable future," is seeing the object (1978, p. 172). Every young child is an extremely capable learner: [H]er behaviour and experiences can have readily identifiable consequences for her future behaviour and experiences. Yet she need not have any (autonoetic) conscious awareness as to the origin of these consequences: [T]here need be no remembering (Lockhart, 1984; Schacter & Moscovitch, 1984). As episodic memory follows semantic memory in normal development (Kinsbourne & Wood, 1975), so autonoetic consciousness emerges from noetic consciousness.

The fourth property of autonoetic consciousness is its selective dependence on particular brain processes: [T]he case of N.N. shows that certain kinds of brain damage may result in its impairment, or loss, without comparable impairment in other forms of consciousness. Correlation with brain mechanisms must be regarded as one of the more important criteria for distinguishing between different kinds of consciousness. If such correlations did not exist, and if differential impairment of different kinds of consciousness had never been observed, classification of consciousness into distinct varieties would remain yet another metaphysical exercise.

The fifth property of autonoetic consciousness concerns its variability among individuals and its variable occurrence in different situations (e.g., Roth, 1980). Individuals presumably vary in the extent to which they "possess" and benefit from autonoetic consciousness in their daily activities, as they vary with respect to other mental characteristics. Similarly, autonoetic consciousness can be expected to vary systematically with the conditions under which it is observed.

Finally, autonoetic consciousness is measurable. Although perhaps a trite point in some ways, it is worth making because of the current state of research on consciousness. If it were not possible to make quantitative statements about autonoetic consciousness, its usefulness as a scientific concept would be greatly diminished.

RECOVERY OF KNOWLEDGE ABOUT PAST EVENTS

I have argued that N.N. possesses neither episodic memory nor autonoetic consciousness. Yet it is a fact that he can make veridical statements about his past. The resolution of this apparent contradiction between the argument and the fact lies in the assumption that people can have and can express knowledge about things that have happened to them even if they can rely only on their semantic memory (Schacter, Harbluk, & McLachlan, 1984; Schacter & Tulving, 1982). That is, even when a person does not *remember* an event, she may *know* something about it. Such knowledge is created in the same way, and it is of the same quality, as the knowledge about the temporally and spatially extended world and its abstract features existing independently of the person.

If it is possible to recover knowledge about past events from either the episodic system or the semantic system, then the phenomenal experience that accompanies the recovery of such information may be one of remembering (autonoetic awareness) or knowing (noetic awareness), or a mixture of the two. It follows, then, that one way of measuring autonoetic awareness could take the form of asking people, when they recall or recognize a previously encountered item, whether they *remember* the event or whether they *know* in some other way that it occurred. The probability of the "remember" judgement can serve as an index of the extent to which autonoetic consciousness is involved in recovery of knowledge about past' events in a particular situation.

Different situations in which autonoetic consciousness can be expected to vary and where its mea-

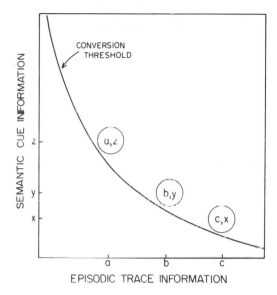

FIGURE 23.1 Schematic diagram of the synergistic ecphory model of retrieval

surement may be informative can be specified in terms of the synergistic ecphory model of recall and recognition (Tulving, 1982, 1983). The central assumption of the model is that both the general nature and specific characteristics of recollective experience (the phenomenal experience of remembering a past event) are determined jointly by episodic and semantic information. A schematic representation of the model is shown in Figure 23.1. The horizontal axis of the coordinate system represents episodic trace information, the vertical axis represents semantic retrieval information, and the two-dimensional space defined by the two axes represents so-called ecphoric information. It is this ecphoric information, an amalgam of episodic and semantic information, that determines the general nature as well as specific content of recollective experience.

The curved line in the diagram represents the *conversion threshold* for a particular level of overt behaviour that serves as an indicant of the rememberer's mental state. This overt behaviour, or memory *performance*, can take different forms. One such form, for instance, is recall of the name of a previously observed event. Another one is recognition, such as identification of a test item as "old." Each type of performance has its own conversion threshold, although

only one is shown in Figure 23.1. The conversion threshold divides the space of ecphoric information into two regions. Ecphoric information above the threshold is sufficient for the required performance, whereas that below the threshold is not.

The model shows how overt memory performance can be supported by different combinations of episodic trace information and semantic retrieval information. A trade-off relation exists between these two kinds of information such that impoverished episodic traces can be compensated for by richer retrieval cues, and vice versa. From the hypothesized correlation between episodic memory and autonoetic consciousness it follows that the kind of conscious awareness that characterizes an act of recollection varies with the nature of the "mix" of trace and cue information—that is, with the location of the bundle of ecphoric information in the sketch in Figure 23.1.

That the three bundles of ecphoric information designated as *a,z*, *b,y*, and *c,x*, representing combinations of corresponding bundles of trace information (*A, B, C*) and retrieval information (*X, Y, Z*), are all above the conversion threshold indicates that the behavioural response (e.g., correct recall) would be equally possible in all three cases. Yet, according to the logic outlined here, the recollective experience underlying or accompanying memory performance corresponding to ecphoric information *c,x* would be expected to be characterized by a greater degree of autonoetic consciousness than *b,y*, which in turn would be expected to represent a greater degree of autonoetic consciousness than *a,z*.

MEASUREMENT OF AUTONOETIC CONSCIOUSNESS

We will next discuss two experiments in which (a) situations were created corresponding to different points above the conversion threshold in the ecphoric space of Figure 23.1, and (b) autonoetic conscious awareness accompanying retrieval in these different situations was assessed.

In the first experiment, 79 university students heard, on a single presentation trial, a list of 27 category names and single category instances (e.g., *musical instrument*—VIOLA; *a fruit*—PEAR). The students' memory performance was subsequent tested in

TABLE 23.2   Recall And "Remember" Judgements in Experiment 1

	Free Recall	Category Recall	Letter Recall
Probability of recall	.51	.35	.10
Probability of recall conditionalized on remaining items	(.51)	.54	.74
Probability of "remember" judgement	.88	.75	.48

three successive tests that yielded three sets of recalled items. The first test was a free-recall test: [S]ubjects were asked to recall as many instances as they could, in any order. The second was a cued-recall test: [N]ames of categories to which the studied instances belonged were given as specific retrieval cues. The third was a cued-recall test: [T]he initial letter of each category instance was given as a cue in addition to the name of the category to which the word belonged.

The logic here is as follows: The ecphoric information (mixture of trace and cue information) of the first set of items, those recalled in *free* recall, corresponds to the ecphoric bundle *c,x* in Figure 23.1: relatively rich episodic trace information combined with relatively impoverished retrieval information. The ecphoric information of the second set of items, those recalled in the category-cued recall *but not recalled in free recall*, corresponds to the ecphoric bundle *b,y* in Figure 23.1: richer retrieval information combined with poorer trace information. The trace information of the second set of items can be assumed to be of lower quality than that of the first set because otherwise these items too would have been accessible for retrieval in free recall. Extending the same logic to the third set of items, those recalled to category names and initial letters, *but not recalled in the other two tests*, we can think of ecphoric information of these items as represented by the bundle *a,z* in Figure 23.1: rather plentiful retrieval information combined with relatively impoverished trace information.

The extent to which subjects' recollective experience was characterized by autonoetic awareness for the three sets of items was assessed by asking subjects, in each of the three tests, to indicate, for each item they recalled, whether they actually "remembered" its occurrence in the list or whether they simply "knew" on some other basis that the item was a member of the study list. The proportion of recalled items for which subjects made "remember" judgements was calculated

separately for the three sets of recalled items, and taken as an estimate of the presence of autonoetic awareness in recollection. The expectation was that the proportion of "remember" judgements would be greatest for free-recall items, next highest for items recalled in response to category names but not previously recalled in free recall, and lowest for items recalled only in response to both category names and initial-letter cues.

The results of the first experiment are summarized in Table 23.2. The three sets of recalled items—those given in free recall, those given in category-cued recall but not in free recall, and those given in the category- and initial-letter cued condition but not in the other two conditions—are designated as free-recall items, category-recall items, and letter-recall items in Table 23.2.

Three descriptive statistics were calculated for each of the three sets of recalled items: (a) proportion of items in the set, (b) this proportion expressed with respect to the items *remaining* to be recalled after the first, or the second, test, and (c) the mean proportion of the items in the set that were judged as having been "remembered" by the subjects. The important data for our present purposes are given by the latter measures.

As Table 23.2 shows, the proportion of "remembered" items was highest for free-recall, next highest for category-recall, and lowest for letter-recall items. These data suggest that the involvement of autonoetic consciousness in recall of past events varies directly with the contribution of the episodic (trace) information to ecphoric information on which recall is based.

The second experiment can be summarized briefly, since its logic was very much the same as that used in the first experiment. "Remember" and "know" judgements were collected from a small group of 10 subjects in two recognition tests, one (for half the items) given in the same experimental session in which 36 to-be-remembered words were presented for study,

TABLE 23.3 Recognition Data and "Remember" Judgements in Experiment 2

Test Items	Measure	Test	
		Day 1	Day 8
Old	Hit rate	.86	.62
	p("remembered")	.83	.55
New	FA rate	.17	.27
	p("remembered")	.45	.40

TABLE 23.4 Distributions of Confidence Judgements for Items Judged "Remembered" and Items Judged "Known" in Experiment 2

Recognized Items	Confidence Judgements			
	1	2	3	Mean
"Remembered"	9	40	143	2.74
"Known"	25	63	35	2.08

the other (for the other half) given 7 days later. The logic here is based on the assumption that the episodic trace information would be reduced in "richness" over the 7-day retention interval, with corresponding decreases in autonoetic awareness, and that, therefore, bundles of ecphoric information underlying recognized items would be more heavily weighted with semantic retrieval information after the longer than after the shorter retention interval. Thus, the expectation was that the proportion of "remember" judgements would decline with the retention interval.

As the data summarized in Table 23.3 show, these expectations were borne out: With the hit rates decreased and the false-alarm rate increased over the 7-day retention interval, the proportion of "remember" judgements for correctly recognized words was lower on Day 8 than on Day 1. We conclude that autonoetic conscious awareness is more clearly present in the recollection of recently encountered events than in that of events encountered a longer time ago.

In the second experiment we also collected conventional confidence judgements from the subjects. As shown in Table 23.4, in which the data for "old" test items are pooled over both short and long retention intervals, there was a tendency for subjects to be more confident about their recognition of those items that they classified as "remembered" than those classified as "known": a positive correlation between confidence and "remember" judgements.

ADAPTIVE VALUE OF AUTONOETIC CONSCIOUSNESS

The results of the two experiments have shown that the distinction between "knowing" and "remembering" previous occurrences of particular events is meaningful to people, that people can make corre-

sponding judgements about their memory performance, and that these judgements vary systematically with conditions under which retrieval of information takes place. The success of the experiments in conforming to the expectations derived from the hypothesized correlation between episodic memory and autonoetic consciousness, and from the synergistic ecphory model, provides support for the assumption that people can retrieve information about personally experienced events without autonoetic "remembering" of the event, simply on the basis of their noetic "knowledge" that the event happened. A new problem arises, however. If recovery of information about past events can occur independently of episodic memory and autonoetic consciousness, why should the episodic system and autonoetic consciousness have emerged at all in the course of evolution? Wherein lies their adaptive advantage?

One possible answer to this question, supported by the data showing positive correlation between confidence ratings and "remember" judgements in our second experiment, is that the adaptive value of episodic memory and autonoetic consciousness lies in the heightened subjective certainty with which organisms endowed with such memory and consciousness believe, and are willing to act upon, information retrieved from memory. Knowledge about environmental regularities certainly has adaptive value. By enhancing the perceived orderliness of an organism's universe, episodic memory and autonoetic consciousness lead to more decisive action in the present and more effective planning for the future (cf. Griffin, 1976; Lachman & Naus, 1984). In this connection, it is worth noting that amnesia has been frequently characterized by the patients' lack of subjective certainty about the mnemonic knowledge that they do in fact possess (e.g., Lidz, 1942; Talland, 1965; Weiskrantz, 1978).

We have often been told that the human brain is the most complicated piece of matter in the universe. We could also say that human consciousness is the most enigmatic manifestation of this piece of matter. Understanding consciousness, its emergence from the brain and its role in human intelligence and in human affairs, can only come, if it ever does come, at the end of a very long scientific journey. What I have tried to do in this paper is to discuss some of the steps with which the journey might begin. . . .

AUTHOR NOTES

This article is a somewhat modified version of an invited paper presented at the meeting of the Canadian Psychological Association, Ottawa, June 1984, in connection with the 1983 CPA Award for Distinguished Contributions to Canadian Psychology as a Science.

Research reported in the article has been supported by the Natural Sciences and Engineering Research Council, Grant No. A8632, and by a Special Research Program Grant from the Connaught Fund, University of Toronto.

The author is grateful for collaboration to Janine Law and Daniel Schacter.

Requests for reprints should be sent to Endel Tulving, Department of Psychology, University of Toronto, Toronto, Ontario M5S 1Al.

ENDNOTES

1. Although the terms "consciousness" and "conscious awareness" (or simply "awareness") are closely related and sometimes used interchangeably, in the present discussion they are used in different senses. "Consciousness" refers to a particular capability of living systems whereas "awareness" refers to the internally experienced outcome of exercising this ability in a particular situation. (Another closely related term, "attention," even though not used in this paper, would refer to the control that the organism, or environmental events, can exert over the direction of consciousness in the selection of "contents" of awareness.)
2. The terms "anoetic consciousness" (Vol. 1, p. 50) and "noetic consciousness" (Vol. 2, p. 11) have been used by Stout (1896) in somewhat different, but related, senses from those used here.

REFERENCES

Anderson, J. R. (1976). *Language, memory, and thought.* Hillsdale, N.J.: Erlbaum.

Atkinson, R. C., & Shiffrin, R. M. (1971). The control of short-term memory. *Scientific American, 225,* 82–90.

Barbizet, J. (1970). *Human memory and its pathology.* San Francisco: Freeman.

Bouman, L., & Grunbaum, A. A. (1929). Einè Störung der Chronognosie und ihre Bedeutung in dem betreffenden Symptomenbild [A disturbance of chronognosia and its meaning in the corresponding syndrome]. *Monatsschrift für Psychiatrie and Neurologie, 73,* 1–40.

Cermak, L. S., & O'Connor, M. (1983). The anterograde and retrograde retrieval ability of a patient with amnesia due to encephalitis. *Neuropsychologia, 21,* 213–234.

Cohen, N. J., & Squire, L. R. (1980). Preserved learning and retention of pattern analyzing skill in amnesia: Dissociation of knowing how and knowing that. *Science, 210,* 207–209.

Craik, F. I. M., & Jacoby, L. L. (1975). A process view of short-term retention. In F. Restle (Ed.), *Cognitive theory* (Vol. 1). Potomac, MD: Erlbaum.

Dennett, D. C. (1969). *Content and consciousness.* New York: Humanities Press.

Dodwell, P. C. (1975). Contemporary theoretical problems in seeing. In E. C. Carterette & M. P. Friedman (Eds.), *Handbook of perception* (Vol. 5). New York: Academic Press.

Ebbinghaus, H. (1885). *Über das Gedächtnis* [On memory]. Leipzig: Duncker and Humblot. (English translation, New York: Dover Press).

Eccles, J. C. (1977). *The understanding of the brain* (2nd ed.). New York: McGraw Hill.

Eccles, J. C. (1980). *The human psyche.* Berlin, Germany: Springer Verlag.

Eich, E. (1984). Memory for unattended events: Remembering with and without awareness. *Memory and Cognition, 12,* 105–111.

Estes, W. K. (1976). The cognitive side of probability learning. *Psychological Review, 83,* 37–64.

Gazzaniga, M. S., & LeDoux, J. E. (1978). *The integrated mind.* New York: Plenum.

Globus, G. G., Maxwell, G., & Savodnik, I. (Eds.). (1976). *Consciousness and the brain.* New York: Plenum.

Gray, J. A. (1971). The mind-brain identity theory as a scientific hypothesis. *Philosophical Quarterly, 21,* 247–252.

Griffin, D. (1976). *The question of animal awareness.* New York: Rockefeller University Press.

Griffin, D. (1984). *Animal thinking.* Cambridge, MA: Harvard University Press.

Hilgard, E. R. (1977). *Divided consciousness: Multiple controls in human thought.* New York: Wiley.

Hilgard, E. R. (1980). Consciousness in contemporary psychology. *Annual Review of Psychology, 31,* 1–26.

Hintzman, D. L. (1978). *The psychology of learning and memory.* San Francisco: Freeman.

Ingvar, D. (1979). "Hyperfrontal" distribution of the general grey matter flow in resting wakefulness; on the functional anatomy of the conscious state. *Acta Neurologica Scandinavica, 60,* 12–25.

Ingvar, D. (1983). Hjärnan, tiden och metvetandet [Brain, time and consciousness]. *Forskning och Framsteg, 39–45.*

Jacoby, L. L., & Witherspoon, D. (1982). Remembering without awareness. *Canadian Journal of Psychology, 36,* 300–324.

James, W. (1890). *Principles of psychology.* New York: Holt.

Jaynes, J. (1976). *The origin of consciousness in the breakdown of the bicameral mind.* Boston: Houghton Mifflin.

Josephson, B. D., & Ramachandran. V. S. (Eds.). (1980). *Consciousness and the physical world.* Oxford: Pergamon.

Kinsbourne, M., & Wood, R. (1975). Short-term memory processes and the amnesic syndrome. In D. Deutsch & J. A. Deutsch (Eds.), *Short-term memory.* New York: Academic Press.

Knapp, P. H. (1976). The mysterious "split": A clinical enquiry into problems of consciousness and brain. In G. G. Globus, G. Maxwell, & I. Savodnik (Eds.), *Consciousness and the brain.* New York: Plenum.

Kuhlenbeck, H. (1965). The concept of consciousness in neurological epistemology. In J. R. Smythies (Ed.), *Brain and mind.* London: Routledge & Kegan Paul.

Lachman, R., & Naus, M. (1984). The episodic/semantic continuum in an evolved machine. *Behavioral and Brain Sciences, 7,* 244–246.

Lidz, T. (1942). The amnestic syndrome. *Archives of Neurology and Psychiatry, 47,* 588–605.

Lockhart, R. S. (1984). What do infants remember? In M. Moscovitch (Ed.), *Infant memory.* New York: Plenum.

MacCurdy, J. T. (1928). *Common principles in psychology and physiology.* London: Cambridge University Press.

Mandler, G. (1975). Consciousness: Respectable, useful, and necessary. In R. L. Solso (Ed.), *Information processing and cognition.* Hillsdale, N.J.: Erlbaum.

Masson, M. E. J. (1984). Memory for the surface structure of sentences: Remembering with and without awareness. *Journal of Verbal Learning and Verbal Behavior, 23.*

Miller, G. A. (1980). Computation, consciousness, and cognition. *Behavioral and Brain Sciences, 3,* 146.

Moray, N. (1959). Attention in dichotic listening: Affective cues and the influence of instructions. *Quarterly Journal of Experimental Psychology, 11,* 56–60.

Moscovitch, M. (1982). Multiple dissociations of function in amnesia. In L. S. Cermak (Ed.), *Human memory and amnesia.* Hillsdale. NJ: Erlbaum.

Natsoulas, T. (1978). Consciousness. *American Psychologist, 33,* 906–914.

Natsoulas, T. (1981). Basic problems of consciousness. *Journal of Personality and Social Psychology, 41,* 132–178.

Neisser, U. (1970). Anticipations, images, and introspection. *Cognition, 6,* 169–174.

Neisser, U. (1979). Review of *Divided Consciousness* by E. R. Hilgard. *Contemporary Psychology, 24,* 99–100.

Nelson, K., & Gruendel, J. (1981). Generalized event representations: Basic building blocks of cognitive development. In M. E. Lamb & A. L. Brown (Eds.), *Advances in developmental psychology.* Hillsdale. N.J.: Erlbaum.

Norman, D. A. (1969). Memory while shadowing. *Quarterly Journal of Experimental Psychology, 21,* 85–93.

Parkin, A. (1982). Residual learning capability in organic amnesia. *Cortex, 18,* 417–440.

Posner, M. I., & Klein, R. M. (1973). On the functions of consciousness. In S. Kornblum (Ed.), *Attention and performance IV.* New York: Academic Press.

Robinson, A. L. (1976). Metallurgy: Extraordinary alloys that remember their past. *Science, 191,* 934 936.

Roth. M. (1980). Consciousness and psychopathology. In D. D. Josephson & V. S. Ramachandran (Eds.), *Consciousness and the physical world.* Oxford: Pergamon.

Schacter, D. L. (1984). *Priming of old and new knowledge in amnesic patients and normal subjects.* Annals of N.Y. Academy of Sciences.

Schacter, D. L., Harbluk, J. L., & McLachlan, D. R. (1984), Retrieval without recollection: An experimental analysis of source amnesia. *Journal of Verbal Learning and Verbal Behavior, 23.*

Schacter, D. L., & Moscovitch, M. (1984). Infants, amnesics, and dissociable memory systems. In M. Moscovitch (Ed.), *Infant memory.* New York: Plenum Press.

Schacter, D. L., & Tulving, E. (1982). Memory, amnesia, and the episodic/semantic distinction. In R. L. Isaacson & N. E. Spear (Eds.), *Expression of knowledge.* New York: Plenum.

Shallice, T. (1972). Dual functions of consciousness. *Psychological Review, 79,* 383–393.

Shallice, T. (1978). The dominant action system: An information-processing approach to consciousness. In K. S. Pope & J. L. Singer (Eds.), *The stream of consciousness.* New York: Plenum.

Sperry, R. W. (1969). A modified concept of consciousness. *Psychological Review, 76,* 532–536.

Stout, G. F. (1896). *Analytic psychology* (Vols. 1 & 2). London: Swan Sonnenschein.

Talland, G. A. (1965). *Deranged memory.* New York: Academic Press.

Tulving, E. (1972). Episodic and semantic memory. In E.

Tulving & W. Donaldson (Eds.), *Organization of memory.* New York: Academic Press.

Tulving, E. (1982). Synergistic ecphory in recall and recognition. *Canadian Journal of Psychology, 36,* 130–147.

Tulving, E. (1983). Elements of episodic memory. Oxford: Clarendon Press.

Tulving, E. (1984). Relations among components and processes of memory. *Behavioral and Brain Sciences, 7,* 257–268.

Tulving, E., Schacter, D. L., & Stark, H. A. (1982). Priming effects in word-fragment completion are independent of recognition memory. *Journal of Experimental Psychology: Learning, Memory and Cognition, 8,* 336–342.

Underwood, G. (1979). Memory systems and conscious processes. In G. Underwood & R. Stevens (Eds.), *Aspects of consciousness: Vol. 1. Psychological issues.* London: Academic Press.

Underwood, G. (Ed.). (1982). *Aspects of consciousness: Vol. 3. Awareness and self-awareness.* London: Academic Press.

Underwood, G., & Stevens, R. (Eds.). (1979). *Aspects of consciousness: Vol. 1. Psychological issues.* London: Academic Press.

Underwood, G., & Stevens, R. (Eds.). (1981). *Aspects of consciousness: Vol. 2. Structural issues.* London: Academic Press.

Weiskrantz, L. (1978). A comparison of hippocampal pathology in man and other animals. In *Functions of the septohippocampal system. CIBA Foundation Symposium.* Oxford: Elsevier.

Wickelgren, W. A. (1977). *Learning and memory.* Englewood Cliffs, N.J.: Prentice-Hall.

Winograd, T. (1975). Understanding natural language. In D. Bobrow & A. Collins (Eds.), *Representation and understanding.* New York: Academic Press.

CHAPTER NINE
Imagery

24 <small>MENTAL ROTATION</small>
Mental Rotation of Three-Dimensional Objects
Roger Shepard and Jacqueline Metzler

24 MENTAL ROTATION

When we carry out some cognitive tasks it feels like we use pictures in our heads or *mental images*. For example, how many windows are in your house or apartment? To answer this question most people recall a mental map of their apartment and, mentally, move through the map as they count windows. Although almost everyone seems to experience something that we call mental imagery, it is difficult to draw conclusions from such introspections. For example, some people report that their mental images are very sketchy and ill defined, whereas others report that their mental images are detailed and crisp. Based solely on these reports, it is impossible to know whether people's mental images really differ, or if some subjects just describe the mental images differently. This impreciseness caused some researcher to question the validity of research on mental imagery.

The debate over the usefulness of mental imagery research reached its peak in the 1970s. Although there was a great deal of research being conducted exploring the details of visual imagery, much of it was vulnerable to questions of experimenter expectations (the experimenter giving subtle cues to the participants about what outcome was expected) or tacit knowledge (the participants using their knowledge of how their visual systems work to "simulate" the results). The paper by Shepard and Metzler (1971) was a breakthrough of a sort because it demonstrated a way in which visual imagery could be studied objectively.

To explore the way in which mental images are manipulated, Shepard and Metzler showed subjects two novel visual stimuli and asked them to determine whether the stimuli had the same shape or different shapes. The shapes (random block shapes) were *rotated* either in the picture plane or in the depth plane. Subjects were asked to decide whether the two stimuli were the same or different as quickly as possible. The results showed that the reaction time increased with the angle of rotation between the shapes. Not only that, but the increase was linear, such that for every degree of rotation needed, there was a regular increase in response time. This suggests that it takes *time* to mentally rotate an image, and implies that mental images are much like real images. Shepard and Metzler further found that every 50 degrees of physical rotation required one second of mental rotation before subjects could respond. This suggests that the rate of mental rotation is at a constant velocity.

This result is very important because it implies that we treat mental images in a very similar way to how we treat real objects. If we were to rotate a real object in the world (like a pen, for example) 180 degrees we would need to physically move it through all the points in between. Thus, it would take longer to rotate something 180 degrees compared to 5 degrees. Of course we could do it slowly or quickly, but there is some limit on the maximum speed we could actually use to perform the task. The argument is that the subjects (who were highly trained) were rotating the objects as quickly as they could and that speed is about 60 degrees per second. Later experiments (Cooper & Shepard, 1973) demonstrated very convincingly that the subjects were indeed "moving" the mental "object" through space.

You may note that Figure 24.2 shows just 180 degrees of rotation, instead of all of the 360 possible degrees. This is because the figure is actually symmetrical; reaction times start to decrease as the angle gets past 180 degrees. What this suggests is that subjects are mentally rotating the object using the shortest path. Thus, if the second object is rotated 200 degrees from the first object, the subjects only rotate it the remaining 160 degrees, not the whole 200 degrees.

Shepard and Metzler's findings have had a large influence on theories of mental representation. The CogLab experiment is very similar to the one used by Shepard and Metzler except the shapes are bits of twisted wire instead of block figures (and there are many fewer than the 1600 trials their subjects saw!).

REFERENCE

Cooper, L. A., & Shepard, R. N. (1973). The time required to prepare for a rotated stimulus. *Memory & Cognition, 1,* 246–250.

QUESTIONS

1. Describe the main results shown in Figure 24.2.
2. What is the difference between the results in the picture plane and those in the depth plane? What does this suggest about mental rotation in these planes?
3. What other processes are necessary in order to carry out the task? Why aren't the researchers worried about these unknowns?

Mental Rotation of Three-Dimensional Objects

Roger Shepard and Jacqueline Metzler

INTRODUCTION

Is it possible that the representation of transformations of objects in the mind is an analogue process, much as such transformations would be in real world? Suppose, for example, you rotate an object such as a coffee cup. The cup will pass through an infinite number of intermediate states as it makes its way toward its destination, say, 90 degrees from its original position. When you visualize this rotation in your mind, does the visual image similarly pass through an infinite number of intermediate states, or does it pass through a set of discrete and potentially countable states that may, nevertheless, be experienced as analogue transformations?

In an ingenious study, Roger Shepard and Jacqueline Metzler provided suggestive evidence for analogue mental transformations of internal representations. Shepard and Metzler showed participants in their study pairs of pictures of three-dimensional objects. Half of the pairs showed the same objects, except that the second figure in each pair represented a rotated version of the first figure. Rotations of the second object in each "same" pair ranged from 0 to 180 degrees with respect to the first object. The other pairs combined nonidentical images. The object in the second position was a mirror image of the object in the first position, again with a range of orientations.

The crucial finding in the study was that the time required to recognize that two objects were the same was a linear function of the degree of discrepancy in angular orientation of the second figure with respect to the first. In other words, people seemed to be mentally rotating the objects to bring them into mental congruence, with a constant rate of rotation across the range from 0 to 180 degrees. These results, then, suggested the use of analogue representations in the mind.

This article is often considered to be one of the most important articles in cognitive psychology, first, because it provided truly compelling evidence for the existence of analogue representations of objects in the mind. Authors rarely can provide such a compelling demonstration of any phenomenon in so short a space! Second, the research employs a simple, elegant, and totally compelling design. One reads the article and wonders why no one thought of the idea before. Often, the best experiments are those that seem so obvious that many researchers wonder why they didn't think of them—but they didn't. Finally, the research showed that reaction-time measures could be used to investigate real-time mental processing of spatial images. Many later researchers would pick up on this idea and extend the use of reaction times to explore the characteristics of mental images.

* * *

The time required to recognize that two perspective drawings portray objects of the same three-dimensional shape is found to be (i) a linearly increasing function of the angular difference in the portrayed orientations of the two objects and (ii) no shorter for differences corresponding simply to a rigid rotation of one of the two-dimensional drawings in its own picture plane than for differences corresponding to a rotation of the three-dimensional object in depth.

Human subjects are often able to determine that 2 two-dimensional pictures portray objects of the same three-dimensional shape even though the objects are depicted in very different orientations. The experiment reported here was designed to measure the time that subjects require to determine such identity of shape as a function of the angular difference in the portrayed orientations of the 2 three-dimensional objects.

SOURCE: Reprinted with permission from Shepard, R., & Metzler, J. (1971). Mental rotation of three-dimensional objects. *Science, 171,* 701–703. Copyright © 1971 American Association for the Advancement of Science.

This angular difference was produced either by a rigid rotation of one or two identical pictures in its own picture plane or by a much more complex, nonrigid transformation of one of the pictures that correspond to a (rigid) rotation of the three-dimensional object in depth.

This reaction time is found (i) to increase linearly with the angular difference in portrayed orientation and (ii) to be no longer for a rotation in depth than for a rotation merely in the picture plane. These findings appear to place rather severe constraints on possible explanations of how subjects go about determining identity of shape of differently oriented objects. They are, however, consistent with an explanation suggested by the subjects themselves. Although introspective reports must be interpreted with caution, all subjects claimed (i) that to make the required comparison they first had to imagine one object as rotated into the same orientation as the other and that they could carry out this "mental rotation" at no greater than a certain limiting rate; and (ii) that, since they perceived the two-dimensional pictures as objects in three-dimensional space, they could imagine the rotation around whichever axis was required with equal ease.

In the experiment, each of eight adult subjects was presented with 1,600 pairs of perspective line drawings. For each pair, the subject was asked to pull a right-hand lever as soon as he determined that the two drawings portrayed objects that were congruent with respect to three-dimensional shape and to pull a left-hand lever as soon as he determined that the two drawings depicted objects of different three-dimensional shapes. According to a random sequence, in half of the pairs (the "same" pairs) the two objects could be rotated into congruence with each other (as in Figure 24.1, A and B), and in the other half (the "different" pairs) the two objects differed by a reflection as well as a rotation and could not be rotated into congruence (as in Figure 24.1C).

The choice of objects that were mirror images or "isomers" of each other for the "different" pairs was intended to prevent subjects from discovering some distinctive feature possessed by only one of the two objects and thereby reaching a decision of noncongruence without actually having to carry out any mental rotation. As a further precaution, the ten different three-dimensional objects depicted in the various perspective

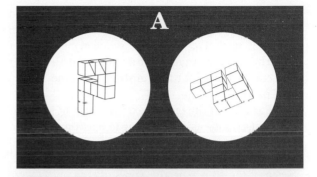

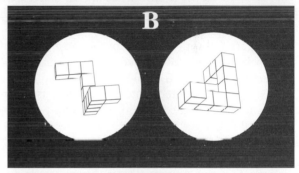

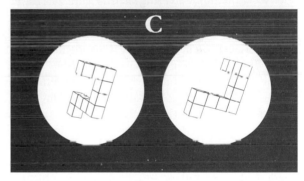

FIGURE 24.1   Examples of pairs of perspective line drawings presented to the subjects. (A) A "same" pair, which differs by an 80° rotation in the picture plane; (B) a "same" pair, which differs by an 80° rotation in depth; and (C) a "different" pair, which cannot be brought into congruence by any rotation.

drawings were chosen to be relatively unfamiliar and meaningless in overall three-dimensional shape.

Each object consisted of ten solid cubes attached face-to-face to form a rigid, armlike structure with exactly three right-angled "elbows" (see Figure 24.1). The set of all ten shapes included two subsets of five;

within either subset, no shape could be transformed into itself or any other by any reflection or rotation (short of 360°). However, each shape in either subset was the mirror image of one shape in the other subset, as required for the construction of the "different" pairs.

For each of the ten objects, 18 different perspective projections—corresponding to one complete turn around the vertical axis by 20° steps—were generated by digital computer and associated graphical output.[1] Seven of the 18 perspective views of each object were then selected so as (i) to avoid any views in which some part of the object was wholly occluded by another part and yet (ii) to permit the construction of two pairs that differed in orientation by each possible angle, in 20° steps, from 0° to 180°. These 70 line drawings were then reproduced by photo-offset process and were attached to cards in pairs for presentation to the subjects.

Half of the "same" pairs (the "depth" pairs) represented two objects that differed by some multiple of a 20° rotation about a vertical axis (Figure 24.1B). For each of these pairs, copies of two appropriately different perspective views were simply attached to the cards in the orientation in which they were originally generated. The other half of the "same" pairs (the "picture-plane" pairs) represented two objects that differed by some multiple of a 20° rotation in the plane of the drawings themselves (Figure 24.1A). For each of these, one of the seven perspective views was selected for each object and two copies of this picture were attached to the card in appropriately different orientations. Altogether, the 1,600 pairs presented to each subject included 800 "same" pairs, which consisted of 400 unique pairs (20 "depth" and 20 "picture-plane" pairs at each of the 10 angular differences from 0° to 180°), each of which was presented twice. The remaining 800 pairs, randomly intermixed with these, consisted of 400 unique "different" pairs, each of which (again) was presented twice. Each of these "different" pairs corresponded to one "same" pair (of either the "depth" or "picture-plane" variety) in which, however, one of the three-dimensional objects had been reflected about some plane in three-dimensional space. Thus the two objects in each "different" pair differed, in general, by both a reflection and a rotation.

The 1,600 pairs were grouped into blocks of not more than 200 and presented over 8 to 10 1-hour sessions (depending upon the subject). Also, although it is only of incidental interest here, each such block of presentations was either "pure," in that all pairs involved rotations of the same type ("depth" or "picture-plane"), or "mixed," in that the two types of rotation were randomly intermixed within the same block.

Each trial began with a warning tone, which was followed half a second later by the presentation of a stimulus pair and the simultaneous onset of a timer. The lever-pulling response stopped the timer, recorded the subject's reaction time, and terminated the visual display. The line drawings, which averaged between 4 and 5 cm in maximum linear extent, appeared at a viewing distance of about 60 cm. They were positioned, with a center-to-center spacing that subtended a visual angle of 9°, in two circular apertures in a vertical black surface (see Figure 24.1, A to C).

The subjects were instructed to respond as quickly as possible while keeping errors to a minimum. On the average, only 3.2 percent of the responses were incorrect (ranging from 0.6 to 5.7 percent for individual subjects). The reaction-time data presented below include only the 96.8 percent correct responses. However, the data for the incorrect responses exhibit a similar pattern.

In Figure 24.2, the overall means of the reaction times as a function of angular difference in orientation for all correct (right-hand) responses to "same" pairs are plotted separately for the pairs differing by a rotation in the picture plane (Figure 24.2A) and for the pairs differing by a rotation in depth (Figure 24.2B). In both cases, reaction time is a strikingly linear function of the angular difference between the 2 three-dimensional objects portrayed. The mean reaction times for individual subjects increased from a value of about 1 sec at 0° of rotation for all subjects to values ranging from 4 to 6 sec at 180° of rotation, depending upon the particular individual. Moreover, despite such variations in slope, the *linearity* of the function is clearly evident when the data are plotted separately for individual three-dimensional objects or for individual subjects. Polynomial regression lines were computed separately for each subject under each type of rotation. In all 16 cases, the functions were found to have a highly significant linear component ($p < .001$) when tested against deviations from linearity. No significant quadratic or higher-order effects were found ($p > .05$, in all cases).

The angle through which different three-dimensional shapes must be rotated to achieve congruence is not, of course, defined. Therefore, a function like those plotted in Figure 24.2 cannot be constructed in any straightforward manner for the "different" pairs. The *overall* mean reaction time for these pairs was found, however, to be 3.8 sec—nearly a second longer than the corresponding overall means for the "same" pairs. (In the postexperimental interview, the subjects typically reported that they attempted to rotate one end of one object into congruence with the corresponding end of the other object; they discovered that the two objects were *different* when, after this "rotation," the two free ends still remained noncongruent.)

Not only are the two functions shown in Figure 24.2 both linear, but they are very similar to each other with respect to intercept and slope. Indeed, for the larger angular differences, the reaction times were, if anything, somewhat shorter for rotation in depth than for rotation in the picture plane. However, since this small difference is either absent or reversed in four of the eight subjects, it is of doubtful significance. The determination of identity of shape may therefore be based, in both cases, upon a process of the same general kind. If we can describe this process as some sort of "mental rotation in three-dimensional space," then the slope of the obtained functions indicates that the average rate at which these particular objects can be thus "rotated" is roughly 60° per second.

Of course the plotted reaction times necessarily include any times taken by the subjects to decide how to process the pictures in each presented pair as well as the time taken actually to carry out the process, once it was chosen. However, even for these highly practiced subjects, the reaction times were still linear and were no more than 20 percent lower in the "pure" blocks of presentations (in which the subjects knew both the axis and the direction of the required rotation in advance of each presentation) than in the "mixed" blocks (in which the axis of rotation was unpredictable). Tentatively, this suggests that 80 percent of a typical one of these reaction times may represent

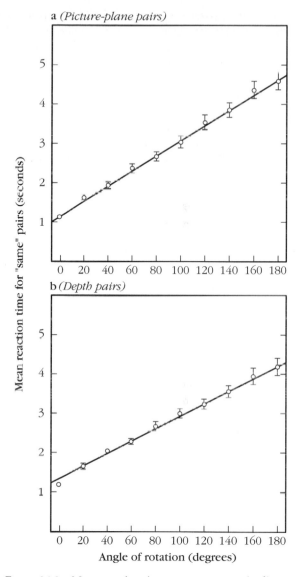

FIGURE 24.2 Mean reaction times to two perspective line drawings portraying objects of the same three-dimensional shape. Times are plotted as a function of angular difference in portrayed orientation: (A) for pairs differing by a rotation in the picture plane only; and (B) for pairs differing by a rotation in depth. (The centers of the circles indicate the means and, when they extend far enough to show outside these circles, the vertical bars around each circle indicate a conservative estimate of the standard error of that mean based on the distribution of the eight component means contributed by the individual subjects.)

some such process as "mental rotation" itself, rather than a preliminary process of preparation or search. Nevertheless, in further research now underway, we are seeking clarification of this point and others.

NOTE

1. Mrs. Jih-Jie Chang of the Bell Telephone Laboratories generated the 180 perspective projections for us by means of the Bell Laboratories' Stromberg-Carlson 4020 microfilm recorder and the computer program for constructing such projections developed there by A. M. Noll. See, for example, A. M. Noll (1965). *Computers Automation 14,* 20.

CHAPTER TEN
Speech and Language

25 CATEGORICAL PERCEPTION

The use of speech and language is one area where humans clearly differ from all other nonhuman animals. It seems to be an ability that sets us apart from all other species. Some theories of speech perception argue that humans have a specialized processor in their brains that is used solely for understanding human speech sounds. This specialization causes speech to be processed in a fundamentally different way from nonspeech. This theory is based in part on the finding that some speech sounds are perceived categorically whereas nonspeech sounds are perceived continuously. Categorical perception means that even though there is a gradual change in the physical stimuli, people hear only two sounds with a sharp change between the categories.

For example, both /d/ and /t/ are stop consonants: To produce these, you close your lips, then open them, release some air, and the vocal chords begin vibrating. Hold your hand on your throat, and say /da/ and then /ta/. The difference between /da/ and /ta/ is the time between the release of the air and the beginning of the vibration. This is referred to as voice onset time (VOT). For /d/, VOT is very short; voicing begins at almost the same time as the air is released. For /t/, the voicing is delayed.

Researchers can construct a series of stimuli in which the VOT changes in small steps. When people are asked to identify these stimuli, they generally have no difficulty: The first few are identified as /d/ and the second few are identified as /t/. What is most interesting is how the middle items are identified. Unlike most other stimuli, people do not report hearing something that is a bit like /d/ and a bit like /t/; rather, they report hearing either /d/ or /t/. This is very different from how you would perceive a continuum of piano notes changing in pitch: You would hear gradual increases in the pitch as the music went in equal steps from one note to another.

There is a powerful way to test any theory that postulates a species-specific ability: Test it in another species. Clearly a chinchilla (a small rodent-like animal) has not evolved a special ability to perceive speech sounds. Thus, if the chinchilla demonstrates categorical perception of speech sounds we can assume that it does not have a special place in its brain for perceiving speech and will probably conclude that there is something about the sound itself that causes mammals (or at least humans and chinchillas) to hear the sounds categorically.

Kuhl and Miller (1975) trained chinchillas to respond to speech sounds using a conditioning procedure in which the chinchillas were rewarded for correctly identifying a variety of different examples of /d/ and /t/. Then, they were asked to identify new sounds that were varied in equal steps along the voice–onset-time continuum between /d/ and /t/. They found that the chinchillas showed the same pattern of performance as the humans: categorical perception. These results suggest that there might be a natural boundary in the stimulus sequence that gives rise to categorical perception.

Since this paper was published there has been a great deal of debate over the correct interpretation of the data. First, Kuhl and Miller did not include a discrimination condition. This is a condition in which two sounds are presented and the subject is asked to determine whether they are the same or different. To definitely demonstrate categorical perception, you really need both the identification task and the discrimination task. In order to show true categorical perception the listener must not be able to tell the difference between stimuli in the same category but should be perfect at discriminating between stimuli that cross the category boundary. This paper does not provide such evidence. Second, some researchers have argued that just because humans and chinchillas exhibit similar behavior does not necessarily rule out a specialized processor in the humans, a possibility that Kuhl and Miller acknowledge. Finally, when one looks at the data more carefully, it might be argued that the chinchillas are showing less categorical perception than the humans. During the change in performance over the category boundary (+30 to +40 ms VOT), chinchillas go from 50% /d/ responses to 25% /d/ responses, whereas humans go from 80% to 20%, a much sharper decrease. Thus the debate on the species-specific nature of speech perception is not yet settled (see Jusczyk & Luce, 2002, for an up-to-date review of the field).

The CogLab demonstration is in two parts—identification and discrimination. In addition, the stimuli are constructed from /p/ and /b/ (varying in VOT) instead of /t/ and /d/. However, the basic result is the same for both stimulus continua.

REFERENCE

Jusczyk, P. W., & Luce P. A. (2002). Speech perception and spoken word recognition: Past and present. *Ear and Hearing, 23,* 2–40.

QUESTIONS

1. Why are chinchillas an appropriate species to compare to humans in these experiments?

2. What was the training method in Experiment 1?
3. What were the results of Experiment 1?
4. What is the significance of the category boundary falling in the same place for humans and chinchillas?

Speech Perception by the Chinchilla: Voiced-Voiceless Distinction in Alveolar Plosive Consonants

Patricia K. Kuhl and James D. Miller

Central Institute for the Deaf, St. Louis, Missouri

ABSTRACT

Four chinchillas were trained to respond differently to /t/ and /d/ consonant-vowel syllables produced by four talkers in three vowel contexts. This training generalized to novel instances, including synthetically produced /da/ and /ta/ (voice-onset times of 0 and +80 milliseconds, respectively). In a second experiment, synthetic stimuli with voice-onset times between 0 and +80 milliseconds were presented for identification. The form of the labeling functions and the "phonetic boundaries" for chinchillas and English-speaking adults were similar.

Neither speech analysis nor speech synthesis techniques have led to a successful account of our perception of speech sounds in terms of invariant acoustic properties.[1] For this reason and others,[1] current theorists have hypothesized that at least some classes of speech sounds are recognized by "special processing."[2,3] Speculation as to the nature of this special-to-speech processing varies: some believe that it involves "phonetic feature detectors" that presumably respond to rather complicated and abstract characteristics of the acoustic signal;[4] others have espoused a "motor theory" of speech perception,[2,3] which suggests that one's tacit knowledge of the acoustic results of articulatory maneuvers somehow mediates the perception of speech. While variously described, these current theories suggest that speech perception is a species-specific behavior, and thus, in large part, a uniquely human ability. As Liberman stated, "Unfortunately, nothing is known about the way non-human animals perceive speech . . . however, we should suppose that,

lacking the speech-sound decoder, animals would not perceive speech as we do, even at the phonetic level."[2]

We asked whether the chinchilla, a mammal with auditory capabilities fairly similar to man's,[5] but certainly without a phylogenetic history of "phonetic knowledge," either acoustic or articulatory, could correctly classify a large number of naturally produced syllables on the basis of the voicing contrast. In experiment 1, we trained four chinchillas, using an avoidance conditioning procedure, to respond differently to a variety of spoken /t/ and /d/ consonant-vowel (CV) syllables. Once trained, these animals correctly classified novel instances of /t/ and /d/ syllables, including syllables produced by new talkers, those produced in new vowel contexts, and computer-synthesized /ta/ and /da/ syllables. In experiment 2, we presented synthetic stimuli that varied systematically from /da/ to /ta/ to the animals trained on natural speech, to animals not trained on natural speech, and to English-speaking adults for identification. The labeling functions and the "phonetic boundaries" were similar for all animal and human subjects.

The voicing feature, which distinguishes voiced (/bdg/) from voiceless (/ptk/) plosives in English, is appropriate for investigations of speech perception by animals since this distinction has been examined in cross-language studies of adults[6,7] and infants.[8,9] The acoustic properties that distinguish voiced and voiceless plosives in absolute-initial, prevocalic, stressed position can be most readily described as a timing difference between the onset of the plosive burst and the onset of voicing,[6] termed the voice-onset time (VOT).

In synthetic speech, VOT can be varied along a continuum to produce plosives in which voicing precedes the plosive burst (prevoiced), begins nearly simultaneously with the burst (unaspirated), or lags behind the plosive burst (aspirated). The VOT is specified in milliseconds; negative values indicate that voicing leads and positive values indicate that voicing lags. In English, prevoiced and unaspirated plosives constitute the voiced phonemic category and aspirated plosives constitute the voiceless phonemic category. When English speakers identify synthetic tokens from the VOT continuum, perception changes abruptly from voiced to voiceless sounds; the VOT at which responses divide equally between voiced and voiceless is termed the "phonetic boundary." These boundaries differ with the place of articulation of the voiced-voiceless pair; the boundaries for labials (/ba-pa/), alveolars (/da-ta/), and velars (/ga-ka/) are approximately +22, +35, and +41 msec, respectively.[7,10] Many languages divide the VOT continuum as we do in English,[6] but in some languages, the division between voiced and voiceless categories occurs elsewhere. For example, in languages such as Kikuyu,[6, 9] prevoiced plosives constitute the voiced category and unaspirated plosives constitute the voiceless category (aspirated plosives do not occur). However, infants 1 to 4 months old discriminate synthetic stimuli that fall on different sides of the English /b-p/ phonetic boundary (VOT of +22 msec) whether they are reared in an English-speaking environment where this boundary is phonemically relevant[8] or in a Kikuyu-speaking environment where it is not.[9] These facts lend themselves to at least two interpretations: either young infants demonstrate this perceptual boundary because their "speech processor" responds to its potential phonemic relevance or because the boundary is a natural psychophysical one that could be demonstrated by a nonhuman as well. While our results do not rule out the first interpretation, they are consistent with the second.

In experiment 1, the CV syllables used during discrimination training (/ti, ta, tu, di, da, du/), were recorded twice by each of four talkers (two male and two female), and dubbed onto a disk pack for use in a digital recorder.[11] The VOT measurements ranged from +40 to +128 msec for /t/ syllables and −200 to +28 msec for /d/ syllables.

The animals were tested in a double-grille cage suspended below a loudspeaker in a sound-treated booth.[5,12] Four chinchillas were deprived of water and trained to lick a drinking tube mounted at one end of the cage for their daily ration of water. Every third lick on the tube produced a drop of water. The animals were maintained at approximately 90 percent of their original weights. It had been demonstrated[12] that an ongoing activity, such as drinking, reduced the number of false alarms and intratrial avoidance responses during discrimination training.

For two animals, /t/ was the positive stimulus and /d/ was the negative stimulus; for the other two animals, these roles were reversed.. On positive trials, the animal was trained to flee the drinking tube and cross the midline barrier to avoid shock. When the animal crossed the barrier, lights positioned at the barrier ends were lit briefly and the stimulus was terminated. Failure to cross the barrier within the 2.5-second trial interval resulted in simultaneous presentation of buzzer and shock until the crossing response was made. On negative trials, no consequences were delivered during the 2.5-second trial interval. If the animal correctly refrained from crossing, the water valve opened, making "free" water available for 1 second, and lights above the drinking tube were lit.

The animals were given 24 trials daily over a 7-month period. Each trial consisted of two presentations, separated by 500 msec, of the CV syllable. The time between trials was varied from 10 to 30 seconds, and the sound levels of the syllables were varied from trial to trial [52 to 66 db, sound pressure level (SPL)]. A masking noise (speech-shaped, 12 db SPL) was continuously presented in the test booth.

The experiment began with a single /tu/ and /du/ syllable; when this task was mastered, variation in the form of tokens (second repetition by the same talker), talkers (identical phonetic token by different talkers), and vowels (different vowel contexts by a single talker) were singly introduced.[13] The criteria for progressing from one condition to the next were that the group's percentage correct remain ≥ 90 percent for two consecutive days and that during this time no single animal's performance was less than 80 percent correct. Failure to make the crossing response on a positive trial and making the crossing response on a

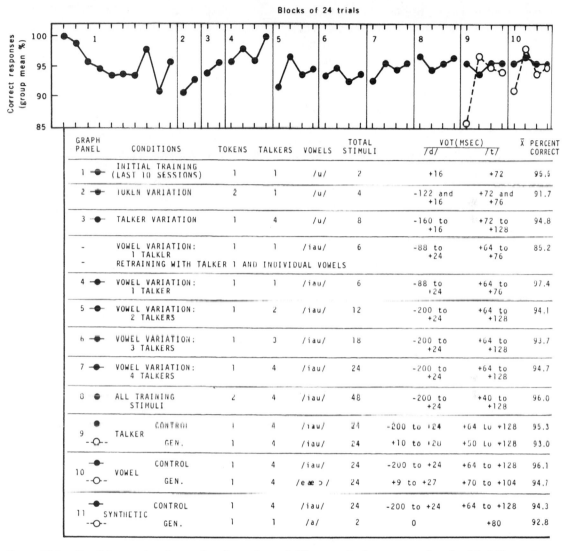

FIGURE 25.1   Conditions and major results of experiment 1. These results demonstrate that the chinchilla can be trained to discriminate /t/ from /d/ in absolute-initial, prevocalic, stressed position in spite of irrelevant changes in the sounds due to level, talker, and vowel (panels 1 to 8). Furthermore, such training generalizes to new talkers, new vowels, and synthetic stimuli (panels 9 to 11).

negative trial were both scored as errors. The group's percentage correct is displayed and the conditions of the experiment are described in Figure 25.1. The only major problem the animals had with the task was mastering the /t-d/ distinction in new vowel contexts; however, after training on individual vowels, beginning with /ta/ and /da/, adding /ti/ and /di/, and finally

/tu/ and /du/, the task was mastered. The successive addition of stimuli produced by talkers 2, 3, and 4 presented no problems.[14]

There were three tests for generalization. The stimuli for talker generalization were the tokens /ti, ta, tu, di, da, du/ produced by four new talkers (two male and two female). The stimuli for vowel generalization were the tokens /te, tae, to, de, dae, do/ produced by the same four new talkers. During synthetic generalization, /da/ (VOT, 0 msec) and /ta/ (VOT, +80 msec) stimuli were taken from the alveolar VOT continuum created by Lisker and Abramson.[7]

On half of the trials during generalization tests, the stimuli presented were those already mastered by the animals. On the other half of the trials, generalization stimuli were randomly presented. In this way, performance on familiar stimuli served as a control for performance on novel stimuli. When control stimuli were presented, all feedback previously in effect was maintained. When generalization stimuli were presented, neither shock nor the buzzer were used, and all other feedback was arranged to indicate a correct response, no matter what the animal did. That is, on all generalization trials, barrier crossings during the 2.5-second trial interval resulted in lighting of barrier lights, and inhibition of the crossing response during the trial interval resulted in availability of "free" water. This procedure tests the animal's ability to correctly classify novel instances from a category without being "taught"; any change in the animal's performance is attributable to experience alone.

Performance on the control stimuli (Figure 25.1, panels 9 to 11, closed circles) remained fairly steady throughout generalization sessions, and all generalization stimuli (open circles) were eventually classified as accurately as their controls. In fact, the continued addition of novel instances of /t/ and /d/ produced increasingly fewer errors during initual sessions (this can be seen by comparing the first open circles in panels 9. 10, and 11).

In experiment 2, two of the four animals in experiment 1 (one for whom /t/ was positive and one for whom /d/ was positive) and two new animals were trained on the "endpoints" of the synthetic continuum (VOT, 0 msec, /d/; VOT, +80 msec, /t/) until the performance of each animal was consistently greater than 96 percent correct. During the next ten sessions, these endpoint stimuli were presented in half the trials and the stimuli between them (VOT, +10 to +70 msec, in 10-msec steps) were randomly presented in the other half. During endpoint trials, all feedback was maintained, but when all other stimuli were presented, feedback was arranged to indicate a correct response. Four English-speaking adults identified the

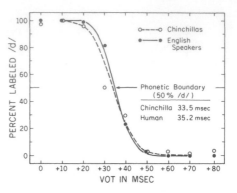

FIGURE 25.2   Mean percentage of /d/ responses by chinchilla and human subjects to synthetic speech sounds constructed to approximate /ta/ and /da/. The animals were trained (that is, given appropriate feedback) on the two "endpoint" stimuli, VOTs of 0 and +80 msec; for all other stimuli (VOTs from +10 to +70 msec in 10-msec steps), feedback was arranged to indicate a correct response to the animal. The labeling gradients and "phonetic boundaries" for human and chinchilla subjects are similar.

same stimuli as /da/ or /ta/. The mean percentage of "d" responses to each synthetic stimulus by human and chinchilla subjects is displayed in Figure 25.2. The stimuli were labeled an equal number of times by both groups of subjects. The two curves, both of which were generated by a least-squares method, are similar both in general form and in the location of the phonetic boundaries; for English-speaking adults and chinchillas the boundaries are 35.2 and 33.5 msec, respectively. Furthermore, training on natural speech was not a necessary condition for placement of the boundary; the mean phonetic boundaries for the two animals originally trained on natural speech and the two that were trained only on the synthetic endpoints were 33.7 msec and 33.1 msec, respectively.

To examine the generality of the correspondence between the labeling functions of our animal and human subjects, we tested two of the four animals and the same four adults with the Lisker-Abramson labial and velar VOT series.[7] The procedure was exactly the same; synthetic stimuli with VOTs of 0 and +80 msec were endpoints for which feedback was in effect while all other stimuli were presented as generalization stimuli. The similarity in the form of the labeling gradients and in the location of the boundaries demonstrated for the alveolar stimuli was again found for the labial and velar stimuli. The boundaries were about +25, +34, and +42 msec for the labial, alveolar, and velar stimuli, respectively, with standard errors of 1.75 msec; these values are in good agreement with those of Lisker and Abramson.[7]

These experiments simply demonstrate that the voiced-voiceless distinction of plosive consonants in initial position, whether in natural speech where the critical features must be abstracted from many others, or in synthetic speech where only the critical features are varied, can be made by a mammal without phonetic mediating devices. While these findings do not rule out the possibility that human listeners process these speech sounds in a highly specialized way, they do demonstrate that uniquely human processing is not essential for these particular tasks, and they suggest that alternative explanations merit further consideration. The fact that the chinchillas respond to the synthetic speech as though an abrupt qualitative change occurs in the short voicing-lag region of the VOT continuum at precisely the place where many languages separate two phonemic categories lends support to the idea that speech-sound oppositions were selected to be highly distinctive to the auditory system. By this reasoning, one might infer that there is at least one other natural psychophysical boundary, located in the voicing-lead region of the VOT continuum, which serves as a basis for the phonemic distinction between prevoiced and voiceless-unaspirated plosives of languages such as Spanish, Thai, and Kikuyu. In any case, further experiments with animals should help to pinpoint which speech-perception tasks require "special processing."

REFERENCES AND NOTES

1. A. M. Liberman, F. S. Cooper, D. P. Shankweiler, M. Studdert-Kennedy, *Psychol. Rev.* 74, 431 (1967). The plosive consonant /d/ is often used as an example. The direction of the second formant (F_2) transition is believed to be a sufficient cue for differentiating place of articulation (/b, d, g/); that is, in the /ae/ vowel context, rising F, transitions produce /bae/, falling F_2 transitions produce /gae/, and those remaining fairly steady produce /dae/. However, the set of F_2 transitions that produce a single plosive, like /d/, across vowel contexts varies extensively; in /di/ the F_2 transition rises, in /du/ it falls, and in /dae/ it remains fairly steady.

2. A. M. Liberman, *Cogn. Psychol.* 1, 301 (1970).

3. K. N. Stevens and A. S. House, in *Foundations of Modern Auditory Theory*, J. V. Tobias, Ed. (Academic Press, New York, 1972), vol. 2, pp. 3–62; M. Studdert-Kennedy, A. M. Liberman, K. S. Harris, F. S. Cooper, *Psychol. Rev.* 77, 234 (1970).

4. P. D. Eimas and J. D. Corbit, *Cogn. Psychol.* 4, 99 (1973).

5. J. D. Miller, *J. Acoust. Soc. Am.* 48, 513 (1970). For differences between auditory capabilities of man and chinchilla, see p. 521.

6. L. Lisker and A. S. Abramson, *Word* 20, 384 (1964).

7. ———, in *Proceedings of the Sixth International Congress of Phonetic Sciences Prague 1967* (Academia, Prague, 1970), pp. 563–567.

8. P. D. Eimas, E. R. Siqueland, P. Jusczyk, J. Vigorito, *Science* 171, 303 (1971).

9. L. Streeter, thesis, Columbia University (1974).

10. At least two acoustic cues appear to contribute to the qualitative change in the perception of the synthetic stimuli as voicing increasingly lags the burst: the presence of aspiration and the absence of a rapid spectrum change at the onset of voicing [K. N. Stevens and D. H. Klatt, *J. Acoust. Soc. Am.* 55, 653 (1974)].

11. B. F. Spenner, A. M. Engebretson, J. D. Miller, J. R. Cox, *ibid.*, p. 427(A).

12. C. K. Burdick and J. D. Miller, *ibid.* 54, 789 (1973).

13. A new variation was introduced by adding only the positive stimuli, then only the negative stimuli, and finally both positive and negative stimuli until performance criteria were met [C. K. Burdick and J. D. Miller, *ibid.* 58, 415 (1975)]. The data plotted in Figure 25.1 are from sessions in which both positive and negative stimuli were presented.

14. Beginning with training on individual vowels, all positive and negative stimuli for a new condition were added simultaneously.

15. Supported by NIH grant NS03856 to Central Institute for the Deaf and NIH grant RR00396 to the Biomedical Computer Laboratory of Washington University. We thank A. M. Engebretson, C. K. Burdick, and R. J. Dooling for their assistance, and we acknowledge the cooperation of the Haskins Laboratories (NIH contract NIH-71-2420) in providing the synthetic stimuli.

26 LEXICAL DECISION

Estimates of the number of words the average adult knows vary between 15,000 and 200,000 words (Nusbaum, Pisoni, & Davis, 1984). However, we generally have very little trouble accessing the meaning of words and we can do it extremely quickly. How do we find a specific word within this mass of information? How are these words organized? Theories of semantic memory propose that there exists a mental dictionary, a *lexicon*, that contains a variety of information about words. This lexicon contains information about a word's meaning (its *semantic* content), its part of language (noun, verb, adjective), and its relationships to other words (What can it follow? What can follow it? How can it be modified?).

The lexicon is similar to a dictionary in that it holds information about words and other components of language. Physical dictionaries generally organize words alphabetically. This arrangement makes it easy to find any word, provided the spelling is known (or can be guessed). Because dictionaries are usually used to find the meanings of known words (or to check if a word is spelled properly), this organization is useful.

In the mental lexicon, however, the most useful features of a word may not be its spelling, but its meaning, and its relationship to other words. If words are arranged in the lexicon by semantic relationships, then words that are related to each other (e.g., chair, seat, table) would be close in the lexicon, whereas words that are unrelated to each other (e.g., chair, dinosaur, broccoli) would be far apart.

The Meyer and Schvaneveldt (1971) experiments tested theories of this type using variants of a lexical decision task. In a lexical decision task, words and pseudowords (e.g., *blar*, or *plome*) are presented and observers determine, as quickly as possible, whether the presented item is a word or nonword. Determining whether the item is a word involves searching the lexicon to see if the item is present. The time needed to make a "word" response indicates the time needed to search the lexicon to find the target word.

Meyer and Schvaneveldt hypothesized that search time would be shorter if the previously accessed word was close to the current target word. Search time would be longer if two words were in very different places in the lexicon. In Experiment 1 they tested this hypothesis by presenting pairs of items, and asked observers to judge whether the two strings were both words or non-words. They expected that the reaction time to the strings would be fastest if the pair of words were semantically associated with one another. The data showed exactly this effect. Experiment 2 was very similar but used a slightly different method. For the sake of simplicity, in the CogLab demonstration words and nonwords are presented one at a time and responses are made to each item successively. However, the end result is essentially the same: Responses to words that are associated with previous words are faster than those that are not associated.

Meyer and Schvaneveldt argued that their result does not necessarily mean that the meaning of a word is retrieved but that words that are similar in meaning are stored close together in the lexicon. They discuss a number of possible theories of accessing words in the mental lexicon. This paper is an important one in that it was one of the first to use procedures such as lexical decision to uncover the structure of semantic memory. Since this paper was published there have been literally hundreds of studies using a variety of methods to explore the structure of semantic memory and the lexicon. A recent review of the literature was provided by McNamara and Holbrook (2003).

REFERENCES

McNamara, T. P., & Holbrook, J. B. (2003). Semantic memory and priming. In A. F. Healy and R. W. Proctor (Eds.). *Handbook of psychology: Experimental psychology, Vol. 4.* (pp. 447–474). New York: John Wiley & Sons.

Nusbaum, H. C., Pisoni, D. B., & Davis, C. K. (1984). Sizing up the Hoosier mental lexicon: Measuring the familiarity of 20,000 words. *Research on Speech Perception Progress Report No. 10, Indiana University.*

QUESTIONS

1. What is the "mental lexicon"?
2. Describe the basic lexical decision task.
3. What is the main dependent variable in the lexical decision task?
4. What is the independent variable in Meyer and Schvaneveldt's experiments?
5. What is the main result of the two experiments?
6. What does this result tell us about the organization of the mental lexicon?
7. Describe the spreading-excitation model. Why do Meyer and Schvaneveldt argue that the data do not require that the subject retrieve the meaning of a word in order to make a lexical decision?

Facilitation in Recognizing Pairs of Words: Evidence of a Dependence Between Retrieval Operations

David E. Meyer and Roger W. Schvaneveldt

Bell Telephone Laboratories, Murray Hill, New Jersey, and University of Colorado

ABSTRACT

Two experiments are reported in which Ss were presented two strings of letters simultaneously, with one string displayed visually above the other. In Exp. I, Ss responded "yes" if both strings were words, otherwise responding "no." In Exp. II, Ss responded "same" if the two strings were either both words or both nonwords, otherwise responding "different." "Yes" responses and "same" responses were faster for pairs of commonly associated words than for pairs of unassociated words. "Same" responses were slowest for pairs of nonwords. "No" responses were faster when the top string in the display was a nonword, whereas "different" responses were faster when the top string was a word. The results of both experiments support a retrieval model involving a dependence between separate successive decisions about whether each of the two strings is a word. Possible mechanisms that underlie this dependence are discussed.

Several investigators recently have studied how Ss decide that a string of letters is a word (Landauer & Freedman, 1968; Meyer & Ellis, 1970; Rubenstein, Garfield, & Millikan, 1970). They typically have presented a single string on a trial, measuring reaction time (RT) of the *lexical decision* as a function of the string's meaning, familiarity, etc. In one such experiment, RT varied inversely with word frequency (Rubenstein et al., 1970). Where word frequency was controlled, lexical decisions were faster for homographs (i.e., words having two or more meanings) than for nonhomographs. To explain these results, Rubenstein et al. proposed that word frequency affects the order of examining stored words in long-term memory and that more replicas of homographs than of nonhomographs are stored in long-term memory.

In another experiment, Meyer and Ellis (1970) measured both the time taken to decide that a string of letters (e.g., HOUSE) is a word and the time taken to decide that it belongs to a prespecified semantic category. When the category was relatively small (e.g., BUILDINGS), the latter type of *semantic decision* was significantly faster than the former lexical decision. However, when the category was relatively large (e.g., STRUCTURES), the semantic decision was slightly slower than the lexical decision. To explain these and other results, Meyer and Ellis suggested that the semantic decision may have involved searching through stored words in the semantic category and that the lexical decision did *not* entail a search of this kind among the set of all words in memory.

The present paper provides further data about the effect of meaning on lexical decisions. To deal with this problem, we have extended the lexical-decision task by simultaneously presenting two strings of letters for S to judge. The stimulus may involve either a pair of words, a pair of nonwords, or a word and a nonword. In one task, S is instructed to respond "yes" if both strings are words, and otherwise to respond "no." In a second task, the instructions require S to respond "same" if the two strings are either both words or both nonwords, and otherwise to respond "different." In each task, RT for pairs of words is measured as a function of the associative relation between the two words.

The two tasks together are designed to give information about the nature and the invariance of underlying retrieval operations. One of their advantages is that the relation between words can be varied while keeping the overt response constant. We reasoned that the response might involve separate, successive decisions about each of the two words. By varying the degree of association between the words, we then hoped it would be possible to test for a dependence between memory-accessing components of the two decisions. Experiment I reports the results of such variation in the context of the yes-no task.

EXPERIMENT I

Method

Subjects.   The *Ss* were 12 high school students who served as paid volunteers.

Stimuli.   The following test stimuli were used: 48 pairs of associated words, e.g., BREAD-BUTTER and NURSE-DOCTOR, selected from the Connecticut Free Associational Norms (Bousfield, Cohen, Whitmarsh, & Kincaid, 1961); 48 pairs of unassociated words, e.g., BREAD-DOCTOR and NURSE-BUTTER, formed by randomly interchanging the response terms between the 48 pairs of associated words so that there were no obvious associations within the resulting pairs; 48 pairs of nonwords; and 96 pairs involving a word and a nonword. Within each pair of associated words, the second member was either the first or second most frequent free associate given in response to the first member. Within each pair of unassociated words, the second member was never the first or second most frequent free associate of the first member. The median length of strings in the pairs of associated words and pairs of unassociated words was 5 letters and ranged from 3 to 7 letters; the median word frequency was 59 per million, and ranged from 1,747 to less than 1 per million (Kucera & Francis, 1967). A separate set of 96 words was used for the pairs involving a word and a nonword. These words were similar to the associated words in terms of frequency, length, and semantic classification. Nonwords were constructed from common words, e.g., MARK, replacing at least one letter with another letter. Vowels were used to replace vowels, and consonants were used to replace consonants. The resulting strings of letters, e.g., MARB, were pronounceable and were equal in average length to the words paired with them. A majority of the nonwords differed by only a single letter from some English word, and the differences were not systematically associated with any one letter position.

In addition to the test stimuli, 24 pairs of words, 8 pairs of nonwords, and 16 pairs involving a word and a nonword were constructed as practice stimuli. Degree of association was not varied systematically among the pairs of practice words.

Apparatus.   The stimuli were generated on a Stromberg Carlson SC4060 graphics system, photographed on 16-mm. movie film and presented on a rear-projection screen by a Perceptual Development Laboratories' Mark III Perceptoscope. The *Ss* responded via a panel having finger keys for the right and left hands. Reaction time was measured to the nearest millisecond by counting the cycles of a 1,000-Hz. oscillator.

Procedure and design.   The *Ss* were run individually during one session involving a series of discrete RT trials. The *S* was seated in front of the darkened screen throughout the session. At the beginning of each trial, the word READY was presented briefly as a warning signal on the screen. A small fixation box, which subtended approximate visual angles of 3°40' horizontally and 1°50' vertically, then appeared during a 1-sec. foreperiod. Following the foreperiod, the stimulus was displayed horizontally in (white) capital letters in the middle of the box, with one string of letters centered above the other. If both strings were words, *S* pressed a key labeled "yes" with his right index finger, otherwise pressing a "no" key with the left index finger. Reaction time was measured from stimulus-onset to the response, which terminated the stimulus display. During an approximate 2-sec. interval when the screen was blank after each trial, *S* was informed of whether his response had been correct.

The session lasted about 45 min. and included a short instruction period and two blocks of 24 practice trials, followed by four blocks of 24 test trials. After each block, *S* was informed of his mean RT and total number of errors for the block, while he rested for

TABLE 26.1 Mean Reaction Times (RTs) of Correct Responses and Mean Percent Errors in the Yes-No Task

Type of Stimulus Pair					
Top String	Bottom String	Correct Response	Proportion of Trials	Mean RT (msec.)	Mean % Errors
word	associated word	yes	.25	855	6.3
word	unassociated word	yes	.25	940	8.7
word	nonword	no	.167	1,087	27.6
nonword	word	no	.167	904	7.8
nonword	nonword	no	.167	884	2.6

about 2 min. This feedback was intended to encourage fast and accurate responses. To further motivate good performance, S was given $3 at the start of the session and then penalized 1¢ for each .1 sec. in mean RT on each trial block, and 3¢ for each error. Whatever money remained at the end of the session served as S's payment for the experiment.

The entire set of practice stimuli was presented during the two practice trial blocks. During the test trial blocks, each S was shown 16 pairs of nonwords, 32 pairs involving a word and a nonword, 24 pairs of associated words, and 24 pairs of unassociated words from the total set of test stimuli. Half of the practice trials and test trials therefore required "yes" responses. Presentation of the test stimuli was balanced, so that each individual stimulus of a given type was presented equally often across Ss; e.g., each pair of associated words was presented a total of six times across Ss, while each pair of nonwords was presented a total of four times. No S saw any string of letters more than once. In displaying both the pairs of associated words and the pairs of unassociated words, the top string (e.g., BREAD) was always a stimulus term from the norm of Bousfield et al. (1961), while the bottom string (e.g., BUTTER) was always a response term. For the stimuli containing at least one nonword, each string was assigned equally often across Ss to the top and bottom display positions. There were thus five types of stimuli, which are listed in Table 26.1 together with their relative frequencies of occurrence. Relative frequencies of these types were balanced within trial blocks to equal their relative frequencies in the total set of test stimuli. The above set of constraints on stimulus presentation was used to construct six lists of 96 test stimuli each. Subject to these constraints, two ran-

dom orders of stimulus presentation were obtained for each list. Each S was then randomly assigned one of the lists presented in one of the orders, so that each list in each order was used for exactly one S.

Results and Discussion

Reaction time and error data from the test trials were subjected to $Ss \times$ Treatments analyses of variance (Winer, 1962). Prior to analysis, an arc-sine transformation was applied to each S's error rates. The reported standard errors and F ratios were computed using error terms derived from the $Ss \times$ Treatments interactions.

Table 26.1 summarizes mean RTs of correct responses and mean percent errors averaged over Ss. "Yes" responses averaged 85 ± 19 msec. faster for pairs of associated words than for pairs of unassociated words, $F(1, 11) = 20.6$, $p < .001$. "No" responses to pairs involving a word and a nonword averaged 183 ± 14 msec. faster when the nonword was displayed above the word, $F(1, 11) = 171.7$, $p < .001$. "No" responses for pairs of nonwords were not significantly faster (20 ± 14 msec.) than "no" responses for pairs where a nonword was displayed above a word, $F(1, 11) = 2.0$, $p > .10$.

The error rates for pairs of unassociated words versus pairs of associated words did not differ significantly, $F(1, 11) = 2.1$, $p > .10$. The error rate for pairs involving a word and a nonword was significantly greater when the word was displayed above the nonword, $F(1, 11) = 18.9$, $p < .005$. The error rate for pairs of nonwords was significantly less than that for pairs where a nonword was displayed above a word, $F(1, 11) = 5.5$, $p < .05$.

TABLE 26.2   Mean Reaction Times (RTs) of Correct Responses and Mean Percent Errors in the Same-Different Task

Type of Stimulus Pair					
Top String	Bottom String	Correct Response	Proportion of Trials	Mean RT (msec.)	Mean % Errors
word	associated word	same	.125	1,055	2.4
word	unassociated word	same	.125	1,172	8.7
nonword	nonword	same	.25	1,357	8.9
word	nonword	different	.25	1,318	11.6
nonword	word	different	.25	1,386	12.0

Error rates were relatively low except for pairs where a word was displayed above a nonword. A possible reason for this exception is considered in later discussion. The pattern of errors suggests that a speed-accuracy trade-off did not cause the observed differences in mean RTs; i.e., mean error rates tended to correlate positively with mean RTs.

The results of Exp. I suggest that degree of association is a powerful factor affecting lexical decisions in the yes-no task. For example, the effect of association appears to be on the order of two or three times larger than the average effect of homography reported by Rubenstein et al. (1970). This effect of association occurred consistently across Ss, and 11 of the 12 Ss showed it in excess of 30 msec. In Exp. II, another group of Ss performed the same-different task to further study the generality of the effect.

EXPERIMENT II

Method

Subjects.   The Ss were 12 high school students who served as paid volunteers. They had not been in Exp. I, but were drawn from the same population.

Stimuli.   The same set of test stimuli was used as in Exp. I. In addition, 16 pairs of words, 16 pairs of nonwords, and 32 pairs involving a word and a nonword were constructed as practice stimuli. Most of these practice stimuli also had been used in Exp. I.

Apparatus.   The same apparatus was used as in Exp. I.

Procedure and design.   The procedure and design were similar to those used in Exp. I, except for the fol-

lowing modifications. The S pressed a "same" key with his right index finger if the stimulus involved either two words or two nonwords, otherwise pressing a "different" key with the left index finger. The complete session lasted about 1 hr. and included a short instruction period, two blocks of 32 practice trials, and six blocks of 32 test trials. Two lists of 192 test stimuli each were constructed. For each list, two random orders of presentation were obtained, subject to constraints like those used in Exp. I. Each of these List × Order combinations was then used for three of the Ss. During the test trial blocks, each S was presented 48 pairs of nonwords, 96 pairs involving a word and a nonword, 24 pairs of associated words, and 24 pairs of unassociated words from the total set of test stimuli. Half of the trials therefore required "same" responses. Because the same-different task was somewhat more difficult than the yes-no task, each S was given $3.50 at the start of the session.

Results

The results were analyzed in the same way as Exp. I. Table 26.2 summarizes mean RTs of correct responses and mean percent errors averaged over Ss. "Same" responses averaged 117 ± 18 msec. faster for pairs of associated words than for pairs of unassociated words, $F(1, 11) = 42.6$, $p < .001$. "Same" responses averaged 185 ± 29 msec. slower for pairs of nonwords than for pairs of unassociated words, $F(1, 11) = 40.7$, $p < .001$. "Different" responses averaged 68 ± 25 msec. faster when the word was displayed above the nonword, $F(1, 11) = 7.3$, $p < .025$.

The error rate for pairs of associated words was significantly less than the error rate for unassociated words, $F(1, 11) = 16.6$, $p < .01$. The difference between error rates for pairs of unassociated words and pairs of nonwords was not significant, $F(1, 11) < 1.0$. For pairs involving a word and a nonword, the error rate did not depend significantly on whether the word was displayed above or below the nonword, $F(1, 11) < 1.0$.

A comparison of mean RTs in the yes-no task (Exp. I) versus mean RTs in the same-different task revealed the following: "Yes" responses to pairs of words averaged 216 ± 68 msec. faster than "same" responses to pairs of words, $F(1, 22) = 10.2$, $p < .01$. The effect of association on "same" responses to pairs of words did not differ significantly from its effect on "yes" responses, $F(1, 22) = 1.4$, $p > .20$. "No" responses to pairs involving a word and a nonword averaged 357 ± 74 msec. faster than "different" responses, $F(1, 22)$ 23.6, $p < .001$. For pairs involving a word and a nonword, the effect of the word's display position on RT interacted significantly with the task, $F(1, 22) = 76.4$, $p < .001$.

DISCUSSION

As a framework for explaining our results, we tentatively propose a model involving two separate, successive decisions. According to this model, stimulus processing typically begins with the top string of letters in the display. The first decision is whether the top string is a word and the second is whether the bottom string is a word. If the first decision is negative in the yes-no task, we presume that processing terminates without the second decision and S responds "no." Otherwise, both decisions are made and S's response corresponds to the second decision's outcome. It is assumed that in the same-different task, both decisions are normally made regardless of the outcome of the first. After both decisions, their outcomes are compared. If the outcomes match, S responds "same"; otherwise, he responds "different."

Now let us consider the RTs and error rates of yes-no responses. The *serial-decision model* explains why "no" responses are faster when the top string is a nonword. This happens because only the first decision is made, whereas both decisions are made when the top string is a word. The model also explains why "no" responses are about equally fast for pairs where

only the top string is a nonword, as compared to pairs where both strings are nonwords; i.e., for either kind of pair, only the first decision is ordinarily made. An occasional reversal in the order of stimulus processing, beginning with the bottom rather than top string, might account for the slightly faster responses to pairs of nonwords.

The relatively high error rate for pairs involving a word above a nonword suggests that processes preceding "yes" responses sometimes terminate prematurely after the first decision. In these cases, S may feel that discovering a word in the top position is sufficient evidence for responding "yes," without making the second decision. This behavior would not be too unreasonable, given the relative frequencies of the various types of stimuli. Such premature termination of stimulus processing, together with an occasional reversal in the processing order, would also explain why "no" responses were most accurate for pairs of nonwords.

The RTs from the same-different task do not provide direct evidence for testing the proposed serial-decision model because both lexical decisions are assumed to be made before all same-different responses. However, the relative invariance of the association effect across the yes-no and same-different tasks suggests that similar processes occur in both tasks. An additional operation, which compares the outcomes of the two lexical decisions for a match, would explain why responses were somewhat slower in the same-different task than in the yes-no task.

Several factors in the present experiments may have induced Ss to process the strings of letters serially. For example, Ss were encouraged to perform with high accuracy and were allowed to move their eyes in examining the stimulus display. Under other circumstances, e.g., with brief stimulus presentation and/or a more relaxed error criterion, Ss might process two or more words in parallel.

If the serial-decision model is valid for the present experiments, then one can use the yes-no data to estimate the time taken in deciding that a string of letters is a word. In particular, let T_{nw} represent the mean RT to respond "no" to a nonword displayed above a word. Let T_{wn} represent the mean RT to respond "no" to a nonword displayed below a word. Then with certain assumptions (cf. Sternberg, 1969), the difference $T_{wn} - T_{nw}$ is a measure of the mean time to decide that the top string is a word. From the results of Exp. I, an estimate of this difference is 183 ± 14 msec. An occasional reversal in the order of stimulus processing would make this difference an underestimate of the true mean.

One can also estimate approximately how much time is required to compare the outcomes of the two decisions before same-different responses. For example, suppose the mean RT of "yes" responses (Exp. I) is subtracted from the mean RT of "same" responses to pairs of words (Exp. II). Then with certain assumptions, the difference of 216 ± 68 msec. is an estimate of the comparison time when the two decisions match. On the other hand, suppose the mean RT of "no" responses to a word displayed above a nonword is subtracted from the corresponding mean RT for "different" responses. Then the difference of 231 ± 76 msec. is an estimate of the comparison time when the two decisions do not match.

What kind of operation occurs during each of the two proposed decisions? One possibility is that visual and/or acoustic features of a string of letters are used to compute an "address" in memory (Norman, 1970; Schiffrin & Atkinson, 1969). A lexical decision about a string might then involve accessing and checking some part of the contents of the string's computed memory location (cf. Rubenstein et al., 1970). Given this model, memory locations would be computed for both words and nonwords, although the contents of nonword locations might differ qualitatively from those of word locations. In essence, we are therefore suggesting that both words and nonwords may have locations "reserved" for them in long-term memory.

The effect of association on RT does not necessarily imply that the meaning of a word is retrieved to make a lexical decision. To understand why, consider the following elaboration of the serial-decision model, which may explain the effect. First, suppose that long-term memory is organized semantically, i.e., that there is a structure in which the locations of two associated words are closer than those of two unassociated words. Evidence from other studies of semantic memory suggests that this assumption is not totally unreasonable (Collins & Quillian, 1969; Meyer, 1970). Let L_1 and L_2 denote the memory locations examined in the first and second decisions, respectively. Second, suppose that the time taken to make the second deci-

sion depends on where L_2 is relative to L_1. In particular, let us assume that the time taken accessing information for the second decision varies directly with the "distance" between L_1 and L_2. Then responses to pairs of associated words would be faster than those to pairs of unassociated words. This follows because the proximity of associated words in the memory structure permits faster accessing of information for the second decision. The argument holds even if the accessed information is (a) sufficient *only* to determine whether a string is a word and (b) does not include aspects of its meaning.

If our second assumption above is correct, then any retrieval operation R_2 that is required sufficiently soon after another operation R_1 will generally depend on R_1. This would mean that human long-term memory, like many bulk-storage devices, lacks the property known in the computer literature as *random access* (cf. McCormick, 1959, p. 103). Recently, Meyer (1971) has collected data in other tasks that are consistent with this notion.

There are several ways in which this dependence between retrieval operations might be realized. One possibility is that retrieving information from a particular memory location produces a passive "spread of excitation" to other nearby locations, facilitating later retrieval from them (Collins & Quillian, 1970; Warren, 1970). A second speculative possibility is that retrieving information from long-term memory is like retrieving information from a magnetic tape or disk. In this latter model, facilitation of retrieval would occur because (a) information can be "read out" of only one location during any given instant, (b) time is required to "shift" readout from one location to another, and (c) shifting time increases with the distance between locations.

The present data do not provide a direct test between this *location-shifting model* and the *spreading-excitation model*. However, the location-shifting model may explain one result that is difficult to account for in terms of spreading excitation. In particular, consider the following argument about the finding that "different" responses were faster when a word was displayed above a nonword. We previously have argued that processing normally begins with a decision about the top string and then proceeds to a decision about the bottom one. Let us now assume that memory is organized by familiarity as well as by meaning, with frequently examined locations in one "sector" and infrequently examined locations in another sector. Recently, Swanson and Wickens (1970) have collected data supporting a similar assumption that Oldfield (1966) has made. Suppose further that before each trial, a location is preselected in the sector where familiar words are stored, which would be optimal under most circumstances (cf. Oldfield, 1966). Then the response to a word displayed above a nonword would require only one major shift between memory locations in the familiar and unfamiliar sectors. This shift would occur after the first decision, changing readout from the familiar to the unfamiliar sector.[1] In contrast, the response to a nonword displayed above a word would require two major shifts, i.e., one from the familiar to the unfamiliar sector before the first decision and one returning to the familiar sector before the second decision. This would make "different" responses slower when the nonword is displayed above the word. Moreover, the assumption that the starting location is in the familiar sector fits with the finding that lexical decisions are generally faster for familiar than for unfamiliar words (Rubenstein et al., 1970); i.e., a major shift between locations is required to access potential information about an unfamiliar word, whereas such a shift would not be required for a familiar one.

The effect of association on "same" responses to pairs of words (Exp. II) is also relevant to a recent finding by Schaeffer and Wallace (1969). In their study, Ss were presented with a pair of words and required to respond "same" if both words belonged to the semantic category LIVING THINGS or if both belonged to the category NONLIVING THINGS. Otherwise, Ss responded "different. Reaction time of "same" responses varied inversely with the semantic similarity of the words in the pair; e.g., "same" responses to a stimulus like TULIP-PANSY were faster than "same" responses to a stimulus like TULIP-ZEBRA. In contrast, Schaeffer and Wallace (1970) found that the RT of "different" responses varied directly with semantic similarity. They attributed the effects of similarity on both "same" and "different" responses to a process that compares the meanings of the words in a stimulus.

The effects of association in Exp. I and II possibly could have been caused by such a comparison process,

rather than by the retrieval mechanisms discussed above. However, if the "meaning" of a word is represented by the semantic categories to which it belongs, then there seemingly is a difference between the same-different task of Exp. II and the one studied by Schaeffer and Wallace (1969, 1970). Logically, Exp. II did not require Ss to compare the meanings of the items in a stimulus; i.e., Ss did not have to judge whether both strings belonged to the same semantic category, e.g., LIVING THINGS. Instead, Exp. II only required comparing the items' lexical status. Moreover, a comparison of meanings would have been impossible for those pairs involving at least one nonword, since the nonword would have no meaning in the usual sense. One might therefore argue that Ss did not compare the meanings of items in Exp. II. The argument is reinforced by the fact that Exp. I (yes-no task), which logically did not require comparing the strings in any way, produced an effect of association like the one observed in Exp. II.

Our reasoning suggests, furthermore, that the findings of Schaeffer and Wallace (1969, 1970) may not have resulted solely from a comparison of word meanings. Rather, their findings could have been caused at least in part by a retrieval process like the one we have proposed. This point is supported by the magnitudes of the similarity effects they observed, which averaged 176 msec. for facilitating "same" responses (Schaeffer & Wallace, 1969) and 120 msec. for inhibiting "different" responses (Schaeffer & Wallace, 1970). In particular, consider the following detailed argument. Suppose that judgments in their task involved two components: an initial retrieval process similar to the one we have proposed, which might be necessary to access word meanings, and a process that compares word meanings (cf. Schaeffer & Wallace, 1970). Suppose further that our experiments required only the first process. One might then expect that whenever both of these processes are used in "same" judgments, they would both be facilitated by semantic similarity. However, when they are used in "different" judgments, similarity would inhibit the comparison process while still facilitating the retrieval process. This would explain why the effect of association on "same" responses in Exp. II (117 msec.) was less than the effect of similarity on "same" responses in the study by Schaeffer and Wallace (1969). Moreover, it would also explain their finding that semantic similarity inhibited "different" responses less than it facilitated "same" responses. Unfortunately, the argument is partially weakened by at least one fact; i.e., their results for "same" versus "different" responses were obtained in separate experiments using somewhat different semantic categories and test words.

Regardless of whether spreading excitation, location shifting, comparison of meanings, or some other process is involved, the effects of association appear limited neither to semantic decisions nor to same-different judgments. At present we do not have ways to test all the possible explanations of these effects. However, procedures like the ones we have described may provide a way to study relations between retrieval operations that are temporally contiguous. We may therefore be able to learn more about both the nature of individual memory processes and how they affect one another.

AUTHORS' NOTES

This paper is a report from work begun independently by the two authors at Bell Telephone Laboratories and the State University of New York at Stony Brook, respectively. We thank S. Sternberg, T. K. Landauer, and Alexander Pollatsek for their helpful comments, A. S. Coriell for preparing the apparatus, and G. Ellis and B. Kunz for running Ss.

Requests for reprints should be sent to David E. Meyer, Bell Telephone Laboratories, 600 Mountain Avenue, Murray Hill, New Jersey 07974.

1. Here we are invoking our earlier proposal that both words and nonwords may have locations reserved for them in memory. We are assuming that from the viewpoint of retrieval, a nonword that is similar to English may be treated as a very unfamiliar word whose location is examined infrequently.

REFERENCES

Bousfield, W. A., Cohen, B. H., Whitmarsh, G. A., & Kincaid, W. D. (1961). *The Connecticut free associational norms.* (Tech. Rep. No. 35) Storrs, CT: University of Connecticut.

Collins, A. M., & Quillian, M. R. (1969). Retrieval time from semantic memory. *Journal of Verbal Learning and Verbal Behavior, 8*, 240–247.

Collins, A. M., & Quillian, M. R. (1970). Facilitating retrieval from semantic memory: The effect of repeating

part of an inference. In A. F. Sanders (Ed.), *Attention and performance III.* Amsterdam, The Netherlands: North-Holland Publishing Company.

Kucera, H., & Francis, W. N. (1967). *Computational analysis of present-day American English.* Providence, RI: Brown University Press.

Landauer, T. K., & Freedman, J. L. (1968). Information retrieval from long-term memory: Category size and recognition time. *Journal of Verbal Learning and Verbal Behavior, 7*, 291–295.

McCormick, E. M. (1959). *Digital computer primer.* New York: McGraw-Hill.

Meyer, D. E. (1970). On the representation and retrieval of stored semantic information. *Cognitive Psychology, 1*, 242–300.

Meyer, D. E. (1971, April). *Dual memory-search of related and unrelated semantic categories.* Paper presented at the meeting of the Eastern Psychological Association, New York.

Meyer, D. E., & Ellis, G. B. (1970, November). *Parallel processes in word recognition.* Paper presented at the meeting of the Psychonomic Society, San Antonio.

Norman, D. A. (1970). Comments on the information structure of memory. In A. F. Sanders (Ed.), *Attention and performance III.* Amsterdam: North-Holland Publishing Company.

Oldfield, R. C. (1966). Things, words and the brain. *Quarterly Journal of Experimental Psychology, 13*, 340–353.

Rubenstein, H., Garfield, L., & Millikan, J. A. (1970). Homographic entries in the internal lexicon. *Journal of Verbal Learning and Verbal Behavior, 9*, 487–494.

Schaeffer, B., & Wallace, R. (1969). Semantic similarity and the comparison of word meanings. *Journal of Experimental Psychology, 82*, 343–346.

Schaeffer, B., & Wallace, R. (1970). The comparison of word meanings. *Journal of Experimental Psychology, 86*, 144–152.

Schiffrin, R. M., & Atkinson, R. C. (1969). Storage and retrieval processes in long-term memory. *Psychological Review, 76*, 179–193.

Swanson, J. M., & Wickens, D. D. (1970). Preprocessing on the basis of frequency of occurrence. *Quarterly Journal of Experimental Psychology, 22*, 378–383.

Sternberg, S. (1969). Memory scanning: Mental processes revealed by reaction-time experiments. *American Scientist, 57*, 421–457.

Warren, R. E. (1970). *Stimulus encoding and memory.* Unpublished doctoral dissertation, University of Oregon.

Winer, B. J. (1962). *Statistical principles in experimental design.* New York: McGraw-Hill.

It seems to make sense that in order to recognize a written word, one must first figure out what each letter is and only then put the letters together to form a word. This idea that visual processing progresses in a step-by-step manner with each step finishing before the next is begun is called *serial processing*. However, if this is the case and processing occurs in a serial fashion, each letter in a word must be recognized before the whole word can be identified. Although this may sound intuitively correct, research has shown that skilled readers can recognize a letter embedded in a word (e.g., E in READ) more accurately than when it is presented as an individual letter (e.g., E by itself). This is called the *word superiority effect*, and was convincingly demonstrated by Reicher (1969).

Reicher started out increasing and decreasing the presentation time of a letter stimulus in a regular manner in order to determine how long it needed to be presented in order for each subject to identify the letter at 90% correct and at 60% correct. The basic idea is that some people needed a longer presentation time than others in order to correctly identify the letters. Then, the actual durations of the letters to be shown to that subject in the rest of the experiment were calculated from those numbers to form short, medium, and long durations. Notice that the presentation duration was different for each subject and varied between 35 and 85 milliseconds. This is a very good way of adjusting for individual perceptual abilities.

After the durations were determined, an isolated letter like K, a word like WORK, or a nonword like ORWK was briefly flashed on a screen and then immediately replaced by a mask of X's and O's. The observer was then forced to choose between whether a D or a K was present in the stimulus that they had just seen. A key component of the experiment was that either of the choices at the end of WOR would create a valid word. Thus, the observer's knowledge that there was a word presented did not automatically tell him or her which letter was presented.

On some trials the subject was told which two possible letters would be presented (precue) and on some no information was given. Finally, Reicher manipulated whether one or two letters, words, or nonwords were shown. Figure 27.1 shows the number of errors in identifying the letters as a function of the three stimulus durations determined separately for each subject in the pre-test. The symbols indicate whether the stimulus was a letter (L), a nonword quadrigram (Q), or a word (W). The number before the symbol indicates whether there was one or two letters, quadrigrams, or words. The most important result is that there were fewer errors in identifying a letter in one or two words (1W and 2W) than when one or two letters were presented (1L and 2L). Thus, detection of K is better when it is part of a word than when it is presented in isolation—the word superiority effect. (Interestingly, the no precue condition was better than the precue condition, although Reicher has no explanation for this.)

This result seems paradoxical. In detecting an isolated letter, there is only one item to focus on. When a word is presented, more letters must be processed before the word can be detected. Thus, it would seem, detecting a letter in a word should be more difficult than detecting a letter in isolation. The data, however, demonstrate exactly the opposite effect.

This finding has been of significant interest to researchers who explore the processes involved in recognizing patterns. These data have been used to argue for the idea that previous knowledge and expectancies affect even very basic letter recognition (Rumelhart & McClelland, 1982). More recent studies have supported this speculation (Ferraro & Chastain, 1997). The CogLab demonstration allows you to participate in a version of the word superiority experiment very similar to that described by Reicher (1969).

REFERENCES

Ferraro, F. R., & Chastain, G. (1997). An analysis of Reicher-task effects. *Journal of General Psychology, 124,* 411–442.

Rumelhart, D. E., & McClelland, J. L. (1982). An interactive activation model of context effects in letter perception: II. The contextual enhancement effect and some tests and extensions of the model. *Psychological Review, 89,* 60–94.

QUESTIONS

1. Why were the durations of the stimuli adjusted for each individual subject?
2. Why is it important in the condition where the stimulus was a word that both alternatives formed a real word?
3. What was the main effect of interest in this study?

Perceptual Recognition as a Function of Meaningfulness of Stimulus Material

Gerald M. Reicher

University of Michigan

ABSTRACT

The present study evaluates a class of models of human information processing made popular by Broadbent. A brief tachistoscopic display of one or two single letters, four-letter common words, or four-letter nonwords was immediately followed by a masking field along with two single-letter response alternatives chosen so as to minimize informational differences among the tasks. Giving Ss response alternatives before the stimulus display as well as after it caused an impairment of performance. Performance on single words was clearly better than performance on single letters. The data suggest that the first stages of information processing are done in parallel, but scanning of the resultant highly processed information is done serially.

Sperling (1960, 1963) and Averbach and Coriell (1961) used a "partial report" sampling technique for testing availability to show that after a very brief visual presentation of a matrix of letters *Ss* initially have more information available than they can report. This suggests that *Ss* have a limited capacity to handle input information so that when they are asked to report all of the items in a stimulus display, they lose information while they are responding. Sperling has called the storage system in which this information loss takes place visual information storage (VIS) and suggests that it is a fast-decaying system for storing sensory information (i.e., information which has not made contact with the central processor or with long-term memory). Presumably, VIS does not contain the information necessary to tell whether a particular figure is a letter or some other figure or whether four letters

make a word or not. A scanning device (SCAN) selects information from the VIS and passes it on for further processing.

Sperling's model is based on an earlier model by Broadbent (1958). Both have a sensory storage system to hold information until the central processor is free to handle it, an attentional mechanism selecting information to be processed while holding the remainder in the sensory storage system, and a limited capacity processing system. In the early version of Sperling's (1963) model, the SCAN took place in a serial manner (the extreme case of a limited capacity processing system) at one letter ever 10 msec. This was suggested by an experiment in which a visual masking field, assumed to erase VIS, followed the stimulus display after various intervals. The function relating time between the stimulus and the masking field to the number of letters correctly reported had a slope of 10 msec. per letter correctly reported.

Estes and Taylor (1966) have also reported data favoring a serial processing model. In Exp. I of their paper they reported a decrease in percentage of correct detections of the letters B or F in a display as the number of elements in the display increased from 8 to 16. They were able to fit to their data a serial model of the following form: During a given time interval, a single item is scanned and classified as signal or noise. The limitation on behavior is imposed by a given probability that during that time interval the remaining traces will pass below threshold. Another possible interpretation of this result is that each item in the display has some probability of being mistaken for the incorrect alternative.

SOURCE: From Reicher, G. M. (1969). Perceptual recognition as a function of meaningfulness of stimulus material. *Journal of Experimental Psychology, 81*, 275–280. Copyright © 1969 by the American Psychological Association. Reprinted with permission.

Sperling (1967) has more recently argued for a parallel, rather than a serial, mode of operation of the SCAN. Although his *Ss* performed better on one particular position of a tachistoscopic display, all of the items in all positions had some probability of being reported correctly even after the shortest times were allowed for processing. This is unreasonable under the hypothesis that *S* completes the processing of one item before he can report any information about a second item and that he uses the same search pattern over trials. Sperling also notes that *Ss* can report the approximate number of items, and the colors, as well as the particular letters which have been cued; he thinks that this fact also suggests parallel processing.

Further support for parallel processing is given by the data of Exp. II of Estes and Taylor (1966). For a fixed display size with redundant target items (i.e., two or four) in the display, one model, postulating the independence of target items, and another model, postulating that a fixed number of the items in the display were being sampled and interrogated at once, both fit the data better than their serial model. Eriksen and Lappin (1965, 1967) and Eriksen, Munsinger, and Greenspon (1966) have also obtained evidence for independent, as opposed to serial, processing of display items.

Thus the evidence on whether early analysis of visual information occurs in serial or parallel is equivocal. Certainly Sperling's (1960) data showing that forgetting has occurred while *Ss* are emitting responses seem to demand that information is being lost while waiting for other information to be handled serially. His model stresses the initial stages of information processing (i.e., VIS) as the locus of information loss associated with the "waiting line" of serial processing. However, it is equally appropriate to assume that the serial processing occurs at some later stage in information processing, such as in identifying or attending previously processed (or analyzed) information. Notice that the term "processing" is being used here to refer to any operation performed on input information and not just to those operations that require attention. Thus far, single letters, the supposed serial elements of perception, have required complete, single-syllable responses and *Ss* have not had the opportunity to say more than one of them at a time. Thus the inferences drawn about time for processing and about forgetting

during processing could as well be made about identifying (categorizing) stimulus input or executing these responses. If *Ss* were given an opportunity to respond to more than one letter at a time, perhaps they would have the same processing time for an *n*-letter unit as for a single letter. In that case it would be necessary to infer that the letters of the *n*-letter unit were processed in parallel. This would still allow the recognition or identification units, the "chunks" (Miller, 1956), to be handled in a serial fashion.

To test these alternatives the present study measured recognition performance on one or two letters, four-letter words, and four-letter nonwords. The informational differences among the tasks were minimized by: (a) requiring a forced choice between two alternative single letters for all conditions; (b) arranging the two response alternatives so that if a word was presented as a stimulus, both the correct and the incorrect alternatives would make a common word, given the other three of the four letters. For instance, if WORD was a stimulus, the alternatives could have been D and K. If a nonword was the stimulus, both of the alternatives made up a nonword.

Three display durations, with masking fields following immediately upon termination of the stimulus, were chosen for each *S* in an attempt to sample three stages of the development of the percept. The basis for inferring development of a percept was improvement at the forced-choice task as a function of increasing duration of stimulus presentation.

In an attempt to reduce the confounding of perceptual effects with memory effects, a condition was added in which the two alternatives were given in advance of the presentation of the stimulus display. With this information, *Ss* would presumably have to remember only the target item so that memory loss would not confound the results.

METHOD

General experimental plan.   Nine *Ss* were extensively tested so that each would contribute 48 observations to each level of all of the major variables: stimulus duration, cueing condition, and type of material. During any particular session, *S* was presented three blocks of trials corresponding to the three stimulus durations. Within these blocks, the order of presentation of the material and the position of the critical letter were random. The Ss were not told and thus had no way of knowing what type of material would be presented on any trial. The stimulus durations for each S were determined separately. One of the six possible orderings of the three durations was chosen at random (without replacement) for each S. The durations were systematically changed after each second session so that each S received all possible orders of the stimulus durations under both the precue and the no-precue conditions. Five Ss received the no-precue condition on the first session of the experiment proper and four received the precue condition. After the first session, these cueing conditions alternated.

Materials and apparatus.   The word stimuli were 216 four-letter words chosen such that each of the words could be changed by one letter to make up a new word. The letter which could be replaced (called the critical letter hereafter) to form a new word, as well as the letter substituted to form that new word, were the two response alternatives in the forced-choice procedure. For example, D and K were the alternatives for the word WORD, with D being the critical letter. The critical letter came from each of the four possible positions of the four-letter words equally often.

The single-letter sets were made up by using the same critical letters in the same position as were used in the word sets. For example, for the word WORD with alternatives D and K there was a letter "D" with alternatives D and K. The quadrigrams were anagrams of the words with the critical letter held in its same position. For example, OWRD was an anagram of WORD, again with D and K as alternatives.

Letters could appear in any one of eight possible positions in a stimulus display of two rows and four columns. A single letter would occur equally often in any of the eight positions. In the two-letter condition the critical letter occurred equally often in each of the eight positions, the other occurring randomly in any one of the four positions of the row not occupied by the critical letter. The same pattern was employed for one and two words and one and two quadrigrams.

A three-channel tachistoscope (Scientific Prototype Model GB) was used for the presentation of stimulus materials. A fixation point was displayed on a blank field, followed by the stimulus display initiated by S after a ready signal from E. This was followed by a visual noise masking field with the two response alternatives directly above or below the position of the critical letter in the prior stimulus display, depending on whether the critical letter had been in the top or bottom row of the display. Underscores were used on the alternative card to indicate the relative position of the critical letter in the stimulus display. For example, ---D/K appearing above the masking field would indicate that the critical letter had been in the top row, fourth column. All channels were kept at 30-ftl. luminance. Stimulus materials were typed on white cards in Bulletin type style. Letters were in uppercase, 3/16 in. high. The stimulus field was less than 2° of visual angle. Because of the necessity of making the alternative letters backwards for the nonstimulus channels of the tachistoscope, the type style was photographed and backwards letters were made on rubber stamps and appropriately placed on the alternative cards. The noise field was made with overlapping Xs and Os of the typewriter.

Procedure.   In Session 1 of the experiment, the duration at which each S performed at 90% accuracy (uncorrected for chance) in identifying single letters from two response alternatives was determined. The test materials were a set of 120 single-letter displays in which all of the letters of the alphabet were used approximately equally often. The incorrect alternatives were chosen randomly. The method for finding the 90% point was a modified up-and-down threshold procedure. Only the last 60 of the trials were used to determine the 90% performance durations. The second session was used to determine the duration yielding 60% performance for each S.

The actual durations used for each S were the duration at which S achieved 60% performance, the duration at which S achieved 90% performance plus 5 msec., and the duration lying midway between these two points. The range of durations over all Ss was 35–85 msec. The mean difference between the longest and shortest durations was 25 msec.

The six types of material were sorted into blocks of 48 stimulus items with each block containing one instance of each type of material with the critical letter in each of the eight positions. The cards were randomized within each block so that type of material and position of the critical item were random. During an experimental session, three blocks—one at each duration—were shown. On alternate days Ss were given the two alternative letters verbally before each stimulus exposure and repeated them. This verbal information before each trial was the only difference in treatment for the condition where Ss had information before the trial (precue) as opposed to the condition where they did not have such information (no precue).

On each trial, S waited until she got a signal from E. During this time the fixation point was visible in the tachistoscope. After receiving the signal, S could initiate the stimulus with a hand switch whenever she was ready. The card with the masking field and response alternatives followed immediately upon termination of the stimulus and remained on for 5 sec. After the appearance of the response alternatives, S responded with the letter which she thought had appeared in the stimulus display. The intertrial interval was dependent upon the time taken to initiate the stimulus and to respond. The E occasionally timed the period between successive initiations of the stimulus and found that this period was generally somewhere between 15 and 20 sec. Inasmuch as one of the possible hypotheses mentioned in the introduction calls for testing of a null hypothesis, confidence judgments were obtained to provide more data on which to base a decision. The confidence judgments ranged from "1" to "4" and corresponded to the following: (1) able to identify the critical letter without reference to the alternatives; (2) able to choose between the two alternatives with better than chance accuracy; (3) not able to choose between the two alternatives with better than chance accuracy; (4) did not see the stimulus display at all.

The instructions to Ss emphasized (a) the way in which the position of the critical item in the stimulus display could be determined from the position of the response alternatives on the card appearing after the stimulus display; (b) that only one of the two responses could occur anywhere in the stimulus display; (c) that before each trial Ss were to look at the fixation point, in a position corresponding to the center of the area where the critical letter might occur; and (d) that one of the two response alternatives was to be given on each trial even if guessing was required. Finally, Ss were shown an example of the sequence of events in the tachistoscope with the stimulus duration increased to 5 sec.

Subjects.   Each of nine paid volunteer female students at the University of Michigan served for fourteen 1-hr. sessions. All Ss were able to read the 20/20 line on an eye chart with each eye, with glasses if they needed them. In addition to the nine Ss, there were three Ss who could not complete the 14 sessions. Three experimental sessions were repeated, two because of illumination changes during a session and one because of E error.

RESULTS

A comparison of the left- and right-hand panels in Figure 27.1 shows that Ss did worse in the precue condition than in the no-precue condition. These conditions were exactly the same except for the advance information regarding the alternatives in the precue condition. The results (frequencies) for all comparisons to be cited were analyzed for significance by a contingency able

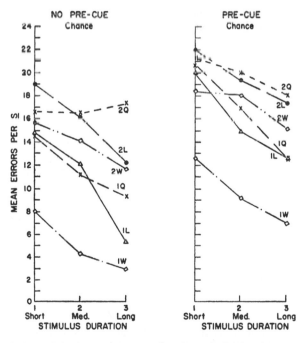

FIGURE 27.1   Mean errors as a function of stimulus duration. (Data are for all Ss combined, 432 observations per data point.)

analysis (Kincaid, 1962).[1] The differences between the precue and no-precue conditions for each type of material (collapsed over stimulus duration) were significant ($p < .01$ for each of the comparisons).

The experiment was successful in collecting data at three stimulus durations with different performance levels ($p < .001$ for all comparisons collapsed over type of material). This is also true when looking at data for individual Ss. Collapsing over the other conditions, it was always the case that the long duration was easier than the short duration for every S.

The comparisons suggested earlier are as follows: Collapsing over stimulus duration in the no-precue condition, performance on one word was better than performance on either one letter ($p < .001$) or one quadrigram ($p < .001$). Performance on two words was better than either two letters ($p < .05$) or two quadrigrams ($p < .01$). The same ordering was true for the results in the precue condition ($p < .01$ for all comparisons). Eight of the nine Ss did better on the single words than on single letters. The one S who reversed this trend was the only S who said that she saw the words as four separate letters which she made into words. All other Ss said that they experienced a word as a word and not as four letters making up a word.

Several other tests were made because they seemed of possible interest, although they are not independent of the tests made above or of each other. Performance on one of each type of material was better than on two of that same type of material ($p < .001$) for all comparisons in both cueing conditions. Performance on one quadrigram was better than performance on two letters ($p < .001$ for each cueing condition). Some Ss reported that the two letters tended to divide their attention so that this type of material sometimes seemed more difficult for them than one quadrigram, which they could sometimes pronounce or make into a word.

The differences attributable to stimulus parameters held up over all serial positions except when the critical letter was in the bottom row in the two-item condition. The most important deviation from the general results was that performance on two words was not better than performance on two letters when the critical letter was in the bottom row. This was true for each stimulus duration.

The confidence scores support the frequency data in that Ss were more confident on words than on the other types of material. However, the difference between one and two of each type of material was not as great as might be expected from the frequency data. Also, the finding that Ss seemed slightly more confident on one quadrigram than on single letters does not support the frequency data.

DISCUSSION

If we accept the assumption made in the past, i.e., that processing time is the critical variable in this task and is a monotonic function of the time between the onset of the stimulus and the onset of the masking field, we must conclude that single words are processed faster than single letters and reject a system for serial processing of sensory information. The Estes and Taylor (1966) fixed sample model suggests that there might be some limit to the number of letters which can be handled in parallel; this data can only suggest that for eight of nine Ss the sample can be four or larger. The result that one S did better on single letters than on words (for all three durations) suggests that the type of scanning that S does may depend on set or strategy. If a person is looking for single letters, he may be able to scan letters rather than whole words. If he is expecting words, the reverse may be true. This would offer no particular problems to a parallel model of processing of sensory information but grave ones for a serial model. In that performance on two of each type of material was worse than performance on one of that same type, the interpretation that coded units or "chunks" might be handled serially remains tenable.

The fact that performance on words was actually better than performance on letters might suggest some difficulty with the assumptions made here. Thinking in terms of a hierarchical system of information processing makes it difficult to understand how a word might be processed faster than the elements of which it is comprised. If the assumption is wrong and some variable besides processing time is important in performance on this task, we would not know whether performance on words was as good as or better than performance on letters because of processing time or because of this other variable.

One possible explanation for the superiority of performance on words is that letters are forgotten more quickly than are words. The attempt to reduce the memory load by giving Ss the response alternatives before presentation of the stimulus display was not successful. The data of the present experiment do not suggest any promising explanations of why prior information interfered with performance. Under somewhat different conditions, the opposite result has been found by Egeth and Smith (1967) and Long, Reid, and Henneman (1960).

A second possibility is suggested by the reports of some *Ss* that a single letter was harder to find in the field of the tachistoscope than four letters. If the process of perception can be broken down into detection and recognition with the completion of the former necessary before proceeding to the latter, the superior performance on words could be explained in terms of their increased detectability due to the greater area taken up by words than by letters.

There are alternatives to hierarchical processing. Cattell (1886) thought that single words were read faster than single letters (in a reading reaction time experiment) because the association between a common word and the name of the word is more frequently made than the association between a letter and its name. Also, Gestalt field effects often suggest that whole figures are more easily seen than the elements of which they are comprised.

Neisser (1967) has recently postulated a theory of the sort considered here. He suggests that there are early passive analyzers which operate on information in parallel and that further "construction" of the percept takes place serially. The construction phase of perception could, presumably, take advantage of a considerable degree of lower level processing. Thus a word or even a "meaning response" could be constructed instead of the separate letters or words of which it is composed.

In conclusion, the present experiment cannot be considered conclusive with respect to the stage of information processing at which serial processing is imposed, but it appears quite clear that the total processing time for multiple-letter arrays need not exceed that for single letters.

AUTHORS' NOTES

This paper is a revision of a dissertation submitted to the University of Michigan in 1968 in partial fulfillment of the requirements for the PhD in psychology. Members of the doctoral thesis committee were: Arthur W. Melton, Chairman; Robert A. Bjork; Edwin J. Martin; Wilfred M. Kincaid; and J. E. Keith Smith. The research was supported by the Advanced Research Projects Agency, Behavioral Sciences, Command and Control Research, Orders 461, and monitored by the Behavioral Sciences Division, Air Force Office of Scientific Research, under Contract AF 49(638)-1736. The revision was written at the University of Oregon with the support of the Advanced Research Projects Agency of the Department of Defense and was monitored by the Air Force Office of Scientific Research under Contract F44620-67-C-0099.

Requests for reprints should be sent to Gerald M. Reicher, who is now at the University of Oregon, Department of Psychology, Eugene, Oregon 97403.

ENDNOTE

1. Kincaid's procedure combines 2 (correct vs. incorrect) × *m* (conditions) contingency tables for each *S* to arrive at a single pooled 2 × *m* table; the test takes into account the consistent differences between *Ss* in a manner analogous to the repeated measurements design in analysis of variance. The *Ss* are treated as individuals rather than as a random sample from a large population, thus limiting statistical generality.

REFERENCES

Averbach, E., & Coriell, A. S. (1961). Short-term memory in vision. *Bell System Technical Journal, 40*, 309–328.

Broadbent, D. E. (1958). *Perception and communication.* Oxford: Pergamon Press.

Cattell, J. M. (1886). The time taken up by cerebral operations. *Mind, 11*, 277–292, 524–538.

Egeth, H., & Smith, E. E. (1967). Perceptual selectivity in a visual recognition task. *Journal of Experimental Psychology, 74*, 543–549.

Eriksen, C. W., & Lappin, J. S. (1965). Internal perceptual system noise and redundancy in simultaneous inputs in form identification. *Psychonomic Science, 2*, 351–352.

Eriksen, C. W., & Lappin, J. S. (1967). Independence in the perception of simultaneously presented forms at brief durations. *Journal of Experimental Psychology, 73*, 468-472.

Eriksen, C. W., Munsinger, H. L., & Greenspon, T. S. (1966). Identification versus same-different judgment: An interpretation in terms of uncorrelated perceptual error. *Journal of Experimental Psychology, 72*, 20–25.

Estes, W. K., & Taylor, H. A. (1966). Visual detection in relation to display size and redundancy of critical elements. *Perception and Psychophysics, 1*, 9–16.

Kincaid, W. M. (1962). The combination of $2 \times m$ contingency table. *Biometrics, 18,* 224–228.

Long, E. R., Reid, L. S., & Henneman, R. H. (1960). An experimental analysis of set: Variables influencing the identification of ambiguous, visual stimulus-objects. *American Journal of Psychology, 73,* 553–562.

Miller, G. A. (1956). The magical number seven plus or minus two: Some limits on our capacity for processing information. *Psychological Review, 63,* 81–97.

Neisser, U. (1967). *Cognitive psychology.* New York: Appleton-Century-Crofts.

Sperling, G. (1960). The information available in brief visual presentations. *Psychological Monographs, 74* (11, Whole No. 498).

Sperling, G. (1963). A model for visual memory. *Human Factors, 5,* 19–31.

Sperling, G. (1967). Successive approximations to a model for short-term memory. *Acta Psychologica, 27,* 285–292.

CHAPTER ELEVEN
Concepts

People have no difficulty identifying each of the 26 letters of the alphabet. These letters vary on multiple dimensions: They can have different heights, different widths, and so on. With items that vary along only one dimension—such as just length—people have great difficulty in identifying more than just three or four items.

A typical absolute identification (or judgment) experiment shows a person a single item and asks the subject to name that item. The name is often just a stimulus number; for example, the stimuli might be a series of line lengths, each one of which is 50% longer than the previous one. The first is 2 cm long, the second is 3 cm, the third is 4.5 cm, and so on. On each trial, one stimulus is shown, and the subject is asked to name it. If the second line length is shown, the correct response is for the subject to say "2". Any other response (e.g., "1" or "3") is incorrect. It is like being shown the letter "B" and asking for its name; if you say "A" or "C," that is incorrect. The task is sometimes called "absolute judgment" and sometimes "absolute identification." The CogLab experiment uses seven line lengths. The shortest line is 100 pixels long, and the remaining line lengths increase by 15%.

Generally speaking, once the number of items reaches about seven or eight, subjects become unable to perform the task without errors; interestingly, errors persist regardless of the range and practice (Shiffrin & Nosofsky, 1994). This finding is particularly important because it seems to reveal a fundamental limit in the ability of the cognitive system to process information. The interesting claim is that people simply cannot learn to identify seven or eight items that vary only on one dimension.

The typical pattern of results seen in this type of experiment is that performance is best on the two endpoints—the shortest and the longest line, in the above example—and performance is worst for the stimulus in the middle of the continuum. Finding best performance on the end points is often described as an "anchor" effect because the endpoints serve as an anchor or basis for making the remaining judgments.

Eriksen and Hake (1957) identify three possible explanations of the anchor effect. The *response attenuation* explanation attributes the result to an artifact: It arises because it is possible to mistake stimulus 4 as either stimulus 3 or stimulus 5, but stimulus 1 has only one item that it is easily confused with, stimulus 2. Thus, the end points are better identified simply because of the task itself. The second possible explanation has to do with *stimulus generalization*. In classical conditioning, for example, a rat that has been conditioned to respond to a 400 Hz tone will show similar responses to tones that are similar in frequency. The more different the tone, however, the less likely the response. A similar idea could explain the anchor effects: The middle item has more similar items than the end items. This explanation differs from the first primarily in that it is a property of the items rather than the method that produces the results.

The third possible explanation arose from reports from subjects. The *subjective-standard hypothesis* states that subjects pick a standard item and make their decision about the current item relative to the standard. Assuming the end points are the most likely standards, then anchor effects would be observed.

The experiments test these three explanations. The stimuli used in Experiment I were designed to have no obvious endpoints. Without endpoints, there can be no artifactual cause and there should be equivalent stimulus generalization. Only the subjective-standard hypothesis predicts anchor effects for the conditions used in this experiment, and anchor effects were indeed seen. Experiment II examines whether possible response factors play a role. It is possible, for example, that people are much more careful about giving extreme values. Imagine when rating things on a scale of 1 to 10 how many 1s and 10s you would give relative to values in the middle. To test this, one group of subjects gave responses of 1 and 20 to the most extreme stimuli, whereas a second group used the end response points to items in the middle of the series. Both groups' data exhibited anchor effects.

Research on absolute identification continues, with researchers examining a variant of the subjective-standard hypothesis. For example, Stewart, Brown, and Chater (2002) examine sequence effects. If you have just seen stimulus 3, you will be more likely to identify the next item correctly if it is stimulus 2 or 4 than if it is stimulus 7 or 8.

REFERENCES

Shiffrin, R. M., & Nosofksy, R. M. (1994). 7 plus or minus 2: A commentary on capacity limitations. *Psychological Review, 101*, 357–361.

Stewart, N., Brown, G. D. A., & Chater, N. (2002). Sequence effects in categorization of simple perceptual stimuli. *Journal of Experimental Psychology: Learning, Memory, and Cognition, 28*, 3–11.

QUESTIONS

1. Give five different sets of stimuli that vary along only one dimension.
2. Technically speaking, stimuli that vary in area might not be unidimensional stimuli. What other dimensions could be changing?
3. If you were in charge of designing a warning system that needed 10 different auditory signals, what would you do to ensure that people could very quickly and very accurately identify the various signals?

Anchor Effects in Absolute Judgments

Charles W. Eriksen and Harold W. Hake

The Johns Hopkins University

One of the most characteristic features of discrimination data obtained by the method of absolute judgments is the prominent anchor effects obtained for the stimuli on the ends of the stimulus continuum. Studies on such dimensions as size, brightness, and hue (1), loudness (5) and pitch (9) have shown that between five and nine stimulus categories can be absolutely discriminated without error along these dimensions. Yet on all of these dimensions, if the judgmental data are scaled on an equal discriminability scale (6), the majority of the discrimination is actually carried by a relatively few stimuli on each end of the continuum. It has been shown that the magnitude of these anchor effects is relatively independent of the number of stimulus and response categories (2).

Despite the prominence and the importance of these end effects, little is known concerning the factors that produce them. Garner (4) suggested that they might in part be due to a *response attenuation effect* that artifactually leads to unidirectional errors on the ends of the stimulus series. In the middle of the stimulus series, *S* can err in either direction in assigning a response to the stimulus while for the end stimuli *S* can err in only one direction. However, Garner (4) as well as Eriksen and Hake (2) have shown that this artifact is not sufficient to account for the observed anchor effects. The accuracy of discrimination for the end stimuli is much greater than can be accounted for on the basis of unidirectional distribution of error.

A second explanation for the anchor effects can be found in the behavior-theory model of discrimination and stimulus generalization. If it is assumed that for each value on the stimulus series a generalization gradient is set up in terms of the particular response that is assigned to that stimulus, there would be for the stimuli in the middle of the series a number of overlapping generalization gradients. Thus the occurrence of a stimulus in the middle of the series would tend to evoke a number of responses. Even if the correct response to that stimulus is assumed to have the greater habit strength, due to such factors as oscillation (7), competing responses would be evoked with a relatively high frequency. However, for the stimuli on the ends of the series, the generalization gradients would be asymmetrical with the result that there would be fewer competing responses and therefore fewer errors. Although there have been no systematic attempts to apply the stimulus-generalization model to absolute judgment data, it is apparent that this model would predict the end effects that are typically found.

There is a third explanation for the anchor effects that has been suggested by Ss' accounts of their subjective behavior and by our own introspections while serving as Ss in absolute judgment tasks. This is the "subjective-standard hypothesis" which, simply stated, says that judgments are never made in a vacuum but are always made relative to a standard or reference level that is subjectively present.[1] The S, when confronted with a series of stimuli in an absolute judgment task, selects a few stimuli in the series that he then uses as standards for judging the remaining stimuli. When a different stimulus is presented S attempts to recall one of these "standard" stimuli and uses it as a reference in judging the presented stimulus. Essentially he transforms the task into a comparative judgment using the recalled value of the selected standard as the comparison stimulus. If it is assumed that Ss select the end stimuli to use as their subjective standards, the observed anchor effects are the expected outcome. The frequent attempt to recall the value of the end stimuli should increase the accuracy

Source: From Eriksen, C. W., & Hake, H. W. (1957). Anchor effects in absolute judgments. *Journal of Experimental Psychology, 53,* 132–138.

of recognition of these stimuli when they do occur. Also the recognition accuracy of the other stimuli in the series should be directly related to the distance of these stimuli from the end stimuli since the effectiveness of a standard is inversely related to the similarity of the standard and the comparison stimulus (8).

In the series of experiments reported below, data have been obtained which are definitely incompatible with the first two theories or explanations of anchor effects. The obtained data lend themselves most readily to an interpretation along the lines of the *subjective-standard hypothesis*.

EXPERIMENT I

Design

It would be possible to test empirically the adequacy of the three theories of anchor effects by means of an endless stimulus continuum. Such an endless continuum is available in the form of visible hues. By using a series of hues that vary from red through green, blue, and back to red again by varying through the purples, one can obtain a stimulus series that has no obvious breaks or end points.

Both the response attenuation and the stimulus-generalization hypotheses would predict that absolute judgments of such an endless continuum would be free of anchor effects. Since for any stimulus on this continuum S would be equally likely to err in either direction in the response he applies to the stimulus, there would be no response attenuation. Similarly, the stimulus-generalization gradients would be approximately symmetrical for each stimulus and thus response competition would be about the same for all stimuli.

The subjective-standard hypothesis would predict, however, that anchor effects would still be present. Subjects would still be expected to select a few stimuli or hues which they would attempt to recall with high frequency to use as standards in judging the other stimuli in the series. The particular hues selected might be expected to vary between Ss, but due to cultural conventions and knowledge about primary colors, this selection would probably not be random.

Actually, it is possible to manipulate experimentally which of the hues Ss are apt to select as their sub-jective standards by manipulating the response assigned to the specific hues. It is common practice to use the number series for responses in absolute-judgment studies since this has the advantage of providing Ss with a familiar set of responses in which the sequential relations are already well known. The assumption in the present study is that in the absence of obvious stimulus values to select as subjective standards, Ss would select their stimulus anchors in terms of the ends of the *number series* assigned them as responses. Thus, whatever hue is assigned the response "1" by E is most apt to be chosen as a subjective standard by S.

In the present experiment two groups of Ss were used. Both groups made absolute judgments of the 20 Munsell hues shown in Table 28.1. Both groups also used the number series 1–20 to identify the 20 different hues, but the groups differed according to which response number was assigned to which stimulus. The Ss in Group I were required to call the 5R stimulus by the response "1," the 10R stimulus by response "2," the 5YR stimulus by response "3," etc., and the number "20" was to be used for the 10RP. In Group II, Ss were instructed to call the 5BG by response "1" and 10BG by response "2," etc. Table 28.1 also shows the response numbers assigned to each stimulus by the two groups of Ss.

Method

Stimuli and procedure. As can be seen from Table 28.1, the 20 hues used in the experimental series were so selected as to form a color circle and to thus provide a stimulus continuum which was endless. The stimuli were constructed by pasting 1-in. squares of Munsell papers in the center of 8×11-in. white cardboards. All hues were of equal brightness and saturation and the different hues were selected so as to be equally spaced on the Munsell system.

During the experimental sessions S was seated at a table and was screened from E by a partition. The stimuli were presented one at a time for S's judgments, in an 8×8-in. aperture in the partition. The sole source of illumination was an overhead McBeth Daylight Lamp.

Prior to the experimental judgments Ss were given eight practice judgments on each of the stimuli.

TABLE 28.1   Munsell Specification of the 20 Stimulus Hues, and Response Numbers Used by *Ss* to Identify Them[*]

Hues	Responses Group I	Responses Group II	Hues	Responses Group I	Responses Group II
5R	1	11	5BG	11	1
10R	2	12	10BG	12	2
5YR	3	13	5B	13	3
10YR	4	14	10B	14	4
5Y	5	15	5PB	15	5
10Y	6	16	10PB	16	6
5GY	7	17	5P	17	7
10GY	8	18	10P	18	8
5G	9	19	5RP	19	9
10G	10	20	10RP	20	10

[*]All hues had a brightness value of 5 and a saturation of 6 in the Munsell notation.

During these practice judgments the stimuli were presented in random order and *S* was informed as to the correct response after each of his judgments. Immediately following the practice session each *S* made 24 judgments of each of the 20 stimuli. During these experimental judgments *S* received no knowledge of the correctness of his judgments. The stimuli were presented in random order with the restriction that each of the 20 stimuli occur three times in each set of 60 judgments. Four duplicates of each of the stimulus hues were used in order to minimize the possibility that *Ss* might employ incidental cues, such as smudges on the stimulus cards, in making their judgments.

Subjects.   Subjects were male undergraduate students at The Johns Hopkins University enrolled in the elementary psychology course where they were required to serve a minimum number of hours as experimental *Ss*. A total of 10 *Ss* were used, 5 in each of the experimental groups.

Results and Discussion

The presence of anchor effects in the present judgmental data was determined by computing the accuracy with which each of the 20 hues was identified. In order to correct for differences in the frequency with which different response numbers were used, accuracy of judgment was computed as the percentage of times each response was used correctly. These percentages

were computed for each *S* in the two groups. In Figure 28.1 these percentages have been averaged by groups for each of the 20 hues.

As can be seen from this figure, both groups show anchor effects in their judgments. For Group I, judgmental accuracy is best for the 5R hue and for the 10RP hue with accuracy also being high for hues close to these values on the hue continuum. It is to be noted that these are the stimuli that *Ss* in this group were

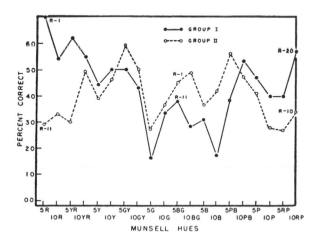

FIGURE 28.1   Percentage of correct responses to each stimulus in the two experimental groups. These measures of discrimination accuracy were computed by dividing the number of times a response was used correctly by the total number of times the response occurred.

TABLE 28.2   Summary of the Analysis of Variance

Source	df	MS	F
Stimuli	19	.0695	.93
Groups	1	.0474	.95
Individuals	8	.0496	
Stimuli × Groups	19	.0743	1.95*
Pooled Individuals			
× Stimuli	152	.0381	
Total	199		

*P < .02.

required to judge by the response numbers "1" and "20," respectively.

Anchor effects are not quite as prominent in the data from Group II, but here again the effects of responses upon accuracy of judgment is quite apparent if a comparison is made of the judgmental accuracy for hues 5R, 10RP, 10G, and 5BG.[2] Hues 5R and 10RP are much more accurately discriminated when they are called by responses "1" and "20" by Ss in Group I than when they are called by responses "10" and "11" by Ss in Group II. Similarly, the hues 10G and 5BG are more accurately judged by Group II Ss who label these hues by the responses "20" and "1," respectively, than by Group I Ss who apply the responses "10" and "11" to these hues. In general, the discrimination function for Group I tends to follow a U-shaped curve while the function for Group II suggests an inverted U function.

The significance of the above effects was tested by means of a modified three-way analysis of variance (groups, stimuli, and individuals). A summary of the results of this analysis is given in Table 28.2. In this analysis the subjective-standard hypothesis is tested by the interaction between groups and stimuli which, as is seen from the table, is significant beyond the .02 level. Since the interaction and its form was predicted, the obtained significance level is on the conservative side. Neither of the two experimental variables was significant by itself. There was no over-all difference between the two experimental groups, nor were the differences between stimuli significant when evaluated by the significant interaction term.

The results of the present experiment quite clearly show that the discrimination accuracy obtained for a specific stimulus is in part at least a function of what response has arbitrarily been assigned to it. This finding is predicted from the subjective-standard hypothesis but is not accountable in terms of either the response attenuation or the stimulus-generalization hypothesis. If anchor effects in absolute judgment data were solely due to either stimulus-generalization gradients or to response attenuation, there would have been no anchor effects in the present judgmental data. The subjective-standard hypothesis not only predicts the obtained anchor effects, but the location of the anchors are consistent with what would occur if Ss selected their subjective standards in terms of salient responses.

EXPERIMENT II

While the results of Exp. I are consistent with the subjective-standard hypothesis, the possibility exists that the response effects upon judgmental accuracy are due to response variables other than those determining Ss' choice of subjective standards. Garner, Hake, and Eriksen (3) have shown that not only can responses be operationally distinguished from perceptual processes, but also that care must be taken to distinguish between response and perceptual effects. Garner has suggested that the results of the above experiment might be due to what he terms response stabilization.[3] That is, responses on the ends of the response continuum may be more stable in that S uses them more carefully or sparingly. Alternatively stated, S may be better able to discriminate among his responses on the ends of the response continuum and thus be able to keep better track of how he has used them.

Volkman has made a somewhat similar suggestion of response effects.[4] He has suggested that in addition to stimulus generalization there is also response generalization along the response continuum. Thus, there would be asymmetrical response-generalization gradients for the end responses corresponding to the asymmetrical stimulus-generalization gradients for the end stimuli, and these response gradients would work in the same manner as has been discussed above for the stimulus gradients in improving discrimination for the end stimuli. This response generalization can be viewed as supplemental to the idea of response stabilization since it is essentially a theory to account for greater stability of the end responses. It was the purpose of Exp. II to determine whether these possible response effects contributed significantly to the anchor effects in absolute judgment.

Method

The method and procedure were identical with those employed in Exp. I with the exception that in Exp. II the stimulus continuum consisted of a series of squares varying in size from 2 to 40 mm. square. There was a total of 20 squares, with the series stimuli increasing in size by steps of 2 mm. on each dimension. Ten additional Ss drawn from the same source were assigned five each to the two experimental groups. The Ss in Group I were instructed to call the smallest square in the series by the response number "1" and the largest square by the response "20" and to assign the intermediate numbers to the intermediate-sized squares in order of increasing size. In Group II, Ss began the number series in the middle of the stimulus series, assigning the number "1" to the square that Ss in Group I were to call "11" and, continuing in this manner, they called the largest square by the number "10" and the smallest by the number "11" with response "20" being assigned to the size Group I was calling "10."

Both the response stabilization and the response generalization hypothesis would predict that increased judgmental accuracy should be obtained for the stimuli identified by responses on the ends of the response continuum. Thus in Group II, increased judgmental accuracy should be obtained for the midsized squares in the series relative to the accuracy obtained for these squares in Group I. The subjective-standard hypothesis, on the other hand, would predict little or no effect of response assignment upon judgmental accuracy in the present experiment. It would be expected that with the opportunity available, Ss would select their standards in terms of the stimulus series where obvious ends are present, rather than from the response series. This is based upon the assumption that salient features present in the stimulus series are prepotent in determining Ss' choice of subjective standards.

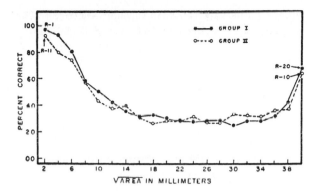

FIGURE 28.2   Percentage of correct responses to each stimulus in the two experimental groups. These measures of discrimination accuracy were computed by dividing the number of times a response was used correctly by the total number of times the response occurred.

Results and Discussion

In Figure 28.2 is plotted the average percentage of times that a response was used correctly for each stimulus by each of the experimental groups. These percentages have been corrected for the total number of times a given response was used by dividing the number of times the response was used correctly by the total number of times the response occurred. As can be seen, there is little or no difference in the judgmental accuracy for individual stimuli between the two groups. While the anchor effects are quite pronounced, they are essentially the same and occur for the same stimuli irrespective of the responses applied to these stimuli. The stimuli called by responses "1" and "20" by Group II are discriminated equally well by Group I Ss who identify these same stimuli by responses "11" and "10."

This lack of effect of responses on the size judgment data is supported by a modified three-way analysis of variance. In this analysis neither of the experimental variables was significant nor did the interaction term approach acceptable levels of significance ($F = .97$, $P > .20$). Thus the results offer no support for the view that response variables, such as response generalization, contribute to any appreciable extent to anchor effects. In view of this, it does not appear very probable that such response variables can be used to account for the results of Exp. I.

Taken together the results of Exp. I and II are sufficient to show that the anchor effects in absolute judgments cannot be understood in terms of response attenuation, stimulus generalization, or even such response characteristics as response generalization or response stabilization. The findings from both experiments, however, are not only consistent with but are predicted by the subjective-standard hypothesis. This hypothesis emphasizes neither the stimulus nor the response factors in absolute judgments, but points out that either stimulus or response characteristics can be important in determining the individual *S*'s choice of stimuli to serve as his subjective standards. In the present studies it has been assumed that the ends of a stimulus continuum or, if they are absent, the ends of a response series, constitute salient perceptual characteristics that in turn determine *S*'s choice of standards.

In addition to describing the anchor-effect data, the subjective-standard hypothesis has several other advantages. The individual differences in discrimination accuracy under the absolute method have seemed somewhat too large to be attributed to differences in sensory acuity. By stressing *S*'s attempt to covertly recall the standards he has selected, this hypothesis not only relates the absolute judgment task to processes important in learning, but it makes the magnitude of the individual differences more reasonable.

SUMMARY

One of the prominent features of discrimination data obtained under the method of absolute judgment is the anchor effects obtained on the ends of the stimulus continuum. Explanations for these anchor effects have been advanced in terms of response attenuation and stimulus generalization. In the present paper an alternative explanation, termed the subjective-standard hypothesis, is presented. This hypothesis states that *S*, when confronted with a series of stimuli in an absolute-judgment task, selects certain stimuli that he then uses as standards for judging the remaining stimuli. When a stimulus is presented, *S* attempts to recall one of these standard stimuli and uses it as a reference in judging the presented stimulus.

In Exp. I two groups of *Ss* were required to judge absolutely a series of hues that formed a circular continuum. The responses consisted of the number series 1–20. The groups differed in what response numbers were assigned to which hues. The results showed that anchor effects were obtained for this circular continuum and that the discriminability of a hue depended in part upon the response number that was assigned to it. These results are interpreted as being at variance with the response-attenuation hypothesis and the stimulus-generalization hypothesis, but were predicted by the subjective-standard hypothesis. The results of Exp. II successfully ruled out an explanation of the results of Exp. I in terms of such response factors as response stabilization and response generalization.

AUTHORS' NOTE

Both authors are now at the University of Illinois.

ENDNOTES

1. An explanation of anchor effects in terms of subjective standards or subjective frames of reference is as old as the problem itself. However, these explanations have seldom been explicitly formulated. The present purpose was to state, in a manner that was experimentally testable, how subjective standards are formed and how they contribute to judgmental accuracy.

2. The effects of the experimental variables in determining anchor effects is somewhat obscured by what appears to be unequal discriminability among the stimulus hues. As can be seen from Figure 28.1, certain hues are much better discriminated irrespective of their location with respect to the anchors. Thus, the hues in the range of 5RP and 10RP show good identifiability while the hue 5G is poorly discriminated by both groups.

3. W. R. Garner. Personal communication. October 3, 1955.

4. John Volkmann. Personal communication. November 11, 1955.

REFERENCES

1. Eriksen, C. W., & Hake, H. W. (1955). Multidimensional stimulus differences and accuracy of discrimination. *Journal of Experimental Psychology, 50,* 153–160.

2. Eriksen, C. W., & Hake, H. W. (1955). Absolute judgments as a function of stimulus range and number of stimulus and response categories. *Journal of Experimental Psychology, 49*, 323–332.

3. Garner, W. R., Hake, H. W., & Eriksen, C. W. (1956). Operationism and the concept of perception. *Psychological Review, 63*, 149–159.

4. Garner, W. R. (1953). An informational analysis of absolute judgments of loudness. *Journal of Experimental Psychology, 46*, 373–380.

5. Garner, W. R. (1952). An equal discriminability scale for loudness judgments. *Journal of Experimental Psychology, 43*, 232–238.

6. Garner, W. R., & Hake, H. W. (1951). The amount of information in absolute judgments. *Psychological Review, 58*, 446–459.

7. Hull C. L. (1943). *Principles of behavior.* New York: Appleton-Century.

8. Hunt, W. A. (1941). Anchoring effects in judgment. *American Journal of Psychology, 54*, 395–403.

9. Pollack, I. (1952). The information of elementary auditory displays. *Journal of the Acoustical Society of America, 24*, 745–749.

29 | IMPLICIT LEARNING

Many areas in cognitive psychology examine explicit learning: You know what you are learning, such as a list of words, a set of facts, or a story, and you know what you have learned. In many situations, however, people can be unaware of what they are learning: Their behavior shows that they have acquired some complex information, but when asked, the person is unable to say what has been learned. Formally, implicit learning refers to acquiring knowledge "about the rule-governed complexities of the stimulus environment . . . independently of conscious attempts to do so" (Reber, 1989, p. 219).

One particular form of implicit learning is implicit sequence learning, in which a person learns a complex pattern but is unable to state what the rule is that governs the pattern. The most interesting—and controversial—part of this definition is that the learned information is unconscious (see, for example, the various chapters in Stadler & Frensch, 1998).

In a typical implicit sequence learning task (also called a serial response time [SRT] task), the researcher is interested in how quickly a person can identify where a stimulus was shown. Subjects are asked to press one of four keys as quickly as they can whenever they see a stimulus, such as an asterisk, appear in any of four locations (labeled A, B, C, and D). If the asterisk appears in location A, the subject is asked to press (for example) the "z" key. If the asterisk appears in location B, the subject is asked to press the "x" key. The experimenter measures the time needed to make each response, and then computes a mean response for a block of trials. There is an underlying pattern that defines the order in which the stimuli appear in the various locations. If the subjects learn this pattern, their reaction times (RTs) will decrease as they experience more blocks. To verify that the subject has learned a pattern rather than just getting generally faster, there is usually a test block. During this set of trials, the pattern is changed. If the subject has really learned the pattern, then RTs should increase during this block.

Given that RTs decrease over blocks and increase during the test block, the subjects can be said to have learned the pattern. A critical question is the extent to which knowledge of the pattern is available to conscious awareness. Destrebecqz and Cleeremans (2001) begin by reviewing some of the evidence relevant to this question. For example, many times, subjects who have demonstrated implicit learning often cannot say what the pattern is (Curran & Keele,

1993). On the other hand, there are some studies in which knowledge of the sequence appears to be available on a conscious level. For example, subjects can be given a recognition test in which they are asked to rate how sure they are that the test sequence was part of the learning sequence. Shanks and Johnstone (1999) found that subjects gave higher confidence ratings for sequences that had been seen compared to ones that had not, and argued that this indicated some awareness of the sequence.

The existing literature, then, seems to have contradictory findings: Sometimes there is awareness of the learned information, and sometimes there is no awareness. Destrebecqz and Cleeremans (2001) make the important point that the findings appear contradictory only if one makes a "process-pure" assumption. This type of assumption occurs when one assumes that a particular task requires only one particular kind of processing. In this case, researchers might think that an explicit task (such as forced-choice recognition) requires only explicit processing and an implicit task (such as sequence learning) requires only implicit processing. If one assumes that both kinds of processing are possible in a given task, then the discrepancy noted above is not necessarily quite so problematic. It could easily be the case that both implicit and explicit processes are used on a recognition task.

Destrebecqz and Cleeremans (2001) use Jacoby's (1991) process dissociation technique to see if they can separate implicit and explicit processes. The basic idea behind this technique is to create two conditions. In one condition, the task is set up so that both processes could contribute to performance; this is the *inclusion* condition. In a second condition, the task is set up so that one process will help performance but the other will not; this is the *exclusion* condition.

The experiment has two parts. First, subjects participated in a sequence learning task, in which the experiments manipulated something called the response-stimulus interval (RSI). This is the time between when a response is made and when the next stimulus is shown. The idea was that only with a relatively large interval would the subjects be able to use explicit knowledge to prepare for the next response. The CogLab demo does not have this manipulation, and also does not have the second phase.

Figure 29.1 shows that both the fast (no RSI) and slow (RSI) groups learned the pattern: There is an overall decrease in RTs, with a sudden increase only for the test block in which the pattern was changed.

In the second phase, subjects were given three tasks. First, they were asked to generate the order in which the pattern had occurred. In the inclusion condition—both explicit and implicit processes are allowed to help performance—they were informed that they should rely on their intuitions if they could not remember. In the exclusion condition—the explicit process is not allowed to help—they were told to generate another sequence of 96 trials but they should avoid any sequences that they had experienced. Explicit processes cannot play a role because if the subjects consciously remember anything about the learned sequence, they are instructed not to use this information. To the extent that they re-create the original pattern, it must have come from implicit processes.

To score performance on the generation tasks, the authors computed the number of generated chunks of three locations that were part of the training sequence. Chance performance is 0.33. The results are shown in the left panel of Figure 29.2 and suggest that subjects had both implicit and explicit information available to them. Evidence for the role of implicit information comes from comparing the fast (no RSI) conditions in both the inclusion and exclusion tests: Performance is above chance but approximately the same (0.40 vs. 0.37). Only implicit information should have been used in the fast condition in the exclusion test. A role for explicit information can be seen by comparing the slow inclusion results (0.55) with the fast exclusion results (0.32).

Finally, there was a recognition test in which the subjects were asked to rate how confident they were that a sequence of dot locations had been seen in the learning phase. As the right panel of Figure 29.2 shows, the subjects were able to distinguish between old and new sequences in the slow condition, in which both implicit and explicit knowledge could play a role. In the fast condition, however, in which the presentation rate was too fast to allow explicit processes to play a role, the subjects were unable to distinguish between old and new sequences.

These data suggest researchers should be careful about making process-pure assumptions. Tasks that seem implicit might benefit from explicit information, and tasks that seem explicit might benefit from implicit information. Previous disputes about whether implicit learning is truly implicit could be resolved by acknowledging that both sources of information could potentially play a role.

REFERENCES

Curran, T., & Keele, S. W. (1993). Attentional and nonattentional forms of sequence learning. *Journal of Experimental Psychology: Learning, Memory, and Cognition, 19*, 189–202.

Jacoby, L. L. (1991). A process dissociation framework: Separating automatic from intentional uses of memory. *Journal of Memory and Language, 30*, 513–541.

Reber, A. S. (1993). *Implicit learning and tacit knowledge: An essay on the cognitive unconscious.* New York: Oxford University Press.

Shanks, D. R., & Johnstone, T. (1999). Evaluating the relationship between explicit and implicit knowledge in a serial reaction time task. *Journal of Experimental Psychology: Learning, Memory, and Cognition, 25*, 1435–1451.

Stadler, M. A., & Frensch, P. A. (Eds.). (1998). *Handbook of implicit learning.* Thousand Oaks, CA: Sage.

QUESTIONS

1. What is the "process-pure" assumption?
2. Why is it important to avoid the process-pure assumption?
3. Why do the authors conclude that awareness is not always necessary for learning to occur?
4. What other information might you have learned in a way analogous to implicit sequence learning?

Can Sequence Learning Be Implicit?
New Evidence with the Process Dissociation Procedure

Arnaud Destrebecqz and Axel Cleeremans

Université Libre de Bruxelles, Brussels, Belgium

ABSTRACT

Can we learn without awareness? Although this issue has been extensively explored through studies of implicit learning, there is currently no agreement about the extent to which knowledge can be acquired and projected onto performance in an unconscious way. The controversy, like that surrounding implicit memory, seems to be at least in part attributable to unquestioned acceptance of the unrealistic assumption that tasks are process-pure—that is, that a given task exclusively involves either implicit or explicit knowledge. Methods such as the process dissociation procedure (PDP, Jacoby, 1991) have been developed to overcome the conceptual limitations of the process purity assumption but have seldom been used in the context of implicit learning research. In this paper, we show how the PDP can be applied to a free generation task so as to disentangle explicit and implicit sequence learning. Our results indicate that subjects who are denied preparation to the next stimulus nevertheless exhibit knowledge of the sequence through their reaction time performance despite remaining unable (1) to project this knowledge in a recognition task and (2) to refrain from expressing their knowledge when specifically instructed to do so. These findings provide strong evidence that sequence learning can be unconscious.

The role that consciousness plays in cognition is one of the most central and long-standing issues in experimental psychology. Differences between conscious and unconscious processing have indeed been explored in many different fields, such as memory (e.g., Jacoby, 1991; see also Kinoshita, 2001), perception (Reingold & Merikle, 1988), conditioning (Clark &

Squire, 1998; Lieberman, Sunnucks, & Kirk, 1998), and learning (e.g., Cleeremans, Destrebecqz, & Boyer, 1998; Shanks & St. John, 1994). Today, these issues benefit from renewed and widespread interest in the study of consciousness—perhaps best exemplified by the "search for the neural correlates of consciousness" now made possible by the increased availability of brain imaging techniques (see Frith, Perry, & Lumer, 1999, for a review).

Despite this wealth of research, the role of consciousness in learning remains intensely controversial (Stadler & Roediger, 1998), with some authors concluding that "human learning is systematically accompanied by awareness" (Shanks & St. John, 1994, p. 394), and others arguing that unconscious learning is a fundamental process in human cognition (Reber, 1993). In this paper, we demonstrate that learning can be unconscious to the extent that the relevant knowledge can influence behavior yet remain unavailable to conscious control. To do so, we apply one of the better methods of assessing awareness—the process dissociation procedure (PDP) introduced by Jacoby (1991)—to the best paradigm through which to study implicit learning—that is, sequence learning.

In a typical sequence learning situation (see Clegg, DiGirolamo, & Keele, 1998), subjects are asked to react to each element of a sequentially structured and typically visual sequence of events in the context of a serial reaction time (SRT) task. On each trial, subjects see a stimulus appear at one of several locations on a computer screen and are asked to press as fast and as accurately as possible on the corresponding key. Unbeknownst to them, the sequence of successive stimuli

SOURCE: From Destrebecqz, A., & Cleeremans, A. (2001). Can sequence learning be implicit? New evidence with the process dissociation procedure. *Psychonomic Bulletin & Review, 8,* 343–350. Reprinted by permission of Psychonomic Society, Inc.

follows a repeating pattern (Nissen & Bullemer, 1987). Reaction times (RTs) tend to decrease progressively during practice but to increase dramatically when the repeating pattern is modified in any of several ways (Cohen, Ivry, & Keele, 1990; Curran & Keele, 1993; Reed & Johnson, 1994). This finding suggests that subjects have learned the pattern and are able to prepare their responses on the basis of their knowledge of the sequence. Nevertheless, subjects often fail to exhibit verbalizable knowledge of the pattern (Curran & Keele, 1993; Willingham, Nissen, & Bullemer, 1989)—a dissociation that has led many authors to consider learning in this situation to be implicit.

Implicit learning has received many different operational definitions, but the most neutral and commonly accepted one simply states that learning is implicit when we acquire new information in such a way that the resulting knowledge is difficult to express (Berry & Dienes, 1993). Accordingly, most empirical studies of implicit learning have taken the form of dissociation paradigms on the basis of the rationale that in order to demonstrate implicit learning, it is sufficient to show that learning is not accompanied by awareness, as assessed by a subsequent test of explicit knowledge.

Such dissociations have often been obtained between performance in the SRT task and sequence knowledge as expressed in verbal reports. However, Shanks and St. John (1994) have convincingly argued that verbal reports do not constitute sufficiently sensitive tests of explicit knowledge, and that the corresponding dissociation findings should therefore be rejected as valid demonstrations of implicit learning. Indeed, verbal reports could fail to detect knowledge held with low confidence or could probe subjects about knowledge that they do not even need in order to perform the task (e.g., knowledge of rules when knowledge of instances is sufficient). As a result, Shanks and St. John, as well as many other authors (e.g., Jiménez, Méndez, & Cleeremans, 1996; Perruchet & Amorim, 1992), have suggested that valid tests of explicit sequence knowledge should involve forced-choice tasks, such as generation or recognition.[1]

With a few exceptions that turned out not to be immune from methodological concerns (see Shanks & Johnstone, 1998), all sequence learning studies using forced-choice tests have demonstrated strong associations between performance on such tests and learning as measured through the SRT task. These findings have prompted many authors to conclude that there is in fact no or very little evidence for implicit sequence learning (Shanks & Johnstone, 1999). This conclusion seems to be at odds with studies showing relatively preserved learning capacities in memory-impaired subjects (see Curran, 1995, for a review). However, only a few such studies have been reported so far. Furthermore, existing results are partly contradictory and often remain open to different interpretations. For instance, according to Shanks and colleagues (Shanks & Johnstone, 1999; Shanks & St. John, 1994), amnesics' performance cannot be taken as a demonstration of implicit learning because, when compared with that of control subjects, their performance is generally not only impaired in forced-choice tasks (taken as an index of explicit knowledge), but also in the SRT task (in which performance is assumed to reflect implicit sequence learning).

Importantly, these debates all tend to be rooted in the questionable assumption that tasks are "process-pure." In this paper, we defend a different position, namely that successful performance on forced-choice tasks cannot be exclusively attributed to the influence of explicit knowledge. In a generation task, for instance, subjects could perform above chance when they believed they were guessing the location of the next stimulus (Shanks & Johnstone, 1998). Likewise, in a recognition task, they could respond on the basis of a feeling of familiarity in the absence of explicit recollection of the sequence (see Reber, Allen, & Reagan, 1985, and Cohen & Curran, 1993, for further discussion). Implicit learning research is therefore cornered in a difficult methodological dilemma, because the most sensitive tests of explicit knowledge also turn out to be those most likely to be contaminated by implicit knowledge (Neal & Hesketh, 1997).

Similar issues raised in the implicit memory and subliminal perception literatures have fostered the development of new methodologies that assume that tasks in general are not process-pure (Merikle & Reingold, 1991; Reingold & Merikle, 1988). For instance, Jacoby (1991) has proposed the PDP as a way to establish the existence of qualitative dissociations between explicit and implicit forms of memory. In stem-completion tasks, for instance (see Jacoby, Toth, & Yonelinas, 1993), the number of word stems completed with previously studied words is compared in two conditions: the *inclusion* condition, in which subjects are asked to use either studied words to complete the stems or, failing recollection, the first word that comes to mind, and the *exclusion* condition, in which subjects are asked to exclude studied words when completing the stems. If studied completions are nevertheless produced in the exclusion condition, such responses can only be interpreted as reflecting the implicit influence of memorized items.[2]

Adaptations of the PDP to sequence learning (Buchner, Steffens, Erdfelder, & Rothkegel, 1997; Buchner, Steffens, & Rothkegel, 1998; see also Goschke, 1997, 1998) and artificial grammar learning (Dienes, Altmann, Kwan, & Goode, 1995) have been previously reported. Buchner and colleagues used the procedure to differentiate between explicit recollection and perceptual fluency in a recognition task subsequent to an auditory version of the SRT task. However, as stated before by Shanks and Johnstone (1999), the perceptual-motor fluency effect cannot be considered as equivalent to implicit influence given that fluency is consciously experienced and that it may be associated with explicit sequence knowledge.

In this paper, we propose a novel adaptation of the PDP to sequence learning in order to disentangle implicit and explicit knowledge acquisition in the SRT task. To assess explicit knowledge after training on the SRT task, we used a so-called "free generation" task—previously shown to be a very sensitive test of sequence knowledge (Perruchet & Amorim, 1992)—and asked subjects to perform this task under both inclusion and exclusion instructions (see below).

Next, to manipulate the extent to which sequence learning is explicit, we hypothesized that response preparation in the SRT task always involves both implicit and explicit components, and that the latter are specifically sensitive to the duration of the response-stimulus interval (RSI)—that is, the interval that separates subjects' responses and the onset of the next stimulus. In other words, our main hypothesis was that the development of explicit knowledge of the sequence depends on the rate of stimulus presentation in the SRT task. On the basis of this hypothesis, we thus compared subjects' performance in two condi-

tions differing only in terms of RSI: In the no-RSI condition, this delay was eliminated in order to prevent explicit preparation to the onset of the next stimulus. In the RSI condition, the RSI was set to a standard 250 msec. Our hypothesis was that suppressing the RSI would exclusively impair explicit sequence learning (but see also Perruchet, Bigand, & Benoît-Gonin, 1997, for a different position). If this were confirmed, we would expect to find that, in contrast to subjects trained in the RSI condition, subjects trained in the no-RSI condition acquire knowledge that, when assessed through our direct tests, would appear to be essentially implicit.

METHOD

Subjects

Twenty-four subjects aged 18–26 years, all undergraduate students at the Université Libre de Bruxelles, were randomly assigned to one of two experimental conditions and paid $10.

Materials

The experiment was run on Macintosh computers. The display consisted of four dots arranged in a horizontal line on the computer's screen and separated by intervals of 3 cm. Each screen position corresponded to a key on the computer's keyboard. The spatial configuration of the keys was fully compatible with the screen positions. The stimulus was a small black circle 0.35 cm in diameter that appeared on a white background, centered 1 cm above one of the four dots.

Procedure

The experiment consisted of 15 training blocks during which subjects were exposed to a serial four-choice RT task. Each block consisted of 96 trials for a total of 1,440 trials. On each trial, a stimulus appeared at one of the four possible screen locations. Subjects were instructed to respond as fast and as accurately as possible by pressing the corresponding key. The target was removed as soon as a key had been pressed, and the next stimulus appeared after either a 0-msec (no-RSI condition) or a 250-msec (RSI condition) interval depending on the condition. Erroneous responses were signaled to subjects by means of a tone. Short rest breaks occurred between any two experimental blocks. Subjects were presented with one of the following 12-element sequences: 342312143241 (SOC1) or 341243142132 (SOC2). Each experimental block consisted of eight repetitions of the sequence. These sequences consisted entirely of so-called "second order conditional" transitions (SOCs; Reed & Johnson, 1994). With SOC sequences, two elements of temporal context are always necessary to predict the location of the next stimulus. Both sequences were balanced for stimulus locations and transition frequency but differed in terms of the subsequence of three elements that they contained. For instance, the transition 34 was followed by Location 2 in SOC1 and by Location 1 in SOC2. In each condition, half the subjects were trained on SOC1 during the first 12 blocks and during Blocks 14 and 15, and on SOC2 during Block 13. This design was reversed for the other half of the subjects. Increased RTs during Block 13 are thus expected only if subjects have acquired SOC knowledge during training over Blocks 1–12.

After the SRT task, subjects were informed that the dots had followed a repeating pattern. They were then presented with a single stimulus that appeared in a random location and asked to freely generate a series of 96 trials that "resembled the training sequence as much as possible:" They were told to rely on their intuitions when feeling unable to recollect the location of the next stimulus. After this generation task—performed under *inclusion* instructions—subjects were asked to generate another sequence of 96 trials, this time under *exclusion* instructions. They were told they now had to try to *avoid* reproducing the sequential regularities of the training sequences. In both generation tasks, subjects were also told not to repeat responses. The stimulus moved whenever subjects had pressed one of the keys, and appeared at the corresponding location after a delay of either 0 or 250 msec, depending on the condition.

After completion of the two generation tasks, subjects were asked to perform a recognition task. Here, we used a procedure identical to that described in Shanks and Johnstone (1999). Subjects were presented with 24 fragments of three trials. Twelve were part of SOC 1, and 12 were part of SOC2. Subjects were asked to respond to the stimuli as in the SRT task, and then to provide a rating of how confident they were that the fragment was part of the training sequence. Ratings involved a 6-point scale (1 = *I'm certain that this fragment was part of the training sequence*, 2 = *I'm fairly certain that this fragment was part of the training sequence*, 3 = *I believe that this fragment was part of the training sequence*, 4 = *I believe that this fragment was not part of the training sequence*, 5 = *I'm fairly certain that this fragment was not part of the training sequence*, and 6 = *I'm certain that this fragment was not part of the training sequence*). It was emphasized to subjects that they had to respond as fast as possible to the dots and that the person achieving the best recognition score would receive a $10 reward. Both ratings and RTs were recorded.

RESULTS

RT Task

Because the two subgroups of subjects presented, in both conditions, with either SOC1 or SOC2, were trained identically, their RTs were combined for subsequent analyses. Figure 29.1 shows the average RTs obtained over the entire experiment, plotted separately for the two conditions. In order to analyze the data, we performed an analysis of variance (ANOVA) with blocks (15 levels) as a within-subjects variable and condition (2 levels) as a between-subjects variable. This analysis revealed significant effects of block [$F(14,308) = 17.094$, $MS_e = 1,110.455$, $p < .0001$] and condition [$F(1,22) = 10.140$, $MS_e = 40,145.88$, $p < .005$]. The interaction also reached significance [$F(14,308) = 2.751$, $MS_e = 1,110.455$, $p < .001$]. However, closer examination of Figure 29.1 suggests that this significant interaction might in fact be attributed to the pattern obtained over the first three blocks of training. This impression was confirmed by an ANOVA conducted on the data after removal of the first three blocks ($F < 1.2$). Overall, subjects were faster in the RSI condition—a result that could be interpreted as resulting either from improved learning or from improved expression of the acquired knowledge.

Most importantly, suppression of the RSI did not prevent sequence learning. Indeed, RTs increased in both conditions when subjects were exposed to the transfer sequence on Block 13. This result was con-

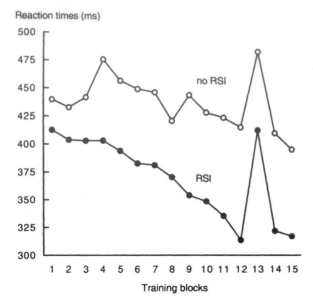

Reaction times (ms)

FIGURE 29.1   Mean reaction times for each training block, plotted separately for subjects trained with and without response-stimulus interval (RSI).

firmed by another ANOVA with block (two levels, Blocks 12 and 13) as a within-subjects variable and condition (two levels) as a between-subjects variable. This analysis showed significant effects of block [$F(1,22) = 35.144$, $MS_e = 2,382.12$, $p < .0001$] and of condition [$F(1,22) = 15.886$, $MS_e = 5,599.197$, $p < .001$]. RTs increased by 100 msec in the RSI condition and by 68 msec in the no-RSI condition, but the corresponding block × condition interaction failed to reach significance ($F < 1.3$). Presenting subjects with the training sequence anew on Blocks 14 and 15 allowed them to recover their pretransfer performance level. On the basis of these findings, we can thus conclude that subjects have learned the training sequence in both conditions. We now examine whether subjects in the RSI and no-RSI conditions differ in their ability to project their knowledge of the sequence in direct tests—that is, whether the corresponding knowledge is best described as implicit or explicit.

Generation Tasks

To measure generation performance, we computed the number of generated chunks of three elements that were part of the training sequence in both inclu-

sion and exclusion tasks. Since the generated sequences were 96 trials long, the maximum number of correct chunks was 94. To obtain inclusion and exclusion scores for each subject, we therefore divided the corresponding number of correct chunks by 94. Since subjects were told not to produce repetitions, chance level was .33.

Figure 29.2 (left panel) shows average inclusion and exclusion scores for both conditions. An ANOVA with condition (RSI vs. no RSI) as a between-subjects variable and instructions (inclusion vs. exclusion) as a within-subjects variable revealed a significant effect of instructions [$F(1,22) = 11.977$, $MS_e = 0.018$, $p < .005$] and a significant condition × instructions interaction [$F(1,22) = 6.918$, $MS_e = 0.018$, $p < .05$]. Condition failed to reach significance. To find out whether generation performance reflects knowledge acquired during the SRT task, one-tailed t tests were used to compare generation scores with those expected at chance level.

Let us first examine the results of the inclusion task. Subjects' performance was above chance level in both conditions [$t(11) = 3.62$, $p < .005$, and $t(11) = 4.33$, $p < .0005$, for the RSI and the no-RSI conditions, respectively]. However, as shown by a planned comparison, the difference in inclusion performance between conditions was only marginally significant [$F(1,22) = 3.511$, $MS_e = 0.028$, $p = .07$]. These results therefore appear to indicate that learning was in fact explicit in both conditions, because all subjects were able to project some of their knowledge about the sequence in the generation task. Similar associations between performance during the choice RT task and corresponding direct measures of sequence knowledge obtained in comparable settings (Perruchet & Amorim, 1992; Shanks & Johnstone, 1998, 1999) have been widely used to reject the idea that learning in such tasks is implicit.

However, a very different conclusion emerges when one also considers exclusion task performance. Indeed, while subjects trained in the RSI condition appear to have been capable of refraining from generating chunks of the training sequence, subjects trained in the no-RSI condition kept generating such chunks above chance level despite being specifically instructed not to do so [one-tailed $t(11) = 3.03$, $p < .01$]. Planned comparisons further revealed that the number of gen-

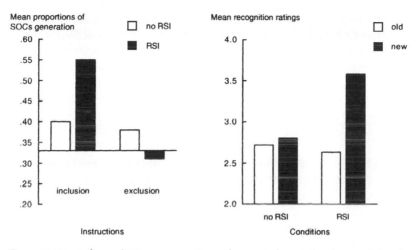

FIGURE 29.2   Left panel: Mean proportions of generated second order conditional transitions (SOCs) that were part of the training sequence, for both conditions, and under inclusion or exclusion instructions. Right panel: Mean recognition ratings given for the 24 test triplets. A high rating (between 4 and 6) is expected for a new sequence, and a low rating (between 1 and 3) is expected for an old sequence.

erated correct chunks decreased significantly from inclusion to exclusion instructions in the RSI condition [$F(1,22) = 18.55$, $MS_e = 0.018$, $p < .0005$] but not in the no-RSI condition ($p > .5$). Hence, it appears that in contrast to RSI subjects, no-RSI subjects had no control over their knowledge of the sequence.

To further explore exclusion performance, we conducted an additional analysis, as follows: For each subject, we computed the number of generated chunks contained in the training sequence (the usual score) and also the number of chunks contained in the transfer sequence (on which subjects have not been trained). The rationale of this analysis is that if sequential knowledge has been acquired implicitly during the SRT task, then it should exert an automatic influence on performance during the generation task. In other words, under exclusion instructions, one would expect subjects to tend to produce the sequential regularities of the training sequence more often than those of some other appropriate control sequence (e.g., the transfer sequence) in spite of the exclusion instructions. This is exactly the pattern of results obtained in the exclusion task performed by subjects from the no-RSI condition, in which they tended to produce more chunks from the sequence on which they had been

trained (37.7) than from the sequence on which they had not been trained (31.6) [one-tailed $t(11) = 1.836$, $p < .05$]. In contrast, subjects should have had control over their *explicit* knowledge, and indeed, we observed that subjects from the RSI condition were able to avoid producing more regular (30.4) than irregular (31.8) triplets when instructed to do so—that is, under exclusion conditions ($p > .3$).

To summarize, learning in the no-RSI condition produced knowledge over which subjects had little control, whereas learning in the RSI condition produced knowledge that subjects could control. If control is taken to reflect availability to consciousness, one can conclude that learning in the no-RSI condition was unconscious. These conclusions are also confirmed by the results of the recognition task, which we describe in the next section.

Recognition Task

Subjects were asked to respond to sequences of three elements and to rate the extent to which they felt these sequences were familiar. Because subjects may tend to respond faster to familiar sequence fragments than to novel fragments, their ratings could reflect feelings of perceptual and motor fluency rather than explicit recollection (see Cohen & Curran, 1993; Perruchet & Amorim, 1992; Perruchet & Gallego, 1993; Willingham, Greeley, & Bardone, 1993, for relevant discussion). To rule out this potential confound, we contrasted RTs elicited by the third element of old and new sequence fragments.[3] An ANOVA with condition (RSI vs. no RSI) as a between-subjects variable and sequence (old vs. new) as a within-subjects variable applied to these data showed that neither factor nor their interaction reached significance (all $ps > .1$). Given that RTs elicited by old and new sequence fragments do not differ in the recognition task, we can assume that perceptual motor fluency does not influence responses in this task—a result that replicates Shanks and Johnstone's (1999) data. Recognition scores can therefore be safely taken to reflect explicit recollection.[4]

Mean recognition ratings for both conditions and for both types of sequences are shown in Figure 29.2 (right panel; recall that high ratings correspond to judgments of novelty and are expected for new sequences). It is clear that subjects in the RSI condition were able to differentiate between old and new triplets. This is obviously not the case for subjects trained in the no-RSI condition. These observations were confirmed by an ANOVA performed on recognition ratings with condition (RSI vs. no RSI) as a between-subjects variable and sequence (old vs. new) as a within-subjects variable. This analysis revealed a significant effect of sequence $[F(1,22) = 6.753, MS_e = 0.477, p < .05]$ and a significant condition × sequence interaction $[F(1,22) = 4.738, MS_e = 0.477, p < .05]$. The effect of condition failed to reach significance. Planned comparisons further indicated that recognition ratings differed significantly between old and new sequences in the RSI condition only $[F(1,22) = 11.402, MS_e = 0.477, p < .005]$. These results are perfectly consistent with those obtained with the generation tasks, and again suggest that subjects trained in the no-RSI condition lacked explicit sequence knowledge.

DISCUSSION

The notion that sequence learning can occur implicitly has been previously rejected on the basis of observed associations between learning and performance on forced-choice tasks used to assess explicit knowledge (e.g., Shanks & Johnstone, 1998, 1999). In this study, while we confirmed the existence of such associations, we also suggested that they need not necessarily be interpreted as evidence that learning is explicit. Indeed, our results indicate that in a generation task performed under exclusion conditions, only subjects trained in the RSI condition were successful in performing the difficult exclusion task as instructed, while subjects trained in the no-RSI condition tended to keep producing chunks from the training sequence in spite of being specifically instructed not to do so. Taken together, these exclusion results can only be interpreted as indicating that in the no-RSI condition, generation performance under inclusion instructions is at least partly subtended by implicit sequence knowledge (Richardson-Klavehn, Gardiner, & Java, 1996), and hence that the knowledge acquired during training on the SRT task must itself be at least partly unconscious. This conclusion is further supported by the inability of the no-RSI subjects to discriminate between novel and familiar sequence fragments in the recognition task. On the basis of these findings, we therefore conclude that sequence learning can proceed unconsciously. In the following, we would like to reflect on the methodological and theoretical implications of our study.

Methodologically our findings demonstrate the importance of taking the contamination problem into account in implicit learning research: Even forced-choice tests—otherwise widely taken to constitute the best available tests of explicit knowledge—turn out not to be immune from implicit influences, and therefore cannot be considered as being exclusively sensitive to explicit knowledge. Other methods designed to address the contamination problem in related fields have resulted in similar conclusions when applied to implicit learning. For instance, Dienes and colleagues (Dienes & Altmann, 1997; Dienes et al., 1995; see also Shanks & Johnstone, 1998), on the basis of Cheesman and Merikle's (1984) studies on subliminal perception, have proposed using subjective rather than objective criteria (i.e., performance on a forced-choice task) to distinguish implicit from explicit learning. Subjective criteria, however, are prone to the same conceptual difficulties as verbal reports are, in that both rely on subjective self-assessments to determine the presence of some knowledge.

Another approach, based on Reingold and Merikle's framework (1988), was introduced by Jiménez et al. (1996), who proposed comparing the relative sensitivity of direct and indirect tasks in order to separately assess the influence of implicit versus explicit knowledge. The main limitation of this approach, however, is that the indirect task (the SRT task) must be assumed to be more sensitive than the direct task (the generation task) in order to demonstrate implicit influences (Toth, Reingold, & Jacoby, 1994). However, it is possible that this condition might not always hold in the sequence learning paradigm (Shanks & Johnstone, 1998, Experiment 3).

In the PDP, as used here, awareness is related to controlled responding. Within this framework, we have been able to demonstrate a qualitative dissociation between implicit and explicit sequence learning. Indeed, as our results indicate, increasing the RSI tends to exclusively improve explicit knowledge acquisition.

Turning now to the theoretical implications of our findings, we note that the PDP is a methodological framework that does not constitute, in and of itself, a process theory. Our findings therefore remain mute with respect to the existence of dissociable memory systems. However, our results suggest a functional dissociation between implicit and explicit learning and should therefore be useful in informing the development of computational models of implicit learning—an important limitation of which is that they have generally tended to remain agnostic about the implicit/explicit distinction.

Our interpretation of this functional dissociation is rooted in three central assumptions. The first is that explicit, conscious knowledge involves higher quality memory traces than does implicit knowledge. "Quality of representation," in this context, designates several properties of memory traces, such as their relative strength in the relevant information processing pathways, their distinctiveness, or their stability in time.

The second assumption is that memory traces continuously influence processing regardless of their quality. Thus, even weak traces, in our framework, while not available to conscious control, are nevertheless capable of influencing processing, but only

through associative priming mechanisms—that is, in conjunction with additional contextual cues. Strong traces, in contrast, are available to conscious control in the sense that they can both trigger responses in the absence of other sources of constraints and be inhibited when required.

Our third assumption is that the development of higher quality representations takes time, both over training and during processing of a single event. Skill acquisition, for instance, involves the long-term progressive development of strong, high-quality memory traces based on early availability of weaker traces. Likewise, the extent to which memory traces can influence performance depends both on available processing time during a single trial and on asymptotic trace strength.

When applied to our data, this framework suggests the following interpretation: People trained with an RSI are given more opportunities to develop and link together high-quality memory traces than people in the no-RSI condition. Because awareness depends in part on the quality of stored memory traces, the former will tend to acquire more explicit knowledge than the latter. Importantly, no-RSI subjects do acquire relevant knowledge about the sequence—but in the form of weaker memory traces that are capable of influencing responses only when contextual information is simultaneously available. This knowledge can thus be expressed in the SRT task as well as in the generation tasks because in both cases responses can be determined on the joint basis of an external stimulus (self-generated in the case of the generation tasks, or produced by the experimental software in the SRT task) and the relevant memory traces. Because these traces are weak and because controlled processing (and hence awareness) requires high-quality traces to be available, their influence on performance remains undetected, and controlled responding is made difficult. The relevant sequential knowledge therefore cannot be inhibited when the generation task is performed under exclusion conditions. Similarly, during recognition, weak memory traces do not allow successful discrimination between old and novel sequences in the absence of perceptual and motor fluency, as was the case in our study.

In conclusion, we believe that our application of PDP to sequence learning provides a useful new tool for investigating the relationships between implicit and explicit learning, and that our results clearly demonstrate that awareness is not always necessary for learning to occur.

AUTHORS' NOTES

A.D. is a Scientific Research Worker of the National Fund for Scientific Research (Belgium). A.C. is a Research Associate of the National Fund for Scientific Research (Belgium). This research was also supported by a grant from the Université Libre de Bruxelles to A.C. in support of IUAP Program P/4-19. We thank Robert M. French, Larry Jacoby, Pierre Perruchet, David Shanks, Tim Curran, Arthur S. Reber, John T. Wixted, and an anonymous reviewer for crucial suggestions and many useful comments on a previous version of this paper. Correspondence should be addressed to A. Destrebecqz, Cognitive Science Research Unit, Université Libre de Bruxelles, Ave. F. D. Roosevelt, 50-CP 122, 1050 Brussels, Belgium (e-mail: adestre@ulb.ac.be).

ENDNOTES

1. In a generation task, subjects are required to indicate the next element of the sequence rather than to react to the current one. In a recognition task, they are presented with small fragments of a sequence and asked to classify them as being part of the training pattern or not.
2. The PDP has raised many controversies. However, these are mainly concerned with the specific measurement model used to obtain *quantitative* estimates of implicit and explicit influences on performance. Different models have been proposed that reflect the hypothetical relationship between both influences. In order to circumvent this issue, we based our adaptation of the PDP on the comparison between inclusion and exclusion performance only (see also Neal & Hesketh, 1997).
3. Recall that two elements of temporal context are needed to predict the next location. Differences in RTs that specifically reflect sequence knowledge can therefore be observed only for the third element of each sequence fragment.
4. On the basis of previous results (Shanks & Johnstone, 1999), it seems that more than three trials are needed to allow perceptual fluency to improve RTs in the recognition task.

REFERENCES

Berry, D. C., & Dienes, Z. (1993). *Implicit learning: Theoretical and empirical issues.* Hillsdale, NJ: Erlbaum.

Buchner, A., Steffens, M. C., Erdfelder, E., & Rothkegel, R. (1997). A multinomial model to assess fluency and recollection in a sequence learning task. *Quarterly Journal of Experimental Psychology, 50A,* 631–663.

Buchner, A., Steffens, M. C., & Rothkegel, R. (1998). On the role of fragmentary knowledge in a sequence learning task. *Quarterly Journal of Experimental Psychology, 51A,* 251–281.

Cheesman, J., & Merikle, P. M. (1984). Priming with and without awareness. *Perception & Psychophysics, 36,* 387–395.

Clark, R. E., & Squire, L. R. (1998). Classical conditioning and brain systems: The role of awareness. *Science, 280,* 77–81.

Cleeremans, A., Destrebecqz, A., & Boyer, M. (1998). Implicit learning: News from the front. *Trends in Cognitive Sciences, 2,* 406–416.

Clegg, B. A., DiGirolamo, G. J., & Keele, S. W. (1998). Sequence learning. *Trends in Cognitive Sciences, 2,* 275–281.

Cohen, A., & Curran, T. (1993). On tasks, knowledge, correlations, and dissociations: Comment on Perruchet and Amorim (1992). *Journal of Experimental Psychology: Learning, Memory, & Cognition, 19,* 1431–1437.

Cohen, A., Ivry, R. I., & Keele, S. W. (1990). Attention and structure in sequence learning. *Journal of Experimental Psychology: Learning, Memory, & Cognition, 16,* 17–30.

Curran, T. (1995). On the neural mechanisms of sequence learning [On-line]. *Psyche, 2.* Available: http://psyche.csse.monash.edu.au/v2/syche-2-12-curran.html.

Curran, T., & Keele, S. W. (1993). Attentional and nonattentional forms of sequence learning. *Journal of Experimental Psychology: Learning, Memory, & Cognition, 19,* 189–202.

Dienes, Z., & Altmann, G. T. M. (1997). Transfer of implicit knowledge across domains: How implicit and how abstract? In D. C. Berry (Ed.), *How implicit is implicit learning?* (pp. 107–123). New York: Oxford University Press.

Dienes, Z., Altmann, G. T. M., Kwan, L., & Goode, A. (1995). Unconscious knowledge of artificial grammars is applied strategically. *Journal of Experimental Psychology: Learning, Memory, & Cognition, 21,* 1322–1338.

Frith, C., Perry, R., & Lumer, E. (1999). The neural correlates of conscious experience: An experimental framework. *Trends in Cognitive Sciences, 3,* 105–114.

Goschke, T. (1997). Implicit learning and unconscious knowledge: Mental representation, computational mechanism, and brain structures. In K. Lambert & D. Shanks (Eds.), *Knowledge, concepts and categories* (pp. 247–333). Hove, U.K.: Psychology Press.

Goschke, T. (1998). Implicit learning of perceptual and motor sequences: Evidence for independent learning systems. In M. A. Stadler & P. A. Frensch (Eds.), *Handbook of implicit learning* (pp. 401–444). Thousand Oaks, CA: Sage.

Jacoby, L. L. (1991). A process dissociation framework: Separating automatic from intentional uses of memory. *Journal of Memory & Language, 30*, 513–541.

Jacoby, L. L., Toth, J. E., & Yonelinas, A. E. (1993). Separating conscious and unconscious influences on memory: Measuring recollection. *Journal of Experimental Psychology: General, 122*, 139–154.

Jiménez, L., Méndez, C., & Cleeremans, A. (1996). Comparing direct and indirect measures of sequence learning. *Journal of Experimental Psychology: Learning, Memory, & Cognition, 22*, 948–969.

Kinoshita, S. (2001). The role of involuntary aware memory in the implicit stem and fragment completion tasks: A selective review. *Psychonomic Bulletin & Review, 8*, 58–69.

Lieberman, D. A., Sunnucks, W. L., & Kirk, J. D. J. (1998). Reinforcement without awareness: I. Voice level. *Quarterly Journal of Experimental Psychology, 51B*, 301–316.

Merikle, E. M., & Reingold, E. M. (1991). Comparing direct (explicit) and indirect (implicit) measures to study unconscious memory. *Journal of Experimental Psychology: Learning, Memory, & Cognition, 17*, 224–233.

Neal, A., & Hesketh, B. (1997). Episodic knowledge and implicit learning. *Psychonomic Bulletin & Review, 4*, 24–37.

Nissen, M. J., & Bullemer, P. (1987). Attentional requirement of learning: Evidence from performance measures. *Cognitive Psychology, 19*, 1–32.

Perruchet, P., & Amorim, M. A. (1992). Conscious knowledge and changes in performance in sequence learning: Evidence against dissociation. *Journal of Experimental Psychology: Learning, Memory, & Cognition, 18*, 785–800.

Perruchet, P., Bigand, E., & Benoît-Gonin, F. (1997). The emergence of explicit knowledge during the early phase of learning in sequential reaction time. *Psychological Research, 60*, 4–14.

Perruchet, P., & Gallego, J. (1993). Associations between conscious knowledge and performance in normal subjects: Reply to Cohen and Curran (1993) and Willingham, Greeley, and Bardone (1993). *Journal of Experimental Psychology: Learning, Memory, & Cognition, 19*, 1438–1444.

Reber, A. (1993). *Implicit learning and tacit knowledge: An essay on the cognitive unconscious.* New York: Oxford University Press.

Reber, A., Allen, R., & Reagan, S. (1985). Syntactical learning and judgment, still unconscious and still abstract. *Journal of Experimental Psychology: General, 114*, 17–24.

Reed, J., & Johnson, P. (1994). Assessing implicit learning with indirect tests: Determining what is learned about sequence structure. *Journal of Experimental Psychology: Learning, Memory, & Cognition, 20*, 585–594.

Reingold, E. M., & Merikle, P. M. (1988). Using direct and indirect measures to study perception without awareness. *Perception & Psychophysics, 44*, 563–575.

Richardson-Klavehn, A., Gardiner, J. M., & Java, I. (1996). Memory: Task dissociations, process dissociations and dissociations of consciousness. In G. Underwood (Ed.), *Implicit cognition* (pp. 85–158). New York: Oxford University Press.

Shanks, D. R., & Johnstone, T. (1998). Implicit knowledge in sequential learning tasks. In M. A. Stadler & P. A. Frensch (Eds.), *Handbook of implicit learning* (pp. 533–572). Thousand Oaks, CA: Sage.

Shanks, D. R., & Johnstone, T. (1999). Evaluating the relationship between explicit and implicit knowledge in a serial reaction time task. *Journal of Experimental Psychology: Learning, Memory, & Cognition, 25*, 1435–1451.

Shanks, D. R., & St. John, M. F. (1994). Characteristics of dissociable human learning systems. *Behavioral & Brain Sciences, 17*, 367–447.

Stadler, M. A., & Roediger, H. L., III (1998). The question of awareness in research on implicit learning. In M. A. Stadler & P. A. Frensch (Eds.), *Handbook of implicit learning* (pp. 105–132). Thousand Oaks, CA: Sage.

Toth, J. P., Reingold, E. M., & Jacoby, L. L. (1994). Toward a redefinition of implicit memory: Process dissociations following elaborative processing and self-generation. *Journal of Experimental Psychology: Learning, Memory, & Cognition, 20*, 290–303.

Willingham, D. B., Greeley, T., & Bardone, A. M. (1993). Dissociation in a serial response time task using a recognition measure: Comment on Perruchet and Amorim (1992). *Journal of Experimental Psychology: Learning, Memory, & Cognition, 19*, 1424–1430.

Willingham, D. B., Nissen, M. J., & Bullemer, P. (1989). On the development of procedural knowledge. *Journal of Experimental Psychology: Learning, Memory, & Cognition, 15*, 1047–1060.

Part of cognitive psychology explores *concepts*. What cognitive events happen when you think about a chair? How is the concept of chair represented in the cognitive system? This is a subtle issue. For example, surely a seat at a formal dining table is a chair, but what about a recliner, a stool, a couch, or a tree stump? The issue is important because the representation of concepts is the basis of everything else we can mentally do with concepts. In a very real sense, how we think and what we can learn is largely determined by how we represent concepts.

An efficient way to represent concepts would be to keep only the critical properties of a concept. This set of critical properties is sometimes called a *prototype* or schema. The idea of prototypes is that a person has a mental construct that identifies typical characteristics of various categories. When a person encounters a new object, he or she compares it to the prototypes in memory. If it matches the prototype for a chair well enough, the new object will be classified and treated as a chair. This approach allows new objects to be interpreted on the basis of previously learned information. It is a powerful approach because one does not need to store all previously seen chairs in long-term memory. Instead, only the prototype needs to be kept.

This paper by Posner and Keele (1968) is one of the earliest studies to systematically explore concept representation in a controlled way. Rather than using an already well-known concept like a chair, Posner and Keele had subjects learn patterns of dots. The patterns were variations of a few prototypes, but the prototypes themselves were not seen during the training phase. Instead, in the training phase subjects learned to classify the variations, with the underlying prototype being the basis for correct classifications.

Although this is a classic paper, the exact method and results are a little difficult to puzzle through. In Experiment 1, there were three groups, each of which received a different training protocol—one or five bits/dot, or the control group that received no training. A "bit" is defined here as one box in a 30×30 matrix. Thus, one bit/dot means that each dot in the pattern was moved over one square in the matrix. One group (Group 1) was given training with very small distortions of the prototype (1 bit/dot). The subjects in Group 5 were shown very large distortions of the prototype: Each dot was changed by five boxes in their matrix. Subjects were asked to identify each pattern as belonging to one of four patterns: a triangle, the letter *M,* the letter *F,* or a random pattern. Each list consisted of 12 patterns, and subjects categorized the patterns until they correctly classified two complete lists of 12 in a row. Group 7 was the control group and received no training. None of the groups actually saw the prototype in the training phase. On the transfer trials, all three groups saw exactly the same patterns: 7.7 bits/dot distortion.

The results for the training phase are expressed in terms of the average number of errors made before the subjects were able to categorize two lists in a row. This number is in the column titled "Original Learning" under the name for the group. Group 1 reached the criterion with fewer errors (4.8) than did Group 5 (12.3). Group 7 did not receive training. So, the group with the smaller distortion from the prototype learned the patterns easier. However, on the transfer trials, in which subjects were given very large distortions, the group that initially learned the patterns with larger distortions performed better than the group that learned with very small distortions (average errors of 4.3 compared to 5.6). Both trained groups did better than the untrained group. (Experiment 2 is very similar to this experiment except that the experimenters manipulated whether the subjects were told whether they were right or wrong in their responses.) This is a very interesting result: Even though it takes longer to learn when the variability in a category is large, the end result is that there is better generalization of learning.

Experiment 3 is the one that the CogLab demonstration is based on. Although it seems like a very complicated experiment, it is actually fairly straightforward. In this experiment, like Experiment 1, subjects were shown a variety of patterns that were distortions of different prototypes. After learning to classify the variants, subjects were shown a variety of dot patterns. In particular, they were shown patterns that had been shown during the training phase ("old distortions"), new variant patterns ("new level 7s and 5s"), and the patterns corresponding to the prototypes ("schema"). Classification and reaction time performance were nearly equal for the previously seen variants *and* the prototypes. Performance was slightly worse for the new variants. This is significant because both the new variants and the prototypes were never seen during testing. To classify dot patterns that were not previously seen, the subjects must be using a mental concept of what corresponds to the different categories. Because performance is better for the prototype patterns than for the new variants, the mental concept is similar to the prototype patterns. The conclusion seemed to be that people created a mental representation that was a mixture of the variant patterns used during training, that is, a prototype.

The patterns in the CogLab demonstration are much more complicated than the simple ones used in Posner and Keele's studies. Nevertheless, performance should be better (faster and more accurate) for the patterns that are based on the prototypes than for new variants.

Posner and Keele's experiment led to an intense investigation on concept formation and representation. Much of that research is consistent with prototype theories. However, aspects of the experimental data (particularly in Posner and Keele's first two experiments) suggest that the prototype theories cannot be the sole basis for concept representation. Many current theories include the possibility that particular examples (or *exemplars*) are also stored (Nosofsky & Zaki, 2002).

REFERENCE

Nosofsky, R. M., & Zaki, S. R. (2002). Exemplar and prototype models revisited: Response strategies, selective attention, and stimulus generalization. *Journal of Experimental Psychology: Learning, Memory, & Cognition, 28,* 924–940.

QUESTIONS

1. In Posner and Keele's experiments, how is the prototype defined?
2. How are the variants constructed?
3. What are the main results of the first two experiments?
4. Why do the first two experiments allow the authors to "reject the idea that only the abstracted prototype is stored"?
5. What is the most important finding of Experiment III?
6. Why is this important?

On the Genesis of Abstract Ideas

Michael I. Posner and Steven W. Keele

University of Oregon

Previous work has shown that Ss *can learn to classify sets of patterns which are distortions of a prototype, even when they have not seen the prototype. In this paper it is shown that after learning a set of patterns, the prototype (schema) of that set is more easily classified than control patterns which are also within the learned category. As the variability among the memorized patterns increases, so does the ability of* Ss *to classify highly distorted new instances. These findings argue that information about the schema is abstracted from the stored instances with very high efficiency. It is unclear whether the abstraction of information involved in classifying the schema occurs while learning the original patterns or whether the abstraction process takes place at the time of the first presentation of the schema.*

When a man correctly recognizes an animal he has never seen before as a dog, he has manifested an ability to generalize from previous experience. What has he learned that allows him to make the classification successfully? This question has been discussed in various forms since Aristotle. Some philosophers suggest a process of abstraction in which S builds up a representation of a figure (e.g., triangle) which is different from the instances he has seen. Others have denied the reality of such composite representations or abstractions. For example, Bishop Berkeley pointed out that he could search his imagination in vain for the abstraction of a triangle which was neither equilateral nor scalene but which represented both of these and all other triangles at once. The philosophical idea of abstract representations entered modern psychology from clinical neurology through the work of Barlett (1932) on schema formation (see also Oldfield & Zangwill, 1942).

In the areas of perception and pattern recognition, psychologists have studied questions related to schema formation. Attneave (1957) demonstrated that pretraining on the schema (prototype) of a set of patterns could facilitate later paired-associate learning. Subsequently Hinsey (1963) showed that pretraining on the prototype pattern is superior to pretraining on a peripheral pattern. However, these studies suggest only that knowing the schema can aid later learning and do not reflect on whether S in fact abstracts information concerning the schema in the course of learning.

Attneave's (1957) study, like most of the subsequent experiments, used stochastic distortion rules to obtain patterns which varied around a prototype. For rules of this type the prototype represents a kind of average or central tendency of the distortions. Following this same line, Posner, Goldsmith, and Welton (1967) showed that the rate at which Ss learned to classify a list of patterns was a function of the amount of distortion of the instances from their respective prototypes. As the amount of distortion increased, so did the variability among instances within a category. This increase in variability served to reduce the rate at which the category was learned. Evans and Edmonds (1966) have developed much the same theme. They also showed that Ss could learn a discrimination between patterns generated from different prototypes without having seen the prototypes. This discrimination could be obtained with or without knowledge of results. These studies indicate very little, if anything, about the use of a schema. That Ss can learn to discriminate patterns without seeing a prototype does not indicate that abstraction is involved or that the schema is itself being learned or used.

Source: Posner, M. I., & Keele, S. W. (1968). On the genesis of abstract ideas. *Journal of Experimental Psychology, 77*, 353–363. Copyright © 1968 by the American Psychological Association. Reprinted with permission.

The philosophical notion of abstract ideas is vague but it does suggest that information which is common to the individual instances is abstracted and stored in some form. In its strongest sense, this might be translated operationally into the hypothesis that the commonalities among a set of patterns are abstracted during learning and that they alone are stored. In the case of patterns obtained by statistical distortion rules, this suggests that S abstracts the prototype. A less extreme hypothesis suggests that S stores the abstracted schema in addition to the individual instances. A still weaker interpretation is that Ss will recognize the schema better than patterns which are similar to the memorized instances but which are not their prototype. This last hypothesis would not necessarily require the abstracting process to take place during learning.

The studies reported in this paper examine various transfer tasks in an effort to understand what S stores during the process of learning to classify distorted patterns. The stimuli are meaningful or nonsense dot patterns which can be distorted by statistical rules. In Exp. I and II, different groups of Ss learned to classify high and low variability distortions of the same prototype. They were then transferred to learning or recognition tasks which involved new distortions not previously seen. In Exp. III all Ss learned to classify distortions of high variability. They were then transferred to the following patterns: old distortions just memorized, the schema of the memorized instances, and control patterns at varying distances from the memorized patterns. Performance in these transfer tasks was used to infer the role of abstraction and of pattern variability in recognition.

EXPERIMENT I

The original learning in this experiment involved instances of four different prototypes. One group had small distortions of the prototypes, while for the other group the distortions were large. After reaching critieron on the original learning task, both groups were transferred to a list of patterns which were more highly distorted than those in either of the two original lists. Previous work (Posner et al., 1967) demonstrated that the transfer list patterns were equal both in physical and perceived distance from the patterns in the two original lists. Since these new patterns are equally similar to the two original lists, any differences between the groups in transfer must be due either to the distance of the memorized patterns from their prototypes or to their distance from each other (variability). If a clearly defined schema was of primary importance in transfer, the small distortion group should show better transfer. If variability is more important, the larger distortion group should show better transfer. A control group with no original learning was used to assess the direction of the transfer effects.

Method

Subjects.   The Ss were 36 introductory psychology students at the University of Wisconsin who received course points for participating in the experiment.

Materials.   The prototype patterns consisted of a triangle, letters M and F, and a random pattern, all made from nine dots within a 30 × 30 matrix. Pictures of prototypes and some of the distortions were previously published (Posner, Goldsmith, & Welton, 1967). From each of the four originals, six distortions were constructed at each of three different levels (1, 5, and 7.7 bits/dot). The detailed statistical rules and distance data have also been published (Posner et al., 1967). The six distortions were arbitrarily divided into two lists of three distortions each. Each list, therefore, consisted of 12 patterns in total, divided into three distortions of each of the four different prototypes (triangle, M, F, and random). Patterns were placed on 2 × 2 slides and each was duplicated three times, thus providing three independent orders for each list.

Procedure.   The 36 Ss were randomly assigned to one of three conditions and to one of the two lists within the condition. All lists consisted of 12 patterns of one particular level of distortion. The conditions were: learning of Level 1 patterns, learning of Level 5 patterns, and no original learning (control). The exact procedure was reported previously (Posner et al., 1967). Briefly, a slide was presented and remained on until S pressed one of four buttons which represented his choice. Then a feedback light indicating the correct button for that slide came on and remained on during the 8-sec. interstimulus interval. The S continued through trials until he correctly classified two complete lists in a row.

After completing the original learning, the two experimental groups were transferred to a list of 7.7-bit distortions. The control group began its session with the 7.7-bit list. The transfer list was learned by all groups in the same way as the original list except that the learning was terminated at the end of six trials.

Results

Table 30.1 shows the basic results of the experiment. The two subgroups within each condition were combined since the sublists were arbitrary samplings of the statistical rule which governed the distortions. As expected, the group at Level 5 made more errors in original learning than did the group at Level 1. This replicated findings reported previously (Posner et al., 1967).

During the transfer task Group 1 made more errors on each of the first six trials than did Group 5. The control group showed more errors on each trial than either of the two experimental groups. Analyses of variance of both the first trial and of all six trials were run. For the first trial the overall effects of groups was significant, $F(2, 33) = 10.6$, $p < .01$. Subsequent t tests showed that on the first trial Group 1 was significantly worse than Group 5 but not did differ from the control group. The analysis of all six trials also showed a significant effect of groups, $F(2, 33) = 32$, $p < .01$. Subsequent t tests showed that Group 1 was significantly worse than Group 5 and significantly better than the control.

Conclusions

The results of this study indicate that transfer from the broader (Level 5) concept was better. This occurs despite the fact that the average distance between corresponding dots and the perceived similarity of the patterns at Levels 1 and 5 to those at Level 7.7 are the same (Posner et al., 1967). Moreover, the minimum distance from Level 5 patterns to any of the new distortions is at least as great, on the average, as the minimum distance of the Level 1 patterns from the new distortions. Thus the superior performance of the groups at Level 5 cannot be due to perceived similarities or actual physical distance between the learned patterns and the new instances. In addition, Ss at Level 1 uniformly reported the correct names of the meaningful patterns, whereas Ss at Level 5 rarely did. Thus having the verbal label does not appear to help as much as practice in classifying patterns which had considerable noise or variability.

The performance of the control group may have been suppressed somewhat due to lack of warm-up prior to the Level 7 list. However, it seems likely that both Level 1 and 5 are showing positive transfer due to their specific learning experience as well as generalized learning-to-learn. The unpaced nature of the learning situation would probably reduce learning-to-learn effects found in the usual anticipation methods. There are two serious objections which could be raised to the differences between groups at Levels 1 and 5. First, is the initial surprise which Ss at Level 1 had when confronted with highly distorted patterns. This is suggested by the finding that Level 1 is not superior to the

TABLE 30.1   Mean Errors to Criterion for Original Learning and Transfer Tasks, Exp. I

Original Learning	Transfer						
	Trial (Mean Errors)						
Errors to Criterion	1	2	3	4	5	6	Mean
Group 1 4.8	8.1	6.2	5.3	5.6	4.4	3.7	5.6
Group 5 12.3	6.0	5.5	4.5	3.7	3.2	3.0	4.3
Group 7 —	8.3	7.8	7.6	6.0	5.5	5.8	6.8

control group on the first trial. Even though Level 1 remains below Level 5 on each trial, it might be argued that a learning procedure confounds initial recognition with later performance. Second, is that Level 5 *Ss* took more trials to learn and it might be argued, therefore, that they have learned methods of how to deal with the storage of information from distorted patterns. Their superior performance would then be due to the appropriateness of the strategies they had previously learned to the new material. Experiment II was designed to eliminate some of these problems.

EXPERIMENT II

In Exp. II the transfer task was pattern recognition rather than learning. It was not necessary for *S* to memorize the new material and thus storage strategies attained in original learning were not appropriate. Since 24 different patterns were shown, performance on each slide was less dependent upon recognition of previous slides than it is in a learning situation. In order to assess the relative influence of new learning during the transfer tasks, groups were run with and without feedback.

Method

Subjects.   The *Ss* were 32 students in introductory psychology at the University of Oregon who received course points for their participation.

Material.   The original learning lists were identical to those used in Exp. I. The transfer material consisted of a list of 24 different slides. The 24 slides were six random samples of the 7.7-bit distortion rule for each of the four original patterns.

Procedure.   The learning procedure was the same as in Exp. I. The *Ss* were divided into two groups. Sixteen *Ss* learned a list at Level 1 and 16 *Ss* learned a list at Level 5. Learning was continued until two successful repetitions of the list were completed. The *Ss* were then given pattern recognition instructions. These instructions indicated that *Ss* should classify each successive slide as rapidly as possible into one of the four categories that they had learned during the original learning task. For half the *Ss* in each condition feed-

back was given after each classification. The other half received no feedback. The *Ss* were shown the transfer list twice in different random orders. The interslide interval was 9 sec.

Results

Table 30.2 shows the mean errors to criterion in original learning and the average error in the pattern recognition tasks for all conditions for each block of four trials. As before, *Ss* in Level 5 took longer in original learning than those in Level 1. There was no significant difference in speed of learning between feedback conditions. Analysis of variance of errors in the pattern recognition task showed that the effect of level was significant, $F(1, 28) = 9$, $p < .01$, and the effect of feedback conditions was also significant, $F(1, 28) = 4.8$, $p < .05$. There were no significant interactions between level and feedback or between either of the two main variables with successive blocks of 24 slides. Table 30.2 also shows the mean errors for successive blocks of four trials in the pattern recognition task. There is a nonsignificant trend for the differences between Levels 1 and 5 to be reduced with practice particularly when feedback is present.

A correlation coefficient was computed between groups at Levels 1 and 5 over the particular slides to which errors were made during pattern recognition. This correlation was .83 indicating that both groups tended to miss the same patterns. A rank order correlation of .97 between distance from the prototype and errors indicated that patterns most distant from the prototype were more difficult to recognize.

Conclusions

The results of this study confirmed those obtained in Exp. I. Once again, *Ss* who had been trained with the high variability patterns did better on transfer than those trained with the low variability patterns. Moreover, they maintained the advantage over the first 24 slides, even though each slide was different. Therefore, it is difficult to argue that the deficiency in transfer for Level 1 *Ss* was due to an initial startle at seeing patterns which were more distorted than those used in original learning. Moreover the transfer task reduced

TABLE 30.2   Mean Errors in Original Learning and Pattern Recognition, Exp. II

Condition	Original Learning	Block of Four Trials												
		1	2	3	4	5	6	7	8	9	10	11	12	Mean
Group 1														
Feedback	3.4	22	16	17	15	13	16	13	12	11	11	11	15	10.8
No Feedback	4.1	16	19	15	14	17	21	17	16	11	10	19	13	11.9
Group 5														
Feedback	16.8	15	12	17	10	14	9	8	15	16	12	9	9	9.1
No Feedback	11.9	16	11	13	13	17	15	14	17	15	9	14	11	10.4

or eliminated the advantage of general learning strategies attained in the original task (learning-to-learn).

However, it could still be argued that the advantage of Level 5 is primarily in the kinds of criterion which *Ss* set for admission of a particular pattern into one of the meaningful categories. The use of three highly familiar categories and one nonsense pattern within the same list may have contributed to this. There is a strong tendency for *Ss* at Level 1 to classify patterns about which they were unsure into the random category. The percentage of random responses made during the 48 trials of pattern recognition were 25.5, 37.5, 33.5, and 42.9 for conditions: 5 feedback, 5 nonfeedback, 1 feedback, and 1 nonfeedback, respectively.

Table 30.3 shows a breakdown of the proportion of correct and false alarm responses during pattern recognition for each of the prototypes. The false alarm rate is obtained by dividing the errors in a category by the number of possible errors. In the case of the three meaningful patterns, Level 5 *Ss* show a higher propor-

tion of correct responses and about equal false alarms. For these distortions, therefore, it is clear that Level 5 *Ss* are showing better discrimination than those trained on Level 1. For the random patterns, Level 1 *Ss* have both more correct responses and more false alarms. When these two measures are combined using a graphical method (Norman, 1964) the Level 5 *Ss* are slightly superior in overall performance. Thus even though Level 1 *Ss* have a higher proportion of correct responses with the random pattern, when false alarms are taken into consideration, they do not show better discriminability.

The strong tendency of *Ss* in Level 1 to use the random category suggests that they were somewhat reluctant to classify distorted instances into one of the meaningful categories. While in this study the main differences between groups seem to be in the ability to discriminate the categories, it would seem reasonable to explore changes in criterion particularly in studies where a forced choice between categories is not required.

TABLE 30.3   Proportion of Correct and False Alarm Responses for Each Category

	Category				
	Triangle	M	F	Random	Mean
Cond. 1					
Correct	.59	.49	.50	.53	.53
False Alarm	.10	.13	.06	.33	.16
Cond. 5					
Correct	.73	.71	.60	.49	.64
False Alarm	.11	.12	.05	.26	.14

TABLE 30.4   Distances from Stored Exemplar Pattern to Each Transfer Pattern

Stored Pattern	Schema	Old Distortion		New Level 7s		New Level 5s		
		2	4	A	B	C[a]	D	E[b]
1	36	73	66	87	89	49	48	51
2	43	0	77	104	98	65	71	59
3	65	88	65	82	60	54	51	56
4	65	77	0	83	87	51	62	55
Mean	52	59	52	89	83	54	58	55
% Errors in Transfer	15	11.5	14.7	42	39	26	28.5	19

[a]List B only

[b]List A only

EXPERIMENT III

The previous two experiments have indicated that Ss do learn something about the variability of instances that they have seen. In both of these experiments, Ss in each group had the same prototypes. If Ss had been storing only the schema, then Level 1 Ss should have shown better performance than Level 5 since it is easier to define the prototype based on Level 1 patterns than based on Level 5 patterns. The results are in the opposite direction, indicating that Ss are learning some information about the individual patterns which they use in their later judgment. In this experiment an effort is made to determine directly whether Ss are also learning information about the prototype.

Method

Subjects.   The Ss were 30 students recruited from the University of Oregon Employment Service and paid $1.50 per hour for their services.

Material.   There were two lists of original learning materials. Each list contained 12 slides. The 12 slides were four distortions of three different prototypes. A set of distortions of the same prototype is called a "concept." The prototypes were different for the two lists and were constructed by placing dots in nine randomly selected positions in a 30 × 30 matrix. The four distortions of each prototype were constructed using the same four random samples of a 7.7-bit distortion rule. Thus the distances from each of the prototypes to its four distortions were identical.

The transfer material consisted of two lists of 24 slides. Three of the slides were the prototypes of the patterns in the learning lists. These represent the schema of each concept. Six slides, two from each of the concepts, were patterns memorized during the original learning (old distortions). Six slides, two from each of the concepts, were new 7.7-bit distortions of the prototypes which had not been seen during learning. Six slides, two from each of the concepts, were new 5-bit distortions of the prototypes. Finally, three slides were new random patterns unrelated to any of the concepts which S had learned.

In Table 30.4 the distances from the four memorized patterns of each concept to the respective transfer patterns are shown. The individual patterns are identified by a number or letter. In the case of the old distortions the two transfer patterns are identical to two of the stored patterns. These distance relationships hold for all concepts in both lists, although the prototypes differ from one concept to another and between the two lists. The distances represent the sum of the vertical and horizontal distances from each dot in the stored pattern to the corresponding dot in the transfer patterns. The numbers are in units of 1/20 of an inch. Previous results have shown that, for a given grain size, the logarithm of this measure is linearly related to perceived distance (Posner et al., 1967).

Procedure.   The 30 Ss were divided randomly into two equal groups and assigned to the original learning lists. Original learning proceeded as described in the previous experiments until completion of two correct classifications of the lists. After the original learning was

TABLE 30.5   Percentage of Errors and Speeds (in sec.) for Classifying Transfer Patterns for Day 1 and Day 2

	Day 1					Day 2				
	Old	Schema	5	7	New	Old	Schema	5	7	New
List A										
% Error	10	13.3	23.3	35	—	9.7	14.4	24.1	36	—
RT	2.04	2.19	2.36	2.52	2.88	1.86	1.88	2.03	2.18	2.81
List B										
% Error	16.1	16.6	30.5	41.7	—	15.8	16.1	25.3	46.9	—
RT	1.97	2.37	2.71	3.22	2.95	1.88	2.06	2.12	2.33	2.38
Average % Error	13.0	14.9	26.9	38.3	—	12.8	15.3	24.5	41.9	—
RT	2.01	2.28	2.53	2.87	2.91	1.87	1.97	2.07	2.28	2.43

complete, Ss were given their respective transfer lists in the pattern recognition procedure described in the last experiment. On the same day as the original learning they went through the transfer patterns twice, for a total of 48 patterns. Twenty-four hours later Ss returned to the laboratory and ran through the pattern recognition tasks four additional times. During the pattern recognition task, no feedback was provided. Both the classification chosen and the speed of classification were recorded. The Ss were instructed to respond accurately, but to try to respond as rapidly as they could when each new pattern was presented. Concepts were randomly assigned to switches for each S.

Results

Original learning required an average of 41 and 34 errors to criterion, for List A and List B, respectively. This difference was not significant. The error and speed data for the pattern recognition task are shown in Table 30.5. Since the lists are replications of each other except for the use of different randomly selected original patterns and the results are similar for the two groups, all 30 Ss were combined in subsequent analyses.

The analyses were performed by sign tests because of the high correlation between successive experiences with the same pattern. Separate analyses were run for Day 1 and Day 2. The results of the sign tests are shown in Table 30.6.

On Day 1, it is clear that Ss show no significant differences in proportion of errors between the patterns which they had just finished learning and the

prototypes which they had never seen. It is also clear that both the old distortion and the schema have a significantly lower error rate than any of the new distortions seen by S. The Level 5 distortions showed significantly better recognition than the Level 7. No error data can be given for the new random patterns since there is not any correct classification for these patterns. On Day 2, there is a slightly lower mean error for the old distortions than for the schemas. However, when the data are analyzed by individual Ss, 16 show a higher proportion of error on the old distortions and only 11 have a higher proportion on the schema. This difference does not reach significance by a sign test. On Day 2, the new distortions all show significantly more error than either the old distortions or schema patterns. Overall, it is clear that the schema patterns show no greater error than the patterns which S had actually seen and memorized.

On Day 1 the old distortions show faster classification times than the schema patterns. This approaches but does not reach significance by a sign test. In every other respect the Day 1 speeds give the same picture as the error data. On Day 2 there is no significant difference between the old distortion and the schema patterns in speed. The other differences on Day 2 are identical to those discussed previously for errors.

A trial by trial analysis of errors and speeds was performed for the schema vs. old distortions. On the very first trial, 21 Ss have longer RTs to the schema while 8 Ss have longer RTs to the old distortions. This is significant ($p < .01$) by sign test. By the second trial

TABLE 30.6   Number of *Ss* with Higher Average Errors or Longer Average Times in Specified Conditions of Transfer

				Error								
			Day 1							*Day 2*		
				Sign Test[a]								*Sign Test*
Old Distort.	9	Schema	9	Tie	12	*ns*	Old Distort.	16	Schema	11	Tie 3	*ns*
Level 7	23	Schema	5	Tie	2	.01	Level 5	24	Schema	4	Tie 2	.01
Level 7	19	Level 5	6	Tie	5	.05	Level 7	24	Level 5	5	Tie I	.01
				Reaction Time								
Old Distort.	11	Schema	19	Tie	0	*ns*	Old Distort.	14	Schema	16	Tie 0	*ns*
Level 5	22	Schema	8	Tie	0	.05	Level 5	23	Schema	7	Tie 0	.01
Level 7	21	Level S	8	Tie	1	.03	Level 7	22	Level 5	8	Tie 0	.05
New Randoms	17	Level 7	13	Tie	0	*ns*	New Randoms	18	Level 7	12	Tie 0	*ns*

[a]All sign test were two-tailed.

the distribution is 14 RTs longer with the old distortion and 16 with the schema, and on no subsequent trial do more *Ss* show longer times to the schema. The error data are similar. On the first trial, 13 have a higher proportion of errors on the schema and 7 on the old distortion. This is not significant by sign test; however, this tendency disappears after the first trial.

The transfer lists contain five general types of patterns. These are the old distortions, schema patterns, the new distortions at Level 7, the new distortions at Level 5, and new random patterns. As described earlier, Table 30.4 shows a breakdown of the various patterns used in the transfer list and their distances from each of the patterns shown in the original list. The schema pattern and the 5-bit distortions have roughly the same mean distance from the four stored patterns. Nonetheless, the schema pattern always shows better performance in terms of mean errors than the 5-bit distortions. The distances from the stored patterns also differed among the three 5-bit distortion patterns used in the transfer lists. The performance on those distortions did not seem to be closely related to their mean distance from the stored patterns. Therefore, mean distance does not prove to be a particularly good predictor in the range of distances which include the schema and Level 5 patterns. However, a comparison of Level 5 patterns with the new Level 7.7 patterns shows that the patterns which have the larger mean distance are recognized more poorly. In summary, the old distortions, schema, and new Level 5 patterns have nearly identical mean distances from the memorized patterns, but the old distortions and schema are better recognized than the Level 5s and are not different from each other.

GENERAL CONCLUSIONS

Abstraction.   In the introduction some operational statements of the old notion of abstract ideas were suggested. The data of the present experiments confirm that some form of this proposition is correct. The weakest operational form of this proposition which is consistent with the present authors' findings is that the prototype (schema) of the stored patterns has a higher probability of recognition than other new patterns contained within the concept. This is confirmed both by the finding that the schema is better recognized than transfer patterns with similar distance relationships (Level 5) and by the finding that, after its first presentation, the schema is as well recognized as the patterns which have actually been memorized by *Ss*. This form of the proposition is consistent with but more explicit than the idea of stimulus generalization. It singles out the prototype of the patterns as unique. In other words, it shows that the maximal generalization for multidimensional patterns of this sort occurs at the prototype even though other patterns are nearly the same average distance from the stored exemplars. Although other patterns may have nearly the same average distance from the distortions, the prototype must share the most common properties with the set of patterns generated from it. This proposition is

READING 30 / PROTOTYPES

stronger than a generalization notion because the schema pattern is, on the whole, as well recognized as the exemplars from which it is abstracted.

The first and second experiments allow the authors to reject the idea that only the abstracted prototype is stored. Clearly the information about the individual patterns must also be present in order for a loose concept (high variability) to give better transfer than a tight concept (low variability). Moreover, the variability is of sufficient importance to overcome whatever advantage the tight concept has from a more clearly defined central tendency. The beneficial effect of variability confirms results in other areas of problem solving (Morrisett & Hovland, 1959) and pattern recognition (Dukes & Bevan, 1967) which argue for the importance of variability during training. It is also consistent with Attneave's (1957) suggestion that part of the process of learning to recognize patterns involves acquaintance with the limits of variability.

Time of abstraction. It is possible to ask when the information is abstracted which allows the efficient recognition of the central tendency. One possibility is that the abstraction of this information takes place during the learning task. This is undoubtedly the notion which philosophers have implied in discussing the genesis of abstract ideas. The present authors cannot either confirm or deny this form of the proposition from the present data. It could be that information concerning the central tendency is stored during learning, but it also could be that the abstraction takes place when the schema pattern is first shown to S. That is, S may not recognize the schema on its first presentation in the direct way in which he identifies the old distortions. Rather he may respond correctly on the basis of a calculation from stored information concerning the exemplars. The finding that RT to the schema is longer than to the old distortions on the first presentation of the transfer list may indicate that S is calculating on the basis of his stored information. However, it could also mean that he has stored abstracted information but that it is not as clearly or completely defined as information concerning the individual exemplars. In either case, once he has seen the schema he recognizes it with the same efficiency as the memorized patterns. If the schema information is not abstracted during learning, then upon its first pre-

sentation S must store it as a particularly good example of its concept and treat it on subsequent trials as equivalent to a memorized instance. One way to demonstrate that abstraction occurs during learning would be to find a situation in which the schema, when first introduced, is recognized as well as or better than the patterns memorized during the original learning.

What is abstracted. In the present study the authors have used the word *idea* in a neutral sense. It is not at all clear what Ss abstract in learning to recognize the transfer patterns. To say Ss learn the central tendency and the variability of the patterns does not tell in what type of a coding system such information is stored. For example, Ss might have an image or mental picture of the individual instances or of the abstracted central tendency. Or perhaps the material is in the form of verbal description, such as has been suggested by various theories of short-term memory (Glanzer & Clark, 1963; Sperling, 1963).

The data obtained here give only a very incomplete answer to these questions. Introspective reports were taken from 15 Ss run in a pilot study with materials identical to one list of Exp. III. These reports suggested that some Ss used verbal rules which related to the patterns. The rules tended to emphasize position of dots, center of gravity, overall orientation of figure, familiar subgroups, and association to familiar objects. The rules were highly idiosyncratic and some Ss verbalized no rules at all. These verbal reports suggest that some of the storage, at least, is by way of rules which are related to the common features of the patterns within a concept. Whether these verbal codes represent all of the information storage or are used in conjunction with other storage codes cannot be determined from the present data.

AUTHORS' NOTE

This research was supported in part by National Science Foundation Grant GB 3939 to the University of Oregon. A preliminary version of Exp. I was included in a report presented at the XVIIIth International Congress of Psychology, August 1966. The authors wish to thank Barbara Kerr, William Eichelman, and Stanley Sue for their help in conducting this research.

REFERENCES

Attneave, F. (1957). Transfer of experience with a class-schema to identification-learning of patterns and shapes. *Journal of Experimental Psychology, 54*, 81–88.

Bartlett, F. C. (1932). *Remembering, a study in experimental and social psychology.* Cambridge: Cambridge University Press.

Dukes, W. F., & Bevan, W. (1967). Stimulus variation and repetition in the acquisition of naming responses. *Journal of Experimental Psychology, 74*, 178–181.

Evans, S. H., & Edmonds, E. M. (1966). Schema discrimination as a function of training. *Psychonomic Science, 5*, 303–304.

Glanzer, M., & Clark, W. H. (1963). Accuracy of perceptual recall: An analysis of organization. *Journal of Verbal Learning and Verbal Behavior, 1*, 289–299.

Hinsey, W. C. (1963). *Identification-learning after pretraining on central and noncentral standards.* Unpublished masters thesis, University of Oregon.

Morrisett, L., Jr., & Hovland, C. I. (1959). A comparison of three varieties of training in human problem solving. *Journal of Experimental Psychology, 58*, 52–55.

Norman, D. A. (1964). A comparison of data with different false alarm rates. *Psychological Review, 71*, 243–246.

Oldfield, R. C., & Zangwill, O. L. (1942). Heads concept of the schema and its application in contemporary British psychology. *British Journal of Psychology, 32*, 267–286.

Posner, M. I., Goldsmith, R., & Welton, K. E., Jr. (1967). Perceived distance and the classification of distorted patterns. *Journal of Experimental Psychology, 73*, 28–38.

Sperling, G. (1963). A model for visual memory tasks. *Human Factors, 5*, 19–31.

CHAPTER TWELVE
Judgment

31   RISKY DECISIONS

This reading reviews several surprising experimental findings about how people make choices and decisions. For centuries, philosophers, mathematicians, and economists had assumed that people made choices and decisions in a rational way. It was generally believed that people would examine the options in front of them, and pick the one that seemed most likely to offer the most benefit (or least discomfort). Of course, rational decision making does not mean that people would always make the correct choices. People could misjudge the probabilities of some events or be uncertain about the actual benefit or discomfort of certain options. It was long assumed that these kinds of "mistakes" were the reasons that people did not always make what were objectively the best choices.

In a series of groundbreaking papers, Kahneman and Tversky demonstrated that people are not always rational decision makers, and that the way people actually make choices cannot be explained as a "mistaken" rational process. That is, a rational decision maker must follow a certain set of rules, and with a series of clever experiments, Kahneman and Tversky demonstrated that people often violate those rules. Typically these demonstrations involve people making decisions in situations where there is not a clear "correct" answer. Thus, the experimenters are less interested in the choices made on a single problem, but are very interested in the pattern of choices across a variety of problems. What they found was that people will choose one option in one problem, but choose a different option in another problem that is essentially the same as the first. It is this change in behavior that violates the rules.

Many of the violations are due to *framing effects*. What are essentially the same problems can be described in a variety of ways. It turns out that, because of other tendencies in human decision making, the way a problem is described can influence the choices people make. For example, it has long been known that people tend to view losses as more significant than gains. Thus, many people will not take an even bet where if a coin comes up heads they win $10 but if the coin comes up tails they lose $10. It seems that the possible loss of $10 is more significant than the equally possible gain of $10. This effect is called *loss aversion*.

A side effect of loss aversion is that people tend to be *risk averse* when options presented to them are perceived as gains. That is, if you have to choose between two advantageous options and one has a certain outcome (e.g., I will give you $10) and another has a probabilistic (risky) outcome (e.g., I will flip a coin and if it comes up heads I will give you $20, but if it comes up tails I will give you nothing), then people tend to prefer the certain option. On the other hand, people tend to be *risk seeking* when options are presented to them as losses. That is, if you have to choose between two undesirable options and one has a certain outcome (e.g., I will take $10 from you) and another has a probabilistic outcome (e.g., I will flip a coin and if it comes up heads, I will take $20 from you, but if it comes up tails I will take nothing), then people tend to prefer the probabilistic option.

It might seem that loss aversion and its side effects could be part of a rational decision-making process. However, Kahneman and Tversky demonstrated that when loss aversion is mixed with framing effects, people violate a basic tenet of rational decision making. The most famous example is the Asian disease problem. There are two versions of this problem (problems 1 and 2), which are almost exactly the same in regards to the choices and outcomes. The only difference is in the presentation of the choices and the outcomes. In one version the choices and outcomes describe how a certain number of people will be saved from an unusual disease. One option is certain (a specific number of people will be saved), whereas the other option involves probability (there is a chance everyone will be saved and a chance no one will be saved). The other version of the problem phrases its options in terms of people dying. Again, there is a certain option and a probabilistic option.

The choices in the two versions are just different ways of saying the same thing. Picking the certain option in either version means a certain number of people will be saved/killed. Likewise, picking the probabilistic option in either version means that there is a chance that no one will die (everyone is saved) and a chance that a certain number of people will die (no one is saved).

Despite these similarities, people choose the options very differently in the two versions of the problem. Because of loss aversion effects, when the options are presented as gains (saving lives), people tend to choose the certain option (to be certain that some people are saved). Risk aversion effects take over. When the options are presented as losses (people dying), people tend to choose the risky option. Risk seeking behavior takes over.

This reading goes on to discuss how people's perception of probability influences decision making and, in combination with framing effects, can lead to more irrational behavior. The examples provided throughout this reading both highlight the basic effects and demonstrate how important these topics are to everyday life. A more in-depth (and mathematical) treatment of these topics is provided in Kahneman and Tversky (1979).

The CogLab experiment asks the participant to choose between two options on every trial. One option always involves a certain amount of money and the other option involves risky (probabilistic) possibilities. Both options involve either gains of money or losses of money. The expectation is that participants will be risk averse when the two options describe gains in money and will be risk seeking when the two options describe losses in money.

This line of work has important implications for economic theories, and it earned Kahneman a share of the 2002 Nobel Prize in Economics. (Tversky's name was not included because Nobel laureates must be living at the time the prize is awarded.)

REFERENCE

Kahneman, D., & Tversky, A. (1979). Prospect theory: An analysis of decision making under risk. *Econometrica, 47,* 263–291.

QUESTIONS

1. How does loss aversion relate to the advice given to business school students to focus on the "bottom line"?
2. What is the difference between "normative" and "descriptive" analyses of decision making?
3. What is the principle of *invariance* that must be part of any rational decision-making process?
4. Given the extremely long odds of their numbers being selected, why do people pay money to play state lotteries?

Choices, Values, and Frames

Daniel Kahneman and Amos Tversky

We discuss the cognitive and the psychophysical determinants of choice in risky and riskless contexts. The psychophysics of value induce risk aversion in the domain of gains and risk seeking in the domain of losses. The psychophysics of chance induce overweighting of sure things and of improbable events, relative to events of moderate probability. Decision problems can be described or framed in multiple ways that give rise to different preferences, contrary to the invariance criterion of rational choice. The process of mental accounting, in which people organize the outcomes of transactions, explains some anomalies of consumer behavior. In particular, the acceptability of an option can depend on whether a negative outcome is evaluated as a cost or as an uncompensated loss. The relation between decision values and experience values is discussed.

Making decisions is like speaking prose—people do it all the time, knowingly or unknowingly. It is hardly surprising, then, that the topic of decision making is shared by many disciplines, from mathematics and statistics, through economics and political science, to sociology and psychology. The study of decisions addresses both normative and descriptive questions. The normative analysis is concerned with the nature of rationality and the logic of decision making. The descriptive analysis, in contrast, is concerned with people's beliefs and preferences as they are, not as they should be. The tension between normative and descriptive considerations characterizes much of the study of judgment and choice.

Analyses of decision making commonly distinguish risky and riskless choices. The paradigmatic example of decision under risk is the acceptability of a gamble that yields monetary outcomes with specified probabilities. A typical riskless decision concerns the acceptability of a transaction in which a good or a service is exchanged for money or labor. In the first part of this article, we present an analysis of the cognitive and psychophysical factors that determine the value of risky prospects. In the second part, we extend this analysis to transactions and trades.

RISKY CHOICE

Risky choices, such as whether or not to take an umbrella and whether or not to go to war, are made without advance knowledge of their consequences. Because the consequences of such actions depend on uncertain events such as the weather or the opponent's resolve, the choice of an act may be construed as the acceptance of a gamble that can yield various outcomes with different probabilities. It is therefore natural that the study of decision making under risk has focused on choices between simple gambles with monetary outcomes and specified probabilities, in the hope that these simple problems will reveal basic attitudes toward risk and value.

We shall sketch an approach to risky choice that derives many of its hypotheses from a psychophysical analysis of responses to money and to probability. The psychophysical approach to decision making can be traced to a remarkable essay that Daniel Bernoulli published in 1738 (Bernoulli 1738/1954) in which he attempted to explain why people are generally averse to risk and why risk aversion decreases with increasing wealth. To illustrate risk aversion and Bernoulli's analysis, consider the choice between a prospect that offers an 85% chance to win $1,000 (with a 15% chance to win nothing) and the alternative of receiving $800 for sure. A large majority of people prefer the sure thing over the gamble, although the gamble has

SOURCE: From Kahneman, D., & Tversky, A. (1984). Choices, values, and frames. *American Psychologist, 39,* 341–350. Copyright © 1984 by the American Psychological Association. Reprinted with permission.

higher (mathematical) expectation. The expectation of a monetary gamble is a weighted average, where each possible outcome is weighted by its probability of occurrence. The expectation of the gamble in this example is $.85 \times \$1{,}000 + .15 \times \$0 = \$850$, which exceeds the expectation of $800 associated with the sure thing. The preference for the sure gain is an instance of risk aversion. In general, a preference for a sure outcome over a gamble that has higher or equal expectation is called *risk aversion,* and the rejection of a sure thing in favor of a gamble of lower or equal expectation is called *risk seeking.*

Bernoulli suggested that people do not evaluate prospects by the expectation of their monetary outcomes, but rather by the expectation of the subjective value of these outcomes. The subjective value of a gamble is again a weighted average, but now it is the subjective value of each outcome that is weighted by its probability. To explain risk aversion within this framework, Bernoulli proposed that subjective value, or utility, is a concave function of money. In such a function, the difference between the utilities of $200 and $100, for example, is greater than the utility difference between $1,200 and $1,100. It follows from concavity that the subjective value attached to a gain of $800 is more than 80% of the value of a gain of $1,000. Consequently, the concavity of the utility function entails a risk averse preference for a sure gain of $800 over an 80% chance to win $1,000, although the two prospects have the same monetary expectation.

It is customary in decision analysis to describe the outcomes of decisions in terms of total wealth. For example, an offer to bet $20 on the toss of a fair coin is represented as a choice between an individual's current wealth W and an even chance to move to $W +$ $20 or to $W - $20. This representation appears psychologically unrealistic: People do not normally think of relatively small outcomes in terms of states of wealth but rather in terms of gains, losses, and neutral outcomes (such as the maintenance of the status quo). If the effective carriers of subjective value are changes of wealth rather than ultimate states of wealth, as we propose, the psychophysical analysis of outcomes should be applied to gains and losses rather than to total assets. This assumption plays a central role in a treatment of risky choice that we called prospect theory (Kahneman & Tversky, 1979). Introspection as

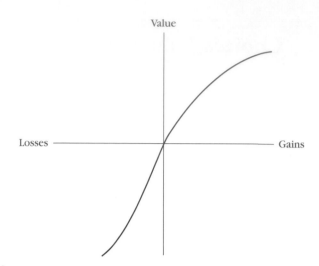

FIGURE 31.1   A hypothetical value function.

well as psychophysical measurements suggest that subjective value is a concave function of the size of a gain. The same generalization applies to losses, as well. The difference in subjective value between a loss of $200 and a loss of $100 appears greater than the difference in subjective value between a loss of $1,200 and a loss of $1,100. When the value functions for gains and for losses are pieced together, we obtain an *S*-shaped function of the type displayed in Figure 31.1.

The value function shown in Figure 31.1 is (a) defined on gains and losses rather than on total wealth, (b) concave in the domain of gains and convex in the domain of losses, and (c) considerably steeper for losses than for gains. The last property, which we label *loss aversion,* expresses the intuition that a loss of $X is more aversive than a gain of $X is attractive. Loss aversion explains people's reluctance to bet on a fair coin for equal stakes: The attractiveness of the possible gain is not nearly sufficient to compensate for the aversiveness of the possible loss. For example, most respondents in a sample of undergraduates refused to stake $10 on the toss of a coin if they stood to win less than $30.

The assumption of risk aversion has played a central role in economic theory. However, just as the concavity of the value of gains entails risk aversion, the convexity of the value of losses entails risk seeking. Indeed, risk seeking in losses is a robust effect, particularly when the probabilities of loss are substantial.

Consider, for example, a situation in which an individual is forced to choose between an 85% chance to lose $1,000 (with a 15% chance to lose nothing) and a sure loss of $800. A large majority of people express a preference for the gamble over the sure loss. This is a risk-seeking choice because the expectation of the gamble ($850) is inferior to the expectation of the sure loss (−$800). Risk seeking in the domain of losses has been confirmed by several investigators (Fishburn & Kochenberger, 1979; Hershey & Schoemaker, 1980; Payne, Laughhunn, & Crum, 1980; Slovic, Fischhoff, & Lichtenstein, 1982). It has also been observed with nonmonetary outcomes, such as hours of pain (Erakar & Sox, 1981) and loss of human lives (Fischhoff, 1983; Tversky, 1977; Tversky & Kahneman, 1981). Is it wrong to be risk averse in the domain of gains and risk seeking in the domain of losses? These preferences conform to compelling intuitions about the subjective value of gains and losses, and the presumption is that people should be entitled to their own values. However, we shall see that an S-shaped value function has implications that are normatively unacceptable.

To address the normative issue, we turn from psychology to decision theory. Modern decision theory can be said to begin with the pioneering work of von Neumann and Morgenstern (1947), who laid down several qualitative principles, or axioms, that should govern the preferences of a rational decision maker. Their axioms included transitivity (if A is preferred to B, and B is preferred to C, then A is preferred to C), and substitution (if A is preferred to B, then an even chance to get A or C is preferred to an even chance to get B or C), along with other conditions of a more technical nature. The normative and the descriptive status of the axioms of rational choice have been the subject of extensive discussions. In particular, there is convincing evidence that people do not always obey the substitution axiom, and considerable disagreement exists about the normative merit of this axiom (e.g., Allais & Hagen, 1979). However, all analyses of rational choice incorporate two principles: *dominance* and *invariance*. Dominance demands that if prospect A is at least as good as prospect B in every respect and better than B in at least one respect, then A should be preferred to B. Invariance requires that the preference order between prospects should not depend on the manner in which they are described. In particular, two versions of a choice problem that are recognized to be equivalent when shown together should elicit the same preference even when shown separately. We now show that the requirement of invariance, however elementary and innocuous it may seem, cannot generally be satisfied.

Framing of Outcomes

Risky prospects are characterized by their possible outcomes and by the probabilities of these outcomes. The same option, however, can be framed or described in different ways (Tversky & Kahneman, 1981). For example, the possible outcomes of a gamble can be framed either as gains and losses relative to the status quo or as asset positions that incorporate initial wealth. Invariance requires that such changes in the description of outcomes should not alter the preference order. The following pair of problems illustrates a violation of this requirement. The total number of respondents in each problem is denoted by N, and the percentage who chose each option is indicated in parentheses.

> Problem 1 ($N = 152$): Imagine that the United States is preparing for the outbreak of an unusual Asian disease, which is expected to kill 600 people. Two alternative programs to combat the disease have been proposed. Assume that the exact scientific estimates of the consequences of the programs are as follows:
>
> If Program A is adopted, 200 people will be saved. (72%)
>
> If Program B is adopted, there is a one third probability that 600 people will be saved and a two thirds probability that no people will be saved. (28%)
>
> Which of the two programs would you favor?

The formulation of Problem 1 implicitly adopts as a reference point a state of affairs in which the disease is allowed to take its toll of 600 lives. The outcomes of the programs include the reference state and two possible gains, measured by the number of lives saved. As expected, preferences are risk averse: A clear majority of respondents prefer saving 200 lives for sure over a gamble that offers a one-third chance of saving 600 lives. Now consider another problem in which the same cover story is followed by a different description of the prospects associated with the two programs:

Problem 2 ($N = 155$):
    If Program C is adopted, 400 people will die. (22%)
    If Program D is adopted, there is a one third probability that nobody will die and a two thirds probability that 600 people will die. (78%)

It is easy to verify that options C and D in Problem 2 are undistinguishable in real terms from options A and B in Problem 1, respectively. The second version, however, assumes a reference state in which no one dies of the disease. The best outcome is the maintenance of this state and the alternatives are losses measured by the number of people that will die of the disease. People who evaluate options in these terms are expected to show a risk-seeking preference for the gamble (option D) over the sure loss of 400 lives. Indeed, there is more risk seeking in the second version of the problem than there is risk aversion in the first.

The failure of invariance is both pervasive and robust. It is as common among sophisticated respondents as among naive ones, and it is not eliminated even when the same respondents answer both questions within a few minutes. Respondents confronted with their conflicting answers are typically puzzled. Even after rereading the problems, they still wish to be risk averse in the "lives saved" version; they wish to be risk seeking in the "lives lost" version; and they also wish to obey invariance and give consistent answers in the two versions. In their stubborn appeal, framing effects resemble perceptual illusions more than computational errors.

The following pair of problems elicits preferences that violate the dominance requirement of rational choice.

Problem 3 ($N = 86$): Choose between:
E. 25% chance to win $240 and
    75% chance to lose $760   (0%)
F. 25% chance to win $250 and
    75% chance to lose $750   (100%)

It is easy to see that F dominates E. Indeed, all respondents chose accordingly.

Problem 4 ($N = 150$): Imagine that you face the following pair of concurrent decisions. First examine both decisions, then indicate the options you prefer.

Decision (i)—Choose between:
A. a sure gain of $240   (84%)
B. 25% chance to gain $1,000 and
    75% chance to gain nothing   (16%)

Decision (ii)—Choose between:
C. a sure loss of $750   (13%)
D. 75% chance to lose $1,000 and
    25% chance to lose nothing   (87%)

As expected from the previous analysis, a large majority of subjects made a risk-averse choice for the sure gain over the positive gamble in the first decision, and an even larger majority of subjects made a risk-seeking choice for the gamble over the sure loss in the second decision. In fact, 73% of the respondents chose A and D and only 3% chose B and C. The same pattern of results was observed in a modified version of the problem, with reduced stakes, in which undergraduates selected gambles that they would actually play.

Because the subjects considered the two decisions in Problem 4 simultaneously, they expressed in effect a preference for A and D over B and C. The preferred conjunction, however, is actually dominated by the rejected one. Adding the sure gain of $240 (option A) to option D yields a 25% chance to win $240 and 75% to lose $760. This is precisely option E in Problem 3. Similarly, adding the sure loss of $750 (option C) to option B yields a 25% chance to win $250 and 75% chance to lose $750. This is precisely option F in Problem 3. Thus, the susceptibility to framing and the S-shaped value function produce a violation of dominance in a set of concurrent decisions.

The moral of these results is disturbing: Invariance is normatively essential, intuitively compelling, and psychologically unfeasible. Indeed, we conceive only two ways of guaranteeing invariance. The first is to adopt a procedure that will transform equivalent versions of any problem into the same canonical representation. This is the rationale for the standard admonition to students of business, that they should consider each decision problem in terms of total assets rather than in terms of gains or losses (Schlaifer, 1959). Such a representation would avoid the violations of invariance illustrated in the previous problems, but the advice is easier to give than to follow. Except in the context of possible ruin, it is more natural to consider financial outcomes as gains and losses rather than as states of wealth. Furthermore, a canonical representation of risky prospects requires a compounding of all outcomes of concurrent decisions (e.g., Problem 4) that exceeds the capabilities of intuitive computation even in simple problems. Achieving a canonical representation is even more difficult in other contexts such as safety, health, or quality of life. Should we advise people to evaluate the consequence of a public health policy (e.g., Problems 1 and 2) in terms of overall mortality, mortality due to diseases, or the number of deaths associated with the particular disease under study?

Another approach that could guarantee invariance is the evaluation of options in terms of their actuarial rather than their psychological consequences. The actuarial criterion has some appeal in the context of human lives, but it is clearly inadequate for financial choices, as has been generally recognized at least since Bernoulli, and it is entirely inapplicable to outcomes that lack an objective metric. We conclude that frame invariance cannot be expected to hold and that a sense of confidence in a particular choice does not ensure that the same choice would be made in another frame. It is therefore good practice to test the robustness of preferences by deliberate attempts to frame a decision problem in more than one way (Fischhoff, Slovic, & Lichtenstein, 1980).

The Psychophysics of Chances

Our discussion so far has assumed a Bernoullian expectation rule according to which the value, or utility, of an uncertain prospect is obtained by adding the utilities of the possible outcomes, each weighted by its probability. To examine this assumption, let us again consult psychophysical intuitions. Setting the value of the status quo at zero, imagine a cash gift, say of $300, and assign it a value of 1. Now imagine that you are given a ticket to a lottery that has a single prize of $300. How does the value of the ticket vary as a func-

tion of the probability of winning the prize? Barring utility for gambling, the value of such a prospect must vary between zero (when the chance of winning is nil) and 1 (when winning $300 is a certainty).

Intuition suggests that the value of the ticket is not a linear function of the probability of winning, as entailed by the expectation rule. In particular, an increase from 0% to 5% appears to have a larger effect than an increase from 30% to 35%, which also appears smaller than an increase from 95% to 100%. These considerations suggest a category-boundary effect: A change from impossibility to possibility or from possibility to certainty has a bigger impact than a comparable change in the middle of the scale. This hypothesis is incorporated into the curve displayed in Figure 31.2, which plots the weight attached to an event as a function of its stated numerical probability. The most salient feature of Figure 31.2 is that decision weights are regressive with respect to stated probabilities. Except near the endpoints, an increase of .05 in the probability of winning increases the value of the prospect by less than 5% of the value of the prize. We next investigate the implications of these psychophysical hypotheses for preferences among risky options.

In Figure 31.2, decision weights are lower than the corresponding probabilities over most of the range. Underweighting of moderate and high probabilities relative to sure things contributes to risk aversion in gains by reducing the attractiveness of positive gambles. The same effect also contributes to risk seeking in losses by attenuating the aversiveness of negative gambles. Low probabilities, however, are overweighted, and very low probabilities are either overweighted quite grossly or neglected altogether, making the decision weights highly unstable in that region. The overweighting of low probabilities reverses the pattern described above: It enhances the value of long shots and amplifies the aversiveness of a small chance of a severe loss. Consequently, people are often risk seeking in dealing with improbable gains and risk averse in dealing with unlikely losses. Thus, the characteristics of decision weights contribute to the attractiveness of both lottery tickets and insurance policies.

The nonlinearity of decision weights inevitably leads to violations of invariance, as illustrated in the following pair of problems:

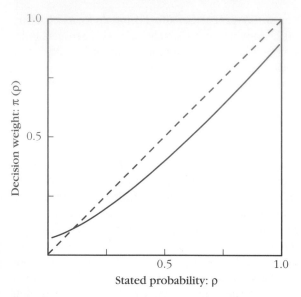

FIGURE 31.2   A hypothetical weighting function.

Problem 5 (*N* = 85): Consider the following two-stage game. In the first stage, there is a 75% chance to end the game without winning anything and a 25% chance to move into the second stage. If you reach the second stage you have a choice between:

A.   a sure win of $30   (74%)
B.   80% chance to win $45   (26%)

Your choice must be made before the game starts, i.e., before the outcome of the first stage is known. Please indicate the option you prefer.

Problem 6 (*N* = 81): Which of the following options do you prefer?

C.   25% chance to win $30   (42%)
D.   20% chance to win $45   (58%)

Because there is one chance in four to move into the second stage in Problem 5, prospect A offers a .25 probability of winning $30, and prospect B offers .25 × .80 = .20 probability of winning $45. Problems 5 and 6 are therefore identical in terms of probabilities and outcomes. However, the preferences are not the same in the two versions: A clear majority favors the higher chance to win the smaller amount in Problem 5, whereas the majority goes the other way in Prob-

lem 6. This violation of invariance has been confirmed with both real and hypothetical monetary payoffs (the present results are with real money), with human lives as outcomes, and with a nonsequential representation of the chance process.

We attribute the failure of invariance to the interaction of two factors: the framing of probabilities and the nonlinearity of decision weights. More specifically, we propose that in Problem 5, people ignore the first phase, which yields the same outcome regardless of the decision that is made, and focus their attention on what happens if they do reach the second stage of the game. In that case, of course, they face a sure gain if they choose option A and an 80% chance of winning if they prefer to gamble. Indeed, people's choices in the sequential version are practically identical to the choices they make between a sure gain of $30 and an 85% chance to win $45. Because a sure thing is overweighted in comparison with events of moderate or high probability (see Figure 31.2) the option that may lead to a gain of $30 is more attractive in the sequential version. We call this phenomenon the *pseudo-certainty* effect because an event that is actually uncertain is weighted as if it were certain.

A closely related phenomenon can be demonstrated at the low end of the probability range. Suppose you are undecided whether or not to purchase earthquake insurance because the premium is quite high. As you hesitate, your friendly insurance agent comes forth with an alternative offer: "For half the regular premium you can be fully covered if the quake occurs on an odd day of the month. This is a good deal because for half the price you are covered for more than half the days." Why do most people find such probabilistic insurance distinctly unattractive? Figure 31.2 suggests an answer. Starting anywhere in the region of low probabilities, the impact on the decision weight of a reduction of probability from p to $p/2$ is considerably smaller than the effect of a reduction from $p/2$ to 0. Reducing the risk by half, then, is not worth half the premium.

The aversion to probabilistic insurance is significant for three reasons. First, it undermines the classical explanation of insurance in terms of a concave utility function. According to expected utility theory, probabilistic insurance should be definitely preferred to normal insurance when the latter is just acceptable (see Kahneman & Tversky, 1979). Second, probabilistic insurance represents many forms of protective action, such as having a medical checkup, buying new tires, or installing a burglar alarm system. Such actions typically reduce the probability of some hazard without eliminating it altogether. Third, the acceptability of insurance can be manipulated by the framing of the contingencies. An insurance policy that covers fire but not flood, for example, could be evaluated either as full protection against a specific risk (e.g., fire) or as a reduction in the overall probability of property loss. Figure 31.2 suggests that people greatly undervalue a reduction in the probability of a hazard in comparison to the complete elimination of that hazard. Hence, insurance should appear more attractive when it is framed as the elimination of risk than when it is described as a reduction of risk. Indeed, Slovic, Fischhoff, and Lichtenstein (1982) showed that a hypothetical vaccine that reduces the probability of contracting a disease from 20% to 10% is less attractive if it is described as effective in half of the cases than if it is presented as fully effective against one of two exclusive and equally probable virus strains that produce identical symptoms.

Formulation Effects

So far we have discussed framing as a tool to demonstrate failures of invariance. We now turn attention to the processes that control the framing of outcomes and events. The public health problem illustrates a formulation effect in which a change of wording from "lives saved" to "lives lost" induced a marked shift of preference from risk aversion to risk seeking. Evidently, the subjects adopted the descriptions of the outcomes as given in the question and evaluated the outcomes accordingly as gains or losses. Another formulation effect was reported by McNeil, Pauker, Sox, and Tversky (1982). They found that preferences of physicians and patients between hypothetical therapies for lung cancer varied markedly when their probable outcomes were described in terms of mortality or survival. Surgery, unlike radiation therapy, entails a risk of death during treatment. As a consequence, the surgery option was relatively less attractive when the statistics of treatment outcomes were described in terms of mortality rather than in terms of survival.

A physician, and perhaps a presidential advisor as well, could influence the decision made by the patient or by the president, without distorting or suppressing information, merely by the framing of outcomes and contingencies. Formulation effects can occur fortuitously, without anyone being aware of the impact of the frame on the ultimate decision. They can also be exploited deliberately to manipulate the relative attractiveness of options. For example, Thaler (1980) noted that lobbyists for the credit card industry insisted that any price difference between cash and credit purchases be labeled a cash discount rather than a credit card surcharge. The two labels frame the price difference as a gain or as a loss by implicitly designating either the lower or the higher price as normal. Because losses loom larger than gains, consumers are less likely to accept a surcharge than to forego a discount. As is to be expected, attempts to influence framing are common in the marketplace and in the political arena.

The evaluation of outcomes is susceptible to formulation effects because of the nonlinearity of the value function and the tendency of people to evaluate options in relation to the reference point that is suggested or implied by the statement of the problem. It is worthy of note that in other contexts, people automatically transform equivalent messages into the same representation. Studies of language comprehension indicate that people quickly recode much of what they hear into an abstract representation that no longer distinguishes whether the idea was expressed in an active or in a passive form and no longer discriminates what was actually said from what was implied, presupposed, or implicated (Clark & Clark, 1977). Unfortunately, the mental machinery that performs these operations silently and effortlessly is not adequate to perform the task of recoding the two versions of the public-health problem or the mortality-survival statistics into a common abstract form.

TRANSACTIONS AND TRADES

Our analysis of framing and of value can be extended to choices between multiattribute options, such as the acceptability of a transaction or a trade. We propose that, in order to evaluate a multiattribute option, a person sets up a mental account that specifies the advantages and the disadvantages associated with the option, relative to a multiattribute reference state. The overall value of an option is given by the balance of its advantages and its disadvantages in relation to the reference state. Thus, an option is acceptable if the value of its advantages exceeds the value of its disadvantages. This analysis assumes psychological—but not physical—separability of advantages and disadvantages. The model does not constrain the manner in which separate attributes are combined to form overall measures of advantage and of disadvantage, but it imposes on these measures assumptions of concavity and of loss aversion.

Our analysis of mental accounting owes a large debt to the stimulating work of Richard Thaler (1980, in press), who showed the relevance of this process to consumer behavior. The following problem, based on examples of Savage (1954) and Thaler (1980), introduces some of the rules that govern the construction of mental accounts and illustrates the extension of the concavity of value to the acceptability of transactions.

Problem 7: Imagine that you are about to purchase a jacket for $125 and a calculator for $15. The calculator salesman informs you that the calculator you wish to buy is on sale for $10 at the other branch of the store, located 20 minutes drive away. Would you make a trip to the other store?

This problem is concerned with the acceptability of an option that combines a disadvantage of inconvenience with a financial advantage that can be framed as a minimal, topical, or comprehensive account. The minimal account includes only the differences between the two options and disregards the features that they share. In the minimal account, the advantage associated with driving to the other store is framed as a gain of $5. A topical account relates the consequences of possible choices to a reference level that is determined by the context within which the decision arises. In the preceding problem, the relevant topic is the purchase of the calculator, and the benefit of the trip is therefore framed as a reduction of the price, from $15 to $10. Because the potential saving is associated only with the calculator, the price of the jacket is not included in the topical account. The price of the jacket, as well as other expenses, could well be included in a more comprehensive account in which the

saving would be evaluated in relation to, say, monthly expenses.

The formulation of the preceding problem appears neutral with respect to the adoption of a minimal, topical, or comprehensive account. We suggest, however, that people will spontaneously frame decisions in terms of topical accounts that, in the context of decision making, play a role analogous to that of "good forms" in perception and of basic-level categories in cognition. Topical organization, in conjunction with the concavity of value, entails that the willingness to travel to the other store for a saving of $5 on a calculator should be inversely related to the price of the calculator and should be independent of the price of the jacket. To test this prediction, we constructed another version of the problem in which the prices of the two items were interchanged. The price of the calculator was given as $125 in the first store and $120 in the other branch, and the price of the jacket was set at $15. As predicted, the proportions of respondents who said they would make the trip differed sharply in the two problems. The results showed that 68% of the respondents ($N = 88$) were willing to drive to the other branch to save $5 on a $15 calculator, but only 29% of 93 respondents were willing to make the same trip to save $5 on a $125 calculator. This finding supports the notion of topical organization of accounts, since the two versions are identical both in terms of a minimal and a comprehensive account.

The significance of topical accounts for consumer behavior is confirmed by the observation that the standard deviation of the prices that different stores in a city quote for the same product is roughly proportional to the average price of that product (Pratt, Wise, & Zeckhauser, 1979). Since the dispersion of prices is surely controlled by shoppers' efforts to find the best buy, these results suggest that consumers hardly exert more effort to save $15 on a $150 purchase than to save $5 on a $50 purchase.

The topical organization of mental accounts leads people to evaluate gains and losses in relative rather than in absolute terms, resulting in large variations in the rate at which money is exchanged for other things, such as the number of phone calls made to find a good buy or the willingness to drive a long distance to get one. Most consumers will find it easier to buy a car stereo system or a Persian rug, respectively, in the context of buying a car or a house than separately. These observations, of course, run counter to the standard rational theory of consumer behavior, which assumes invariance and does not recognize the effects of mental accounting.

The following problems illustrate another example of mental accounting in which the posting of a cost to an account is controlled by topical organization:

Problem 8 ($N = 200$): Imagine that you have decided to see a play and paid the admission price of $10 per ticket. As you enter the theater, you discover that you have lost the ticket. The seat was not marked, and the ticket cannot be recovered. Would you pay $10 for another ticket?

Yes (46%)   No (54%)

Problem 9 ($N = 183$): Imagine that you have decided to see a play where admission is $10 per ticket. As you enter the theater, you discover that you have lost a $10 bill. Would you still pay $10 for a ticket for the play?

Yes (88%)   No (12%)

The difference between the responses to the two problems is intriguing. Why are so many people unwilling to spend $10 after having lost a ticket, if they would readily spend that sum after losing an equivalent amount of cash? We attribute the difference to the topical organization of mental accounts. Going to the theater is normally viewed as a transaction in which the cost of the ticket is exchanged for the experience of seeing the play. Buying a second ticket increases the cost of seeing the play to a level that many respondents apparently find unacceptable. In contrast, the loss of the cash is not posted to the account of the play, and it affects the purchase of a ticket only by making the individual feel slightly less affluent.

An interesting effect was observed when the two versions of the problem were presented to the same subjects. The willingness to replace a lost ticket increased significantly when that problem followed the lost-cash version. In contrast, the willingness to buy a ticket after losing cash was not affected by prior presentation of the other problem. The juxtaposition of the two problems apparently enabled the subjects to realize that it makes sense to think of the lost ticket as lost cash, but not vice versa.

The normative status of the effects of mental accounting is questionable. Unlike earlier examples, such as the public-health problem, in which the two versions differed only in form, it can be argued that the alternative versions of the calculator and ticket problems differ also in substance. In particular, it may be more pleasurable to save $5 on a $15 purchase than on a larger purchase, and it may be more annoying to pay twice for the same ticket than to lose $10 in cash. Regret, frustration, and self-satisfaction can also be affected by framing (Kahneman & Tversky, 1982). If such secondary consequences are considered legitimate, then the observed preferences do not violate the criterion of invariance and cannot readily be ruled out as inconsistent or erroneous. On the other hand, secondary consequences may change upon reflection. The satisfaction of saving $5 on a $15 item can be marred if the consumer discovers that she would not have exerted the same effort to save $10 on a $200 purchase. We do not wish to recommend that any two decision problems that have the same primary consequences should be resolved in the same way. We propose, however, that systematic examination of alternative framings offers a useful reflective device that can help decision makers assess the values that should be attached to the primary and secondary consequences of their choices.

Losses and Costs

Many decision problems take the form of a choice between retaining the status quo and accepting an alternative to it, which is advantageous in some respects and disadvantageous in others. The analysis of value that was applied earlier to unidimensional risky prospects can be extended to this case by assuming that the status quo defines the reference level for all attributes. The advantages of alternative options will then be evaluated as gains and their disadvantages as losses. Because losses loom larger than gains, the decision maker will be biased in favor of retaining the status quo.

Thaler (1980) coined the term *endowment effect* to describe the reluctance of people to part from assets that belong to their endowment. When it is more painful to give up an asset than it is pleasurable to obtain it, buying prices will be significantly lower than selling prices. That is, the highest price that an individual will pay to acquire an asset will be smaller than the minimal compensation that would induce the same individual to give up that asset, once acquired. Thaler discussed some examples of the endowment effect in the behavior of consumers and entrepreneurs. Several studies have reported substantial discrepancies between buying and selling prices in both hypothetical and real transactions (Gregory, 1983; Hammack & Brown, 1974; Knetsch & Sinden, in press). These results have been presented as challenges to standard economic theory, in which buying and selling prices coincide except for transaction costs and effects of wealth. We also observed reluctance to trade in a study of choices between hypothetical jobs that differed in weekly salary (S) and in the temperature (T) of the workplace. Our respondents were asked to imagine that they held a particular position (S_1, T_1) and were offered the option of moving to a different position (S_2, T_2), which was better in one respect and worse in another. We found that most subjects who were assigned to (S_1, T_1) did not wish to move to (S_2, T_2), and that most subjects who were assigned to the latter position did not wish to move to the former. Evidently, the same difference in pay or in working conditions looms larger as a disadvantage than as an advantage.

In general, loss aversion favors stability over change. Imagine two hedonically identical twins who find two alternative environments equally attractive. Imagine further that by force of circumstance the twins are separated and placed in the two environments. As soon as they adopt their new states as reference points and evaluate the advantages and disadvantages of each other's environments accordingly, the twins will no longer be indifferent between the two states, and both will prefer to stay where they happen to be. Thus, the instability of preferences produces a preference for stability. In addition to favoring stability over change, the combination of adaptation and loss aversion provides limited protection against regret and envy by reducing the attractiveness of foregone alternatives and of others' endowments.

Loss aversion and the consequent endowment effect are unlikely to play a significant role in routine economic exchanges. The owner of a store, for example, does not experience money paid to suppliers as losses and money received from customers as gains. Instead, the merchant adds costs and revenues over some period of time and only evaluates the balance. Matching debits and credits are effectively cancelled prior to evaluation. Payments made by consumers are also not evaluated as losses but as alternative purchases. In accord with standard economic analysis, money is naturally viewed as a proxy for the goods and services that it could buy. This mode of evaluation is made explicit when an individual has in mind a particular alternative, such as "I can either buy a new camera or a new tent." In this analysis, a person will buy a camera if its subjective value exceeds the value of retaining the money it would cost.

There are cases in which a disadvantage can be framed either as a cost or as a loss. In particular, the purchase of insurance can also be framed as a choice between a sure loss and the risk of a greater loss. In such cases the cost–loss discrepancy can lead to failures of invariance. Consider, for example, the choice between a sure loss of $50 and a 25% chance to lose $200. Slovic, Fischhoff, and Lichtenstein (1982) reported that 80% of their subjects expressed a risk-seeking preference for the gamble over the sure loss. However, only 35% of subjects refused to pay $50 for insurance against a 25% risk of losing $200. Similar results were also reported by Schoemaker and Kunreuther (1979) and by Hershey and Schoemaker (1980). We suggest that the same amount of money that was framed as an uncompensated loss in the first problem was framed as the cost of protection in the second. The modal preference was reversed in the two problems because losses are more aversive than costs.

We have observed a similar effect in the positive domain, as illustrated by the following pair of problems:

Problem 10: Would you accept a gamble that offers a 10% chance to win $95 and a 90% chance to lose $5?

Problem 11: Would you pay $5 to participate in a lottery that offers a 10% chance to win $100 and a 90% chance to win nothing?

A total of 132 undergraduates answered the two questions, which were separated by a short filler problem. The order of the questions was reversed for half the respondents. Although it is easily confirmed that the two problems offer objectively identical options, 55 of the respondents expressed different preferences in the two versions. Among them, 42 rejected the gamble in Problem 10 but accepted the equivalent lottery in Problem 11. The effectiveness of this seemingly inconsequential manipulation illustrates both the cost–loss discrepancy and the power of framing. Thinking of the $5 as a payment makes the venture more acceptable than thinking of the same amount as a loss.

The preceding analysis implies that an individual's subjective state can be improved by framing negative outcomes as costs rather than as losses. The possibility of such psychological manipulations may explain a paradoxical form of behavior that could be labeled the *dead-loss effect*. Thaler (1980) discussed the example of a man who develops tennis elbow soon after paying the membership fee in a tennis club and continues to play in agony to avoid wasting his investment. Assuming that the individual would not play if he had not paid the membership fee, the question arises: How can playing in agony improve the individual's lot? Playing in pain, we suggest, maintains the evaluation of the membership fee as a cost. If the individual were to stop playing, he would be forced to recognize the fee as a dead loss, which may be more aversive than playing in pain.

CONCLUDING REMARKS

The concepts of utility and value are commonly used in two distinct senses: (a) experience value, the degree of pleasure or pain, satisfaction or anguish in the actual experience of an outcome; and (b) decision value, the contribution of an anticipated outcome to the overall attractiveness or aversiveness of an option in a choice. The distinction is rarely explicit in decision theory because it is tacitly assumed that decision values and experience values coincide. This assumption is part of the conception of an idealized decision maker who is able to predict future experiences with perfect accuracy and evaluate options accordingly. For ordinary decision makers, however, the correspondence of decision values between experience values is far from perfect (March, 1978). Some factors that affect experience are not easily anticipated, and some factors that affect decisions do not have a comparable impact on the experience of outcomes.

In contrast to the large amount of research on decision making, there has been relatively little systematic exploration of the psychophysics that relate hedonic experience to objective states. The most basic problem of hedonic psychophysics is the determination of the level of adaptation or aspiration that separates positive from negative outcomes. The hedonic reference point is largely determined by the objective status quo, but it is also affected by expectations and social comparisons. An objective improvement can be experienced as a loss, for example, when an employee receives a smaller raise than everyone else in the office. The experience of pleasure or pain associated with a change of state is also critically dependent on the dynamics of hedonic adaptation. Brickman & Campbell's (1971) concept of the hedonic treadmill suggests the radical hypothesis that rapid adaptation will cause the effects of any objective improvement to be short-lived. The complexity and subtlety of hedonic experience make it difficult for the decision maker to anticipate the actual experience that outcomes will produce. Many a person who ordered a meal when ravenously hungry has admitted to a big mistake when the fifth course arrived on the table. The common mismatch of decision values and experience values introduces an additional element of uncertainty in many decision problems.

The prevalence of framing effects and violations of invariance further complicates the relation between decision values and experience values. The framing of outcomes often induces decision values that have no counterpart in actual experience. For example, the framing of outcomes of therapies for lung cancer in terms of mortality or survival is unlikely to affect experience, although it can have a pronounced influence on choice. In other cases, however, the framing of decisions affects not only decision but experience, as well. For example, the framing of an expenditure as an uncompensated loss or as the price of insurance can probably influence the experience of that outcome. In such cases, the evaluation of outcomes in the context of decisions not only anticipates experience but also molds it.

REFERENCES

Allais, M., & Hagen, O. (Eds.). (1979). *Expected utility hypotheses and the Allais paradox.* Hingham, MA: D. Reidel Publishing.

Bernoulli, D. (1954). Exposition of a new theory on the measurement of risk. *Econometrica 22,* 23–36. (Original work published 1738.)

Brickman, P., & Campbell, D. T. (1971). Hedonic relativism and planning the good society. In M. H. Appley (Ed.), *Adaptation-level theory: A symposium* (pp. 287–302). New York: Academic Press.

Clark, H. H., & Clark, E. V. (1977). *Psychology and language.* New York: Harcourt Brace Jovanovich.

Erakar, S. E., & Sox, H. C. (1981). Assessment of patients' preferences for therapeutic outcomes. *Medical Decision Making, 1,* 29–39.

Fischhoff, B. (1983). Predicting frames. *Journal of Experimental Psychology: Learning, Memory, and Cognition, 9,* 103–116.

Fischhoff, B., Slovic, P., & Lichtenstein, S. (1980). Knowing what you want: Measuring labile values. In T. Wallsten (Ed.), *Cognitive processes in choice and decision behavior* (pp. 117–141). Hillsdale, NJ: Erlbaum.

Fishburn, P. C., & Kochenberger, G. A. (1979). Two-piece von Neumann-Morgenstern utility functions. *Decision Sciences, 10,* 503–518.

Gregory, R. (1983). *Measures of consumer's surplus: Reasons for the disparity in observed values.* Unpublished manuscript, Keene State College, Keene, NH.

Hammack, J., & Brown, G. M., Jr. (1974). *Waterfowl and wetlands: Toward bioeconomic analysis.* Baltimore: Johns Hopkins University Press.

Hershey, J. C., & Schoemaker, P. J. H. (1980). Risk taking and problem context in the domain of losses: An expected-utility analysis. *Journal of Risk and Insurance, 47,* 111–132.

Kahneman, D., & Tversky, A. (1979). Prospect theory: An analysis of decision under risk. *Econometrica, 47,* 263–291.

Kahneman, D., & Tversky, A. (1982). The simulation heuristic. In D. Kahneman, P. Slovic, & A. Tversky (Eds.), *Judgment under uncertainty: Heuristics and biases* (pp. 201–208). New York: Cambridge University Press.

Knetsch, J., & Sinden, J. (in press). Willingness to pay and compensation demanded: Experimental evidence of an unexpected disparity in measures of value. *Quarterly Journal of Economics.*

March, J. G. (1978). Bounded rationality, ambiguity, and the engineering of choice. *Bell Journal of Economics, 9,* 587–608.

McNeil, B., Pauker, S., Sox, H., Jr., & Tversky, A. (1982). On the elicitation of preferences for alternative therapies. *New England Journal of Medicine, 306,* 1259–1262.

Payne, J. W., Laughhunn, D. J., & Crum, R. (1980). Translation of gambles and aspiration level effects in risky choice behavior. *Management Science, 26,* 1039–1060.

Pratt, J. W., Wise, D., & Zeckhauser, R. (1979). Price differences in almost competitive markets. *Quarterly Journal of Economics, 93,* 189–211.

Savage, L. J. (1954). *The foundation of statistics.* New York: Wiley.

Schlaifer, R. (1959). *Probability and statistics for business decisions.* New York: McGraw-Hill.

Schoemaker, P. J. H., & Kunreuther, H. C. (1979). An experimental study of insurance decisions. *Journal of Risk and Insurance, 46,* 603–618.

Slovic, P., Fischhoff, B., & Lichtenstein, S. (1982). Response mode, framing, and information-processing effects in risk assessment. In R. Hogarth (Ed.), *New directions for methodology of social and behavioral science: Question framing and response consistency* (pp. 21–36). San Francisco: Jossey-Bass.

Thaler, R. (1980). Toward a positive theory of consumer choice. *Journal of Economic Behavior and Organization, 1,* 39–60.

Thaler, R. (in press). Using mental accounting in a theory of consumer behavior. *Journal of Marketing.*

Tversky, A. (1977). On the elicitation of preferences: Descriptive and prescriptive considerations. In D. Bell, R. L. Kenney, & H. Raiffa (Eds.), *Conflicting objectives in decisions. International Series on Applied Systems Analysis* (pp. 209–222). New York: Wiley.

Tversky, A., & Kahneman, D. (1981). The framing of decisions and the psychology of choice. *Science, 211,* 453–458.

von Neumann, J., & Morgenstern, O. (1947). *Theory of games and economic behavior* (2nd ed.). Princeton, NJ: Princeton University Press.

32

Philosophers like John Locke have argued that humans are inherently logical beings; that is, they naturally know and can follow the rules of logic. However, to the contrary, experimental research has shown systematic biases in the logical reasoning of most humans, even those with a great deal of education (like college professors!). The overwhelming tendency we have is to search for evidence that will verify a rule (prove that it is true) instead of working to falsify it (prove that it is false). However, these conclusions are based on experiments in which the subjects had no experience in or knowledge of the domain in which they were reasoning. They were given abstract rules and rules that have no basis in their actual experiences.

This paper discusses a reasoning task that has come to be known as the "Wason selection task" after Peter Wason, one of the authors of this article. The task seems to be relatively simple, but most humans have some difficulty solving it correctly. In the classic form of this problem, the subjects are asked to test the truth of a rule such as "Every card which has a D on one side has a 3 on the other side" and are told that each card has a letter on one side a number on the other. When given the cards, D, K, 3, and 7, slightly under half of the people studied will correctly choose to turn over the D. A relatively large number of subjects will choose to turn over the 3 card, which actually gives you no information (the rule did not say that if it had a 3 on one side it would have a D on the other). The K card similarly gives no information. Finally, very few of the subjects will correctly decide to turn over the 7 card, which is the only one that could actually falsify the rule (if it had a D on the other side).

Although Wason and Shapiro's Experiment I shows no effect of experience with the problem, Experiment II demonstrates that, in situations that are realistic (their "thematic" condition), people do actually reason significantly better than they do when the materials are abstract. Thus it is not the logical structure of the problem that makes it difficult—it is the arbitrariness of some of the materials. The abstract material is arbitrary in that any rule could be specified. In thematic or realistic situations, only a limited number of rules are possible. To use the example in the reading, when traveling from one place to another it is usual to use cars or trains, but one could possibly use things like horses or feet. However, there is an upper limit on the choices to be used in the situation. In the abstract case there are an infinite number of possible abstract symbols that could represent the problem and there is no meaningful link among the alternatives.

This experiment has led to a great deal of research using the Wason selection task with meaningful materials (see Evans & Newstead, 1995, for a review). More recent findings have suggested that as long as the hypothesis being tested activates a set of rules called "permission rules," the familiarity of the materials has no effect on performance (Cheng, Holyoak, Nisbett, & Oliver, 1986; Smith, Langston, & Nisbitt, 1997). Permission rules are of the form that "If an action is to be taken, then a precondition must be satisfied." The thematic materials in Wason and Shapiro's Experiment II activate the permission rules ("Every time I go to Manchester I travel by car" is reinterpreted as "In order to go to Manchester, I must travel by car"), whereas the abstract materials ("Every card which has a D on one side has a 3 on the other side") are not reinterpreted.

The CogLab Wason selection task experiment is most similar to Experiment II of this paper. You should find that you do much better on the meaningful materials than on the abstract materials.

REFERENCES

Cheng, P. W., Holyoak, K. J., Nisbett, R. E., & Oliver, L. M. (1986). Pragmatic versus syntactic approaches to training deductive reasoning. *Cognitive Psychology, 18,* 293–328.

Evans, J. St. B. T., & Newstead, S. E. (1995). Creating a psychology of reasoning: The contribution of Peter Wason. In S. E. Newstead and J. St. B. T. Evans (Eds), *Perspectives on thinking and reasoning: Essays in honour of Peter Wason.* Hove, UK: Lawrence Erlbaum Associates.

Smith, E. E., Langston, C., & Nisbett, R. E. (1997). The case for rules in reasoning. In W. M. Goldstein and R. M. Hogarth (Eds.), *Research on judgment and decision making: Currents, connections, and controversies.* Cambridge, MA: Cambridge University Press.

QUESTIONS

1. Why is it so difficult to follow logical principles in the Wason selection task?
2. Under what circumstances is it easier to make logical choices?
3. What are the three hypotheses discussed by Wason and Shapiro to account for the beneficial effects of thematic materials on reasoning?

Natural and Contrived Experience in a Reasoning Problem

Peter C. Wason and Diana Shapiro
University College London

INTRODUCTION

This study is about the effects of two kinds of experience on a deceptive reasoning problem. In the first experiment the experience is introduced as part of the procedure, and in the second it is inherent in the material used.

Previous experiments (Wason, 1968, 1969a) have established that it is very difficult to decide what information is required to test the truth of an abstract conditional sentence. For example, given the sentence: *Every card which has a D on one side has a 3 on the other side* (and knowledge that each card has a letter on one side and a number on the other side), together with four cards showing respectively D, K, 3, 7, hardly any individuals make the correct choice of cards to turn over (D and 7) in order to determine the truth of the sentence. This problem is called the "selection task" and the conditional sentence is called "the rule."

The rule has the logical form, "if p then q," where p refers to the stimulus mentioned in the antecedent (D); $\bar{p}$, i.e. not p, refers to the stimulus which negates it (K); q refers to the stimulus mentioned in the consequent (3); and $\bar{q}$, i.e. not q, refers to the stimulus which negates it (7). In order to solve the problem it is necessary and sufficient to choose p and $\bar{q}$, since if these stimuli were to occur on the same card the rule would be false but otherwise true.

The combined results of four experiments (see Table 32.1) show that the subjects (students) are dominated by *verification* rather than *falsification*. On the whole, they failed to select $\bar{q}$, which could have

TABLE 32.1   Frequency of the Selection of Cards in Four Previous Experiments ($n = 128$)

p and q	59
p	42
p, q and $\bar{q}$	9
p and $\bar{q}$	5
others	13

falsified the rule, and they did select q, which could not have falsified it although this latter error is much less prevalent.

EXPERIMENT I

The previous experiments have been concerned with the stability of the errors and their resistance to correction by "remedial procedures." After the subjects had performed the selection task they had to evaluate the cards independently, i.e. turn them over and say whether the rule was true or false in relation to each. The present experiment is concerned with the prevention of error. The subjects are made familiar with the other side of the cards before the selection task is performed.

This prior experience is introduced by two methods. The "construction" method requires the subject to imagine, or project, a value on the other side of a card which would make the rule true, or make it false, in relation to it. In effect, positive and negative instances of the rule are constructed. The "evaluation"

SOURCE: Wason, P., & Shapiro, D. (1971). Natural and contrived experience in a reasoning problem. *Quarterly Journal of Experimental Psychology*, 23, 63–71. Reprinted by permission of The Experimental Psychology Society.

method simply requires the subject to turn over the card and say whether the rule is true, or false, in relation to it. The construction method clearly involves an imaginative act, and hence a greater degree of involvement than the evaluation method. It was accordingly predicted that it would be associated with superior performance in the subsequent selection task.

Design

Two independent groups were used: the construction group and the evaluation group. Both carried out their respective tasks on 24 cards in relation to a given conditional rule. They then performed the *initial selection task* with four more cards in relation to the *same* rule. A new conditional rule was then presented together with a further four cards. This *transfer selection task* was designed to assess the extent to which specific knowledge, gained in the prior experience, would be generalized.

Subjects

Twenty-four undergraduates (paid volunteers) of University College London were allocated alternately to the groups and tested individually. They had no previous experience with tasks of this type.

Procedure

Before presenting the rule all the subjects were first handed 28 cards, and instructed to inspect them to ensure that each had a letter of the alphabet on one side and a number on the other side.

They were then presented with the following rule: *Every card which has a vowel on one side has an even number on the other side.* Twenty-four of the 28 cards were then presented, one at a time, the remaining four being reserved for the transfer selection task. In the construction group they were instructed to name a value on the other side of each card which would make the rule true (or make it false). They were, however, told that it would be in order to say that no value on the other side would make the rule either true or false. In the evaluation group they turned over each card and said that it made the rule true (or false). Similarly, they were told that it would be in order to say that a card was irrelevant to the truth or falsity of the rule.

The eight possible ways of permuting the logical values were each represented three times in the series of 24. They were presented successively in the following pairs, where the value given first refers to the symbol uppermost: $(pq, p\bar{q})$ $(\bar{p}\bar{q}, \bar{p}q)$ $(qp, q\bar{p})$ $(\bar{q}\bar{p}, \bar{q}p)$. All the subjects received the cards in the same order, and within a pair the order of presenting the two cards was constant, but the pairs themselves were randomized in a different order within each of the three blocks of eight cards. In the construction group, where only the uppermost symbol was presented, the instruction for the first card within a pair was to name a symbol to make a verifying instance, and for the second card to name a symbol to make a falsifying instance.

In both groups the subjects were told they were wrong if they failed to evaluate (construct) $p\bar{q}$ and $\bar{q}p$ as falsifying, and if they did evaluate (construct) $\bar{p}q$ and $q\bar{p}$ as falsifying. This was to ensure that they did appreciate the falsifying instances of a conditional rule, but did not confuse them with the falsifying instances of an equivalence rule. The $\bar{p}q$ and $q\bar{p}$ instances do falsify an equivalence rule in the form: "if, and only if p then q."

For the initial selection task four cards (E, Z, 6, 7), taken from the 24 used in the prior experience, were placed on the table in a random order. The subjects were instructed that the rule now applied to these four cards taken as a whole, i.e. no longer independently. They were told "to select those cards, and only those cards, that would need to be turned over in order to discover whether the rule was true or false." No comments were made about these selections, and the subjects were not allowed to turn over any of the cards.

For the transfer selection task the following rule was presented: *Every card which has a D on one side has a 3 on the other side,* together with the four cards (D, K, 3, 5) which had not occurred in the series of 24, but had been included in the 28 originally inspected. The instructions were similar to those given for the initial selection task.

Results

Table 32.2 shows the frequency of correct and incorrect solutions, the first number in each cell referring to the initial selection task and the second to the transfer selection task.

TABLE 32.2   Frequency of Correct and Incorrect Solutions

	Correct	Incorrect	N
Construction	5 (6)	7 (6)	12
Evaluation	2 (2)	10 (10)	12
Totals	7 (8)	17 (16)	24

As predicted, there is a trend in favor of the construction group, but it falls short of statistical significance. The performance overall is unimpressive, particularly in the evaluation group. It will also be noted that the difference between the two selection tasks is negligible: knowledge is generalized to the extent that it has been gained. The two types of error, i.e. the selection of q and the omission of $\bar{q}$ are examined separately in Tables 32.3 and 32.4.

Table 32.3 shows that both groups do better in omitting q than in getting the solution correct. But the frequency of this particular error also increases the difference between the groups in the predicted direction. On the transfer selection task it is significant ($P = 0.05$, one-tailed, Fisher-Yates exact test).

It may be inferred from Table 32.4 that the proportion of subjects in both groups who select $\bar{q}$ is greater than ever obtained initially in previous experiments. But it is also evident that none of the frequencies differ from chance expectancy. However, it may be inferred that the trend, showing the construction group superior on the correct solution, is entirely due to a greater tendency to omit q rather than one to select $\bar{q}$ . . . .

It may be concluded that the putative experience of logical structure, introduced procedurally, is rela-

TABLE 32.3   Frequency of Selecting q

	q Selected	q Omitted	N
Construction	2 (3)	10 (9)	12
Evaluation	7 (8)	5 (4)	12
Totals	9 (11)	15 (13)	24

TABLE 32.4   Frequency of Omitting $\bar{q}$

	$\bar{q}$ Omitted	$\bar{q}$ Selected	N
Construction	7 (5)	5 (7)	12
Evaluation	6 (6)	6 (6)	12
Totals	13 (11)	11 (13)	24

tively ineffective in enabling insight to be gained into the problem. It is reasonable to inquire whether "natural" experience, inherent in the subjects' everyday knowledge, may be more successful in inducing insight. It was predicted that when the material is realistic ("thematic"), as opposed to abstract, the selection task will be significantly easier.

EXPERIMENT II

Design

Two independent groups were used: the "thematic group" and the "abstract group" which differed solely in the terms in which the problem was presented.

Subjects

Thirty-two first year psychology undergraduates of University College London were allocated alternately to the groups and tested individually. They had no previous experience with tasks of this type.

Procedure

The thematic material represented a journey made on 4 different days of the week. Before presenting the rule about these journeys the subjects were given 16 cards which they inspected to ensure that each had the name of a town on one side and a mode of transport on the other side.

They were then presented with the four selection task cards, taken from the 16 originally presented, and arranged in random order on the table. They were instructed that they would now only be concerned with these cards. On two of them a different destination was written, i.e. "Manchester" and "Leeds," and on the other two a different mode of transport, i.e. "Car" and "Train." In addition each had a different day of the week in smaller type at the top.

The rule was then presented as a claim made by the experimenter about four journeys she had made on the four different days indicated on the cards. One variant of this rule was: *Every time I go to Manchester I travel by car.* Three other variants, derived from permuting the items on the cards, were also used. The presentation of all four was systematically rotated between the subjects to control for any possible preconceptions about the relation between destinations and modes of transport.

It was explained to the subjects that for each journey the destination appeared on one side of the card and the transport used on the other side. They were then instructed to say which cards they would need to turn over to decide whether the experimenter's claim was true or false. They were encouraged to take their time before answering.

A similar procedure was followed in the abstract group. Sixteen cards with a letter of the alphabet on one side and a number on the other side were first inspected. Four of these, D, K, 3, 7, were used for the selection task. The rule: *Every card which has a D on one side has a 3 on the other side,* was then presented as a claim made by the experimenter about the arrangement of letters and numbers on the cards. The subjects were instructed that this rule applied only to the four cards, and that they were to say which they would need to turn over to decide whether the claim was true or false.

Results

Table 32.5 shows the frequency of correct and incorrect solutions.

The prediction that the thematic group would perform better than the abstract group is clearly confirmed by the distribution of the frequencies in Table 5 ($P = 0.004$, one-tailed, Fisher-Yates exact test). It is evident that representing the problem in the form of a realistic situation had a dramatic effect on the subjects' ability to gain insight into it. There may, however, be several reasons for this result.

DISCUSSION

The results of the two experiments show the relative failure of procedurally introduced experience and the relative success of realistic material in allowing insight to be gained into the problem.

TABLE 32.5 *Frequency of Correct and Incorrect Solutions*

	Correct	Incorrect	N
Thematic	10	6	16
Abstract	2	14	16
Totals	12	20	32

It could, of course, be argued that if the experience, introduced in Experiment I, had been more intensive, or if only the falsifying contingencies had been used, then performance would have been improved. But the purpose of the experience was only to acquaint the subjects with the logical structure of the problem, and not to train them to make particular responses. Previous results (Johnson-Laird and Wason, 1970b) have shown that various factors, such as cognitive load, may affect the appreciation of the task, and over-learning of the contingencies might be one more variable affecting performance. The point is that understanding the contingencies did not allow this knowledge to be used with maximum efficiency in the selection tasks. This result may seem incredible to anyone unacquainted with the difficulty of the problem. The reasons for it will not be discussed until the effects of thematic material on the task have been considered because these help to explain it.

Three hypotheses about different aspects of the thematic material used in Experiment II could account for its beneficial effects. First, the terms used in the thematic material, the towns and modes of transport, are concrete as opposed to the abstract terms which consisted of letters and numbers. It is well known that concrete material is better remembered than abstract material, and that in syllogistic reasoning familiar terms inhibit fallacious inferences (Wilkins, 1929). Thus in Experiment II the concrete terms may have been symbolically manipulated more readily and more appropriately than the abstract terms. This hypothesis might be tested by using concrete terms with an arbitrary connection, e.g. "Every card which has *iron* on one side has *apple* on the other side," where metals and fruits are known to occur on either side of the cards.

Second, it may be the concrete relation between the terms, rather than the terms themselves, which is beneficial. In the thematic material the relation which connects the terms is "traveling," as opposed to "the other side of the card" which connects the abstract material. This hypothesis could be tested by using abstract terms with a concrete relation between them, e.g. "Every time I go to K I travel by 3," where letters and numbers are known to stand for towns and transport respectively.

Third, the thematic material, unlike the abstract material, forms a coherent, unified whole: a claim about journeys supposed to have been made on four different days. Hence the subjects may have been more inclined to distribute their attention equally on its components, i.e. the four cards. They would thus be liberated from fixations on those cards which correspond to items mentioned in the rule. Cyril Burt (personal communication) has even suggested that thematic material enables the subjects to concentrate on the situation depicted, unfettered by the presence of the cards. This does not, in itself, explain why thematic material is helpful. But if it is assumed that knowledge about such material is represented in the brain in schemata, which may be activated by appropriate cues, then the solution to the problem may be simply "read off" by reference to this stored information.

The abstract material has no unifying link: each card is distinct and separate rather than being parts of a whole. The subjects are instructed that the rule refers only to the four cards, but in spite of this they may have construed it merely as a formula. They may, in fact, have regarded the cards as items in a sample from a larger universe, and reasoned about them inductively rather than deductively. In doing this they may have implicitly followed the Bayesian rule which assumes that the probability of a generalization is increased by repetition of confirming instances. Hence they might not have been disposed to consider the potential relevance of $\bar{q}$. There was some introspective support for probabilistic reasoning of this kind. It would follow, of course, that the experience of the problem's logical structure, introduced in Experiment I, would not have disabused the subjects of this particular misconception.

In fact, the difficulty of the abstract selection task may be due, not to the failure to recognize the correct solution, but to the failure to generate alternatives in order to derive the correct solution. In other words, abstract material may inhibit the realization of the necessity of combinatorial analysis rather than hindering the performance of such an analysis. The meaninglessness of the rule may tempt the subjects to interpret it, not as a rule, but as a sentence to be matched against instances. With thematic material it is gratuitous to talk about combinatorial analysis: the activation of stored knowledge spontaneously generates "real" alternatives. This hypothesis might be tested by comparing thematic and abstract material, but presenting

all the possible solutions in a list from which one has to be selected, thus obviating the need for a combinatorial analysis. It would then be predicted only that the correct solution would be located more quickly with thematic material than with abstract material without a difference in its relative frequency.

Finally, the present results support the suggestion (Wason, 1969b) that it is not so much the logical structure which makes the abstract problem difficult, as the structure which the subjects impose upon the problem. Its difficulty does not lie in the fact that inferences of the kind demanded "hardly ever occur in real life"—a criticism sometimes voiced of the early experiments. On the contrary, when the task is made realistic it becomes appreciably easier. What makes the abstract task difficult is the arbitrariness of material which seems to defy the reasoning process. A more precise definition of the impediments involved must await further investigation.

AUTHORS' NOTE

The experiments in this paper form part of research to be reported in a thesis to be submitted for the degree of Ph.D. of London University by the second author, under the supervision of the first author. We are most indebted to our colleague, Dr. P. N. Johnson-Laird, for invaluable critical comments and suggestions, and also to the Medical Research Council for a grant for scientific assistance.

REFERENCES

Johnson-Laird, P. N. and Tagart, J. (1969). How implication is understood. *American Journal of Psychology*, **82**, 367–73.

Johnson-Laird, P. N. and Wason, P. C. (1970a). A theoretical analysis of insight into a reasoning task. *Cognitive Psychology* **1**, 134–148 .

Johnson-Laird, P. N. and Wason, P. C. (1970b). Insight into a logical relation. *Quarterly Journal of Experimental Psychology*, **22**, 49–61.

Wason, P. C. (1968). Reasoning about a rule. *Quarterly Journal of Experimental Psychology*, **20**, 273–81.

Wason, P. C. (1969a). Regression in reasoning? *British Journal of Psychology*, **60**, 471–80.

Wason, P. C. (1969b). Structural simplicity and psychological complexity. *Bulletin of the British Psychological Society*, **22**, 281–84.

Wilkins, M. C. (1929). The effect of changed material on ability to do formal syllogistic reasoning. *Archives of Psychology*, No. 102.

AUTHOR INDEX

SUBJECT INDEX

schema, 386
semantic memory, 310, 342
sensory memory, 150, 164, 180
serial position effect, 180, 253
serial response task, 372
short-term memory, 199, 207, 216, 253
signal detection theory, 97, 98, 99
Simon effect, 22, 23
size constancy, 80
span of apprehension, 164
spatial awareness, 128
spatial cueing of attention, 27, 28
speech perception, 334
split-brain patient, 127, 128
spotlight theory of attention, 27
stimulus generalization, 363
stimulus persistence, 166. *See also* visual persistence
stimulus suffix effect. *See* suffix effect
stop consonant, 334
strong cue, 241, 242
Stroop effect, 46, 47
subjective standard hypothesis, 363
suffix effect, 180, 181

tacit knowledge, 326

threshold, 97, 98
trigram, 199

visual attention, 109, 110
visual illusions, 80, 81
visual imagery, 326
visual masking, 151, 152
visual perception, 62, 63, 134, 109, 128
visual persistence, 151
visual scribe, 216
visual search, 109, 110
visual sensory memory, 164, 166
visual spatial sketchpad, 216
voice onset time, 334
von Restorff effect, 253, 259
VOT. *See* voice onset time

Wason selection task, 415, 416
weak cue, 242
Wheatstone bridge, 81
word length effect, 217, 227
word superiority effect, 151, 352, 353
working memory, 207, 215
working memory capacity, 227